Cradles of Conscience

Cradles of Conscience

Ohio's Independent Colleges and Universities

EDITED BY

JOHN WILLIAM OLIVER JR.,

JAMES A. HODGES,

AND

JAMES H. O'DONNELL

THE KENT STATE UNIVERSITY PRESS

KENT & LONDON

Library of Congress Cataloging-in-Publication Data

Cradles of Conscience: Ohio's independent colleges and universities /
edited by John William Oliver Jr., James A. Hodges, and James H. O'Donnell.

p. cm.

Includes bibliographical references and index.

ISBN 0-87338-763-5 (alk. paper) ∞

1. Private universities and colleges—Ohio—History.

I. Hodges, James A., 1932–

II. O'Donnell, James H., 1937–

III. Oliver, John William Jr.

LB2328.52.U6 C73 2003

378'.04'09771—dc21

2002073025

British Library Cataloging-in-Publication data are available.

To Geoffrey Blodgett (1931–2001),
and to all the gifted teachers and scholars in Ohio's
independent colleges and universities.

Contents

Preface and Acknowledgments ix

Introduction *by James A. Hodges* 1

Antioch College *by Scott Sanders* 8

Ashland University *by John L. Nethers* 23

Baldwin-Wallace College *by Norman J. Clary* 39

Bluffton College *by Perry Bush* 52

Buchtel College *by George W. Knepper* 64

Capital University *by James L. Burke* 78

Case Western Reserve University *by Dennis Harrison* 91

Cedarville University *by Murray Murdoch* 109

The University of Dayton *by Erving E. Beauregard* 120

Defiance College *by Randall Buchman* 134

Denison University *by G. Wallace Chessman* 144

The University of Findlay *by Richard Kern* 158

Franciscan University *by John Carrigg* 172

Franklin University *by Kelli Nowlin and Helga Kittrell* 186

Heidelberg College *by David Gerard Hogan and Kimberly Roush* 194

Hiram College *by David R. Anderson* 208

John Carroll University *by MaryAnn Janosik* 217

Kenyon College *by Perry Lentz* 226

Lake Erie College *by Margaret Gross*   243

Lourdes College *by Nancy J. Brown*   254

Malone College *by John W. Oliver*   263

Marietta College *by James H. O'Donnell III*   276

College of Mount St. Joseph *by Kimberly J. M. Wilson*   288

Mount Union College *by John Saffell*   299

Mount Vernon Nazarene University *by Paul D. Mayle*   312

Muskingum College *by William Fisk*   324

Notre Dame College *by Patricia E. Harding*   338

Oberlin College *by Geoffrey Blodgett*   358

Ohio Dominican University *by Camilla Mullay*   364

Ohio Northern University *by Paul M. Logsdon*   380

Ohio Wesleyan University *by Richard W. Smith*   392

Otterbein College *by Elizabeth MacLean*   404

The University of Rio Grande *by Ivan M. Tribe*   421

Tiffin University *by Michael A. Grandillo*   442

Urbana University *by Lisa Oda Fede*   453

Ursuline College *by Anna Margaret Gilbride*   462

Walsh University *by Joseph Torma*   476

Wilberforce University *by Erving E. Beauregard*   489

Wilmington College *by Larry Gara*   509

Wittenberg University *by Richard T. Ortquist*   523

The College of Wooster *by James A. Hodges*   539

Xavier University *by John LaRocca*   551

Appendix: Defunct Colleges and Universities *by Erving E. Beauregard*   558

Contributors   569

Index   574

Preface and Acknowledgments

The idea of collecting the histories of Ohio's independent colleges arose from an interest in the story of Malone College, where I taught from 1966 to 1998. A school in transition from a Bible to a liberal arts college, Malone was fertile ground for seeds of change. But was this story unique or was it similar to the histories of Ohio's other colleges, most of which were founded in an earlier era? Is there a pattern colleges commonly follow? How, if at all, is the original identity of the college likely to affect what it becomes over time?

This book only became possible after two past presidents of the Ohio Academy of History—Jim Hodges of the College of Wooster and Jim O'Donnell of Marietta College—committed themselves to this project. In addition, the project required help from dozens of historians who set about to explain the mission of the founders of each school and how and why each has changed over time. Finally, we are indebted to John Hubbell and Joanna Hildebrand Craig of The Kent State University Press, who agreed to serve as our publishers, and to the Ohio Foundation of Independent Colleges for their generous support.

Jim Hodges thanks Denise Monbarren and Elaine Snyder of the Special Collections room of Andrews Library and faculty secretaries Dale Catteau and Charlotte Wahl, as well as Damon Hickey, director of Libraries at The College of Wooster, who helped in the early days to put this book together. James O'Donnell thanks Mabry O'Donnell and the librarians at Marietta College.

John William Oliver Jr.

Introduction

Thinking about Ohio's Independent
Colleges and Universities

JAMES A. HODGES

In 1998 John Oliver, a historian at Malone College, thought it would be interesting to gather together some historical essays on the founding and development of Ohio's private, or independent, colleges. John argued that Ohio, as the most eastern state of the Northwest Territory, exploded in growth throughout the nineteenth century, and from the beginning the people of Ohio sought colleges and universities. As the essay on defunct colleges chronicles, many of the early institutions failed to thrive. Nevertheless, Kenyon College (1824), Denison University (1831), Ohio Wesleyan University (1832), Marietta College (1835), and Muskingum College (1836) persisted and were, by the 1880s, joined by many others that grace the state.

Ohio today has more independent colleges than other state except for Pennsylvania. These schools educate tens of thousands of Ohioans and students from every state in the nation and from all over the globe. How were they founded and by whom? What happened to their founding missions and how did they meet the twists and turns of challenges of financial crises, different arguments for educational mission, changing student interests, the increasing secularity of American society, the crises of the American war experiences, the cultural conflicts of the 1960s, and the cyclical nature of the American economy? How do they now see themselves and their meaning for their students and constituencies in the twenty-first century?

John enlisted James O'Donnell and me, both of us former presidents of the Ohio Academy of History, to join him in assembling a group of contributors who would write short interpretative essays about individual colleges or universities. The essays, presented here in alphabetical order by college, came about as the three of us found willing contributors. The contributors are in preponderance historians who teach or taught at the colleges they write about. But these authors are also archivists, a librarian, a public relations professional, and other college- or university-affiliated people who agreed to join this effort. The nature of the essays varies from the comprehensive chronologically arranged essays to those that develop singular thematic treatments. Each, however, provides an interesting look at the college or university. We trust that they are accurate and useful essays as well as mostly affectionate in tone. The authors were given no rigid formula of fact and topics selection to follow, only a hopeful request that they give clear insight as to what human forces brought the colleges and universities into being, what the major events or circumstances were that informed the history of their institution, and what distinguishes the institution at the turn into this century. We believe this to be a useful collection of informative and knowledgeable stories about these lively Ohio places.

The clearest theme that dominates the essays and drives the title of the book has to do with founding ideals. Except for two (Ohio Northern and Franklin Universities), all the institutions were founded by people of distinctive Christian faith with the clear conviction that a college or university was needed to prepare men and/or women for the ministry or for a life of Christian service. From that point the stories develop quite differently from campus to campus. At each school there was through the decades an evolution of the founding mission. At some the strong Christian identity slowly melded into a late-twentieth-century view of the college or university as a place of academic excellence for education in a diverse and complex secular world. At others various leaders and crises confronted the college with modernity, but the search for an overt primary religious mission remains, although sometimes muted and explained by the contingencies of attracting students and supporters to an attractive educational program for a far more secular world. Some schools retain a firm commitment to religious education with such things as mandatory Bible courses, mandatory attendance at devotional meetings, religious enrichment programs to stimulate spiritual growth, prohibition against the use of alcohol, dress codes, and moral codes of personal behavior. A majority celebrate their church ties as a historical tradition with only a few or no symbolic practices on campus. All these institutions share the idea that education consists of more than the accumulation of knowledge; they argue passionately for educating the whole person and providing access to a moral and aesthetic world beyond the merely selfish individual.

What is common among these schools is that a mission of conscience peculiar to their identity and their circumstances was present at the beginning and still remains. The essays' explanations of the colleges' reasons for being, despite the wide diversity—Protestant to Catholic, mainstream religious ideals to more conservative ideals, a continuing strong church affiliation to a slight one or none at all—show one sign of commonality: the trustees, the administrators and faculty, and the immediate constituents—and they alone—decide what they are and what they might be. Even the most secular schools dedicated to academic achievement and distinction as a dominant goal labored mightily to remain connected in some way to the past religious and moral conscience that brought them into being.

The essays commandingly demonstrate that these schools depended heavily on presidential leadership to establish themselves and then to weather all sorts of crises. For example, Perry Lentz sees two different Kenyon Colleges: the Old Kenyon under the control of the bishops of the Ohio Protestant Episcopal Church and the Kenyon College that, under the dynamic and forceful leadership of William Foster Peirce (1896–1937), would become a nationally recognized liberal arts college. In some ways Peirce's leadership traits can be seen in the history of many of the schools profiled in this collection. Peirce, in his forty-one years at Kenyon, did not depend on some vague vision; he thought that "Kenyon must believe in itself if it is to induce others to believe in it." Loyalty to Kenyon College dominated his presidency; he was a partisan in the struggle for Kenyon's present and future.

The essays bring attention to such leadership, principled and visionary but also pragmatic for the place and time. A transforming leadership can be seen at Capital University in the thirty-eight-year presidency of Otto Mees (1912–46), who skillfully negotiated the school's growth and changes through the modernity shoals of the first half of the twentieth century. For exemplary purposes of this phenomenon, consider in the essays the triumphant careers of Israel Ward Andrews at Marietta College (1855–85), Charles E. Miller at Heidelberg College (1902–37), A. E. Smith at Ohio Northern University (1905–30), William Henry McMaster at Mount Union College (1908–37), Alfred B. Bonds Jr. at Baldwin-Wallace College (1955–81), and Glenn L. Clayton at Ashland University (1946–77).

Sometimes the impact of important presidential leadership could be measured in shorter years, as the tenure of Kevin McCann of Defiance College (1951–64), who led a college of only 200 students to financial stability, steady and increased enrollment, and reaccreditation. A common pattern of leadership was that just when things were adrift, an energetic and thoughtful leader set the institution on the right path. At Wooster Louis Edward Holden (1894–1915) raised the funds to build the core of the modern campus after the school's major academic building burned in 1901; Howard Foster Lowry (1944–77) established a thoughtful and compelling curriculum that still serves the school well; and Henry Jefferson Copeland (1977–95) artfully guided the school through the financial and cultural challenges peculiar to the 1980s and early 1990s. The essays concerning Lourdes, Notre Dame of Ohio, Ohio Dominican, and Ursuline tell us about the consistent leadership that facilitated the adaptations their colleges made to the world around them. But nothing sums up the importance of presidential leadership better than one of the earliest examples of it in Ohio—the literal college-saving exertions of the famous Horace Mann at Antioch College, its first president, who used his own resources to keep the college alive (and who worked himself to death in 1859).

Those interested in program development will find these essays useful. Most of the early colleges founded in the early or middle of the nineteenth century adopted the prevailing classical curriculum of the eastern colleges, with Yale being a popular model. The title of "college" or "university" often meant little in practical ways, as these schools were small and the various departments or branches of knowledge were staffed with one to three professors. Some schools, such as Ohio Wesleyan and Denison, kept the "university" designation, though over the years they became four-year liberal arts colleges. Some four-year colleges in the late nineteenth and early twentieth centuries established small programs that granted master's degrees and doctorates, but the practice died out with the coming of professional graduate schools. Many survived in the nineteenth century and up to the first decade of the twentieth century by having affiliated preparatory schools (high schools). Case Western, which began as two separate four-year colleges that merged in 1967, became a national research university in which its graduate schools actually dominate the university.

What these essays teach is that these schools have often pragmatically made their way through the thickets of knowledge gauging the academic market and deciding what they could do to attract supporters and students while at the same time remaining true to, or at least in touch with, their sense of why they exist. Today they all offer four-year baccalaureate degrees of several kinds with majors and minors in a bristling number of academic divisions full of proficient scholar-teachers.

The importance of the faculty and the roles they played in founding the schools and their contributions to keeping these schools alive and enriching their presence emerge in some essays. In these brief histories one can see the faculty change from devout ministerial-trained B.A.s and M.A.s from schools like those they taught in to the professional, discipline-trained Ph.D.s out of the graduate programs of large public and private universities. The essays also discuss how, in the second half of the twentieth century, the schools and their faculties responded in positive and swift manner to the new fields of knowledge and to the new interdisciplinary nature of the social and natural world. Otterbein College's current program, as outlined by Elizabeth McLean, is the best example of such changes prevalent throughout these institutions.

The schools changed their academic programs despite the continual financial burdens they often faced. Every school needed financial support beyond just tuition fees. The schools at first depended on the churches for funds and on the few people who had brought them to life. Then, as they accumulated alumni, they broadened their appeals to wherever they could find support. As early as 1859 the Reverend Thomas Hill, a Unitarian minister and the second president of Antioch College, observed, as he attempted to cast Antioch's appeals to a broader audience, that the founding group, the Christian Movement, was "slow to pay and quick to demand privilege." Official church support over the years lost importance, and each school developed its own body of supporters and set out on an unceasing search for financial support. What is fascinating is how, just at critical moments, presidential leadership, a generous donor, and determined faculty support and sacrifice emerged to give these places a future. Make no mistake about it, these schools exist because committed people saw them as needed places they loved.

Openness characterized these institutions from the first. While most from the very beginning admitted women, following the early practice of Oberlin, Mount Union, and Antioch, some schools, such as Ohio Wesleyan and Denison, admitted women much later. Interestingly, Kenyon College waited until 1972 to become co-educational, a decision that Perry Lentz called the "most significant" in the college's history, and one of the "happiest." And even though the Catholic women's colleges were founded and developed by women for women, they too have in recent years opened their programs to men. Early on Oberlin had a significant number of African American students. Elsewhere, apparently, no college or university prohibited their enrollment, but black students were small in numbers and isolated in white seas. Nevertheless, the colleges responded quickly to the changing cycles of race relations in the post–World War II years. Amid the civil rights revolution of the 1960s and beyond, the schools recruited black students vigorously, and many established black study courses and programs.

Despite the strong denominational feelings that produced these schools, not a single one developed a specific denominational test for admittance. Most underscored their acceptance of students of different faiths, even if at the beginning most of the faculty remained in the faith and the governing boards came exclusively from the ranks of the faithful, a practice that has all but disappeared. Usually, at first, all students had to attend daily or weekly chapel and attend on Sunday a church of their choice. Most at the beginning required biblical study courses, and many still do. The trend was always toward tolerance and even religious ecumenicalism. At the turn of the twentieth century Protestant schools had students from all faiths, and daily chapel or any kind of required religious devotion practices had disappeared. At the Catholic schools students of all faiths were welcomed, and the Catholic identity never got in the way of traditional educational goals.

The diversity of admission to these schools so often thought of as "private" and the strong attention to classroom instruction and the faculty and student bonds produced an inordinate number of leaders. Ohio Wesleyan University's long history produced both Union Civil War generals as well as Confederate, as did Marietta College. Richard Smith's essay recounts some truly impressive achievements of Ohio Wesleyan graduates. Indeed, most of the essays tell us that accomplished Americans of distinct fame in politics, education, business, academia, and many other endeavors came from the ivy-covered halls of these colleges. Despite the dominance in numbers of students enrolled in public universities, the authors of these essays clearly would argue that the independent institutions more than justify their history and continuance in today's complex society.

These colleges' and universities' histories never happened outside the pulls and tugs of American life at large. The fortunes of these institutions were often at the mercy of events beyond their control. The pre–Civil War colleges saw the war threaten their enrollments and their fragile support. World War I, with its brief history for this country, barely impacted them; but World War II severely challenged them as enrollments fell drastically. Several of the essays note that the avoidance of great pain, if not survival, depended on the officer training programs that the U.S. military service placed on the campuses (although one wonders just how swiftly faculty members adapted to teaching navigation and how many planes and ships lost their way). Many authors note the importance of the GI Bill in giving a needed jolt to admissions and even in changing the nature of student life. As the Ashland University essay notes, "They had seen the world and they were more worldly." The Vietnam War did not create a fiscal crisis, but it did challenge on many of the campuses the purpose of education, control of student life, and the meaning of authority. One great result of this was the end, in varying degrees, of in loco parentis for these residential colleges. What jumps out of these essays often is the active and involved nature of student life in the second half of the twentieth century. The Ivory Tower was never a reality, and clearly students at these independent colleges have always been encouraged to participate in the world around them.

History shows that these schools were not immune to the shifts in the economy around them. The "panics" of the 1870s and the 1890s set back many a college. The colleges prospered in the golden years of 1900 to 1918 and boomed in the 1920s. But the Great Depression of the 1930s was a dark period, with salaries cut in half, few new buildings constructed, and survival often an issue. The early 1950s also saw a brief challenge to enrollment as GIs left the campuses and the postwar boom was a few years short of filling the classrooms. In some ways, too, the postwar American economic miracle also challenged the schools because it created a huge demand for higher education. So to compete with public schools, these private colleges and universities had to vary their curriculum, modernize their mission, and create new programs not envisioned by their predecessors.

There are some light moments in these histories of these schools. Most touch on the pleasantries of student life amid ideas, parties, and sports. You can discover the Purple Eagles of Ashland University, the pride of Mount Union's recent athletic success, and the improbable story of Franciscan University in Steubenville. You can read about how Antioch College was twice up for sale and discover why Denison University in the 1850s sued William T. Denison, for whom the school was named, for $10,000. Would you believe that in 1980 half of Urbana College's students were incarcerated? Find out which university, well into the twentieth century, had no paved road to its campus and which college on an April day in 1953 in less than two hours changed its affiliation from Presbyterian to Baptist. Discover why Mount Vernon Nazarene College has a day set aside in the spring for students, staff, faculty, and administrators to join together to plant flowers and trees.

The editors hope that readers will come to their own insights about particular places that interest them. These essays tell vivid stories of hopes and dreams, defeats and victories, and success over sometimes long odds. These schools followed the dictates of conscience and developed their own sense of how to educate. Over the decades societal changes economically and ideologically buffeted these colleges and universities, forcing them to change and adapt. But as the essays argue, they still see themselves as independent places with their own distinctive ideals that they hope to convey to their students. They see themselves as modern cradles of conscience just as strongly as did their nineteenth-century founders. At the beginning of the new millennium, they have achieved an impressive stability as a group and enormous status as state and national institutions, and they have every reason to expect that they will flourish in the future.

Antioch College

Establishing the Faith

SCOTT SANDERS

As Ohio commemorates its bicentennial in 2003, Antioch College celebrates its own sesquicentennial. The approach of such a milestone becomes all the more monumental against the backdrop of Antioch's distinguished, colorful, if not occasionally unfortunate, past. Scattered among its many successes—a distinctive liberal arts curriculum combining work and study, a revolutionary program of education abroad, and a unique participatory governance system, just to name a few—are the pitfalls of its history that can provoke wonder at how it has survived at all. Over its 150 years Antioch has endured bankruptcy, an auction, three suspensions, and a near-sale to the YMCA, and that's just half the story. Its propensity for controversy—a concomitant trait of intellectual freedom—is legendary, and while generally known for amiable disagreement in its last seventy-five years, its first were marked by sectarian strife that repeatedly threatened its existence. Despite such impediments, the college never lacked enthusiasm for its work, and at no time were its high aspirations, its quarrelsome ways, or its financial exigency more evident than in its earliest years.

Antioch was born out of a heated dispute between the founders of Meadville Theological School (now the Meadville/Lombard School of the University of Chicago) in Pennsylvania. Established in 1844 by two ostensibly like-minded Protestant sects, the Unitarian Association and the Christian Connexion (hereafter "the Christians"), Meadville was intended, as one Christian leader declared, to educate "young men who intended to preach the gospel—not of Calvin, nor of Wesley, but of Jesus." At issue was a statement by Henry W. Bellows, a prominent Unitarian minister of New York, that "the Christian denomination with its thousand ministers [Christian clergy actually numbered about half that figure], almost identical in opinion with us, if we will take charge of their theological education, will become

Earliest known photograph of the Antioch College Campus, ca. 1860

one with ourselves." The response to such condescension was perhaps best put in the Reverend John Ross's letter to the editor of the *Christian Palladium* in July 1845: "We have not yet approximated sufficiently near to denominational Unitarianism to grow giddy in view of the awful gulf below or the vast elevation above us." Fearing they might be "swallowed up" by their Unitarian friends, in 1848 the Christians withdrew from Meadville and struck out to establish a college of their own.

The dispute over Meadville merely scratched the surface of the differences between the Christians and Unitarians. The Christians professed a simple ecumenical faith, declaring "the Bible, our only creed; Christian character, our only test of fellowship and communion; private judgment, the right and duty of all men; our aim, the union of all Christians and the conversion of sinners." An amalgam of former Presbyterians, Methodists, and Baptists, their nondenominational position afforded wide latitude for their religious beliefs and left perhaps too much room for disagreement. Many distrusted any form of ministerial education at all, believing it inherently denominational and therefore "un-Christian."

The Unitarians, while similar in outlook to the Christians—both rejected creeds, valued freedom of worship, and believed in the essential goodness of humanity—more strenuously denied the divinity of Christ and sought enlightenment in sources other than Scripture. Also, they valued greatly their history of nonconformity and intellectualism in religious thought. By seeking to preserve this unique identity, Unitarians of the nineteenth century appeared sectarian in comparison to the Christians.

Beyond their theological disagreements, the two sects represented two distinct constituencies. The Unitarians represented a well-educated, individualistic, urban congregation, the Christians were mostly rural, salt-of-the-earth folks more interested in tent revivals, prayer meetings, and mass conversion than the scholarly, introspective form of worship the Unitarians represented. Most importantly for the development of Antioch history, the Unitarians had money while the Christians had none.

Finances aside, the Christians went at the founding of their new college with missionary fervor. At their annual General Convention in October 1850 at Marion, New York, they resolved to raise a sum of $100,000 "as the standard by which to measure [their] zeal and effort." An endowment of $50,000 was stipulated, which would be raised with the sale of 500 scholarships, much like a stock certificate in the college providing the investor the benefit of free tuition for one student, of $100 each. The convention further decreed that the college be located in the most healthful, inexpensive, and accessible place that also pledged the most money. Though not broadly supported at the convention, an influential minority of liberal Christian ministers provided for a nonsectarian college with no theology in its curriculum. The economics of building separate colleges motivated the Christians to found a coeducational institution. Both their lack of agreement on and commitment to these novel principles would create great tension for them and even greater problems for their college.

One issue all in attendance at the Marion Conference agreed on concerning the college was its name: Antioch, after the biblical Syrian city where, as written in Acts 9:26, the term "Christians" first appeared. Though possibly apocryphal, having not been revealed until 1913, the origin myth of the name Antioch is nonetheless worth retelling. Joseph Badger, an elder in the Christian Church and by 1850 paralyzed and dying, was asked to provide a motto to put over the door of the college library. Unable to speak, Badger replied in a scribbled note: "The disciples were called Christians first at Antioch. Call the College Antioch." The storyteller, his daughter, described it as the last act of his life, even though he died nearly two years after the Marion convention where the name was unanimously approved.

As to location, early consensus held that the college should be somewhere in western New York. Ohio took the lead in fund-raising, however, thanks largely to the efforts of the fanatical elder John Phillips of Lebanon, and it became the favorite as the apparent "seat" of the Christian Church. The publicity surrounding the proposed school aroused much interest across the state and engendered the kind of intercommunity rivalry common in the West as neighboring towns competed to deny one another internal improvements to insure their own prosperity.

"Judge" William Mills, who gained his "office" through the mediation of a few local disputes, had already achieved a measure of success at this sort of contest for the tiny Greene County village of Yellow Springs, his adopted hometown. Born in Connecticut in 1814, Mills had come west with his family in 1819. In 1827 his father, Elisha, purchased a rustic hotel near the iron-laden spring that gives the town its name and moved there from Cincinnati. By the 1840s William was the leading citizen among barely 150 residents, and he had big ideas. In 1845 he successfully wrested the route of the Little Miami Railroad away from nearby Clifton to Yellow Springs, with almost immediate impact. Thanks to Judge Mills, the railroad, and vast quantities of native limestone (from which lime, a key ingredient in concrete and fertilizer, is extracted), by 1852 Yellow Springs had developed into an important commercial center with a population of 1,500. Mills intended his town to become an educational center as well.

Though as many as eight Ohio towns considered themselves in the running, Lebanon and Yellow Springs were the strongest candidates, and they fought it out in the local newspapers over the issue. In February 1852 the editor of the *Xenia Torchlight* attacked the editor of a Lebanon paper, probably the *Western Star,* for referring to Yellow Springs as "a barren poverty-stricken oak knobs country, which produces only hazelnuts and a plant not good for cows." By then, however, the outcome was already beyond doubt, as Mills had presented the case for Yellow Springs (in typical western hyperbole, he claimed the area so healthful that its residents had to go elsewhere to die) along with a gift of twenty acres and a pledge of $30,000, rendering the *Western Star*'s barbs as so many sour grapes.

For their college president the Christians settled on the Honorable Horace Mann of West Newton, Massachusetts. Mann was one of the most famous people of his time, known as a brilliant public speaker (he was a perennial orator in Boston on the Fourth of July), an eloquent defense attorney (in 1848 he defended the sea captain Daniel Drayton in a landmark test of the Fugitive Slave Laws), and an outspoken antislavery congressman (attacking slavery as a "bedside institution"). A career reformer, he had championed such causes as temperance and proper care for the insane as well as abolition, but he received his greatest acclaim as a pioneer of American public education.

Massachusetts had formed the first State Board of Education in American history in 1837, and it in turn appointed Mann its first secretary. He threw himself into the job with characteristic fervor, publicizing the conditions of Massachusetts's common schools in *The Common School Journal* and in his twelve monumental *Annual Reports on Education.* Mann served the board indefatigably until 1849, often with little regard for his own well-being or for the feelings of those educators whose methods he found flawed or inadequate. When it came to advancing the cause, Mann let nothing stand in his way.

By 1850, as America's most recognizable educational reformer, Mann had become a natural candidate for a college president. He received an offer for the presidency of "a Missouri college" (possibly Marion College in Palmyra) as early as 1839, but he declined. In 1849 Mann refused a similar offer from Girard College in Philadelphia, founded as a school for orphaned boys in 1848 from a bequest from wealthy banker Stephen Girard, promising Mann a fine house and "light duties." He was, after all, still a member of Congress with responsibilities to the Massachusetts Eighth District.

Christians who heard Mann at a March 1852 speaking engagement in Rochester, New York, probably first recommended him for the presidency. The honor of approaching him for the position went to Elder Eli Fay, chair of the college committee. Though attracted by Antioch's nonsectarian and coeducational principles, an unsure Horace Mann vacillated and sought the counsel of friends and colleagues. In a letter to Lexington schoolmaster Cyrus Peirce, he asked, "Confidentially, what would you think of your humble servant's complying with a request to preside over this [college]?" Dr. Samuel Gridley Howe, a reformer and adventurer (he fought in the Greek revolution) perhaps most famous for being married to the suffrage leader Julia Ward Howe, told him, "You are of vastly more importance to the Institution over which you are invited to preside than it is or ever will be to you." Ultimately he convinced himself to take the job as an opportunity to mold the young minds (and morals) of the West, and on September 17, 1852, he accepted the unanimous election to the presidency of Antioch College.

That same day the Sub-Committee of Antioch College assembled to elect a faculty. They believed strongly that Antioch's professors should be of the Christian denomination since most of the students would presumably be of that persuasion. Of the six inaugural faculty positions, four were bestowed on Christian ministers (described as so zealous they would do the job for nothing), and the other two went to Mann's niece and nephew, Rebecca and Calvin Pennell. Mann had several conditions for acceptance of his new post, one of which that he have the right to choose two professors so at least some of his teachers would be familiar with his methods. Mann further demanded full control over the curriculum, high standards of moral conduct, and a house worthy of a college president. The founders also pledged to him a liberally endowed college free of financial worry and a handsome annual salary of $3,000.

In charge of constructing the campus was an influential and colorful Christian carpenter with the memorable name of Alpheus Marshall Merrifield. Dubbed the "Master Builder from Massachusetts," Merrifield had long supported the college project, he served on the committee that established Antioch and contributed $1,000 to its construction. He also supported the founding of a separate theological school, to which he gave an additional $500. Though untrained as an architect, he possessed extensive building experience and, perhaps most importantly, he thought in grandiose terms. Merrifield designed an imposing physical plant to support 1,000 students, employing a mix of the Greek, gothic, and Romanesque revival styles popular for institutional buildings of the day. The plans, which still survive in the

Antioch archives, called for a main building (its floor plan in the shape of a cross), flanked by "male" and "female" dormitories, and a president's house. Facing east toward the railroad and Yellow Springs's unique and picturesque glen, the sight of Antioch Hall (lauded incorrectly at the time as the largest structure on the highest ground in Ohio) rising above the broad lawn of Front Campus would be an impressive one for any rail traveler.

As Merrifield set about hacking the campus out of the thick forests of Yellow Springs, Mann convened the first meeting of the Antioch College faculty at his West Newton home in early November 1852. Though he would later discover otherwise, Mann wrote to Christian minister Austin Craig of the broad range of agreement among his teachers, "not only as to theory but in practical matters. We were all teetotalers; all anti-tobacco men; all anti-slavery men; a majority of us believers in Phrenology. . . . We agreed entirely in regard to religious and Chapel exercises, etc. etc." The primary source of future disagreement on the faculty was the founding principle of nonsectarian education and the one that most influenced Mann's decision to take the job. The Christians' professed ecumenism worked against Antioch in this case, as many of their constituents, including members of the faculty and board of trustees (specifically one A. M. Merrifield), opposed the notion of a college that would not advance the theological views of its own denomination. Indeed, from the outset of the college project a counterreformation was at work to turn Antioch into a Christian seminary.

The curriculum formed at that meeting was as progressive as any other of the day. It reflected the president's interest in phrenology, the early behavioral pseudoscience that formed the basis of all his educational efforts. The curriculum emphasized the sciences, history, and literature over the classics (though Latin and Greek were required, elective courses could be substituted for advanced classical language) and Mann's disdain for emulation, the tendency of students to compete for prizes, which he believed fostered unhealthy rivalries and hindered the learning process. Other modern elements included courses in didactics (teacher training), required physical education (for male students only), and a rudimentary form of independent study. Moral and ethical instruction was provided throughout, as well as lessons in personal hygiene and the development of oratorical skill.

The following year was a heady and busy one, particularly for Master Builder Merrifield. He not only supervised the project, but he also handled all the hiring and purchasing of materials. As their chief representative in Yellow Springs during construction, the founders had added "College Treasurer" to his other duties. In keeping accounts, however, Merrifield was well beyond his expertise; and it was during this time that the first signs of Antioch's financial misfortunes appeared. As pledges of money poured in, he declared the $400 annual fee to employ an accountant to be an unnecessary waste of money. He apparently knew more about wasting money than the nuances of bookkeeping. Though he projected initial building costs at $50,000, the final bill more than doubled that figure.

Merrifield's inadequacies aside, many of the road agents appointed to sell the scholarships intended for the endowment did so at dangerously low prices. In far too many cases they demanded only the 6 percent annual interest up front on a $100 note. In return for their support of the college, scholarship holders received a tenth of a vote to elect trustees and one student enrolled in perpetuity, neither of which could any institution of the time expect to fulfill on six dollars a year. Factor in the Christians and their general observance of the poverty of Christ in their own lives, and the inspiring educational dream of Antioch College stood in stark contrast to its numbing fiscal reality.

Nevertheless, Merrifield had set a feverish construction pace, instructing th laborers to work even on the Sabbath. Yet when Mann arrived with his wife, Mary, and their three sons in September 1853, the campus was in a chaotic state. The main building was sheathed in scaffolding, its familiar towers not yet in place, and South ("Gents") Hall was barely framed; only North ("Ladies") Hall had windows. The president's house did not exist except as a drawing in Merrifield's sketchpad. The Manns moved into a suite of rooms in North Hall as the unfinished "little Harvard of the West" and its undaunted president prepared for their mutual inauguration, set for October 5, the same day the Christians had passed their resolution to establish a college.

Three thousand spectators (described by Mary Mann as "a motley multitude that would have made a splendid show if their costumes were as brilliant as they were various") attended Horace Mann's inauguration. Yellow Springs, then a village of perhaps 1,500, was simply not equipped to accommodate such a great host, and many visitors had had to spend the previous night in their carriages. In appreciation he delivered a marathon address of 27,000 words, lasting perhaps two hours. As Mrs. Mann wrote to her father, the speech was "a fine dish of discourse to the music of eight to ten babies who cried about all the time." The Reverend T. Starr King said it contained enough inspiration to make a college flourish in the Sahara.

By that time a vigorous promotional campaign had produced nearly a thousand applications, the vast majority from Ohio. Few survived the harsh entrance examinations imposed by Mann, however, and only eight students advanced to the first college class. About 250 applicants qualified for enrollment in a Preparatory Department that in its long association with the college always boasted a significantly larger registration until the 1920s.

Overwhelmingly from Ohio, the first student body had a rough-hewn quality that appalled the vastly more cultured Manns; however, a core of students was possessed of a greater maturity, and their seriousness set high standards of scholarship. For example, Eli and Mahala Jay, two of the original eight college freshmen, had transferred from Oberlin College. Dissatisfied with its somewhat limited coeducation, they were attracted by Antioch's promise of equal treatment of the sexes. In particular Mahala wanted to read her graduation essay atop the college platform at her commencement, a right Oberlin then extended only to its male graduates. The Jays and other students like them—older, more experienced, and idealistic—helped guide, and periodically had to force, Antioch in living up to its own coeducational values.

The college faculty suffered from a lack of faith either in full coeducation or in their students' ability to carry it forward. There persisted among them notions of an inferior female intellect and disagreement on the morality of educating men and women together. Women were restricted from otherwise required instruction in physical education. At least one preparatory teacher did not permit his female students to deliver papers before the class from memory. President Mann himself expressed an inconsistency in his belief. He spoke often of "the Great Experiment," in almost biblical terms, but when confronted with the reality of college-educated women let loose on the world, he confided that, had he known this result, he might have "reconsidered presiding over a coeducational institution." It ultimately took the effort and will of its students to make Antioch deliver on its promise.

As they shaped its core values, Antioch students also, ironically, helped bring down its financial house of cards. The first operating budget allowed a maximum one-third of the 500 students to "hold" scholarships, but more than half of the first scholars held such notes. Inexpensive tuition (just eight dollars per year) and room and board contributed almost nothing to a paltry $6,000 annual income, and with no endowment the college opened with a deficit. It took just eighteen months to accumulate $75,000 in debts. Based on Antioch's original articles of incorporation, state law held the scholarship holders responsible for the debts of the college. Most of them cried foul, as they heaped their collective wrath upon Horace Mann, blaming him for the collapse. They judged his constant lecture touring across the state as neglect of his duties, though he quietly put most of the fees he earned into the meager Antioch treasury. Little did they know how much of his own money he had diverted to its coffers and how many IOUs he had received from the college treasurer for his salary.

Mann, of course, had little to do with Antioch's bedeviling finances. Ohio's depressed economy and the high interest rates in the 1850s made recovery increasingly difficult. Gifts of funds from influential eastern friends, including Peter Cooper, Henry Bellows, and Moses Grinnell, failed to reverse the debt. William Mills, the dynamic Yellow Springs man who had brought Antioch to town, would lose his entire fortune to a wash of claims against the college and the bubble of local land speculation burst by the Panic of 1857. The final insult came from Mills's own brother-in-law, Antioch trustee and local limestone magnate Joseph Wilson, who subsequently had Mills evicted from the grand mansion he had built in the center of town.

Mann received his greatest challenge not because of Antioch's financial problems but for his fierce nondenominationalism. From the time he agreed to serve as Antioch president, he had to defend his religious views against Christian criticisms. He had to respond to innumerable letters that sharply questioned his disbelief in the Trinity, even though the founders guaranteed him safety from such attacks. Upon revealing a plan (before the congregation of the First Christian Church of Yellow Springs) to teach all religions to Antioch students, he inadvertently galvanized the forces of religious conservatism, and they resolved to rid themselves of this president who sought to "Unitarianize" Antioch.

The debate over a literary or theological college had raged in the editorial pages of the monthly *Christian Palladium* since the Marion convention in 1850. Did not every other Protestant denomination advance their aims through higher education? A great majority of the Christian faith regarded establishing a seminary as a responsibility to the denomination. Master Builder Merrifield shared this view, and he took out his frustrations on the Manns by delaying completion of the president's house while constructing the campus. He pulled laborers and materials for the job constantly, and the stately home remained uninhabitable until the fall of 1854. A year before, Mann had written to his friend Samuel Downer in Boston that "Ohio growths are rapid growths; but this does not hold true of our house, which has not yet grown up to the chamber-floor." After finally completing the house, Merrifield neglected Mrs. Mann's request for a fence to protect the fruit trees and flowers she had brought from home, and the livestock that freely roamed the campus quickly consumed them.

Key insiders assisted the outside forces arrayed against Mann and the liberal educators: Merrifield, who by his time sat on the board of trustees, set about garnering enough votes on the board to remove the president, mathematics professor Ira Allen agreed to serve as Mann's replacement. In town the mutiny was led by Elder Derostus F. Ladley of the Christian Church, who if he did not think Mann an infidel at least said as much on one occasion, and to a lesser extent William Mills, who perhaps saw too much of his rapidly dwindling political capital at risk to oppose the plot.

The coup might have succeeded but for circumstance. The trustees met to appoint a new principal of the preparatory school in September 1856. Mann proposed acting principal John C. Zachos, who would go on to become a famous educator himself. The conservative faction supported a more politically reliable choice, Henry Burlingame, who had recently resigned from the college faculty. The board twice elected Burlingame (the president demanded a recount after the first vote), and a sectarian victory appeared imminent, but their candidate declined to serve, and Mann won by default.

A financial crisis further unraveled the plot, for by spring 1857 Antioch faced certain bankruptcy. The trustees had no alternative but to release the faculty outright. They chose soon thereafter to keep the college open while they sought its pecuniary redemption and to rehire all the instructors save two, the Reverend James Doherty, because of incompetence, and the pretender Allen. The following December Merrifield resigned from the board in disgust, never to return to the college he built, except once for two weeks in 1858 to exhort local parents to send their children to any other school but Antioch. There the plan died but for a final, pointless act, the publication in 1858 of *A History of the Rise, Difficulties and Suspension of Antioch College,* Allen's scathing diatribe against the Mann regime. In a battle of words Mann and his supporters had the advantage, however, and they soundly discredited *Rise, Difficulties and Suspension* as slander in *A Rejoinder to the Pseudo-History of Antioch College by Professor Allen,* edited by the Reverend Eli Fay, Mann's strongest advocate on the board.

Though the liberals now controlled the direction of the college, they fared little better than anyone else at controlling its finances. Past the point of desperation, they divested Antioch of its ruinous scholarships, brought suit against the holders of hundreds of delinquent notes, and tripled the cost of tuition. In a particularly dramatic moment a group of trustees and Mann himself put forth great sums of their own to retire one $20,000 claim against the college. Unable to satisfy another $27,000 suit, however, the board assigned Antioch College for its debts and put the property up for public auction. Antioch went on the block in Cincinnati on April 19, 1859. Francis A. Palmer of New York City, a friend of Antioch, a trustee, and president of the Broadway Bank, bought the college for $40,000 without an opposing bid. Palmer then turned control of a reorganized Antioch over to a new board of trustees. A new charter forbade the contraction of debt.

The spring of 1859 wore terribly on Horace Mann, who bore much of the responsibility of the reorganization ordered by Palmer. He carried an ever-increasing teaching load as members of his faculty defected for teaching positions at other institutions that actually paid them for their work. His many years of self-sacrifice for the causes dear to his heart—the common school, the abolition of slavery, the nurturing of Antioch—had caught up with him, and his often-fragile health had worsened. Exhausted, he tendered his resignation to the board in June, only to accept his unanimous reelection. He just never could say no.

Though he scarcely possessed the strength, Mann ascended the college platform one last time at the commencement of the class of 1859 to deliver the baccalaureate address. Harried as usual, he had not quite completed the speech. As he made his concluding remarks, he told the story of Admiral Nelson at the Battle of Trafalgar and then closed with the most fateful and stirring words conceived in an entire lifetime of legendary oration: "I beseech you to treasure up in your hearts these my parting words: Be ashamed to die until you have won some victory for humanity." It was the last public statement Horace Mann ever made.

Through the month of July he declined rapidly under the strain of endless meetings and searing summer heat. He ate little and hardly slept despite constant fatigue. On July 28 he wrote a brief note accepting a small payment, perhaps another gift to help keep Antioch solvent: "Dear Sir, Rec'd thirty-five dollars on acct. I am very sick." His illness proved so severe that before his correspondent, a Mr. Warner of Wrentham, Massachusetts, received the receipt, Mann had already died on August 2. He was buried on the Antioch campus, a spot marked since 1883 by an obelisk that bears his parting words. In 1860 Mary Mann had his body disinterred and reburied in the North Burial Ground in Providence, Rhode Island, next to Mann's first wife, Charlotte, who had died during childbirth in 1824.

The day before he died, Mann knew he neared the end, and he received a stream of visitors. Despite his delirium he spoke to each one, and true to form he managed an admonition for many on how to live their lives. To the moment of his death he thought of others, and of his college. He gave instructions to contact Henry Bellows, the Unitarian minister whose comments on the Christians started the idea of Antioch back in 1848, and urge him to take over the presidency. "More than any man I know of," Mann pronounced, "[Bellows] can carry [Antioch] on with zeal and energy, he must come and do it."

By his death, Antioch's first president began its transformation into a Unitarian college. Henry Bellows declined to serve as successor as Mann had hoped. Instead he found Antioch a new president. The Reverend Thomas Hill, a Harvard-educated Unitarian minister and husband to Dr. Bellows's cousin, Anne Foster Bellows, agreed to leave his pastorate in Massachusetts to fill the post. An astronomer and mathematician as well as a theologian, Hill was scholarly and serene in contrast to his fiery predecessor. In the raising of funds Hill found even less success than Mann with the Christians, as many of them strenuously objected to a Unitarian presiding over the college they founded. Equally frustrated with their poor stewardship of Antioch, he once wrote of the Christians as "slow to pay and quick to demand privilege." He made great inroads, however, in gathering support from other prominent Unitarians before returning to Harvard in 1862 to serve as its president. The college soon closed until operating costs and an endowment were raised. The board of trustees then resolved to determine which denomination would control Antioch. The Christians and Unitarians entered into an agreement whereby each had an equal opportunity to raise enough funds to reopen the college and establish a $50,000 endowment. The side that failed would forfeit its seats on the board, leaving the other in charge. In this contest the Christians had no chance. In 1865 the Reverend Edward Everett Hale, the most prominent American Unitarian (A.U.) of his time, presented Antioch with an endowment of $100,000, more than twice the prescribed figure. The Christians withdrew their meager support, and Antioch passed into Unitarian hands.

The college continued to operate on little more than the interest of that same $100,000 well into the twentieth century. Enrollment remained small throughout the period: there were no graduates in the Class of 1880. In 1881 the trustees voted to suspend operations for three years while they scrounged for funds. The Reverend J. B. Weston, a member of the first graduating class, served his third interim presidency during that time as little more than a caretaker. The board was returned to the Christians the following year under the auspices of the Christian Education Society, to whom the trustees gave the right to nominate the faculty. They reopened the college, though perhaps only to transfer Antioch's endowment to another institution, possibly Union Christian College in Merom, Indiana. In 1883 they entertained such a proposal only to discover restrictions placed on the money caused it to revert to the Unitarians if ever diverted.

Failing to raise any additional capital, though they managed to lose some, the Christian Education Society dissolved in 1898 when the board rescinded its faculty appointments. This decision put an end to the perennial sectarian strife, though money continued to be a problem. But for the lively presidency of future Ohio congressman and senator Simeon D. Fess (1906–17), which enjoyed strong enrollment in the Summer Normal program and featured an annual Chautauqua held on the college grounds, Antioch barely remained operational.

By 1919 the board was strongly considering selling Antioch. The Young Men's Christian Association, seeking to establish a college of its own, had approached the trustees with a $50,000 pledge to take over the campus. The trustees accepted and even elected a provisional president, YMCA educational director Grant Perkins. They did so on a mere promise of money, which spoke volumes about their desperate view of the situation.

Unitarian representation on the board of trustees had shrunk to one seat by that time, and as the trustees pondered the YMCA offer that seat came open. The American Unitarians in turn appointed its energetic lay vice president, Arthur E. Morgan, to look after its interests. Morgan, a flood-control engineer, was directing the construction of the Miami Conservancy District, a system of earthen dams to solve the Miami Valley's chronic flooding problems. A product of the Progressive Era, Morgan brought to the job a strong sense of social responsibility, establishing public parks rather than reservoirs behind the dams and providing permanent low-cost housing for construction workers and their families. Morgan also had ideas about education: he wanted young people to get a broad range of instruction in the classroom, but he saw great educational value in real-world experience. Morgan himself had never finished high school and attended the University of Colorado for only six weeks, but he had been a logger, a surveyor, and a miner before starting his own engineering company. At the time of his appointment as an Antioch trustee, he and his wife, Lucy, pondered building a school on a farm they had bought in the

Berkshires in Massachusetts (a farm that became the internationally famous school of modern dance, Jacob's Pillow).

The YMCA proposal evaporated once they discovered they were unable to raise the money and complete the sale, and the trustees began to look for a new president. Morgan had proposed an idea he called "industrial education" that afforded students a traditional education in the classroom and experience working in business and industry. Perhaps most importantly for Morgan, through the program's work component students could earn money to pay for college. It soon became clear to the rest of the board that Morgan was the best candidate for college president. After much modification by more qualified educators Morgan had hired, his ideas translated eventually into a cooperative plan of alternating work at a job and study on campus. Based on the "Schneider plan" then in place in the University of Cincinnati Engineering Department, the Antioch version applied to the entire curriculum and all majors. Morgan began to aggressively promote "the New Antioch" and to cultivate the support of industrialists and business leaders. The effort paid off. In 1921 the college reopened to its highest enrollment yet, 203; and by 1927 it rose to over 700. The nature of work-study meant that only half of the students were on campus at any one time; thus the program actually helped to stabilize Antioch's long precarious finances.

The Antioch reestablished under Arthur Morgan has since gained national prominence for its often-creative approach to higher education and campus governance. By encouraging invention and providing space for it, Antioch has contributed to the founding of important local industries in Vernay Laboratories (precision fluid handling products), Morris Bean, Inc. (aluminum casting), and the Yellow Springs Instrument Company (sensor technology). In 1930, by invitation of Arthur Morgan, the Samuel Fels Foundation launched its landmark longitudinal study of human development in a farmhouse adjacent to the campus that continues to this day under the management of Wright State University. In the natural splendor of its thousand-acre Glen Helen—a gift of Hugh Taylor Birch, a wealthy Antiochian of the 1860s who as a boy knew Horace Mann—Antioch created a model for outdoor education. In 1941 members of the faculty put their liberal anti-Communist views on the line in a small political journal called the *Antioch Review,* now a literary publication and widely regarded as one of the nation's finest "little magazines." Beginning in 1954, with strong support from President Samuel Gould, later architect and first chancellor of the State University of New York system, Antioch Education Abroad set standards for cross-cultural study.

The second half of the twentieth century saw Antioch enjoy its greatest period of intellectual ferment, endure some of its most significant challenges, and undergo its most dramatic changes. In the years following World War II there matriculated at Antioch future leaders in education (Warren Bennis), literature (Mark Strand), law (A. Leon Higginbotham), science (Stephen Jay Gould), civil rights (Coretta Scott King), politics (Eleanor Holmes Norton), and even television (Rod Serling). Beginning in 1963 with the acquisition of the Putney Graduate School of Education in Vermont, the college embarked on an expansion of almost missionary fervor that would see it grow to a mind-boggling network of thirty-five campuses, clusters, and field centers by 1975. With substantial funding from the Rockefeller Foundation, from 1965 the Antioch Program for Interracial Education and its student-led successor New Directions attempted the college's most radical admissions efforts to increase its cultural pluralism. Those same students would shut down the campus in Yellow Springs for six weeks in the spring of 1973 when cuts in federal financial aid threatened to terminate their educations. In 1978, having developed or taken over several graduate programs from New England to the West Coast, including the inventive School of Law in Washington, D.C., the board of trustees reincorporated the entire institution as Antioch University. The system remains in place today as a federation of five independent campuses, including the original Antioch College in Yellow Springs.

None of it might have happened without the tireless efforts of Horace Mann. He kept a poverty-stricken college afloat in its formative years on little more than willpower. He fought the forces of religious bigotry that sought to subvert the founding principles that he knew would make it a significant institution. He gave Antioch most all his time and money, neither of which he possessed in great abundance, to keep it from slipping into financial oblivion. In a sense, Mann died so that Antioch might live. Its 150th anniversary would have surely satisfied his martyr's complex.

SUGGESTED READING

Robert L. Straker (Class of 1925) was perhaps the most thorough historian of Antioch College during the nineteenth century. His *Unseen Harvest: Horace Mann at Antioch College* (Antioch Press, 1955), a brief study of operations in its early years, and *Horace Mann and Others* (Antioch Press, 1963), a series of biographical essays, are both well researched if a bit dated. "A Brief Sketch of Antioch College: 1853–1921," an unpublished pamphlet composed for the Antioch Centennial celebration in 1953, is highly detailed and informative and available on the Antioch College website. *Horace Mann at Antioch* (1938), by Joy Elmer Morgan, was written for the National Education Association in observance of the 100th anniversary of public education in 1936. Several biographies of Horace Mann exist, the most authoritative one written by Jonathan Messerli, *Horace Mann* (Knopf, 1971). Antioch is a featured institution along with Reed and Swarthmore in Burton R. Clark's comparative study *The Distinctive College: Antioch, Reed and Swarthmore* (Aldine, 1970). *Connected Thoughts: A Reinterpretation of the Reorganization of Antioch College in the 1920s* (University Press of America, 1997), by Stephen R. Herr (Class of 1983), presents an interesting if controversial view of the Arthur Morgan era that makes extensive use of Morgan's own personal papers housed in the Antioch Archives. *Antioch College: Its Design for Liberal Education* (Harper, 1946), by Algo D. Henderson and Dorothy Hall, is an administrative study by an Antioch president of the first twenty-five years after the reorganization in 1921. The memoir of James P. Dixon's presidency, *Antioch: The Dixon Era 1959–1975* (Bastille Books, 1991) by Edla Mills Dixon (Class of 1941), gives one view of the changes at Antioch through the turbulent 1960s and early 1970s. *An Antioch Career: The Memoirs of J. Dudley Dawson* (Antioch University, 1995) recounts a near-seventy-year association with the college of a longtime Antioch administrator. *Notes from a Pragmatic Idealist: Selected Papers, 1985–1997* (Antioch University, 1997), by Alan E. Guskin, is a series of essays and speeches by the former president and chancellor of Antioch University. *Not Just A Matter of Degree: 20-Plus Years at Antioch Los Angeles* (Antioch University, Southern California, 1996), by Harvey Mindess, is a memoir by a former psychology professor and one of the original faculty members at one of the three remaining West Coast Antioch campuses. *Five Experimental Colleges: Bensalem, Antioch-Putney, Franconia, Old Westbury, Fairhaven* (Harper and Row, 1973), edited by Gary B. MacDonald, includes an essay on the graduate school of education known today as Antioch New England written by former director Roy P. Fairfield. Doctoral dissertations on Antioch include Harvard F. Vallance, "Connected Thoughts: A History of Antioch College" (Ohio State University, 1936); George C. Newman, "The Morgan Years: Politics of Innovative Change—Antioch College in the 1920s" (University of Michigan, 1978); and Steven R. Coleman, "To Promote Creativity, Community and Democracy: The Progressive Colleges of the 1920s and 1930s" (Columbia University, 2000), which includes a study of Antioch during the Morgan era.

Ashland University

Patterns of Expansion

JOHN L. NETHERS

Ashland College was established by a Christian denomination, the Brethren, that grew out of the Reformation and the Anabaptist movement of the 1500s and 1600s. Many of these religious dissenters, including the Brethren, the Mennonites, and the Amish, were primarily of Germanic origins. They were driven from Europe by religious, military, and political persecution, frequently finding refuge in Holland. In the 1730s they began migrating to America, settling predominantly in Pennsylvania.

Experiencing countless hardships in the East because of their seemingly odd religious practices and because of the shortage of good farmland, they began migrating westward to set up their own separate communities. With the organization of the Northwest Territory in the 1780s and 1790s and subsequent creation of new states like Ohio in 1803, the West provided a refuge and a new home for these religious pioneers. The life of the Brethren consisted of two dynamic verities: religion and education, the church and the school—heart and mind. Even from their early history these Brethren had some college-trained men among their leaders. By the second half of the twentieth century the Brethren had become interested in establishing an institution in northeastern Ohio for educating ministers and other students, since many of their members had settled in the region.

When northeastern Ohio was suggested in the 1870s as a possible college location, the Brethren also considered Akron, Canton, Danville, and Louisville. Ashland, a town of only 2,000 and relatively isolated from the "evils" of urban society, seemed like an ideal setting and a wholesome environment, both for the sons and daughters of Brethren as well as other likely applicants from the surrounding area. Dr. Edward Jacobs, the tenth president, observed, "Perhaps as influential a group of ministers as could be found within the whole church lived in Ashland and Wayne counties." So within this constituency, at the Maple Grove Church near Ashland, a

Founders Hall–Administration Building

meeting was called in March 1877 in order to consider the matter; this gathering was "remarkably well attended."

Subsequently, a meeting was called later in the year for the purpose of asking the citizens of Ashland if they were interested in a college locating in their community; if so, they must subscribe to the amount of $10,000. Furthermore, the proposed college must offer and provide teacher training for the public schools, a department of science, a "classical course of high character," and "advantages of a higher education to young people—for both boys and girls." It was understood that this new institution would be a training facility for potential ministers and religious leaders, especially of the Brethren faith. To these requirements the citizen leaders of Ashland enthusiastically agreed.

Following the Board of Incorporation in 1878, a fifteen-member board of trustees was formed. After a charter was granted by the State of Ohio, efforts proceeded to find a president. Dr. S. Z. Sharp, a Brethren evangelist who had organized and participated in many love feasts within the area, became the first president. (Love feasts, usually an annual occurrence, are a tradition among Brethren when, at the time of communion, they have "washing of the feet" and also share dinner, the latter being symbolic of the Last Supper.) In 1878 Sharp and Brother Ezra Packer, who had been instrumental in seeing the need for a college, began soliciting funds and asking for pledges among congregations in Ohio, Indiana, Illinois, and Michigan for the purpose of erecting buildings. Fourteen acres of the original twenty-eight-acre building site were purchased for $2,900, and Founders Hall was constructed. George Washington Cramer, who later became a leading church architect in New York, designed Founders Hall. His fee was $100, which he later contributed to the college funds. This three-storied edifice with its impressive central tower, made of bricks from the clay soil right on the campus, was the central academic and administrative building until October 1952, when it was destroyed by fire.

Most of the promoters of this new endeavor were not experienced in creating a college. Thus they had overlooked the need for student housing. It was known, however, that some students would commute. While Founders was being erected someone asked, "Where shall the students be accommodated with lodging and board?" The trustees therefore borrowed $15,000 and constructed a boarding hall. The dormitory, known as Allen Hall, at first housed both men and women but ultimately only women; it was demolished in the 1970s to make room for the eight-story Memorial Library.

The first term began on September 17, 1879, with sixty students present; by the close of the college year there were 102 students. There were eight faculty members, including the "teaching" president. President Sharp received a salary of $750. The initial 1879 college catalog, under "General Information" and "Religious Exercises," informed the students that the college was "thoroughly Christian but not sectarian" and that the college "inculcates the spirit of plainness and economy in dress and manner of living and aims to adorn the mind rather than the body." Furthermore, it stated that "students who are members of the Brethren are required to attend Sunday School and Prayer Meeting services held in the College Chapel"; and all students were required to attend daily morning chapel, and non-Brethren students should attend their own churches on Sundays. The 1884–85 catalog noted that "this church is an advocate of plainness in dress though not a particular form and simplicity in manner of living. . . . One of the distinctive features of Ashland College, therefore, is that rich and poor meet upon the grounds of equality; that worth, not dress, is valued and respected, that economy, not extravagance, is fostered, and that a desire for usefulness, not show, is promoted." Ashland has always made plain its purposes and convictions.

Although the early years of the college opened with promise, serious problems soon faced the new institution. In 1881 a sharp theological division between the conservative and the progressive Brethren caused difficulties for the fragile institution, but staunch supporters among the progressive element won control and managed to maintain the college. In 1888 the college went into receivership, owing $41,000; the faithful trustees, however, paid off the debt and the college passed legally under the direction of the Brethren Church, and in August 1888 a new charter was issued and the name was officially changed to Ashland University. It remained a university until 1926, when it was designated a college; but in 1989 it officially changed its name back to Ashland University.

In 1896 financial problems again hindered the college's progress, and it was forced to close for two years. But with the debt liquidated, it opened again and has been in continuous operation since. Upon his arrival the new president, Dr. J. Allen Miller (1898–1906), besides being confronted with financial problems, "found two buildings on a bleak, desolate campus of thorns and briars." Another critic noted that the "grounds were covered with weeds, blackberry bushes, and baldwin apples." Supposedly Miller and his wife "knelt in prayer, pledging their lives to the enrichment of youth and asking God's blessing upon their efforts."

The fall term in 1898 opened with five faculty members with a curricula consisting of economics, English, history, Latin, language, literature, mathematics, music, philosophy, and theology. The academic year was divided into three ten-week terms. Classes met five times a week with forty-five minutes "allowed for each recitation." The catalog for 1900 revealed the additional offerings of French, Greek, German, natural sciences, bookkeeping, typewriting, and both vocal and instrumental music. The total enrollment varied between fifty and seventy students.

During the eight years of Miller's leadership, the college's significant progress and growth gave the institution a "new" beginning. The campus was made more attractive, trees were planted, especially evergreens, which came to characterize the hilltop school and are noted in the singing of the *Alma Mater:* "Remember among those pine trees upon the hill so blue." Greatly adding to the enrichment of the institution was the erecting of a much-needed gymnasium in 1902 at a cost of $6,000, joining Founders and Allen Halls. The gymnasium, funded through a gift from a member of the board of trustees, was a "tile building, with only a dirt floor and balcony around the playing area for spectators, appeared as fine as Madison Square Garden to those sports-loving fans. . . . A few years later a wood floor was installed, making the building more commodious." In that same year a "large ceremony was held to celebrate the record enrollment of over 100 students." Up to then it had fluctuated between thirty and forty students. The college in 1902 was now free from debt and had an endowment of $2,500.

By 1904 there were forty-five graduates, and at that year's commencement a notice was sent requesting "all alumni . . . to meet at Ashland on June 14 at 10:00 in the College for the purpose of effecting an organization." As a result the first reunion of alumni and students was held with 243 present. The commencement speaker at that year's address ascertained that "he who has never been a senior and a graduate has missed one of the supreme joys, and he who does not attend an occasional Commencement misses [out] on one of the best opportunities for reviving the golden glow of youth."

Furthering its commitment to the training of ministers, the university's Bible department was designated a seminary in 1906. Since that time the seminary has been an integral part of the university; according to the constitution and by-laws, it is a division of the university and not owned by the Brethren Church.

The university had only one dormitory, Allen Hall, and it housed both men and women. When it first opened women occupied the first floor and the men the second and third, but a few years later the women were housed in the front half and the men in the rear half of the hall, separated by a wooden wall. Fuel was supplied by coal, and the "dormitory management kept a record of the weight of each pail of coal . . . and the sum added to the student's account each month." Cleanliness was a serious problem due to the absence of adequate toilet and bath facilities. Toilets were outdoor wooden structures located some distance away from the dormitory; the men's facility was dubbed "Mother Jones." Coal oil–lit dormitory lamps and crude boardwalks were the way of life, but in 1910 campus life was modernized with the installation of gas lights and heating stoves in each room. At the same time, running water and new bathrooms, even though crude, made life more comfortable. Walking became less hazardous as the boardwalks were replaced with brick.

With the advent of World War I and the administration of Dr. W. D. Furry (1911–19), a men's military unit took over the dormitory and the college enrollment increased from 100 to 500 students. During World War I church support was lethargic, finances critical, and the buildings sorely in need of improvement. Thus, the trustees solicited churches and the community for funds. The resulting financial enrichment led to the building of a library and the installation of a modern heating plant in Founders Hall.

With the resignation of Dr. Furry in 1919, Dr. E. E. Jacobs (1919–35) assumed the presidency. Jacobs was known as an intellectual, a great scientist, and an excellent administrator, and Ashland was fortunate that he remained in office for sixteen years. New academic departments were added, including music, speech, and business, and a successful endowment campaign was launched. A new library was constructed, Miller Hall, and the holdings expanded from 3,000 to 14,000 books. Further restructuring occurred with the establishment of the publicity and alumni offices.

The university had been recognized as a teacher training institution by the State Department of Education as early as 1925, but a significant accomplishment was securing in 1930 full accreditation by the North Central Association of Colleges and Secondary Schools and the Ohio College Association. (Actually, prior to the mid-1920s there was little concern by colleges to have their teacher programs certified.) Further improvement in the academic programs was the creation of a summer school and the beginning of Saturday classes, especially for teachers, who needed to upgrade their training and gain certification. In the spring of 1930 the Theological Seminary was enlarged and the offerings within the department expanded.

During the administrations of Dr. C. L. Anspach (1935–39) and Dr. E. G. Mason (1939–45) there were reorganizations of the academic philosophy and the standardization of courses that permitted the institution to reenter the North Central Association and the Ohio College Association. A major building addition to the college was the gift in 1940 of a palatial residence known as the Myers Memorial Home. Within a block of the campus, Myers became the music building, a location that greatly enhanced the department. The faculty now numbered fifteen with doctoral degrees and thirty-two with master's degrees, a key factor in maintaining accreditation. During the 1920s enrollment fluctuated between 100 and 200 students, but by 1931–32 it had grown to 454. However, during World War II, with many students going off to war, the mostly female student body dropped to around 100. Nonetheless, the "doors were kept open" with the total academic program maintained. As one critic observed, "Ashland College was born in the midst of crisis and has weathered many crises throughout her history, [but] crises have been conceived as challenges [to] its leaders, faculty, students and community."

When Mason resigned in 1945, Dr. Raymond W. Bixler, a member of the history department, was selected as president. Although presidents generally had been members of the Brethren faith, Bixler was a Methodist; he served for only three years before happily returning to the teaching faculty. During his administration the influx of returning veterans boosted the enrollment from 100 to over 600, the largest to that time. This required the addition of married veterans' housing, designated Glenn Haller Court, in the form of twelve Quonset huts, which made for a "lively little community." After the veterans left, these buildings proved to be both a blessing and a sore spot; they were used by various departments until the last two were torn down in the late 1980s to make room for parking. Without question, the influx of veterans with their GI Bill of Rights, often commuters and over twenty-one, brought challenges to conservative traditions. As was frequently said, "They had seen the world and they were more worldly."

In the autumn of 1948 Dr. Glenn L. Clayton, a thirty-seven-year-old history professor from Ohio State University and a member of the Brethren faith, was inaugurated as the college's youngest president. He remained for twenty-nine years, and during his presidency enrollment grew from 300 students to over 3,000, and in 1970 the largest freshman class in Ashland's history was enrolled with 1,000 students. In 1950 Clayton presented a ten-year plan that included more buildings, additional faculty, increased enrollment, and curriculum advancement. Another significant project of the plan was to substantially increase the financial endowment of the college. This was successfully achieved through vigorous and persistent efforts. As with many private and independent colleges, Ashland could not exist without the generosity of alumni and friends, as it has always depended heavily on grants, donations, and private and corporate giving.

The college's long desire for a chapel was met in 1950 when the National Women's Missionary Society of the Brethren Church funded the building now known as University Memorial Chapel. It was completed in 1952 at a cost of $176,000. That same autumn a great tragedy shook the college community. On the night of October 20 the oldest building and the hub of the campus, Founders Hall, was destroyed by fire. Albert T. Ronk observed in his *History of the Brethren Church* that "nothing remained but smoking embers. . . . The loss seemed a catastrophe. . . . Yet, that fire might have been a benefit in disguise." A week later, in an all-night session, the trustees and the president made a momentous decision. After much deliberation and despite considerable argument for closing the college forever, they determined to take the insurance money and rebuild. Fortunately, the college remained open that autumn term by utilizing classroom space in the new chapel and some additional community facilities. Ronk sensed that "sympathizers among Ashland College friends, Brethren and non-Brethren alike, thrust hands deep into pockets to provide funds to carry on." Consequently, the $98,000 insurance money from Founders was used for the building of a student union, which was started the next March and opened that October; it also provided temporary classroom space.

A new Founders Hall was completed in 1954, incorporating the foundation stones and chimney from the old structure. To meet the immediate needs of student housing, several surplus army barracks were erected. Under various programs entitled "Programs for Quality" and a complimentary philosophy "Accent on the Individual," the institution changed from a commuter college to a residential campus.

After erecting the new Founders and student union, college buildings "seemed to spring up like mushrooms." Beginning in 1956, with Edward E. Jacobs Hall, and lasting until 1968, four additional residential halls were built—Myers, Clayton, Clark, and Kilhefner—as well as four fraternity houses, known as Fraternity Circle. In addition, rapidly appearing on campus were a new library (a few years later being converted to Patterson Student Center); the Charles F. Kettering Science Center; the Redwood Dining Hall; Kates Gymnasium; Conard Field House; Hoffman Natatorium; the Arts and Humanities Building and adjoining Hugo Young Theater; and Myers Convocation Center. Capping off this building program was the tearing down of Allen Hall and in its place the building in 1972 of the impressive eight-story, centrally located Memorial Library.

Since the 1960s Ashland has offered off-campus college credit classes at the nearby Mansfield State Correctional Institution and, beginning in the 1970s, at the Grafton Correctional Institution. The affiliations, classroom facilities, and academic offerings have varied over the years, but Ashland is compensated by the Ohio Department of Rehabilitation and Corrections, although it receives some funding from the federal government. This unique program is offered to inmates who can pass the GED equivalency tests and is essentially an aspect of their rehabilitation. It has been a meaningful and beneficial program to the university in terms of financial support, as well as complementing its humanitarian mission.

The college also saw parallel growth in the theological seminary, and in 1958 it moved from the main campus to the John C. Myers Home on Center Street, two blocks away. Under the direction of Dean Joseph R. Shultz, a seminary library and the first chapel were completed in 1964. Soon thereafter the Myers and Miller gardens and property were purchased and became part of a six-acre campus. Campus apartments and the Ronk Memorial Chapel were built in 1970 and additional classrooms in 1973. With this expansion program and the improvement in both faculty and programming, the seminary was fully accredited by the Association of Theological Schools in 1969. Its enrollment grew from eighteen to nearly 500 students. In 1976 the seminary added a fully accredited doctor of ministry program.

As Ashland College entered the 1960s and the period of the Vietnam conflict, it was confronted by the civil unrest that beset the entire nation. As President Clayton noted, "Ashland was not exempt from these disturbing trends." He further asserted, "Our student body was no longer regional . . . but reflected a cross-section of urban and rural homes from many states and was sure to feel the impact of broad national movements . . . [and the] new morality and rising tides of change." Although the invasion of Cambodia in April 1970 led to a "wave of student unrest, protest, and violence on many campuses," Ashland was relative free of turmoil at this time. But the tragic and infamous event at nearby Kent State University on May 4, 1970, in which four students were killed, caused sympathy pains to be felt on many campuses, including Ashland. As a result of a student-faculty march from the campus through downtown Ashland and other demonstrations, the college closed for two days.

Further complicating matters, the college had scheduled a well-advertised major lecture for May 10 with the arrival of comedian Bob Hope. Eight thousand tickets had been sold and among the guests to attend was Governor James Rhodes. Hope, sympathetic to the war, symbolized the conflict to its supporters. Knowing that he was coming to the Ashland campus for a major address, students from other colleges started flocking to the area by May 8 amid rumors that there would be a major antiwar demonstration. Townspeople, especially those living near the campus, were greatly disturbed by the "demonstrators who were bedding down in their yards." The situation on campus became highly volatile, and the mayor and city officials alerted the college administration that they "doubted their ability to keep order." Adding to the tension was the discovery of a homemade bomb hidden in the student union's men's room.

The college administration, realizing the inflammatory environment, awakened the students on the morning of May 9 at 2:00 A.M. and told them "to vacate the campus and not to return until [May] 20th." The institution was then shut down.

Only a few security and administrators were permitted on campus. Bob Hope was informed of the situation, and he agreed not to come, graciously returning the $15,000 speaking fee. Fortunately, the campus was quiet the rest of the summer.

In the early 1970s the college joined other private colleges facing declining enrollments and financial crises. Factors such as unemployment, a precarious economy, changing demographics, and the increased attractiveness of public institutions of higher learning strongly undermined the financial stability of numerous colleges, even threatening some with closure. For Ashland this meant, among other things, tight fiscal management and a reduction in faculty and administrative personnel.

After serving so admirably as president for twenty-nine years, Dr. Clayton resigned in 1977, realizing that a "change of administration might be for the best interests of the college." He was succeeded by Dr. Arthur L. Schultz, who became enmeshed in the college's financial crisis. After two rather stormy years he stepped down in 1979, and Dr. Joseph R. Shultz, the dean of the seminary, became Ashland's twenty-fifth president. Shultz, helped by two most successful capital campaign efforts, "A Time of Opportunity" and a "Partnership in Excellence," brought in much-needed capital. The various departments were reorganized into five schools: the Schools of Arts and Humanities, Business Administration, Economics and Radio/TV, Education and Related Professions, and Sciences. Then in 1981 a School of Nursing was added. In 1976 the Master of Education program began, followed in 1978 by a Master of Business Administration program, both of which have enjoyed phenomenal growth. The college also established a number of branch campuses.

Two important academic programs attached to Ashland University are the John M. Ashbrook Center for Public Affairs, named for a former Ohio congressman and American political conservative, and the Gill Center for Business and Economic Education. Both were established in the 1960s but have greatly expanded since. The Ashbrook Center is "an academic forum for the study, research and discussion of the principles and practices of American constitutional government and politics." It annually hosts a series of campus lectures and conferences, publishes scholarly monographs and books, and provides internship opportunities for students interested in careers related to public affairs. The Gill Center programs are designed primarily for business people, teachers, and students to enhance their understanding of economics and the private enterprise system. Both centers reach out to the public and are looked on as excellent public relations for the university.

In 1970 the seminary began its satellite extension, and the institution followed with a combined total of fourteen program centers. This seemingly created a "new Ashland College." The enrollments in these graduate programs, together with the seminary, by 1989 comprised nearly 50 percent of the total enrollment. Enrollment, off- and on-campus, reached over 4,000, the highest in its history. There were now more than eighty academic majors with six undergraduate degrees and six graduate degrees.

During this economic crisis an innovative program was the establishment of a high school academy. Its major purpose was to bring in needed revenue and to attract students to "fill up empty dorm and classroom space." Fully accredited and professionally staffed" with fifteen faculty members, it lasted from 1981 to 1985. The high school had its own classrooms, housing, faculty, and administration. At first there was much enthusiasm and optimism, but at its peak it had only sixty-five students registered; however, it had two graduating classes, five students in the first and seventeen in the second. It collapsed primarily because it failed to bring in sufficient funds and students.

In 1989, after a two-year feasibility study, the board of trustees voted to officially change the name to Ashland University, which was formally announced at that year's May commencement. This designation was the result of much debate. The change, undoubtedly, more appropriately represented the role the institution played in higher education, but also it was an "aspect in the development of a strategic plan that [called] for the consideration of several new programs for the 1990s." Thus, the university was still to maintain a genuine concern for it historic undergraduate mission of liberal arts and professional studies but at the same time develop further graduate programs.

In the past two decades the university budget has grown from $11 million to $70 million. Much of this growth has occurred under the administration of Dr. G. William Benz, a Presbyterian who assumed the presidency in May 1993. Soon after, under the slogan "A Vision Worth Pursuing" and the prevailing philosophy of "Accent on the Individual," Benz outlined programs for the enhancement of the institution. These changes are apparent in the university's greatly increased financial strength and stability; significant growth in enrollment, particularly with respect to graduate and nontraditional students; strengthened academic programs; major increase in donor support; and improvements and additions to facilities and the physical plant and an upgrading in the appearance and upkeep of the campus.

The new state-of-the-art Hawkins-Conard Student Center was dedicated in the fall of 1996. During the mid-1990s the main campus and the satellites were equipped with the technology for teaching and learning in the information age. Governance changes were instituted by converting five academic schools into the Colleges of Arts and Sciences, Business and Economics, and Education, with each headed by a dean.

In January 1998 the Ohio Board of Regents granted authorization for Ashland to offer the Doctor of Education in educational leadership; in June fourteen doctoral students were admitted to the program. In the same year the university became affiliated with the Council of Graduate Schools, the largest national council representing the interests of graduate education. The institution now offers master's degrees through the Colleges of Education and Business and Economics and the Ashland Theological Seminary and doctoral degrees in the College of Education and Ashland Theological Seminary.

In the mid-1990s an environmental science program was established to "provide specific environmental training for students who wish to pursue a career in environmental science or in biology, chemistry or geology with an emphasis in environmental science." A popular and expanding program, it recognizes that many scientific investigations and research projects today and in the foreseeable future deal with environmental problems. This program has been augmented with the addition of three different parcels of land within a few miles of the campus. Referred to as "environmental preserves," they encompass eighty-three acres and are different in terms of the terrain and wildlife. The program has been further augmented by an environmental lecture series funded through several grants.

The Ashland Theological Seminary, with the opening 1999 autumn semester, registered 760 students and is the twelfth largest seminary in the United States and Canada and the largest in Ohio. The student body represents more than seventy denominations and/or religious organizations from almost every state in the nation and fourteen foreign countries. The seminary also offers extensive programs at its campuses in Cleveland and Detroit, plus selected courses in Columbus and Akron.

Ashland University competes in intercollegiate athletics. As with other programs, many changes have occurred since their introduction in the 1920s. Amusingly, because of the restriction on football exacted in the will of major donor Lydia Fox of Miamisburg, football in the earlier years had been forbidden, but in a 1923 meeting of the board of trustees this ban was lifted. As early as 1905–6 the college had sponsored basketball and baseball teams; however, they competed mainly against noncollege competitors such as YMCAs. In 1929 Ashland joined the Ohio Athletic Conference. There was much enthusiasm for the football team as they won six out of seven games in that inaugural year. Thus, a longtime landmark was added to the campus in Redwood Stadium. Not only used for recreational purposes, it was the facility for commencements and local high school football games. It was torn down in the mid-1960s to pave way for two new dormitories; however, especially at homecoming, alumni reverently and nostalgically reflect on the heroics at the old facility. Finding itself in need of a new football field, the college and the city school system joined efforts in 1964–65 to build Community Stadium, which lies a few blocks south of campus.

Late one night in October 1926 a fire destroyed the original gymnasium that had served the college since 1902. Shortly thereafter a new gymnasium appeared, which was considered a "show case" when erected in 1927. Besides hosting many heated collegiate basketball games, it functioned as a community facility for nearly thirty years. Finally the "old" gym was abandoned in 1966–67 and used as a storage facility until it was torn down in 1990.

By the mid-1960s, with the need for additional space, a new athletic complex, Kates Gymnasium and the adjoining Hoffman Natatorium, were constructed. Within the next several years the athletic facilities were complemented with Conard Field House and the Wurster Fitness Center. The university, with the growth of women's athletics and with competition in twenty intercollegiate sports, is contemplating building further recreational facilities.

In the spring of 1948 Ashland dropped out of the Ohio Athletic Conference, joined the NAIA's Mid-Ohio Conference for eighteen years, and played in the Division II Heartland Collegiate Conference until 1990, when it affiliated with the Midwest Intercollegiate Conference (MIFC) for football and the Great Lakes Valley Conference (GLIAC) for all other sports. The two conferences merged in 1995.

Without a doubt, the strongest tradition is the heritage of the purple and gold eagles. (Purple and gold have been the college colors since 1900.) The college's athletic teams competed as the Purple Titans from 1928 until the autumn of 1933 when the college became the Purple Eagles as the result of a contest sponsored by *The Collegian*. The name "Purple Eagles" was supposedly inspired both by FDR's National Recovery Act's symbolic blue eagle and the national bird. Stuffed and wooden eagles, eagle jewelry and jackets, and a whole array of eagle paraphernalia adorn the shelves at the university bookstore. The most visible, striking, mysterious, and controversial are the imposing eagle statues spread around the campus that were once the corporate symbol of the Case Implement Company. In the 1970s the company gave the university the molds for the eagles and donated the eight-foot eagle that had adorned their corporate headquarters in Columbus. This eagle, called Old Abe, is painted purple and gold and perches boldly atop a four-foot round metal world in front of Kates Gymnasium.

Whereas literary societies, such as Pierian, Dallas, Philomathean and Hesperian, once were an active part of student life, today the social fraternities and sororities—the so-called Greeks, who appeared on campus in the 1960s—address the needs of numerous students. The Greek activities, especially the competition among these various organizations, certainly add liveliness to campus life.

Unlike today, when there is an excessive amount of ready entertainment, the students, especially prior to World War II, provided for their own—YMCA and YWCA, gospels teams, literary societies, scavenger hunts, popcorn- and candy-making parties, unscheduled ball games, and a few faculty chaperoned dress-up parties. Students were informed that "dancing, card playing, billiard-playing, and visiting any billiard soloon [*sic*] or any immoral place are forbidden." Furthermore, "The university is a place for work. Young persons seeking chiefly social enjoyment

✓ ed INLEX

____ On Inlex   ___ Not on Inlex   Date: _____

____ On Inlex   ___ Not on Inlex   Date: _____

C.I.P.   ___ Yes   ___ No

TITLE: _____

SERIES TITLE: _____

CALL #: _____

UPDATE: ___ Yes ___ No   Call #: _____

_____ other library   _____ replacement

✓ ed Bibliofile

___ On Bilbiofile   ___ Not on Bibliofile   Date: _____

___ On Bilbiofile   ___ Not on Bibliofile   Date: _____

___ Collection Code   ___ Media Code   ___ Location Code

should look elsewhere to gratify their wishes . . . as their presence tend to demoralize those of higher aspirations." Despite the rules, supposedly "cards were secreted into ingeniously-contrived spots."

Although numerous colleges banned students (especially underclassmen) from bringing cars to the campus, Ashland, although it was discussed by various administrations, never officially prevented freshmen from having cars. Evidently this was because the college had many commuters, as well as students from outside Ohio, especially after World War II. Nevertheless, President Clayton emphasized that automobiles were "greatly discouraged."

When the college was founded, smoking was prohibited on campus, as it was forbidden by the teachings of the Brethren Church. In fact, smoking was not permitted on campus until the 1960s; of course, it was frequently hidden. By the 1990s growing concerns about the dangers of cigarette smoke brought a ban on the campus sale of cigarettes and limited smoking to specific campus areas. At the request of the student government and with a ruling by the board of trustees, there was no smoking in residence halls beginning in the academic year 2000–2001. Alcoholic beverages were forbidden on campus prior to 1960. With an increasing number of student requests from 1970 until 1990, alcoholic beverages were eventually permitted on campus. Then, with the stricter state restrictions on the usage of alcohol by underage college students and the dangers of institutional liability, the trustees ruled that beginning in 1990–91 no alcohol would be permitted on campus.

The entire Ashland community is enriched culturally and socially because of the university. The Departments of Music and Fine Arts, for example, since the birth of the college, have provided activities and entertainment for town and gown. The university radio/television department, through WRDL 88.9 FM and WRDL TV 2, also serves the Ashland community. A communicative arts major in the field of radio and television was established in the 1960s. This popular major offers a range of laboratory experiences for students through the campus radio and television stations. Besides airing college activities, both the radio and TV stations carry a wide variety of community events, which contribute toward good public relations. Moreover, the university contributes substantially to the local economy. The Ashland Chamber of Commerce estimates that the total dollar impact of the university on the local community is "countless millions." With over 600 full-time employees and many part-time, the university is among the three largest employers in Ashland County. And since 90 percent of these employees live in the nearby area, most of the $25 million annual payroll is spent in the Mansfield-Ashland community. In 1995 these employees paid $315,000 in city taxes.

From an institution of fewer than 100 students and ten to fifteen faculty members and three buildings on fourteen acres during its first few years, the university has grown to nearly 6,000 students, 220 full-time faculty, and thirty-five buildings on more than 100 acres. With a minimal number of offerings in those early years, Ashland now offers more than seventy majors, including hotel and restaurant management, radio and television, international studies, toxicology and environmental science, and sports medicine. And with only 25 percent of the faculty having doctoral degrees in the 1950s, the university faculty with doctorates is now over 80 percent. In 1906 the college had an annual budget of $7,000; it now is nearly $70 million. And what was once just one campus, Ashland now offers programs at thirteen other sites throughout Ohio. In the college's early years the student body was generally Brethren, but today according to the "Report of the President, 1998–99," the university has nearly 2,000 full-time students of diverse religious and ethnic backgrounds on the main campus. Some 85 percent come from Ohio—from sixty-two of the state's eighty-eight counties—while the remainder come from twenty states and twenty-five countries.

Ashland University, although not as strongly tied to the Brethren Church or as dependent upon it for financial support as at the time of its founding, still has a deep commitment to the Christian faith and its affiliation with the Brethren Church. Neither Ashland University nor the Theological Seminary is owned by the Church but, rather, by the board of trustees, which has to have half of its thirty-nine members as Brethren. Entering students do not have to take a pledge to any religious affiliation, neither are they required to attend chapel service; and belonging to any college religious organization is voluntary. The original required daily chapel services later became a three-time-a-week requirement and then weekly; in 1968–69 the requirement was dropped altogether. In 1999 there was instituted a midweek voluntary chapel service. Sponsored by the Department of Religious Life, the service offers participants a twenty-five-minute inspirational service conducted by persons of various Christian traditions. In 1999–2000 more than 400 different students identify with these student activities; of course, some participate in several organizations. All undergraduate students must take a three-semester-hour credit in religion to meet the graduation requirement, but this requirement is met by a variety of nondenomination religious study courses.

The 1998–99 mission statement for Ashland University states that it "is a mid-sized regional teaching university historically related to the Brethren Church. Our mission is to serve the educational needs of all—undergraduate and graduate, traditional and non-traditional, full and part time—by providing educational programs of high quality in an environment that is both challenging and supportive." Furthermore, the programs "emphasize both the importance of liberal arts and sciences and the need to provide initial and advanced preparation in selected professional areas—including business, education and theology—which enables our students to lead meaningful and productive lives in the world community." The university is built on a "long-standing commitment to Judeo-Christian values that stresses the importance of the each individual." Ashland University enters the new millennium with a spirit of optimism and a commitment to its rich heritage.

Suggested Reading

Several general histories of Ashland County provided useful material: H. S. Knapp, *A History of the Pioneer and Modern Times of Ashland County* (J. B. Lippincott, 1863); George William Hill, *History of Ashland County* (Williams Bros., 1880); A. J. Baughman, *History of Ashland County* (S. J. Clarke, 1909); and Betty Plank, *Historic Ashland County*, vols. 1 and 2 (Ashland County Historical Society, 1987–95). A most valuable source on the relationship of the Brethren Church to Ashland University was Albert T. Ronk, *History of the Brethren Church* (Brethren Publishers, 1968). The sesquicentennial booklet *Ashland, Ohio: Past and Present in Word and Picture* (1965) proved useful.

Clara Worst Miller and Glenn E. Mason, *A Short History of Ashland College 1873–1953* (Brethren Publishers, 1953), provided an insightful view of that period. Duncan R. Jamieson and Kristine M. Kleptach, *The Eagles of Ashland* (Ashland University Press, 1994), and Joseph R. Shultz, *Ashland from College to University* (Landoll, 1995), were of topical usage. President Glenn L. Clayton's two-volume, unpublished survey "Whispering Pines and Purple Eagles: A Personal View of Ashland College, 1948–77" conveys an account of his administration. Clayton, who has a doctorate in history and is still working at the college, gives penetrating insight into the functioning of the university during his lengthy association with it.

Many useful articles were found in the Ashland University Library archives: S. Z. Sharp, "The Origin and Early History of Ashland College: 1878–1882 (n.d); "Ashland College Songs," *Ashland College Bulletin* vol. 19 (Oct. 1945); "Traditions and Customs," *The Key* (1946–47); "Fifty Years of A.C. Presidents," *Ashland Collegian*, Oct. 20, 1948; "The Changing Shape of Ashland College," *Brethren Evangelist* (Feb. 1978); "A Historical Vignette: Founder's Day Centennial Worship Service" (Feb. 19, 1978); and "What College Should I Attend," *Brethren Evangelist* (Oct. 1998). Several official university publications were also useful: *Accent Magazine* (Winter 1997; Spring, Summer, Winter, 1999); the undergraduate and graduate catalogs (1998–99); and the president's annual reports (1996–99).

A few articles from the local *Ashland Times Gazette* were valuable: "Traditions at Ashland College," Feb. 22, 1978; "AU President Looks at Past, Future at Start of Year," Aug. 25, 1999; "Students Back to Class Today," Aug. 30, 1999; "University Acquires Equipment to Enhance Video/TV Curriculum," Sep. 18, 1999; "AU's Strength Built upon Continuous Improvement," (Sep. 18, 1999); and "Yesterday, Today, Tomorrow," Dec. 30, 1999. A few electronic sources were of value as well in preparing this article; see the websites for Ashland University, the Church of the Brethren, and the Ashland Park Street Brethren Church.

During the year 1999 and through the spring of 2000 interviews were conducted on the campus with many Ashland University personnel, some of whom are retired: James A. Barnes, Glenn L. Clayton, Robert C. Cyders, Mary Ellen Drushal, William H. Etling, Frederick J. Finks, Michael Gleason, William J. Goldring, Steven M. Hannan, Susan B. Heiman, Al King, Fred Martinelli, William W. Mast, Mary Alice Mielke, Mia Preston, Donald Rinehart, David Roepke, Joseph R. Shultz, Stanford K. Siders, Thomas Stoffer, Ralph V. Tomassi, William B. Weiss, and Robert G. Zinkan.

Baldwin-Wallace College

A Microcosm of America

Norman J. Clary

To examine the history of Baldwin-Wallace College is to see a microcosm of the changes of American life across time. The college has been representative of much of the evolution of American college education and has also shared in the achievements and the problems in the country's development. The college evolved through several stages from what was at first a primary school called the Berea Seminary, chartered in 1837, which was expanded in 1838 into an academy of both primary and secondary levels called the Berea Lyceum School. In its origin the institution was part of the movement of various American religious denominations to found communities to promote the pursuit of religious life and the study of the liberal arts and, frequently, the acquisition of practical and vocational skills. From these beginnings the lives of Berea as college and town intertwined. The aim of this account is to trace the stages of the college's evolution as it reflected the development of the country.

The town was founded in 1836 as a Methodist communal association by James Gilruth, Henry Sheldon, and John Baldwin. Sheldon and Baldwin were from Connecticut and Gilruth was from western Virginia. All were devout Methodists and, like their denominational peers, were against the use of tobacco or liquor. Like most northern Methodists, all three were opposed to slavery. While Sheldon and Gilruth were preachers, Baldwin had taught school. All three farmed, and in 1828 Baldwin began farming with property on both sides of the East Branch of the Rocky River, where Baldwin Lake in Berea is today.

In 1836 the three men, who had met each other through their Methodism, founded the Community of United Christians and named it for the New Testament town of Berea. By the spring of 1837 about thirty families had joined. The purpose of the community was to promote "holiness," cleanse the members of sinfulness,

From left: Josiah Holbrook, John Baldwin, and Wilhelm Nast

relieve the oppressed of the "human family," and spread "useful knowledge." The members immediately built a meetinghouse large enough to seat everyone and also to house their school, the "Berea Seminary," for which they received a charter from the state on March 14, 1837, the earliest of several foundation dates for what would become Baldwin-Wallace College. The school opened in the meetinghouse on April 3 with twenty-four children taught by the Reverend John L. Johnson. Unfortunately, the inflated land prices of 1836 and then the Panic of 1837 hurt the little community economically, causing the first Berea's decline.

Sheldon then appealed to Josiah Holbrook of New England and New York City, founder in 1827 of the lyceum movement, through which he became one of the foremost educational reformers of his time. Holbrook came west to help refound the community and school. Sheldon had visited Holbrook in 1834 in Baltimore and had learned that more than 3,000 towns across the northeastern United States were participating in his lyceum movement. Indeed, the 1837 charter of the Berea Seminary referred to Berea as a "lyceum village." In accordance with Holbrook's concept, each lyceum village was linked with an academy, or lyceum, that would provide instruction in literature, religious principles, science, and skilled craftsmanship and would train teachers to serve at additional lyceums. In addition, the lyceum villages were expected to promote adult education through libraries, science museums, and public lectures by such notable figures as Ralph Waldo Emerson, Daniel Webster, William Lloyd Garrison, Charles Dickens, and Susan B. Anthony, who in fact did lecture on the lyceum circuit.

In 1837 Holbrook accepted the invitation to come to Ohio because he wanted to create a model village for his lyceum association and saw the great economic potential of the Berea and Cleveland area. With his eldest son, Alfred, he marked out the streets for a revived Berea. The village green laid out by the Holbrooks is now the grassy area between the college's Marting Hall and the Conservatory of Music. It is still known as the Lyceum Village Square and is listed, along with Marting Hall, in the National Registry of Historic Places. The Berea school founded by Holbrook in 1838, sometimes called the Lyceum School and sometimes the Berea Seminary, the name of the first school, was the real beginning of Baldwin-Wallace College.

The study of literature was emphasized, but true to the American way and Holbrook's concepts the school included the practical by making employment available to students at a small "factory" doing the highly skilled work of making terrestrial globes for sale. Holbrook's second son, Dwight, was the manager. The Lyceum's building was the meetinghouse that had been used by the first Berea. Holbrook's son Alfred was the principal of the little Lyceum. Both he and his father were graduates of Yale College and were originally from Connecticut, like many other early Bereans and settlers throughout the Connecticut Western Reserve.

The meetinghouse, said Alfred Holbrook, was "a rickety, unfinished, cheerless building" unfit for a school. So in its place John Baldwin, who was on the verge of becoming extremely wealthy through the quarrying of the large deposits of fine sandstone on his farm for high-quality grinding wheels and building stone, erected a two-story sandstone building. It was located on Factory Street (now part of South Rocky River Drive) on the west side of the Factory Triangle (now a little park in downtown Berea known as "the Triangle"). The lower floor was occupied by the factory and store, and the upper floor housed the Lyceum School. Alfred soon married a cousin, who was also a teacher, and both taught in the Lyceum. In 1841 Sheldon converted the school from a community-owned institution into a joint-stock corporation. However, the economic depression of the early 1840s frightened away investors. Meanwhile, a new public school called the Central School competed successfully with the Lyceum. And as the Central School succeeded, the Lyceum school declined.

When the private Lyceum fell into financial collapse, John Baldwin quickly gave the academy a financial rescue for rebirth in 1845. It had a faculty of four, including Holbrook, and a new location on land donated from Baldwin's farm along the east side of Rocky River at the southern edge of Berea. The reborn academy, chartered on December 20, 1845, was renamed the Baldwin Institute and unlike the Lyceum was linked to the Methodist Church Conference. For that reason and because of the new name, the year 1845 has been used ever since as the foundin date of Baldwin-Wallace College, even though the institution is really older, traceable back to 1838 and even 1837. While respecting the Methodist claims and traditions, one may view the Holbrooks, in addition to Sheldon and Baldwin, as the primary contributors to the college's foundations and the Lyceum as the true forebear of the college. Both Baldwin and Alfred Holbrook were among the trustees of Baldwin Institute. Baldwin repeatedly entreated Holbrook to continue as principal of the academy, now called the Baldwin Institute, but he declined because he believed that the Methodist Church leaders would prefer to have a minister head a Methodist school. Instead, he accepted the position of assistant principal. The Reverend Holden Dwight, principal of the defunct Norwalk Academy (founded by Sheldon in 1834), was appointed principal. Baldwin erected a building, North Hall, at the new location, and classes opened on April 9, 1846. The Baldwin Institute was in part a resurrection of the Norwalk Seminary. The Methodist Church of Northern Ohio now looked at the Baldwin Institute as the academic affiliate.

Although he dressed like a backwoods rustic, John Baldwin was an able entrepreneur. He soon developed not only a quarry but also a grindstone factory, a flourmill, a saw mill, and woolen mills. These provided jobs for students and invigorated Berea economically and also enabled Baldwin to have the means to found and support more schools: Baker University and its town, Baldwin City, Kansas, in 1856, along with mills there to help support the school; Baldwin Seminary in Baldwin, Louisiana, a two-year vocational school to teach freed African Americans; and Baldwin High School for Boys and Girls in Bangalore, India. At all the schools he founded he always insisted on his policies of no liquor and admission to all regardless of nationality, creed, race, religion, or gender. He and his wife, Mary Chappell Baldwin, were so devoted to freedom and equality that they set up at their house in Berea the first "Underground Railroad" stop in the township, part of the famous network across northern America that helped fleeing slaves escape to Canada.

Other men would soon form quarry companies at Berea, and one of them, James Wallace, a wealthy man from Detroit and a Baldwin Institute trustee, promised that if the institute would add a division for higher education, he would construct for this "university" a stone building on the Lyceum Village Square. The new principal of Baldwin Institute, the Reverend James Wheeler, was pleased with the idea, and the institute acquired a new charter in 1855 permitting it to become Baldwin University with Wheeler as its first president.

Despite the new name it was still a small school, like all American colleges then. For an actual university education one had to go to Europe after graduation from a college in America. Even so, the university required the study of Latin, Greek, Greek history, algebra, geometry, and Bible study for the first year of its curriculum. In the second year the curriculum included Latin and Greek, geometry, trigonometry, English ("rhetoric"), general science ("natural theology"), and Bible study. In the third year the required courses were Latin and Greek literature, chemistry, geology, physics, English, logic, aesthetics, and economics. And the fourth-year courses were Latin and Greek literature, astronomy, philology, English literature, history, religion ("evidences of Christianity"). This Classical Curriculum was in accordance with German and, later, French practice. There was an alternative curriculum, abbreviated to three years, Scientific Course that actually had fewer science courses but no Greek or Latin. Having such a second curriculum also followed the European model. Electives included French, German, Hebrew, Italian, piano, voice, guitar, melodeon (a small reed organ), and drawing. In 1857 a Commercial Curriculum was begun, offering courses in bookkeeping, banking, shipping, and mining. The promised Wallace Hall was completed in 1857 on the Public Lyceum Square. In 1859 five students, including one woman, were the first graduates of Baldwin University. Its enrollment was 269 in its first year of existence, and it soon reached 400.

From 1861 to 1865 the Civil War engendered strong feelings of patriotism at the school, but it also caused a precipitous drop in the male enrollment as young men went into military service. After the war the university recovered slowly and always had a small enrollment and financial difficulties. In 1858 the school had begun the building of a stone chapel on the primary campus on the south side of Berea. Financial support for the building came from James Wallace and another quarry and mill owner, Fletcher Hulet. The architecture was copied from the general design of the Oberlin College Chapel that was built in 1855. Construction was suspended during the Civil War, and work proceeded so slowly after the war that the chapel was not finished until 1878. Named Hulet Hall, it had classrooms on the first floor and, like the Oberlin chapel, a sanctuary on the second.

Financial difficulties were especially acute in the 1860s and 1870s. In 1874, during the depression that followed the Panic of 1873, President William D. Godman even suggested that the university should close and give its assets to his alma mater, Ohio Wesleyan University (also the source of his honorary doctorate). After the Berea townspeople hanged and burned him in effigy from a tree in his front yard, Godman soon departed. The university struggled on, with enrollments through the rest of the century remaining between 175 and 250, the great majority of whom were in the Preparatory School, the heir of the Lyceum School. The Preparatory School included not only an academy but also the normal department, or teacher training department, which was the way teacher training in Europe and America was structured during that time. In spite of the financial difficulties, a large stone dormitory, Ladies Hall (in fact housing gentlemen as well), was slowly erected starting in the mid-1870s.

Unfortunately, the location of the main campus of Baldwin University had become untenable by the early 1890s because quarries now extended dangerously close to the foundations of the campus buildings. Incessant noise and dust from the quarries may also have contributed to enrollment problems. Consequently, the campus had to be abandoned. Despite the precarious physical and financial situation of the tiny university, ways were found to build two beautiful stone buildings on a new campus north of Bagley Road: Recitation Hall, or Wheeler Hall (1892), and a library building (1893). Before the disappearance of the old campus, two buildings there, including Ladies Hall, were torn down and moved stone by stone to the new campus, where Ladies Hall became, with help from the Carnegie Foundation, Carnegie Science Hall.

The university achieved success also in the establishment of a link with another educational institution in the Cleveland area. From 1897 to 1913 what would become Cleveland-Marshall Law School was connected to Baldwin University and from 1913 to 1926 to Baldwin-Wallace College. The law school began in 1897 as the Baldwin University Law School, organized by several judges and attorneys, including Willis Vickery (1857–1932), a Shakespeare scholar of national renown, and Frederick C. Howe (1867–1940), the recipient of a Ph.D. from the John Hopkins University, partner in law with the sons of President James Garfield, and leader of the Progressive movement in Cleveland and Ohio. Another law school merged with the law school in 1899, and the united school took the name Cleveland Law School, which was still connected to the university. It was Ohio's first evening law school and, true to the Baldwin way, the first to admit women.

While Baldwin University struggled along financially during the Civil War, its seven-year-old German department did so well that in 1863 the department became the nucleus for a separate college, German Wallace College. The man whose idea it was to create the German department, and even a college especially for German-American Methodists, was the Reverend Dr. Jacob Rothweiler, born in 1823 in Berghausen in the state of Baden. He came with his family in 1839 to New York City, where so many immigrants from Germany were joining the American Methodists that they were organizing a German Methodist branch of the denomination. Rothweiler joined the new organization, which sponsored him as a missionary to German Americans in Ohio. When he visited Berea in 1856, he proposed to President Wheeler that the new Baldwin University create a German department because of the many German Americans in Cleveland, Cincinnati, Detroit, and Buffalo.

Actual departments of modern languages were quite unusual then, but instant support for the proposal for a German department came from the Reverend Wilhelm Nast (1807–1899) of Cincinnati, who was a trustee of Baldwin University from 1859 to 1865. Born in Stuttgart, Germany, he had attended the Blaubeuren Seminary in eastern Württemberg, near Ulm, and then the University of Tübingen, intending to prepare for the Lutheran ministry. While at Tübingen he was the roommate of David Friedrich Strauss, who would soon become an influential figure among those modern biblical scholars searching for the "historical Jesus." Nast, in contrast, followed a more traditional interpretation of the Gospels. He came to America in 1828 and served as librarian and professor of German at West Point and then as professor of Greek and Hebrew at Kenyon College. In 1835 he joined the Methodist Church and became a missionary to German immigrants in Cincinnati and, later, in Kentucky and other states. A published scholar and acknowledged father of German Methodism in

America, he would give vital support to Ludwig Jacoby, the founder of the first American Methodist mission to Germany. Strong agreement with Rothweiler's proposal for a German department at Baldwin University came also from the Cincinnati Methodist Conference and the Northern Ohio Methodist Conference.

Meanwhile, Dr. Rothweiler received financial support for a German department from his old friend of Detroit and Berea, James Wallace. John Baldwin also supported Rothweiler's proposal, promising to grant students studying German the use of Baldwin Hall as a residence. In its first year the enrollment of the German department totaled twelve and soon expanded. Rothweiler was the professor of German from 1859 to 1864. Most of the support for scholarships for German American students at the university came from German Americans in Cincinnati.

With the growing success of the German department, the German Methodist Conference, led by Wilhelm Nast, decided to promote Rothweiler's idea for the establishment of a German Methodist College. In response Wallace, trustee and treasurer of the university and mayor of Berea, donated the already-constructed Wallace Hall, the Lyceum Village Square, and some of his own funds to establish the college named after him. Soon after German Wallace College was chartered in 1863, John Baldwin gave Baldwin Hall on the Baldwin campus to the new institution. Enrolling forty students in 1864–65, the college continued to expand after the end of the Civil War. In 1864 Nast became the first president of the board of trustees of the college; he remained a trustee until 1895 and served as president of the college from 1864 until 1893.

Despite the move to the new campus, Baldwin University continued to be financially weak, while German Wallace, with its special niche in the market for students, grew steadily stronger. Seeing the financial difficulties of Baldwin University, Methodist leaders encouraged the two colleges of Berea, with their common roots, to merge. They did unite in 1913, forming Baldwin-Wallace College. United the faculty numbered more than thirty and the student body well over 300. The great majority of the students were from German Wallace. The president of German Wallace College and graduate in 1898 of the college, the Reverend Dr. Arthur L. Breslich, became president of Baldwin-Wallace College. George F. Collier, the registrar and dean of the faculty of Baldwin University from 1896 to 1913 and also professor of English and an expert on Shakespeare, became registrar and dean of Baldwin-Wallace.

Included in the newly united college was the Nast Theological Seminary, located in Marting Hall. In the first year of German Wallace College its trustees had founded a chair in biblical studies. President Nast had expanded the program and then had founded the Theological Seminary for graduate study, offering the B.D. degree, the preeminent graduate degree in "divinity" studies. After his death in 1899 the little school was named the Nast Theological Seminary in his honor.

Although the Baldwins had been abolitionists and supporters of the "Underground Railroad," even after World War I there were no African American students at the college. That was typical of American colleges in the North and South for years to come. And there was racism at the college, particularly among the students. In Marting Hall, at a party of one of the student "literary societies," while the women guests were dressed in beautiful dresses in the fashion of the time, and the young men wore suits and ties, some of the men were made up in minstrel-style blackface. The chapter room of the society was hung with burlap and animal skins to make it seem "more realistic" as a cabin in the Old South. Using a racist pejorative written in a mock southern dialect, the student newspaper reported a quartet in blackface "captivated the audience." Neither the members of the society nor the reporters for the student newspaper, *The Exponent,* seem to have had any sense that they were an illustration of the enormous American tragedy. Minstrel-style "entertainments" continued at the college into the 1920s and perhaps beyond, as they did across America.

Toward students from China and other Asian countries, however, the college's attitude was quite different. Two factors account for this. First, there had been Methodist schools in China for many years, served in part by missionaries who were graduates of German Wallace College. Second, on May 13, 1908, the United States informed China that about two-thirds (or $12 million) of the Boxer Rebellion indemnity to the United States would be remitted to China if it would use the money for scholarships to send students to American colleges. Thus, between 1901 and 1940 some 7,900 Chinese students attended American colleges, including Baldwin-Wallace. Students and faculty members of Baldwin-Wallace welcomed Chinese students. In 1921, for example, the Chinese students, all male, were the guests of a literary society for women students. During October of that year Professor Frederick Roehm invited the Chinese students of the college to his house in celebration of the tenth anniversary of the "Double Ten," the beginning of the Chinese Revolution, October 10, 1911. There were students from eleven other foreign countries, including Egypt, Sweden, and Hungary, where there had been a small Methodist mission among German Calvinists at Srbrobran in the Voyvodina since 1898.

During the early years of the new college there were a number of study programs. Those graduates of June 1917 completed the following courses of study: seventeen in the liberal arts and sciences, twenty-two in piano and organ; fourteen in the normal department, which included the new (1913) home economics department; five in the academy (the descendant of the Lyceum School); twenty-six in the academy's branch at the Cleveland Law School, the Cleveland Preparatory School, a night school in downtown Cleveland that offered students a way to meet the state's requirement of a high school diploma for admission into a law school; and fifty-eight in the law school.

Baldwin-Wallace's early-twentieth-century development was hindered by the great wave of hostility toward German Americans during World War I. The resultant nationalism led to the removal of the president, Dr. Arthur Breslich, who was also professor of Hebrew and author, in 1913, of the words to Baldwin-Wallace's original *Alma Mater*. In January 1918 he was "relieved" of his position by the college trustees following the campus uproar that included marches, petitions, and disruption over his attempt to lead the annual college Christmas service in singing "Silent Night" in German. Claims that his patriotism was half-hearted, mainly from persons with Baldwin University roots, were turned over to the head of the Cleveland office of what was developing into the Federal Bureau of Investigation. But there were no grounds for charges against Breslich.

The repressive actions of nationalists toward German Americans in 1917–18 were paralleled by the Prohibitionists' success in achieving passage of the Eighteenth Amendment in December 1917 (ratification in 1919), designed to prevent everyone from drinking alcoholic beverages. The temperance movement had always been strong in Methodism, and in 1917 it was claimed that half the students at the college had volunteered to assist in the campaign for the amendment.

Following the unfortunate termination of Dr. Breslich, the college appointed to its presidency the Reverend Albert Storms, whose honorary doctorate was from Drake University. Storms, a professor of history, worked successfully to end discord at the college. Even so, in 1926 the Cleveland Law School ended its affiliation, which had begun in 1897. The separation was caused by disagreements over the control of finances and appointments at the law school.

After the Wall Street crash of October 1929, the United States rapidly entered the Great Depression. Everyone at the college received a 45 percent cut in salary, but there were no firings of faculty members. In spite of the Depression the college managed to survive. Because of declining enrollments, however, the Nast Theological Seminary did cease to exist in 1935. The Conservatory of Music, however, continued to thrive. In 1899 Professor Albert Riemenschneider (German Wallace Class of 1899)—son of scholarly professor of philosophy and college president (1893–1908) Dr. Karl Riemenschneider—had founded the German Wallace music school. Fourteen years later he founded the conservatory by combining the music departments of the uniting colleges. Director of the conservatory from 1913 to 1948, he was also an outstanding organist who installed in 1914 the great Austin pipe organ with its sixty ranks and four manuals in the conservatory's concert hall. In 1933, during the depths of the Great Depression, he and his wife, Selma, founded the annual Bach Festival and the important Bach Library. The library became the heart of the Riemenschneider Bach Institute formed in 1969 to coordinate research by scholars from around the world who use its archives. The institute sponsors symposiums and since 1970 has published a scholarly journal, *BACH*.

Similarly, the college, as a whole as well as the American nation, would pass through difficult years to achieve greater strength. From 1934 to 1948 the president of the college was the Reverend Dr. Louis C. Wright, who had received the Ph.D. from Boston University in 1917. Following graduation he was director of the YMCA and worked with American soldiers in France. From 1920 to 1934 he was pastor at the Epworth-Euclid Church in Cleveland. During the fifteen years of the Wright administration the United States went through the Depression and the Second World War to emerge as the most powerful country, militarily and economically, in the world. At the college student enrollment tripled and finances improved greatly. During the war a Navy V-12 unit was established at the college on July 1, 1943, to offer education to officer candidates. More than 850 men went through the program, which ended on November 1, 1945. Also during the early period of the war, more than 300 Army Air Corps officer candidates were trained in the War Training Service at the college.

After the war veterans flooded the campus. Their tuition, books, and room and board were covered by the Serviceman's Readjustment Act of June 1944, popularly known as the GI Bill of Rights. Not wanting to lose this opportunity for a major enrollment increase, the college dropped the semester system and on September 23, 1946, began the quarterly system, thus offering more opportunities per year for veterans to enter, which also meant a more intensive study program. At the same time attendance at chapel programs and services was made voluntary. Even though there were three presidents from 1948 to 1955, and two of them were acting presidents chosen from the faculty, enrollment continued to increase.

Beginning in 1955 the college entered a new era of leadership under Alfred B. Bonds Jr. From Arkansas, he held an A.B. from Henderson State Teachers College and an A.M. from Louisiana State University and had served in the U.S. Department of Education. He soon brought Dr. Fred Harris to the college as dean of the faculty. The college education and professional life of the two men was in teacher training. Dean Harris was a specialist in elementary education. Both men believed that the college needed strong, authoritarian leadership, and they would have a large impact on the college, particularly on the Humanities Division.

President Bonds was excellent at raising money from both private and government sources at a time when money was becoming readily available. To form the inner circle of the college's trustees, he selected outstanding Cleveland business and banking figures, such as Dr. Jacob Kamm, the brilliant but modest financial expert, businessman, author of books on investment, professor of business administration and reformer of the curriculum of the Division of Business Administration, and later member of the Ohio Board of Regents. With the American economy booming through the postwar period, and with enrollment increasing from 1,300 students in 1956 to 2,400 in the 1960s, President Bonds carried through an extensive building program which included the new library building, the college union, the art and drama center, and many dormitories. Also, the ratio of female students to male was improved from 1:2 in the 1950s to 1:1 in the 1960s, as it was in colleges across America in this time.

Not all parts of the college would thrive, however. The "shift from academic merit to student consumerism is one of the . . . greatest reversals of direction in all the history of American higher education," Clark Kerr of Berkeley wrote in 1980. For William H. Whyte, writing in 1956, the crucial shift was the dislodging of the liberal arts and sciences by technical and vocational education as the center of the university, a shift much desired by parents and businessmen, whatever they might claim. Bonds and Harris led Baldwin-Wallace in following these trends. Thus, Dean Harris decided to reduce sharply the required hours for the humanities in the core curriculum. The change was accomplished in two phases, in 1965 and in 1968–69. Amazingly it was not foreseen by any but a few that these changes were going to reduce the need for faculty members in the humanities. The times seemed so good that there was no fear.

In the late 1960s, during the years of the nationwide movement against the war in Vietnam, an increasing number of students and faculty at the college joined in "silent vigils" in Berea to protest the war and also participated in the "Mobilization Against the War" in New York and the march on the Pentagon. Some protested out of pacifist convictions; others believed the war was not in the U.S. interest, was a massacre of the Vietnamese people, and was resulting in needless and tragic deaths of American soldiers. No one was against American soldiers. All distrusted the government's claims regarding the war. Meanwhile, the civil rights movement helped to bring a growing number of African American students to the college.

At the college the democratic spirit of the sixties would finally appear in the elimination of much of the authoritarian form of leadership of the Harris era. Richard Miller, who held an Ed.D. from Columbia University, became the dean of the faculty in 1969. Not only did Miller dismantle much of the Harris governance system, but he also persuaded President Bonds to allow the faculty to elect the person who would preside over faculty meetings and proposed the creation of several faculty-elected committees for the faculty. While these changes did not lessen the administration's strength, it did gave an opportunity for many more faculty members to participate on committees instead of just a few persons handpicked by the dean. In addition, Dean Miller accepted the proposal to have the dean grant departments the right to elect their heads, or choose a rotation procedure, with final approval by the dean, for three-year terms, instead of having chairpersons appointed by the dean. The faculty approved these proposals enthusiastically and virtually unanimously. Immediately faculty morale rose. Also, Dean Miller dropped Harris's merit-pay system and introduced a much better teacher evaluation form. He proposed a faculty grievance committee. One of the college lawyers, the elegant and aristocratic young Mr. Lopez, explained to the committee that in informality lies injustice. Drawing extensively from the guidelines of the American Association of University Professors, he drafted the committee's rules, which became part of the college by-laws and helped to restrain the department heads.

Before he was dismissed by President Bonds, Dean Miller, for all the help he gave the faculty, allowed a serious problem to continue to develop for the humanities faculty. He and the executive assistant, James Harvey, had unwisely approved the requests of many departments in the humanities to add more members. Unfortunately, with the reduction of the required hours in the humanities for the core curriculum, there was a grave danger of overstaffing. The lack of a salary schedule was another problem. There was, and would continue to be, a significant difference between the salaries of those in the humanities and those in some other divisions. For full professors the gap would become astonishing, however respectable the average salary in rank might be. Also, a gender gap in salary for senior faculty persisted. Dean Miller had wanted a salary schedule, calling for an elected Faculty Salary Schedule and Budget Committee, but after his departure the word "schedule" was dropped from the name of the committee, and a salary schedule was never created.

The solution to these problems in the thinking of some was a faculty union. They argued that only with the system of collective bargaining would faculty be assured of fair play in salary and job security. They pointed out that with many professors working an overload, plus the fact that the college had hired more faculty while cutting the required hours in the humanities, and with enrollment in the humanities in decline generally, faculty jobs were in jeopardy. But in 1973 the faculty voted against collective bargaining. In 1974 sixteen tenured faculty members were fired. All had supported the campaign for a union. Almost all were in the humanities, including Dr. H. D. Rowe, head of the English department and leader of the campaign. The administration said it was done because of "financial exigency." Conservative faculty concluded that one should never oppose the administration. For the prounion faculty the primary struggle was not as much with the administration as with the conservative faculty.

In 1975 Dr. Neal Malicky came to the college as dean of the faculty. He would be president from 1981 to 1999. He held a Ph.D. in political science from Columbia University in the field of international relations. Under his guidance total enrollment grew by 45 percent to about 4,500. With help from the American economy and with the support of the outstanding financial experts of the college trustees, Dr. Malicky increased the endowment from $13 million to $114 million. He was able to raise average faculty salaries to the top quintile in the annual survey of the American Association of University Professors, although inequality in rank would persist. In the 1980s he started a special program of "merit scholarships" to attract more students with high academic achievement and potential, regardless of their financial need. At the same time he kept the tuition of the college at a relatively low level among private institutions.

In the 1980s Malicky established the Office of Multicultural Affairs so that the college could better serve African American students, whose numbers had increased steadily from the 1970s. In 1992 he supported a community operation begun by students in 1986 to coordinate student volunteer projects, including an adult literacy program, intensive work with the homeless, and a tutoring program for "at-risk" youths. Participation in this social service also benefited the volunteers because it helped them to mature.

For over 160 years the college and its parent, the Lyceum School, have been a microcosm of America, following trends and sharing in difficulties and triumphs of the country, from the movement to establish church-related schools through the abolition movement, the Civil War, economic expansion and depression, two World Wars, tremendous increase in college enrollments, racism and struggles to end racism, increase in admission of women students, the antiwar movement of the sixties, the assault on the humanities in the 1960s and 1970s, and the increasing emphasis on vocational and professional education. After a history of struggle and achievement, Baldwin-Wallace can look forward with hope.

SUGGESTED READING

For further reading see Clyde Feuchter, et al., *A History of Baldwin University and German Wallace College* (Baldwin-Wallace College, 1945); Walter F. Holzworth, *Men of Grit and Greatness* (Holzworth, 1970); David Lindsey, "A 'Backwoods Utopia': The Berea Community of 1836–1837," *Ohio Historical Quarterly* 65 (July 1956): 272–96; A. R. Webber, *The Life of John Baldwin, Sr., of Berea, Ohio* (Caxton Press, 1925).

Bluffton College

Progressive Anabaptism

PERRY BUSH

In the 1999–2000 academic year Bluffton College celebrated its centennial birthday with a good deal of enthusiasm. By any measurement of institutional health—steady increases in student enrollment, state of its beautiful physical plant, and growth of endowment—the college was clearly thriving. Yet perhaps the institution's greatest area of vitality came in its quite conscious understanding of its own mission and purpose.

This is a sense of identity, which, for lack of a better phrase, I have characterized as "progressive Anabaptism." The term is a loose one and must be allowed some flexibility. "Progressive" works better for the first half of the college's story, when its most important early leaders were progressives in every sense of that term in its historical context of early-twentieth-century America. Captivated by mainstream culture inside and outside academia, they were determined to construct a college that would help drag their Mennonite people, some of them quite reluctantly, into the "enlightenment" of modern life. Such an agenda had by its nature much potential for conflict with church traditionalists, who were likely to see such an agenda for the potentially dangerous course it was.

By midcentury, however, the national political movement of progressivism had about played itself out. Subsequent leaders of the college became more discreet in terms of their political leanings, and, at any rate, an overtly political reading of "progressive Anabaptism" diminishes the term. In describing leaders from midcentury on—such as presidents Lloyd Ramseyer, Robert Kreider, and Elmer Neufeld—the proper stress is on the second part of the phrase. The college became explicitly Anabaptist partly because of pragmatic necessity and partly because of a growing commitment to reach out and include students beyond the confines of traditional Mennonite ethnoreligious peoplehood. Instead, they would invite all sorts of Christians

The Kobzar

to come to the college for instruction both in the liberal arts and also in Mennonite precepts such as peace, service, and matters of justice—understandings that, in true Anabaptist fashion, students would be invited, but not forced, to accept. By the 1990s such understandings had been creatively fermenting for long enough to lend a particularly directed and purposeful quality to the college's celebration of its centennial.

Mennonite historians point to a general revival, or "quickening," that occurred among U.S. Mennonites in the latter years of the nineteenth century. Traditionally a conservative, rural people resistant to change, in these decades many Mennonites began to welcome selected aspects of a burgeoning outside society as a means for their own reform and renewal. Mennonites soon began enterprises such as their own Sunday schools, revival meetings, foreign missions, and hospitals. At the same time they began to make the transition from German to English as their primary language. They also founded their own colleges, establishing seven different institutions of higher education between 1890 and World War I.

These dynamics were certainly at play in the Central, Eastern and especially Middle Districts of what was then emerging as a separate Mennonite denomination, the

General Conference Mennonite Church (G.C.M.C.). In the 1860s ambitious G.C.M.C. church leaders in central Ohio had already mounted one unsuccessful attempt at creating a Mennonite college in the American Midwest. Located in Wadsworth in southern Medina County, the Wadsworth Institute, in its short life from 1868 to 1879, had a few moments when it looked as if it might flourish. By the early 1870s, upwards of fifty students came each year for classes in theology, English, and some sciences (with all instruction conducted in German). The college foundered on the rocks of financial failure, hastened by a bitter conflict between the school's president and its leading theology professor. Yet the kinds of impulses represented by Wadsworth would not go away and two decades later resulted in the creation of a more enduring Mennonite college. The momentum particularly emanated from a determined young Noah C. Hirschy, a Wadsworth graduate and assistant pastor of the town of Wadsworth's First Mennonite Church. Raised by Amish immigrant parents on an Indiana farm, Hirschy from a young age had been captivated by the life of the mind. In 1900 his intellectual aspirations resulted in bachelor's degrees in both art and divinity, a master's in theology, and, in 1907, a doctorate in Old Testament studies from the University of Bern in Switzerland. Hirschy demanded the same kinds of opportunities for his people. Together with other ambitious Mennonite intellectuals, by the 1890s he had thrown himself into what would become a successful campaign to found another Mennonite college to serve the G.C.M.C. churches east of the Mississippi.

Convinced by Hirschy's arguments that "Christian, positively Christian schools is the need of the hour" (and also, somewhat ironically, by assurances that Mennonite colleges might provide an additional hedge against the pressures of assimilation), in 1898 the G.C.M.C.'s Middle District Conference officially approved the creation of Central Mennonite College. Its charter purposes would be modest, aimed largely at Bible instruction; the college would also, Hirschy pledged, operate "entirely without debts." After considering attractive offers from town boosters in Goshen and Berne, Indiana, the church agreed to locate the new institution near the small town of Bluffton in northwest Ohio, principally in order to center it amidst the large Mennonite settlement on the border of Allen and Putnam Counties.

Significantly, from the beginning the college's founders understood that while the college would be Mennonite, it "shall be open to all." In his soaring two-hour speech at the groundbreaking of the college's first building, incoming president Hirschy played on the same themes. He pointed to Menno Simons as among the "mighty cloud of witnesses" beaming down approval from Heaven on that historic day in June 1900, also declaring, "let our college be an American college." Classes began that November with nineteen students clustered around five professors. By the spring of 1904 the student body had expanded to more than seventy students. While most were enrolled in the academy as high school students (not until 1914 would the institution function as a real college), students were immersed in a heady curriculum of Bible, languages, and the sciences and also enjoyed a rich extracurricular life of literary societies, choral music, and faculty teas.

Beneath the shiny veneer of high academic culture, however, a number of problems were layered. Even more than other church institutions, colleges tend to be founded by the innovators, ambitious and talented young people who became enamored of academic culture in their training at elite universities and then determined to share these delights with the uninitiated in their home churches. By their nature early church colleges thus had the potential for conflict with denominational traditionalists, who distrusted such high ideals and remained committed to the old, unvarnished faith of the fathers. As a rural, ethnoreligious people constantly on guard against cultural adaptations as signs of pride and "worldliness," Mennonites proved particularly susceptible to the kind of conflicts that innovations such as higher education could bring into their midst.

This Noah Hirschy would soon discover. Headstrong, self-righteous, unbending, and a little vain, Hirschy, in the eight years of his troubled presidency, fought a running battle against the leadership of the local Swiss Mennonite Congregation, which several times brought the college to the brink of closing. By the end of its first decade, with the capable Bible scholar Samuel Mosiman having replaced Hirschy as president, Central Mennonite College stood exhausted and nearly bankrupt. In 1912 it would be overwhelmed by the energies of a new generation of Mennonite academics who would provide both reinvigoration and renewal.

Somewhat ironically, the impetus came from the head of a rival Mennonite institution, Noah Byers, president of Goshen College in Indiana. Like many other Mennonite educators, Byers thought that rather than maintaining three struggling colleges, it made a lot more sense for his church to unite its energies behind one of them and really make it go. From the beginning Byers signaled his receptivity to considering another locale. In several unpublicized meetings and then public gatherings in the winter and spring of 1913, a growing number of educators and lay people from five different Mennonite groups laid plans to create a college that would unite their efforts and jointly serve the young people from all their different groups. Central Mennonite would become a new institution, Bluffton College, and would clearly be the Harvard of the Mennonite world. It would offer not only a bachelor's degree but a Master's of Divinity as well, available through the creation of the first Mennonite seminary.

As the central focus for the educational efforts of the Mennonite churches, the planners were confident that they could attract to Bluffton a veritable all-star lineup of academic talent, led by Byers himself who would come to serve as Mosiman's dean. They quickly induced a half-dozen leading scholars from the other Mennonite colleges to transfer to Bluffton, where they busied themselves with the same central task. In their early years, historian James Juhnke has written, all the Mennonite colleges "took on a creative but difficult task: to reconcile traditional, rural Mennonite values with American democratic society and its progressivism."

The new cohort of educators at Bluffton reveled in Byers's description of themselves as "United Progressive Mennonites." The appellation seems accurate in at least two senses. First, these scholars were certainly progressives in that they were innovators in the church. Take, for instance, Bluffton's new star history professor, Goshen transfer C. Henry Smith. In his lifelong quest for academic excellence, Smith defined "the whole object of education" as an effort to "break up old habits of thought." Both his writings and speeches were peppered with disdainful references to images like "superannuated ministers" and "outworn church workers." He had tasted the life of high culture and found it good, and much of his life's mission would be to expose his Mennonite people to these fine fruits as well.

In the context of their day, this adoption of mainstream American academic culture meant that the educators at Bluffton embraced progressivism in a second sense as well as the political/cultural orientation dominating national society. Byers, Smith, Mosiman, and others identified closely with national progressivism. Mosiman even dabbled in state Democratic party politics and brought his friend, Ohio governor James Cox, to campus to give a rousing oration on progressive principles in 1913. Bluffton College's leaders worked tirelessly to immerse hundreds of Mennonite young people in a progressive variant of Anabaptism that would take young Mennonites and others attracted to the same vision and graft Mennonite tradition onto the best of what their society offered. In so doing they would produce cultured, refined young Mennonites armed for a lifetime of service to their church and their society, two spheres that were not seen to be in conflict. Mennonites no longer had to be seen as odd members of some isolated religious sect; instead they could take an honored and legitimate place in outside society, a society to which they had much to offer.

Under this defining call of progressive Anabaptism, Bluffton College blossomed in the teens and twenties, even while continually facing down the rising expressions of dissent from Mennonite conservatives in the pews. The progressivism that informed such efforts was expressed in both inward and outward directions. Inwardly, the educators at Bluffton created a rich student culture around a host of related activities—plays, literary societies, intercollegiate debates and sports, active campus chapters of the YMCA and YWCA. From all this a growing number of students (numbering more than 300 by 1924) received not only academic credit but the deeper inculcation into what was widely called "the Bluffton spirit."

Outwardly, the vision of progressivism Anabaptism could be functional as well. Seeking funds for a new men's dormitory in the 1920s, President Mosiman declared that the building would be a "memorial to Lincoln" and "employed as an incentive to the development of patriotism and good government." Indeed, it was not just Lincoln Hall but the entire enterprise at Bluffton, he informed another potential donor in 1920, that could be a "mighty factor" in the "process of Americanization."

Yet, as Mosiman's overt nationalism indicated, the vision also had some problems. In their rush to accept the best of outside culture and assimilate it into their own Mennonite tradition, many of the zealous educators at Bluffton adopted a bit too much. Some periodically expressed, for example, the racism of national progressivism. Even more ominously for a Mennonite college, many in the Bluffton academic community embraced with varying degrees of enthusiasm the ultimate crusade of national progressivism, the First World War. Given the air of patriotism permeating the campus, large numbers of Bluffton students and faculty entered both noncombatant and regular military service. Under Mosiman's leadership the college actively pushed liberty loans and thrift stamp sales and also the patriotic war work of the YMCA. Young women energetically gathered supplies for the Red Cross.

Such open violations of the traditional Mennonite precept of pacifist nonresistance fueled the outrage of many church traditionalists. As a result, by the early 1920s the college found itself at the center of bitter and destructive theological conflict that raged for more than a decade. As early as 1919 conservatives had raised accusations that theological "modernism" permeated the college. While these charges would only intensify for the next dozen years, they were blatantly unfair.

Mosiman and his fellow educators at Bluffton may have been innovators and progressives, but (with the possible exception of Bible professor Jacob Quiring) they retained a pietistic evangelical theology that was a far cry from theological modernism. Fundamentalist attacks left Mosiman sputtering with anger. "I am at a loss to know where all the bunk comes from," he wrote a supporter, "unless it be from a diseased, debased or perverted imagination." However, the uncritical acculturation of Mosiman and his colleagues gave conservative Mennonite critics much material to work with, and they used it with vigor and determination.

Fundamentalist charges inflicted painful damage. In 1924 the conservative Mennonite Church publicist John Horsch, for example, published an explosive polemic, *The Mennonite Church and Modernism.* This pamphlet labeled a number of Bluffton leaders—including Mosiman, Byers, and Smith by name—as dangerous modernists, "traitors" who were betraying the church into the hands of religious liberalism. "Bluffton is the citadel of religious modernism among the Mennonites of America," he insisted. Horsch followed this blast with another pamphlet repeating the charges, which he mailed free of charge to every Mennonite minister in the country. In 1929 G.C.M.C. fundamentalists in Berne, Indiana, prepared and distributed their own pamphlet, *Evidences of Modernism at Bluffton College,* laying out their charges.

In the end, combined with the financial devastation of the Great Depression, the fundamentalist attacks killed Bluffton's Witmarsum Seminary and nearly succeeded in killing the college. After peaking at 371 students in 1930, the college's enrollment dropped rapidly, hitting a low of 185 in 1936. By 1934 the college found itself a quarter-million dollars in debt (over $3 million in 1999 dollars). The college's first major attempt at academic accreditation met with a rude and sarcastic dismissal by two NCA investigators. In 1934 beloved old President Mosiman was forced from office under angry accusations of financial mismanagement; his successor lasted three years before the emotional strains of the office brought him to the edge of a nervous breakdown.

To be sure, all was not grim at the college in the 1930s. No matter how perilous the financial conditions appeared (and they were), Mosiman and his professors could not help but take pride in the initiative and leadership of a number of Bluffton's students. As the Depression deepened and the war clouds gathered, they spoke and acted with courage and conviction on behalf of issues of peace and social justice. Acting in keeping with the founding vision of the college were such stalwart Mennonite activists as Vivienne Mussleman, Carl Landes, and Martha Graber as well as non-Mennonites like Betty Keeney and Ralph Locher. Locher would follow up a sterling student record with a law degree and a political career that included a term as mayor of Cleveland and service as chief justice of the state supreme court. In the early 1930s a passionate young socialist named John Keller, who brought in socialist presidential candidate Norman Thomas to speak on campus, spearheaded student activism. Keller also pushed hard against what he perceived as the complacency of some of his fellow students. The emotional difficulties of the later 1930s were somewhat lightened by the wit and laughter of a sparkling student named Phyllis Driver, who ran a campus gossip column and starred in theatrical productions. She later married fellow student Sherwood Diller and blossomed nationally, years later, as the famous comedienne Phyllis Diller.

Even so, the 1930s blasted through Bluffton College as years of nearly unrelenting disaster. In the end the college's ambitious dream of 1913, the "union movement" of Mennonite colleges, was never realized. Goshen would remain the dominant Mennonite college east of the Mississippi, with Bluffton a discredited left-wing substitute. Over the next several decades the percentage of Mennonites in the Bluffton student body slowly declined. By the later 1930s it once again stammered toward the verge of collapse.

Yet all the power and momentum of Depression economics and fundamentalist attack could not dismantle the integrity of the progressive Anabaptist vision that had shaped the college's founding. During World War II and into the postwar years a new generation of Bluffton leaders and faculty would correct the flaws of the earlier vision and reconstruct this progressive heritage into a serviceable vehicle for

Mennonite higher education. Most centrally this reconstruction of progressive Anabaptism took place in the capable hands of a doughty Bluffton alum and former football team star named Lloyd Ramseyer.

Given the dismal state of the college's affairs in 1938 when Ramseyer assumed Bluffton's presidency, his accomplishments appear almost breathtaking in retrospect. Within a year he had the college operating once again in the black and managed to balance the budget for every year but one in a presidency that stretched until 1965. After the collapse of enrollment during World War II (the student body dipped to seventy students in 1944), he slowly rebuilt both student and faculty numbers and also the college endowment, to the point that in 1953 the college achieved a dream that it had pursued since its infancy: accreditation by the North Central Association.

More to the point, even as the nation devoted itself once again to the cause of world war, Ramseyer rededicated the college to the ways of peace. Privately he admonished friends for buying war bonds. Publicly he invited several Japanese American students to come from relocation camps to study at the college. He would allow neither Bluffton's wartime student newspaper nor the yearbook to publish army or navy advertisements. He realized that the ranks of WWII conscientious objectors in the Civilian Public Service (C.P.S.) were promising faculty recruitment grounds for a peace church college. Throughout the war he wooed promising young alumni and other scholars lodged in the C.P.S. labor camps, an effort that resulted in the long Bluffton College postwar professorial careers of a number of former objectors. In his weekly chapel talks and annual baccalaureate addresses, Ramseyer harnessed a personal kind of evangelical piety to a number of oft-repeated themes. He denounced student drinking and smoking, railed against American racism decades before Little Rock or Birmingham, condemned war as sin, and continually called students to lifetimes of service.

Pursuing peace in a nation mobilized for total war was a policy fraught with danger, but it was a risk that Ramseyer faced willingly. When a local military manufacturer requested permission to use an empty campus building, Ramseyer pushed the board of trustees to tell them no, thereby inviting the wrath of the surrounding village of Bluffton. As the Cold War later hardened and the nation embarked on an anti-Communist crusade, Ramseyer publicly stood by a young history professor, Larry Gara, who was charged with urging nonregistration with the 1948 draft law. Ramseyer testified at Gara's trial and proclaimed the college's solidarity through Gara's subsequent prison term, even as evidence mounted that the stand cost the college measurable financial support. (Gara went on to teach history at Wilmington College.)

Finally, in November 1944, as World War II entered its final phases, Ramseyer articulated a vision that could carry the college a long way in the postwar world. He conceded to the board of trustees that the great "union movement" that had given birth to the college was dead. As it stood leaders at Bluffton faced an uncertain future as they tried to build on a constituency of three small church conferences with a total membership of 12,000 people. What kind of future could they hope to construct in the face of such obstacles?

The president had just one glittering idea. He suggested that "we enlarge our constituency by making this a center of a certain type of thinking, a certain brand of educational and religious philosophy which is different." The guiding "distinctive things . . . must coincide with Mennonite principles, but not be confined to Mennonites." In a way Ramseyer seemed to be thinking aloud. "Having found these principles," he wondered, "how can we capitalize upon them to attract others than Mennonites who would be interested in these ideals?"

The vision was hazy, but it shone with promise. As it turned out, he did not have to look far for the guiding principles he hoped to find; as a Bluffton College alumnus, he had them all along. This vision had come to him from the teachings of his mentors, confident progressives such as Smith, Byers, and Mosiman. In the postwar decades Ramseyer worked closely with other alums on the faculty who had absorbed the teaching of the earlier generation. Through them—and through the efforts of compatriots who shared the vision like Robert Kreider and Elmer Neufeld—the flaws of the prewar progressivism were slowly ground away and a serviceable progressive Anabaptism retained. It would be rooted in the traditional Mennonite precepts of peacemaking and service to others. Partly out of pragmatic necessity and partly because of the particular historical trajectory of Bluffton College, the vision would be shared with an increasingly nonethnic, non-Mennonite student body, and aimed at a national society that a progressive, outward-focused heritage had rendered a little less distant and a little more approachable.

For the next half-century Bluffton College continued along the same trajectory mapped out in 1944 by Ramseyer and his colleagues. To be sure, there were some other significant turning points. As was the case with many American colleges and universities, the demographic, political, and cultural watershed of the 1960s registered its own deep impact on the college. Driven by the great postwar "baby boom," the college's own student population more than doubled beginning in the mid-1950s. By 1960 enrollment hurdled the old barrier of 400 students and accelerated, growing at an average of 10 percent a year to a peak of nearly 800 students in the fall of 1969. To feed, house, and educate these new students, the college built three new dorms and large additions on its old ones, added huge extensions to the library and the gym, and in 1967 dedicated the expansive and handsome Marbeck Center, which housed the student center, lounge, bookstore, and cafeteria, after Anabaptist leader Pilgram Marbeck.

It was in these years that the Mennonite percentage of the student body declined rapidly from 24 percent in 1967 to 15 percent five years later, a percentage that the college has roughly maintained since. The decline was not the result of declining Mennonite commitment to the college; in 1972 a good 65 percent of the faculty remained Mennonite, along with a vast majority of administrators and trustees. Through the early and mid-1960s Mennonite students came to the college in increasing numbers as well, but the numbers of non-Mennonites increased even faster. Increasingly—in line with the heritage of progressive Anabaptism—it was many of these non-Mennonite students who pushed the cutting edge of peace and social justice activism.

The larger student body by itself brought marked cultural changes. As a matter of course the campus lost the kind of "extended family" sensibilities of a tiny college, and for the first time it became possible to attend Bluffton College without knowing everyone by name. The campus also witnessed a number of the political and cultural changes peculiar to the 1960s. On the one hand, because of the particular peace and justice commitments of the faculty and administration, the college managed to escape much of the personal and political confrontations common at other schools of the era. Decades before the college had admitted students to membership on significant faculty and trustee committees. Now student peace activists found a number of their pacifist professors voicing full agreement with their antiwar analyses. Likewise, from 1965 to 1972 they encountered former history professor and academic dean Robert Kreider as the president. Kreider himself had been a conscientious objector during World War II and greeted peace and justice student activism with enthusiastic sympathy. On the other hand, student pressure in the 1960s changed the campus ineradicably nonetheless. One student, Baldemar Velasquez, launched a consuming crusade of farm labor organizing. In the process he founded an enduring farm worker labor union that persists to this day, but at the time he antagonized many local farmers (many of them Mennonites and firm supporters of the college). Bluffton College student feminists denounced what they saw as endemic campus sexism. In the early 1970s the Black Student Union capped several years of intense racial activism by mounting a boycott of classes and athletic events until the college evinced a greater commitment to black student recruitment and cultural support.

The more enduring legacy of student activism of the era came, however, in the transformation of many long-standing student traditions and the destruction of the college's in loco parentis mode. Vociferous student pressure quickly did away with class initiation rituals, compulsory chapel and class attendance, "family-style" meals in the cafeteria, campus-imposed dress codes, student curfews, and the like.

A second turning point, in a more sober way, arrived with the larger student demographic downturn of the later 1970s. Student enrollments fell dramatically, dipping back under 600 by 1975 and hovering in the mid-500 range through the 1980s. Not surprisingly, college finances proved a nagging problem. In his short presidency from 1973 to 1978, Benjamin Sprunger made some real progress in putting the college back on safer financial footing (though his campaign to reorient the college in a more conservative evangelical direction met angry resistance of many professors). Elmer Neufeld, the college's capable president from 1978 to 1995, spent nearly two decades paying off the $3.5 million debt inherited from the 1960s. Neufeld's presidency was remarkably successful for a number of reasons. A widely respected Mennonite church leader, Neufeld had spent decades in the thick of Mennonite peace activism, had served as Bluffton's academic dean, and began his presidency deeply committed to the progressive Anabaptist mission of the college that had been fermenting for three-quarters of a century. He believed, commented one of his administrators later, that "we're here to serve not just Mennonites, but all kinds of students."

Impelled by such a vision, Neufeld called students to Christian service vocations and peace commitments that dovetailed with their (and his own) evangelical theology. In so doing, in the 1990s Neufeld and his successor, Lee Snyder, led the college—somewhat unexpectedly—into another great era of expansion. For a variety of reasons, both internal and external, the college began to boom under Neufeld, a trend that was maintained and furthered by Snyder and her staff. Beginning in the later 1980s student enrollments climbed yearly, breaking the 1,000 mark in the fall of 1995, a peak the college has maintained since. In the decade following 1988 the college more than doubled its operating budget and quadrupled its endowment from more than $3 million to more than $12 million. Girders for new buildings once again rose over campus—a new football stadium, a handsome visual arts center, a state-of-the-art recital hall and a new dormitory (named for Lloyd Ramseyer). Finally, in the spring of 2000 the college put finishing touches on a stunning new centerpiece for the campus, a soaring four-story academic center that, with an eye to the institution's birthday, the trustees named Centennial Hall.

Nonetheless, even with all the changes, what remains most striking is the degree of continuity that the college has maintained with its original founding vision, and especially with the mission as reshaped by President Ramseyer and his colleagues in the years during and following World War II. Bluffton College remained a self-consciously Christian college. Upwards of 250 to 300 students (easily a third of all residential students) voluntarily pack its weekly chapel services. At the same time, such students (the vast majority of them from beyond the boundaries of the college's founding church) received a thorough grounding in basic Mennonite precepts such as justice, peace and service to others. And people began to notice. In 1995 a visiting team of church officials described the college as "a peace church emphasis in more or less an evangelical Christian setting."

Indeed, for a number of reasons—its own increased selectivity of new faculty, for example, and also a new focus on academic assessment—in the 1990s the college seemed to grow more conscious of its mission than ever before. It spoke to this new consciousness most dramatically, for example, when workmen painted the key words of the college's mission statement along the ceiling beams in the Marbeck cafeteria. Neufeld phrased the fundamental point perfectly. "Bluffton should not be seen as somehow less than Mennonite for its diversity," he declared to alumni in 1996, "but rather *more than Mennonite* . . . with a stronger Christian peace church witness growing out of this experience."

In the end, perhaps a small stone statue best encapsulates what the college has been about. Decades ago college officials set on a prominent place on campus the figure of a Russian minstrel singer called a Kobzar. The figure had been sculpted by a near-legendary figure on campus, a Russian Mennonite refugee named John Peter Klassen, who had fled Stalin's intense persecution of Ukrainian Mennonites and had arrived on campus in 1924, where he taught art to generations of students for the next thirty-four years. Klassen originally intended his Kobzar statue to be a gift from the Mennonites to the Russian people because "they were good to us." To his immense disappointment, Soviet authorities refused the piece. Klassen later sculpted a small statue of the seated Kobzar from memory. It still remained his gift to a people outside, a symbol that could bridge the gap between Mennonites and other people no longer beyond the boundaries of their world. The small minstrel singer sits today in a brick courtyard in front of Marbeck Center. In his figure and founding purpose, the statute still embodies the kind of vision that has propelled Bluffton College for a hundred years, and now beyond.

Suggested Reading

The most recent analytical summary of Bluffton College's history is found in Perry Bush, *Dancing with the Kobzar: Bluffton College and Mennonite Higher Education* (Pandora Press, 2000). Also see the three previous histories of the college: Von Hardesty, *A Narrative of Bluffton College* (Bluffton College, 1975); Members of the Faculty, *Bluffton College: An Adventure in Faith, 1900–1950* (Berne Witness Press, 1950); and C. Henry Smith and E. J. Hirschler, eds., *The Story of Bluffton College* (Bluffton College, 1925). For more information on Bluffton in the 1913–45 years, with a particular focus on the church conflicts of the 1920s, see Perry Bush, "United Progressive Mennonites: Bluffton College and Mennonite Higher Education, 1913–1945," *Mennonite Quarterly Review* 74 (July 2000). On the same focus in other Mennonite colleges, see Paul Toews, "Fundamentalist Conflict in Mennonite Colleges: A Response to Cultural Transitions?" *Mennonite Quarterly Review* 60 (Jan. 1986): 38–57. On the Mennonite "quickening" and the larger background that produced so many Mennonite colleges, see James Juhnke, *Vision, Doctrine, War: Mennonite Identity and Organization in America* (Herald Press, 1989).

Buchtel College

From Universalism to the University of Akron

GEORGE W. KNEPPER

A visitor to the campus of the University of Akron, a comprehensive state university of more than 20,000 students, has little reason to know that it evolved from Buchtel College, a small, church-related institution. Approaching the university's administration building, Buchtel Hall, the visitor passes a statue of John Richards Buchtel that is situated alongside the central campus walkway, Buchtel Common. By now the visitor may well have deduced that the name Buchtel was somehow central to the university's history, and the visitor would be right.

Buchtel College was established in May 1870 by the Ohio Universalist Convention, the coordinating body of Universalist congregations in Ohio. Since the end of the Civil War Universalists had contemplated building an academy or seminary in Ohio where their sons and daughters could receive instruction in an environment compatible with their beliefs and practices. Ohio was brimming with church-related schools sponsored by an impressive diversity of Christian bodies; now it was to be the Universalists' turn.

Universalists were Protestant Christians who believed in universal salvation and in a single manifestation of the deity. They shared the "liberal religion" with Unitarians. Since most Christian bodies were Trinitarian—believing in a triune God of Father, Son, and Holy Spirit—Universalists often found themselves regarded as less than fully Christian. It was difficult for them to make their case because they were relatively few in number, they did not proselyte, and they had no elaborate ecclesiastical structure to lead the way. Intellectually they were well prepared to defend their Christian view thanks to their colleges, each with a theological school—Tufts at Medford, Massachusetts; St. Lawrence at Canton, New York; and Lombard at Galesburg, Illinois.

By 1868 the Ohio Convention had formulated a plan. Ohio Universalists were to subscribe $50,000 for a denominational school, probably an academy or seminary,

Enthusiastic Universalist leaders open Buchtel College, 1872

to be located in the town or city that would provide at least $10,000 in additional funds. The Reverend Henry Miller was hired to manage the enterprise. By the spring of 1870 Miller had the $50,000 subscription in hand and set about selecting a site for the new school.

There were three serious bidders. Oxford was rejected because it already had all the schools it could handle. Kent had a history of fever outbreaks that made it an "unhealthy place." Mount Gilead, seat of Morrow County, centrally located, was healthy and had a strong Universalist congregation, and it promptly subscribed $10,000. Miller was ready to recommend it when another key player in the enterprise, the Reverend Andrew Willson, pastor of the Universalist church in Kent, asked for a delay until wealthy businessmen in nearby Akron could be sounded out.

In 1870 Akron was a booming industrial city of 10,000 people, many of whom worked in its farm machinery, clay products, match, and milling industries. A newcomer to the city in 1873 described Akron as "a brisk young city . . . enterprising in business, public spirited, large minded, up to date, and bound to win." John R. Buchtel was its representative man. Buchtel, a leader in farm machinery manufacture and in many related business enterprises, was a Universalist who had worshiped with Willson's Kent congregation during a hiatus in the life of the Akron church. Though Buchtel had shown no interest in the school project, Willson, Miller, and others now enlisted the Reverend George Messenger, a retired Universalist minister and friend of Buchtel, to write to him on behalf of the school enterprise. Messenger must have been persuasive, for Buchtel changed plans already made for his philanthropy and lent his support to the securing of the Universalist school for Akron. But Buchtel and his local supporters were not interested in a secondary school. The Akron High School was already doing good work. They asked for a college. "A college it shall be," said Henry Miller, but "Akron and Summit County have to pay for it accordingly." An additional $60,000 had to be raised to secure the college. Buchtel responded handsomely, pledging $31,000 for building and endowment. One hundred local citizens and thirteen businesses pledged an additional $31,000, and Akron won its prize.

On May 31, 1870, trustees of the Ohio Universalist Convention met at the Summit County courthouse, constituted themselves and others whom they invited to act with them as "corporators," and voted unanimously to locate the college in Akron. To complete incorporation they needed a name for their college. Many suggestions were put forward and rejected before it was suggested that Buchtel be called in for advice. When asked his opinion Buchtel replied, "Gentlemen, this is to be your college, not mine. I mean to help it financially as I may be able. If I live and am prospered, I intend to give the college someday one hundred thousand dollars. You may call the college what you please." The corporators responded unanimously; the school would be named Buchtel College.

The Reverend Henry Canfield, one of the trustees involved and from whose recollections we have this story, wrote: "If anyone reading these lines is moved to say or think that John R. Buchtel bought the name of the college for himself, let me say such person has no just conception of the spirit of the occasion. If we had felt that he had made a bid for the name, it would have been given reluctantly, if at all." John Buchtel, wrote Canfield, was a "great hearted man" seeking to provide for others the formal education that had been denied him. A few weeks later the Ohio General Convention unanimously endorsed the work of the college corporators and passed a resolution giving a vote of confidence to their work and to Mr. Buchtel by gratefully recognizing "the wisdom that gives the institution his name."

The corporators now selected a board of trustees to lead the college venture. Among the trustees were five Universalist ministers and fifteen laymen, eight of the latter being Akron residents. The board's makeup was significant, for the local laymen, including John R. Buchtel, as president of the board, were strong and influential men who soon dominated affairs and tended to overshadow Universalist influence, eventually moving the college ever more closely toward local interests.

As the trustees organized, work progressed on a previously selected campus site. The chosen spot was the Spicer Hill Cemetery of slightly over one acre in size, located on high ground about half-mile east of Akron's downtown commercial district. The cemetery had been abandoned and bodies removed to Akron Rural Cemetery (Glendale Cemetery) because the soil on Spicer Hill held water, and relatives of the dearly departed were distressed at the thought of their loved ones floating through eternity.

Though unfit for graves, Spicer Hill was well suited for a college building. It was thought to be a healthy site due to its altitude (some misinformed enthusiasts claimed it was the highest point in Ohio) and because wells could tap an underground stream of pure water, a source that also served local breweries. The cemetery reportedly had been cleared, but the first students occupying the college building found an occasional bone after a heavy rain. One student recalled, "I remember the early years of the college, before the trees were planted and every rainfall gouged out deep runnels in the clayey soil and disclosed full many a human bone," a sight that spooked the prep school youngsters living in the college dormitories.

While the site was being prepared, Thomas W. Silloway of Boston was selected to design the college building, and his plans were promptly approved and implemented. On Independence Day 1871 elaborate cornerstone-laying ceremonies were held on the college grounds. The featured speaker was Horace Greeley, editor of the *New York Tribune*, a Universalist widely known for his strong views on the conduct of the Civil War that often conflicted with President Lincoln's. His popularity led enthusiastic Akronites to string a banner along the parade route that read "Greeley for President." A year later, when the great man did indeed run for the presidency, Akron claimed first honors in putting him forward.

Following Greeley's lengthy speech, a reception was held on the grounds of Buchtel's nearby residence. There Greeley gave an impromptu defense of Universalism, concluding with the observation that "we of the Universalist faith are out of the great body of Christian churches at the present time, not because we deserve to be, but because they say we are not orthodox. Our case is similar to that of members of colored churches. Being denied admission to churches of their white brethren, they build for themselves. So we, denied admission to the churches of our orthodox brethren, build for ourselves." The crowd then called on Buchtel for remarks, which he made in "one of his off-hand unreportable speeches," assuring his listeners that the college would be "first class" in every respect. He reassured Trinitarians, "We don't intend to pull a shingle from a single church." He harbored no antipathy toward any church in the city. When he hired a man, he did not inquire into his religion but into his qualifications. This institution was to qualify men for work, "and women too," for he wanted them to be on equal terms with the men (cheers!). He believed in educating all, black and white, of both sexes. The day's activities ended on this felicitous note.

By September 1872 the great college building was ready for students although some finishing work was still in progress. Architecturally it was a combination of Doric, Gothic, and Norman styles, a mix not especially attractive to modern tastes. This massive structure was five stories high, 240 feet wide, and 54 feet deep. It was symmetrical with men's dormitory rooms in East Hall and women's in West Hall, the two wings connected by a central section containing classrooms, dining facilities, and, of course, a large chapel on the upper floors. In its first years, before trees and landscaping softened its outline, it loomed stark and somewhat forbiddingly over the city. It was to many rural students the grandest building they had ever seen.

As the building (commonly called Buchtel College or Buchtel Hall) moved toward completion, a presidential search was under way. Henry Blandy, a lay member of the board of trustees, was traveling to the East Coast on business, so his fellow trustees charged him with visiting New England in order to find a president suitable for the college's needs. In today's world, it would be incomprehensible to take such an important task so casually. Blandy consulted with Universalist leaders and, following their lead, recommended the Reverend Sullivan McCollester, the learned pastor of the Universalist church in Nashua, New Hampshire. At the time it was commonly assumed among leaders of sectarian schools that a college-trained minister of the faith would have the intellectual qualities, and likely the personal ones as well, necessary for a college presidency. At any rate, McCollester visited Akron, where he was interviewed "to the eminent satisfaction of all present." He got the job.

In late-nineteenth-century America the presidential role in church-related colleges was fairly well defined. The president should be an ordained minister of the sponsoring denomination: he was to preside over the faculty, which in turn determined the curriculum, standards, and discipline of the institution. The president served as a court of appeals from faculty disciplinary actions; raised money; kept the school in the public eye by preaching and speaking in churches, denominational meetings, and on public occasions; presided at commencements and other special events; led daily chapel exercises; preached Sunday sermon; and was expected to teach classes, usually a course in mental and moral philosophy. It was important that he be well read and well traveled and that he command respect, if not affection. McCollester met these criteria handsomely.

At Buchtel College the president was two steps removed from day-to-day business affairs. A financial secretary handled the accounts, but major business decisions (and some minor ones) were rendered by the trustees. As president of the board of trustees from the school's founding until his death in 1892, John R. Buchtel played a central role in college business. Unlike many donors for whom colleges have been named, Buchtel gave generously of himself as well as of his money—about $500,000 in all, an enormous amount for the time.

This earnest native of a Stark County farm had little formal education. As a young adult he farmed successfully using "scientific" agricultural techniques. He then became a farm machinery salesman, rising to establish and head the Akron plant of the Buckeye Mower and Reaper Company. Coincident with his role in starting Buchtel College, he was appointed by Governor Rutherford B. Hayes to the board of newly established Ohio Agricultural and Mechanical College (later Ohio State University). As one of three "managing trustees," he recommended the Neil farm, two miles north of Columbus, as the campus site, partly because it had a fine spring of clear water that he fancied. He secured Jacob Snyder of Akron to design the first building and, most significantly, supported those trustees who from the start wanted a broad curriculum that transcended a narrow focus on agriculture. All in all, this was an admirable performance from a man with Buchtel's educational background.

Buchtel and his wife, Elizabeth, were childless, and they embraced students as a surrogate family. Students were fond of them, referring to John as "Uncle Johnnie," but not to his face. Buchtel faithfully attended college events and, late in life, when crippled by a stroke, students carried him in a chair up the many steps to the college chapel so that he could attend the exercises.

One is not surprised, then, to learn that he personally recruited Buchtel College's first faculty member, Carl Kolbe, editor of the *Akron Germania*, the local German-language newspaper. He presented Kolbe to the board with typical informality, "Gentlemen, this is the man who is going to teach our boys and girls Dutch." Years later, when Kolbe tried to resign due to a work overload, Buchtel showed up on Kolbe's front porch before 6:00 A.M. one bitter winter morning and demanded that Kolbe return to the college. Kolbe returned, became a campus legend, and when he died in 1905 the campus shut down for three days in mourning.

Kolbe was joined on the first faculty by five other new instructors, three of whom were fired after the first year. The college appeared determined to live up to McCollester's promise that there would be no compromise with collegiate standards. "Some bearing the name college are not even first class academies," said McCollester. "Ripe scholarship can no more be the outgrowth of second rate institutions than oaks and elms can be the product of hot houses." Buchtel College emphasized effective teaching, so it was a bonus when several early faculty members also won distinction for their research. Dr. Charles Knight, for example, initiated the world's first collegiate course in rubber chemisty, which led ultimately to the University of Akron's dominant role in polymer research.

The tiny faculty faced a daunting task. Forty-six collegiate students and 171 preparatory students were present for the opening of classes in September 1872. Universalists dominated the collegiate ranks but were less prominent among the younger students, among whom local access rather than denominational loyalty determined enrollment. Young ladies were well represented in a student body that ranged in age from ten-year-old Vincent Tomlinson to mature adults, including a Civil War veteran (who had served several campaigns as a drummer boy) who came to college in 1873.

Many collegiate students came from out of state. First to arrive were the Parmenter brothers, Charlie and Fred, from Vermont. Though the college building was not quite finished when they arrived, they were cared for by President McCollester, who personally helped nurse them through an illness. Later the boys went hunting for pigeons in Copley Swamp with Buchtel and President McCollester. Fred wrote his parents, "Mr. Buchtel is a jolly good fellow. He is full of fun and always seems to be as happy as a clam in high water." Not all went well, however. "We have pretty poor fare in the victuals line," wrote Fred. "I guess they will do better after they get straightened round a little. If they don't we shall come home—that is all." Thus omnipresent student dissatisfaction with institutional food arrived with the first students.

Food would be an issue throughout the college's history, but it was secondary to behavior standards beholden to nineteenth-century morality. In the late nineteenth century a "decent fellow" could be concerned about the nature of his neighbor's behavior. In common with many Protestant denominations, Universalists regarded smoking, drinking, swearing, and failure to attend Sunday services as signs of moral weakness. Frank Wieland (Class of 1890) recalled the day a Kappa Kappa Gamma sorority meeting broke up in shock when the young ladies observed a student smoking a cigarette. "He was from Oil City, Pennsylvania, a Godless place," wrote Wieland, tongue in cheek, "and did not know that smoking was considered sinful at Buchtel."

The college minimized chances for questionable behavior by requiring a certificate of good moral character for admission and then enveloping its charges within a cocoon of rules and regulations common to all church-related colleges of that time. "No student shall fire gunpowder in the college building or on the premises, or engage in card playing or any form of gambling in the college or in the city, or visit liquor saloons or billiard rooms," one proscription intoned. An especially onerous restriction said, "Young men and young women are not allowed to take walks or rides together without permission." Since men occupied rooms in the east end of Buchtel Hall and women the rooms in the west end, special care was taken to keep them apart. But student ingenuity and resourcefulness were in plentiful supply at Buchtel, and occasional trysts were arranged, sometimes in the chapel situated between the men's and women's dormitories. On the whole, behavior was well controlled. In 1876 a board committee reported that college work was being conducted in excellent fashion with good discipline, solid work, and a high level of moral and religious outlook. The trustees were gratified.

The collegiate courses of study (degree programs) were demanding for their time. For admission to the four-year classical course, a student must have competence in Latin and Greek grammar and "prosody"; some familiarity with selected writings of Xenophon, Homer, Caesar, Virgil, and Cicero; as well as algebra, English grammar, U.S. history, ancient and modern geography. These requirements were essentially the same as Yale's, to which Buchtel liked to compare itself A less ambitious two-year philosophical course was soon upgraded to four-year status with more stringent requirements. This course led to the Bachelor of Philosophy degree, unlike the Bachelor of Arts degree associated with the classical course. A scientific course was the only one not to require Latin; it emphasized the natural sciences and led to the Bachelor of Science degree. These programs were in constant flux throughout the nineteenth century. A radical innovation for its time was the introduction of the elective system in 1882, much to the dismay of old-line purists.

Slowly the college acquired the supporting resources such as library, laboratories, specimens, and collections featured by established schools. Rote learning, which featured daily classroom recitations, did not encourage use of auxiliary resources. The "library" initially consisted of a few glass-fronted cases in which books were displayed under lock and key. A major step forward occurred when General Lucius V. Bierce, a prominent Akronite, gave the college his substantial personal library, collections of fossils and presidential signatures, and the sword of Major Hume, a British officer killed by Bierce's troops during a filibustering invasion of Canada in 1838. As the curriculum developed new flexibility and the college responded to the needs of a rapidly expanding industrial society, rote learning lost its primacy, and students were encouraged to make use of the library and other support materials.

The original college building lacked anything resembling a scientific laboratory, but growing interest in the physical and natural sciences demanded suitable facilities. Charles Knight, professor of physics and chemistry, and Edwin Claypole, professor of geology, led the charge. Knight and his students created laboratory space in the basement of Buchtel Hall while Claypole had his students devise their own scientific apparatus from whatever was at hand. Although the resulting equipment was primitive, it proved an effective learning experience.

Extracurricular activities at Buchtel were similar to those found in colleges everywhere. Literary societies, originally segregated by sex but later integrated, had their own rooms and "libraries." They competed with one another in staging plays and other performances; contemporary accounts report that the results were often extremely amateurish. Fraternities and sororities made an early appearance and quickly supplanted literary societies as focuses of student entertainment and competition. Delta Tau Delta and Phi Delta Theta led the way in fraternities, while Kappa Kappa

Gamma and Delta Gamma were first among sororities. Inevitably splits developed between "Greeks" and nonaffiliated students. These splits mirrored to a degree some town and gown splits. Just as unaffiliated students perceived Greeks as condescending, so "townies," especially boys, thought campus men acted superior, although contact between the two was limited largely to occasional athletic contests.

To provide for its students' physical well-being, the college erected Crouse Gymnasium in 1888, describing it with typical collegiate hyperbole as "the finest west of the Alleghenies." Buchtel Field (1892) extended opportunity for outdoor physical activities, and it was soon used for intercollegiate sports. A football team was first fielded in 1891, and basketball, initially played by women, followed a decade later.

Early intercollegiate contests were entirely managed by students. With faculty approval students even hired coaches, the most famous of whom was football's John Heisman. Buchtel joined other Ohio schools in one or another athletic association, none of which had much stability or credibility until colleges took matters of finance, scheduling, and facilities out of student hands and assigned such duties to a faculty manager of athletics or to a faculty board of control.

As Buchtel College matured in the last decades of the nineteenth century, strains developed between the college and the local Universalist congregation. President McCollester had helped revive that congregation, which included Mr. and Mrs. Buchtel, and the locals met for services in the college chapel. The Reverend George Weaver's arrival in 1873 as pastor of the local congregation seems to have focused town and gown dissatisfaction. The record suggests that the more liberal outlook of the campus irritated some conservative spirits in the local congregation. The immediate cause of town and gown split, however, seems to have centered on fallout from the decision of Reverend Weaver's children to withdraw from Buchtel.

"Disaffected students" had been nursing grievances for some time when pastor Weaver permitted his daughter to withdraw from Buchtel and return to St. Lawrence, which she had previously attended. Weaver's son was permitted to enroll at Tufts College because he wanted "to attend a more noted institution." Weaver's children were also among some students who petitioned the board to remove President McCollester, for reasons not stated in the records. This action "created a feeling of alienation between the president and the pastor and their friends." The chasm broadened and deepened until "the church people withdrew from the college chapel." President McCollester had but recently received a strong vote of confidence from the board, but in the face of this furor he resigned in 1878. Weaver resigned his ministry of the local congregation as well, leaving local and collegiate Universalists without leadership.

The void was briefly filled when the Reverend Everett L. Rexford was hired as president and local pastor, and he helped heal, temporarily as it proved, the rift between college and campus. He thrived on intellectual debate, however, contributing to stresses with Universalism and creating controversy within the Akron community. "Like the ocean petrels," wrote one observer, "he seemed at times to hover . . . over the stormiest waters." In a running debate with an esteemed local Episcopalian leader, he attracted criticism to the campus and its professed objectivity, charges that made Rexford realize that he should choose between the academic world and the pulpit. He chose the latter, resigning in 1880 to assume the pastorate of an out-of-state Universalist church.

Rexford's successor, the Reverend Orello Cone, was a noted biblical scholar from the theological school at St. Lawrence University. It took all of Buchtel's formidable persuasive powers to attract him to campus, but once there Cone served longer than any other Buchtel president (1880–96). In the first dozen years of his presidency the college enjoyed some of its most successful years. By 1892, however, things were coming apart. The college experienced a monumental loss in that year with the death of John R. Buchtel. Throughout the school's twenty-two years he had sustained it through one crisis after another with his funds and his leadership. Shortly after his death the national economy faltered, and from 1893 through 1897 the nation experienced what has been called "the first industrial depression." It hit Akron with exceptional vigor, and the loss of local funding coupled with diminishing Universalist support brought near-collapse to the college.

Universalist support for the college had been declining for some time. College leaders had been slow to cultivate money sources in the East where Universalist influence was strongest, and denominational membership had plateaued in Ohio. Universalists made up an ever-smaller part of the Buchtel student body. From 1878 to 1896, on an average, just 36.6 percent of the student body, college and prep, was Universalist, and by 1896 the number had diminished to 19.7 percent. If collegiate enrollment alone had been counted, the Universalist representation would have been somewhat larger. Nearly all of the endowment money (and there wasn't much) was Universalist in origin, but building funds, prize money, and scholarships increasingly were funded by local sources.

Even before the economic crisis of the 1890s, the Ohio Universalist Convention appealed to the college leadership to reinvigorate denominational ties. In 1896 Dr. H. L. Canfield presented to the college board a memorial urging consideration of closer Universalist ties. "We have no desire to make the college a proselytizing institution nor to make its management offensively denominational. We only ask that it shall record the respect due to the people by whose sacrifices it was founded and the church whose interest it was builded to conserve."

Some of the discontent centered around President Cone. He was more interested in scholarly competence than in Universalist orthodoxy when recommending faculty appointments. While considering a Buchtel alumna, Mary Jewett, for the chair in English literature, he wrote to her that he was under much pressure to hire a Universalist, "but I shall not allow myself to be influenced by the mere fact of religious belief or association. I shall recommend the best qualified candidate regardless of Theological opinions." The trustees did the hiring, however, so Cone wrote again to Jewett asking her to attend the Universalist church as an example to the girls. "Could you give us a part of your heart, at least, in case you should find our preacher acceptable?" She could, and she did, until resigning from the college to assume a new career in medicine.

Cone's academic specialty, the critical examination of the Scriptures, also caused contention. The use of history, archeology, and language study as a basis for assessing the Bible offended traditionalists who were not ready to see old truths reexamined. But Cone's struggles with Universalism affected his stewardship far less than did the depression's severe economic problems. The industrial city of Akron was hit uncommonly hard with extensive unemployment and with the demise or restructuring of much of its economic base. Since the college's student and monetary support came increasingly from the city and Summit County, hard times for the city were reflected in hard times for the college. Enrollment dropped, student organizations folded for lack of members, teachers took pay cuts and several left, and efforts to secure financing failed. Morale was at its nadir.

Amid these troubles President Cone suffered yet another blow. Once more student unrest undermined a president. Students circulated a petition to trustees claiming that Cone was not a suitable leader: he was too reticent, he was not a sports enthusiast. Some alumni joined with their own petitions of grievance only to be countered by still other alumni arguing on Cone's behalf. This unrest was the coup de grace. Cone resigned in March 1896, briefly assumed a pastorate in Kansas, and then resumed work congenial to his interests and talents on the faculty of the St. Lawrence University Theological School.

The trustees now turned to Dr. Charles M. Knight, the highly respected professor of physics and chemistry, to serve as interim president until Cone's replacement could be found. He was the only nonclergyman to serve as president while the school was under Universalist auspices. Knight proved a popular choice, and many wanted him to assume the presidency permanently, but he saw his true vocation in the classroom and laboratory, to which he returned after one year in office.

Once again a Universalist pastor was selected to head the college. Ira Priest, pastor of the local congregation, was chosen to heal the rifts in local Universalist ranks. He was acceptable to both liberal and conservative sentiment, and he appeared to have good prospects for leadership since the depression had abated and Akron was again booming industrially. But the fates ruled against him. Inadequate finances continued to be a severe problem. It cost the college between $125 and $140 a year to educate students who paid but $40 a year in tuition. As this problem was being addressed, the college suffered a near-fatal blow. On December 20, 1899, a devastating blaze burned Buchtel Hall to the ground, destroying nearly all of the school's property and possessions.

Immediate steps were taken to rebuild, but where would the money come from? Insurance brought in a portion of the rebuilding costs, but the main source of funds was local. Akron civic leaders pledged their support, and contributions for rebuilding poured in from students, faculty, alumni, and the local citizenry, including the pennies of children. Ohio Universalists pledged support, and old quarrels were forgotten in the emotional weeks following the fire. Classes resumed on January 4, 1900. Crouse Gymnasium was partitioned into classrooms, laboratories, a library, and a chapel. Nearby buildings were pressed into service. Books and equipment were donated. Housing for collegiate women had to be arranged. (The college had closed its men's dormitory rooms some years earlier.)

If one were to select a point at which Buchtel College became less a Universalist enterprise and more a city enterprise, one would do well to choose those weeks in 1900 when heroic efforts were being made to resurrect the school's programs. Ohio Universalists, devastated by the loss, pledged $100,000 toward rebuilding, but this money was beyond their ability to deliver. The denomination had lost those things that had created and sustained emotional ties—books, records, mementos, personal belongings, and the great old college building itself that was so full of memories. Into this growing vacuum of sentiment and support Akron influences moved with ever more confidence, which was further enhanced by the construction of two new buildings.

The new Buchtel Hall, much smaller than its predecessor, was dedicated in 1901. It was strictly a classroom and office building. It serves today as the administration building of the University of Akron. A new building for Buchtel Academy (the preparatory school) was dedicated at the same time, but it, too, was essentially a classroom building. Much work remained before the college's needs could be met. The new facilities coincided with new leadership. President Priest resigned in 1902. The healing he had promoted at the beginning of his tenure had been undermined by the trauma surrounding the tragic fire, and he had to bear the additional burden of discontented students and alumni as well as sniping from certain Universalist sources.

Priest's successor, the Reverend Augustus B. Church, was not only pastor of the local congregation, but he also had taught at the college on a part-time basis and thus was a familiar figure on campus and in the community. Handsome and outgoing, he had the temperament to pour oil on troubled waters. Church was the first Buchtel president to exercise powers now common to college presidencies. He took a leading role in day-to-day administration, including finances. Although his role was different, he faced same old problems that had dogged his predecessors, foremost of which was the chronic need for additional funding for operations and for capital improvements. He had some success with the latter, securing funds to build the college's first science building, complete with modern laboratories, and he helped secure funds for a small women's dormitory.

As these changes were occurring, the Universalist era at Buchtel College came to an end. The fire and its aftermath had swung the management of affairs closer to local interests. Akron was again thriving industrially and demanded skilled personnel for its workforce, employees with specific skills not traditionally emphasized in liberal arts curricula. The old courses of study were united under a liberal arts rubric that led to a single Bachelor of Arts degree. Business-related courses and additional science courses were added to the curriculum, and some of these courses were taught in the evening to accommodate working people.

In June 1907 the Buchtel College trustees, anxious to participate in the financial benefits offered by the Carnegie Foundation for Pensioning Teachers, voted to sever ties with the Universalist church as required by the Carnegie program. The Ohio Universalist Convention endorsed the move, and surprisingly little dissent from Universalists appears in the records. Perhaps this small, none-too-affluent denomination was relieved to escape the annual pleas for funds to support a school in which its sons and daughters were now but a small part of the student body.

For the next six years Buchtel operated as a private college with a self-perpetuating board. Its last Universalist clergyman president, Augustus Church, died in November 1912 and was succeeded by a layman, young Parke Rexford Kolbe, whose father had been Buchtel's first professor. Kolbe provided the insight and drive to move the college into its next organizational phase.

The Buchtel trustees realized that new sources of funding were imperative to keep the school alive. To secure this funding they offered the college and all its assets to the city of Akron to be operated as a municipal university following the successful model of Cincinnati. The city council accepted the offer, and in December 1913 the new Municipal University of Akron was formed with Parke Kolbe as its first president. Kolbe led the way toward the immediate establishment of a college of engineering plus new courses in commerce and secretarial science. In accordance with the transfer agreement, the name Buchtel College remained on the college of liberal arts (later arts and sciences), as it does to this day.

Akron grew slowly as a municipal university until post–World War II enrollment surges made it clear that the municipal tax base could not meet the institution's expanding needs. Salvation was at hand, however, from Governor James A. Rhodes's plan to assist higher education in Ohio. The University of Akron became "state assisted" on July 1, 1963. Just four years later, on July 1, 1967, President Norman P. Auburn led the university into full state university status.

One can only speculate about the astonishment that nineteenth-century Universalists would have felt to see their small, struggling, but proud college transformed into a large, sophisticated multiversity. Surely they would approve of the university's teaching and learning mission, but one suspects they would regret the loss of moral and ethical instruction so much a part of the Universalist tradition.

What was Buchtel College's legacy? From the first commencement in 1873 through 1913 it awarded 465 baccalaureate degrees, 47 percent of them to women. More than twice that number attended collegiate courses at one time or another but did not graduate. The preparatory school provided mostly local students with an extraordinary education that served them well when they entered some of the best colleges in the land.

Despite internal dissension, Buchtel College extended to its students and to the community a sympathetic view toward social reform initiatives, women's rights especially. From the outset women were well represented on the faculty. These were adventuresome women, many of whom left teaching to assume roles in less traditional occupations. Two women served as college trustees at a time when few institutions could make that claim. John R. Buchtel's liberal view toward race persisted, although the college had but one "colored" student of record.

Buchtel graduated no president, governor, senator or Nobel laureate, but its sons and daughters established enviable records in many useful fields of endeavor, a testament to the foresight of Universalism in Ohio.

Suggested Reading

George W. Knepper, *New Lamps for Old: One Hundred Years of Urban Higher Education at The University of Akron* (University of Akron Press, 1970); George W. Knepper, *Summit's Glory: Sketches of Buchtel College and The University of Akron* (University of Akron Press, 1990); Albert I. Spanton, ed., *Fifty Years of Buchtel 1870–1920* (Akron Alumni Association, 1922); Russell E. Miller, *Light on the Hill: A History of Tufts College 1852–1952* (Beacon Press, 1966).

Capital University

A Lutheran University of Service to Many

JAMES L. BURKE

Capital University has undergone considerable change from its establishment by the Evangelical Lutheran Church leaders in 1830. The church elders believed that a seminary to educate future pastors was needed in Ohio to keep students and potential pastors closer to home. The Theological Seminary of the Evangelical Lutheran Synod of Ohio, founded on June 9, 1830, was opened in Canton, Ohio, on October 1, 1830. The following year the school was moved to Columbus. The site for the school was on South High Street near what became the second location of the Capital University Law School. On March 2, 1850, the Ohio General Assembly granted Capital University a charter, and on September 12, 1850, classes began for a dozen students. Thus, from its 1830 seminary origins the university has grown into a complex, 4,000-student, multicollege institution.

Pastor Wilhelm Schmidt had six students that first year in Canton. Apparently he taught for two years without receiving any pay. After the second year Pastor Schmidt received a salary of $250 per year. Classes were taught in German. Only men were admitted until 1918. In 1831 the Lutheran Church leaders decided to move the seminary to Columbus, where Pastor Schmidt had received a call to serve four congregations. Also, Columbus Lutherans had outbid those in Canton by $500 in providing $2,500 to move the seminary to Columbus. The first site for the seminary was on Third Street, but the location soon was moved into a two-story building on South High Street near the second site of Capital University's future law school. Students had to find their own housing since financial problems prevented the entire building from being completed until 1841. One of the students wrote, "The students rented two log huts near the Seminary, formerly occupied by Negroes. Here we six studied in a small room sitting around a table with a tallow candle standing in the center. We rolled the beds in which we slept under the low roof of

View of the Old Dormitory from the Corner Gate

the hut. As the majority were very poor and had no source of income, six of us undertook to board ourselves in the cellar of the Seminary building, which in the beginning cost each 49 cents a week." A second building was constructed for the seminary in 1832 when the enrollment was a total of nine students. The seminary was fairly firmly established, and the Church officials wanted to establish a collegiate institution. In 1844 they initiated an effort to establish what was known as the Germanic College; however, severe financial constraints caused partly by an economic recession at the time doomed the effort.

Even as private colleges at the present face the continuing problems of finances and attracting students, so also did the seminary in its early years. Moreover, an argument developed about educational philosophy. Should the teaching consist of an extremely conservative orthodox view, or should a milder form of Lutheranism be learned? Apparently the conservatives prevailed in this debate. After Pastor Schmidt died in 1839 from typhoid fever, the college and preparatory school struggled to attract students and funds for the next several years. However, on March 2, 1850, the Ohio General Assembly granted the school a charter, and Capital University was established "as a corporation for the promotion of religion, learning, and morality." Capital University students were able to take courses in Greek, Latin, mathematics, history, science, and philosophy. The university enrolled between two and five students that year. The university took its name from Ohio's chief city and the seat of state government. The first president of Capital was Reverend William M. Reynolds.

The college, the preparatory school (known as "the Academy"), and the grammar school enrolled about 125 students. In 1850 the school was moved to a location on East Town Street between Fifth and Sixth Streets. The famous Hungarian patriot Louis Kossuth and the well-known singer Jenny Lind visited the school. Jenny Lind donated $1,500 toward establishing a professorship.

Student life in those days must have been demanding as the students immersed themselves in German, Greek, Latin, logic, and psychology in an effort to provide for more than a purely professional training. All instruction was provided in German, and it was not until 1866 that a course in English composition was taught. Resident students went to bed at 10:00 P.M. and arose at 5:00 A.M. Classes began at 8:00 A.M. with a lunch break at noon and then classes resumed until 5:00 P.M. Even in those days students had rules and regulations by which to abide. In the mid-1850s students were prohibited from smoking or chewing tobacco and from spitting on the floors. There were no organized college athletics, although some students gained their physical exercise by periodic fights between the town and gown groups.

By 1850 it was obvious that if Capital were to continue to develop it would need a new building to attract more students and serve a larger enrollment. Recurring themes in the college's development appear throughout its history. In 1852 a member of the university's board, Ohio's attorney general, and a prominent physician in Columbus, Dr. Lincoln Goodale, donated four acres of land on North High Street only a short distance from Broad Street and High Street for a new building site (currently the location of the Greek Orthodox Cathedral of the Annunciation). Completed in 1853, the new structure was large enough to serve as both a recitation hall and as a dormitory for the next twenty-three years. The building housed sixty residents and one professor. Most students attended the preparatory school for one year followed by three years in college and two years in the seminary, if they so chose. The university remained at the site until it was moved to the present location in Bexley in 1876. Capital had its first graduating class in 1854; during that same year the Reverend Christian Spielman was chosen as the university's second president.

Institutions of higher education have always witnessed controversy over various issues. In the years during the 1850s a concern surfaced over whether the president was too secular for the more conservative Lutherans. Many non-Lutherans served on the board, and some Lutherans feared that the university would lose its unique German Lutheran heritage. In some respects that issue is still a concern 150 years later. Many church-related colleges have had to struggle with this problem in an apparently increasingly secular society. This controversy probably added to the declining enrollment to fewer than forty students by 1857 as well as to a financial crisis. Another concern that emerged fairly quickly was whether Capital was to be a liberal arts college or a professional training college. This issue continued well into the twentieth century. Currently Capital has blended the two purposes effectively to develop a liberal arts education with a preprofessional curriculum.

Over and over again in critical times, a person has emerged to save an institution from ruin. The German-born Reverend William F. Lehmann, who had been one of the first students in the seminary, became the president in 1857. Lehmann served faithfully in that capacity until his death in 1880. In 1859 ten students were enrolled in the university; in 1867 there were thirty students in attendance; and by the time of President Lehmann's death the enrollment had reached more than 100 students in the grammar school, in the collegiate department, and in the seminary. President Lehmann led the university during critical times in the nation as well as for the college. The Civil War caused a decline in student numbers once again, but President Lehmann revitalized the college by starting at the foundation of any university. He expanded the faculty by bringing well-respected professors to Capital. After the war the enrollment began a modest increase in enrollment, but in 1897 there were still only forty-three students. Other than continuously trying to raise funds from the various Lutheran congregations, another issue for President Lehmann was to relocate the college from the "distractions" of downtown Columbus. However, the Church and the college leadership decided to remain in Columbus. A Mr. F. Michel offered the university a fifty-acre site in a cornfield just east of Alum Creek about four and a half miles east of the Goodale location in an area that would eventually become the City of Bexley. The Christ Lutheran Church congregation was being organized across the road, so it was a natural site for the two Lutheran institutions. In May 1876 wagons were used to transport the college to the new building. The main building on the location, named after President Lehmann, housed students, classrooms, and offices. Originally Lehmann Hall was a red brick structure, but in the early 1900s gray-colored stories were placed on the outer walls. Lehmann Hall stood on the campus until it was razed in 1988. The other building was Leonard Hall, which still exists as part of the Conservatory of Music. College costs in those days were $40 a year for tuition, $10 a year for room, and $2 a week for board.

Dormitory life in Lehmann Hall was grimly austere. The rooms were unfurnished except for several cupboards and a wood-burning stove. Students had to carry wood from a wood pile between the dorm and Leonard Hall. The stoves were the reason for all of the chimneys on the rooftop of Lehmann Hall. Lehmann Hall students finally had hot water in 1892. Natural gas was installed in 1893, and it was not until the 1897 that the first bathroom was built in Lehmann Hall. In 1882 the first telephone was installed in the building. Fresh water was a problem for students, since the wells were near the horse stables and the outdoor plumbing. Finally, in 1900

Lehmann Hall residents acquired city water. At one time Lehmann Hall housed the cafeteria, a clinic, a gymnasium on the fourth floor, and a hamburger stand in the basement, as well as all of the administrative offices.

Financial problems continued for successive presidents. In 1878 the university debt was $17,000. A fund-raising effort was conducted among the local Lutheran congregations, and while little cash was collected the university received many bushels of apples and potatoes.

However, Capital University was firmly established by the turn of the century. Recitation Hall was completed in 1891. Loy Gymnasium and Auditorium (named after President Lehmann's successor, Matthias Loy) was built in 1906, and Rudolf Library was completed in 1915. The presidents over the next several years included the Reverend Drs. Matthias Loy, C. H. Schutte, William F. Stellhorn, and L. H. Schuh.

In 1911 another controversy regarding the future of Capital arose over whether to separate the college and the seminary. Some believed that the university had developed the reputation of being a "preacher factory" and that that label discouraged other students from enrolling in the college. Some wanted a totally separate seminary building. Also, the curriculum slowly was beginning to include more liberal arts education. More science classes were included, and instruction in music had begun in 1889.

The time of considerable modernization in the early years of Capital University came during the presidency of Otto Mees (1912–46). Capital truly began to develop into a liberal arts university during this period. Schenk Divinity Hall was completed in 1923. A new auditorium was constructed in 1926, named after President Mees, and a new dormitory was also finished in 1926. A School of Music was started in 1918, and in the fall of 1928, under the direction of the Reverend Dr. Ellis Snyder, the Chapel Choir was organized. This choir would receive national and international acclaim. The choir performed in the White House in 1931 for President and Mrs. Hoover. The choir continues today as a fine representative of the university.

A major event in Capital's history occurred in 1918, when the board approved admitting up to twenty-five women students. Five women did enroll in 1919. The women were educated in separate classrooms, and a women's dormitory, Troutman-Ackermann Hall, was completed in 1926. A room in Lehmann Hall was provided for the women as a lounge and as a place to study between classes. For some time the men ate first at the boarding clubs; and even when men and women ate together, they sat on opposite sides of the tables.

By 1916 the enrollment had increased to 243 students with fourteen professors, and by 1948–49 there were 1,081 students on campus.

Capital has an athletic tradition about which to be proud. The football team won a regional national championship in 1970, and the women's basketball team won back-to-back national championships in 1994 and 1995. The foundation for Capital's intercollegiate athletics began in 1889 with six baseball games. Capital defeated both Ohio State University and Ohio Wesleyan University that year. In 1894 the first football games were played, including a game that would begin the long-standing rivalry with nearby Otterbein College. A basketball schedule began in 1907–8. Playing space has always been a problem for Capital athletic teams due to a lack of land for the university. In 1921 the university purchased land to develop an athletic field on the east side of the campus. Prior to that purchase the baseball field was south of Lehmann Hall. Students on the south side of Lehmann Hall had good views of baseball and football games that were played between Lehmann Hall and what is now Mees Hall. In 1940 a football stadium, which bears the Bernlohr name, was completed. The Bernlohr brothers, Fred and Bill, were excellent student-athletes and, later, instructors and coaches at Capital. In 1951 Alumni Gymnasium was completed, and athletic events moved out of Loy Gymnasium. At the turn of this century Capital completed the largest fund-raising campaign in its history to build a new health, recreation, and athletic facility. Bernlohr Stadium and Alumni Gymnasium were torn down in the spring of 2000 to make way for the new Capital Center, which opened in 2001. The Capital Center has a new football stadium, and the playing field has an artificial surface A multipurpose field house has an indoor track, a variety of playing courts, training rooms, classrooms, and faculty offices. And a new basketball performance arena replaces Alumni Gymnasium. Capital has continued its membership in the nationally respected Ohio Athletic Conference since 1927.

For many years Capital was known as a "preacher-teacher" institution with a good choir and music program. That label has been expanded due to the presence of a law school, a graduate business program, a nursing school, a conservatory of music, and an adult degree program, and Capital's teacher-education program became highly respected for its quality students. In 1922 W. L. Young was in charge of the "Normal Course" to prepare students to teach, and in 1924 a two-year course was established to train teachers, and a separate program to train church workers was started. In 1926 a Bachelor of Science degree in education was approved. In 1922 the North Central Accrediting Association gave approval to Capital's education program. Currently the education department accredited by N.C.A.T.E. continues to graduate excellent teachers who begin their field experiences in their second year.

The Great Depression years of the 1930s were difficult times for Capital university. Although the enrollment remained fairly steady, many sacrifices were made by the faculty and the staff to keep the college open. Faculty members accepted a 30 percent salary reduction in 1932, and many taught summer school classes for no payment. In 1932 the American Association for University Professors did not approve Capital's standing because of the low salaries; however, by 1935 the A.A.U.P.

did recognize the college. Many Capital students worked in the New Deal National Youth Association projects to earn money to remain in college. By 1937 a fund-raising effort permitted salaries to return to normal, but still low, levels.

A paradox appeared during those troubled financial times. President Mees launched a fund-raising campaign in 1936, which was so successful that a new wing and a new reading room were added to the Rudolf Library by 1938, and there were enough funds to begin planning for a new science hall.

No sooner had the Great Depression begun to ease than World War II started. During the war the Fifth College Training Detachment of the U.S. Army Air Corps lived and trained at Capital for six-month sessions from February 1943 through June 1944 for over 250 Capital and non-Capital people. During the war the number of classes was reduced, but the basic courses continued as usual for about 750 students. Several of Capital's faculty left the classroom to serve in the armed forces in Europe or in the Pacific. Twenty-two Capital alumni or students died during World War II.

In 1946 Harold L. Yochum became the ninth president of the university. He served in that capacity into 1969. Yochum received his undergraduate degree from Capital in 1923 and his divinity degree from the Evangelical Lutheran Theological Seminary in 1928. He came to Capital in 1946 from the Michigan district of the American Lutheran Church, where he had been serving as president. During his presidency at Capital the enrollment increased threefold, the campus doubled in size, three new buildings were constructed, and a law school and a nursing school became part of the university. Capital's tradition of blending a liberal arts education with prepro-fessional training was firmly established during President Yochum's administration. Half of the buildings on campus were constructed or almost totally remodeled during Yochum's tenure. After World War II a housing shortage occurred due to the influx of veterans. While seven temporary barracks were being constructed, many of the male students were housed in Loy Gymnasium. Two two-story barracks located on either end of Bernlohr Statdium were for families, and the one-story barracks were for single men. Two barracks were torn down to make way for Alumni Gymnasium in 1951. One barracks was located just north of Rudolf Hall; the other two were located between Mees Hall and Troutman Hall, where Saylor Hall stands currently. The enrollment was limited to 1,000 students until new dormitories could be built. A new student union–dining building, a new science hall, and a new gymnasium were built. These were not easy tasks because President Yochum disdained accepting any federal funds for the constructions. Apparently he wanted to be certain that Capital would remain independent in its decision making. Therefore, Dr. Yochum, almost by himself, but with the assistance of his vice president, proceeded to raise the funds for the new projects. President Yochum reorganized the administration and added four vice presidents to his staff. The burden of being the single major administrator was simply too heavy for one person in the 1960s. In addition,

President Yochum firmly believed that Capital University should become an integral part of the Columbus community. He was actively involved in many community endeavors while continuing to write, preach, and oversee the well-being of the university. He established a precedent that his successors have continued.

An important decision in the life of Capital occurred in 1959 when the college and the seminary became separate administrative entities. The seminary had grown considerably in numbers, from 103 in 1948 to 231 in 1957. The undergraduate enrollment had continued to grow, and one person could not adequately administer both institutions. Moreover, the leaders of the American Lutheran Church had decided that it wanted its seminaries to be separate from its colleges.

A brief explanation of two of the denominations of the Lutheran Church is in order here. The Lutheran Church in the United States has several denominations. The various Lutheran immigrant groups to America in the seventeenth and eighteenth centuries organized congregations and then combined into synodical organizations. Two of the major Lutheran denominations were the American Lutheran Church (A.L.C.), which supported Capital, and the Lutheran Church in America (L.C.A.). The relatively minor differences between the two denominations were based on ethnic differences and geographic location. The L.C.A. congregations were predominantly German people who settled in the eastern part of the United States, while the A.L.C. congregations were composed of German and Scandinavian peoples who settled in the Midwest. In 1988 the two congregations merged to form the Evangelical Lutheran Church in America (E.L.C.A.).

In addition to the separation of the university and the seminary in 1950, a School of Nursing was established, and in 1966 the Franklin University Law School became the Capital University School of Law. In 1967 the university surpassed the 2,000-student enrollment level with the inclusion of the law school. As the university continued to grow, Capital continued to search for new land to acquire for the landlocked campus. In 1968 the university purchased 12.7 acres of land on Nelson Road, formerly the site of the Columbus Academy. This purchase added land for a baseball field and a practice area for football and soccer. Also, the building contained a gymnasium, a natatorium, and classrooms.

Another important development during this time started in 1960 when professors were recognized for their outstanding teaching. The Praestantia Award was bestowed on a professor selected by faculty and third- and fourth-year students. The award was established to emphasize that excellence in teaching was the primary responsibility for Capital professors. The Praestantia Award continues to be a highly regarded honor. Moreover, in 1961 the first awarding of tenure to faculty occurred.

President Yochum retired in 1969, and a search was conducted for the next president. Dr. Thomas Langevin, the first nonclergyman, was selected as Capital's tenth president. Langevin, a Nebraska native, came to Capital from Pacific Lutheran University, where he had been the vice president for academic affairs since 1965. The ten-year administration of President Langevin spanned the rapidly changing American scene of the Vietnam War, the civil rights movement, the counterculture era, the men's rights movement, and the gay rights movement, to name only a few of the developments. It was a time of more liberal demands on college campuses. Students wanted more voice in campus governance designing the curriculum and changing dormitory rules and regulations among other demands. Even the traditionally conservative Capital students held a small demonstration after the Kent State shootings in May 1970.

The overall number of students continued to grow because of increased enrollments in the Schools of Nursing and Law, but enrollment had begun to shrink in the other undergraduate schools. Financial demands of the university increased accordingly. In 1969 more than 2,000 students were enrolled; but by 1979 that number had increased to more than 2,600. Like many other private colleges, Capital needed to increase its endowment to weather difficult financial times, and the effort to balance student financial aid with escalating tuition costs became a major concern. Adding to the financial problems was a $5,500,000 long-term indebtedness carried over from previous years as well as the construction of a new library. President Langevin stopped all new construction temporarily and worked on increasing student enrollment and the university's endowment. The Battelle Hall of Science and Nursing was completed as President Langevin was leaving office.

Because President Langevin believed that Capital needed to be recognized within the Columbus community even more than before, he devoted a considerable amount of his time to civic activities. Two very important developments occurred during this period that would have a positive influence on Capital's development. The law school, located on the north side of Main Street in a converted former automobile dealership building called the Willaman Building, started a full-time day program in 1969, but the school lacked adequate space, including library shelves. Although some wanted to see the law school remain on campus, a building was leased on South High Street on the north edge of German Village near the site of Capital's first location in Columbus. Moreover, the new building was near the downtown county court house complex where law school students could take advantage of the legal environment. The other development during this time was the establishment of an adult degree program. Capital purchased the "University Without Walls," now called the Adult Degree Program (A.D.P.), from the Union for Experimenting Colleges and Universities in 1979. The U.W.W. would have centers in Cleveland, Dayton, and Columbus. Many people older than traditional college-age students wanted to complete a college degree but not within the confines of the usual college schedule. The A.D.P. provided some credit for experiential learning and offered classes during nontraditional hours. The program began in January 1979 with 126 students statewide; by 1999 more than 880 A.D.P. students were enrolled in degree programs. In the spring of 1974 another program was started that reached out to the Columbus community. The Graduate School of Administration was created to offer a Master of Business Administration degree. Moreover, a concerted effort was made to increase the minority student enrollment and to employ more women in all positions at Capital. Slowly the number of minority students began to increase toward 10 percent of the total student body, and by 1979 the number of African American students reached that figure. Capital was indeed becoming a complex small university.

In an effort to meet the changing times, a more liberal visitation policy was adopted whereby men could be in women's dorm rooms until 5:00 P.M. on Fridays, Saturdays, and Sundays. And in 1971 alcohol was permitted in the dorm rooms, but state and local laws regarding minors were to be observed. Some conservatives within the Lutheran Church did not look with favor on many of these changes.

Budgetary problems were concerns to almost all private colleges during this period of increasing inflation and declining potential students for colleges at the undergraduate level. Attempting to balance the budget and pay off the university debt was a major task for a college of over 2,600 students. President Langevin retired in 1979 after having served the university for ten years.

In 1979 the Reverend Dr. Harvey Stegemoeller—a Texas native, a Lutheran clergyman, and president of a Lutheran college—became the eleventh president of Capital University. Dr. Stegemoeller faced a major task of balancing the budget, reducing the debt, increasing the endowment, improving the campus physical environment, and strengthening the relations with Lutheran Church congregations. He traveled to more than 300 different American Lutheran Church congregations almost every Sunday for nearly three years to preach and to talk about Capital University.

In 1988 the American Lutheran Church and the Lutheran Church in America merged to become the Evangelical Lutheran Church of America. The E.L.C.A. was the fourth-largest Protestant denomination in America. At first glance the merger appeared to be a benefit financially for Capital; however, church support for a Lutheran college was confined to certain synods. As Capital's overall enrollment and budget began to increase, church financial support as a percentage of the budget decreased perceptibly. However, by 1981 the undergraduate enrollment had increased by 25 percent in part because of increased recruiting efforts of faculty, staff, and alumni and due to the strengthened relationship with the Lutheran congregations. In addition, President Stegemoeller's "Spit 'n Polish" program was initiated to improve the appearance of the campus, and additions to Science Hall and to Alumni Gymnasium were completed. The old Rudolf Library was converted into the Kerns Religious Life Center with a beautiful new chapel, offices, and classrooms. Some university properties were sold, and Lehmann Hall, the first building on campus, was closed and eventually demolished in 1988–89. Faculty and staff salaries were frozen in 1979 and in 1980. The endowment began to increase, and the university's $1,800,000 operating deficit was eliminated by 1987. The university indebtedness began to decline due to good management and to effective fund-raising. Salaries began to increase gradually starting in 1982.

Many academic changes occurred during this era as well, including the establishment of new majors in computer science, criminal justice, and sports medicine and of a master's degree in education, to mention only a few. Capital students were encouraged to apply for internships within the Columbus community and in Washington, D.C., as well as to study abroad.

One part of Capital's unstated, but recognized, mission was to provide a college education for first-generation college students. The university was established to provide higher education for students here in Ohio. Only a small percentage of those students' parents were college educated. Throughout the years nearly half of Capital's undergraduates have been first-generation college students. At present about 40 percent of the undergraduate students are first-generation college students. Capital has continued to reach out to these students.

When President Stegemoeller retired in 1987, Capital University was in good shape financially. The budget had been balanced for ten years, and the modest endowment had increased by $5 million. The relationship with the Lutheran Church was strong, the physical environment of the campus was attractive, the enrollment had surpassed the 3,000-student level, and the quality of the students and of the faculty was highly competitive with those in other private colleges in Ohio. President Stegemoeller's successor would write that new financial, academic, and programmatic integrity characterized the administration of Harvey Stegemoeller.

In 1987 Josiah Blackmore, the dean of the Capital University Law School, was appointed interim president, and a year later he became Capital's twelfth president. Dr. Blackmore was the first non-Lutheran to serve as president of Capital. He was able to build on the efforts of his predecessor and move Capital forward in many areas. The university enrollment increased by 1,000 students during his tenure and moved beyond the 4,000-enrollment level in 1995–96, thus becoming the largest Lutheran institution of higher education in the country. Moreover, faculty and staff salaries increased accordingly, the endowment tripled, the Conservatory of Music building was totally renovated, the entire campus was wired for computer use, over fifty million dollars in gifts was committed to the university, and the law school moved to a spacious building on East Broad Street in downtown Columbus. "Building on Promises," the $25 million fund-raising campaign was oversubscribed by $5 million. The law school fund-raising campaign surpassed its goal. In the summer of 1995 more than six acres of additional property, located west of the Trinity Lutheran Seminary, were purchased. This acquisition will provide space for future campus expansion.

Capital has continued to be a Lutheran university but one to serve people of all faiths and beliefs. Lutherans no longer comprise the largest number of students on campus, but the university's Lutheran heritage continues to be exceptionally strong. Another change in recent years is that more and more students wish to live on campus. The number of resident students has increased from about 50 percent ten years ago to over 80 percent currently. However, because of the increased enrollment third- and fourth-year students may live off campus.

In recognition of the growing number of African American, Asian, Hispanic, and other minority students, the Office of Minority Student Activities and Multi-Cultural Affairs was created in 1989. Support services and student organizations were established to help these students adapt to college life. Moreover, each year, beginning in 1990, the Capital University community celebrates the birthday of Martin Luther King Jr. with a campuswide day of activities.

In addition to all of the other programmatic changes at Capital, an office for international programs was established to assist students in finding study-abroad opportunities. Also, the office has recruited overseas to attract more international students to study on Capital's campus, and an English as a Second Language program continues to attract many international students to the Bexley campus.

President Blackmore retired as president at the end of the 1997–98 academic year. His presidency left Capital in fine shape as it moved into the twenty-first century. In addition to the campaign to have a new law school building, President Blackmore's administration began the largest single-project fund-raising campaign in the university's history, building a new health, education, recreational, and athletic facility, which was completed in 2001. All of these financial activities occurred while the university had positive budgetary surpluses. In honor of his services to Capital University, the library was named for Josiah Blackmore.

During the 1998–99 academic year the provost and vice president for academic affairs, Ronald Volpe, served as the interim president while a national search was conducted for Capital's thirteenth president. In 1999 Dr. Daniel A. Felicetti, the president of Marian College in Indianapolis, Indiana, was selected as Capital's new president. While President Blackmore was the first non-Lutheran to be a president of Capital University, President Felicetti is the first Roman Catholic to hold that position. President Felicetti resigned in May 2001. From May 2001 through March 2002 Dr. Paul Doure, the retired president of Concordia College in Moorehead, Minnesota, served as the interim president. In November 2002 the board elected Dr. Theodore Frederickson, the dean of the graduate school of business at the University of St. Thomas in St. Paul, Minnesota, as its fourteenth president.

Capital University had a long tradition of serving students, friends, community, and the Lutheran Church since its inception at Canton, Ohio, in 1830. The road of service has not always been smooth or easy, but countless numbers of students have been better prepared to serve others because of their association with Capital University. The late George Dell, Professor Emeritus of English, captured the essence of the meaning of the university when he wrote these words for Capital's "Alma Mater":

> Thy swords are we, and shields to guard thy glory;
> Thy lamps are we to beacon far and near;
> Thy pens are we to write in deathless story
> Lives that shall honor thee, o mother dear.

Suggested Reading

The author gratefully gives thanks to the late professor of English, David Owens, who wrote *These Hundred Years: The Centennial History of Capital University* (Capital University, 1950). Most of the information on Capital's early history comes from Professor Owens's book. Another history was located in the 1915 *Capitalian* in "Historical Sketch of Capital University and the Theological Seminary." Additional information came from a speech by former president of Capital University, Thomas H. Langevin, on May 8, 1974, to the Newcomers Society in North America (copy found in the Capital University Archives). Gilbert F. Dodds wrote "The Century of Capital University," *Bulletin* of the Franklin County Historical Society (Jan. 1950). See also James Burke, *Chronicle of Change: Capital University, 1950–2000* (Blue Pencil Creative Group, 2002).

Case Western Reserve University

From Liberal Arts and Applied Science
to a National Research University

DENNIS HARRISON

The history of Case Western Reserve University is not easily told, embracing as it does two quite different educational institutions: Western Reserve University (f. 1826) and Case Institute of Technology (f. 1880). The former, established to prepare its students for the ministry and professional positions through a traditional classical curriculum, contrasts sharply with Leonard Case Jr.'s instructions to create "an institution of learning to be called the 'Case School of Applied Science,' located . . . in Cleveland, in which shall be taught by competent professors and teachers, mathematics, physics, engineering—mechanical and civil, chemistry, economic geology, mining and metallurgy, natural history, drawing, and modern languages."

The lives of the founding fathers of these two institutions were as distinct as the institutions they created. David Hudson, founder of Western Reserve College, was born on a New England farm in the eighteenth century. Originally a free-thinker in the tradition of Thomas Paine, Hudson experienced a religious conversion and became a devout Congregationalist. He was also a man of action who led an exploration party into the untamed West to found the village that bears his name. He made his fortune in Hudson and thereafter went on to found the Hudson Congregational Church, a grade school, and then Western Reserve College. His intention was that the college would produce a learned ministry, and to this end the trustees established a theological department in 1830.

Leonard Case, founder of the Case School of Applied Science, was born in Cleveland in 1820 and was a graduate of that most traditional of American colleges, Yale. He was the beneficiary of great wealth that he inherited from his father, Leonard Case Sr. Leonard Case Jr.'s health was as poor as his wealth was great, and throughout his life he shunned business pursuits, politics, and an active social life to enjoy a small core of close friends and devote his energies to intellectual pursuits and

About the time of their 1887 ether drift experiment, Albert A. Michelson (*left*) and Edward W. Morley

philanthropy. Along with many other Americans, David Hudson and Leonard Case Jr. shared an optimistic faith in higher education.

Western Reserve College was one of many denominational colleges founded in Ohio in the nineteenth century. Beyond a vague commitment by its early trustees to the creation of additional professional schools, there was little to indicate that one day it would develop into a great university and center of research. Anyone attempting to predict its future course would safely have guessed that it would continue as did so many other liberal arts colleges in Ohio as a relatively small institution centered on an undergraduate student body. A pessimist might have predicted its early demise—a not uncommon end for these early colleges. Instead, it developed a graduate school and numerous professional schools and became the largest private university in Ohio. It was modeled in large part after the universities of Germany, which so greatly impressed the few Americans fortunate enough to study in them. These Americans found that the seminars and laboratories, the emphasis on original research and publication, and the commitment to intellectual freedom placed them at a level far above even the best American colleges. Their commitment to the sciences likewise surpassed that of American or English colleges, which resisted any modification of the traditional classical curriculum of Latin and Greek, the classics, simple mathematics, and rhetoric.

Case School of Applied Science (renamed Case Institute of Technology in 1947) diverged sharply from the typical nineteenth-century American or English college in that it offered a curriculum centered on the sciences. However, it too focused largely on an undergraduate curriculum and emphasized the applied aspects of science over theory or pure research. That these two institutions would one day federate to become the largest private research university in Ohio was hardly fore-ordained. Their common destiny resulted, however, from decisions that, in their cumulative effect, transformed both institutions. This history is the story of those decisions and of the men who made them.

The first indications that Western Reserve College might take a path different from the typical denominational college came early, at the outset of the administration of George Edmond Pierce, who became the second president of the college in 1834. Pierce was an impressive figure who stood well over six feet tall and weighed more than three hundred pounds. He had graduated from Yale with honors in 1816, at a time when the college offered a curriculum unusually rich in scientific and mathematical studies. He then taught mathematics briefly before entering Andover Theological Seminary. Thereafter he served as a Congregational minister until he came to Hudson.

President Pierce brought a personal interest in science and mathematics to the college, and, by combining this interest with a talent for securing extraordinary faculty, he established a tradition of preeminence in the sciences that continues to this day. Pierce's success places the college in the tradition of a small number of late-eighteenth- and early-nineteenth-century American educational institutions that stepped beyond the bounds of the traditional classical curriculum.

Two appointments by Pierce signaled the introduction of the new emphasis on the sciences at Western Reserve College. The first was that of Elias Loomis, who taught mathematics and natural science at the college from 1836 to 1844. The second was that of Professor Samuel St. John, who was professor of chemistry, mineralogy, and geology from 1838 to 1852. The college faculty, which consisted of six professors in 1836, now included two members with exceptional qualifications for the teaching of science. During these same years entrance requirements were strengthened and, to the surprise of many, admissions increased.

After graduating from Yale Loomis remained at his alma mater as a tutor in astronomy. In 1835 Loomis and a colleague were the first Americans to sight Halley's Comet and calculate its orbit as it reappeared in its periodic cycle. Before Loomis began teaching at Hudson, the trustees authorized him to spend a year visiting European universities and observatories and provided him with an appropriation of $4,000 for the purchase of scientific equipment. (The impact of this sum can be better appreciated when one realizes that it amounted to half the cost of any building then standing on the campus.) Upon his arrival in Hudson, Loomis immediately drafted plans for an observatory to house the newly purchased equipment, and only two months later construction began. This observatory was the first to be built in the West and only the third in the nation; neither Harvard nor Yale boasted an equivalent facility.

Loomis was well versed in the fields of physics, astronomy, and mathematics. Two years later, intent on a more comprehensive program, the college secured

Samuel St. John to teach the fields of chemistry, geology, and mineralogy. St. John was also a graduate of Yale and went on to study law, medicine, and science at American and European schools. Like Loomis, St. John received a leave of absence to continue his studies in Europe and an appropriation of $2,500 to purchase scientific equipment. Shortly after he arrived in Hudson, a second new building, the Athenaeum, was constructed to house this equipment and to provide expanded facilities for the teaching of science. In 1851, while at the college, St. John published the first geological textbook to appear in Ohio. He expanded on the glaciation theories of Louis Agassiz and, in applying them to Ohio, stimulated extensive interest in glacial phenomena throughout the state.

In its earliest years the college was composed of a liberal arts college, a theological school, and a preparatory school offering secondary education. In 1853, during a period of financial exigency, the theological department would be closed, lifting from the college the financial burden of its students, most of whom did not pay tuition. The preparatory school would remain in Hudson until it closed in 1903, two years after the university withdrew its financial support.

The last of the Hudson-era "departments," and the only one surviving to this day, is the Medical Department, which was founded in 1843. The college had always had intentions of founding a medical college, and when a medical college opened in Willoughby in 1839 the trustees reiterated this intention, publishing a notice "that it has been and still is the intention of the Board to establish a Medical Department." Here the matter rested until early 1843, when dissension among the faculty at Willoughby resulted in the resignation of all but one faculty member. Some of the dissident faculty secured a building in Cleveland with the intention of founding a medical college. In August they met with the trustees, and it was agreed that the college would award degrees to the graduates of the school that became the Medical Department of Western Reserve College. Classes began in November 1843, and sixty-seven students enrolled.

The college's control over its Medical Department was limited at best. The faculty assumed complete responsibility for the administration of the school and received neither salaries nor financial support from the college. The building, library, and equipment were all provided at the personal expense of the medical faculty. Any profits that resulted were divided among them; and while Samuel St. John did journey to Cleveland to teach chemistry and medical jurisprudence, the only other contribution of the college came at the conclusion of the term when the trustees approved the diplomas to be awarded and the president collected a small fee for signing each diploma.

This arrangement was not unusual. In the early nineteenth century medical colleges were sometimes affiliated with a college but often were not. Where they existed, the affiliations were typically weak. By the end of the century, however, as scientific advances greatly enhanced the value of a university affiliation to a medical school, universities would take a more active role in the administration of their affiliated medical schools.

When the Medical Department opened, a medical course in the United States typically involved a minimum of three years' study with a preceptor—essentially a physician who accepted students in a training program that was a medical apprenticeship. Many practicing physicians never attended a medical school. Instead, they received a license following a successful examination by a county or state medical board at end of the preceptorship. Those students who elected to undertake some study at a medical college or secure a medical degree attended lectures at one or more schools in the course of their preceptorship. Entrance requirements to medical colleges were minimal, standards were often low, and students usually matriculated without prior attendance at a liberal arts college.

The curriculum in Cleveland was typical for the time and consisted of a series of lectures delivered over sixteen weeks. Students who expected to receive a degree were required to repeat these same lectures during a second year. The majority of students, however, neither repeated the lectures nor received a degree. Those who did stand for the degree were required to submit a thesis and undergo an oral examination by a committee composed of faculty members and physicians from the local medical society. A successful candidate received both a degree and a license to practice medicine.

Despite President Pierce's success in recruiting faculty and securing a Department of Medicine, his administration ended in a financial debacle that led to his resignation in 1855. His successor, Henry Lawrence Hitchcock, returned the school to fiscal health and went on to further strengthen the science faculty. In 1856 Hitchcock secured Charles A. Young to teach mathematics and astronomy. Young had graduated first in his class at Dartmouth at the age of eighteen. At Hudson he taught mathematics and astronomy and continued the seminal meteorological observations initiated by Professor Loomis. Young remained at the college for ten years. His later career was spent at Dartmouth and Princeton, where in 1881 he wrote the capstone of his career, *The Sun*, which became a standard in the discipline and was translated into many languages.

Hitchcock's greatest success was to secure Edward W. Morley as professor of chemistry. Morley was an experimental scientist of exceptional ability who spent his entire career at Western Reserve. He was also a gifted teacher with a talent for innovation. At a time when only German universities and a few leading American colleges in the East used laboratories in scientific instruction, Morley designed a laboratory for his students' use. Morley excelled at precise measurements. His finest work consisted of determinations of the composition of air and of the atomic weight of oxygen and hydrogen and the ratios at which they combine to form water. His magnum opus, "On the Densities of Hydrogen and Oxygen and on the Ratio of their Atomic Weights," published by the Smithsonian Institution in 1895, was the culmination of eleven years of ingenious, painstaking research. It was quickly translated into German, and Wolcott Gibbs, professor of chemistry at Harvard, characterized it as "by far the finest piece of exact chemical investigation with which I am acquainted."

Morley was elected president of the American Association for the Advancement of Science in 1895 and of the American Chemical Society in 1899. In 1902 he was nominated for the Nobel Prize in chemistry and, in a reportedly close vote, finished second to the great German chemist Emil Fischer. In 1907 he received the Davy Medal from the Royal Society. Beyond these professional accolades, Morley lay claim to great popular fame based on his collaboration with the physicist Albert Michelson when the latter taught at Case School of Applied Sciences.

In the 1870s, under the leadership of President Hitchcock, the college continued to enjoy a reputation for high standards and a strong science program. But it remained a far cry from a modern university. Its exclusive focus on the undergraduate student and the weak connection of the school with the Department of Medicine in Cleveland bore but a faint resemblance to a modern university's emphasis on graduate studies, research, and professional education.

Had the college remained in Hudson, it is unlikely that anything resembling a modern university would have arisen so far from a metropolitan area. Earlier proposals to move it to Cleveland had foundered on the opposition of the Hudson community. In the late 1870s, however, several new factors emerged. Where once the college had been the sole institution of higher education in northern Ohio, it was now one of nine other similar institutions. Among these was Buchtel College, which was only twelve miles away in Akron. The slightly more distant University of Wooster, founded by an important faction within the Presbyterian Church, competed for the support of Presbyterians who had become a financial mainstay of the college in recent years. In the face of these developments, the trustees, who had just led the college out of troubled financial waters, were receptive to proposals for innovative and even radical change.

By the 1870s the bulk of the financial support of the college came from Cleveland rather than Hudson, and population trends overwhelmingly favored Cleveland in any consideration of relocating the college. Beyond the desire of the founders to locate the college among the virtuous yeomanry of Hudson, it should be noted that in 1826 they placed the college in a county (Portage) with a population 60 percent larger than Cuyahoga County. But by 1880 Portage and Summit counties together had barely one-third the population of Cuyahoga County, and yet Cuyahoga County was without an institution of higher learning.

In effect, the trustees had an opportunity to reposition the college as the primary institution of higher learning in a city that was northern Ohio's foremost industrial center at a time when it was experiencing an explosive growth in population. This growth continued into 1920, when Cleveland was the fifth-largest American city. Hudson, a community based on agriculture, had been overtaken by one of the new industrial cities of America, and control of the college was passing into the hands of a new group—urban capitalists, financiers, and industrialists who were predisposed to support the practical arts and sciences and who did not hesitate to reach out and capture an established college located in a nearby village.

The trustees determined that an endowment of $400,000 and an additional $100,000 for buildings would be needed to relocate the college to Cleveland. Amasa Stone, a Cleveland businessman, made an initial commitment of $100,000. Shortly thereafter an announcement was made that Leonard Case Jr., recently deceased, had made provisions to found a polytechnic institute in Cleveland bearing the Case family name. Amasa Stone, whose relationship with the Case family was stormy and competitive at its best, then pledged the full $500,000 to the college. In return Stone required that the college be renamed after his son, Adelbert, and secured the right to name a majority of the board of trustees. Conceived in personal rivalry, the two institutions would continue as rivals for seventy-five years before federating in 1967.

The townspeople of Hudson and the college's alumni bitterly opposed the move and were never reconciled to it. Nevertheless, the move to Cleveland exponentially expanded the financial support available to the college and was an essential step in its transformation into a university.

Even as the trustees contemplated a move from Hudson, events were unfolding in Cleveland that would link the destiny of Western Reserve College with that of an institution that did not yet exist. In 1877 Leonard Case Jr., convinced that existing colleges were ignoring the sciences and practical arts, decided to found a technical and engineering school in Cleveland. The purpose and financing of the school were laid out in a trust deed, which set aside the bulk of his fortune to support the institution he envisioned. When he died in 1880 his close friend and adviser Henry Abbey formed a corporation, appointing fifteen prominent Clevelanders to its board and thereby bringing Case School of Applied Science into existence. The men selected to establish and govern the school were wealthy bankers, businessmen, and lawyers associated with the steel and iron ore shipping industries and with major railroads such as the New York Central and the Nickel Plate Railroad. One of the original trustees, Jeptha Wade, was the president of the Western Union Telegraph Company. Another, Henry Payne, was a banker who was instrumental in the founding of what became the American Steel and Wire Company.

The newly established board had numerous ties with the existing board of Western Reserve College and included two men who also sat on the Western Reserve College board. Rufus P. Ranney, the first chairman of the Case board, was a lawyer and jurist who had briefly attended Western Reserve College. In 1871 Ranney was awarded the first honorary degree granted by the college. Samuel Williamson was a graduate of Western Reserve College and was elected to the board of Western Reserve University in 1882 while serving as an incorporator of Case School of Applied Science. Truman P. Handy endowed a professorship in philosophy at Western Reserve in 1865 and had served as a trustee of the college since 1866.

Since the endowment with which Leonard Case Jr. established the school consisted of real estate that the trustees intended to hold for appreciation, they faced a shortage of cash in the early years of the institution. Although they considered delaying the opening of the school until the income from the endowment increased, the trustees elected to open the school immediately, if modestly. Thus the first classes offered in 1881–82 met in older buildings that had been in the Case family for years and included the family stable, which was modified to house a modest laboratory. In this, its first year, the school had fifteen students and five faculty.

The trustees did not intend to remain in rented quarters for long and were searching for a permanent location at the same time that Western Reserve College decided to move to Cleveland. Under the terms of its agreement with Amasa Stone, Western Reserve College was required to secure the land for the new buildings that Amasa Stone had committed to build. The two institutions agreed to seek funds for a single plot of land they would share. Amasa Stone envisioned the two institutions existing in "harmony," and the Case board expected that placing the two institutions side by side would allow them to share expensive resources such as libraries, equipment, and even faculty. Between them, the two institutions raised more than $70,000 from individual donors and purchased forty-three acres of land in what came to be known as University Circle. The donors included representatives of Cleveland's emerging industries—petroleum, iron ore, shipbuilding, and railroads—as well as bankers and financiers. The most famous among them was John D. Rockefeller. In purchasing a single plot of land and placing the two institutions side by side, the trustees of the two institutions linked the schools indissolubly until federation in 1967.

Even as they sought to secure a site and minimize the financial impact of creating a physical plant, the Case board began to recruit a faculty worthy of its decision to concentrate its limited funds on personnel. In this they succeeded beyond any reasonable expectation—the quality of this early faculty is remarkable. Among them was John Nelson Stockwell, professor of astronomy, who was a self-educated farm boy from the outskirts of Cleveland. He was an astronomical and mathematical genius whose interest in astronomy was first tweaked in 1844 when he observed an eclipse of the moon. He taught himself mathematics and science and found his metier when he taught himself French and calculus in order to read the four-volume, 4,000-page work *Mecanique Celeste* by the renowned French astronomer Pierre Simon La Place. Stockwell taught at Case for six years and successfully served as the de facto administrative head of the school until 1886 when the board hired Cady Staley as the school's first president. In the course of his career Stockwell drifted away from teaching into research and writing. His magnum opus on the orbits of the planets was published in 1872 by the Smithsonian Institution.

Another of the founding faculty was Charles Frederic Mabery, professor of chemistry. Mabery received his undergraduate degree from the Lawrence School at Harvard at a time when the school had instituted laboratories modeled directly on those in use by German universities. He then received one of the first doctorates awarded by Harvard's graduate school. Mabery published chemical treatises relating to petroleum, aluminum, bromine, and electrochemistry. Among his students were Albert Smith, who later succeeded Mabery as professor of chemistry, and Herbert H. Dow, who founded the chemical company that bears his name.

John Eisenmann, who taught civil engineering, was an eclectic figure who drafted Cleveland's building code and designed the Cleveland Arcade. (In 1975 the Arcade was the first building in Cleveland to be placed on the National Historic Register.) Other designs by Eisenmann included "Case Main," the first building on the Case campus, and the pennant-shaped state flag of Ohio. Although he served only four years on the faculty, he played a critical role in these early years, since a majority of the students who attended Case became civil engineers and worked under his tutelage. When Albert Michelson needed an accurate measurement of the course on which he measured the speed of light, he turned to Eisenmann for this critical work.

Finally, the board secured Albert A. Michelson as professor of physics. Michelson was a former naval cadet and midshipman who was on the faculty of the U.S. Naval Academy in 1878 when he astonished the world with his measurement of the speed of light. Michelson accepted his position at Case while conducting research in Germany, where he first attempted to detect the "ether," the supposedly undetectable medium that nineteenth-century physicists believed was necessary to transmit waves of light through space. Once he arrived at Case, Michelson refined his earlier determinations of the speed of light and produced a figure that was the accepted standard until he further refined his work forty-three years later. Michelson entered on a series of collaborations with Edward Morley of Western Reserve, which led to one of the most famous scientific experiments the world has ever known: the Michelson-Morley ether drift measurements.

This collaboration alone would justify the trustees' hope that in positioning the two institutions side by side the interaction of the two faculties would lead to a richer, more productive environment. Michelson and Morley worked together in a laboratory in the Case administration building until the building was destroyed by fire in 1886, endangering Michelson's equipment. Fortunately, bystanders rescued his interferometer and it was transferred to the Adelbert dormitory, where Michelson and Morley completed their famous experiment in 1887. The two scientists next intended to use the interferometer to set an international standard for the meter based on light waves, but Michelson left for Clark University, effectively ending the collaboration. He taught there briefly before transferring to the University of Chicago, where he was on the faculty when he became the first American scientist to receive a Nobel Prize.

The history of the college immediately following its move to Cleveland is characterized by controversies over declining enrollment, coeducation, and presidential prerogatives. The president, Carroll Cutler, a reformer by nature, began admitting women to the college on his own authority in 1874. After the college moved to Cleveland enrollment did not meet expectations, and the faculty and trustees concluded that the presence of women in Adelbert College limited its appeal to men and urged Cutler to close the college to women. Cutler refused and stood alone against the trustees and faculty until his resignation in 1886. The Reverend Hiram Haydn, a member of the board, took the presidency on an interim basis. Haydn ended coeducation in Adelbert College but, in an unexpected turn, went on to play a leading role in founding the College for Women established in 1888 and renamed Flora Stone Mather College in 1931. The college enrolled women until it merged with Adelbert College and Cleveland College in 1971.

When Haydn accepted the position of interim president, he already had a successor in mind, Charles F. Thwing. The trustees, led by Haydn, had tried already to secure Thwing's services, but Thwing remained committed to a pastorate he had only recently accepted. Three years later, however, Thwing accepted a renewed offer of the presidency, came to Western Reserve in 1890, and served for an unprecedented thirty-one years.

Thwing was only thirty-six years old when he came to Cleveland. He was a Rooseveltian character of great energy and optimism who inspired those around him. He had chosen to attend Harvard because he was attracted to the elective system that its reforming president, Charles W. Eliot, had only recently introduced. After graduating Phi Beta Kappa, he went on to earn a theology degree from Andover Seminary. When Thwing arrived in Cleveland he found that his "university" consisted of a men's and a women's undergraduate college loosely conjoined to each other and to the Medical Department and with virtually no sense of a common identity or destiny. In the three short years following his inauguration, he gave life to the concept of a university, welding the disparate schools into a single entity, Western Reserve University. In these same years he established the Graduate School, the School of Law, and the School of Dentistry. Later in his term Thwing added a School of Library Science (1904), a School of Pharmacy (1908), and a School of Applied Social Science (1915). During this same period, 1890–1915, enrollment increased from 246 to 2,118, and the faculty grew from 40 to 415. Four buildings became twenty-two while the endowment increased more than sevenfold and the number of volumes in the library increased sixfold.

From their founding, many of these schools set an extremely high standard. When it opened, the School of Law offered a three-year program of study and was the first law school in the West to do so. In 1911 the school became the third in the United States, after Harvard and Columbia, to require a bachelor's degree for admission. As a result, the school stood first in the state in the percentage of its students passing the Ohio bar exam. The law school also benefited from strong support among the trustees; and when its founding endowment proved elusive, the trustees stepped in, securing the necessary funds for a new building and an extensive library.

The example of the Medical Department is similarly instructive. The late nineteenth and early twentieth century witnessed a revolution in medical education as schools across the nation upgraded their requirements and standards in order to keep pace with technological and scientific advances. The Medical Department of Western Reserve University took a leading role in these changes and rose to greatness as a result. The department built a new building in downtown Cleveland, strengthened entrance requirements, improved the clinical facilities, and secured an endowment. Rival medical schools could not compete, and in 1914 the department emerged as the sole medical school in northern Ohio.

The move to Cleveland, however, brought to the surface tensions that threatened to separate the Medical Department from the university. First, the Medical Department, led by its dean, the obstreperous and authoritarian Gustav Weber, refused to affiliate with the newly renamed and "upstart" Adelbert College. In 1884, in order to accommodate the department, the trustees incorporated a separate entity, Western Reserve University. The historically tenuous links of the department with the university were further tested when Dean Weber refused to allow President Haydn to preside at the meetings of the medical faculty. Haydn, the first president to attempt this, fought back, securing precedents from Harvard and the University of Pennsylvania demonstrating that at both schools the president of the university presided at meetings of the medical faculty. Next Haydn secured the backing of the board of trustees, which asserted the legal right of the president to preside at all faculty meetings.

At this point, Charles F. Thwing arrived and immediately grasped the helm, presiding at all the meetings of the medical faculty. Dr. Weber then boycotted these meetings until his resignation two years later. On his resignation the trustees further asserted their authority and ended the long-standing custom by which the medical faculty selected its dean. Thereafter the president, with the approval of the trustees, appointed the dean of the Medical Department.

The earliest of a series of advances that strengthened the curriculum dates from the expansion of the traditional sixteen-week curriculum to twenty weeks in 1871. Further advances occurred in 1894 when the optional twelve-week spring term became mandatory and in 1896 when the Medical Department introduced a four-year curriculum, an increase of one year. It was the first medical school in Ohio to do so and the eleventh of some 170 medical colleges then existing in the United States. In 1909 admission standards were strengthened when the Medical Department required a bachelor's degree for admission. The only two other schools with a similar standard were Harvard and Johns Hopkins. In these same years the faculty improved the curriculum by introducing extensive laboratory and course work in the basic sciences. In 1913 the department was renamed the School of Medicine of Western Reserve University.

As a result, in 1910, when Abraham Flexner published his famous rankings of American medical schools (which led to the closure of nearly half the medical schools in the country), Flexner told Thwing that the Western Reserve University Medical Department was the best medical school in the United States after Johns Hopkins. One immediate result of the Flexner report was the merger of the only other regular medical school in northern Ohio with its rival at Western Reserve University. (A homeopathic school of medicine continued in Cleveland until 1914.)

Following Thwing's retirement in 1921, additional professional schools and a third undergraduate college were founded. The most innovative of these was Cleveland College, the undergraduate college that was blessed with the fervent enthusiasm of its dean, A. Caswell Ellis, and the vision of a guardian angel, Newton D. Baker. Baker was a trustee of Western Reserve University who was imbued with the progressive spirit of Cleveland mayor Tom L. Johnson, who took his campaigns to the people in a large tent that traveled around the city. During World War I Baker served as secretary of war, and with the war's sudden end he created a model system of secondary and higher education for the doughboys stranded in postwar Europe. At its height, thousands of soldiers enrolled in higher education.

Baker was convinced that this model would transfer back to Cleveland, and he campaigned tirelessly to secure the necessary financial support to found Cleveland College and implement a program of higher education for adults. When the college opened in 1924, it was separately incorporated from the university and was affiliated with Case School of Applied Science. The fifteen-member board of directors included five trustees from the university and four from Case.

Dean A. Caswell Ellis arrived in 1926. He was an evangelist for adult education who envisioned Cleveland College as a venue for older, primarily part-time students who would shun the adolescent culture of freshman hazing, fraternities, and football games to concentrate on careers and academics.

The college's downtown location made it easily accessible to working adults, and by 1929 6,000 students were enrolled in the college, many of whom attended part-time while working. Enrollment continued to swell until the Great Depression, but by 1933 enrollment had fallen by one-third and President Vinson of Western Reserve University was ready to close the college. At this point Baker intervened and personally saved the college by abandoning all his other outside interests to focus solely on raising funds for Cleveland College. As a result, the college survived the Depression and, during the immediate postwar years, would enroll as many as 12,000 students. In the 1950s enrollment again dropped and the college was moved to University Circle in an effort to reduce expenses. By the time it closed in 1973, the unique role it played in the education of adults and working students had largely passed to Cleveland State University and Cuyahoga Community College.

The School of Nursing traces its history to 1898 when it was founded as the Lakeside Hospital Training School for Nurses. At this time Lakeside Hospital was moving to a location much nearer the School of Medicine's new building in University Circle. The original affiliation agreement between the hospital and the university dates from this time and virtually transformed Lakeside Hospital into a university hospital. (The incorporation of University Hospitals, including Lakeside Hospital, did not take place until 1926.) Soon after the move Lakeside Hospital established the school and cooperated with the faculty of the School of Medicine in training nurses.

The early history of the program is rife with conflict between the hospital administration and the program's teaching staff. The former considered the primary responsibility of the trainees to be the provision of nursing care to patients, while the latter saw them as students to be educated. In these early years the students effectively functioned as the full-time nursing staff of the hospital and were expected to find time for their studies only after fulfilling their obligations to the hospital. As late as 1925 the dean of the school struggled to limit the student nurses to a forty-eight-hour week comprised of nursing care and studies.

In 1920 the Cleveland Hospital and Health Survey recommended that the nurse training program affiliate with the university. Shortly thereafter Frances Payne Bolton, a wealthy Clevelander who had a lifelong interest in nursing education, came forward with a pledge of $500,000, and the nursing school joined the university in 1923. It was at this time that University Hospitals incorporated, and the medical school and hospital complex were constructed adjacent to the existing university campus.

The most recently established professional school at the university is the School of Management, which dates from the 1967 federation of Case Institute of Technology and Western Reserve University. Before this both institutions had programs that awarded bachelor's and master's degrees in business administration. The program at Western Reserve originated with Cleveland College, which offered business degrees from its founding in 1925. At Case School of Applied Science, a Department of Engineering Administration was established in 1931, and the first management degrees awarded date from 1949.

Because Case School of Applied Science was never a liberal arts college or a university, it never developed the same pattern of professional schools as Western Reserve University did, and its graduate program remained informally structured for many years. In effect, its engineering students were in a professional school that was conducted on an undergraduate level side by side with a core of departments—physics, chemistry, mathematics, etc.—that also produced graduates. Informal graduate study leading to the master's degree began in 1895 and consisted of additional course work and research projects supervised by the faculty. This pattern was revamped in 1931 shortly after William E. Wickenden came to Case as its third president. Graduate education was formalized and the standards for both the master's degree and the Ph.D. codified. Case School of Applied Science awarded its first doctoral degree in 1939. Graduate education became an increasingly important component of the curriculum, and in 1947, Wickenden's last year at the school, a total of 217 graduate students comprised 13 percent of the student body. A formal graduate division administered by a dean only came into existence in 1955.

Throughout Wickenden's tenure the academic credentials of the faculty, many of whom had more practical experience than formal education, were upgraded and more emphasis was placed on formal education and the doctorate. From its inception, the school had offered a variety of courses beyond engineering and science. For example, in his original trust deed Leonard Case Jr. stipulated that the school offer instruction in modern foreign languages. Courses in English, economics, and history were offered as early as 1885, and, in the early years of the twentieth century, the first courses in drama and literature appeared in the curriculum. The Wickenden administration specifically stressed the importance of the humanities for engineering students and further increased the role of the humanities in the curriculum at Case. Thus, under Wickenden the curriculum and the faculty at Case came to more nearly resemble that at Western Reserve.

These tendencies continued during the administration of Case president T. Keith Glennan, who personally raised large sums of money to support the further introduction of the humanities into the curriculum. During these years the institute established a Division of Humanities and Social Studies as well as a graduate program in the history of science and technology. During Glennan's administration the typical Case student took 20 percent of his course load in social studies and humanities courses.

When the trustees of Case School of Applied Science and of Western Reserve College, along with Amasa Stone, placed the two institutions side by side, all the parties intended that the two institutions would be mutually supportive. That this was often the case is evidenced by their joint control of Cleveland College and by the Michelson-Morley experiment. Nevertheless, the history of the two institutions also includes strong athletic rivalries and other, more petty ones. An instance of the latter is best captured in Case president Charles S. Howe's request for a flag pole of 115 feet—a height chosen in order to top the flagpole of Adelbert College by some fifteen feet.

Despite these all-too-natural rivalries, the contiguous campuses of the two schools encouraged proposals for cooperation or federation, and indeed many instances can be cited of administrators at both institutions and many outside observers urging closer cooperation or even a merger. Invariably these proposals generated little response, until Robert Vinson succeeded Charles Thwing as president in 1923. Vinson was a man who welcomed change, and shortly after his arrival the two schools created a blue ribbon commission under the auspices of the Cleveland Foundation. This commission recommended that Case and Reserve combine in a single university that would invite other educational institutions to join with it in the creation of a grand, new, and enlarged university.

The commission published its recommendations in 1925 as a "Survey of Higher Education in Cleveland," and a "Greater University Committee" of trustees from both institutions met and recommended the formation of the "Greater University." In April the trustees of Case approved the recommendations of the committee. In the meantime, however, President Howe had come to believe that in any merger, the smaller, more specialized Case would lose its identity. When the trustees of Western Reserve insisted that the name of the new university must continue as Western Reserve University, Howe took the occasion to make his point with the trustees of Case, and the proposal died a sudden death. At the time, Eckstein Case, a cousin of Leonard Case Jr. and a key administrator at Case since 1887, ventured his opinion that "something may happen in about fifty years."

By the 1960s a number of new elements influenced the efforts to unite the two schools. Higher education was an increasingly expensive proposition that required a level of support beyond the capability of wealthy individuals and even corporations. Since World War II the federal government and foundations had increased their support of higher education dramatically and the dependence of private universities and colleges on this support increased accordingly. The sometimes precarious position of private colleges was underscored in 1965 when Fenn College, in downtown Cleveland, finding itself at a competitive disadvantage after Cuyahoga Community College opened, became Cleveland State University. This occurred just as Glennan was preparing to retire and influenced Glennan and others to consider a union of Case and Reserve. Then, as Case Institute of Technology began to search for a new president, a succession of candidates inquired into the possibility that Case and Western Reserve might merge. Next, John W. Gardner, the newly appointed Secretary of the U. S. Department of Health, Education and Welfare and the former president of the Carnegie Foundation, suggested a merger. Glennan and John S. Millis, president of Western Reserve, met with Secretary Gardner, who was a friend of both men, and a new commission was formed. The Carnegie Corporation, the Cleveland Foundation, and the Greater Cleveland Associated Foundation provided $400,000 to finance this commission. Henry T. Heald, president of the

Ford Foundation, led the commission, which recommended the federation of the two universities under a single president and a single board. Despite considerable opposition in some quarters, the merger went ahead.

It not only had the strong support of Glennan and Millis as well as that of Glennan's replacement, incoming Case president Robert Morse, but also that of a majority of the trustees at both institutions, who believed that the federation of the two institutions was critical to their continued success. In July 1967 the two schools federated and Morse became the first president of Case Western Reserve University. The president, however, became an early casualty of federation and resigned in October 1970 amid growing deficits, declining enrollment, and protesting students.

His successor was Louis A. Toepfer, who had been the dean of the School of Law. In Toepfer's first year as president the university incurred a deficit of over $4 million. Two years later the budget was balanced and has remained so to this day. Toepfer accomplished this despite declining enrollment, high inflation, and a precipitous decline in the region's industrial base. In the process he eliminated many weaker programs and closed the University Press. The student protests that had disrupted academic life and undermined his predecessor now faded as quickly as they had once flared up, and in 1974 Toepfer reported that the students "were returning to their studies with an air of sobriety and dedication."

Toepfer was unable to reverse the continued decline in undergraduate enrollment, but the financial impact was softened by strong enrollment in the graduate and professional schools. Under Toepfer and his successors the financial basis of the new university gradually shifted so that a larger proportion of its income derived from endowment and research grants. When Toepfer became president 9.6 percent of income came from endowment funds. This number increased to 16.7 percent by 1999–2000. Research income, which was 34.1 percent in 1968–69 grew to 41.7 percent in 1999–2000.

A sustained increase in undergraduate enrollment did not occur until the late 1980s, when Agnar Pytte became president. Pytte worked hard to improve the quality of undergraduate student life and increased undergraduate scholarship aid. These steps came at a time when the image of Cleveland was improving and technical education was increasingly in demand. As a result, the quality of incoming students improved even as the undergraduate enrollment returned to the levels of the early 1970s.

Although enrollment in graduate and professional schools remained strong in these years, individual professional schools underwent crises. Despite their strong reputations, the Mandel School of Applied Social Sciences and the School of Dentistry experienced enrollment declines in the 1980s related to reduced employment opportunities for their graduates. Both of the schools successfully adapted and underwent strong recoveries. The School of Library Science, however, faced problems that were deemed insurmountable and closed in 1986 after eighty-three years of operation. This was in line with national trends that led to the closing of well-known library science schools at other private universities, including the University of Chicago and Columbia University.

From the perspective of the twenty-first century, it can be seen that many of the difficulties faced in the post-federation years were endemic to higher education and were exacerbated by the economic decline of heavy industry in the Midwest. Had federation not occurred, it is unlikely that either school would have weathered the storms of those turbulent years as favorably. Certainly, over the course of the entire twentieth century both institutions fared well under federation. In 1900 the combined student bodies and faculties of the two schools totaled 984 students and 159 professors. A century later 2,140 faculty members instructed 9,614 students from ninety-six countries. The recent report "The Top American Research Universities" ranks CWRU as twentieth among thirty-four private research universities and lists it thirteenth in federal research dollars received and eighteenth in the number of faculty who are members of the national academies. Private contributions to the university in the year 2000 reached a record high of 109 million dollars in cash and 131 million in commitments while the university's endowment and trusts reached $1.55 billion. Clearly Case Western Reserve University enters a new century stronger than ever.

SUGGESTED READING

Thomas F. Campbell, *SASS: Fifty Years of Social Work Education* (Press of Case Western Reserve University, 1967); Clarence H. Cramer, *Case Western Reserve University: A History of the University, 1826–1976* (Little, Brown and Company, 1976); Clarence H. Cramer, *The Law School at Case Western Reserve University: A History, 1892–1977* (Case Western Reserve University, 1977); Clarence H. Cramer, *The Story of Dentistry and the School in University Circle* (Case Western Reserve University, 1982); Clarence H. Cramer, *The School of Library Science at Case Western Reserve University: 75 Years, 1904–1979* (Case Western Reserve University, 1979); Clarence H. Cramer, *Case Institute of Technology: A Centennial History, 1880–1980* (Case Western Reserve University, ca. 1980); James E. Cutler and Maurice R. Davie, *A Study in Professional Education at Western Reserve University, the School of Applied Social Sciences, 1916–1930* (Western Reserve University Press, 1930); Margene O. Faddis, *A School of Nursing Comes of Age: A History of the Frances Payne Bolton School of Nursing* (Francis Payne Bolton School of Nursing, Alumni Association, 1973); Frederick Clayton Waite, *Western Reserve University: The Hudson Era* (Western Reserve University Press, 1943);

Frederick Clayton Waite, *Western Reserve University: Centennial History of the School of Medicine* (Western Reserve University Press, 1946); Frederick Clayton Waite, *History of the School of Dentistry of Western Reserve University* (Western Reserve University, 1940).

Cedarville University

Keeping the Faith

Murray Murdoch

The most unique feature of Cedarville University is its century-long commitment to orthodox biblical Christianity, a course spanning two denominations and eight presidents. Four of those presidents had a clear vision of the mission and four did not. Indeed, throughout Cedarville's history there have been three key ingredients that have been essential to maintaining this mission: first, a firm attachment to a specific church constituency; second, strong executive leadership; and third, a solid relationship with the local community. When these three ingredients were in place, the institution prospered. When these ingredients were not in place, the institution struggled.

People of Scotch-Irish descent who settled in the Ohio Valley and formed the General Synod of the Reformed Presbyterian Church in North America founded Cedarville College. In 1885 the General Synod appointed a committee of five men to choose a site for a college in the Cedarville area. The Reverend J. F. Morton, Thomas Gibson, R. Park, Hugh McCollum, and H. H. McMillan signed the corporation papers on January 20; six days later, on January 26, 1887, a charter for Cedarville College was granted by the State of Ohio.

For a while it seemed the college would never get off the ground. The trustees were frustrated in their attempts to raise support and would have given up had the General Synod permitted it. In late 1891, however, the college received a sizeable bequest that enabled the trustees to move toward making the college a reality. A Cincinnati pastor, Dr. David McKinney, was named the first president, and on September 19, 1894, the college opened its doors.

At the time of his selection McKinney was the pastor of the First Reformed Presbyterian Church of Cincinnati. A graduate of the University of Pennsylvania and the Reformed Presbyterian Seminary in Philadelphia, he was an articulate, energetic,

Founder's Hall, the oldest building on campus

and slightly dour young man in his mid-thirties. He was to maintain his role as pastor while devoting two days per week to the college.

Following McKinney's selection as president, the board determined to "present the interests of the proposed college to citizens of the village of Cedarville, and in particular to the graduating class of Cedarville High School." Next, they decreed that the institution would be coeducational and that a "circular and prospectus of the college would be prepared." By June the trustees were ready to advertise the opening of Cedarville College in the *Xenia Gazelle* and the *Cedarville Herald.*

Thirty-six students enrolled for the first semester, with one additional student entering for the second semester. Seventeen of the thirty-seven first-year students were from the village of Cedarville, and another seventeen were from other areas of Greene County. This strong community emphasis would characterize Cedarville College through most of its years as a Presbyterian institution.

McKinney continued to provide strong executive leadership until 1915 when both he and the trustees began to recognize the need for a resident administrator. Another major factor leading to his resignation was the merger of his congregation with the First Presbyterian Church of Cincinnati, the new body belonging to the Presbyterian Church in the U.S.A. Thus, McKinney was no longer a part of the General Synod of the Reformed Presbyterian Church. This change in his "church relations" concerned him so greatly that he resigned not only as president but also as trustee of the college.

Following McKinney's resignation, the board of trustees moved quickly to promote Welbert Renwick McChesney, the first faculty member hired by the trustees (1894), to the presidency. In the early years of his presidency McChesney launched a fund-raising campaign for an endowment and building program. By 1921 the student body had reached 135. Despite the war, a financial campaign more than doubled the modest endowment from $109,000 to $242,000, and the college was able to build a new Science Hall. But faculty salaries remained low and finances continued to be a concern.

Late in the 1920s the board of trustees took a step that undermined one of the key elements in the success of the institution. In 1928, in an attempt to broaden their financial base, college officials asked the General Synod of the Reformed Presbyterian Church to release them from the denomination, allowing them to seek support from the Presbyterian Church in the U.S.A. The Reformed Presbyterians agreed to the request, and the governance passed into the hands of a self-perpetuating board of trustees.

The Presbyterian Church in the U.S.A. already had a college in Wooster. Although Wooster's president, Dr. C. F. Wishart, publicly supported Cedarville's request for financial support, he ultimately shifted his position in private letters to denominational leaders, fearful that the church could not support two colleges. As a result, the college never formed an official tie with the Presbyterian Church in the U.S.A., leaving it with no church constituency.

By this time in the history of churches in America, there was a battle raging in every denomination between the fundamentalists and the modernists. That same battle raged in denomination after denomination and within the Presbyterian Church in the U.S.A. The Cedarville administrators gradually began to make concessions to the new theology. This led to conflict between McChesney and the trustees, and several decisions were made that eroded the power of the president. In 1939 President McChesney lost his wife and one month later resigned as president of the college. With his resignation the college lost the strong executive leadership it so desperately needed.

The third president of Cedarville College, Walter Kilpatrick, had graduated from Cedarville before attending seminary. He was a young man who was not prepared for the challenge of administering a college. Kilpatrick shocked the trustees in 1942 by asking for a leave of absence just when the board was preparing to launch a $100,000 fund-raising campaign. But the board granted the leave because Kilpatrick was going to become assistant director of the European Student Relief Fund. Kilpatrick stated that this organization would help "prisoners of war of all nationalities, but especially those of the United Nations interned in Germany." The board felt that by allowing their president to render this "great Christian service," they would receive a landslide of positive publicity. Unfortunately, the publicity received was anything but positive. Kilpatrick left Cedarville early in 1943 and went to Toledo. While awaiting his passport, he was arrested on a morals charge. Following his arrest, Kilpatrick was released on a $2,500 bond paid by his brother-in-law and was then committed to a sanitarium for treatment and observation. Soon he was indicted by a Lucas County grand jury on the charges of rape and felonious assault. The *Cedarville Herald* reported that Kilpatrick entered a plea of guilty and was given an indeterminate sentence.

In a special meeting held after Kilpatrick's conviction, the board of trustees accepted his resignation as president and asked Ira D. Vayhinger, who served as acting president, to continue in that role until June. But the damage to Cedarville College was immense. This local disaster, coupled with the United States's involvement in World War II, forced the board of trustees to give up the campaign for $100,000.

By 1943 the major factors that would bring the board of trustees to the verge of closing the doors of Cedarville College were all in place. Strong church ties had been lost in 1928, the power of the president had been limited by trustee action, and the Kilpatrick situation had eroded community support. Since the trustees had a strong desire to see the institution continue, they approached several denominations about a merger. But conversations with the Nazarenes, the Church of Christ and Christian Union, and the Southern Baptists came to naught.

Ironically, at approximately the same time, Cedarville College began to fade in its commitment. There was a fledgling night school, the Baptist Bible Institute of Cleveland (B.B.I.), being developed in Cleveland to train people for the ministry. Then in 1946 the leaders decided to start a day school organized to provide an education framed in the context of orthodox Christianity. The institute's founding pastors had broken away from the American Baptist Convention over the issue of modernism versus fundamentalism. This new fellowship of churches was called the General Association of Regular Baptist Churches (G.A.R.B.C.). This new group was committed to the inerrancy of Scripture, the deity of Christ, and the cardinal doctrines of the Christian faith.

When the B.B.I. made a commitment to a day school, their circumstances changed drastically. Though the Hough Avenue Baptist Church housed the classes, more buildings were needed, but property was difficult to purchase because Western Reserve University was expanding and could obviously outbid the small Baptist Bible Institute.

At this time Dr. James T. Jeremiah was pastoring in the city of Dayton when Harold Engle, a former Cedarville resident, began attending Jeremiah's church. Aware of Cedarville's plight, Engle asked Jeremiah if he knew of any "Regular Baptist" school that might be in need of property. Jeremiah was familiar with the needs of B.B.I., so he arranged for a committee of trustees from that institution to meet with him and Engle in Cedarville. After that preliminary visit, the trustees of B.B.I. and Cedarville met again. As the meeting with the representatives of Cedarville College continued, Jeremiah was well aware of the prevailing attitudes in the G.A.R.B.C. Knowing the sensitivity of the Regular Baptists issues concerning fundamentals, he understood that in order to succeed, a new direction for the Bible institute would require the support of the pastors and people in the G.A.R.B.C. He was not at all sure that a merger would be supported. As the discussion of "merging" began, he leaned toward Harold Engle and whispered, "I don't think Regular Baptists can merge." Engle smiled at his young pastor and replied, "Preacher, you had better wait a minute and see what they mean by 'merge.'"

As the discussion developed, the love that the Presbyterian trustees had for their institution became obvious. These men were willing to turn the campus over to someone who had the strength, desire, and burden to carry on for the cause of Christ. Consequently, as a self-perpetuating board, they devised a plan by which the Presbyterian trustees would gradually resign, allowing representatives from the new group to be elected. By exchanging the boards in this manner, it would be possible for Cedarville College to continue functioning under its charter, and the college's mission could go on uninterrupted. Jeremiah recognized the unique opportunity; this was clearly a "merger" that even Regular Baptists could accept!

After describing their plight, the Cedarville trustees asked the B.B.I. representatives to share their vision for the future. The Baptists outlined their hopes of building an institution that would not only prepare young men and women to enter vocational Christian ministry but would train young people for leadership in every academic discipline so that they could go out and be "salt and light in a world that was lost." As they explained their mission, the room fell silent, a silence finally broken by the chairman of the Presbyterian Board of Trustees, Earl McClellan (Class of 1913). McClellan rose and said, "Gentlemen, this is what Cedarville College always was meant to be."

Within a week both boards met and approved the merger. The attorneys worked out the final details, and all the Baptist trustees traveled to Cedarville for a joint meeting of Presbyterians and Baptists. This historic meeting took place on April 4, 1953. The first step was for the Presbyterian trustees to delete the article in their by-laws that required a majority of their board to be members of the Presbyterian Church in the U.S.A. Once that by-law was deleted, the next step was to read the individual letters of resignation from eight Presbyterian trustees. The motion was made to accept their resignations and passed unanimously. Then two of the Presbyterians moved and seconded that nine Baptists be added to the board of trustees. That motion also passed unanimously. Next, the final group of Presbyterians resigned, and their resignations were accepted. Then the final group of Baptists was elected. Finally, the chairman and the other officers of the board resigned. The

Presbyterians had removed themselves from the board of trustees. In the matter of one and a half hours, Cedarville College concluded its tenure as a Presbyterian institution and began its existence as a Baptist college.

The move from Cleveland was made during the summer, and the Baptists began classes in the fall of 1953. The early days of the new administration did not go well. Dr. Leonard Webster, the first Baptist president, informed the trustees in December that the college had debts of $24,074.83, with about $2,500.00 cash on hand. Before the trustees could recover from the shocking financial news, Milner read a letter from faculty member Arthur Williams expressing his dissatisfaction with Webster and resigning in the "best interest of the school." Webster defended his differences with Williams, but Milner then read another letter signed by several members of the faculty indicating that they also would resign if Williams were to leave. Suddenly, the board was faced with a crisis that threatened to turn their dream into a nightmare.

Webster was forced to resign, and James T. Jeremiah was named "acting president." Later he resigned his pastorate in Dayton to assume the presidency, during which the three key ingredients needed to maintain the mission were restored. The General Association of Regular Baptist Churches provided a growing and committed constituency, "Pastor-President" Jeremiah reestablished strong executive leadership, and eventually the college gradually regained the support of the local community. Jeremiah's vision for a Christian liberal arts college moved Cedarville into a unique niche, since the other schools approved by the Regular Baptists were Bible schools. In those early days, Jeremiah picked up the milk for the students' breakfast, personally supervised maintenance work, and hired faculty and administrators. He drew heavily on the expertise of the people he hired and worked with the trustees much like a pastor would work with a church board.

Under Jeremiah's leadership, the three-year Bible institute curriculum was replaced with a four-year Bible major. As faculty was added, the liberal arts programs began to develop. During the first decade there were two important events that greatly aided the college. The first occurred in June 1958 when the twenty-seventh annual conference of the General Association of Regular Baptist Churches met in Columbus, just forty-five miles from Cedarville. Eight hundred messengers from across the United States attended. Jeremiah arranged for several buses to bring the Regular Baptist pastors to Cedarville on the Wednesday afternoon of the conference. His wife, Ruby, prepared a luncheon for all the pastors and church people who would come. The response was tremendous. The next month the *Baptist Bulletin* reported: "On Wednesday afternoon the Association made a trip to Cedarville College. A crowd of over 650 were served a lovely lunch and enjoyed a sightseeing tour of the buildings and grounds." This occasion introduced hundreds of people to Cedarville College.

In those early years of appealing to Regular Baptists for support, Jeremiah, the "pastor-president," learned many important lessons. One of the most significant related to finances. Appealing to churches across the nation for funds required a different approach than in dealing with a local congregation. Jeremiah "learned that you don't send out letters of despair if you want a response. The answer to that kind of thing is 'If they are that bad off, why should I give to something that's going to die?'"

This knowledge began an important part of the second key event introducing Regular Baptists to Cedarville College. In 1958 the *Baptist Bulletin*, the official organ of Regular Baptists, was a struggling journal. Jeremiah recognized the value of that publication in circulating word of Cedarville College. He entered into a verbal agreement with the editor to place a Cedarville advertisement on the back of the *Baptist Bulletin* each month. For years every issue carried such an advertisement. With the passing of years the quality of those advertisements was testimony to the development of Cedarville College; Regular Baptists watched the school's progress on the back of their national magazine.

Under Jeremiah's leadership Cedarville College gradually stabilized and then began to grow. By the mid-sixties, the student body had reached 500, and the growth pattern continued into the seventies. Facilities were expanded, the faculty grew, and Cedarville became the strongest academic institution supported by the General Association of Regular Baptist Churches. The college sought North Central accreditation despite the fact that many in the fundamentalist community believed that an institution that required faculty to sign a doctrinal statement could not be accredited. When Dr. Clifford Johnson and Dr. James T. Jeremiah traveled to Chicago to deal with final questions, everything progressed nicely until one North Central representative looked at President Jeremiah and said, "If we give you accreditation, what would you do if someone on your faculty told you he didn't believe your doctrine anymore?" Jeremiah looked him directly in the eye and said, "We'd fire him." Silence engulfed the room until the man smiled, nodded, and said, "That's exactly what ought to happen." North Central examiners recognized the value of an institution maintaining its mission.

By the late seventies Jeremiah began to realize that the college needed new leadership because the next step in the development of the institution would be a giant one. He felt it would take ten years to accomplish some of the things that needed to be done and said, "I didn't think that I wanted to start something that I couldn't finish." Consequently, on June 4, 1977, at the conclusion of the commencement exercises, Jeremiah announced that he would be stepping down as president after the next academic year. He indicated the desire to return to a ministry of evangelism and Bible teaching for the remainder of his active years.

As the 1977–78 school year came to a close, it was natural for everyone to begin assessing the impact of Jeremiah's years as president of the college. The statistics below indicate the strong executive leadership Jeremiah provided. From 1953–54 to 1977–78 the number of students grew from 100 to 1,250; the number of buildings from 8 to 37; acreage from 15 to 180; the annual budget from $95,000 to $4,580,000; and total assets from 325,000 to $9,700,000. Under Jeremiah's leadership Cedarville College had become a dynamic force in the field of Christian higher education. The institution stood firmly committed to the principles of historic fundamentalism. As an approved school of the G.A.R.B.C., Cedarville took a firm position "for the Word of God and the Testimony of Jesus Christ."

By the end of Jeremiah's quarter-century of leadership, the three key ingredients in the success of Cedarville College were firmly in place: the church tie, strong executive leadership, and the respect of the local community. Yet Jeremiah was on the verge of making what may have been his greatest contribution. After choosing to step down, Jeremiah gave his full support to the newly selected president, evangelist Paul Dixon. Although he was a strong leader himself, Jeremiah had the wisdom to never second-guess his replacement. At the same time, Dixon exhibited strong loyalty to now-chancellor Jeremiah. Through the years he frequently referred to the opportunity he had to build on the base so firmly established by his predecessor.

The selection of Paul Dixon as president was a surprise to many, including Dixon himself. A graduate of Tennessee Temple University and a local evangelist, he had preached in many Regular Baptist churches but had no background in higher education. But in many respects Dixon and Jeremiah were alike: both were loyal to the Regular Baptist Movement and biblical fundamentalism, firmly committed to local churches, sympathetic to the needs of pastors, believers in quality education within a Baptist framework, and desirous of making that education available to the Bible-believing community.

But there were also huge differences between the two. In the 1970s Dixon praised Jeremiah for his quarter-century of leadership and then described himself as someone who had never managed anything except his own life and family. He admitted that the greatest challenge he faced was "starting as a novice in higher education and having to learn on the job." Further, the two men were different in their styles of leadership. Both were strong executives, but Jeremiah related to the board of trustees in a collegial manner and involved them in the decision-making process. Jeremiah never voted when the board of trustees voted, and he seldom put pressure on the board to move in a particular direction. When he selected his administrative team, he gave them a great deal of freedom in how they would develop their particular areas. The administrative committee frequently voted on actions that were to be taken. Jeremiah was the pastor-president. Dixon, however, presented a much more aggressive pattern of executive leadership. He outlined specific goals and objectives to the board and aggressively sought their adoption. He provided strong leadership both for his board and for his administrators and faculty. Dixon was and is much more an entrepreneurial executive.

There was also a significant difference in their approach to fund-raising. Jeremiah centered most of his fund-raising activity in the local churches, encouraging them to include Cedarville in their budgets and to contribute to the various fund drives. While Dixon continued to seek support from the churches, he broadened the financial base significantly. He began to contact businessmen and foundation leaders, particularly those who believed in the free-enterprise system, challenging them to support an institution that took no government aid because of their religious convictions. Gradually Dixon increased the financial base of Cedarville, expanding the budget and constructing new buildings.

At the same time Dixon maintained the institution's firm commitment to fundamentalism. He repeatedly said that the Chapel service was "the heartbeat of every Christian institution." From the outset of his administration, he sought to bring to campus leading speakers from around the nation. He addressed the student body and faculty nearly every Monday in chapel. His passion for "the Word of God and the Testimony of Jesus Christ" was clear to all, and his commitment to the roots of the institution was unchallenged. During the years that followed, the Cedarville faculty became leaders in the development of the integration of Scripture and knowledge, and the quality of education continued to improve.

Dixon's aggressive leadership was never more clearly manifested than in the first year of his presidency. In the fall of 1978 enrollment dropped at Cedarville for only the third time in the twenty-five years of Baptist operation. The Dixon administration came face to face with the difficulties of the new age in education. The decline from 1,250 to 1,185 students had serious budgetary implications. When his research uncovered the impending recession in higher education, Dixon was stunned: "I did not understand what higher education was about to go through. I had no idea what I was getting into relative to those pressures."

The Cedarville administration immediately began a comprehensive review at virtually every level: admissions, recruitment, public relations, and development came under careful scrutiny. Though Dixon had little experience in these areas, his entrepreneurial concept of leadership became immediately apparent. When he realized that the number of traditional college-aged individuals would decline 26 percent over the next decade and a half, and that the decline would be as high as 40 percent in some of the major areas from which the college drew its students, he concluded that decisive action was needed. But where many institutions met the crisis by cutting programs and budgets, Dixon's approach was much different. Because he was totally convinced that Cedarville was a special place, a rarity in Christian higher education, Dixon refused to recommend entrenchment. Instead, he launched an aggressive expansion program that encompassed every area.

At Dixon's urging the trustees made dramatic improvement in faculty and staff salaries. New positions were added in the areas of student recruitment, student services, and development. Consultants in key areas supplemented institutional planning. The president became vigorously involved in fund-raising, placing an emphasis on new constituencies. As a result Cedarville College entered a period of remarkable growth. While most colleges battled declining enrollments, Cedarville grew 53 percent, from 1,185 students in 1978 to 1,800 students in 1986. This extraordinary success was a result of careful planning and the dynamic leadership of Paul Dixon.

At this point the decision was made to level enrollment temporarily in order to guarantee the quality of both programs and facilities. However, it became increasingly difficult to keep a cap on enrollments as the demand for a Cedarville education continued to grow. During the 1980s all existing programs were greatly strengthened, including the Department of Business Administration. A successful nursing program was added and planning for an engineering program began. New buildings and programs continued to be brought on board, and by the 1985–86 academic year, the annual budget had reached $11,750,000. By this time Dixon received his doctorate in higher education planning, and the degree of strategic planning in place at Cedarville was a manifestation of his education.

Dixon frequently told the faculty and student body that "anything done in the name of Jesus Christ ought to have quality stamped all over it." Dixon's commitment to this excellence was clearly seen in the manicured lawns and well-maintained buildings of the college. But never was it more clearly seen than in the construction projects that dominated the closing years of the twentieth century. The $16 million Dixon Ministry Center houses a 3,400-seat chapel, which can be expanded to seat 4,000. The Ministry Center also houses the Departments of Music and Christian Ministry. Music professors have well-equipped studios for the individual instruction of students. In the fall of 2000, the students returned to campus and quickly occupied the new Stevens Student Center. This new $21 million facility houses numerous offices: the campus post office, the book store, the cafeteria, the president's dining room, and a state-of-the-art 400-seat theater.

Under the Dixon administration Cedarville also has been a leader in technology. It was one of the first campuses in the United States to place a computer in every dormitory room and launch a campus network linking faculty, staff, and students. Recently, Cedarville received the CAUSE Award as the leading technology campus of any U.S. institution with a budget under $160 million. Cedarville was named in *U.S. News and World Report* one of the outstanding educational values in this region. The average ACT Score for Cedarville students has moved from 20 in 1979 to 25.6 today. The university is able to enroll only one-third of the students who apply for admission.

On September 1, 2000, Cedarville became a university. Limited graduate programs were introduced and several new faculty positions were added. Forty-one denominations are represented in the student body, with students coming from every state in the United States and fourteen foreign countries. The budget now exceeds $46 million, and the forty buildings and 418 acres of the campus are valued at almost $90 million.

Thus, Cedarville stands as a marvelous testimony to what can be accomplished when an institution is faithful to its mission. Cedarville entered the twenty-first century committed to the same values that were the foundation of the institution well over a century ago. Throughout both the Presbyterian and Baptist years, the key to success has been to maintain the mission.

Suggested Reading

An overview of Cedarville's Presbyterian background can be found in the *Dictionary of the Presbyterian and Reformed Tradition in America*, ed. D. G. Hart and Mark A. Noll (Intervarsity Press, 1999). For an overview see Mark A. Noll, Nathan O. Hatch, and George M. Marsden, eds., *The Search for Christian America* (Helmers and Howard, 1989). Much of the early history of the General Association of Regular Baptist Churches is covered in J. Murray Murdoch, *A Portrait of Obedience: The Biography of Robert T. Ketcham* (Regular Baptist Press, 1979). The issue of colleges moving from their commitment is covered in *The Dying of the Light: The Disengagement of Colleges and Universities from their Christian Churches*, by James Tunstead Burtchaell (Eardmans, 1998).

For a detailed history of Cedarville College, see J. Murray Murdoch, *Cedarville College: A Century of Commitment* (Cedarville College Press, 1987). Recently Gregory K. Belliveau authored *Say to the Mountain: The Life of James T. Jeremiah* (Regular Baptist Press, 1999).

The University of Dayton

The Creation of a Modern Catholic University

Erving E. Beauregard

The origins of the University of Dayton lay in the convulsions of the French Revolution of 1789. The government's imposition of the Civil Constitution of the Clergy drove underground and then into exile Father William Joseph Chaminade, honorary canon of St. Andrew's Cathedral at Bordeaux. After he returned from Spain he determined to overthrow the de-Christianization of France that he ascribed to the Revolution. He wholeheartedly agreed with the proposition trumpeted by Monseigneur Jean Brumauld de Beauregard, Bishop of Orléans: "Love God and serve the King" and promote the education of the various social classes.

To forward his stand Chaminade founded the Society of Mary (S.M.), a congregation of priests and lay brothers known as Marianists. As Superior-General Chaminade carefully guided his following. He rejected modernism as anti-Christian but adopted the egalitarian ethos of the French Revolution by insisting that religious renewal work from the bottom up. Profoundly influenced by aesthetic developments in literary romanticism, Chaminade emphasized the heart as the affective source of divine wisdom and faith as a unifying force in a world of perplexing diversity. Chaminade promoted a teaching ministry that would extend beyond spiritual formation to include commercial education, crafts, agricultural programs, and special curricula for teachers in normal schools.

Headquartered in France, the Society of Mary survived the anticlericalism of the revolutions of 1830 and 1848. By that time, Father Leo Meyer had become one of Chaminade's "most cherished disciples." Reaching maturity as a priest in the 1820s, Meyer absorbed the ideas of Catholic thinkers who were focusing on the reintegration of religion and culture. A priest of the Diocese of Strasbourg, Meyer in 1837 joined the Society of Mary rather than the Society of Jesus. Meyer was influenced by two "ecstatic women" (one of them later founded a religious community known as the

Chapel of the Immaculate Conception

Daughters of the Divine Redeemer) who prophesied he would do missionary work in America. In late 1848 Bishop John B. Purcell of Cincinnati asked Father George J. Caillet, Chaminade's successor as Superior-General, to send Marianist teaching brothers for three parishes in Cincinnati. In 1849 Caillet selected Meyer to head the mission.

In July 1849 Purcell sent Meyer to assist Father Henry Juncker, pastor of Emmanuel Church in Dayton. Meyer purchased seventy-five acres (later it came to 125 acres) from John Stuart, reputedly a descendant, via France, of the Scottish dynasty. Meyer signed the mortgage for 125 acres at $12,000 with a 6 percent annual interest, using his medal of St. Joseph to seal his promise to pay. Meyer named the property "Nazareth," as if it were Mary's motherhouse for those brothers and priests committed by a fourth vow to Mary Immaculate. Nazareth would focus on fighting secularism in America, thus carrying on Father Chaminade's crusade from the days of the French Revolution. In America this could be seen as a battle against Protestanism in the 1840s and 1850s. At Nazareth on July 1, 1850, Meyer opened St. Mary's School for Boys. Following prescribed rules, Meyer had sent the prospectus for approval to Purcell (now Archbishop). Purcell returned the prospectus with only the insertion "none but Catholic boys are admitted." Purcell insisted that St. Mary's be totally Catholic because, in his view, the two Catholic academies in Cincinnati that included Protestants had emerged as a mixed blessing. Meyer "loyally" accepted the restriction and adhered to it until the end of his administration. Thus Meyer dissented from the enlightened position of Father Chaminade, who wrote to a parish priest in France who wished to exclude non-Catholic pupils; Chaminade said, "Yours is a restricted view. Let us be Catholic, very decidedly, even to the shedding of our last drop of blood, but let us also be kind and moderate, that is to say, truly charitable toward all and meek without the least trace of bitterness, as St. Paul urges us."

The school opened with fourteen middle-class, German-American students aged nine to twelve years. The teachers numbered three: two German-speaking Marianist brothers from France and a young Irish American diocesan priest. By 1853 the enrollment reached twenty boarding students and thirty day students. During 1850–52 and 1860–75 Brother Maximin Zehler headed the school, which had become St. Mary's Institute. Zehler was a subordinate of Father Leo Meyer, Provincial-Superior of the Marianists in America. Meyer perceived the institute as subservient to the interests of the Marianist motherhouse, which, like the institute, was located at Nazareth in Dayton.

During the 1850s St. Mary's Institute confronted formidable problems. On December 27, 1854, a fire destroyed the central house at Nazareth, including the boys' dormitory, classrooms, and several rooms of the Marianists. (Classes resumed in September 1856.) In 1855 the United States suffered a severe depression and high inflation, and Meyer could not pay the semiannual premium on the debt. The debt problem brought serious repercussions. Meyer became preoccupied with the farming economy at Nazareth. Thereupon he imposed a quasimonastic asceticism on St. Mary's Institute. One brother reported to the Marianist Superior-General in France that the boarding students and brothers "sleep on straw," the students "sweep the classrooms, etc. [other maintenance work]. Often food is set before them which you would hardly give a beggar. Some have acquired the reputation of uncleanliness, for avarice, for trickery." Moreover, other actions by Meyer had antagonized the parish clergy of Dayton and Archbishop Purcell.

Nevertheless, Meyer had saved Nazareth, including St. Mary's Institute, through his program of austerity. Thanks to his business acumen, he reduced the debt through the sale of property at Nazareth, and in 1862 he made the final payment to John Stuart. Because Meyer had succeeded without financial assistance from the Marianist general administration, Brother Zehler could only lament Meyer's recall to France in 1862.

After Leo Meyer's departure, modest growth characterized St. Mary's Institute. One hundred students enrolled in 1860, college preparatory courses began in 1861, and a year later a novitiate and normal school for Marianist candidates opened. By 1869 St. Mary's had 210 resident students and forty boarders. In the quarter-century after 1860 construction was completed of Zehler Hall, Liberty Hall, the Chapel of the Immaculate Conception, St. Mary Hall, and St. Joseph Hall. St. Mary Hall, then the city of Dayton's tallest building, was dubbed "Brother Zehler's Folly" because of his alleged megalomania in persisting in its construction. In 1882 St. Mary's Institute was incorporated and empowered to confer degrees under the laws of the State of Ohio.

By 1886 the pioneering work of Father Meyer and Brother Zehler was carried on by Brother John A. Waldron. First educated at St. Mary's Institute, he then studied in Paris from 1883 to 1886 at Stanislas College under the direction of the Society of Mary. Stanislas, according to a writer, was "undoubtedly the foremost Catholic school in France and perhaps in the world."

At Stanislas, Waldron made contact with Marianists who had lived with Father Chaminade, thus absorbing the original spirit of the Marianists' founder. At the same time, Waldron gained exposure to the French culture.

Upon his return to the United States in 1886, Waldron was assigned to St. Mary's Institute as vice president where he overshadowed two successive presidents. The French-trained Waldron was a foe of the secularism he had witnessed in the anticlericalism of the Third Republic. In this sense he was a true heir of Chaminade and Meyer. As vice president Waldron expanded and coordinated the program of studies at St. Mary's, designing a program for the bachelor of arts degree, the stress being on the classics. To assure efficient instruction, he labored enthusiastically in assisting faculty members in detailed preparation of their next day's classes. During Waldron's tenure St. Mary's conferred its first degree (bachelor of science) in 1899. Students highly esteemed him for his warm interest in them and lamented his departure.

In the early twentieth century innovation continued at the institution. In 1912 it became St. Mary's College but changed to St. Mary College in 1915. Activities in harmony with the vision of Chaminade, Meyer, and Waldron marked the college.

On June 25, 1901, the first bachelor of arts degrees were granted to five students. In 1902 the college underwent reorganization into four departments: classical, scientific, academic, and preparatory. In 1905 the commercial department began, becoming the Department of Commerce and Finance in 1921, then the Division of Business Organization in 1924, and ultimately the School of Business Administration. Debuting between 1909 and 1920 four engineering departments joined to form the School of Engineering. In 1915 the Marianist training program (novitiate and normal school) was moved from the campus to Mount St. John's (present-day Bergamo Center). In 1920 the Division of Education opened, offering evening and Saturday classes to serve adult members of the area. In 1922 the College of Law appeared, also with evening classes. Other graduate programs ensued, and a summer session was inaugurated in 1923 that joined the College of Law in being coeducational.

In 1920 a momentous change took place under the leadership of Father Bernard P. O'Reilly, Provincial of the Marianist Province of Cincinnati, owner of St. Mary College. He had been president of the college (1909–18) and would be again (1923–32). O'Reilly heard that a movement was afloat to establish a four-year state institution to be called "the University of Dayton." Believing that such a secular body would become a serious threat to the future of St. Mary College, he hurried to Columbus, where he secured support for incorporating St. Mary College as the University of Dayton on September 2, 1920.

The nativism that flourished in Ohio after the First World War was manifested against the new school in the activities of the Ku Klux Klan. According to one of Dayton's Klan newspapers, the University of Dayton "stands like a giant fortress upon a high hill overlooking the surrounding country," with a Reserved Officers Training Corps program that had been established to train a Catholic army to fight religious wars against American Protestants. The Klan worked fervently to frighten faculty and students at the university. In December 1923 the Klan burned a cross on campus and also set off twelve bombs. The bombs caused no injuries because there were few students on campus at that time. Many Daytonians disapproved of such an outrage because they remembered when St. Mary's College sheltered six hundred refugees during the city's great flood of 1913.

For some decades the University of Dayton carried on as a small institution. The student body hailed from Dayton and environs; some came from places where they had attended Marianist high schools, including Hawaii. In 1935 the university inaugurated a college for women with sisters of Notre Dame de Namur in charge, but in 1937 that unit closed because all divisions of the university were opened to women, thus making the institution fully coeducational. The Great Depression caused the College of Law to cease in 1935, but in 1939 the Graduate School opened. The Marianists comprised the board of trustees and administration of the university. The faculty consisted overwhelmingly of Marianist priests and brothers. The curriculum remained largely unchanged for some time. The course of study produced Charles J. Pedersen (summa cum laude, Class of 1926) who became a Nobel Prize laureate in chemistry in 1987.

World War II had a marked impact on the University of Dayton. The enrollment, 900 in 1945, rose to 2,400 in 1947, half of whom were veterans. To teach such students, many laity, men and women, joined the faculty. A building program ensued.

In the late 1960s a mighty crisis engulfed the University of Dayton. It caught the attention of both the Roman Catholic and secular worlds. It may be characterized as involving the soul of the institution and its future. The perilous situation contained diverse ingredients: Scripture and Church tradition, the Roman Catholic Church's teaching authority and individual conscience, dogma and freedom of inquiry, hierarchical jurisdiction and university autonomy, institutional administration and faculty bodies, students and clergymen, and national and local media. Intellect and emotions darted throughout the campus.

Developments at both the university and the world at large coalesced to bring the explosion. Despite an occasional setback, such as the Korean War, the university's enrollment increased. Thus arose the need to provide an adequate faculty that became mainly lay as the Society of Mary could not supply the required numbers from its ranks. At the same time a profound happening took place in the Roman Catholic world. Pope John XXIII's insistence on the principle of *aggiornamento* (that the Church should develop and change with society and history) permeated the Second Vatican Council, 1962–65. This outlook of openness and reform would lead to a furious response at the University of Dayton.

Controversy erupted in the philosophy department. There the emphasis involved neoscholasticism, which "functioned primarily as an ensemble of agreed-upon answers to various kinds of speculative questions, the validity of which one accepted on authority, which provided a rational grounding for Catholic beliefs and attitudes and served as the source of organizing principles for practical action." Neoscholasticism was grounded on Thomism; at the University of Dayton "Thomistic" textbooks were used.

The Second Vatican Council allowed airing philosophies other than Thomism. Some faculty members in the philosophy department at Dayton felt the time was propitious and proper to speak and write on new insights. However, the majority within the department echoed Cardinal Alfredo Ottaviani, who represented the minority view at the Second Vatican Council: rigid adherence to standpatism on church doctrine. The struggle between the two camps would determine, in the case of the University of Dayton, whether there was truth in George Bernard Shaw's assertion that a "Catholic university is a contradiction in terms."

The controversy can be traced to 1960–61, when the philosophy department hired Professor Joseph L. Dieska, a Thomist, and Assistant Professor John M. Chrisman, the first non-Thomist. A former seminarian, Dieska held bachelor's, master's, and doctoral degrees from Slovak State University, where he taught 1944–48. He also had headed the Slovak Christian Democratic Party of Freedom and accepted the rule of Monsignor Josef Tiso, president of the pro-Nazi Slovak state. (Dieska fled Czechoslovakia upon the Communist takeover in 1948.) The youthful Chrisman earned his A.B. at the University of Portland, where Thomism reigned, and then a master's degree at the University of Toronto, where his Thomism was punctured.

Chrisman had a few like-minded colleagues in the philosophy department. In 1962 Assistant Professor Eulalio R. Baltazar was hired. He had earned two bachelor degrees in agriculture and philosophy in his native Phillippines. Leaving a Jesuit seminary, he obtained a doctorate in philosophy at Georgetown University. When Baltazar arrived in Dayton, he was a non-Thomist and a follower of Father Teilhard de Chardin. Instructor Lawrence P. Ulrich joined the department in 1964. He had bachelor's and master's degrees from the Catholic University of America.

Dieska and his fellow conservatives dominated their overwhelmingly male department. They opposed opening up the curriculum to non-Thomistic thought. They informed the administration that the non-Thomists were advocating "false teachings." The Thomists assailed Baltazar's chapter on contraception that he contributed to a book. The Thomists strongly opposed allowing the Philosophy Club to sponsor a discussion, "Birth Control—A Time to Evaluate," on October 19, 1965. Claiming to represent the majority (Thomists) of the department, Father Richard J. Dombro, assistant professor, called on the university president, the Reverend Dr. Raymond J. Roesch, to forbid the meeting. Roesch would not. Dombro attended the meeting and then sent a report to Roesch, claiming the discussion involved attempts to undermine the Magisterium (the Church's teaching authority). Dombro accused Chrisman, the club's moderator, of disagreeing with the papal teaching on contraception and saying that popes contradict one another. Dombro recommended that Roesch do things that would allow the philosophy department to muzzle the Philosophy Club. (This meant that the Thomists would prevail, since they were the majority in the department.) Roesch did not reply. Believing that the president was ignoring their complaints, the conservatives launched their attack off campus.

Their ally, Father Francis Langhirt, a Marianist living on campus, sent a missive to Archbishop Karl J. Alter of Cincinnati. (Dayton lay within Alter's canonical jurisdiction.) Langhirt accused Chrisman and Baltazar of endorsing situation ethics during a lecture in spring 1966 and also Chrisman of advocating abortion in some cases. Alter forwarded Langhirt's letter to the university administration and asked for an explanation. Thus, Alter ignored the very words he had uttered at a Xavier University commencement: "A Catholic University has complete freedom to explore the entire field of knowledge and to transmit to the students its findings, unrestricted by the Church, just as any other university in the land."

Alter's action drew no response from the administration, but on October 15, 1966, the attack renewed. Hired in 1965 by Dayton to teach philosophy, Assistant Professor Dennis Bonnette had an A.B. from the University of Detroit and an A.M. from Notre Dame. Claiming that "a crisis of faith" was developing at the university, Bonnette asked Alter to fulfill his duties allegedly as required by Canon Law. Bonnette charged four faculty members with publicly—either in talks on the Dayton campus or in writing—revealing their explicit disagreement with Roman Catholic doctrine. Bonnette claimed that Baltazar defended philosophical pluralism, questioned the church's infallibility in its formulation of theology, defended birth control and situation ethics, and denied the dogma of purgatory. Bonnette charged that Chrisman advocated birth control and situation ethics and denied the dogma of purgatory. Bonnette stated that Ulrich and Instructor Randolph F. Lumpp of the theology department were partisans of situation ethics. Bonnette sent a carbon copy of his letter to the Apostolic Delegate to the United States, Archbishop Egidio Vagnozzi, an ally of Cardinal Ottaviani, head of the Sacred Congregation for the Doctrine of the Faith, formerly the Congregation of the Inquisition. Vagnozzi called Alter, who immediately telephoned Roesch and asked the university to investigate. Thus Alter again disregarded his own words about academic freedom at a Catholic university.

Roesch consulted his administrative council, exclusively Marianist. He asked Bonnette to acquaint all with his charges, requested Bonnette to substantiate the charges, and directed each of the four accused to answer the charges. Roesch concluded that the scenario could end in either Bonnette admitting his error and publicly recanting or Bonnette could persist in the charges, in the case of the latter, the administration could establish an ad hoc committee to investigate the details of the situation.

The two sides complied. Bonnette sent a six-page letter to Roesch and a copy to each of the accused. Baltazar defended himself in an eleven-page letter, Chrisman in seven pages, Ulrich and Lumpp in four. Thereupon Roesch consulted "a competent canonist" and several outside theologians. Roesch found the accused innocent "of teaching and advocating doctrines contrary to the magisterium of the Church." Roesch added that Alter concurred.

On December 6, 1966, Assistant Professor of Philosophy Thomas J. Casaletto read "A Declaration of Conscience on the Doctrinal Crisis at the University of Dayton" on Dayton's WHIO radio station. The declaration stated that "the University of Dayton has conducted a classic whitewash" and "was issued to defend ourselves from those colleagues on the faculty who revealed and confessed publicly their incompetence in the field of philosophy and their deviation from fundamental principles of Catholic doctrine." The declaration was signed by eight members of the philosophy department: Bonnette, Casaletto, Dieska, Dombro, Hugo A. Barbic, Allen V. Rinderly, Paul J. Seman, Edward W. Harkenrider, and also Father Langhirt.

The Faculty Forum entered the fray (the Forum was a consultative body of sixteen elected faculty members and four appointed administrators) and censured the declaration's signatories "for conduct unworthy of members of the University of Dayton faculty." It demanded that the eight faculty members rescind publicly or fully substantiate their charge of incompetence against the four; otherwise, they should resign from the faculty. According to the vice president for public relations and development, the eight rescinded their charges. However, Bonnette affirmed that the signatories never withdrew their charges involving "a substantial number of even more serious issues," listed in the declaration. Dieska announced formation of a National Committee for Defense of Catholic Doctrine, with Bonnette as secretary-general.

The controversy raged all the more. The eight accusers appealed Roesch's decision to Alter. They were supported by six Roman Catholic pastors in Dayton, including the dean of the Dayton Deanery. On January 9, 1967, Alter appointed a "fact-finding commission": Monsignor Robert Tensing (chairman) and Father Robert Hagedorn of Mount St. Mary's Seminary, Cincinnati; Father Donald McCarthy, chaplain of the Newman Center, University of Cincinnati; and Father Henry Kenny, S.J., philosophy department, Xavier University. The Dayton chapter of the American Association of University Professors (A.A.U.P.) deplored Alter's action and the intimidating conduct of the commission. The university's student council also lambasted the formation of the commission. Immediately Roesch criticized the student council. The executive committee of the Dayton A.A.U.P. chapter hurled volleys at Roesch's statement, noting that it was outrageous to haul the accused before an inquisition at Cincinnati and to summon still other persons from the university to defend their teaching.

The Tensing commission sent a seventy-five-page report to Alter on February 13, 1967. The Very Reverend Dr. James M. Darby, chairman of the Dayton Board of Trustees, announced that the report cleared the accused of any charge of heresy. However, Tensing retorted that the report contained "substance to the charges that some professors had taught against the Magisterium." Alter never publicly released the full report, and his successors, Archbishops Joseph L. Bernardin and Daniel E. Pilarczyk, refused this author permission to see it. Darby's copy cannot be located in the Marianist Provincialate Archives at the University of Dayton.

The accused felt they were ill-treated by Alter's commission. The competence and mind-set of Tensing, Hagedorn, and McCarthy were questioned. There was not enough time allowed for proper explanation of their views. Further questions included: who were the accusers from off-campus? Why did a fact-finding commission render judgments? Why did the commission imply that philosophical and theological research had no place at an undergraduate level?

On March 1, 1967, President Roesch addressed his faculty on the controversy. He defended Alter's actions. He said genuine academic freedom must flourish at the

University of Dayton, but those who teach should confine themselves to areas of their competence and that appropriate respect must be given to the Magisterium according to the guidelines that the university ad hoc committee would formulate. The audience responded with a standing ovation. Casaletto accused Roesch of paying lip service to Tensing's commission while rejecting its basic findings.

The ad hoc committee's report appeared to be muddled. It asserted the university's independence of "all outside authority" but "presumably because the individuals who composed it were conscientious Catholics, it could claim to respect the teaching authority of the local bishop." The report also asserted the university community's commitment to secularization, that is, "to come of age . . . means a new freedom for men to perfect the world in a non-religious way." Roesch ignored that bold statement. Philip Gleason comments: "Yet the episode represented an important landmark. Never before had a formal faculty committee at a Catholic university flatly recommended secularization as the policy to follow."

The accused four were retained. Later three voluntarily departed. Four of the faculty accusers angrily left. Of the other conservatives, one exited because of denial of tenure and three stayed at the university until retirement.

President Roesch encountered other problems. Assistant Professor of History Philip A. Grant arrived in 1966 from St. John's University of New York, where he had been dismissed because of participation in a faculty strike. Grant worked strongly to establish a faculty chapter of the American Federation of Teachers. A small group formed a union. However, the administration refused recognition. Denied tenure, Grant left in 1969. A large group of students supporting him confronted Roesch at a faculty meeting, but the president did not budge.

Various conflicts arose in Roesch's long administration. Students demanding curriculum liberalization staged a sit-down strike outside his office. Students demanding the end of campus R.O.T.C. disrupted a meeting of the Academic Senate. (Compulsory R.O.T.C. was abolished in 1969.)

Alleging the university would not permit its workers to unionize, some students and others caused a rumpus during the dedication of the Roesch Library on September 25, 1971. (Governor John J. Gilligan and Archbishop Paul F. Leibold of Cincinnati graced that ceremony.) The biology department bowed to the provost, Father Thomas A. Stanley, when he forbade an experiment involving human semen. (Stanley was one of the defenders of the accused in the "heresy trial" of the 1960s.) An African American Marianist brother, Joseph M. Davis, a graduate of Dayton and the Catholic University of America and first executive director of the National Office of Black Catholics, criticized Dayton as "hopeless," a "haven for bigoted, racist attitudes and they had some bad situations there." (Davis later became a Marianist priest.)

In the midst of these events, during Roesch's presidency, 1959–79, there occurred a number of significant accomplishments. First of all, the university successfully met the challenge posed by Wright State University and Sinclair Community College. The establishment of those two institutions siphoned off much of the University of Dayton's clientele in the area. There resulted intensive efforts to recruit students from other parts of Ohio, other states, and even from a few foreign countries. These drives and careful management of the budget, including modest faculty salaries, allowed the university to carry on. Indeed, financial campaigns led to continuing the building programs of previous presidencies, and the Roesch Library and the Arena were erected.

Some other happenings of 1959–79 bear mentioning. The lay board of trustees was abolished, and the board of trustees became predominantly lay with twenty-four members to Marianists' nine. (The trustees are nominated and removable by the members of the University of Dayton Corporation, which is controlled by the Marianist Province of the United States, the owner of the university.) The university adopted a number of documents of the A.A.U.P.; however, the university still clings to restrictions found in the A.A.U.P. Statement on Academic Freedom in Church-Related Colleges and Universities. The Academic Senate began operation; combining legislative authority, legislative concurrence, and consultation, it comprises administrators ex officio and elected faculty and student members. The School of Law saw rebirth, and a doctoral program in biology debuted. The undergraduate curricula permitted more choices for elective subjects. The trimester system and the campus radio station began. Inability to compete on the top level of intercollegiate football led to inaugurating nonscholarship teams. For a time a unique situation involved the University of Dayton providing undergraduate education for members of the Society of the Precious Blood and the Society of Missionaries of Africa (White Fathers).

In August 1979, Brother Raymond L. Fitz became the seventeenth president of the university. He was the second Marianist brother to head the institution, Maxmin Zehler having been the first. Fitz, at thirty-seven, was the youngest president. Possessor of a doctorate, he had served on the university's civil engineering faculty. President Roesch had prepared him for the presidency through an apprenticeship. From August 1978 to August 1979 Brother Fitz received initiation into the university's administrative structure, while during the remainder of that year, as a member of the American Council on Education's Administrators Fellows Program, he participated in seminars and extensive visits to seven campuses to witness their operation and programs.

The new president had the longest tenure in the university's history. (His term lasted to June 30, 2002.) Strength, compassion, and faith characterize Brother Fitz. His endeavor was to place Dayton at the pinnacle of Catholic universities. One component of the plan was involvement of faculty, such as by implementing a volume-based budgetary process to provide incentives to operating units. The latter was first applied by Dr. John O. Geiger, the first lay provost at Dayton.

Fitz also firmly supported technology; indeed, technology is the backbone of the university's master plan, Vision 2005. The university aggressively pursues "wiring" the campus along with student housing off campus. The campus is fully networked. All entering first-year students must purchase a computer.

Technology exists to advance the University General Education Program. The program both provides a base in humanities for all students, coupled with a clustering of courses on a particular theme. This program reflects "best practice" in terms of purposely integrating information from different disciplines to encourage students to reflect on and synthesize perspectives from various sources. The College of Arts and Sciences is responsible for implementing the program and works in close cooperation with the professional schools.

Progress continues in various units. The School of Business Administration features an Investment Seminar in which undergraduates may use university money to make investments; the school enjoys strong relationships with key civic leaders and the loyalty of its alumni. The School of Education has sturdy linkages with the K-12 community and with their professional development schools. The School of Engineering seeks to enroll more minority students and has 23 percent women as undergraduates. The School of Law's program combines a traditional core curriculum with innovative professional skills training and distinctive offerings such as the Program in Law and Technology.

The university maintains a unique unit, the Research Institute. Its research opportunities help in general economic development via funding derived from federal, state, and major industrial firms. It stimulates faculty and student research, in addition to the research conducted by its own principal investigators. It provides a very important link with the business community as a technological source for new projects and services in the greater Dayton area.

Noteworthy are the Marian Library and the International Marian Research Institute. Recognized as the world's largest and most comprehensive collection of printed materials on Mary, the Marian Library aims to further study and research and to promote well-founded devotion to Mary. The International Marian Research Institute serves a diverse, international student population including laity, religious, and clergy, both men and women. Affiliated with the Pontifical Theological Faculty Marianum in Rome, the academic program offers a certificate and a number of advanced pontifical degrees.

The university sponsors other facilities. The Institute for Pastoral Initiatives aims to use the university's resources to network with various Church agencies for the initiation of pastorial services on an international basis. The Center for Business and Economic Research conducts research and forecasting on local and regional issues. The Center for Catholic Education attempts to support Catholic education through programs and services across the country. The Center for Competitive

Change is national in scope, focusing on management changes in manufacturing and the education necessary to undertake those changes.

There are several more university components. The Center for Family and Community Research focuses on how families and communities can best meet the challenges of a changing society through application of the knowledge gained through research to the social systems of the local community. The Center for International Programs is responsible for development and implementation of internalization strategies to advance the university as a more internationally oriented institution. The Center for Social Concern works to develop programs that enable students to get involved in both short-term and long-term projects that raise student consciousness of social issues and social justice.

Two more university parts deserve mention. The Campus Ministry Office makes a concerted effort to empower students to get in touch with their spiritual selves, to reflect on their experiences, and to provide opportunities for serving others. It embodies much of the university's spirit as it attempts to build a community that "learns, leads and serves." The English Language and Multicultural Institute offers English as a Second Language instruction, cross-cultural communication and management seminars, multicultural classroom teaching techniques, and special language programs. It provides an ideal opportunity to increase multiculturalism and builds a base for international study within the university.

Other than organic, what is the connection between the present-day University of Dayton, Ohio's largest private institution of higher learning, and its ancestor, St. Mary's School for Boys, facility for fourteen students in 1850? The fundamental tie embraces the owner, the Society of Mary, and its founder, Father Chaminade. The narrow purpose of the original school—elementary education for white Roman Catholic boys—has been replaced by higher education for the academically qualified regardless of gender, race, or religion. This egalitarianism harmonizes with the purpose of Chaminade, who approved that principle of the 1789 French Revolution. However, Chaminade's disapproval of that movement's secularism became ingrained in St. Mary's School and its successors, culminating in the statement that the University of Dayton exists "under the influence of religion."

The bond of Chaminade and Dayton also encompasses other areas. Just as Chaminade espoused love of country, so does the university, as exemplified by sponsorship of R.O.T.C. and the Research Institute through its contracts with governmental agencies. Chaminade's endorsing of "the teaching of worldly knowledge" and his application thereof equates with the university's activities in the College of Arts and Sciences and the Schools of Business Administration, Education, Engineering, and Law. Chaminade and the university agree on flexibility with regard to practices in teaching. Chaminade's stress on service to humanity correlates with the multiple centers and institutes of the university. The mystically inclined affirm that the University of Dayton is endowed with the spirit of the Blessed William Joseph Chaminade, whose beatification occurred in 2000.

Edward H. Knust and Frank Deibel, "Hallowed Memories" (1950), unpublished manuscript, University of Dayton Archives; William O. Wehrle, "A History of the University of Dayton" (1937), unpublished manuscript, University of Dayton Archives; Jean-Claude Delas, *History of the Constitutions of the Society of Mary* (Marianist Press, 1975); Joseph J. Panzer, *Educational Traditions of the Society of Mary* (University of Dayton Press, 1965); George Ruppel, *The Marianist Story* (Marianist Publications, n.d.); Christopher J. Kauffman, *Education and Transformation: Marianist Ministries in America since 1849* (Crossroad, 1999); John Brueck, "Chronicles of Nazareth" (University of Dayton Archives, 1888); Henri Lebon, *Our First Century 1817–1917,* ed. Lawrence Cada and Michael Lux, trans. John Dockter (Marianist Resources Commission, 1975); John E. Garvin, *The Centenary of the Society of Mary* (Brothers of Mary, 1917); Andrien Dansette, *Religious History of Modern France,* 2 vols. (Herder and Herder, 1961); Vincent R. Vasey, *Chaminade: Another portrait,* ed. Joseph Steffanelli and Lawrence Cada (Marianist Press, 1987); John M. Graves, *Father Leo Meyer's 13 Years at Nazareth,* rev. ed., ed. Joseph H. Lackner (Marianist Press, 1997); Paul C. Goelz, "John A. Waldron: The Man and the Educator" (M.A. thesis, University of Dayton, 1945); Erving E. Beauregard, "An Archbishop, a University, and Academic Freedom," *Records of the American Catholic Historical Society of Philadelphia,* 93 (Mar.–Dec. 1987); Mary Jude Brown, "The 'Heresy Affair' at the University of Dayton, 1960–67: The Origins of the 'Affair' and Its Context" (M.A. thesis, University of Dayton, 1999); Jerome Murphy, "A History of Coeducation at the University of Dayton," unpublished manuscript (University of Dayton Archives, 1975).

The University of Dayton   133

Defiance College

Created to Serve, and Still Serving

Randall Buchman

In the mid–nineteenth century church and community leaders throughout Ohio were creating colleges to prepare young people in the liberal arts to enter the theological, medical, and legal fields as leaders in their communities and their denominations. The feeling among these founders was that young people needed to be well versed in the liberal arts and guided by the prevailing Christian ethic of their denomination.

In northwest Ohio, the last frontier in Ohio, the leaders of the Defiance community also wanted a college as well as a preparatory school, a normal school, and a vocational school. Since the community was less than twenty years old, funds were lacking. To raise the funds for their college-seminary-preparatory school, they sought help from the state through a charter that would grant them unsold canal lands. On March 23, 1850, the founders, who claimed no denominational affiliation, were granted a charter to form the Defiance Female Seminary. The state also made 1,283 acres of canal lands in Paulding and Defiance Counties available to the trustees to raise funds for the college, but it took years to accumulate the money to begin the institution.

Early in 1875 they had secured enough financial support to purchase nine acres of land north of the Maumee River from William C. Holgate for $1,200, and even then it was not until 1884 that funds were sufficient to erect a building on the campus. In 1886 Defiance Hall, a three-story Queen Anne–style building, was opened to the first five students. Although the charter proclaimed a female college, the first class had two males. The administration and faculty outnumbered the student body by three. The first public notice of the college being open to students appeared in the spring of 1886. It read: "DEFIANCE NORMAL COLLEGE, Defiance, Ohio, Summer Term Will Open May 26, 1886, Tuition—$1.00 per week."

During its first ten years the college struggled through five presidents, roller coaster enrollments, and financial difficulty. During this period the curriculum

Serrick Center

stressed normal, commercial, and college preparatory courses. The resident student body was housed in a two-story, wooden, twelve-room, coed dormitory. Women roomed on the first floor and men on the second. The balance of the students commuted from the community.

In the spring of 1896, the trustees called to the presidency Dr. John R. W. Latchaw, an ordained clergyman of the Christian Church. He thought the college should increase its offerings in the arts and sciences to enrich the vocational career thrust of its curricula. Latchaw was convinced that religious affiliation would help solve the problems of financial support and enrollment. When he learned of the pending disaffiliation of Antioch College from the Christian Church, he explored avenues with the Ohio Christian Convention to affiliate the college with that denomination. To aid this process, he brought Dr. Peter W. McReynolds, another Christian Church minister, to become the college's dean. These men believed that a denominational connection would broaden the curriculum, increase the area from which to recruit students, and ensure financial security. Unfortunately, during Latchaw's efforts to secure financial support from the Ohio Christian Convention, he was enticed to become the president of the university which that denomination planned to start in Muncie, Indiana, and in the summer of 1902 he resigned.

Dr. Peter W. McReynolds succeeded him in December 1902. The affiliation with the Christian Church was completed, and the charter granted by the state was revised. The new charter changed the name to Defiance College and established it as a private church-related college. The denomination controlled the board of trustees of the new college. The name changed, but the thrust of the college remained the same as stated in its first catalog: "The bright student and backward plodder will find within its walls welcome and inspiration. It appeals to all young men and women, regardless of their age, regardless of their present condition, who have a thirst for knowledge and a desire to make themselves better and stronger." Admission to the collegiate courses required certain college preparatory studies as background. Those who lacked this background could qualify by making up their deficiencies in the program of the academy. That same catalog announced course offerings in the following areas: collegiate courses leading to baccalaureate degrees, college preparatory studies in the academy, teacher education courses in the normal department, biblical studies in a department offering both degree and nondegree programs, and courses in a business department that included secretarial arts. Most of the students at this time did not pursue bachelor's degree studies.

In those early years the catalog carried the following statement about the business department: "The business department is essentially professional, it aims to meet the most exacting demands of the business world. The student who graduates from the department has reason to be proud of his chosen vocation." In regard to shorthand and the advantages of the Defiance College program, the early catalogs stated, "The advantages of attending a shorthand school with large numbers of literary students in good standing is not be overlooked."

The student body went through significant changes at the same time. The resident student body increased as students from southwestern Ohio, where the Christian Church had a large following, enrolled in the college. Campus activities increased with the advent of YMCA and YWCA groups, and literary societies emerged as the arts and sciences became a vital part of academia. A new dormitory was built to satisfy the growth of the student body.

The Christian Biblical Institute of New York was brought to campus in 1907 and resulted in the first influx of easterners onto the campus. During the tenure of Dr. McReynolds (1902–17) enrollment grew, the campus expanded, five new buildings were added, and the curriculum in the sciences and arts was enlarged. The college dropped the preparatory division and sought accreditation by North Central Association of Colleges. In the fall of 1917 McReynolds was killed in an automobile accident, and the board of trustees once again turned to the presiding dean of the college and named Albert C. Caris as its next president.

As the student body became more cosmopolitan, sororities and fraternities replaced literary societies. The campus had clubs from the various parts of the nation from which the students came. The New Yorkers, the Keystone Club, the Hoosier Club, and the Daytoners indicated the broad spectrum of the student body's geographical composition.

By the time of World War I the college had became a focal point of the community. The community of Defiance supported May Day activities, theatrical and musical performances, visiting lecturers, and athletic events. The local schools depended more and more on the college to educate and supply teachers and leaders. During World War I the campus was used as an army training center.

In the late twenties and early thirties, when the nation's economy became less stable, the support of the Christian Church dwindled and the college was forced to use endowment funds to continue operations. This eventually brought about the loss of North Central accreditation. Once again the resident student body declined and became narrowly regional. Enrollment vacillated between 90 and 250 students. Faculty and administration often received less than half of their contractual salaries.

After the merger of the Christian Church and the Congregationalists in 1931, many of the new denominational leaders urged the trustees to merge with Oberlin or Marietta, two Ohio schools with strong Congregational ties at that time. The college leaders leased space in one of its buildings to a local dentist for his office and laboratory. Serious consideration was given to the community's offer to purchase one of the dormitories for use as a new hospital, but the leadership of the college held firm to the need for a college in the community. During the thirties student activities and course offerings were curtailed. Often athletic teams had to find their own transportation to away contests. On the happier side, the economic struggle drew the student body and faculty closer together into a common bond as they struggled to continue the educational process. The result of the external forces at work and the reduced number of students was a prevailing attitude of a "campus family" that carried the college through the darkest part of the Depression.

At the end of the decade, the college experienced a mild resurgence of students, especially from New England and northeastern Ohio, where Congregationalism flourished. This resurgence was short-lived with the entrance of our country into World War II. During the war years, the enrollment of males declined. But as secondary education opened more female positions, the college continued to refine and developed the Department of Education. As the enrollment grew, the college developed a strong teacher education program that was to be the hallmark of the college for the next forty years. Once again in a time of national crisis, the student body and faculty developed ties beyond the classroom. Community projects, drives for the war effort, and service to the needy in the community became an integral part of college life.

When the war ended, hundreds of veterans arrived on campus using the GI Bill to further their education. Many of the programs that had been curtailed because of the war were revived and expanded. To serve the physical needs, Hickory Hut, Tin Town (barracks secured from a local prisoner of war camp), and Sessions Hall annex (a wooden classroom building) were quickly constructed. Athletics, fraternities, yearbook staffs, and other groups were revived. Because many of the students were older, or married, they were much more resourceful in meeting their social and educational needs. Campus events brought people of varying ages together. Faculty and students intermingled, forming lifelong professional bonds. Although the academic offerings were dominated by the teacher education program, preprofessional programs with a strong arts and sciences base emerged. For many, the college also became a stepping stone to professional and graduate schools.

The returning veterans revitalized many of the extracurricular activities and added a few new ones. Campus dances, yearbooks, homecoming parades, choir, and orchestra all regained their role in student life. Political party clubs and mock presidential conventions also became part of campus life. Organizations that involved the students in community affairs expanded their activities. The GIs left their mark not only on Defiance but on all of higher education with a college education now reaching a broader segment of our nation's population. The GI in the classroom opened a freer dialogue between students and professors, and that communication and those relationships between the learner and the teacher became a vital part of the educational process.

As rapidly as the enrollment swelled to 800, so did it decline as the GIs graduated. By 1950 the college needed to regain its programs for the typical college-age student body. The student body had declined to fewer than 200 and deferred maintenance had left the facilities in a destitute condition. Once again, as so often since its founding, the college faced a serious financial problem. The board of trustees sought advice from the president of Columbia University, Dwight David Eisenhower. His administrative aide was Kevin McCann, who had been on the general's staff in the Pentagon. McCann had been a journalist and newspaper editor prior to his association with Eisenhower. McCann asked Eisenhower to recommend him as president, and in 1951 Kevin McCann became the thirteenth president of Defiance College.

McCann's challenge was to establish financial stability, reaccredidation by North Central, and a remaking of the physical plant. Defiance, like many Ohio colleges, benefited from the college-age population boom. The East Coast students who were denied admission to many of the eastern schools for lack of language requirements and grades matriculated at Defiance. First-generation students from western Ohio and northwest Ohio also found the environments of the college and community to their liking.

These students sought degrees in fields that would place them in the workforce immediately upon graduation. They were young people who came from rural homes and small towns, regardless of eastern or midwestern origins. Teaching was by far the dominant career sought. Others sought professions in social work, religious education, business, and preprofessional courses. The government programs of the 1950s, student loans, the National Defense Education Act, and low cost pushed Defiance to the forefront for first-generation students and large segments of minorities as compared with other private church-related colleges in Ohio.

McCann made major strides in financial stability and academic respectability, and through his efforts enrollment increased at a steady pace. His closeness to Eisenhower brought people of distinction in the political, educational, and entertainment world onto the campus. These national and world leaders came to share in the excitement of the growth of the college. The concept of family and community service was an extension of the settings from which most of the students emerged. When President Eisenhower laid the cornerstone to the college's new library, the entire community gave him an "All-American" welcome. On two occasions McCann was granted leaves of absence to join the Eisenhower administration as a speechwriter and aide.

Faculty members with regional reputations in their fields developed strong programs in the sciences and humanities. The college received accreditation from North Central in 1961 and continued to expand its strong teacher education reputation. Some of the vocationally oriented programs such as home economics and industrial arts were removed from the curriculum.

In the late 1950s and early 1960s eight new buildings were constructed for academic and housing needs. Athletic facilities were relocated to an additional forty acres of land purchased by the college. In the early 1960s the enrollment approached the 1,000 mark. McCann stepped down in 1964 and W. Noel Johnston was selected by the board of trustees to be the new president.

President Johnston was faced with a serious crisis when he came onto campus. Defiance Hall, the major classroom building and administration center, was destroyed by fire. During the remainder of the 1960s not only was a "new" Defiance Hall built, but also constructed or developed were the Weaner Physical Education Center, an addition to Enders student union, the McCann Center addition to the library, and the alumni athletic fields.

When a 1957 merger of the Congregational, Christian, and Evangelical and Reformed Churches formed the United Church of Christ, the college reaffirmed its church ties. A unanimous faculty deemed it significant that the heritage of church affiliation be retained.

In 1967 the Schauffler College of Cleveland and Oberlin merged with Defiance College to form the Schauffler Division in Social Work and Religious Education. These service-oriented programs easily merged into the academic offerings of the college. Schauffler College, like Defiance, had been organized to meet the needs of its geographical region. Founded to respond to the needs of the immigrant population of Cleveland, Schauffler's social work and Christian education programs had impacted that urban community positively. During the postwar era it had relocated at Oberlin

College until Oberlin no longer wanted to place its emphasis in these fields. The leadership of Schauffler chose Defiance because of its long traditions of service-oriented education and its affiliation with the United Church of Christ and its antecedents. Teacher education, social work and Christian service all had an experiential component with a liberal arts base integrated into their course of study. Members of the Schauffler Board of Trustees merged into the controlling body of Defiance and endowment funds were co-mingled.

The college granted the local congregation of the United Church of Christ land to construct their new church on campus. It was completed in 1968 and has become an integral part of the campus; it is used for community religious services, concerts, recitals, and all-campus convocations. The local congregation and the college community often share a common experience in community service.

The Vietnam War drove enrollments to all-time highs, and in 1971 1,100 students attended Defiance. McReynolds Hall was built through a financed contract with the builder. Twenty-five years later the college owned the dorm. In 1965 the college instituted the 4-1-4-semester plan to enhance its experiential learning thrust. The plan created two four-month semesters in which the student was enrolled in at least four courses and a single course was offered in January for one month. This afforded the students and faculty an opportunity to expand the academic offerings to sites throughout the world. Over 65 percent of the student body was involved in off-campus studies. Education, business, social work, and accounting majors had an opportunity for hands-on learning during the "Winter Term." Students were involved in field trips in foreign-language studies, archaeology, governmental internships, theater, psychological studies, independent research in scientific centers and libraries. On-campus studies concentrated on extensive laboratory work, art projects, theater productions, forensic research, marketing seminars, and other concentrated learning. Creativity experimentation and real-life experiences were the guiding factors in this innovative approach that put the college on the cutting edge of this learning concept.

During this period student unrest reflected concerns over civil rights issues and Vietnam. Winter Term allowed many students to join in nationwide activities. These young people became campus leaders in the student response to world and national issues. As these concerns increased, the college and its student body responded to the need for more student involvement in college policy.

The academic programs of the college were adjusting to the growing needs of the community. Evening programs were created to meet the needs of the industrial and corporate components of the community. Courses were offered at work sites between shifts, and credit for work experiences was instituted. College faculty and corporate executives team taught courses. Programs to enable people who had not completed their degree earlier were also developed. These programs helped the college deal with the decline in college-bound "traditional" students.

As the Vietnam War came to an end and enrollment in many of the eastern schools became less selective, the student body at Defiance changed. The student profile was still predominately first-generation midwesterners with a mix of midwest urban, reentry students, and inner-city minorities. Into this blend was mixed the small-college type of student athlete. The nature of campus life was changing because the average age of the students went up and because the number of commuters, working students, and part-time students increased. Campus residents continued to be involved in the traditional small-college activities—sororities, fraternities, forensics and theater, small musical groups, and intercollegiate athletics. The creative curriculum using the 4-1-4 calendar and several nationally recognized programs such as forensics, museum studies, and social work brought attention to the college so it was still attractive to bright second-generation students from the eastern states. This core group set the pace in the academic and social activities among the resident students.

In the mid-1970s the college called Marvin J. Ludwig to its presidency. Dr. Ludwig had been a career international YMCA leader, serving seventeen years in Africa. Under his guidance the college developed even more a sense of community responsiveness. It explored the possibility of a merger with a newly created community college and assessed the needs of higher education in the northwest corner of the state. A decision was made for Defiance to remain an independent, church-related, liberal arts–based college that would work in a cooperative manner with the new community college. In response to the local challenge, the academic offerings in business administration were expanded and a co-op education program was established in business and social work. Programs in computer science and in criminal justice were created and offerings in sports medicine and sports management were instituted. Moreover, the evening program was expanded and a weekend college created in the fall of 1993.

The enrollment leveled at 700–800 and the college went into two major capital campaigns to upgrade all aspects of the campus in 1981. A new academic building for social work and the social sciences, as well as religious education, was erected and called Schauffler Hall (to perpetuate the name of Schauffler College). A new wing was added to the science facility and also a second gymnasium was constructed to meet the needs of student recreation and sports medicine and management.

In the mid-1980s the college started preparations for a master's program in education as well as a feasibility study of what type of a master's program in business was needed. The college calendar returned to the former two-semester year with three mini summer sessions to retain the uniqueness of the January term and a more flexible calendar for part-time graduate students. The college's strong long-time program in teacher education paved the way in the fall of 1991 for North Central Accreditation of a master's degree in education. The aim of the degree was to improve the quality of instruction and knowledge of subject matter rather than administrative credentials. Leadership and expert teaching through enhancement of skills and competencies make up the core of the curriculum offerings.

As the decade of the nineties started, the second major capital campaign was in progress. A new campus learning center, Pilgrim Library, and outdoor athletic facilities were built. The master's in Business Organizational Leadership program was being formalized; this degree emphasizes leadership, communication, and the practical application of knowledge and is equally appropriate for profit, nonprofit, and governmental organizations.

In 1995, on the retirement of Dr. Ludwig, the college called James T. Harris to become its sixteenth president. Dr. Harris led the college in an extensive self-study of its mission. With his guidance the college was able to discern its great tradition as an institution of higher learning that has always focused on careers that rendered a service to humanity and offered up graduates who often were leaders in volunteer agencies in their communities. He envisioned a college that would make "service learning" and character development intentional and the focal point of its mission. Defiance College had always prepared teachers, religious educators, ministers, social workers, criminal justice people, and preprofessional people for a career to serve their community and fellow humans in the Christian tradition.

Defiance College has never been a traditional liberal arts college in the manner of most church-related liberal arts colleges in respect to its founding and nurturing. The college's curriculum has included more career-oriented educational programs through the years than would be found in the curricula of most other church-related liberal arts colleges. It has always done well what it professes to do, and in many of the areas it has been on the cutting edge. Its role in the total spectrum of higher education is unique in Ohio. As the college struggled, enrichment of its mission drove it from a secular college to a college related to the Christian mission to serve. The mission to serve, and prepare its students to serve, has made it into one of the nation's leaders in service learning. This prevailing attitude has driven the college and created its niche in Ohio's story of private higher education.

It is only fitting as Defiance College celebrates the 150th anniversary of its charter that the college and its president, Dr. James T. Harris, were recognized by the Templeton Foundation both for the Templeton Honor Roll and Presidential Leadership. To quote the Templeton publication, "Defiance College's strong commitment to character development and the strength of its program make it a model for colleges and universities nationwide." To know, to lead, to serve, and to understand has driven this career-oriented liberal arts–based college throughout its history.

A visual glimpse of Defiance College can be gleaned in *Making a Difference for 150 Years: A Pictorial History of Defiance College,* by the Office of Communications at Defiance College. Other articles to read are "A History of Defiance College," an alumni magazine article in a 1958 issue of *Today;* and "History of the Defiance College" in the alumni directory for 1987. All of these can be found in the Pilgrim Library on the Defiance College campus.

Denison University

Challenge and Response

G. WALLACE CHESSMAN

You left Columbus about thirty minutes ago in your year-old sedan with your wife and two teenage children, and now you've turned off Interstate 70 onto Route 37 headed north seven miles to Granville, Ohio, the village home of Denison University. As your car crosses Raccoon Creek and climbs the hill on South Main to the stoplight at Broadway, you see the churches on each corner of this major intersection. There's also the business block to the east, private homes to the west, and the entrance to College Hill just ahead. The light turns green, so you drive up another block on North Main to College Street; there on the wall ahead, at the start of the road uphill, a prominent stone plaque proclaims that here is "Denison University: A Christian College of Liberal Arts."

You will find that this is a centennial plaque erected in 1931 to mark 100 years since this college was established. And it suggests the first major question one should ask: under what circumstances was Denison founded and what was its original mission? Specifically, who were the founders, what kind of school did they aim to establish, and why did they choose the Granville location?

Before 1831 there was no Baptist college west of the Allegheny Mountains. Because the Ohio Baptist Education Society had recently been formed, its founders wished to foster a trained ministry in the frontier West. "Let us locate a school in Ohio under our patronage," read its declaration to local churches in 1830, "where not only the correctness of the present translation of the scriptures will be inculcated, but where the Holy Oracles may be read in the language in which they were originally written by men who were inspired to write as they were moved by the Holy Ghost."

The Society at first envisioned a seminary that would be (like the original plan of Hamilton College in New York) "chiefly if not exclusively for the training in secular and sacred learning" of ministerial students. But in May 1831, at a crucial Soci-

Swasey Chapel

ety meeting in Lancaster, Ohio, a distinguished Massachusetts visitor, the Reverend Jonathan Going, favored "the New England Plan," where colleges would offer "common learning" to all students and "theological instruction" would be given "separately" in that locality or elsewhere.

Society members responded favorably; this plan would be easier to implement and would provide needed teachers as well as preachers. The two Granville men present were especially pleased when Going asserted that their village, founded in 1805 by a company of pious settlers from the vicinity of Granville, Massachusetts, would be an excellent site for this "New England Plan" institution.

By 1831 Granville's 1,800 inhabitants already supported four churches and an active temperance movement. Also located in the town were a foundry, a bank, several mills, and distilleries in a thriving local economy linked by road, river, and canal to Ohio's developing commerce. The village met the Society's prescription that the location "be not too far removed from the center of the state." Its citizens, moreover, already had pledged $1,650 toward the $3,300 needed to purchase a 200-acre farm for the college. No other delegation at the Lancaster meeting could match that offer.

The Society had been anxious to have a farm location so that the students could "labor a portion of their time, to aid the expenses of education." Yet the members assembled in that May of 1831 were so hesitant to incur an initial debt of $1,650 that Granville's two delegates finally "agreed to purchase the farm and present it to the society for educational purposes." That pledge, together with Jonathan Going's "New England" blessing, counted heavily as thirty of the thirty-three members then voted for Granville.

Riding horseback north the twenty-seven miles toward home, Granville's two delegates no doubt worried about their bold offer to double the subscription, but such fears soon proved groundless. As Society members reconvened the next afternoon at Granville to view the farm site, thoughts were all for moving ahead quickly. Their constitution had been revised to emphasize the school's broad literary aim, and now a new committee would seek a classical teacher for principal of the preparatory school, "where the learned languages and higher branches of English education may be taught."

By October 3, 1831, the Reverend John Pratt, thirty-one-year-old graduate of Brown University and Newton Seminary, had been elected principal of the Granville Literary and Theological Institution at an annual salary of $600. On November 23 he arrived in Granville, encumbered with books and baggage, only to find that the remodeled farmhouse could not be ready until spring. Everyone was so eager to begin studies, however, that Pratt decided to begin the initial eleven-week term in the village's still-unfinished Baptist church on West Broadway at Cherry Street. After inaugural exercises in the morning, Pratt met with his first students at 2:00 P.M. on December 13.

Twenty-seven of the first term's thirty-seven students were residents of Granville, and only two were not Ohioans; but they were all disappointed when a fire destroyed the nearly reconstructed farmhouse and delayed transfer of operations to the 200-acre farm for another seven months. And though Pratt soon brought in three professors to help him teach the six-year curriculum to a growing student body, the burden of debt became so heavy that he resigned the presidency in despair in 1837. The nation and Granville itself were also in financial crisis, but fortunately Jonathan Going agreed to return and take up leadership of this school that would hold its first commencement in 1840 for three classical scholars. Although Going died in 1844, his New England plan was clearly in place, and in 1845 the Granville Literary and Theological Institution officially was renamed Granville College.

When the Reverend Silas Bailey took over as president in 1846, the institution had a new Alumni Society and was about to pay off its debts. Yet by early 1850 a crisis loomed. The trustees had neither funds for upkeep nor badly needed new buildings. And though the population and the denomination in Ohio were rapidly growing, enrollment from the state was "but slowly increasing," and the number of pious students applying was "even on the decline." Business and industry in Granville had declined seriously since the early 1830s, as had the supply of students. Indeed, by 1851 President Bailey himself had come to believe that the college would have to be moved to a more promising location in Ohio.

The mission of Granville College was still to educate young men, "preachers and teachers," to be "a useful institution" that was "suited to the wants and calculated to promote the welfare of a rapidly growing and free country." But could those aims be better achieved at a different location in the state? President Bailey thought so, but leading members of his faculty disagreed. John Pratt had come back on the staff shortly after resigning the presidency in despair in 1837, and with his long-time colleague Professor Paschal Carter he "now opposed removal so strongly that a trustee committee concluded that faculty reorganization would be unavoidable."

Soon the debate raged both locally and within the Ohio Baptist denomination. The only community to make a definite offer for relocation was Lebanon, which had lost out to Yellow Springs in the bidding for Antioch College. The proponents of removal were so strong, however, that the Granville advocates finally went to a special Baptist state convention in Cleveland in October 1852 proposing to raise $50,000 to equip and endow the college. Though they did win a vote of confidence, the amount prescribed to be raised within two years was increased to $125,000.

After Silas Bailey resigned to become president of Franklin College in Indiana, the Reverend Jeremiah Hall, pastor of the Granville Baptist Church and founding principal (1846–51) of Norwalk Academy, took over fund-raising leadership and, in July 1853, the presidency. It was Hall who reported to his trustees the following October that William S. Denison, a prosperous farmer in adjoining Muskingum County, had pledged $10,000 toward the endowment on condition that the Ohio Baptist Education Society received forty perpetual scholarships for its beneficiaries.

The trustees thereupon recalled, as Hall may have explained to Denison out on his farm, that their board once had pledged to name the institution for any donor of $10,000. They also decided to adopt the title of university, because the college would now have four departments, not just the preparatory and the classical but also the scientific and the agricultural. And less than a year later, in a most significant step, they voted to move Denison University off the farm onto "the land A. P. Prichard now offers to sell us in the immediate vicinity of the town of Granville." Those twenty-four acres on College Hill are still the vital center of today's Denison.

Transfer of the college site to the hill overlooking the village would be a welcome change. No one liked the "unmeasured mile of unmeasured mud" between the college farm and town. Nor did the students relish being stopped by Raccoon Creek when it ran swift and deep after a storm. And the manual labor program that the founders had promoted to help poor boys meet expenses and to produce "sober and industrious habits" had soon proved too difficult to supervise and too expensive; by the fall of 1837 its cooper's shop was shut and the farm work abandoned.

The agricultural department proposed for the university reflected the background and interests of some students, but it would also soon be abandoned. Only the new scientific area, where the faculty and trustees had approved a three-year course of study leading to the degree of Bachelor of Science, proved a valuable addition, with several graduates annually by 1860.

The new frame church of the Granville Baptists, on the southwest corner of Main and Broadway, had been built in 1849 and would now accommodate college services. Jeremiah Hall would oversee the transfer to College Hill of the three-story frame building that had housed classes and students since 1836. That move and the erection of a four-story brick building on the prospective academic quad would cost $23,000. In the two years allotted since 1852 the university reported a subscription of $65,000, much less than the $125,000 goal yet still significant enough to win the endorsement of the Ohio Baptist Convention. Denison University in Granville had survived its first major crisis.

To raise a subscription through financial pledges was one thing; to collect them in hard cash was quite another. And these were turbulent years in America's history. The late 1850s witnessed an economic recession, and then the slavery controversy drove the nation into a Civil War that recruited young men out of the classroom into combat. In 1861–63, through two years of sharply reduced enrollments and salaries, the Denison faculty somehow maintained instruction, but in June 1863 a tired and discouraged Jeremiah Hall resigned. The college was fortunate in that trustee Samson Talbot (Class of 1853), pastor of Dayton's First Church since 1856, agreed to succeed him. Under Talbot's leadership a decade of marked progress lay ahead. This second major crisis in this institution's history would also bring change.

The Denison board found that only $39,000 out of the total of $82,000 pledged to 1863 proved collectible. So many of these collectible funds were in the form of notes that the trustees had to borrow on them; from 1853 to 1863 they spent $6,500 in interest on bank loans and $8,500 for a collecting agency. Annual income, in the meantime, suffered from the scholarships issued in the 1847–854 period, forcing the board by 1860 to draw $2,300 from the endowment to meet current expenses.

Most troubling of all, William Denison revealed in 1858 that he would not pay the $8,000 remaining in his $10,000 pledge because the university had not raised the sum of $125,000, as prescribed in October 1852 by the Ohio Baptist Convention. The trustees were appalled, since they had legally adopted the name of Denison University, awarded the forty scholarships to the Ohio Baptist Education Society, and received the convention's blessing in 1854 after raising $65,000 in pledges. So they took the issue to court and soon won a judgment that William Denison would have to honor his full pledge. Indeed, by the mid-1860s he would even be paying penalties and interest fees as well.

President Talbot survived that embarrassing development because his fellow trustees fulfilled their promise "to stand by him." Led by Ebenezer Thresher and Eliam E. Barney of Dayton, some thirty Ohioans contributed more than three-quarters of Denison's first permanent endowment fund of $100,000. By 1873, at Talbot's untimely death, the university also had another four-story brick structure for classrooms and dormitory (later Talbot Hall). A further $75,000 in endowment was built up by Eliam Barney's gifts, including an endowed chair (the college's first) in moral and intellectual philosophy as a memorial to his deceased daughter, Maria Theresa.

Talbot regarded the union of piety and intellect as the college's vital center. Students had to attend chapel every morning, Monday through Friday, and seats were assigned at the Baptist church each Sunday. In a book review published in 1872 he also opposed Darwinism, arguing instead for a special creation of man by God's unique revelation. Ultimately, however, instruction at Denison accommodated Darwinian evolution without the struggle some denominational colleges endured.

President Samson Talbot had opposed the fraternities that sprang up at Denison after the Civil War, and in 1872 his trustees followed Ohio Wesleyan in outlawing the recruitment of pledges. But by 1881 President Owen, himself a fraternity member, informed the trustees that "Kenyon, Wooster, Delaware and Marietta" now "tolerated if not encouraged" such organizations and that the Denison faculty also believed its old ban should be repealed. Social life was changing generally across Ohio; the trustees approved the faculty's recommendation.

One other important area into which Talbot stepped was coeducation. In the late 1850s Denison trustees had pigeonholed the suggestion that women be admitted, but the founding of a Young Ladies' Institute (Y.L.I.) in the Baptist Church of Granville in 1859, by Nathan Burton and his wife, Sarah, and its transfer in 1861 to the old Female Seminary campus once run by Baptists (1832–38) and then by Episcopalians, opened up new possibilities. In 1868 the Y.L.I. principal, Marsena Stone, turned over direction to the Reverend Dr. Daniel Shepardson and his wife, Sarah, who favored a closer relationship with Denison. And after Talbot and faculty approved, two senior women were admitted to the college course in logic. The Shepardsons were the real promoters of coeducation, to the point where one of the students in the logic course, Grace Lyon, in 1889 requested a Bachelor of Philosophy degree from Denison on the ground that she had completed all the requirements that a man fulfilled for that degree. But not until 1900 would she and several other qualified women graduates officially become Denison alumnae.

President Talbot's most important contribution to his alma mater was his leadership in establishing its post–Civil War financial strength. Yet he also advanced the role of science at Denison significantly by appointing Lewis E. Hicks (Class of 1868) as professor of natural science in 1870. Having done graduate work with Harvard's famous Louis Agassiz, Hicks at once began to delight students with lectures (instead of classroom recitations based on readings) and trips to surrounding sites for their geology and natural history courses. By 1872 he also had a new department of natural science and $200 for chemical apparatus and materials for a new course in that vital area. Not until 1883 could he obtain a microscope. By then the faculty had lengthened the scientific course for a B.S. degree to four years. They also pleased the students by approving a "non-Greek" curriculum of "such scientific and philosophical studies as they may select" in seeking a new degree of Bachelor of Philosophy.

Hicks disappointed everyone by accepting a professorship at the University of Nebraska in 1884, but the march of science at Denison continued under his successor from the University of Minnesota, Clarence Luther Herrick. That expansion of science would contribute to Denison's next major crisis, the battle over whether the institution was to be a college or a university.

Since Professor Herrick soon had several graduates engaged in research projects, he was gratified when, in 1887, the trustees approved the award of an M.A. or an M.S. degree for one year's resident study or two years' nonresident study under the direction of Denison faculty. President Daniel B. Purinton (1890–1901), even extended that to a Ph.D. and fashioned a "university administration" of six colleges. The next two presidents wrestled with the question of "college" versus "university" until the 1920s, when Denison would finally become a four-year coeducational college with a "university" name.

Although the Denison faculty had understood how their institution had acquired its name back in the 1850s, they began to worry about it as more universities with graduate programs arose after the Civil War. So when Herrick's research efforts led to trustee approval of a Denison master's degree, it appeared that a solution was at hand. The first degree thus awarded went to William Dexter Tight (Class of 1886), who had stayed on a year to do special work in geology and natural history as Herrick's devoted disciple. And when Herrick resigned in 1889 to take a professorship at the University of Cincinnati, it was Tight who assumed his teacher's old duties. Herrick left behind the journal of science he had founded along with the Denison Scientific Association.

In 1890 the trustees selected a new president who became a strong "university" advocate. Son of a Baptist minister, Daniel B. Purinton had earned his B.A. and

M.A. at the University of West Virginia and had taught there in the field of metaphysics since 1873. He was not an ordained minister, as his predecessors had all been, yet the reductions he soon initiated in classical language and math requirements for the B.A. were favored by ministerial students as well as prospective lawyers, teachers, and even businessmen.

Undergraduate enrollment of men and women did increase dramatically in the early 1890s, as it did generally in American higher education. To enhance Denison's usefulness still further, Purinton introduced a university extension program that by 1892 had centers in Newark, Zanesville, and Canton and offered as many as eleven different series of weekly lectures available at "moderate" cost. By the fall of 1893 the new forty-four-room Barney Science building was under construction, Herrick was returning to resume his valuable instruction, and the M.A. program was advancing so well that Purinton projected Ph.D. awards in physical science and philosophy.

Unfortunately, a nationwide depression and Clarence Herrick's serious illness weakened Purinton's plans that winter. Within a few years, as Denison professors moved to better positions elsewhere, President Purinton complained that state universities had developed into "seats of educational privilege and power" while his own work was "being seriously hindered by reason of financial limitations." Of the leading Denison scientists of the 1890s, only Clarence's younger brother, able biologist C. Judson Herrick, was to stay on in Granville, until 1907 when he left for the University of Chicago.

Before Purinton himself resigned to return to the University of West Virginia as president, he did effect a key administrative change at Denison by organizing six departments, each headed by a principal or dean, under one university. This made sense for Granville College (for men) and Shepardson College (for women), which would now have the same board of thirty-six trustees. It also made some sense for two other departments, Doane Academy (the prep school) and the Conservatory of Music. But to establish the School of Art and the School of Military Science on similar bases strained the imagination; the latter did not long survive his departure, while the School of Art by 1913 succumbed to demands for greater efficiency and higher standards.

In choosing the Reverend Emory W. Hunt in 1901, the trustees seemed to be leaning back toward a "college," for Hunt had gone from the University of Rochester (B.A., 1884) and Crozer Theological (B.D.) into the parish ministry. In his first annual report as president in June 1902, he even asserted that "it ought to be our purpose to make it [Denison] a first-class college in every respect and to resist the tendencies toward work which properly belongs to the university."

The faculty had already stopped the Ph.D. in physical science in February 1901, so it was easier to eliminate the doctoral programs altogether by dropping the philosophical course as well. There would never be a Ph.D. Denison graduate. University extension courses also disappeared, as did the branches of the Conservatory of

Music in nearby cities. And in 1903, influenced by antimilitarist sentiments and declining student interest, the trustees directed that the School of Military Science be closed and the equipment returned to the government.

Hunt nonetheless expanded the scientific fields that Purinton had promoted. Botany became a separate department in 1904, and the next year chemistry broke off from physics. Hunt brought in able scholars for these new areas. As he told the trustees in 1909, "I find the superior scientific equipment of Denison is very attractive, and renders it easy to interest the best men for . . . positions in our teaching force." The Hunt administration spun off new departments also as expansion carried over into greater variety and specialization in the curriculum. Expand, departmentalize, specialize—in many ways Denison still seemed to be dancing to the university tune, and that was ironic for a president who had originally sought to stress the general over the particular, the broad foundation over the professional training, and the college over the university.

Nevertheless, disagreement over Denison's true status remained strong. The faculty in 1907 recommended that the name be officially changed to Denison College, but the trustees declined because of "some color of a breach of faith" with earlier donors and because of the possibility that "at no very distant day, it may become a university in fact." Award of a prized charter (Theta of Ohio) to Denison by the Society of Phi Beta Kappa in 1911 quieted some doubts about direction, but not for long. By 1913–14 a variety of outside agencies placed the Granville institution in the second (U.S. Bureau of Education) or third class (the Board of Education of the Northern Baptist Convention) among American colleges and universities. Though he had often been called "the best all-round college president in Ohio," by 1913 Emory Hunt had indicated that he was ready to give over leadership to a younger man who could try to meet the more demanding educational standards. And as his successor told the trustees during his first year, "Ours is the task of making a better college and doing it with less money if possible."

In choosing Clark W. Chamberlain as president in 1913 the trustees selected an alumnus (Class of 1894) and a physicist who had taught at Denison and then Vassar (1909–13). Though he at once eliminated Purinton's School of Art and reversed Hunt's "divide and specialize" tendency, his administration would soon have to expand offerings in religion, psychology, and the social sciences in particular to keep up with curricula prescribed by the new Association of American Colleges.

Perhaps also to meet major criticism by outside educational agencies, President Chamberlain sought to reduce teaching loads. He also raised standards by requiring written final exams each semester, encouraging the faculty to improve its grading system, and promoting better faculty organization. And though a Northern Baptist Convention fund drive in the early 1920s only realized $525,000 for Denison out of its expected $3,500,000, that still did provide the $200,000 needed to complete the new $1,200,000 fund for teachers' salaries.

Despite these achievements, however, Clark Chamberlain became more unpopular year by year with students as well as faculty. Some found him cold, others thought him not trustworthy, and still others tired of his repeated promises of a "Greater Denison" without enough visible fulfillment. In the spring of 1922 dissatisfaction suddenly erupted into open opposition over the dismissal of Sidney I. Kornhauser, a popular professor of biology who was Jewish. Kornhauser had replaced a professor going on leave in 1919. He was a capable zoologist and a popular instructor in an era when many religious and political conservatives were coming to attack the teaching of evolution. When he refused to resign quietly in 1922, Chamberlain dismissed him, citing the trustees' declaration of 1913 that Denison was a denominational college and that its instructors "should not only be proficient in their departments but . . . should be men of the highest Christian character." Ironically, that declaration had probably been adopted back in 1913 to reassure the Denison constituency that the appointment of a scientist (Chamberlain) as president did not mean a departure from the college's commitment to piety as well as learning. But its use against Kornhauser touched off a controversy that would not subside for years.

There had been a growth of "unreligious tendencies" at Denison ever since the Purinton administration changed the catalog's wording from "required to attend" to "expected to attend" church twice each Sunday. Yet it was not until Hunt's hearty Christian leadership gave way to Chamberlain's dour formality that religious discipline among students eroded quite openly. The social climate was changing nationally, too, especially after World War I, and reform preachers further fed youthful discontent with the established order. In the wake of the Kornhauser dismissal, one recent graduate even argued in the *Alumni Bulletin* that Denison's Baptist connection should be severed and the college's direction radically altered.

That was too extreme a solution for most Denisonians, but twelve faculty members formed a local chapter of the American Association of University Professors, which by 1938 would win a definite policy on academic tenure. Alumni leaders also won trustee permission by 1929 to have six graduates regularly elected to the thirty-six-member board, even though they might not be Ohioans or Baptists. And as the magnificent 1,200-seat chapel opened in 1924 on College Hill beside the astronomical observatory that trustee Ambrose Swasey of Cleveland also had given to Denison, Clark Chamberlain prepared to vacate his presidential office the next year.

Before Chamberlain's successor took over in 1927, however, faculty and trustees almost resolved that old "college or university?" question. Management of separate records had become so difficult that the men's and women's colleges were formally merged into one coeducational institution by October 1927. Competition from high schools had cut Doane Academy's enrollment below forty by the mid-1920s, so the trustees suspended its operation. That left the Conservatory of Music, which could now support a bachelor's degree, as the sole remnant of Purinton's university structure.

In the meantime, by November 1926, after months of study, faculty and trustees agreed to eliminate the B.S. and the B.Ph. degrees, leaving just the Bachelor of Arts still in place for all entering students by 1927–28. Latin and Greek were also eliminated from the B.A. requirement, a last step away from that old classical program aimed at prospective preachers. Denison University, despite its name, had become a coeducational college of the liberal arts.

Chamberlain had rocked this "cradle of conscience" in Ohio's Granville: in 1931 the new centennial plaque at the college entrance would proclaim that Denison University was "a Christian College of Liberal Arts." The Reverend Avery A. Shaw would support that as president (1927–40), as would his successors Kenneth I. Brown (1940–50) and A. Blair Knapp (1951–68); but by the mid-1960s a newly nondenominational, pluralistic character of the college was emerging. And at the same time three decades of academic reform aimed at "General Education for all" were starting to fade into an era of greater student choice.

A native of Nova Scotia who had completed his ministerial training at Rochester Theological in 1896, Shaw came to Denison from fourteen years at Emmanuel Baptist Church in Brooklyn, New York. For him the Christian religion could not be just a department; it had to become "the enlivening and integrating spirit of the whole institution." When two years of faculty meetings failed to resolve their questions about what a Christian college was, Shaw reduced the heading on official stationery to simply "Denison University." And he often presided at the half-hour chapel services on Mondays and Wednesdays, where his "soft, quiet religion touched a deep note in everyone." In 1939, after the North Central Association criticized Denison for "penalizing students by reducing their study hours for excessive absences from chapel," the faculty changed the system to award a half-credit hour per semester toward the 124-hour graduation requirement if the student attended three-quarters of the services. To meet some student objections of too many chapels, in 1939–40 Shaw began to turn a few of them into secular convocations.

Presidents K. I. Brown and Blair Knapp were not ministers, but they both promoted religious activities on campus. In 1942 Brown established a Denison Christian Emphasis Program (D.C.E.P.), which soon consolidated the two weekly chapels into a one-hour Monday event, and then initiated a voluntary 9:40 A.M. "Deni-Sunday" service. The D.C.E.P. program also launched numerous campus projects as well as special three-day visits each semester by religious leaders. And though the Deni-Sunday option closed down by 1950, Blair Knapp in the fall of 1954 initiated a new chapel service on alternate Thursday evenings and appointed the Granville Baptist Church's great preacher, the Reverend Harry H. Kreuner, to be the first dean of the chapel. By the next year Kreuner was preaching every Thursday night, and well over half of the student body was attending.

So down through the 1950s Shaw's focus on piety was progressing. But what was the link with learning? Denison had returned fully to collegiate status when the faculty voted in 1930 not to award master's degrees after 1930–31. And back in 1926 they had moved toward general education by dividing the departments into three "groups" (languages, sciences, and all other) and requiring that students take twelve hours in each of the two groups in which they were not majoring. Now Shaw not only revived the art department and fostered a theater arts program but also then cheered in 1937 as a new "group" requirement of three hours was approved for the arts (art, music, and dramatic art). Specialization was in full retreat.

Under K. I. Brown and Blair Knapp general education advanced further. Brown did revive the B.S. degree, but by 1946 the faculty had introduced "core courses" into the "group" system, thereby stiffening and broadening Denison's liberal arts training. And when instructors found that many seniors coming into the four-hour capstone course in philosophy and religion were "essentially illiterate" in both these vital areas, in 1953–54 a new introductory three-hour core course was added to study "great events and ideas in the religion and philosophy of men in the Western World." With most students sharing these General Education Program courses in their first two years at Denison, they almost seemed to be listening to Jonathan Going or Samson Talbot.

Moreover, the college's Baptist affiliation eroded. Three decades of more liberal membership rules had reduced Ohio Baptist influence on the board of trustees. Then a major Baptist fund-raising effort for Denison also fell short, and the possibility of a Ford Foundation challenge grant of $1,500,000 was so great that the board pledged in 1962 to remove "patronage of the Baptist denomination" from its constitution and to change rules so that "the majority of the Board may be of any denomination."

Denison received that grant, and by 1964–65 its catalog simply stated, "Denison aspires to be a community of intellectual excellence and Christian ideals." In the 1967–68 edition that one reference to "Christian" became "religious," and the campus by the 1970s was debating whether that Christian entrance plaque should be removed, changed, or kept. The trustees thereupon reaffirmed the college's Christian character but emphasized Baptist individualism and the commitment to religious pluralism within the modern college. The plaque remained, unchanged. The catalog by 1980–81 just substituted "moral" for "religious."

In the meantime the General Education Program that had developed over three decades to the 1960s also changed significantly. Faculty wanted to specialize more; black studies and women's studies developed; computers invaded instruction; and the heritage of other continents and peoples challenged Europe's dominance. Diversity was growing along with the expansion from 1,250 students in the 1950s to more than 2,000 today. Like American colleges generally, Denison was moving out of that "core course" era into a modern world with a global economy and greater career concerns.

After the 1960s trustees and faculty were of all faiths, and the Denison Christian Association was the Denison Community Association. A dean of the chapel still led a weekly service, but academic credit was gone and student attendance was down. Denison presidents came from diverse academic backgrounds, and in 1989 Michele Tolela Myers became the first woman to lead the college. Before resigning in 1998, she would raise many millions in endowment and make all the fraternities nonresidential.

Graduate record exams were long gone, as were most senior comprehensive exams, but the Honors Program's seminars flourished, as did student research projects. And though Avery Shaw might say again, "We have lost the universal in the particular," Knapp could reply that modernization was inevitable. Modernization has changed this institution in significant ways, obviously, yet Denison has always sought to be "a useful institution" that is "suited to the wants and calculated to promote the welfare of a rapidly growing and free country." That was its goal through the four major crises this essay has examined. It also figured in that recent decision to make the fraternities nonresidential, a revolutionary step strongly opposed by many fraternal alumni yet still taken in order to make campus life for everyone less turbulent and more democratic.

That democratic impulse has been apparent as the college gradually became fully coeducational and increased the enrollment of minority and foreign students from about 1 percent of the student body in 1965 to about 9 percent today. And though student scholarship is honored annually at commencement, since 1985 there has also been a special convocation each spring where Presidential Medals are awarded to as many as nine seniors who have demonstrated not only "exemplary intellectual achievement" but also distinction in some combination of "service to the community; contribution to the arts; enlargement of our global perspective; athletic fitness and achievement, leadership; contribution to community discourse."

Contribution to community has been the direction in which this college has always encouraged students to be more active. And today the Denison Community Association (D.C.A.) promotes that as strongly as the YMCA and the YWCA once engaged their members in evangelistic endeavors. Piety is not dead; it just focuses more on concern for others of all ethnic, economic, sexual, and religious backgrounds. And though past presidents like Jonathan Going and Samson Talbot and Emory Hunt would be sorry that so few ministerial candidates enroll today, they would approve of Denison's continuing effort to foster a democratic society of shared concerns and academic excellence.

At the same time they would understand why this college has always sought to keep abreast of educational change. Thus they would be pleased that the Honors Program, led by philosophy professor Tony Lisska, is enrolling so many more students in its ambitious intellectual activities. Yet, as Baptist leaders of years past, they would also honor that centennial plaque at the college entrance, as many devout graduates still do today.

When President Michele Myers announced in November 1997 her intention to become the ninth president of Sarah Lawrence College in Bronxville, New York, Denison trustees launched their search that led, by May 1998, to their unanimous choice of Dale T. Knobel as her successor. Knobel had spent a freshman year at Granville before going on to Yale (B.A.) and Northwestern (Ph.D.). Then he served almost two decades on the history faculty at Texas A&M University and entered the administration as executive director of the university's 2,000-student honors program. He completed his service at Texas A&M as associate provost. As provost and dean of the faculty at Southwestern University in Georgetown, Texas, he was well prepared and truly eager to lead this institution back in his native Ohio.

SUGGESTED READING

The following sources were published by the Denison University: S. Carman Augustine, *Memorial Volume of Denison University, 1831–1906* (1907); G. Wallace Chessman, *Denison: The Story of an Ohio College* (1957); G. Wallace Chessman and Wyndham M. Southgate, *Heritage and Promise: Denison 1831–1981* (1981); G. Wallace Chessman, "Historically Yours" column in *The Denisonian* (1994–); Thomas F. Gallant, *Doane Academy: A Story of Preparatory Education, 1831–1927* (1993); Thomas F. Gallant, *Shepardson College and Its Heritage* (1996); Francis W. Shepardson, *Denison University, 1831–1931: A Centennial History* (1931). See also William T. Utter, *Granville: The Story of an Ohio Village* (Granville Historical Society, 1956).

The University of Findlay

A Vision of Collegiate Education in Northwest Ohio

RICHARD KERN

The story of the University of Findlay begins in the late nineteenth century with an account of a small American denomination working with a village in northwestern Ohio to establish a college. Ironically, the church did not have the resources or the educational tradition to support the institution adequately; nor for many years did the village seem to care about it. Consequently, the college's survival rested in the hands of a relatively few dedicated supporters in the church and the community. These fragile underpinnings help explain a significant portion of the university's history. All in all, fifteen presidents have aided in the struggle for survival, growth, and conservation, in some form, of the religious commitment of the school's founders. Theirs were the hands which, either gently or with vigor, rocked the "cradle of conscience" now known as the University of Findlay.

It should be understood that the University of Findlay was founded as a Christian liberal arts school. The early presidents were ministers, religion occupied an honored place in the curriculum, Greek and Hebrew were emphasized, chapel was required, and students found their consciences finely honed as they responded to intellectual demands placed on their lives by a pervasive environment drawn from the Judeo-Christian tradition. Yet in the year 2003, while chapel services are no longer a part of daily activities and theology is no longer deemed "the queen of the sciences," religion courses remain popular, and there are numerous Christian organizations on campus promoting the faith.

Findlay College (after July 1, 1989, the University of Findlay) emerged in the 1880s, established by articles of incorporation certified by the State of Ohio in February 1882. The cornerstone of "Old Main" was laid in May 1884; in September 1886 classes first met, and in June 1889 the college proudly graduated its first class.

The origins of the college can be traced to the desire of the Church of God (since

Old Main reigns as the original campus building, xonstructed during 1882–86.

1975 the Churches of God, General Conference) to have a college in which to train its youth, and to the desire of residents of the village of Findlay to enhance their community with an institution of higher education.

The Church of God originated in the Harrisburg, Pennsylvania, area in the 1820s. John Winebrenner, a German Reformed Church pastor much concerned with what he felt was the lack of true Christian spirit in his four-church parish near Harrisburg, adopted certain revivalistic techniques (popularly known as "new measures") in order to remedy the situation. A portion of his Harrisburg congregation withdrew from the parent body in 1825, adopting the biblical name "Church of God" for their group. By 1830 a number of like-minded churches had been organized in eastern Pennsylvania and a Church of God eldership was formed. The new denomination expanded with the westward-moving population, especially among those of German extraction. Local elderships were established as far west as Iowa by 1848, and a general eldership, made up of the rapidly increasing number of local elderships, was established in Pittsburgh in 1845. In Ohio an eldership was organized as early as 1836, and a Church of God was meeting in Findlay by the mid-1850s.

Early in the history of the Church of God, John Winebrenner and other ministers often expressed the need for an institution to train Church of God ministers and laymen in the teaching and practices of the church. Until his death in 1860, Winebrenner used the columns of the church paper, *The Gospel Publisher,* and its successor, *The Church Advocate,* to promote the educational interests of the church.

When the General Eldership met at Findlay, Hancock County, on May 24, 1881, there were several propositions that came to the floor touching on the subject of a college for the Church of God. They were referred to the committee on education, which urged that the board of education of the General Eldership be instructed to "secure at once a suitable place for said school" and then "to provide whatever means may be required for the opening of same."

After considering a site in Smithville in Wayne County and finding it inadequate, the board adjourned to meet in Findlay, where some residents were preparing an offer to induce the Church of God to locate its college there. Several local booster committees of "wide-awake businessmen" were formed to raise money and to otherwise persuade the church to consider the advantages of their community.

On June 22, 1881, an article appeared in *The Church Advocate* entitled "Our College, Where Shall It Be Located?" The author, who was both a resident of Findlay and a member of the local Church of God, paraded the virtues of the village before the readership of the paper. He noted that the sanitary conditions of the town "cannot be excelled," perhaps in response to rumors that Findlay was more or less in a malarial swamp. He continued: "We have broad streets, well lighted with gas by night and finely shaded by day. Our sewage system is complete and perfect. In point of morality our town is far in advance of any town in northern Ohio." In sum, Findlay was an excellent location for the church's college.

At a meeting at the Hancock County courthouse on July 8, 1881, attended by interested citizens and the board of education of the church, the residents of Findlay involved in the college project offered the Church of God $20,000 plus the college grounds if the institution were located in Findlay. In response the board accepted the offer because no other communities had expressed interest. After viewing several possible sites, the board chose as the college's future location more than ten acres of land on Main Street, about a mile north of the courthouse, worth in excess of $10,000. On August 1, 1881, John Gable, chairman of the board of education, sent a letter from Pennsylvania in which he officially notified the citizens of Findlay that the church's college would be built in the village on the chosen site.

On January 25, 1882, the executive board of the General Eldership met in Findlay to formally establish the long-hoped-for institution. At that meeting "Findlay College" was officially chosen as the school's name, in appreciation of the support the village was giving the project. Articles of incorporation were then approved and filed with the Ohio secretary of state. As provided in the third article, Findlay College was to be "a Public College of learning for the promotion of such branches of science, art, and literature, and for such theological instruction as the Trustees of such corporation acting under the advice and direction of the General Eldership . . . may from time to time elect." Clearly, its founders envisioned the college as a liberal arts institution open to all, with special provision for theological education, and under the ultimate control of the Church of God.

The first Findlay College board of trustees, made up of eighteen representatives from the church and community, met on February 8. Most of the board (twelve of the eighteen) were members of the Church of God; a majority (ten of eighteen) were also from Ohio, fulfilling Ohio law. Almost all the trustees were business and professional men; rather unusual for the time was the fact that only three were ministers.

At a special meeting of the board of trustees in October 1882, architectural plans for the college by M. Rumbaugh of Mansfield were approved. "Old Main" was to be "a building 171 feet 8 inches in length by 107 feet 3 inches in depth, four stories in height, exclusive of attic, and including basement, with a main corridor in each story, running the entire length of the building with two stairways through the entire building, located, one to the North and the other to the South of the chapel entrance." The trustees believed that such a building should not cost more than $50,000 and that it would be a "massive and imposing one, a credit to the organization that projected it and also a matter of pride to our town where it is located."

Stone for construction began to arrive in November 1882. In June 1883 the trustees accepted the construction bid of $49,000 from Pierce and Coleman of Dayton, and the contract for erection was drawn up and signed on August 16, 1883. Work on the building was begun at once. The cornerstone was laid on May 25, 1884, and Old Main was opened for classes—for seventy or so students—on September 1, 1886.

In reporting the opening day exercises the *Findlay Courier* confidently announced September 1, 1886, as "An Auspicious Day in the History of a Promising Institution." Optimism was in the air. In January 1886 Findlay's "Great Karg Gas Well" had come in with an explosion heard five miles away, helping to inaugurate a gas and oil boom in Findlay and Hancock County. Some speculated that Findlay was about to become "the great inland city of America," and the college administration made arrangements to have Old Main become the first college building in the nation, if not the world, to be heated with natural gas. Between 1880 and 1890 the population of Findlay quadrupled as new businesses came to town in response to the offer of cheap fuel. In such circumstances the college could only benefit.

It did—for a short time. What was hidden beneath the euphoria of the founding of Findlay College was the stark reality of prospects for its continuing support. The Church of God simply did not have the population, financial base, or educational tradition to adequately maintain an institution of higher education, at least as originally envisioned. Of the perhaps 20,000 Church of God members (at most) in 1880, only 2,000 were in Ohio, and probably well over half of the remainder were basically uninterested in the "college project." The droughts and weather-related catastrophes in the western farm belt in the 1880s, and the Panic of 1893–97 drove many Church of God farmers and businessmen into bankruptcy, making previous good-faith pledges uncollectible. Then, too, the Findlay community's support, so essential to the college's founding, was considerably diminished when the "inexhaustible" gas pool under the town proved exhaustible. Bust followed boom. The county's population dropped, even though the discovery of quantities of oil eased the slide somewhat. Businesses failed and money became scarce.

In late 1886 the board of trustees had taken out a $7,000 loan, secured by a mortgage on the college property, to pay off the contractors. In 1886, when college collections were still good, it probably was thought a reasonable move. A few years later, with the contraction of the economy, the debt loomed larger and larger, haunting every meeting of the board. By the 1890s talk of the college being forced to close because of a severe financial crisis was heard both on campus and off. The debt was finally paid off about twenty-five years later, but some semblance of economic stability for Findlay College would not be found until well into the twentieth century.

In November 1884 the board of trustees elected John Roland Harris Latchaw as the first president of Findlay College. Born in 1851 in Venango County, Pennsylvania, Latchaw was raised on a farm in Iowa. He received A.B. and M.A. degrees from Hillsdale College in Michigan in 1881 and 1887, and in 1881 he became pastor of the Barkeyville Church of God in the West Pennsylvania Eldership. While there he established Barkeyville Academy, a school that gave precollege training to many who went on to leadership positions in the Church of God.

In Findlay Latchaw's responsibilities included raising money for the completion of Old Main, building an endowment, establishing a curriculum, and hiring a faculty and "the general supervision of the College grounds." Later, he became pastor of the recently formed (1887) College Church of God.

The 1886–87 curriculum designed by Latchaw involved the establishment of seven departments: collegiate, theological, music, art, elocution and oratory, preparatory, and English and normal (a commercial department was added a year later). The collegiate department was further divided into classical, philosophical, and scientific courses of study that offered, respectively, the bachelor of arts, bachelor of philosophy, and bachelor of science degrees. The theological department included both the equivalent of a postgraduate seminary program offering an M.A. degree and an "elective" course for students without a college degree. There was no tuition charge for theology students, nor were there any "denominational distinctions" in the department. Latin was a requirement for all who took collegiate degrees. Greek and Hebrew were also offered, especially for those in theological studies.

To teach courses during the 1886–87 academic year, President Latchaw put together a faculty of twelve, including himself (as professor of ethics and psychology). The college year was forty weeks, divided into fall, winter, and spring terms. Tuition was eight dollars a term, and all students were expected to attend daily chapel services.

President Latchaw's earliest years at the college were successful by most standards. The building was completed, and the student body increased significantly. In June 1889 the first annual commencement was held, with two graduates in the collegiate department. Latchaw looked forward to a time in the not-too-distant future when Old Main would be serving between 2,000 and 3,000 scholars. Then the gas pool underneath Findlay began to play out, and the national economy began to sputter. Internally, the Church of God began to reveal its displeasure that a number of its ministerial students at the college were joining other denominations upon graduation. Moreover, there was the matter of the continuing mortgage on the college building and the fact that the board of trustees had to borrow from its small endowment to cover annual operating deficits. By the early 1890s the "extravagances" of Latchaw and the board had become a source of contention in the church. Latchaw, for his part, noted that the Church of God was sending neither its students nor its money to the college in significant amounts. (During the Latchaw years probably no more than 10 percent of the student body was from the Church of God.) The president routinely emphasized that it was not for the board of trustees to cut back on the college program, which was hardly extravagant, but for the Church to give what it had originally pledged to the endeavor. Finally, with pressure increasing from the Church, on July 1, 1893, Latchaw resigned as president. During a service in the college chapel the following month, he renounced the authority of the General Eldership and quit the church. Shortly thereafter he became pastor of a Baptist church in Zanesville. By 1896 he had been elected president of Defiance College.

The next four presidents of Findlay College were primarily concerned with the survival of the institution. Latchaw's immediate successor was the Reverend William Nelson Yates, one of Latchaw's former students at Findlay. Born in Westmoreland County, Pennsylvania, he had attended Barkeyville Academy and, in 1887, enrolled at Findlay College. While at the college "Nockemstiff" Yates was responsible for its first "yell" ("Hic, Haec, Hoc! Free from Smoke! Now You Know, Findlay College! O! Hi! O!). He received his bachelor's degree in 1891 and an M.A. in theology in 1894. In 1889 he was called to the pulpit of the Front Street Church of God in Findlay. The board of trustees named him acting president of Findlay College in July 1893. Yates accepted the position reluctantly, knowing that there was no easy way out of the college's critical financial situation. In late spring 1894 the board elected Yates "permanent president" in appreciation for his efforts to raise money to pay off the college debt. But the Panic of 1893–97, then in full swing, made his job ever more difficult. In November 1894 the college's financial secretary reported that the annual deficit for 1894–95 would be close to $4,500. On March 19, 1895, Yates (close to a "nervous breakdown," according to one source) resigned, effective in June of that year. He eventually returned to Pennsylvania, where he enjoyed a lengthy career as an honored pastor in the East Pennsylvania Eldership of the Church of God.

Following Yates's resignation, at the insistence of the faculty, the Reverend Charles Trout Fox—professor of philosophy, German, and Latin and a minister of the College Church of God—was elected acting president of the college by the board of trustees in June 1895. He was born in Westmoreland County, Pennsylvania, in 1857. His B.A. and M.A. degrees were from Allegheny College in Meadville, Pennsylvania, in 1881 and 1888. After five years of teaching in the public schools in western Pennsylvania and one term at Barkeyville Academy, he became one of the original faculty members at Findlay in 1886.

Fox's election as acting president prevented a strike by the faculty, which had endured several years of nonpayment and underpayment of salaries. But there was little he could do under the circumstances. The church wanted the college run more economically, but the board of trustees was loathe to dismantle the existing academic program and faculty in favor of something less costly. By March 1896 the college debt had risen to $18,825, including a "new debt" (running expenses since June of 1894) of $7,200. With the handwriting on the wall, a number of the longtime faculty assembled by President Latchaw left and were not replaced.

In desperation, the board of trustees presented a "Memorial" to the General Eldership, asking "whether the school shall continue to run or close." The General Eldership ordered the board to keep the college open and promised it would assist financially. In return, the executive board of the General Eldership would "supervise" the college board. Findlay College, which had been church related, now became church controlled—a relationship that would continue through most of the twentieth century. The trustees then offered the position of acting president to Fox for another year, at what was probably a reduction in salary. Fox refused the offer and rejoined the full-time faculty, apparently with the support and good wishes of the church. In 1897 he was made dean of Findlay College, continuing in that position until 1929, four years before his death.

The Reverend Charles Manchester succeeded Fox as president. He was born in 1858 near Rockford, Illinois, and graduated from Park College, Parkville, Missouri, receiving his A.B. in 1883 and his master's degree in 1887. He attended McCormick Theological Seminary in Chicago and Oberlin Theological Seminary in Ohio, receiving his B.D. from the latter institution in 1884. From 1892 to 1896 he was principal of Barkeyville Academy. Although the college board of trustees elected Manchester acting president in 1896, the executive board of the General Eldership disapproved the board's action and instead selected for Manchester the title "President of the Faculty." He also served as pastor of the College Church.

Manchester worked well with the church and the board and benefited from the return to prosperity following the Panic of 1893–97. In July 1897 the board of trustees reported that the school was operating as economically as possible, and in June of 1898 it was reported that "for the first time" the college "has lived within its income." By 1904 the debt was down to "a few thousand dollars." With the approval of the church the board elected Manchester acting president in 1897, president in 1900, and president "without date" in 1892.

As president, Manchester was pleased by the recent electrification of Old Main with current from the nearby street railway powerhouse. He gratefully received a $25 gift for the college library from President William McKinley about a month before the latter's assassination in Buffalo in September 1901. In 1903 Manchester supervised the movement of the gymnasium from the basement of Old Main to the southeast wing of the first floor. On a more somber note, he was president when some in the Church of God began to question the theological orthodoxy of some on the college staff. A special concern to those enmeshed in the fundamentalist-modernist controversy was Charles T. Fox, who styled himself as a "progressive fundamentalist."

Indicating that he would prefer being a pastor or teacher of theology, Manchester resigned in June 1904. He later became principal of the Fort Scott Collegiate Institute in Kansas and, still later, professor of public speaking at Defiance College.

The board of trustees selected as the college's fifth president the Reverend Charles Ira Brown, president of the board. He was born in 1861 in Woodbury, Pennsylvania, and attended Dickinson Seminary in Williamsport. In 1888 he became a pastor in the East Pennsylvania Eldership. As three presidents before him, he ministered at the College Church.

Reverend Brown's primary focus was establishing the financial credibility of Findlay College, and to that end he inaugurated a number of successful fund drives. One of these was an effort to match with $37,500, a $12,500 challenge grant made in behalf of the college library by philanthropist Andrew Carnegie. Unfortunately, M. K. Smith, secretary and sometime-treasurer of the board and the treasurer of the General Eldership, had been investing college endowment monies in highly speculative stock. When the price of the stock fell in 1912, the college lost heavily—probably in excess of $15,000. How much President Brown knew of Smith's investment activities is unknown. But, with the loss coming on his watch, the popular president resigned as a matter of principle in May 1913. Shortly after his resignation, he was appointed to the Ohio Civil Service Commission. Later he moved to Defiance, where he became editor of the *Crescent News*.

Brown's successor was the Reverend William Harris Guyer, an ordained minister in the West Pennsylvania Eldership. Born in Bedford County, Pennsylvania, in 1870, he attended normal school in New York and Pennsylvania and graduated from

Barkeyville Academy in 1895. In 1895 and 1896 he was a student at Findlay College and completed his work there by correspondence in 1906. He joined the faculty at Findlay as professor of theology and history in 1912 and was elected president of the college in May 1913. Guyer was the last president of the institution to serve as pastor of the College Church. Guyer was an "event" in the life of the Churches of God, the town of Findlay, and at Findlay College. Widely sought after as a speaker throughout Ohio, he was an avid reader and had a passion for motoring everywhere in his Willys-Knight.

While finding money to carry on the work of the college was always a concern to Guyer, and there were small annual deficits some years, the financial crises faced by the first five presidents had clearly passed. During Guyer's term a sense of optimism pervaded the campus. He increased the college's permanent endowment from $104,000 to $277,000, and there was notable growth in the physical plant for the first time since 1886. Approximately six acres were purchased to the north of the main campus for an athletic field, and a small gymnasium was erected just to the north of Old Main. By 1926 the faculty had expanded to twenty-six, and in 1926–27 more than 500 students were enrolled. Guyer died as the result of a heart attack on July 22, 1926. Mourned by the entire Findlay community, his funeral, attended by approximately 4,000 people, was held on the south lawn of the campus.

To replace Professor Guyer the board of trustees unanimously elected Harvey L. Allen, superintendent of schools from Guthrie, Oklahoma, on August 19, 1926. Allen was born in Missouri in 1888. He received his undergraduate degree from Kendall College in Tulsa and his M.A. from Oklahoma University in 1917. Though raised in a Church of God family (his father was a thirty-year minister in the church), he was the first president of Findlay College who was a layman and a professional educator and the first one born west of the Mississippi River.

When Allen took office he found that both the college and the church were debating how the college might be accredited by the Ohio College Association and the North Central Association without the school losing its denominational character. Allen made a number of recommendations, including the addition of Ph.D.s to the faculty (even if not Church of God) and $100,000 to the permanent endowment. He also urged the church to relinquish some of its control of the institution and to accept the principle of accreditation regardless. Having made his recommendations, on June 5, 1929, Allen promptly resigned. The board accepted his resignation and expressed its appreciation for his service to Findlay College, however brief. Allen returned to Oklahoma, later serving as chancellor of Tulsa University for three years.

Allen's successor was Homer Dunathan, a 1917 graduate of Findlay College and, in 1927, of Teacher's College of Columbia University. He was born in Mendon, Ohio, in 1893 and, like the preceding presidents, was a member of the Church of God.

Before coming to the college Dunathan had worked as a school superintendent in two public school systems, assisting them to prepare for their accreditation. He was elected president by the board of trustees in June 1929.

Dunathan benefited from President Allen's effort to acquaint the church with the necessity of accrediting their college, especially if it were the church's desire to maintain a four-year liberal arts institution in Findlay. At its meeting in Martinsville, Illinois, June 10–13, 1929, the General Eldership agreed to Dunathan's (and Allen's) recommendations, which included upgrading the faculty by hiring several "sectarian" (non–Church of God) Ph.D.s to head departments and to let some unqualified Churches of God personnel go. Clearly the denominational character of the college was diminished. But in return Dunathan was successful in getting accreditation by the Ohio College Association in 1931 and by the North Central Association in 1933.

The president's next challenge was guiding the college through the Great Depression. Repairs and maintenance were deferred; nonessential budget items were ignored. Faculty salaries were cut by 40 percent. Dunathan proved adept at getting some extra monies from the Churches of God, the federal government's National Youth Administration, and from Mr. and Mrs. O. D. Donnell, president of Findlay's own Ohio Oil Company. The college survived.

Then came the "Great Fire" on May 27, 1938, which damaged each of the thirty-some rooms and hallways in Old Main. Dunathan arranged for year-end classes to meet at nearby Glenwood Junior High School or the college conservatory. Commencement exercises were held on the college's front lawn, and the president then led a campaign that managed to pay off the fire debt.

The United States formally entered World War II in December 1941. Enrollment dropped drastically, and the college debt once again began to increase. Dunathan, with a feeling that he had done what he could at Findlay, in April 1943 accepted a lieutenant's commission in the navy. The board of trustees granted him a leave of absence until the end of the war when, in February 1946, his resignation was accepted. Guiding the institution as acting president from 1943 to July 1, 1947, was Dean Carroll A. Morey, who led the college with barely 100 students (mostly women) in 1943–44 and with its largest liberal arts enrollment to that time, 412 in 1946–47, courtesy of the GI Bill. When a new president took office on July 1, 1947, Carroll Morey happily returned to "deaning" and teaching chemistry.

The college's tenth president was Dr. H. Clifford Fox, professor of history at the University of Dubuque. He received his A.B. at Findlay College in 1920 and his Ph.D. from the University of Iowa in 1941. He was born into a Churches of God home in western Pennsylvania in 1895 and was ordained into the Church's ministry in 1947. Fox, like his predecessors and successors, was strongly committed to Christian values in education. At his investiture on November 9, 1947, he emphasized his conviction that "out of Christian college halls must come the leaders who will reshape the world nearer the will of God."

Unfortunately, Dr. Fox inherited a difficult situation in 1947. The Depression and war years had severely taxed the resources at the college, and in 1948 the North Central Association removed Findlay from its accredited list. The association found the endowment and dormitories inadequate, salaries too low, and "a weak and improperly managed and poorly used library." Dr. Fox spent the rest of his presidency struggling to achieve reaccreditation. He was unsuccessful, but he did start the college on its way to a much firmer foundation. When he retired on February 1, 1959, new dormitories were being built, enrollment was increasing, and a Findlay businessmen's advisory committee had been established to develop a base for a fiscally sound and growing institution.

During most of his administration Dr. Fox had suffered from arthritis, which often made a wide range of presidential activities difficult for him. With his approval, the board of trustees appointed Dr. Ollie James Wilson as executive vice president of the college in June 1958. On February 1, 1959, Wilson was then named the eleventh president of Findlay College, and Fox was made president emeritus and professor of history. Fox died in an automobile accident on November 24, 1959.

Dr. Wilson was born in 1909, in Warbranch, Kentucky. His B.S. was from Union College, Kentucky, in 1935 and his Ed.D. from the University of Kentucky in 1951. He did further academic work at the University of Chicago and Ohio State University. During World War II Wilson served in the army in the Pacific Theater, and after suffering a serious injury he retired as a colonel in December 1945. Prior to his arrival at Findlay he was professor of speech at Morris Harvey College in West Virginia. He was the first president of Findlay College who did not have a Church of God background.

Immediately after assuming the presidency Wilson set about preparing the college for accreditation. The faculty was upgraded, 10,000 new books were added to the library, new buildings (a dormitory, student union, and science hall) were erected on campus, and, because the North Central Association objected to the control exercised by the church over the board of trustees, Wilson persuaded the church to relieve the executive board of its veto power over board actions. Also at the suggestion of North Central, Winebrenner Theological Seminary, a part of the college since 1942, was separated to begin its life as a totally independent institution. The president's whirlwind of activity resulted in Findlay being once again accredited in March 1962.

Although Wilson was generally popular in both the Findlay community and the church, his authoritarian style of leadership—which some detractors traced back to his army experience—led to considerable dissatisfaction on the part of many faculty and students. With his service injury causing recurring health problems and hospitalization, he resigned on August 31, 1963. Eventually he joined the staff of Western Kentucky University and, in 1975, retired from there as professor emeritus.

Succeeding Dr. Wilson was Dr. Ivan Frick, who had been named assistant to Dr. Wilson in January 1963. Frick was born in 1928 in New Providence, Pennsylvania. He was a minister in the Churches of God and a graduate of Findlay in 1949 (A.B.), Lancaster Theological Seminary in 1952 (B.D.), Oberlin Seminary in 1955 (S.T.M.), and Columbia University in 1959 (Ph.D.). Prior to becoming Dr. Wilson's assistant, he was chairman of the division of humanities. On April 9, 1964, he was elected the twelfth president of Findlay College.

Because of campus problems associated with Dr. Wilson's administration, a North Central team visited Findlay in 1963 and voted to place the institution on probation, noting a severe morale problem and the "lack of an efficient and effective administration cadre." Calling on his ministerial and human relations skills, Dr. Frick worked to remediate those and other problems. Consequently, North Central lifted the probation in 1966, and in 1969 it continued the college's accreditation for a ten-year period.

Under Dr. Frick the financial situation at Findlay improved significantly, new dormitories were built, and a new library and physical education center were dedicated. The president's (and his administration's) willingness to maintain a dialogue with students kept disruptions at Findlay minimal during the campus activism in the 1960s and early 1970s. Discontinuing a tradition dating back to 1886, required attendance at chapel services was dropped during the 1969 academic year. Effective November 14, 1971, Dr. Frick resigned the presidency of Findlay College and became president of Elmhurst College in Illinois.

Glen R. Rasmussen, the fourteenth president of Findlay College, was born in Chicago in 1921. He received his B.A. and M.E. degrees from Wayne State University in Detroit in 1947 and 1949 and his Ph.D. from the University of Michigan in 1953. He came to Findlay from his post as vice president for academic affairs at Morningside College, Sioux City, Iowa. A Lutheran layman, Rasmussen assumed the presidency of Findlay College on March 1, 1972.

A major theme in Rasmussen's administration was balancing liberal education and vocationalism. Various improvements continued to be made in the liberal arts curriculum. Dr. Jean Nye's bilingual/multicultural major, begun in 1980, was particularly noteworthy. At the same time new ground was broken at Findlay with the introduction of an Intensive English Language Institute for international students in 1975, an equestrian studies program in 1976, a weekend college program in 1979, a computer science major in 1980, and a pre-veterinary medicine in 1982.

In 1976, under Dr. Rasmussen's direction, a committee began to rethink the goals and mission of Findlay College. Its report acknowledged the role of the Churches of God in founding the institution and the "rich Judeo-Christian heritage and traditions" on which the school was based. It then went on to suggest "ideal goals" for Findlay that promoted more of a humanistic approach within the religious and ethical context associated with the history of the institution.

On campus Dr. Rasmussen was deeply appreciated by the faculty for his interest in things academic, and they regretted his decision to resign as president, effective August 31, 1982. He retired to North Carolina.

After a lengthy search the board of trustees announced on April 19, 1983, that Kenneth E. Zirkle would become the fifteenth chief administrator of Findlay College. Born in Meadville, Pennsylvania, in 1940 (one of eight Findlay College presidents from that state), Zirkle graduated from Edinboro State College with a B.S. in 1962, from Rutgers University with an M.Ed. in 1965, and from Pennsylvania State University with a Ed.D. in 1973. He came to Findlay from the State University of New York College at Cortland. Assuming office in August 1983, Zirkle indicated his intention to continue Findlay's sound fiscal policies, "to build on the school's excellent academic reputation," and to enhance the relationship between the college and the town and with the Churches of God, General Conference. During his twenty years in the presidency (the longest-serving president in the history of the school), Dr. Zirkle managed to realize his intentions, and then some.

Taking as his motto "I know one thing for sure; if you don't change, you're backing up," the president led the institution through an epochal decade in its history. From 1990 to 2003 the main campus (twelve acres in 1890) increased to sixty acres, and five new buildings were constructed; the student body increased to more than 4,500 and the faculty to 160 (both essentially doubling in size); seven new graduate programs and more than ten new undergraduate programs were added; the endowment grew from $4.5 to $19.6 million; and athletic programs boasted twenty-six intercollegiate sports.

Dr. Zirkle frequently emphasized the importance of the Judeo-Christian heritage in the life of the institution. At the same time, he was successful in getting the General Eldership to agree to give up its domination of the board of trustees, one of the most significant achievements of his administration. He also was instrumental in changing the name of the institution to "the University of Findlay" on July 1, 1989.

The founders of Findlay College in 1882 envisioned a college in which the liberal arts would be presented within the context of an informed Christian conscience. How that was to be accomplished was sometimes unclear, and compromises had to be made by one administration after another as the college struggled for survival. But the basic vision did endure, informing generations of students, and today it remains a key concept in the life of the institution.

Suggested Reading

Richard Kern, *Findlay College: The First Hundred Years* and *John Winebrenner: 19th Century Reformer,* as well as miscellaneous recent printed materials from the Office of University Relations, the University of Findlay.

Franciscan University

And Catholic Orthodoxy

John Carrigg

The College of Steubenville opened its doors on December 10, 1946, and graduated its first class in June 1950. The dream of Fathers Daniel W. Egan and Regis Stanford had been realized: a Catholic college dedicated to community service in a dominantly Protestant area had been founded, had flourished, and had produced its first class. Those seventy men and women in the class of 1950 became the first of a band of alumni now numbering more than 10,000.

What these two founding Franciscans and those who were to follow them were to accomplish was simply astounding. Steubenville was a most unlikely place to found a college. A mill town with a reputation so unsavory it was off limits to soldiers in World War II, it would become the locale of a little college that would struggle in obscurity for many years and then suddenly burst onto the scene like a meteor and establish itself as a model Catholic college with a national reputation.

The beginnings were humble. Bishop John King Mussio, newly installed in the fledgling Diocese of Steubenville, had been searching for a religious order to found a college in Steubenville.

The Jesuits were approached but would not consider it without upfront money that the diocese did not have. The bishop then turned to the provincial of the Third Order Regular of St. Francis, Archbishop John Boccella, who had offered to help the bishop in his new role. Boccella was enthusiastic about the idea of founding a new college, and within a year of the bishop's request sent Father Daniel W. Egan to Steubenville with the mandate to found that college.

Father Dan arrived in Steubenville on June 2, 1946, a total stranger and went to work on his new assignment. A native of Boston, the forty-year-old Egan had given up a successful career as an accountant to join the Third Order Regular of St. Francis in 1928. He was ordained to the priesthood in 1935 and soon established himself as

a scholar and orator and served as dean and later vice president of St. Francis College in Loretta, Pennsylvania.

At Steubenville he faced a daunting task. An administration building had to be found, faculty and staff hired, students recruited, schedules organized, a catalog written, speaking engagements met, and meetings with town leaders kept. Since the Franciscans had agreed to assume all the costs of the project, Egan went shopping with $350,000 of borrowed money. He first purchased the old Knights of Pythias Hall, a two-story brick building at 420 Market Street in downtown Steubenville to house the administration offices, classrooms, and a chemistry laboratory. The basement of that building, once the notorious Walker Nightclub, became the library. Main campus was now located in a building that cost $70,000, not including renovations. On North Fourth Street two houses were purchased, one to serve as the monastery and the other across the street as the biology building. Behind it, in 1948, a two-story barracks secured from Wright Patterson Air Force Base was located as a classroom building structure called the Liberal Arts Building. These three buildings were rather grandly called the North Campus. Finally, two additional houses were purchased in the north end of Steubenville to serve as residence halls for a handful of boarding students; they were known as the Alpha House and the Delta Sigma Fraternity House. An interval of fifteen minutes between classes was necessary for the walk from Washington Street to the North Campus.

The college operated under the charter of St. Francis College in Loretta, Pennsylvania, until 1948, when it was granted articles of incorporation by the State of Ohio. Another milestone was achieved in 1949 when the college became the forty-eighth member of the Ohio College Association. Membership in this organization placed the college on equal footing with other institutions of higher learning in Ohio. The challenging hurdle of full accreditation by the North Central Association was achieved in 1960 during the leadership of Father Kevin Keelan's first administration (1959–62).

Early in September 1946 Father Regis Stanford arrived in Steubenville to help Father Dan Egan. The two priests proved to be an exceptionally effective team. In their black clerical garb they became a familiar sight in downtown Steubenville—Father Regis always buoyant, Father Dan the more sober because of his burdensome responsibilities.

On opening day December 10, 1946, 258 students registered, seven of them women. Most of the students who entered were veterans of World War II. Nearly all were from the local area and could not afford to go away to school; but empowered by the GI Bill, they found the College of Steubenville the answer to their dreams of higher education.

The college offered a rather old-fashioned liberal arts curriculum that was apparently more of a wish list by Father Dan and obviously influenced by the Jesuit *Ratio Studiorum*. To graduate, all students had to take twelve hours of theology and twelve hours of philosophy; six hours of Latin, Greek, or mathematics; six hours of lab science; six hours of history, literature, and modern language on the intermediate level in addition to the usual major degree requirements for a total of 138 hours.

Student preference soon modified these offerings, or led to their abandonment. Greek was dropped from the catalog in 1950. Latin was listed throughout the fifties with an impressive array of offerings in Ovid, Virgil, Cicero, Horace, and St. Augustine. Father Leonard Sardo taught Latin, but there were few takers and it was phased out, only to make a comeback in the early nineties under the direction of Sister Regina Pacis. Non-Catholic students were exempt from the theology requirement but had to take an equivalency—Basic Truths 101 and Character Formation 102 and six hours of social psychology. Major programs leading to the B.A. degree were offered in economics (business administration or accounting), English, history, political science, social science, and sociology. Those leading to the B.S. degree were biology and chemistry. In 1951 education and engineering became major fields of study and attracted a large number of students. Education soon became the leading major until the 1980s, when theology pulled abreast and then passed it.

Classes were offered in the evening and on Saturday to accommodate students employed at daytime jobs. Tuition was low, deliberately set at ten dollars a semester hour to make the college accessible to people in the community. The Community Institute, later called the Egan Institute, was a series of lectures offered by the faculty to the public on a variety of popular subjects; it attracted large crowds.

The Catholic commitment of the college was clearly stated in its first catalog: "The purpose of the college was to educate men and women so that they were properly prepared for life in this world and the next. The student is taught not only his duties to himself but also his rights and duties to Christian society." It further stated that "teachers of the highest moral character each thoroughly trained in his particular branch of learning, each dedicating his life enthusiastically to the teaching of Catholic culture impart this training." Finally, the Franciscan influence is most important of all in the founding of the college: "The philosophy of life of St. Francis of Assisi ennobling work and study motivates and directs the lives of the Franciscan fathers conducting this college and is communicated by word and example to those coming under their influence."

The fact that prominent members of the early faculty were not Catholic may have eased the concern of non-Catholics who read the catalog and felt uneasy about teachers "enthusiastically dedicated to teaching Catholic culture." Despite this diversity among the faculty respect for the Church was assumed. Professors were urged to begin their classes with a prayer, and many did. The year always began with Mass in the chapel next to the administration building.

Loyalty rallies were a feature of the early years of the college. While Yale was turning to the Left, at least according to William F. Buckley in his *God and Man at Yale*, the college was turning to the Right. These gatherings included highly patriotic speeches and vehement denunciation of communism and all its works. They were usually held on the front steps of the Main Campus at 420 Washington Street and must be viewed against the background of events in the world at that time. The Soviet Union appeared unstoppable as it dominated all of Eastern Europe, including Eastern Germany and Czechoslovakia. In June 1948, when the Soviet authorities cut off access to Berlin except by air, the United States responded with the Berlin airlift. NATO was formed and inluded all the nations of Western Europe and the United States against the Soviet Bloc. While all this was going on the Hiss trial occurred. Alger Hiss, a top government official, was found guilty of perjury in connection with his role as a Soviet spy. When North Korea invaded South Korea, we joined the United Nations action to repel the invaders.

The fifties were difficult years for the college because its facilities were so humble, its financing so precarious, and its campus virtually nonexistent. It must have vexed the spirit of Father Dan to face this scene optimistically, yet his spirit never flagged or failed. Indeed it must have lifted when a successful long-range fund drive begun in 1952 enabled him to purchase forty acres of hilltop land one mile from downtown Steubenville on which to build the new campus. In 1954 Father Dan turned the presidency over to Father Regis Stanford so he could devote full time to planning the new campus.

If the fifties was a time of struggle it was also, for various reasons, a time of growth for the college. First, it was the only college for miles around, the nearest located forty miles away in Pittsburgh. Bethany College was only twenty-five miles from Steubenville, but it had its own long-established clientele and did not depend on commuters. The college could therefore successfully serve as a community college for those young men and women in the Ohio Valley who could not afford to go away to college.

Second, Father Dan was able to assemble an excellent faculty. He wisely took advantage of the refugee scholars fleeing from Communist tyranny. Most of them possessed a Ph.D. and were serious scholars in the old-world tradition. Some were overqualified to be teaching undergraduates, but they added luster to the faculty.

Prominent townspeople also generously lent their assistance and deserve mention for their service to the infant college. Attorney Samuel Freifield, a brilliant scholar of the law and a leading member of the bar in Jefferson County, became a friend of the college from the beginning and helped in so many ways with his time, advice, and money. He was the first chairman of the board of advisers and developed a warm relationship with Father Dan and Father Regis. Emma Carter Zeis, a prominent local philanthropist, strongly believed the college was an asset to the community. Every year during the 1950s she held an elegant party for all the graduates on the lawn of her home on Franklin Avenue (now the Jefferson County Historical Society). She was unstinting in her praise of the college; and as part of the old Steubenville elite and a member of St. Paul's Episcopal Church, she did her best to promote it to the community.

Michael Starvaggi, of Weirton, West Virginia, an Italian immigrant who became a leading industrialist by dint of brains and hard work, was responsible for securing the hilltop campus. Later he underwrote the cost of the Starvaggi Building, which housed the library and nursing department for many years and today is the administration building. His wife, Angeline, shared her husband's ardent support of the college and was active for many years in the College Women's Club.

Graduation exercises, during the downtown phase, took place in the Steubenville High School Auditorium. Baccalaureate Mass was held in St. Peters Church across the street from the high school. The seventy who graduated in 1950 made up the largest class until 1960. Professor Edward Kelly acted as grand marshal in those years and after his death in 1981 was succeeded by Professor John Korea, who holds that position at this writing. Three graduations were held outdoors on the hilltop campus (1962–64) until both baccalaureate and graduation were moved to the spacious Diocesan Community Arena in 1965. Seeking to keep college activities on the campus, the 1987–92 graduations were held in the Big Tent; but the new Finnegan Fieldhouse became the graduation site in 1993, easily accommodating 300–400 graduates and their guests.

The college enjoyed a warm relationship with Bishop Mussio, who was a frequent celebrant at the Baccalaureate Mass in those days. He received the honorary Doctor of Laws degree in 1956 and gave the commencement address. He ended his career in 1977 with a farewell address in which he urged the graduates to hold fast to their faith and not be taken in by New Age rhetoric.

One of the major events in the early history of the college was the establishment of Founder's Day, which would become the occasion of conferring the Poverello Medal on a worthy person or organization that demonstrated the Christ-like charity of St. Francis of Assisi. This medal became the college's highest nonacademic honor. The first Founder's Day was held on December 7, 1949, in the ballroom of the Fort Steuben Hotel. Alcoholics Anonymous was the first recipient of the medal. Sister Agatha of the order of Sisters of Charity, who had founded a clinic for alcoholics at St. Vincents hospital in Akron, Ohio, received the medal on behalf of AA. Father Dan Egan also chose Founder's Day to announce the first board of advisers. Twenty-one in all, eight Catholic and thirteen non-Catholic, these advisers were important community members. A Founder's Day banquet has been held every year since that first one. Some of the more famous recipients of the medal include Birgit Nilson, the great Metropolitan Opera soprano; Arthur Rooney, owner of the Pittsburgh Steelers; and Mother Teresa of Calcutta.

In the midst of the planning for a new campus, Father Dan Egan died of suffocation in a fire that broke out in the monastery on March 30, 1959. This dreadfully shocking event was a great loss to the college and the community.

An extremely important part of college life dating back to its opening days was the athletic program. The intercollegiate football and basketball teams were christened the Barons for Baron von Steuben, the namesake of Steubenville. But almost immediately Sister Bonaventure, a Franciscan nun and an English professor, produced the Baron in the form of a medieval jester dressed in the college colors green and gold. The college song, "Hail Steubenville" was written by Fred Warring of the famed Pennsylvanians, with the lyrics by Father Walter Plimmer, a friend of Warring. The somewhat difficult piece did not catch on, but in recent graduations a college choral group has sung it well and will hopefully give it new life.

Both of the sports teams did not have equal success. Football had one good year, the first in 1947 with a record of 4-4-1 The high point of the season came with the last game, when the Barons upset undefeated St. Francis, our sister college, 13-6. After that it was all downhill, and the program was abolished in 1950 because of cost. Basketball was much more successful. With the arrival of Paul Brownlee in 1952 and Jim Smith two years later, the Barons were virtually unbeatable. Hank Kuzma was the coach in those glory days when the Barons won fifty-six home games in a row. The 1958 team, with a record of 24-1, was proclaimed the number-one small college team in the nation by the Associated Press. Ultimately those costs were too high also, and when the program was abolished in 1981 the college withdrew from intercollegiate sports.

The move from downtown to the new campus began early in 1960 with groundbreaking on a half-dozen buildings. In the summer of 1961 the college community bade adieu to the downtown and moved to the hilltop. Although it was a distance of only about a mile, it was psychologically as good as a hundred. The college would never again be as close to or as involved with the town as it had been in those first fifteen years.

The 1960s were boom years for the college. The campus by 1969 consisted of ten structures: Marian Hall and Holy Trinity dormitories for women; St. Thomas More and St. Francis for men; the Holy Spirit Monastery; Starvaggi for administration offices and library; Egan and Stafford for classrooms, laboratories, and faculty offices; AntonIan, the college dining hall; and Christ the King Chapel. In 1974 the J. C. Williams Center was opened. The expansion occurred during the presidencies of Father Kevin Keelan (1959–62, 1969–73) and Father Columba Devlin (1962–68).

As enrollment grew, the total each year was greater than the preceding one. By 1962 resident students outnumbered commuters and women outnumbered men. Total enrollment was 1,085 in 1968, and by 1970 it peaked at 1,333. Because finding room for all those students was a problem, floors were added to the dormitories to accommodate them. The expansion resulted in all debts being paid and income exceeding expenditures. The board of trustees was created in 1966 to assist the president in the governance of the college. But there was a downside to those years of boom. The spirit of the sixties, hostile to the Catholic way, washed up over the college, affecting both faculty and students. A significant sign of the decline in the school's Catholic identity was the paucity of students at one opening-day Mass, where there were probably a half-dozen students and eight faculty members.

Then came the decline as enrollment went into a tailspin and bottomed out in 1978, with an enrollment total of 550 full-time students. With the abolition of the draft, students were not flocking to college to avoid service in Vietnam. The college was no longer the only community college. Competition from four nearby state-supported institutions offering lower tuition had a severe impact on enrollment. As a result, dormitories closed and deficit financing replaced the surpluses of the sixties. A "For Sale" sign went up in front of one of the dormitories. In those bleak years every faculty meeting was a crisis with announcements of cutting and eliminating and doing without. Faculty and staff were laid off. The history and political science department went from seven professors to three. Fall registration was a time of intense anxiety with enrollment figures being constantly checked and rechecked. A class with ten students enrolled was considered decent.

To staunch the flow of blood the curriculum was revised to make it more attractive to the students. Philosophy and western civilization were dropped as requirements; theology was reduced to six hours; and the students could select from a wide range of offerings in communications, humanities, social sciences, and natural sciences to satisfy their general degree requirement. Conceivably, a student could graduate without taking a course in history or philosophy!

It was also a period of student protests and violent demonstrations against the war in Vietnam. The college had little of that. There was just one mild antiwar protest involving about thirty students in 1969. There was, however, a serious press for open dorms. Father Kevin said "no" to that demand and gave his reason: "Some are of the opinion that unless we change our beliefs we will not survive as a college. I am of the opinion that unless we reconsecrate ourselves to the truth of our beliefs we do not deserve to continue as Catholic and Franciscan."

Faculty morale also suffered. Early in 1974, in Father Kevin's last year as president, a poll of the faculty was taken to determine if the college was living up to its Christian name. Seventy-five percent of the faculty responded to a long questionnaire probing its commitment. The faculty was evenly divided; half said it was, the other half said no. Three faculty members were asked to comment on the results. Father David Tickerhoof emphasized the importance of faculty support for the college's Christian commitment: "We must not be dishonest in terms of our vision and goals. We have a right to select those who would teach in accordance with the design of the [Christian] community. Those who would not fit in this community. . . . have other places to teach."

In the midst of this crisis Father Michael Scanlan became the college president. A graduate of Williams College and Harvard Law School, a most unusual preparation for the role he was to play, he served in the air force and then entered the T.O.R.s in 1957. Dean from 1962 to 1968, he was prominent in the Catholic charismatic renewal, a movement identified with healing and speaking in tongues and for its strong support of Catholic orthodoxy and the magisterium. His ardent supporters in charismatic communities all over the country were willing and eager to send their sons and daughters to the college.

Early in his presidency Father Mike made it clear that the thrust of the college was going to be robust Catholicism. When students petitioned him to postpone the Sunday Mass to late in the afternoon so they could sleep off the night before, he told them there would be Sunday morning Mass, he would be the celebrant, and they would have plenty of time for prayer and contemplation. One his first moves, symbolic of new confidence and leadership, was to take down the "For Sale" sign in front of the dormitory.

The question is often asked, "How did he do it?" The answer is simple: he led with the courage of his convictions. He truly believed that a university could be God centered and at the same time committed to intellectual life of a high order. An examination of his essays that appear in the university publication *Franciscan Way* under the heading "From the President" invariably reveal a deeply religious commitment to the Catholic faith. In the summer 1997 issue he quotes from the university mission statement that the college was to be an "intellectual and faith community, integrating faith and learning in and out of the classroom" with "no artificial separation of the intellectual and faith life."

The theology faculty and all the friars at Franciscan University were the first to take the oath to uphold the magisterium in its teaching as required by *Ex Corde Ecclesiae* (1989). Father Mike had in his favor the fact that the faculty was not so locked into secularity that he had to go to war with it. There were a few dissenters to the strong Catholic direction that Father Mike was leading, but they left within a few years of his arrival.

While presidential leadership was certainly crucial in the turnaround of the college, equally important was what was going on in the classroom. Father Mike interviews every potential faculty member and makes it clear that the mission of the college is Catholic and orthodox and hands the candidate a copy of the mission statement of the university. If the potential faculty member is not comfortable with that he would not be happy teaching there. It rarely comes to that, because before he reaches Father Mike the candidate has been interviewed by the department head and the dean, both of whom are committed to the Catholic mission. The result is that the faculty is dominantly Catholic.

Transforming student life and making it part of the spiritual renewal resulted in the household concept. Father Mike described how this came about: "In the first four months I spent quite a bit of time visiting with students. As I talked with them one question emerged: 'In your dorms do you know the people across from you? On either side? Down the hall?' The answer was usually 'no.' Time after time students had never had a personal conversation with their neighbors or could not remember their names. I thought this absurd. As I mingled with students it became clear to me that renewal at the college had to begin with changing their sad and lonely lives." The first households were established in the fall of 1975. Rather than grant open dorms as a remedy for loneliness and alienation, Father Mike drew from his experience as seminary rector to introduce small-group living. "We needed a family spirit but it was a stretch to call it a little family. I thought the word 'household' best expressed sharing a common life." By definition, households are groups of men and women who gather under a common agreement to live out their daily Christian life together. The members agree to keep certain commitments, usually shared prayer, recreation, and Lord's Day celebration. They typically live on the same dorm wing and often eat meals together, attend Mass, and pray together regularly. Initially households were mandatory. Today they are optional, but more than 50 percent of resident students join them. Each household has a religious name, such as Precious Blood or One in the Spirit. The best aspect of households is that they work, said Father Mike. "With households, you have a solid base to overcome loneliness and identify with other people in their struggles as well as their joys." The wholesome life resulting from life in the households was manifested in growing attendance at daily Mass and the long lines outside the confessional. Sunday Mass was standing-room only.

The summer conferences for priests and deacons had much to do with the Scanlan revival. The first conference for priests was held in the summer of 1975 and was attended by more than 500 priests. Since the conferences began twenty-five years ago, it is estimated that 12,500 priests, deacons, and seminarians have attended these conferences to get their "spiritual batteries" recharged. They liked what they saw and heard and returned to their parishes to sell Steubenville.

Also influential are the youth conferences that take on the form of a giant pep rally for the Faith. Beginning with one session in 1976 attended by 1,000, they grew to two sessions in 1994 attended by 5,800 to three sessions in Steubenville in 2000 and parallel sessions in seven different cities around the country, with attendance of over 20,000. A significant number of students who attend the rallies enroll in Franciscan University. When the word was out that Steubenville was the center of Catholic orthodoxy, Catholic parents—appalled at what was happening elsewhere—sent their sons and daughters to the university.

The climb in enrollment began in the 1980s and by 1999 had exceeded 2,100. Students were coming from all fifty states and from many foreign countries. Three graduate programs were added to the curriculum: business administration, theology, and education. At the same time the bachelor's degree in nursing was established.

The college was now a university, and on April 22, 1979, at the University Dedication Day ceremony, Father Michael stood on the platform with two former presidents, Father Columba and Father Kevin. Father Columba addressed the gathering: "I believe the transformation that has taken place on this campus over the past few years is totally due to the dreams, the vision and the trust of Father Michael. I can see only good things in the days and years ahead for the institution under Father Michael."

Since that dedication master's programs have been added in counseling, philosophy, educational administration, and nursing. Under the leadership of Father Mike and John Green, the new vice president and treasurer of the university, the financial health of Franciscan was stabilized. An anonymous donor assumed the short-term debt of the university. Another anonymous donor underwrote the aesthetic improvement of the road that cut through the heart of the campus, which was evacuated in 1983 and replaced with a circle, steps, and a long walkway enhanced by a lovely lawn that added immeasurably to the beauty of the campus. Another anonymous donor underwrote this improvement. The Vacarro Baseball Field, completed in 1984, is hailed as one of the finest in the country.

The university also attracted many students who were deeply involved in the pro-life moment. Every January huge numbers of Franciscan students take part in the pro-life march in Washington, D.C., on the anniversary date of *Roe v. Wade*. In January 1999 nine busloads of students attended the rally. A Human Life Studies minor was added to the curriculum in 1995. An eternal flame burns over the grave of an unborn child, and a grave of seven aborted babies lies next to the Portiuncula. Governor Robert Casey of Pennsylvania was honored for his courageous stand for the life of the unborn and received an honorary degree from the university in 1994. He commended the university for its Tomb of the Unborn Child and told the graduates, "It must be very hard sometimes to hold to your conscience in such a culture. I am honored to be in the presence of young people who have the courage to do that, and I salute you."

It is not surprising that out of the spiritual life fostered on the campus religious vocations emerge. Students and staff founded the Franciscan Sisters Third Order Regular in 1988. A survey conducted in 1980–2000 revealed that seventy-nine priests were ordained in that period and 117 women joined religious orders. Most of these priests and nuns trace their vocation to the atmosphere on the campus of Franciscan University. Father Todd Molinari (Class of 1990) said he did not start thinking seriously about a vocation to the priesthood until his sophomore year at the university: "I began to go to spiritual direction with Father Gus . . . it became apparent that I had a vocation to the priesthood."

More than 700 Franciscan University alumni work around the country as directors of religious education, Catholic school teachers, youth ministers, and leaders of programs for adults preparing to join the Church. For those who would say we are running a seminary, Father Mike has an interesting question: "If Catholic Universities do not produce the future priests, sisters and brothers, the loyal and scholarly Catholic theologians and philosophers, the Catholic business and professional people taking the high road of moral behavior, and the Catholic parents of the succeeding generation's Church leaders, who will?"

It goes without saying that Pope John Paul II is extremely popular on the campus. Father Mike presented him with a spiritual bouquet from the students of F.U.S. and a honorary degree in 1986. One of Father Mike's most cherished memories goes back to a visit to Rome on March 30, 1996, when he heard from the Holy Father, "I am very grateful to you." A "Strong in the Eighties" fund drive was launched in 1981, the first successful million-dollar campaign in the school's history. The fruit of this campaign was a second building program on the hilltop campus. The John Paul II library, housing more than 200,000 volumes, was dedicated in 1987. A former skating rink adjoining the campus was acquired in 1988 and today is known as the St. Joseph Center, which houses classrooms, offices and meeting rooms.

A replica of the chapel rebuilt by St. Francis of Assisi, the Portiuncula was erected in 1987. A short time later a creche with life-sized figures was built. Overlooking it all is a huge steel cross that was erected in 1991. The magnificent Finnegan Field House was opened in 1992. It holds two basketball courts, two racquetball courts, a weight room, and an exercise room. With seating capacity of 2,000, baccalaurete and graduation exercises are held there. In 1997 the St. Clare and St. Kolbe resident halls were opened, and the Saints Cosmas and Damien Science Building was underwritten by a fund drive that exceeded $18,700,000. A former motel on University Boulevard, adjoining the campus, was purchased as a dormitory for pretheological students. The value of the hilltop campus buildings is placed at $55,000,000. In 1994 two of the university's economists, Joseph Zoric and Michael Welker, performed a study of the economic impact of Franciscan University on the area. They concluded the total impact was in excess of $100 million.

Father Mike's presidency is also credited with the great strengthening of the intellectual life of the university. The faculty was enhanced with the addition of such well-known scholars as John Crosby and Patrick Lee in philosophy and Regis Martin, Mark Miravalle, Alan Schreck, and Scott Hahn in theology. And since the charismatic approach was not everyone's choice, Father Mike appointed a number of traditional Catholics. Theology and philosophy departments enjoyed enormous growth and attracted huge numbers of students. Theology has 400 majors, the largest in the university and in the country. A major achievement was the founding of the Society of Catholic Social Scientists by Dr. Stephen Krason of Franciscan University and Dr. Joseph Varacalli of State University New York. In 1991 the university opened a branch in a former Carthusian monastery in Gamin, Austria, seventy-five miles west of Vienna. Every semester since then, 75–100 students attend classes in this delightful setting and have a chance to travel widely in Europe.

By the 1990s the university was attracting national and international attention. It was a curious phenomenon: a Catholic university really committed to the Catholic faith with a stellar academic program. Church leaders have showered Father Scanlan with praise and have visited the university and received honorary degrees: "I don't know a better university in the U.S. or anywhere else in the world," said the late John Cardinal O'Connor. Archisbishop Charles Chaput of Denver called Franciscan "the best known college of its kind in the country and throughout Europe" and said," I believe in the mission of this school." Francis Cardinal Arinze of Nigeria and Christoph Cardinal Schonborn of Austria have visited the campus. Both Arinze and Schonbom are considered papal candidates, and if either should assume the throne of St. Peter, the one American Catholic university they would know well is Franciscan University.

The university was cited in 1990 by *National Review* as one of the top universities in the country and, as well, every year since 1992 in *U.S. News World Report*'s "Guide to America's Best Colleges." In 1997 Franciscan University was named to the John Templeton Foundation Honor Rolls for Education in a Free Society, one of thirteen colleges and universities so honored. Franciscan was cited in the 1999 "Templeton Guide to Colleges that Encourage Character Development" for its Great Books Honors Program, for its Works of Mercy (more than 500 students are involved in helping inner-city children, prisoners, handicapped adults, and the elderly), and for its households and chapel ministries, both of which promote a vigorous spiritual life on the campus.

In February 1999 Father Scanlan announced he would retire from the presidency. The trustees voted to name him chancellor, which would free him from the daily grind but would give him continued influence in the life of the university. Whether he stays or moves on, he can look back on a record of stunning achievement.

The trustees then chose Father Terence Henry as the fifth president. Father Henry, no stranger to the university, had served on the board of trustees since 1993. He came from St. Francis College in Loretta, Pennsylvania, where he had been vice president of mission and ministry and taught in the continuing education department. He had twenty-five years in education as a history teacher at Bishop Egan High School in Philadelphia and, later, as principal and then as president of the new combined high school.

At his inauguration in October 2000 Father Henry took the oath of fidelity, promising to uphold the Catholic Church's teaching in matters of faith and morals. In his years as a teacher and administrator, he won a wide reputation for rapport with students and faculty, and under him the news from Franciscan University of Steubenville continues to be good. Enrollment is at capacity with 2,700 students.

The university was again cited as one of the top universities in the country by *National Review, U.S. News and World Report,* and the John Templeton Foundation. In addition, all six editions of *Barron's Best Buys in College Education* feature Franciscan as one of its "300 myth-breaker schools" that offers "fine academic programs" and "a spiritual environment" at an affordable price.

In 2001 Franciscan University received a $600,000 award from the Fides et Ratio grant committee. The grant furthers the university's mission to educate students who desire to understand their faith as integral to their educational experience.

SUGGESTED READING

The Baronette, 1946–83; *The Troubador,* 1983–; *Franciscan Way,* 1990–; Father Michael Scanlan, *Let the Fire Fall* (Franciscan Press, 1993). See also the *Steubenville Herald Star* (1946).

Franklin University

Serving Nontraditional Students

KELLI NOWLIN AND HELGA KITTRELL

Founded in Columbus in 1902 under YMCA sponsorship as the School of Commerce, Franklin University has since become a leading educator of working professionals in central Ohio. For nearly 100 years Franklin University has served nontraditional students seeking to advance their education. Franklin provides student-centered lifelong higher education and has earned a national reputation for its unmatched student services. The recurrent theme throughout Franklin's history is the university's primary concern for the individual student. More than 6,000 students annually attend Franklin University to earn associate's and bachelor's degrees in fifteen undergraduate programs and master's degrees in four graduate programs.

The typical Franklin student is a full-time professional who has many other obligations, including work and family, and who has generally transferred from another institution. Many Franklin alumni have attended classes in the evenings, on weekends, and at other hours considered unusual for the times. Students range in age from eighteen to eighty and come from all walks of life. More than 500 international students, representing nearly seventy different countries, also call Franklin University home.

Franklin University has been a pioneer in meeting the needs of people who have the ambition to continue their education in combination with other responsibilities. The university is committed to providing flexible, innovative, and responsive education at an affordable cost to those who seek it. And Franklin continually assesses the needs of students and employers and responds with educationally sound programs.

During its early days the YMCA schools were comprised of the Day and Night Mechanical Schools, Evening High School, Evening School of Commerce, Evening Technical School, and Evening Law School. Classes offered in the School of Commerce included blueprint reading, mechanical drawing, and agricultural science.

The Clock Tower in front of Fisher Hall

Classes were scheduled mostly in the evenings so that students could retain full-time jobs. This remains true of Franklin today.

The School of Commerce started with just a few students studying bookkeeping. In 1913 a two-year college course in accounting was offered, and by 1917 forty men were studying accounting. A number of unrelated courses like exporting, advertising, and insurance were offered as the need arose. By 1920 production engineering, accounting, banking and finance, marketing, and business administration were offered in four-year evening programs leading to a Bachelor of Commercial Science degree. Overall, the curriculums and courses offered were devoted to preparing students for their work life.

The Evening Law School, which was named the Law School of Franklin University in 1948, offered its first courses in 1902, opening with five part-time instructors and fourteen first-year students. In 1965 the law school was transferred to Capital University, where it remains today. In 1921 the university was conferred degree-granting authority by the State of Ohio. The first formal commencement was in 1923, with twenty-four students in the graduating class. In 1933 the name Franklin University was adopted, and the university was organized as a separate branch of the Columbus YMCA.

Franklin University separated from YMCA sponsorship in 1964, incorporating under Ohio law as a not-for-profit, independent educational institution governed by its own board of trustees. The board is composed of thirty business, industry, and community leaders who are charged with being actively involved in setting the policy for the university. In addition to the trustees, a board of advisers is made up of many nationally respected members of the professional world.

Dr. Joseph F. Frasch became the university's first president in 1951 and served until 1977. Previously, a board of governors headed the university. Frasch shepherded the university's growth from an institution of fewer than 600 part-time students housed in the YMCA building to a university of more than 4,000. The underlying success and growth of the university is largely attributed to the functional educational philosophy of Frasch in seeing the union between practicality and philosophy. He started the trend that many other educational institutions and educators copied: he carried his belief to his position as an administrator. In theory he believed that the best administrator was one in constant contact with the students. And he could be found everywhere students could be—in classrooms, the cafeteria, hallways, parking lots. Frasch also believed that serious, interested students should be able to "experience the helping hand of education" when the road got rocky. He felt strongly that education is to serve and assist students to become productive members of the community.

The university's second president, Dr. Frederick J. Bunte, began his career at Franklin as a faculty member. He taught an array of courses from sociology to history. When Bunte received his Ph.D. in 1972, he was one of the few on campus at the time. But his commitment to lifelong learning would not let him stop there. Two years later he earned an associate's degree in business administration from Franklin.

While serving as dean of Academic Affairs, Bunte spearheaded major changes in academic programs and faculty governance that enabled Franklin to be granted full accreditation by the North Central Association of Colleges and Schools in 1976. He was chosen as the university's second president in 1978. During Bunte's reign as president, the university saw major changes. It became the largest independent university in the central Ohio area and the fourth largest in the state in the number of students enrolled. The campus itself grew with the additions of a library, a television studio, and an art gallery, which was later named the Bunte Gallery. Bunte also saw the opening of Phillips Hall in 1980. President Bunte may be best remembered for his commitment to Franklin University students and his ability to "look down the pike" and create programs responsive to a changing community's needs.

Dr. Paul J. Otto took over the reins as president in 1986. Otto has been at the forefront of numerous initiatives and great change. He is credited with supporting the continued growth of the downtown campus, developing suburban campuses, increasing course delivery options to students, initiating the creation of the Franklin University Graduate School, and building the Community College Alliance. The alliance provides students from nearly 100 community colleges across the nation and in Canada the opportunity to complete their bachelor's degrees from Franklin through a combination of onsite and online courses.

Franklin University put its beliefs in writing in 1992 with the development of seven Relationship Management Principles. Among these principles is a commitment to service, trust, effectiveness, and lifelong learning. "The customer is not always right, but the customer is always the customer," says President Otto, even when the customer is a student. Franklin prides itself on eliminating many of the frustrating barriers to achieving educational goals by providing easily accessible support through its Student Services Associate (S.S.A.) program. Based on their major, each student is assigned a S.S.A. who guides them from application to graduation. The associates help students clarify their educational goals, assist in course scheduling, and serve as a liaison between students and other departments in the university.

Franklin students rarely find themselves waiting in line to pay their fees, schedule their classes, or meet with their S.S.A. And all student services are housed in one building, making it easy for students to take advantage of "one-stop shopping." New undergraduate students can apply and register for classes in just one hour.

Franklin University received national recognition for its Relationship Management Principles in 1999 when it was featured in *The One to One Manager,* by business experts Don Peppers and Martha Rogers, alongside companies like General Electric, American Airlines, Nabisco, Xerox, and Hewlett-Packard. Franklin also received the Outstanding Institutional Advising Program award in 1994 from the National Academic Advising Association. In addition to those honors, Franklin was honored by the National Association of College and University Business Officers (N.A.C.U.B.O.) for applying relationship management in education. Franklin was the only Ohio winner and was among prestigious institutions like Johns Hopkins and Cornell University.

Franklin University's philosophy of "learn today, apply tomorrow" has been a constant since its origination nearly 100 years ago. For professionals aiming to keep up with the demands of the job, it has become essential to gain knowledge and applicable skills throughout the degree process, not just after graduation. Franklin's programs are designed to put students in a better position to advance their careers in the most effective and efficient ways possible. Franklin also keeps close ties to the business community to ensure that the curriculum keeps up with the changing business world. The university uses advisory boards to measure interest in proposed programs as well as to provide feedback on curriculum enhancements. The advisory boards are made up of key personnel from local businesses and government institutions as well as others critical to the industry.

In line with its commitment to students, Franklin opened its first suburban campus in Dublin in 1995, and after phenomenal success it targeted the northeastern suburb of Westerville in 1999. These full-service campuses have increased options for busy professionals who wish to fit higher education into their lives. In all, thousands of students are working on undergraduate or master's degrees at these convenient suburban locations. Many of the major area courses in a variety of undergraduate programs are featured at the suburban campuses, and an M.B.A. degree can be completed in its entirety. The Northwest Campus features all the amenities of Franklin's Main Campus, including computer labs, student advisers, placement testing, makeup exams, and free parking. After opening to just fifty-eight students in the fall of 1995, the Northwest Campus today hosts more than 1,000 students per term and is still growing.

The Northeast Campus in Westerville is a 47,000-square-foot facility that includes fifteen classrooms, two computer labs equipped with Internet access and the Columbus Metropolitan Library's Discovery System, the Teaching and Learning Center, a cafe, a library, free parking, and video conferencing with the downtown campus. The Northeast Campus was a result of student interest from surrounding communities, students who expressed a desire to receive a quality, affordable education that was convenient to work or home. The number of students at the Northeast Campus has increased each term, and predictions are that enrollment will continue to grow.

As it had since its opening nearly ninety-one years earlier, Franklin University once again listened to the needs of the community and created the Franklin University Graduate School in 1993. The graduate program has seen tremendous growth in recent years and now serves nearly 1,000 students annually. Classes are filled virtually through word of mouth, and its commitment to applied learning has made it a preferred program in the central Ohio community. The charter class of the Master's of Business Administration program had 120 students enrolled, now central Ohio's largest M.B.A. program. When an online counterpart to this program was introduced, 2,000 students enrolled from more than five states. The Master of Science in Marketing and Communication is the only one of its kind in central Ohio, and one of only a few in the country, that blends these two traditionally separate disciplines. Its charter class recently graduated with a curriculum including market research, e-commerce, and international and multicultural communication. Like all Franklin programs, this initiative resulted from the demands of the workplace, where marketing, advertising, public relations, sales and communication continue to intertwine.

Franklin's Master of Science in Computer Science is the result of the rapidly growing computer industry that faces a critical shortage of computer science programmers and technology managers. This M.S. is a natural outgrowth of Franklin's undergraduate computer science program and encompasses everything from software engineering and algorithm analysis to operating systems and computer networks. Franklin's other master's program, the Master of Science in Human Services Management, is a highly specialized graduate degree that targets professionals who work in the area of child welfare; city, county, and state governmental service agencies; and nonprofit organizations. Graduates of the program are well versed in numerous areas, including fiscal management, project evaluation, managing diversity, and marketing for nonprofit organizations. Students in Franklin University's Graduate School experience not only a strong academic curriculum but professors well versed in their fields who have impeccable credentials and a wealth of hands-on experience. Professors in the Graduate School, as well as throughout the university, practice what they teach at some of the area's most prominent organizations.

Franklin University's role in higher education was redefined when local two-year technical and community colleges began to experience tremendous growth. Suddenly there was increased competition for first-time students, and Franklin once again responded to the needs of the community by shifting its focus from educating first- and second-year students to an institution serving continuing transfer students who brought some previous college experience. Today the majority of Franklin students come to the university with some transfer credit and continue work toward their college degrees.

In the summer of 2000 Franklin University introduced the new Balanced Learning Format (B.L.F.). Students in the B.L.F. take one six-week onsite or online class at a time, which frees them from juggling a variety of assignments from numerous professors. This format is the latest of several delivery options Franklin offers, giving students more choices than ever. In addition to the short time frame, what makes these courses unique is that each B.L.F. course is created with a student manual, an instructor manual, Web support for students taking classes onsite and a Web version of the course for students who prefer taking the class via the World Wide Web.

A brief introductory course is essential to the success of students taking B.L.F. courses. This introductory course teaches the effective use of technology used in the courses and in business, such as email, bulletin boards, white boards, chat rooms, and Web research. Many students also discover that this course helps them become more independent learners, another necessary skill for lifelong learning. Faculty members teaching in the Balanced Learning Format also are required to complete a development course, or workshop. In this course faculty members learn to use technology effectively in teaching and communicating with students and how to facilitate a student-centered learning environment.

In anticipation of the future of higher education, Franklin began partnering with community colleges across the nation in 1998. Students in this program begin by earning an associate's degree from a partner community college. Their junior- and senior-year course work includes "bridge courses" taught at community colleges integrated with forty credit hours via online bachelor's degree program delivered by Franklin University. The bachelor's degree conferred is from Franklin. Faculty members in the C.C.A. Program use a variety of communication technologies to enhance the learning environment, from faxes and CD-ROMs to email, chat rooms, and bulletin boards. Franklin's C.C.A. Program eliminates the typical disadvantages of many distance learning programs, including students who feel isolated and experience insufficient instruction and a lack of interactivity. Through the C.C.A. Program the community colleges make accommodations and services available to the students throughout the degree process, and Franklin offers chat rooms, bulletin boards, and email to encourage one-on-one communication with instructors. Degrees currently offered through this program are business administration, technical management, computer science, management information systems, health care management, and public safety management. Partner schools are located in Colorado, Illinois, Indiana, Ohio, Michigan, Missouri, New York, North Carolina, Tennessee, West Virginia, Wisconsin, and Canada, and more states are expected to be added as the program grows.

More than 31,000 Franklin University alumni reside in nearly every state and in many foreign countries. They are entrepreneurs and hold a variety of important positions in all fields. Two such successful alumni are Harry C. Moores and Stanley M. Ross. Both raised on farms, they met in an accounting class and on graduating in 1903 formed a partnership. They used their farming background and their accounting knowledge to start the Moores & Ross Milk Company. This company prospered through the years and in 1924 moved into the milk-based infant formula business, making Franklin Infant Food, known to most now as Similac, produced by Ross Laboratories, a division of Abbott Laboratories. Upon Stanley's death in 1945, his son, Richard M. Ross, became president. Richard Ross served on Franklin University's board of trustees from 1978 until his death in 1993.

Thousands of traditional and nontraditional students alike have passed through the doors of Franklin University, hoping to make their futures better with a solid foundation of education. They leave Franklin not only more educated but better people. They contribute to the communities in which they live in numerous ways, and what they learned at Franklin contributes to their lives in uncountable ways. Franklin University's philosophy is a simple formula: know the diverse needs of students and then provide them with what they need to increase their personal potential. Franklin has been doing just that for nearly 100 years and plans to carry out that philosophy for the next 100.

Suggested Reading

Joseph Frederick Frasch, "An Evaluative Survey of Franklin University" (Ph.D. diss., n.d.); Mary Rogers and Don Peppers, *The One to One Manager* (Doubleday, 1999), 38–45; *Shaping the Future—Celebrating One Hundred Years* (Franklin University, 2000).

Heidelberg College

College for the Common Folk for 150 Years

DAVID GERARD HOGAN AND KIMBERLY ROUSH

A denominational need for frontier preachers and the desire of a small town for legitimacy combined to create Heidelberg College. The German Reformed Church and the people of Tiffin, Ohio, pooled their resources to start a college in the countryside, giving hundreds of professors and thousands of students a wonderful place to teach and learn. Never large, expensive, or elite, Heidelberg taught the common people of Ohio. In the 150 years since the college's birth, Heidelberg graduates have gone forth to pastor churches, teach in one-room schoolhouses, conduct local business, and heal the sick. Though most of their names are now long forgotten, these men and women helped build Ohio's economy, educate generations of children, and contribute to the betterment of society.

Heidelberg College's early roots run back to 1833, when the recently formed Ohio Synod of the German Reformed Church resolved to establish a seminary to train ministers for serving both its existing congregations and those it hoped to establish throughout the new western frontier. The synod first opened a school in Canton, Ohio, but closed it just a year later when its only professor resigned because of low enrollment. Two more seminaries were founded in the early 1840s and were again quickly abandoned because of insufficient student interest. In 1846 the synod began exploring the idea that a seminary would be more viable if combined with a college offering a classical curriculum. This idea became a firm plan by 1849 when a committee of three church leaders was appointed with the assignment of "soliciting proposals from different localities looking towards the permanent location of an institution." This committee investigated placing the school in the Ohio communities of Xenia, Worthington, and Tiffin. But at its April 1850 meeting the synod chose the Fairfield County village of Tarlton as the home for its new college and seminary.

Founder's Hall

Cholera and schoolmaster S. S. Rickly strongly influenced the synod's decision in favor of Tarlton. Rickly had moved his family from Columbus to Tarlton in 1849 during a major cholera outbreak, and there he "found a number of young men whose parents desired to afford them a better opportunity for education than they could obtain in the public schools, and yet without sending them from home." Shortly after his arrival Rickly opened his own private school and "soon had every desk occupied by diligent students." Rickly not only reported on his own success to the synod during the April 1850 meeting, but he also brought an offer from Tarlton to host a new college. The town fathers pledged land valued at $800 and $7,200 in subscriptions from village merchants. The synod members voted to accept their offer, founding Tarlton College and rewarding Rickly's efforts by naming him their school's first president.

Almost immediately, however, the Columbiana Classis, a division of the synod not represented at the April meeting, protested that the location selection process violated the synod charter. Other factions expressed concerns that the new college would be located too close to competitor institutions in neighboring towns, predicting another quick demise. Other synod members objected on the basis that Tarlton was primarily a Methodist community and thus an undesirable location for a Reformed Church seminary. Considering this mounting dissatisfaction within the church over the choice of Tarlton, selection committee member Jeremiah Good decided that the search should be reopened and once again sought bids from other towns.

The Seneca County town of Tiffin was among the locations reconsidered. The search committee originally had discounted Tiffin, based on committee member Henry Shaull's opinion that Tiffin was more concerned "with railroads than colleges." Despite Shaull's initial objections, Jeremiah Good traveled to Tiffin in early September 1850 to speak with town representatives, convincing them about the economic and cultural advantages of having a college in their midst. Good told Tiffin leaders that such a school would become a "great luminary from which radiations of intelligence will be defused in every direction." Impressed with Good's proposal, Tiffin pledged $11,030 to the new college if it located in their town. This pledge exceeded those from other competing towns, so the synod voted in late September to move their official location from Tarlton to Tiffin.

Since the college was not going to be situated in Tarlton, the synod deemed that a name change was in order. They decided on the name Heidelberg College at the same meeting where they approved the location change. Heidelberg was significant in two ways: the Heidelberg catechism was important in the theology of the Reformed Church, and Heidelberg University was the oldest and among the most respected schools in Europe. Perhaps synod members thought that borrowing on the legitimacy of the German university could only aid in its success, possibly observing the already flourishing institutions in the Ohio villages of Athens and Oxford. Regardless of their motivation, Heidelberg College was officially incorporated by an act of the Ohio General Assembly on February 13, 1851. The synod now had its seminary and college.

Once chartered, Heidelberg College got off to a rather slow and inauspicious start, with no campus, five students, and a faculty of two brothers, Jeremiah and Reuben Good. Without buildings of their own the Goods rented third-floor rooms above businesses in a block of South Washington Street known as Commercial Row. Though modest in facilities, the Goods founded a highly progressive school for that era, freely admitting both women and African Americans as regular students. Also, rather than appealing to an economic elite, they sought to offer "additional courses of instruction designed to meet the particular wants of different classes of the community." In November 1852 the town of Tiffin deeded a parcel of land to the college, consisting of grazing land near the intersection of East Perry, East Market, and Greenfield Streets. A cornerstone was laid for the first campus building on May 13, 1852, but classes were conducted in the rented rooms on Commercial Row for the next year and a half.

The Goods and their growing student body finally moved up the hill to the new building, a stately four-story red structure intended to house classes and both student and faculty living quarters. Though occupied, this building was not completely finished until 1858 because of persistent fund-raising difficulties. (Now called "Founder's Hall, this original building is still in use today, housing the college's communication and foreign language programs.) These funding problems also extended beyond issues of bricks and mortar, since the faculty was paid poorly and sporadically throughout the decade.

After numerous false starts the Reformed Church in Ohio finally could train its ministers. In Heidelberg's first graduating class in 1854, ten of the twelve graduates were seminarians, who were then sent off to serve synod churches. The church appointed Reformed minister Reverend Emanuel Vogel Gerhart as president to oversee this training. Further reinforcing this emphasis on the church, the college also adopted the motto "Religion and Education Are the Safeguards of Our Nation" and stressed strict moral values. By 1879 Heidelberg president George W. Williard proudly observed that "more than one-third of those who have graduated are now in the active duties of the ministry, whilst nearly all the alumni are filling honorable and influential positions, showing that the moral and religious influence exerted on them whilst in College was of a healthful character."

Despite this overt religious influence, secular disciplines soon comprised most of Heidelberg's offerings. The college offered varied courses of instruction in the 1850s, including classical, preparatory, teacher's, scientific, farmer's, and ladies'. The 1851–52 catalog describes the farmer's curriculum as "embracing four years, and including a practical and thorough knowledge of the English branches, the Natural Sciences, Mechanics, and Scientific Agriculture." The college discontinued this farmers course by 1860 and also abolished the ladies' curriculum, "there being no special necessity for it, as the ladies took the same studies the gentlemen did, and recited with them." By 1871 the catalog stated that "the Curriculum has been revised and enlarged so that it now embraces all the subjects usually taught in the oldest and best established colleges." Following still other national trends, the college soon pared down to a more streamlined curriculum, offering just classic and scientific courses.

Heidelberg's steady growth in the 1850s abruptly halted with the outbreak of the Civil War. A professor at that time explained, "The most trying of her past experience was in 1861, when one student after another enlisted in the army, and fought for the 'Stars and Stripes.' Some of them never returned to complete their course of study." The seminary's graduating class in 1863 numbered only one, which exceeded the number of graduates from the college. Though Heidelberg endured several difficult years during the war, support from the town and synod remained strong. Enrollment soon rebounded after the war ended and Heidelberg began a new era of expansion.

In 1866 college leaders asked the townspeople of Tiffin to donate funds to build an eleven-room president's home to show their appreciation for the school. Tiffin responded generously, completing the president's new home in 1868. Growing enrollment also signaled a need for additional student housing. Postwar prosperity greatly enhanced the college's endowment, finally moving the trustees beyond the point of constantly worrying about survival to the confidence needed for strengthening and expanding the institution. With money in hand they authorized the college's third building, a ladies' boarding hall, described as a "great accommodation and convenience for all concerned." Soon after this boarding hall was successfully completed in 1873, President Williard started formulating plans for yet another campus building. Finally, in 1881, the college's trustees voted unanimously to construct a large classroom and office building at the hefty cost of $40,000. To pay for this project Heidelberg's financial agent again appealed to the town, to the synod, and to thousands of Sunday school children in Reformed churches across Ohio. Each child was urged to purchase bricks for the new building, donating two cents for each brick. Once it was completed in 1886, the final price tag for this new building exceeded over $60,000. Named "College Hall," this building project faced a final shortfall of $24,000, which President Williard quickly alleviated by securing additional pledges.

In this expansion era of the 1880s Heidelberg built new programs in addition to new buildings. The Conservatory of Music opened in 1886, followed the next year by new Departments of Art and Business. As a result, the campus experienced rapid enrollment growth during this period, growing from 182 students in 1886 to 290 in 1888. Heidelberg even added new dimensions in 1889 when the Reverend John Kost, then the chancellor of the University of Florida and an influential member of the Reformed Church, offered to donate his valuable collections of fossils, stuffed birds, mammals, minerals, and other items. One of his conditions for donating these collections was that the trustees agree to construct a suitable museum in which to house them. Kost also requested that Heidelberg change its charter to become a university, appointing him as chancellor. The board of trustees readily agreed to the re-chartering and to his hire but temporarily balked at the museum, finding that neither the synod nor the citizens of Tiffin would fund such a specialized building at that time. Nevertheless, Kost moved his collections to Heidelberg and accepted his position as the new university's first chancellor. Kost's hiring, however, over the longtime and much-revered president George Williard, caused great controversy within both the synod and the Tiffin community. Large factions within both of these groups believed that Williard rightfully should remain as the school's leader and vowed to thwart further funding efforts. Petitions circulated in the town and in churches across the state, but the school's governing body, now reorganized as a university board of regents, held its ground, and Williard resigned after twenty-four years as Heidelberg's president. The regents hired Dr. John Abram Peters to replace him as president. Williard's departure did not quell the fighting, with Kost's opponents continuing to call for his ouster. Trying to make peace, Kost twice offered his resignation to the regents, who rejected it both times. On his third submission in 1891, however, the regents accepted his letter, ending two years of conflict.

Though Kost's appointment caused strife in the community and the church, his insistence on the college rechartering to university status launched Heidelberg into a dramatic new phase of restructuring and growth. Heidelberg grew physically, acquiring extensive property adjacent to the original campus and greatly expanded as an institution by offering graduate coursework and awarding master's and doctoral degrees. This dramatic shift in mission not only reflected Kost's ideas but also a major trend in higher education during that era. Borrowing the concept of graduate education from Germany in the latter half of the nineteenth century, Ivy League schools and other select universities soon led the way in making graduate degrees the single gauge for academic credentials. Heidelberg chose to offer such advanced degrees in order to both remain competitive with other institutions and to further enhance its academic reputation.

Two years later the university also adopted another popular convention of that era by forming the Heidelberg Athletic Association in October 1892, which fielded an intercollegiate football team that fall, beating neighboring Findlay College in its first game 20-0. Needing school colors for this new team, the faculty voted to adopt "the Reformation colors," of red, orange, and black. To better accommodate these new academic and athletic programs, Heidelberg constructed still another large brick building to house offices, a much-needed gymnasium, and the museum space to finally display Kost's various collections. Making this new building even more functional, board of regents member George Bareis outfitted the gymnasium area with shower rooms and lockers and paid for the purchase of athletic equipment, including dumbbells, Indian clubs, a vaulting horse, climbing ropes, and parallel bars. Heidelberg now had a state-of-the-art athletic facility, allowing the school to mandate a physical exercise requirement for all students, in addition to providing training for the burgeoning intercollegiate teams.

Despite these advancements, the 1890s proved to be one of Heidelberg's most difficult periods. A severe recession early in the decade caused the entire country to struggle financially and resulted in dangerous revenue problems for the university. New faculty, departments, and buildings meant additional expense in the best of times and significant hardship during such an economic crisis. Heidelberg struggled to meet its higher costs while faced with shrinking income. Expenses for one year exceeded $12,500, while receipts totaled less than $8,500. To make ends meet the regents even spent $36,000 out of their endowment funds to complete payments on the new museum and gymnasium building, critically depleting the university's reserves. Local banks refused to loan money to the university, and the depressed economy caused many donors to default on their pledge payments. Lingering dissatisfaction over the hiring of Chancellor Kost and the sudden resignation of President Willard also caused some donors to withhold their contributions.

Heidelberg found itself in a dilemma, facing financial disaster if it attempted needed expansion yet needing to compete with the new programs offered by other Ohio colleges. Concerned about possible closure, the synod again came to the school's aid, initiating a new fund-raising campaign. Donor enthusiasm also increased in 1900, centered on Heidelberg's Semi-Centennial celebration. The university ultimately survived that decade of economic hardship, beginning the new century with a healthier endowment and a much brighter future.

Compounding their economic difficulties during the 1890s, administrators and regents faced a student rebellion over the issue of allowing fraternities on campus. Not satisfied with the existing literary societies on campus, a group of Heidelberg students sought to organize local chapters of national social fraternities. The faculty, the administration, and the board of regents all expressed their opposition to these new local chapters, observing "that such societies as fraternities tend to weaken discipline and are prejudicial to the interests of the students." School leaders asked those students involved to sign a promise to abandon their plans to organize these chapters. These organizers refused, and controversy raged on campus until finally twenty-nine disgruntled students and one faculty member left Heidelberg in protest. The students immediately enrolled in the College of Wooster, where they were welcomed into the Wooster chapters of the same fraternities banned by Heidelberg. Never again did Heidelberg students lead a serious drive to bring such national fraternities to campus. Instead, students strengthened their existing literary societies and periodically branched off from these groups to form new campus literary clubs.

The school's fiftieth anniversary in 1900 was both a significant milestone and a turning point. Now on the road to financial stability, university officials took pride in their curricular offerings and growing reputation. During that celebration year President Peters reflected on the new curricular offerings, expanding tuition, and the plans for a campus library. As a challenge to the future, Peters declared his goal for a "Greater Heidelberg." Unfortunately, President Peters did not live to see this new library or any part of a greater school, dying of pneumonia just the following year.

As a result of his sudden death, the start of the new century also brought a new president for Heidelberg University. In 1902 Heidelberg inaugurated theology professor Charles E. Miller as its sixth president and acting chancellor, beginning his administration that would last thirty-five years. Almost immediately Miller proposed a new $150,000 capital campaign to the regents, outlining ambitious plans for further expansion and improvement. By fall he had raised almost one-third of that amount from just six donors. Never doubting that this goal was within reach, Miller spent the winter of 1903–4 traveling 15,000 miles to virtually every Reformed church appealing for donations from the pulpit. The synod pledged money, as did once again the people of Tiffin. One year after the campaign began, Miller proudly announced to a packed theater in downtown Tiffin that "the entire amount has not been raised, but has been guaranteed."

Enjoying the comfort of a healthy endowment and building capital, Miller began an era of unprecedented expansion. His first project was to construct a new dormitory on Greenfield Street, a three-story building given the name Williard Hall. Dedicated in 1908, with reformer Jane Addams featured as guest speaker, this new women's dormitory was built with locally quarried gray limestone blocks designed in modern English gothic style. Months later Heidelberg purchased nearby Keller Cottage and other neighboring homes, to provide more students housing. In 1910 President Miller secured a generous grant from industrialist Andrew Carnegie's foundation to build a handsome limestone library. Over the next two decades, President Miller continued his building spree, adding Laird Science Hall, a men's dormitory, and the College Commons, all in the same stately style topped with identical red roof tiles. Now, almost a century later, these gothic buildings continue to define the architecture of the campus and are all still used daily.

In addition to spending his expanding endowment funds on brick and mortar, Miller established three new faculty chairs and hired a dean of women. He also led academic reforms, in 1914 adopting a new liberal arts curriculum that offered either an arts emphasis, leading to a Bachelor of Arts degree, or a scientific course of study, earning a Bachelor of Science degree. During this same period, however, Miller eliminated programs and streamlined offerings. In 1908 he discontinued the Theological Seminary due to consistently low enrollments and closed down the commercial department in 1917. The seminary merged with the Ursinus School of Theology, assuming the new name of Central Theological Seminary and relocating to Dayton. The commercial department had earlier combined with the Tiffin Business College in 1896, using a separate building in downtown Tiffin.

Despite a rapid growth in enrollment after the turn of the century, Miller deemed that commercial education was "contrary to the spirit and purpose of Heidelberg, and hinders us in our great work." Though officially severed from Heidelberg in 1917, the commercial department continued to exist in Tiffin, in 1918 incorporating as an independent proprietary school, Tiffin Business University. After various name changes over the years, this same business school still thrives today as neighboring Tiffin University.

Heidelberg continued to streamline programs well into the 1920s, dropping both their graduate degree offerings and rechartering again to resume college status in the summer of 1928. Miller pushed for this change with the regents, citing a regional trend among other comparable schools and that the name "college" better reflected Heidelberg's present mission and numbers of degrees conferred.

The start of World War I disrupted life at Heidelberg. Many male students immediately left school to join the military in 1917, dropping enrollment from 650 to 484 that year and then down to 331 in 1918. The War Department organized a Students Army Training Corps on campus to prepare the remaining male students to qualify as army officers. Fortunately the U.S. involvement in the war was quite brief, so many of Heidelberg's soldiers soon returned from Europe, resuming their studies.

By 1920 both enrollment and fund-raising returned to their prewar momentum, with Miller announcing a generous gift of $75,000 from Goodyear Corporation president and former Heidelberg student Frank A. Seiberling to build a new gymnasium. Soon other gifts arrived, including a surprise pledge of $150,000 from oilman John D. Rockefeller given through the General Education Board. Earmarked for improving faculty salaries, Rockefeller donated the money contingent on matching funds from Heidelberg for that same purpose. Rockefeller's gift was soon followed by the "princely sum" of $160,000 given by Tiffin businessman Lewis Selle. Inspired by this good fortune, Miller set the endowment goal even higher, announcing his plans to reach the $1 million mark. The enthusiasm surrounding the school's seventy-fifth anniversary celebration only helped his fund-raising efforts, with alumni, students, and church members giving generously. The prosperity and inflation of the 1920s caused the endowment to swell, but the good times abruptly ended with the stock market crash in 1929.

America's economy plummeted in the two years following the crash of the stock market. Bank failures, widespread unemployment, and mortgage foreclosures plagued the land, and Heidelberg was not immune. Between 1931 and 1934 faculty salaries fell by 25 percent, and President Miller reduced his own by a third. The board of trustees mandated a new faculty retirement age of seventy, which some professors angrily protested. Unable to meet tuition payments, many students left school. As the stock market tumbled, so did Heidelberg's proud endowment of the 1920s. Building plans came to an abrupt halt. Frank Seiberling's recent gift of $75,000 in Goodyear stock shrank to a fraction of its original value, suspending the gymnasium construction, which finally took place twenty years later. Shrinking resources brought a multitude of problems to the Heidelberg campus.

In addition to the college's financial woes, Miller contended with a growing rebellious spirit within the student body. All across the country the ongoing economic crisis led to sharp political division and conflict between conservatives and advocates of extreme change. Many Americans argued that the status quo was insufficient and demanded reforms. Others believed the established order to be sound, optimistic that "prosperity is just around the corner." Radicalized by these national debates, a group of Heidelberg students suddenly demanded increased freedoms and control over campus decisions. Specifically, these students called for an end to the college's ban on card playing, dancing, and smoking tobacco.

Personnel issues also came into the fray, with students openly criticizing certain faculty members and administrators during public mass meetings. After much debate Miller finally relented on the dancing and cards but kept his restrictions in place on tobacco. His concession, however, did not quell the many controversies, which continued to escalate, eventually to the point of serious violence. In the early hours of June 1, 1935, someone exploded a dynamite bomb against the front of President Miller's home on Greenfield Street, causing extensive damage but no injuries. Though police never arrested a suspect in the case, or even ascertained a motive, the incident underscored the hostilities on campus at that time. The trustees affirmed their support for Miller, but he chose to retire less than two years later. After thirty-five successful years as president, and now seventy-years-old, Miller believed that Heidelberg needed a change in leadership.

In 1937 Clarence E. Josephson succeeded Miller, becoming Heidelberg's seventh president, and inheriting severe economic and social problems. Josephson assumed the Heidelberg presidency at a difficult time, starting the job during the most desperate year of the Depression. Undaunted he immediately confronted the college's revenue shortfall by opening evening classes for adults at the Tiffin YMCA and reorganizing the faculty's retirement program. Addressing other concerns, Josephson also took a firm stand against the growing dissension on campus, using his opening speech to call for a stronger Christian culture at Heidelberg.

Serving until 1945, his administration was one of constant crisis, going directly from economic disaster to world war. The coming of World War II did restore prosperity to the campus, but it also once again called away most of Heidelberg's male students and virtually eliminated freshmen applications from young men. Most healthy males enlisted in the military by late 1941, causing enrollments to dwindle. The college itself, however, was not so wholly committed to the war effort. Though Josephson described the war as a moral Christian duty, several students, faculty members, and trustees declared themselves conscientious objectors and urged that Heidelberg be officially opposed to American involvement.

Respectfully acknowledging their antiwar position, Josephson and the board of trustees chose instead to issue a formal invitation to the War Department to use the college's facilities. The school extended this offer to both assist in the war effort and, not insignificantly, to receive desperately needed income. The government accepted the offer, opening an Army Specialized Training Program on campus, housing 270 soldiers in the empty men's dormitories and feeding them in the College Commons. Designed to train highly skilled technicians, Army officers ran the program, but Heidelberg professors taught many of the science and technical classes. As the program grew larger, the Army built numerous temporary barracks on the lawns of the campus, making the college more resemble a military post. This convenient arrangement between Heidelberg and the federal government continued until the end of the war when the training unit disbanded. Though an inconvenience in some ways, hosting these soldiers kept the college financially afloat during what otherwise would have been disastrous years. With the generous rental fees paid by the military, and the continued strong female enrollment during the war, Heidelberg ended 1945 in fine fiscal standing. With stability restored, Josephson left the college that same year to accept a senior government position in Washington. He was followed at Heidelberg by Dr. Nevin C. Harner.

The United States experienced unprecedented prosperity after the war, and higher education boomed. At the beginning of the 1946–47 school year, Harner announced a record enrollment of 660, including 275 war veterans. The spring semester found 685 students in the classroom. Coming to Heidelberg through the tuition and stipend benefits of the GI Bill of Rights, many of these returning soldiers and sailors were older than traditional prewar Heidelberg students, often from more diverse ethnic and class backgrounds and married. Their war experience, age, and family responsibilities caused these new students to approach their studies with greater seriousness, frequently disregarding the literary societies, sports, and other extracurricular activities. To house all these new students—up to 817 by 1948—the college used the barracks erected by the army during the war and accepted a 6,000-square-foot metal gymnasium from the Federal Works Administration. To build more permanent accommodations, Harner called for a new capital campaign to add needed facilities, quickly raising almost a half-million dollars. Soon after his fund-raising success, however, Harner decided to end his presidency after less than three years, citing ill health.

The board of trustees unanimously chose William Terry Wickham as Harner's successor, ushering in the college's first layman to serve as president. From the very start of his administration, Wickham demonstrated exceptional leadership skill and strength, eventually guiding the school through over two decades of turbulence and growth. During his inauguration he announced a seven-point development and academic plan to advance the college into its second century. Wickham also immediately began erecting new buildings, long delayed because of the Depression and wartime hardship. As a first step he directed the construction of a new facility for the Conservatory of Music. Wickham then announced his goal to finally build the long-awaited gymnasium, to be named for donor Frank Seiberling. Presiding over the centennial celebration activities in 1950, he nurtured the endowment to $1,143,000, allowing for even more building. During Wickham's twenty-one years in office, the college also built four modern dormitories, a dining hall, a health center, a science center, and purchased an elementary school adjacent to campus from the Tiffin City School Board for use as classrooms and offices.

Though these new buildings added needed space to the Heidelberg campus, Terry Wickham initiated even greater changes in the curriculum and college community.

Keeping pace with national trends and strengthening admission criteria, he mandated either the SAT or ACT exams for all incoming freshman. Upon arriving at the college, these freshmen participated in the new General Studies program, designed to better link together different areas of study. To expand students' social and cultural awareness, Wickham implemented a semester-long exchange program with several traditionally African American colleges and a yearlong program in Heidelberg, Germany. Athletics also became more important to campus life during Wickham's administration, as the school fielded a wide variety of new intercollegiate teams, including baseball, tennis, and golf. In addition to sports, the music program was a point of great pride for the college, featuring its nationally acclaimed choir, led by Professor Ferris Ohl.

Enrollment remained strong throughout Wickham's years, though fluctuating sometimes due to the size of the college-bound cohort. At the time of his retirement in 1969, Heidelberg's dormitories strained to accommodate more than 1,200 full-time undergraduates, the result of strong birth years during the baby boom. The endowment also continued to swell, and the future of the college seemed bright.

Organizational changes added even more to Heidelberg's growing prosperity. A new denominational affiliation with the United Church of Christ further enhanced the college's pool of potential students and its list of possible contributors. Formed through a merger of the Evangelical and Reformed Church with the Congregational Christians in 1957, this new combined denomination covered a much broader geographic area and a more ethnically diverse membership. (Heidelberg still continues its affiliation with the United Church of Christ today, but many of the overt religious manifestations, such as mandatory chapel attendance, have long ago disappeared.)

Unfortunately, new problems greatly disturbed this era of prosperity. Turbulence plagued the 1960s, with many American campuses exploding in protests and riots. All across the country students decried the Vietnam War and racial inequality, leading marches, seizing and burning campus buildings, and temporarily closing down their colleges. Unrest came to Heidelberg later than to most other schools, beginning in late 1969 when the Black Student Union brought a list of demands to newly inaugurated president Leslie H. Fishel. These students insisted that the college immediately initiate programs and hirings designed to bring more black faculty and students to Heidelberg. A noted scholar of African American history, Fishel sympathized with the group's goals but firmly rejected any ultimatums. Serious racial tension followed Fishel's refusal, but it quickly was overshadowed by the growing outcry against the war.

The shooting of four students at Kent State University by the Ohio National Guard finally propelled Heidelberg students into action. They organized and held a march around campus on May 5, 1970. President Fishel urged faculty and administrators to participate in the march; he ordered the flags flown at half-mast for the students killed and suggested that the war be discussed in every class. Student leaders next called for a total campus strike, effectively closing down the college for the next three days. Once again President Fishel supported this student-led movement, even sending letters to all their parents calling the strike "a well-managed student effort to devote time to . . . the critical problems of war, racism, poverty, population, and environment which plague us all." Protest activities continued until the May 24 commencement weekend, when most of the students returned home for their summer break. Fishel praised the student action for being peaceful and dignified. Renewed opposition to the war occurred two years later when the Student Senate coordinated a two-day "moratorium," including teach-ins, a candlelight march into Tiffin, and protest messages sent to President Richard Nixon.

The end of the war reduced student activism at Heidelberg, allowing Fishel more time and energy to run the college. Rather than just constantly reacting to crises and demands, he could now work to improve programs and formulate ideas for the future. Fishel began by implementing a Management by Objectives program in 1971, attempting to prioritize long- and short-term goals. The next year he ordered the development of an affirmative action program to foster greater ethnic and gender diversity among the faculty. Keeping pace with technology, he brought in the college's first computer system. In addition to these progressive policy changes, Fishel also built a theater and a maintenance facility and expanded the music conservatory.

Though he successfully led the college through stressful times, the college faced serious economic problems in the late 1970s with a shrinking freshman applicant pool. Tuition driven since its founding, Heidelberg had expanded its facilities, programs and faculty during the enrollment heyday of the late 1960s and early 1970s. As the baby boomers dwindled in number, enrollment took a sharp drop, from 1,265 in 1969 to 866 ten years later. At the same time, contributions from the church decreased, increasing the revenue shortfall. The operating budget bottom line fell from a $2,714,000 gain in 1973–74 to a $436,576 loss just four years later. The board of trustees asked Fishel to reduce the number of faculty and to find other ways to cut expenses. Losses continued, placing the college in an increasingly precarious financial position. Finally, after years of both success and failure, Fishel stepped down from his presidency in June 1980.

Succeeding Leslie Fishel as president in the summer of 1980 was not an enviable position. When the trustees chose William Cassell for the job, many doubted that the college could ever financially recover. As a career fund-raiser and most recently president of the College of Idaho, the trustees hoped that Cassell could balance the budget and restore the college's fiscal strength. Conditions worsened, however, and in early 1981 auditors from Ernst and Whinney suggested the possibilities of "merger or dissolution." In light of this critical situation, Cassell took the extreme action of using endowment funds to cover needed operating expenses. In addition to spending endowment money, he fired professors, and the college reduced its admission requirements, welcoming in more international students and lower-achieving American applicants. Deficits, however, plagued the college until 1985, when its annual ledger finally returned to the black. Cassell repaid an outstanding loan the following year, then kept the college flourishing for the next decade. He looked abroad for still more revenue, seeking more and more international students from all around the world and even opening a branch campus in Japan. Under Cassell's leadership the college also began graduate programs in both business and counseling, in addition to creating an extension site for returning adults in suburban Toledo. By the time he left office in 1996, Heidelberg was not only financially stable but had also greatly expanded its program offerings.

Prosperity and stability still prevailed as the college approached its sesquicentennial celebration in 2000. Combined undergraduate and graduate enrollments reached record highs, and the bull market of the late 1990s significantly boosted Heidelberg's endowment. Most importantly, the college continues the tradition which it started a century and a half earlier of educating individuals who go forth to make our society strong. Though living in a radically different world than in 1850, these Heidelberg graduates still teach children, conduct business, and preach from church pulpits. True to its origins, the college continues successfully preparing Ohioans for meaningful careers and fulfilling lives of service.

Suggested Reading

E. I. F. Williams, *Heidelberg: Democratic Christian College, 1850–1950* (George Banta Publishing, 1952); Philip Harner, *Heidelberg College: In Service and in Faith, 1850–2000*.

Hiram College

A View from the Hill

DAVID R. ANDERSON

From its inception, Hiram College was marked by independence, tolerance, and the struggle for survival. Founded in June 1849 by a meeting of Campbellites in South Russell, the Western Reserve Eclectic Institute, as it was first known, opened its markedly Greek revival doors to students in November 1850. The relatively isolated village of Hiram in northeast Portage County had been chosen as the location, according to an early circular, "in the midst of a farming population, as moral and accommodating as any other—and a location as salubrious as any in the world." Amos Sutton Hayden, a young preacher-musician from Cleveland, was named principal and joined two other men and three women to form the first faculty of the fledgling school. Their students were male and female, an important distinction in that time. Norman Dunshee, a member of the first faculty, remarked in 1857 that "the fountain of knowledge should be open to all—male and female—and freely dispense its blessings, irrespective of cast or condition."

The Eclectic Institute, like so many Ohio secondary institutions, was established by a Protestant denomination in order to encourage the formation of an educated laity. The Campbellites (who were influenced by the egalitarian teachings of Alexander Campbell in the 1820s) had attempted to create an American church on ecumenical principles to overcome the splintering of Christianity into rival denominations. Sectarian proselytizing, characteristic of many nineteenth-century educational institutions, went against the grain of the founders of the Western Reserve Eclectic Institute. A. S. Hayden articulated this most clearly in the first catalog: "It is important to state, explicitly, that nothing is to be taught in this Seminary under color of these Biblical lessons, or otherwise, partaking in the least degree of sectarian character." This has remained fundamental to the college's mission from its opening day.

Old Main, also called Hinsdale Hall, 1850–1969

The founders chose for the school's official seal a dove bearing an olive branch alighting on an open book, with the rays of the rising sun in the background. The motto "Let There Be Light" accompanied the image. Appropriately, the original classroom building faced east, and students and faculty were reminded daily of the need for enlightenment.

Until 1867 the Eclectic's charter did not allow for the granting of full college degrees, so it was necessary for students to complete their education at degree-granting institutions. For some of the students this meant spending a year or two at Oberlin or Western Reserve College in Hudson. Other students went East, among them James A. Garfield of Orange, near Chagrin Falls, who, along with several of his Hiram contemporaries, chose Williams College in western Massachusetts. When he graduated in 1856, the twenty-five-year old Garfield returned to Hiram to become principal of the Eclectic. His leadership and example, perhaps more than that of any other person, marked the young school and its successor college. His own teacher from the Eclectic years was Almeda Booth, a person of remarkable intellect who saw in Garfield the makings of an important figure in American life.

Garfield's tenure as principal was marked by serious issues of economic viability for the school and strong dissension over the issue of abolition. The Disciples of Christ (as Campbellites came to be known officially), unlike many northern religious groups, held ambiguous views on slavery. For instance, Bethany College—a sister Disciple college in Virginia—seemed by many in the Disciple brotherhood to support slave ownership. For many students and several faculty at the Eclectic, the unwillingness of Disciple institutions to speak for abolition caused enormous consternation and pain.

It was not until the outbreak of the Civil War in 1861 that Garfield came to declare himself unequivocally opposed to slavery. He organized a company of Hiram village men, made up to a large extent of male students from the Eclectic Institute, as Company A of the 42nd Ohio Volunteer Infantry and went off to war in the fall of 1861. By the time the men were mustered out in late 1864, their ranks had been dramatically depleted; an inordinate number of them fell from disease or battle, and few of the living returned to college life, so that the institute was permanently changed.

Garfield left Hiram in 1863 for a life in politics, culminating in his election as the twentieth president of the United States in 1881. He maintained strong ties with the college until his untimely death in September of the same year by an assassin's bullet. During his last visit to Hiram as president-elect, he addressed the students from the heart: "May the time never come when I cannot find some food for mind and heart on Hiram Hill!" Other than Woodrow Wilson at Princeton, no American president has been as closely associated with a college than James A. Garfield and Hiram.

The Western Reserve Eclectic Institute attained collegiate status in 1867, and the name was changed to Hiram College. Burke Aaron Hinsdale, the college's first president, was important both as a pedagogue and as an historian (his groundbreaking work *The Old Northwest* appeared in 1888). He introduced a modern collegiate curriculum. Just as important for the college, his close friendship with Garfield, who had been his teacher, confirmed in him the need for independent status from interference in affairs of the college by the Church. Despite his strong feelings, he himself felt compelled to serve as part-time preacher to the local Disciples congregation. His struggle to create financial stability for the institution was barely successful, and he left Hiram in 1883 first to become superintendent of the Cleveland schools and then to complete a distinguished career as professor of the history of education at the University of Michigan.

College life in Hiram was similar to that of most American colleges of the period in that its social life was dominated by literary societies that had been founded in the Eclectic years. The societies functioned also as libraries until 1901 when their collections were combined to create a centralized college library. What extracurricular activities that existed were circumscribed by elaborate rules designed to subdue the biological imperatives of adolescents. Hiram students celebrated home-grown holidays that lived on well into the second half of the twentieth century: Campus Day in the fall, when students' natural gusto was harnessed to clear the campus of leaves, and Sugar Day in the spring, when a local sugar bush was commandeered for students and faculty to boil maple syrup together.

Idiosyncratic, however, was the custom of "perching," which referred specifically to a woman's sitting on a rung of the wooden fence that surrounded the campus while being courted by a beau. "Perching" remained synonymous with dating in Hiram until the 1960s. Alex Lee, a student from China in 1909, was so impressed by the term that he felt "afraid when I shall return to China people will say to me that all my time spent in the United States is in vain, for I have not yet learned even how to perch." As late as 1941 a student wrote that "of all Hiram traditions, perching is the most ancient and the most honored. Something about the air in Hiram makes boys prefer to be with their girls out in the open air than in any other place." The final death knell for perching was sounded in a student essay in 1972: "The grand old custom of perching has gone the way of other campus traditions; with the advent of open dorms nobody has to go to the graveyard in order to be alone."

Another example of the feistiness of the Hiram student body is indicated by the search for a team name and mascot in the 1920s. A few sports writers persisted in calling Hiram teams the Disciples. When "Hiram" became the name on the vaudeville stage for many a country bumpkin, Hiram students cringed at being called everything from "Farmers" to "Mudhens" (perhaps appropriate for football players but hardly dignified enough for basketball players who had, after all, brought home the winning trophy from the St. Louis World's Fair Universal Exposition Olympic Games in 1904). In 1928 the fierce little terrier was finally chosen to represent the college, and Hiram players have been called Terriers ever since.

In the late nineteenth century and in the early twentieth century the curriculum became more recognizably one shared by most colleges and universities, so that in 1914 Hiram was accredited by the North Central Association of Colleges and Universities. Two Hiram students, Miner Searle Bates in 1916 and Steven Kemp Bailey in 1937, were named Rhodes Scholars, a testament to the intellectual rigor of those decades. It was not until 1971 that the College was awarded a Phi Beta Kappa chapter, Mu of Ohio.

Nevertheless, as early as 1890 a writer in the college newspaper declared that "probably not the least valuable feature of Hiram life is the spirit of independence which prevails here. It is always desired that students should think for themselves."

Independence was expressed also by student rejection of national fraternities and sororities in favor of the old literary society structure that remained local and free of outside control. In 1906 the board of trustees reaffirmed its own independence by certifying to the Carnegie Foundation for Advancement of Learning that "Hiram College is non-sectarian and non-denominational in teaching and in selection of trustees, administrative officers and faculty."

Hiram students felt compelled, however, to put into action the humanitarian lessons they were learning in the classroom. George Bellamy (Class of 1896) recognized the need for social action to help the urban poor of Cleveland, whose numbers had burgeoned as the city attracted low-paid labor—many of them recent immigrants—for the rapidly expanding steel industry. Though the appeal of the pastoral life in rural Ohio no doubt tempted Hiramites to avoid the city and its problems, Bellamy and a group of his classmates established Hiram House, one of the earliest settlement houses, in the notorious Sixteenth Ward.

The physical plant of the college expanded from the solitary, original 1850 building (renovated and Victorianized in 1886) to include an auditorium/gymnasium (1895), a library and observatory (1901), and a science facility (1928), and dormitories slowly replaced the boardinghouses where students had found lodging in the village. But the hilltop campus remained small and unimposing until a building boom in the 1960s.

The beginning of the Great Depression coincided for Hiram with the administration of Kenneth I. Brown, who was named president in 1930. At thirty years of age Brown was only five years older than Garfield had been when he assumed the office of principal. Brown's inauguration on October 10, 1930, suggested anything but the privations that faced the nation. In his inaugural address he spoke of the origin of the peculiar name of the village and the college: "Was it not Hiram, King of Tyre, when that Phoenician realm was mistress of the seas and invincible from land—was it not Hiram that supplied the cedars of Lebanon for the construction of the royal palaces of David and of Solomon and for the building of Solomon's temple, and whose fleet for its furnishing fetched the gold of Ophir and of Tarshish?" His vision of biblical splendor for the tiny Western Reserve village was easily matched by the enthusiasm for Hiram that was shown by Vachel Lindsay, the populist American poet (famous for "The Congo" and "General William Booth Enters Heaven") and former Hiram student (1897–1900), who received one of the very few honorary degrees the college has ever awarded.

Lindsay composed a striking poem for the inauguration, "The Ezekiel Chant," two stanzas of which follow:

Now on this hill apart, we watch
The future through the stars astream,

Far from the towns we therefore see
In special forms Ezekiel's dream.

We see the colors of his mind
In maple sugar groves turned red;
In autumn winds through chestnut boughs
Hear special words the prophet said.

He further captured in exuberant prose written for the 1932 *Spider Web*, the college yearbook, what was for many Hiram students and alumni the special spirit of the place: "Let us plainly remember that Hiram is first of all a superb example of unspoiled Americanism. He who EXPRESSES Hiram will be an AMERICAN ARTIST. The simplicity, the willingness to be simple; the outdoors quality and the willingness to be rural; the religious tradition and the willingness to be devout; the studious tradition and the willingness to value a book, and be in earnest."

Out of the efforts to remain financially solvent in the 1930s arose one of Hiram's most interesting contributions to the pedagogy of postsecondary education. In order to make it possible for financially pressed students to attend college, Brown proposed and the faculty approved the Hiram Intensive Study Plan, which was a salient characteristic of a Hiram education for nearly thirty years. Beginning in 1934 students took nine-week intensive courses one at a time; faculty, likewise, taught one course at a time. Since this made it possible for students to enter and leave the college as their finances allowed, the Intensive Study Plan was enthusiastically embraced by students and most faculty. Though it was succeeded at Hiram by the Quarter Plan in 1961, it is still used by Cornell College in Iowa and Colorado College. It has recently returned to Hiram in the form of three-week intensive courses required of both students and faculty twice a year at the end of the fall and spring semesters.

The war years exacerbated many of the enrollment and financial problems that had always plagued Hiram. With a majority of male students removed from the campus, the college was hard pressed to maintain its program. In 1943 and 1944 a contingent of 250 Army Air Corps students was assigned to Hiram and replaced the missing scholars to provide a welcome respite from what were otherwise hard times. Eventually twenty-four of the regular students lost their lives in World War II, including women. A surge of postwar enrollment brought the college in 1946 to a record enrollment of 385, a number that for the later twentieth century would have seemed impossibly small for sustaining an educational institution.

In the centennial year of 1950 there was cause for optimism; enrollment stabilized, money was raised for a modern dormitory, theater students spent their summer plying the Ohio River aboard the showboat *Majestic* (which they did until 1958), and a group of students traveled to Europe to study for a term with a Hiram faculty member. The 1950 European trip became the basis for a study-abroad program that over the next fifty years would take Hiram students and faculty to every continent to study Hiram courses. From 1970 on students studied with Hiram history and English faculty in Cambridge, England, every fall. Language students have lived and studied with their mentors in Europe, Mexico, and Central and South America. Biologists have explored habitats as varied as the Scottish highlands and Costa Rican rainforests. Art students have lived in France, Italy, Japan, and New York City while studying with Hiram faculty. Locales as disparate as Zimbabwe and Russia have been utilized as off-campus sites. In 1954 the *Saturday Evening Post* dubbed Hiram "the Happiest College in the Land," focusing to a large extent on the goodwill that was engendered by the foreign-study program.

The baby boom, with its surge of college-age students beginning in the 1960s, affected Hiram dramatically. Physically, the college and village of Hiram had remained substantially unchanged for more than a century; when new buildings had been added in the early years of the twentieth century, buildings were moved to other locations in the village to make way for them, so that the New England character remained constant. A surge of building during the sixties, however, created dramatic alteration to the historic fabric. A music building and an art building were added to the campus. Many historic residences were razed (rather than moved) to make way for three new dormitories and a student union An empty lot is all that remains of the handsome Greek revival farmhouse of a college founder, Zeb Rudolph, in the parlor of which his daughter Lucretia married James A. Garfield.

In 1969 the original building of the Western Reserve Eclectic Institute was demolished and was replaced by a contemporary classroom building of little architectural interest or distinction. Planners had determined that colleges like Hiram should look to the future rather than becoming mired in the past. Elmer Jagow, president of the college from 1966 to 1985, remarked in his opening address in 1966 that "young people are impatient with colleges and universities that are nothing more than 'ivied' Disneylands or 'academic zoos' with pacing professors in their study or cubicles."

The shadow of Berkeley fell over much of American higher education. The contradictions inherent in decisions to rid an institution of the visible manifestations of its past became apparent. Could or should a college with more than a century of contribution to higher education simply turn its back on its links to the past? Hardly had the dust settled from the removal of Old Main than efforts were initiated to restore the historic buildings that remained; today the Hiram campus is, ironically, a model for the sensitive conversion of old structures to academic use. Bonney Castle, Bancroft House, Pendleton House, Bowler Hall, the Hiram Inn, Jessie Smith House, and Mahan House are beloved icons of the commitment of the college to historic preservation.

Despite its rural isolation, Hiram was not spared the student unrest of the late sixties and early seventies. In the spring of 1969 African American students occupied the main classroom building to call attention to their grievances. Assisted by Title IX of the Civil Rights Act of 1970, female students were finally able to participate in intercollegiate sports. Students demanded and were afforded a larger say in decision-making bodies in the institution.

The tragic events of May 4, 1970, at Kent State University deeply affected the Hiram community because of the proximity of that campus. Students demonstrated their solidarity with their Portage County neighbor by voting to strike, which was endorsed by faculty and administrators by a nearly unanimous vote. Given the volatility in nearby communities, it was a courageous decision. A statement at the time made clear that "peace is the emphasis being placed on the five-day strike. Both student leaders and administrators see peaceful protest as the most effective way of achieving their goals."

There were varied responses to the dramatic changes that were taking place in society. Helped by a major grant from the National Endowment for the Humanities, the faculty introduced the New Curriculum in 1969, which fundamentally rethought first-year courses and general education. Interdisciplinary study was particularly encouraged, which led in the 1980s to another NEH funded program, "Regionalism in the Humanities," involving a significant number of faculty and students. The results drew national attention to the college, and, though much revised, elements of the programs are still an important part of a Hiram education at the beginning of the twenty-first century.

In 1973 Hiram's enrollment peaked at an all-time high of 1,320 students. Forecasters, though, predicted an eventual shortfall of college-age students toward the end of the decade. To ensure a steadier influx of new students, in 1977 the Hiram Weekend College was introduced to provide nontraditional, adult students with the identical curriculum leading to the B.A. of its other undergraduates. It was the first program of its type in Ohio and only the second in the nation (after Mundelein College in Chicago). Between 1932 and 1937 an attempt had been made to establish a branch campus in Warren, Ohio, to address some of the same needs as the Weekend College, but it foundered with the economic uncertainties of the Great Depression. By extending educational opportunity to otherwise neglected constituencies, the Weekend College has, in its twenty-five years, proven to be a significant participant in the ideals put forward by the founders of the college in 1850.

A successful $42 million capital campaign, the first in nearly half a century, concluded in 1997. It provided for a striking new library (graced with the restored original college clock from Old Main) and a sorely needed modern science facility. The oldest dormitory, Bowler Hall (1879), was thoroughly renovated and remains as one of the most sought-after residences on the campus.

Students, faculty, and alumni in recent years have embraced, as seldom before, the idea that Hiram College is rooted in a historical tradition that informs the present. Part of the mission statement, which was adopted by the trustees in 1990, states that the college is a "mentoring community [that] honors our historical traditions and environment." Now more than halfway toward completion of a second century (the college celebrated its sesquicentennial in 1999–2000), Hiram's place in postsecondary education in Ohio and in the nation is secure. Kenneth I. Brown wrote concerning Hiram in his book *A Campus Decade,* "No one studying the educational life of America will question the meritorious role which Hiram has played. Northeastern Ohio and especially the city of Cleveland have profited by the wise leadership of Hiram-trained men and women. And far beyond the state, beyond the oceans and below the Gulf, the influence of Hiram, standing for scholarship and character, has spread." Sixty years later Brown's valedictory words to Hiram retain the ring of truth.

Suggested Reading

Kenneth I. Brown, *A Campus Decade* (University of Chicago Press, 1940).

John Carroll University

Coeducation and Conscience

MARY ANN JANOSIK

"Individuals shape institutions and institutions shape society." Father Glynn's quotation, taken from the *Spiritual Exercises of St. Ignatius,* is particularly fitting when examining the history and community of John Carroll University, nestled in the upper-middle-class residential suburb of University Heights, Ohio, ten miles east of Cleveland. John Carroll University, one of twenty-eight American colleges and universities operated by the Society of Jesus, was founded in 1886 as St. Ignatius College. A continuous degree-granting institution since that time, the college was renamed John Carroll University in 1923, after the first archbishop of the Catholic Church in the United States. Originally located on Cleveland's west side, the university was relocated to University Heights in 1935, where it continues to grow and expand physically, intellectually, and spiritually.

In its 117-year history John Carroll University has expressed and often embodied many of the social and political issues that challenged the American Catholic Church in general and Catholic higher education in particular. The ongoing historical debate over whether being a good Catholic is complementary or contradictory to being a good American has penetrated the university's castlelike walls, but it has not impeded its development as a viable American Catholic institution either. As the university enters its second century and a new millenium, it can proudly attest to having overcome obstacles, met challenges to its meaning and development, and embraced American ideals without compromising Jesuit tradition.

Situated in sixty acres that house eight residence halls and five academic buildings (including the newly renovated Grasselli Library and Breen Learning Center), John Carroll University offers fifty-eight bachelor's and master's degree programs. Full-time undergraduates consistently number around 3,400, with the student body

totaling somewhere near 4,500. Seventy-five percent of those who enter as fresh-men graduate, earning the university a first place in both average graduation rate and freshman retention rate among Midwest regional schools.

A stable and distinguished faculty complement the university's steady enroll-ment and matriculation. Of the 228 full-time and 164 part-time faculty, 89 percent hold a doctoral degree or the highest degree in their field, 62.9 percent are tenured,

20.2 percent are on tenure track. Only 17 percent are visiting faculty, and eleven faculty members are Fulbright scholars. The small student-faculty ratio (15:1) promotes quality learning in an environment that focuses on the total person. Faculty members are not only professionally qualified but also student oriented, and they value interpersonal relationships equally with academic achievement.

As a Jesuit university John Carroll University draws its intellectual and educational resources from more than four centuries of the teaching and administrative experience offered by the Society of Jesus. Jesuits on the John Carroll University faculty and in its administration help impart the unique character and value of a Jesuit education and, together with other religious and lay faculty and staff, share the educational practice of service to its students and the community.

What John Carroll University's faculty, administration, and staff express is what sociologist Andrew Greeley called the "dialogical imagination of [American] Catholics" (*Catholic Myth* [1990]: 45–47). Greeley's dialogic, like theologian David Tracy's analogical imagination, "are phrases used to describe a distinctively Catholic way of understanding the world. Using the works of Thomas Aquinas, Martin Luther, John Calvin, and Max Weber, both Greeley and Tracy define the fundamental difference between Catholics and Protestants as one that emphasizes the needs of the community over the wants of the individual. A Protestant vision of the world centers on the distance between God and man, while the Catholic imagination celebrates God's presence in the world. That world, and the individuals who make up its various communities, is flawed. It is here, between its mission to imbue educational values consistent with the Jesuit tradition and its desire to remain competitive as a viable American institution of higher learning, that John Carroll University bridges the gap between individual achievement and community responsibility. In doing so, the University begins to address critical ideological issues about how its mission can encompass a definition of "community" that goes beyond the original intentions of Jesuit teaching and learning without losing its fundamentally Catholic core.

As a university John Carroll is committed to communicating and expanding the treasury of human knowledge with the individual autonomy and freedom of thought appropriate to any university, secular or religious. As a Catholic university it is further committed to "seek and synthesize all knowledge, including the wisdom of Christian revelation." In seeking this integration of knowledge, the university community is enriched and encourages scholarship that represents the pluralistic society in which we live. All members of the university community can participate freely and openly in the intellectual, moral, and spiritual dialogue necessary to the search. Within this dialogue, philosophical and theological questions play a critical role, and students have the freedom to find, design, and live a value system based on the following: respect for and critical evaluation of the facts; intellectual, moral, and spiritual values that enable them to cope with new problems; and the sensitivity and judgment that prepare them to engage in responsible social action.

In a Jesuit university the presence of Jesuits and others are inspired by Ignatius Loyola, founder of the Society of Jesus, through his *Spiritual Exercises*. The source of Jesuit life and activity, the Spiritual Exercises reflect the value system of the Gospels and bring to education "a rationality appropriately balanced by human affection, an esteem for the individual as a unique person, training in discerning choice, openness to change, and a quest for God's greater glory in the use of this world's goods" (*The Jesuit Tradition*).

The educational priorities expressed through Ignatius's *Spiritual Exercises* speak to the notion of educating the whole person and, in the last quarter of the twentieth century, represented something new to Catholic higher education—what historian Philip Gleason has identified as the American Catholic struggle with modernity. In his book *Contending with Modernity: American Catholic Higher Education in the Twentieth Century,* Gleason presents the history of Catholic higher education in terms of challenge and response: "external cultural and ideological challenges and internal Catholic religious responses." Seeing the debates over Americanism and modernism early in the twentieth century as the impetus for debates that would culminate during the 1960s, Gleason identifies the struggle of Catholic higher education in terms of the Church's institutional and ideological confrontation with modernism.

For example, while Catholic colleges and universities, like their secular and other denominational counterparts, expanded their graduate programs during the 1920s and 1930s, these programs were primarily intended to prepare future teachers for colleges and secondary schools. Graduate education at Catholic universities and colleges did not focus on research and creative scholarship, even though there was a growing consciousness to move in that direction (Carey, 142). What Gleason suggested here is that, prior to the 1960s, Catholic higher education (and perhaps even Catholic education in general) was more internally focused, more insular in its mission directed more to preserve its own community rather than extend beyond its own ideological parameters. At John Carroll University (and other Jesuit schools) college traditions, celebrations, rgulations, and the physical setting all contained conscious (or unconscious) assumptions that shaped the campus culture and community. Those traditions were essential to carrying out the values intrinsic to a Jesuit education.

Too, the neoscholastic antimodernism that became the philosophical core of the Catholic mind-set between the two world wars gave Catholic education "a firm and unified sense of its identity in the world," forcing Catholic higher education to become internally static, challenging modernity rather than growing with it. For some Catholics this insular institutional organization was necessary to protect against the anti-Catholicism that resurfaced during the 1950s. For others insularization was just the thing that would keep Catholic higher education from coexisting with its secular counterparts.

And although Gleason contends that the 1950s marked a decade of relative continuity in the American Catholic Church, it was also a period that "awakened some Catholic intellectuals to a kind of self-criticism that called for institutional and intellectual changes that were more consistent with democratic and American values" (Carey, 143). Gleason also identifies other forces that called for change in thinking among Catholic intellectuals: the new scholarship—especially debates over intellectual excellence inspired by John Tracy Ellis—and the breaking apart of the scholastic synthesis, reinforced postwar Catholic liberalism and prepared the way for more radical changes that would occur in the next decade.

Thus, the Catholic notion of community and its relationship to American culture would undergo dramatic reinterpretation in the post–Vatican II era, not so much to change the ideological foundations of the Church but rather to integrate Catholic values into American society at large. The profound effects of the institutional, cultural, religious, and ideological revolutions of the 1960s climaxed "the transition from an era in which Catholic educators *challenged* modernity to one in which they *accepted* modernity." At John Carroll University the acceptance of modernity followed closely the intellectual ferment described above.

In specific, the acceptance of modernity can be seen drastically in its decision in 1968 to become a coeducational institution. Following the lead of Georgetown University and joining more than half of the twenty-eight Jesuit institutions that adopted coeducation in the 1960s and early 1970s, John Carroll University adopted coeducation in 1968. The university's decision to do so took place within the context that Catholic higher education had been more sexually segregated than its Protestant or secular counterparts. Even though coeducation in America began in 1833 at Oberlin College and spread to more than two-thirds of American colleges and universities by the turn of the twentieth century, Catholic institutions of higher education did not embrace this overwhelming trend.

The first Catholic university to admit women was Marquette University, which did so in 1909. Other Catholic colleges and universities were slow to follow, claiming that Catholic tradition and culture supported single-sex education. Because the Church taught that men and women have unique roles in life and education should be separate and appropriate to their spheres of activities, the goal of education for women was "the development of the future mother and homemaker." To this end women needed to be taught by women along the lines demanded "by women's nature" (Shields, 37).

For some Catholic educators the female domestic ideal disavowed any need for higher education. For others fear that coeducation would encourage promiscuity or relationships with non-Catholics became a strong argument in favor of single-sex schools. The Catholic tradition of single-sex education was further reinforced by the single-sex nature of religious orders, many of which had established Catholic colleges and universities in the United States. In addition, there was also concern that coeducation would drive men and women away from religious vocations, particularly men, since entry into seminaries reached a peak in the mid-1960s. Between 1945 and 1965 the American Catholic Church experienced an unprecedented growth in membership, in vocations to religious orders and the priesthood, and in enrollments in parochial primary and secondary schools. This growth would later have an impact on the governmental policies made for Catholic schools' funding, on increased competition between public and private schools, and how Americans (Catholic and non-Catholic) viewed Catholic education. As Catholicism broadened to embrace some of the social and moral issues of its time, so did Catholic institutions of higher learning. But the changes (both real and perceived) brought on by decisions to become coeducational also brought new conflicts and challenges.

At John Carroll the arrival of women on campus was met initially with skepticism and concern. Skeptical that women could compete with men in disciplines such as business, philosophy, and history, many faculty and administrative staff feared that the curriculum would need to be watered down in order for women to succeed. On a more practical level, the need to rearrange dorm assignments and create single-sex classes for courses in physical education created other logistical challenges.

One John Carroll faculty member, who began her career as a physical education instructor for the newly admitted women, had said that the presence of women on campus in classrooms, dormitories, and dining halls left many male faculty uncertain about the future of the college. Concerns ranged from the notion that male students would become disenchanted with the inclusion of women and turn away from what had been a traditionally male-focused Jesuit education to the perception that women on campus (students, faculty, and administrative staff) would somehow alter the definition of what Catholic education meant.

In both areas the fears proved unwarranted, and the university not only survived its coeducational status but thrived. By opening its doors to men and women, religious and lay, Catholic and non-Catholic, John Carroll University accepted modernity and widened its community sphere. No longer would Catholic education be synonymous with simply becoming a better Catholic but, now, with becoming a better human being. In this way the ideological core of the Second Vatican Council, its spirit of ecumenism through a kind of democratization of the Church, allowed the opportunity for greater participation from its followers and a broadening of its concept of community. The "Catholic Imagination" could no longer apply only to Catholics but to a greater commitment to the human community that binds us all.

Since 1968 John Carroll's curriculum mirrors its mission to educate the whole person, echoing the words of its founder: "Freedom and independence, acquired by united efforts, and cemented with the mingled blood of Protestant and Catholic fellow-citizens, should be equally enjoyed by all." As head of the missions in the provinces of the United States (1784–90), John Carroll made clear the Church's spirit of ecumenism and need for the inclusion of all people in a common spirit of freedom and friendship. Two hundred years later the Jesuit mission at the university founded in his name continues to do the same.

John Carroll's student, staff, and faculty handbooks speak to its commitment to educating the whole person. Prospective visiting and adjunct faculty are oriented to this vision as intensely as full-time faculty and staff. Workshops are held to introduce students, faculty, and staff to the values outlined by the Jesuit tradition and the application of those values in the classroom. Students are required to take a range of courses to acquaint them with social and moral issues that challenge the world community, not just their immediate world. Faculty members are expected to be sensitive to increasingly important issues involving diversity, multiculturalism, and alternative lifestyles. The education department, for example, requires all teacher education majors to take a course entitled "Multiculturalism in a Pluralistic Society" as an introduction to the many social and cultural issues faced in today's classroom. Some faculty members who teach this course invite representatives from a variety of ethnic, cultural, and religious backgrounds to share their experiences with students. At one recent class meeting, members of Cleveland's Gay and Lesbian Alliance spoke to students about the individual challenges they face as gays and lesbians. The appearance of gay and lesbian Catholics in this multicultural class gave John Carroll's students the opportunity to engage in a dialogue with individuals practicing a lifestyle choice seemingly at odds with the Catholic Church. In this way the opportunity to examine the facts about diverse populations and to compare them with their own stereotypes and misperceptions became a learning tool, one that will better prepare them, as future educators, to engage in responsible social action.

Subtle curriculum changes like this one have been underscored by solid administrative and faculty support for a diverse population and an overall embracing of a renewed sense of community that goes beyond American Catholics. In the late 1990s John Carroll University launched its own Institute of Catholic Studies, which focuses on both the traditional spirit and history of the Catholic Church worldwide as well as on contemporary issues, ideas, and challenges to the faith in the twenty-first century.

Additional recognition from national and regional surveys has helped to solidify John Carroll University's success in moving from a tradition, same-sex Jesuit institution to a diverse coeducational university that propagates Catholic values through an intense, critical examination of other ideologies and values. In September 2000 *U.S. News and World Report* ranked John Carroll University fourth-best among Midwest regional universities, tying it with Bradley University and the University of Dayton. John Carroll University has been listed in the publication's top-ten rankings of midwestern regional universities since 1989. The rankings were based on an analysis of the school's academic reputation, percentage of classes with fewer than twenty and fewer than fifty students, student-faculty ratio, percentage of full-time faculty, student selectivity, and alumni giving rates. *U.S. News and World Report* also named John Carroll University one of the Midwest's best values in college education, sharing fifteenth place with Creighton University, a Jesuit school in Nebraska.

Responding to the news of John Carroll's high rankings, John Gladstone, associate academic vice president for enrollment services, said, "John Carroll University continues to offer the very best education to a highly qualified student population. As our demographic reach continues to grow, so too does the good news about this excellent university. In areas of academic reputation, student satisfaction and affordability, John Carroll is shining brightly. *U.S. News and World Report*'s recognition of these facts is gratifying."

Gladstone's comments represent a keen awareness of John Carroll University's growth in the years since it adopted coeducation. It also suggests that while the university continues to move in sync with modern American social issues, more work is needed to increase student diversity on campus, not just in curriculum or class discussion. The person to spearhead that movement perhaps best personifies an optimism that the university will, too, achieve this goal.

In 2000 the John Carroll community welcomed the Reverend Edward Glynn as its new president. Father Glynn's appointment came after the tragic and unexpected death of Father Michael Lavelle in 1997, a well-liked and beloved leader of the university. A Pennsylvania native, Glynn's introduction to the Jesuit tradition came from a hometown parishioner whose "kindness enable him to attend [the] nearby Scranton Preparatory School." He later graduated from the University of Scranton and earned additional degrees at Fordham University, Woodstock College, Yale Divinity School, and the Graduate Theological Union in Berkeley, California. He entered the Jesuit Noviate in 1955 and was ordained in 1967.

Father Glynn's career is much like the Jesuit educational tradition the university endorses, for he embodies the quest for lifelong education of the whole person. Professional experiences in teaching, writing, and administration have taken him from Gonzaga High School in Washington, D.C., to Gonzaga University in Spokane, Washington, and from *America Magazine* to Georgetown University. Prior to his appointment as president at John Carroll University, he served on its board of trustees (1987–90) and was homilist at the inauguration Mass for the late Father Lavelle. The son of a prizefighter and a lifelong Boston Red Sox fan, Glynn is a genuine Renaissance man, one who understands the common man, inspires greatness in all he meets, and aspires to emulate the Spiritual Exercises that he values so dearly. His concept of the institutional mission embraces the individual, the institution, and their place within society as a whole. In the coming years, his most important directive will be maintaining the high standard of excellence that has come to be associated with John Carroll University, more than just the "Jesuit University in Cleveland."

The double-edged sword faced by Catholic educational institutions in the United States—the delicate balancing act that suspends them between the rock of Catholic doctrine and a hard place of a competitive curriculum— is not new to John Carroll University. During the past thirty-five years the university has accepted its most critical challenge: adopting coeducation while maintaining the strong philosophical foundation rooted in the Jesuit tradition. In doing so the university has not only demonstrated the viability of Vatican II's ecumenism but has shown that in America individualism can work hand in hand with community and that being a good Catholic is not inherently in conflict with being a good American. The two, in fact, can coexist quite compatibly. The proof is right here on John Carroll University's campus.

SUGGESTED READING

Alice Gallin, *Negotiating Identity: Catholic Higher Education since 1960* (Notre Dame University Press, 2000); Alice Gallin, ed., *American Catholic Higher Education: Essential Documents* (Notre Dame University Press, 1992); Michael Galligan-Stierle, ed., *Gospel on Campus* (1996); Donald Gavin, *John Carroll University: A Century of Service* (Kent State University Press, 1985); Philip Gleason, *Contending with Modernity: Catholic Higher Education in the Twentieth Century* (Oxford University Press, 1995); Michael J. Hunt, *Catholic Colleges: A New Counterculture* (Thomas More Press, 1993); MaryAnn Janosik, "Black Patent Leather Shoes Really Do Reflect Us: Family, Community, and Traditional Values in Two Generations of Hollywood Film," *U.S. Catholic Historian* 13 (Fall 1995): 97–116; William P. Leahy, *Adapting to America: Catholics, Jesuits, and Higher Education in the 20th Century* (Georgetown University Press, 1991); David Murphy, ed., *What I Believe: Catholic College Students Discuss Their Faith* (Paulist Press, 1985); Patrick J. Murphy, ed., *Visions and Values in Catholic Higher Education* (Sheed and Ward, 1991); David J. O'Brien, *From the Heart of the American Church: Catholic Higher Education and American Culture* (Orbis Books, 1994); Susan L. Poulson, "From Single-Sex to Coeducation: The Advent of Coeducation at Georgetown 1965–1975," *U.S. Catholic Historian* 13 (Fall 1995): 117–38.

Kenyon College

From the Kenyon of the Bishops to the
Kenyon of the Presidents

PERRY LENTZ

At 1:30 on the afternoon of Memorial Day 1892, William Foster Peirce descended from the No. 3 train of the C.A. & C. at Gambier, Ohio. Before him was a small sandstone station standing just southeast of a forested hill. A gravel highway ran northward, paralleling the hill, and then turned left to ascend it. On the crown of the hill he saw a massive stone building adorned with spires and a second stone building a hundred yards beyond. Peirce was at Gambier to interview for a position. He set out up the road.

He was twenty-four, tall, lean, and had the eagle profile of the New England Protestant aristocracy. He was from Chicopee, Massachusetts, had graduated from Amherst in 1888 with a degree in philosophical studies, and had entered graduate school at Cornell. He had married Louise Fagan, a fellow graduate student. With his doctoral degree in history and political science in prospect, he had taken a temporary position at Ohio University. His year there, in an atmosphere reeking with humidity and soft coal, had been miserable. He was homesick for the East, but he was nonetheless walking toward an interview at another Ohio college—one that, he knew, had been founded seventy years earlier by Bishop Philander Chase of the Protestant Episcopal Church. And he also knew that those seventy years had not been kind to it.

Chase had been a giant in stature, temper, and command. The Diocese of Ohio had been established in 1818, and Chase was its first bishop. From the outset he had been confronted by a shortage of clergymen. Episcopal priests could not be persuaded to cross the Allegheny mountains; there had been only a half-dozen in the entire diocese. "Unless," he wrote, "we can have some little means of educating our pious young men here, and here being secure of their affections, station them in the woods and among our scattered people," there was "no hope in the continuance of the Church in the West." In Worthington on a June evening in 1823, Chase's

Old Kenyon in the mist

son had mentioned that he had heard of a glowing account of "the American Church, and particularly of Ohio," in a British journal. Chase sat upright, struck by a "thought . . . as from Heaven." *"I will apply to England for assistance."*

The leading bishops of the Church were immediately hostile. The presiding bishop, William White of Pennsylvania, did not want an American bishop to appear before British churchmen as a "beggar." Bishop John Hobart of New York was developing the General Theological Seminary in New York and did not want a rival. They warned Chase that if he persisted they would destroy his prospects.

He had nonetheless sailed in October, carrying, among other introductions, one from Henry Clay addressed to Admiral James Lord Gambier. Clay and Admiral Gambier had met at Ghent during the negotiations that ended the War of 1812. Improbably, the rakehell Clay and the dour and pious Gambier—"Gloomy Jimmy"—had become friends. Down to the moment that Chase called on Gambier at his Buckinghamshire estate, he had been blocked at every turn. Warned off by Hobart, no one would meet him.

But Gambier, albeit with some misgiving, honored Clay's introduction. That was all the bishop needed: his personal presence, his sincerity, and his powers of persuasion won over the admiral in the course of a weekend. Gambier formally introduced Chase to other devout Britons: Lord Kenyon, Lady Rosse, Hannah Moore,

George Marriott. The magnetic power of Chase's presence would remain vivid in the minds of these people and their families for generations. They subscribed some $30,000 to his project.

On December 29, 1824, the General Assembly of Ohio passed an "act to incorporate the Theological Seminary of the Protestant Episcopal Church in Ohio," and Kenyon College came into being. It was founded to be "the very best of colleges," offering a general education foundational to theological study but valuable to any man. It was temporarily housed in Chase's own farmhouse in Worthington while the bishop set about finding a permanent location for it in the Ohio "wilderness," where its students would be isolated from "vice and dissipation." He finally selected a site on a broad hill in Knox County, five miles from Mount Vernon, and purchased a great tract of 8,000 acres.

He conceived of an empire of different schools, on the model of Oxford or Cambridge, and his first construction was the building for Kenyon College, gothic, steepled, and of fortress-thick stone. Thus Bishop Chase's unquenchable personal powers had brought the institution into being, but his vision had far exceeded his funds, and even his energies. For five years and more the great building stood in a wasteland of brush, stumps, mud, and cabins. And the personal powers that had created Kenyon led to catastrophe in Chase's administration of it. He contended that he held absolute, ex officio authority over faculty. They challenged him; and when the Diocesan Convention of 1831 supported their challenge, Chase abruptly quit his diocese, exiling himself from Gambier forever.

But the bishops who succeeded him were also men of authority and power. His immediate successor was Charles Pettit McIlvaine, a clergyman of renowned oratorical and intellectual brilliance, famously committed to the evangelical movement in the Episcopal Church, committed to its Protestant rather than its Catholic tradition. Under Bishop McIlvaine Chase's overwhelming and underfinanced schemes were reduced: he recruited David Bates Douglass, a military engineer on the faculty at West Point, to take over the presidency and to direct the work. Douglass defined a small, manageable portion of Gambier Hill as the College Park; he laid out Middle Path from the Kenyon College building to the College Park gates and planted hard maples alongside it. Meanwhile McIlvaine made his own mendicant's visit to Britain and returned with the funds and plans enabling the construction of Bexley Hall Seminary at the northern edge of the village.

Under McIlvaine's episcopacy the institutions at Gambier became bastions of low-church piety, stressing the Word rather than the sacraments. In 1854 he appointed Lorin Andrews to the presidency, a man of the Kenyon Class of 1842 who was admired throughout the state because of his effective labor in establishing its public school system. Enrollment in the institutions at Gambier soared to over 200, and Kenyon was considered to be preeminent among "western" colleges. It educated Rutherford Hayes, Edwin Stanton, and Supreme Court justices David Davis and Stanley Matthews. Because of the power of his writings against the Oxford Movement, McIlvaine himself was known throughout the Anglican world, saluted publicly by the Prince of Wales, and selected privately by Abraham Lincoln to preach the cause of the Union in the pulpits of the British Isles. But the effect of the Civil War on the college was catastrophic. Andrews died of fever contracted while on operations in 1861 as colonel of the 4th Ohio Infantry; enrollment plummeted.

McIlvaine died in Italy in 1873; his body lay in state for four days in Westminster Abbey. His successor was Gregory Thurston Bedell, who had come out to Ohio from the Church of the Ascension in New York City. So revered was the "saintly" Bedell that that New York congregation gave him funds sufficient to construct both an academic building, Ascension Hall, and a chapel for the college whose oversight he had inherited from McIlvaine.

But during the decades when the college was directed by these great Episcopal bishops, one constant had remained: grinding impoverishment. Schemes to secure financial stability collapsed, one after the other. The college sustained itself by student tuition and by selling off portions of its great holdings in land. And, even worse, during the third quarter of the nineteenth century the institutions on Gambier Hill had been riven by the schisms that had beset the Anglican communion. And during the last quarter those institutions had lost their unique significance when the evangelical tradition in the Episcopal church had vanished into the liberal, intellectual, accommodation-seeking "broad-church" movement.

So that afternoon Peirce found himself looking at what seemed more a park than a campus, at vast lawns beneath ancient locust, oak, maple, and elm trees. The formal buildings, ivy covered, were at great distances—a hundred yards or more—from one another. To his left was Ascension Hall, Tudor and massive; beyond it was the gothic, spire-studded Old Kenyon, with "Kenyon" spelled in the slate of its roof. Directly across from him was Rosse Hall, in the Greek revival style, and to his immediate right was Hubbard Library, new, small and arched. The chapel was to his right front, with the cross atop its clock tower gleaming in the May sunlight. And that, except for a few white frame houses, was all. Northward, beyond a stone-and-chain fence, he could see a small village. He was to meet the president of the college at the hotel there, and he walked that way.

In 1892 Kenyon was a church college, and it was run as though it were a small Episcopal parish—and a poor one. It had no endowment; its wealth, estimated at $600,000, was contained in its land and buildings. Its officers had never practiced strict bookkeeping; its operations depended on what money came in from student tuition; it ran deficits each year and regularly "balanced" its books by failing to pay faculty salaries. Its president presided over three institutions, and two of them, Kenyon College and Bexley Seminary, were drastically underenrolled. The third, the Kenyon

Military Academy, had been founded to supply students to the college, but less than one in a dozen of its cadets went on to enroll at Kenyon. On that afternoon there were 134 cadets at K.M.A., forty-three students at Kenyon, and a score at Bexley Hall.

The president was Theodore Sterling, the scientist on the college's faculty. His predecessor, William Bodine, had managed to change the college's constitution so that authority no longer rested with the Bishop of Ohio. But Sterling's own presidency was on tenuous ground. Desperate for students, he often admitted boys who were not prepared, sometimes from the junior class at the military academy. Less than half those entering the college lasted the course.

Old Kenyon could accommodate ninety students, but it had no plumbing; coal fires heated the rooms, and the young men studied by lamplight. The college did not provide board; students contracted for their meals with families in the village. In some years the enrollment sank below thirty. There were eight faculty members.

Although by history and sectarian definition it was an Episcopal college, in its educational enterprise Kenyon was an entirely typical example of the vast majority of the nation's denominational colleges, which were synonymous with American higher education in the nineteenth century. Kenyon devoted itself to educating the full man, of which the intellectual man was only a part; it devoted itself to producing men capable of moral conduct and citizenship in the fullest sense. Character was more important than intellect and consisted of gentlemanliness—the term was used without embarrassment—and the Christian virtues.

The faculties at such colleges believed that they knew "the good" and that their essential responsibility was to instruct their students therein. Boys seeking admission to Kenyon had to pass examinations in Greek, Latin, geography, literature, and mathematics. The college offered separate bachelor's degrees in classics, philosophical studies, and science, but the curriculum for each was entirely set. A freshman candidate for philosophical studies, for example, would study German, Latin, mathematics, English, and the Bible each term (Christmas, Easter, and Trinity Terms). Instruction was through exemplification, repetition, and recitation. Ascension Hall had eight recitation halls where students were called on daily to recite. (The word "classroom" was unknown.) Instruction in the natural sciences, a modest part of the curriculum even for candidates for the Bachelor of Science degree, was conducted in a single corner room. At denominational colleges a course entitled "Mental and Moral Philosophy," a course in ethical issues and practices, was required all seniors and was traditionally taught by the college's president. But Sterling was the single scientist on Kenyon's faculty, and so Peirce had been invited to interview for the Spence Professorship of Mental and Moral Philosophy.

Student life was neither innocent nor edenic. Cheating, or "cribbing," on examinations was widespread. Corporate vandalism was common, such as wrecking furniture to "stack"—barricade— the recitation halls. Women passing Old Kenyon evoked the cry "Heads out!" at which men would rush to the windows. Discipline was always larded with appeals to each man's sense of honor and to the college's reputation for gentlemanliness. (Five national fraternities, thought to teach and to validate gentlemanliness, were housed in Old Kenyon.) These appeals were consistent with the formal education the students were receiving, and they tended to work. The college would soon establish an "Honor System" that would encompass both academic and social conduct.

Students had to attend daily chapel service and two services on Sundays. Recruitment was through the Church, through family ties, and by word of mouth. Almost all of the students were from Ohio; over half were Episcopalians, and the rest were Protestant. There were almost never any students from minority backgrounds, and there were no women. Athletics were significant. Kenyon's color was mauve, with its teams called "the Mauve." In 1892 the football team, which included K.M.A. cadets, had tied Ohio State for the state title.

The college's appeal to Peirce was immediate and transforming, and he would spend the rest of his life articulating it. Part of it, he said, lay in the way this "western" institution was marked by "the culture, the traditions, [and] the beauty" that "characterized the best of the Eastern colleges." He was captivated by the location of such monumental buildings—heroic and antique—in this pastoral setting. The smallness of the college appealed to him, even its poverty. He admired the fact that "there is no life for the students except what they make for themselves," a situation that developed self-reliance and community spirit and that reminded him of "ancient Athens and medieval Florence." He admired its "refinement," its commitment, both despite and because of its poverty, to elegance and greatness. "The student may tramp knee-deep in snow," he wrote, "but he does it with the music of the Canterbury chimes in his ears." The constellation of such things accounted for the loyalty the college generated in its faculty and its students.

Kenyon also struck him, he said, as "a beauty in distress." His love for the college may have overwhelmed his own marriage, or have compensated him for the lovelessness of it. He was completely absorbed—intellect, heart, and soul. For 250 years his family had been Congregationalist, but a year after joining the Kenyon faculty Peirce converted to the Episcopal Church. In 1894 he dropped his graduate work and entered the priesthood. He was a great favorite with the students, famous for his Latinate phraseology, orotund and self-mockingly pompous. He played tennis for the college. Because of his lean physique, the students nicknamed him "Fat."

In 1896, in his twenty-eighth year, the trustees of the college offered him its presidency. Peirce had been in Cincinnati. He arrived back by train at 2:40 on a morning in mid-April and was greeted by the entire student body. They yoked themselves into the harness of his buggy and hurtled him around Gambier Hill. Roman candles soared into the postmidnight skies. He was deposited at last in front of Old Kenyon in the light of a roaring bonfire. "President Peirce is all right," the students cheered, in that turn-of-the-century fashion. "I hardly know whether I am all right or not," he said, "but these moments have been truly the happiest ones in my life."

Four decades later, in the spring of 1937, Kenyon students again honored "Fat" Peirce with a buggy ride around the campus. At sixty-nine he was still erect and athletic. For forty-one years he had served the college as its president. Each year he had represented it at sixty or seventy occasions away from Gambier Hill, but he had always made sure to be in town to do the lecturing in American history on Rutherford Hayes (Class of 1842), "a man of sterling integrity and impeccable veracity." He had garnered seven honorary degrees. A year earlier he had announced his retirement, to take effect on his seventieth birthday this June. Although there was reason enough in his age and prodigious length of service, there were other factors as well. For the last five years he had been separated from his wife, a final divorce was at hand, and he had become friends with a divorced woman named Edith Bruce. His position was now uncomfortable for him and for the Church. So on this buggy ride his successor was seated beside him, Gordon Keith Chalmers, called to Kenyon after three years as president at Rockford College.

During Peirce's presidency the college had remained poor. Its endowment in 1937 was only $3.5 million—but at least it now had an endowment. His presidency had also been marked by extraordinary catastrophes. In 1897 Rosse Hall, the college's assembly hall and gymnasium, burned. Peirce defiantly held the graduation in front of the roofless shell. In 1905 a train on the trestle below the hill killed a fraternity pledge, and the incident received national coverage. In 1906 the Kenyon Military Academy burned; three cadets died, and K.M.A. was never rebuilt. In 1910 Hubbard Library burned. When the United States entered the Great War in 1917, the majority of students withdrew to enlist. Recognizing opportunity amidst calamity, Peirce joined the Red Cross and served with the French, keeping Kenyon College before the public by getting himself quoted and photographed. The impact of the Great Depression on the college was brutal. Its enrollment dropped by a quarter, and its deficit increased proportionately.

Through all of this Peirce's college not only endured but prevailed. The college under his guidance not only survived such horrendous events, but also emerged as an institution far superior to what anyone could have anticipated in 1892 or 1917 or 1929. And more importantly, he also had shepherded it through the most defining transformation in its history.

How he had accomplished this almost defies explanation. If Chase's virtues were Herculean, Peirce's were Protean. He was a man of wit, vigor, and rolling eloquence with an extraordinary capacity for new knowledge and a shrewd eye for publicity. He was not a visionary. Philander Chase could envision a new reality, an Oxford in the Ohio wilderness. Peirce was a partisan instead, a servant. His imagination responded to the "Kenyon of To-Day"—of any day: to the Kenyon of 1896 ("a thoroughly first-class institution"), of 1906 ("buildings worthy of comparison with those on the banks of the Isis or the Cam"), or of 1932 ("the best year in Kenyon's history"). When Kenyon enrolled 128 students, that was the ideal size, and Kenyon would "make no 'bid' for greater numbers"; twenty-five years later "the college numbering perhaps three hundred is best for educational work." There was policy in this: "Kenyon must believe in itself," he had said in 1896, "if it is to induce others to believe in it." Thirty years later an alumnus left an alumni gathering "with a sense of having attended the best College in the world, as one always does after a Kenyon dinner at which President Peirce speaks."

Perhaps he was not even devout in any way that would pass a fundamental, or sanctifying, muster. During his presidency he tightened or loosened Kenyon's ties to the Episcopal Church as he found them to be of greater or less pragmatic value. He continued to argue for required chapel for collegial rather than Christian reasons. In his retirement he would even claim that he had entered the priesthood because he knew the college would expect its president to be a clergyman. (The historical record does not quite bear this out.)

The central and enduring fact of his professional life was his loyalty to Kenyon College; he was not a man for all seasons, but a man for each season. In the pictures of him as president in the 1890s and 1900s he is always in a clerical collar; in those from the 1920s and 1930s he is wearing striped trousers and a swallowtail coat; in those from the 1930s he is in a suit of professor's tweed or businessman's blue. Sometimes he wore these beneath an aviator's helmet; he often had the college's flight instructor fly him to speaking engagements, and at sixty-nine he earned a pilot's license.

In his private life he was a "wonderfully fine person," keeping "simplicity of living" and not "spoiled with all the adulation" he received. (This personal note was written to him, after his resignation, from a faculty wife who had lived for years in gossip-inspired dread of him.) But at every moment and in every season, in whatever dress the occasion required, he had represented the college. His priesthood gave him access to pulpits; his presidency gave him access to board rooms and preparatory school assemblies. When he held the lectern at conventions of Episcopalians or of educators, people vacated other rooms to hear his legendary eloquence.

You cannot locate one single defining moment of his presidency or one single crucial decision. The ruinous events that befell the college had kept it small and poor, but they had also reinforced those particular virtues that had first drawn his allegiance: the closeness of its physical and emotional landscapes; its determination to achieve greatness and "refinement" on its isolated hilltop; the fact that individual faculty members and individual students could directly enhance the character of the college. For four decades he embodied those virtues actively, vigorously, and eloquently. He gave Kenyon a presence, one with whom both captains of industry and potential students could converse.

Thanks to Peirce's own example of commitment to and delight in the enterprise of teaching at Kenyon ("Gentlemen, Rutherford Birchard Hayes was a man of sterling integrity and impeccable veracity"), and thanks to his personal selection of similarly motivated men for his faculty, the "classroom," the pedagogical nexus between student and teacher, had become (and would remain) central to the life of the college. Kenyon students expected to be taught and cherished both the excellencies and eccentricities of the faculty, men who gloried in those expectations.

To the students he was "Mr. God," a commanding presence, elegant and not "a back slapper"—not someone with whom to trifle—but open and kind, someone to whom you could hopefully apply in a time of crisis. He knew every one of them by name.

Kenyon was still a men's college and enrolled only 300 students. But unlike the college across whose lawns Peirce had walked in 1892, the college through which he and Chalmers were drawn that afternoon in 1937 is recognizable. During the forty-one years of Peirce's presidency the Kenyon of the great bishops—of Chase and McIlvaine and Bedell—had become the Kenyon of the great presidents, of Chalmers and of those who would follow him. The man who had abandoned his graduate work to enter the priesthood was the man who had presided over the transformation of Kenyon from a substantially religious college, threadbare but no more uncertain about its mission than is lichen on stone, to an entirely secular one, more secure in its physical and financial conditions but vigorously and nervously alert to its place in the competitive academic world, inevitably open to chance and to change.

This transformation exactly exemplifies the greatest paradigm shift in the history of American higher education, wherein the nineteenth-century paradigm of the Protestant denominational college was replaced by the twentieth-century paradigm of the research university. In those nineteenth-century colleges the humanities had been central, and the faculties had seen themselves as conservators of culture and morality, devoted to producing Christians (if possible), or at least citizens. But from the turn of the century the practical and theoretical triumphs of science had advanced scientific methodology—research—as the superior way of knowing reality. The scientific model had become central to academic institutions. Each new scientific theory destroys the preceding, and in research universities faculty are always seeking "the cutting edge." In the twentieth-century paradigm of the research institution there may be various competing "goods" or "truths" but no permanent "good" or permanent "truth." Morality itself becomes a subject of "value-free" intellectual debate. The various disciplines of the fine arts, liberated from antique moral issues, also burgeon. The research university is devoted to producing people (if possible) of individual and original intellect, or at least skeptics. By the 1930s, for any American college seeking national distinction—seeking to hire the best faculty, and to offer an educational program of broad appeal—the model would have to be that of the research institution.

The emphasis in the college's academic courses had shifted from "recitation" to response and from the lecture to the seminar. The designation "recitation hall" was no longer used. Elocution had been dropped from the curriculum, as had ethics. Departments of Biology and Political Science had been added. Economics and psychology had been established on new bases.

Peirce himself was no longer a professor of "Mental and Moral Philosophy" but of history. The academic year was no longer divided into terms denominated by Christian seasons but into the "first" and the "second" semesters.

The faculty had increased fourfold. Their salaries were regularly paid and were competitive, and they were enrolled in the Teacher's Insurance and Annuity Association and in the pension fund of the Carnegie Foundation. The college had added an entire professional administration: a dean of the college and a dean of students; directors of admissions and of public relations; and a registrar, a physical education staff, an alumni office, a security force, an engineer, a physician, and a food service. Steam heat, electricity, and plumbing had long since arrived. The Park had become a "campus," and open lawns had filled with sandstone buildings. Two great new dormitories had been added, the first named after Bishop William Leonard and the second after politician Mark Hanna. Facing Ascension was a new building devoted to the natural sciences. A new library had been built, as had a president's house, a natatorium, and a theater. And the college's newest, most monumental building was Peirce Commons and the Chase tower above.

In 1937 Kenyon was recruiting nationally, advertising itself through profusely illustrated publications, and hosting spring visits for prospective students. Students were admitted on the basis of letters of recommendation, high school transcripts, and performance on standardized national tests. Eighty percent of entering students stayed the course through graduation. The college offered only one degree, the Bachelor of Arts, but there were no longer any required courses. A student did have to demonstrate that he could "speak and write good English" and that he had "a reading knowledge of one foreign language." There remained a chapel requirement, but it had been reduced to nine Sunday services a semester; Catholic and Jewish students could make separate arrangements. Aside from those requirements and a required year of "Physical Training," the graduation requirements were similar to those sixty-five years later. Each man had to complete two semesters of work in six of eight fields, had to complete a major, and had to conclude that major by passing a comprehensive examination. Students could undertake an Honors Program in their major, and an outside examiner assessed the results. There was a foreign studies program in France. To direct students through this array of possibilities, each faculty member advised five or six entering students and an equal number of majors.

The disciplinary problems facing the college had shifted in character. There were fewer instances of the kind of class-prank destructiveness of forty years before. The problems were now in the realm of individual behavior—drunkenness, vandalism, and a dwindling respect for others. For the first quarter of the twentieth century the Honors System had been a keystone in Peirce's belief that a college education should build the entire man, instructing him in ethics and honor. Then it had suddenly collapsed. In 1931 the faculty had been forced to reclaim authority over the students' social conduct; in 1932 the student council had requested that the faculty revoke the Honor System entirely as it was no longer effective in academic matters.

A number of reasons were advanced for this collapse. The seismic shift in American morality during the "Roaring Twenties," the baneful influence of Prohibition, the loosening of admissions standards during the Depression all may have contributed, but a principal reason also lay in the changing character of the institution. Aside from academic dishonesty, the paradigmatic research institution professed no interest in the way students led their lives.

Editorials in the student newspaper lamenting the decline of "gentlemanliness" became, as the educational program of the college moved away from moral instruction, increasingly elitist. "The gentleman" became, in the Kenyon of the 1920s and 1930s, a social rather than a moral term— "big pockets," according to a characterization of Kenyon in a Denison University newspaper, rather than "high morals." The football team had become woeful, and the baseball team had had to cancel a season. But the college had begun winning championships in swimming, tennis, and polo. In 1923 "Royal Purple" replaced mauve as the team color, and the nickname "Lords" first appeared.

Kenyon was still subtly shaped by the legacy of the bishops in its enduring sense that a Kenyon education could benefit the entire person and the consequent regulation that all students must live in the college's residence halls. But the college's central argument about the value of a liberal arts education was now based on a skeptical perception of reality. If indeed there are "truths" but no "truth," "goods" but no "good," any specific knowledge a student acquires from an education is far less important than the ability to be continually acquiring new knowledge—to be intellectually flexible in the face of the chaos of reality and the uncertainty of career. And the specific benefits of residential life had become somewhat hard to pin down (after another four decades they would become subsumed in a sweeping but entirely imprecise phrase, "the Kenyon experience").

In the winter of 1949 Old Kenyon burned horrifically, taking the lives of nine students. Its rebuilding began immediately. The architects numbered the stones so that it could be precisely replicated. The "new" Old Kenyon presents the same exterior facade, and the aura of the bishops' world still hovers; but its undergirding reality is completely different, built of twentieth-century steel rather than nineteenth-century oak. But then the college that Peirce delivered to President Chalmers in 1937 had already become a modern college, and Chalmers and his successors have been able to develop it accordingly, unclouded by ecclesiastical definitions.

The letter offering Gordon Chalmers the presidency invited him "to make Kenyon a leading place of learning." A Rhodes Scholar, thirty-three years old and widely published in political philosophy, he set about it, making his decisions with cavalier indifference both to the counsel of others and the cost of things. In 1937 he recruited John Crowe Ransom away from Vanderbilt and introduced him to his new, and startled, Kenyon colleagues. In 1939 the *Kenyon Review* was established. Kenyon College, which had once been a bastion of McIlvaine's stress on the profound quality of the Word as a way of knowing God, thereby became a bastion of Ransom's stress on the profound quality of literature as a way of knowing reality. The English department became, and remains, the college's largest; the written word is taken with seriousness unmatched at any other American college. The Kenyon Bookstore is the college's de facto student union.

Chalmers brought international conferences to the college and the Kenyon School of English. He began the assiduous recruitment of African American students and created "the Kenyon Plan," which developed into the national Advanced Placement Program. He accomplished what the invitatory letter set before him, and Kenyon was listed among the finest of the nation's men's colleges. He died unexpectedly, of a cerebral hemorrhage, in 1956.

The presidency of his successor, Franz Edward Lund, was comparatively lackluster. The faculty had had enough of presidential dictatorship, no matter how inspired. The physical condition of the college was urgent, and its financial condition was desperate. In 1967 Kenyon had to end its support of Bexley Hall Seminary. The institution moved to Rochester. Other lineaments of the college's church heritage have likewise fallen away. The chapel requirement was ended; the Anglican ivy was removed from the buildings; the cross is no longer carried at formal occasions; the position of college chaplain has been erased.

The hard decisions confronting Lund "drove him," he confessed, "inward." Men serving beneath him—among them Bruce Haywood, who was the dean of the college, and Samuel Lord, who was its financial officer—provided the genuine leadership. Only by doubling the size of the student body, they determined, could the college sustain its quality. The prospect of recruiting another 500 men was doubtful, so they persuaded the trustees to create "a college for five hundred women which would have its separate campus but which would share Kenyon's program and facilities." The decision was the most significant in the college's history since Bishop Chase decided to sail to England—and the happiest.

Kenyon's definition as a men's college had always been one of President Peirce's main presentational points. "It remains," he wrote in 1906, "practically alone among Western colleges in maintaining the old-fashioned tradition of separate education and in making no provision for the education of women." But aside from the "distractions" attendant upon "coeducation" in 1926, Peirce offered no rationale beyond tradition. When the decision was finally taken to "make provision for the education of women," the college's alumni mounted no serious objection. The step was obviously necessary for preserving its essential qualities and virtues. William Foster Peirce passed away in 1967 at age ninety-nine. There is no record of his own objection to this monumental decision, nor is it imaginable, given his history of ferocious commitment to making Kenyon the best conceivable college in any given "Day," that he would have objected.

Lund resigned in 1968 and William Caples (Class of 1930), a permanent trustee and a vice president of Inland Steel, replaced him. He was a decisive and confidently genial man, thoroughly familiar with the college's circumstances and with American commerce and thoroughly experienced in addressing financial matters and in handling authority. He provided the discipline that the college needed during the 1970s. But his most significant contribution was in setting aright, at last, Kenyon's finances. From the outset of his presidency—from the Friday afternoon of his first weekend, when the Gambier bank would no longer extend credit and it appeared that the college would not be able to issue end-of-the-month paychecks— Bill Caples attended intensely to its financial condition, ultimately with a success unparalleled in Kenyon history. From the second year of Caples's term down to the present moment, "the college has never had a deficit year."

The Coordinate College for Women admitted its first class in 1969. Its "separate campus" was on the northeast edge of Gambier Village and was built of brick rather than stone. The models the college had in mind were "Brown-Pembroke" or "Hobart and William Smith." Its hope was that someone might come forward with a major financial contribution to be honored in the naming of the new women's college. But that hope proved as foundationless as the belief that the women would wish to have sororities. In 1972 Kenyon College became coeducational.

The decision to admit women was of incalculable significance in developing the character of the college. The (voiced) idea that women would choose fields of study different than those selected by men proved entirely false; the (unvoiced) fear that their presence would slacken the intensity of the college's classrooms proved laughably erroneous. "It was as if you had invited the Pittsburgh Steelers to join your touch-football league." In recent years well over half the student body has been female, attrition has been negligible, the women's teams (the "Ladies," an appropriate honor for Lady Rosse, whose portrait in Rosse Hall gazes across the college's main lawn) have excelled, and the general quality of student life has been so enhanced that on the evening of their graduation Kenyon students more typically weep than rejoice. But in historical perspective that decision was only the most signal in the college's long history of coping with its financial condition by increasing the size of the student body. The quality of its admissions staff has become crucial to the institution's intellectual health and, hardly less, its offerings in athletics and the fine arts. The tendency to be ever-expanding is inevitable. Since 1969 a dozen new residences for students have been built or acquired. The college enrolled 1,500 in 2001.

And, inevitably, to the college's disciplinary problems have been added those accruing to a coeducational institution. But no one at Kenyon, faculty or staff or student, ever suggests that its formal educational enterprise—the one awarding grades of "A" or "D"—ought to be directly involved in addressing such problems. As generally happy as are these current years, the virtues of "residency" in the college remain hazily defined. But looming in that haze are two monumental Kenyon traditions. There is the compelling tradition, fostered by Chase's and Douglass's geography, that the Kenyon faculty will be accessible to their students. And, fostered by Peirce, there remains the tradition that that faculty will be close witnesses to their students' extracurricular accomplishments—in drama and the arts, in athletics, in religious community (Catholic, Jewish, Protestant), and in social service (in Hospice of Knox County, for example, or at Wiggin Street Elementary School), a witness that has been inspiring in cases beyond counting.

Philip Jordan became president in 1975. Jordan graduated from Princeton and Yale and had been a professor of history and then the dean of the faculty at Connecticut College. The politicization of the American academy arrived at Kenyon during his tenure and darkened much of it. Fortunately he was a man of public eloquence, energy, wide capacity, and the stature that comes from intelligence and integrity. From the outset of his presidency he challenged the faculty to present their work to a wider world than that surrounding a Kenyon "lectern." When enrollment fell short of budgetary expectations, his administration honored the faculty's sabbatical leave program above all others. He insisted on greater professional range and conduct in the college's hiring processes—an insistence that, decision by decision, has gradually produced a more stable and yet more variegated faculty. The impetus toward "professionalism" (in the current meaning of the term, of course, which would have been meaningless to the bishops in their day) took increasingly visible form as departments were relocated in separate buildings and as old stipulations that the faculty had to be literally "in residence" (had to live, in the early twentieth century, within five miles of Old Kenyon) vanished.

Robert Oden, educated at Harvard and Cambridge, was called to the presidency in 1995. He had been a legendary professor of religion at Dartmouth and then headmaster at Hotchkiss. He brought buoyant enthusiasm, energy, and a soaring, oft-reiterated belief that Kenyon is, and so should always recognize and carry itself as, one of the nation's preeminent small colleges. As was true of Peirce in his day, a joyous delight in the college's particular virtues was a staple of President Oden's public statements and addresses, and he brought elegance and esprit to the college's occasions and undertakings. Under the title "Claiming Our Place," he led the most ambitious capital campaign in Kenyon's history, which added $116 million to its endowment. His decision in the late winter of 2002 to accept the presidency of Carleton College ended a seven-year tenure in which he either achieved or established—only time and the exertions of his inheritors will tell—what a senior professor of political science has termed "a golden era" in the history of Kenyon College. In July 2003 Georgia Nugent, a professor of classics and a dean at Princeton, became the eighteenth president of the college.

During his tenure Oden moved the faculty even farther in the direction of the research institution model. The college now aspires to reduce the teaching load to 3-2 across the faculty, reducing its members' formal commitment to teaching by a sixth. Semester-long sabbatical leaves in advance of the tenure decision have been instituted. In 1998, at his urging, the faculty voted overwhelmingly for the principle that, for the first time in Kenyon's history, formal publication will be expected at the time of decisions about tenure and promotion.

And the trends begun during Peirce's oversight of the college's transition from the paradigm of the denominational college to that of the research institution were especially accelerated. During the last fifty years, Kenyon has averaged adding a new science building every decade. In the spring of 2001 the college dedicated a new science complex, the final precedent step being the demolition of its chemistry building, which had been dedicated in 1962. During the last three decades and at the same pace, departments in the fine arts also have acquired new buildings and spaces. (The list of its outstanding twentieth-century graduates centers heavily in the arts and literature: Paul Newman, Allison Janney, Bill Watterson, Jim Borgman, Graham Gund, Robert Lowell, James Wright, Peter Taylor, Ed Doctorow, and P. F. Kluge.)

In contrast, during those decades most departments in the humanities and social sciences were relocated to white frame buildings that used to be faculty homes. Even as the new science complex was being dedicated—the foyers in the mathematics and physics building are floored with polished stone in which fossils can be discerned—the English department and the *Kenyon Review* were presented with another 150-year-old, and fraying, wooden house.

President Oden also initiated what will be the largest single construction project in the college's history, a vast new fitness, athletics, and recreation center into which will move (along with very much else, since a fifth of its students participate in varsity athletics) the Kenyon men's and women's swimming teams, who constitute the greatest dynasty in the history of the National Collegiate Athletic Association.

This new building will replace two current structures—one of them only twenty years old—and will enclose eight acres under a great glass roof. It is called by some, among them those who are perhaps not inclined to favor the project, "the Crystal Palace." But that name is not inappropriate, given that Bexley Hall was designed by Henry Robers, who was in fact the architect of the Crystal Palace in the London Exposition of the 1850s.

The heritage from the denominational college of the great bishops can still be glimpsed in the closeness of its communities and in the loose but ubiquitous belief that an education on Gambier Hill will benefit more than just the intellect. The qualities established under the paradigm of the research institution and the years of its great presidents are much more visibly apparent—in its sophisticated new facilities and in its ability to enlist a superlative and varied faculty and to attract a fine, generally devoted, and increasingly variegated student body. But how much further can the college be pressed into the latter mold until the legacy of the former becomes threatened?

Nevertheless, the qualities of the college that enlisted Peirce's loyalty a century ago were not necessarily located in its administrative or educational regimes. They were derived instead from the intersection of a particular landscape and a particular human record of aspiration, endeavor, and experience. These qualities endure and continue to give Kenyon its particular cast and character. The mutual respect between students and faculty is still extraordinary, as is the centrality of the educational enterprise. Individual initiative and commitment can still affect the whole, students still walk to class beneath the sound of Canterbury chimes.

SUGGESTED READING

The standard histories of Kenyon College are two: George F. Smythe's *Kenyon College: Its First Century* (Yale, 1924), and Thomas B. Greenslade's *Kenyon College: Its Third Half Century* (KNA,1975). Also of interest is *The Kenyon Book*, a scrapbook of materials edited and privately published by William Budd Bodine (1892), one of the college's devoted clergyman-presidents. Another striking and much-sought volume is *A Dusty Path* (Kenyon, 1964), a history of the college rendered through significant pictures and passages from Kenyon's first 140 years, compiled by John Hattendorf for inclusion in his class's 1964 yearbook but also published separately.

The fascinating career of Charles Petit McIlvaine is developed in detail in Diana H. Butler, *Standing Against the Whirlwind: Evangelical Episcopalians in 19th Century America* (Oxford, 1995). For the career of William Foster Peirce, see Christopher Barth, *Seeking the Kenyon Ideal: The Modernization of Kenyon College under the Administration of William Foster Peirce,* (Kenyon, 1993). Its excellent survey of the subject is enhanced by a chapter of oral history in which students from the college during the last years of Peirce's presidency recall the man. P. F. Kluge's *Alma Mater* (Addison-Wesley, 1993) presents in fascinating detail, from the dormitory rooms to the deliberations of the senior staff, the academic year 1991–92 at Kenyon College.

Lake Erie College

A Success Story for Early Women's Education

MARGARET GROSS

A phoenix does not always rise in the same place as its fiery death. Thus, when the Willoughby Female Seminary in Willoughby, Ohio, called Mount Holyoke's "first godchild in the West," burned in 1847, it was resurrected as Lake Erie Female Seminary in Painesville, fifteen miles to the west. The Honorable Charles A. Avery, one of the founders of Lake Erie Female Seminary, in a Founders Day address in 1898, said, "You must understand, the Seminary did not come to us, we had to go for it. Many towns wanted it, but the decision gave it to us. But first we must tell what we would do." What they did was this, the citizens of Painesville offered $20,000 and land to locate the school there.

Six local citizens signed the petition for the school and their pledge of money "for the object of promoting the Education of Females." Then when the committee appointed to decide the fate of the seminary announced its decision, Avery said, "They gave many reasons for their decision: the locality, the character of the people being largely New Englanders, the different churches to accommodate the preferences of the young ladies. Painesville also made a proposition to furnish a suitable building, grounds and a pledge of sixty thousand dollars."

The original founders were all well-known Painesville citizens. Timothy Rockwell produced pig iron at the Concord Furnace Company. He was also a trustee of Western Reserve College, an incorporator of the Western Reserve Teachers Seminary, and a trustee of Willoughby Female Seminary. Silas Trumbull Ladd ran a general store with Rockwell. Judge William Lee Perkins had been a trustee of the Willoughby Seminary. He had been a lawyer for fifty years and at one time served as Lake County prosecutor. Reuben Hitchcock, judge of the Lake County Common Pleas Court, was president of the Cleveland and Mahoning Railroad, had been president of Willoughby Medical College, and was later a trustee of Willoughby Female Seminary. Aaron

LAKE ERIE FEMALE SEMINARY.

Wilcox served as mayor of Painesville several times and was president of the society that operated the Painesville Academy. Charles Austin Avery, who had set his name to the largest subscription, was a self-made man who came from Connecticut by canal and lake boat to Conneaut and by covered wagon from there to Painesville with only one dollar.

The stated objective of the seminary was to promote thorough and complete female education, and for that purpose the system of instruction, the principles of government and the general principle of management were to be substantially after the plan of Mount Holyoke Seminary. That institution in South Hadley, Massachusetts, had "introduced the ideal of quality education for the daughters of middle class through a proposal of a publicly endowed, nonprofitmaking boarding seminary with high educational standards and domestic work done by its members." This domestic work was designed to reduce expenses and also to prepare the young ladies for their future duties as wife and mother. Also stressed was the girls' health, and they were expected to exercise daily through a one-mile walk. A further objective of the seminary was to train teachers, and the students were encouraged to teach several years before marriage. The first faculty were from Mount Holyoke, and indeed until 1951 all the principals or presidents were women graduates from that institution.

Entrance requirements for the new Lake Erie Female Seminary were for girls over fifteen years of age who were prepared "for a careful examination in English Grammar; Green's Analysis of the English Language; Modern Geography; History of the United States; Stoddard's Intellectual Arithmetic; Davies' University Arithmetic; Robinson's or Davies' Elementary Algebra; Cutter's Physiology; Watts on the Mind; Andrews' and Stoddard's Latin Grammar and Reader." The seminary was organized for three years of instruction with the following curriculum:

Junior Year: Latin, Ancient Geography, Playfair's Euclid, Ecclesiastical History, General History, Robinson's Algebra, and Gray's Botany.

Middle Year: Latin, Day's Trigonometry, Stockhard's Chemistry, Olmsted's Natural Philosophy, Alexander's Evidences of Christianity, Olmsted's Astronomy, Rhetoric, and Paley's Natural Theology.

Senior Year: Latin, Haven's Mental Philosophy, Butler's Analogy, Hitchcock's Geology, Wayland's Moral Science.

Instructions were also given in vocal music, linear and perspective drawing, and French.

As the seminary opened, the main building was not yet completed. Nevertheless, it opened with 127 students. Enrollment was listed as nine seniors, twenty in the middle class, sixty-seven juniors, and seven unclassified students. The majority were from Ohio, but students also came from New York, Illinois, Texas, Michigan, Pennsylvania, Massachusetts, and Indiana. Since all teachers and students lived in the same building, they were considered "family," and "all the members of the school aid to some extent in the domestic work of the family. The portion of time thus occupied is so small that it does not retard their progress in study but rather facilitates by its *invigorating influence*" (emphasis added). The religious, albeit nonsectarian, emphasis of the seminary was stressed in the catalog, and the young ladies were not to receive visitors on the Sabbath, nor were they to spend any Sabbath away from the seminary.

Tuition and board was $160, $140 for daughters of clergy. Girls were to furnish their own napkins and towels, one pair sheets and pillow cases, one blanket, a carpet if desired, and one table or dessert spoon (why spoon only?). She was to provide suitable clothing for the climate. Books and stationary could be purchased at the seminary, but girls were encouraged to bring their own reference books, including a Bible commentary and dictionary and Bible, as the Bible lessons for the year were to be from the Old Testament. Enrollment during the first ten years ranged from sixty-nine (Civil War times) to 155, and the largest classes were always the first-year junior class. In 1881 preparatory students were included.

The 1880–81 catalog said, "The Seminary does not prepare students for College, because the requirements for admission to its own course represents college aims and methods, if not the full amount of college work." Yet in 1898 a charter was granted to Lake Erie Seminary and College. In June of that year the institution granted the last seminary diploma and the first Bachelor of Literature degree.

The tone of the college for over forty years (1868–1909) was set by two remarkable women. The first was Mary Evans, a petite dynamo from Mount Holyoke who served as principal of the seminary and then president of the college. In addition to her administrative duties, she taught ethics, philosophy, and biblical literature. After a tour of Europe and a study of art history in Paris, she added a course in that subject to her repertoire. Part of a tribute to her given at her memorial service read, "Realizing the importance of her position, she never lost an opportunity to point us on to the loftiest ideals, to aid us in nobler judgments, and to open before us visions of larger usefulness and worthwhileness of life. . . . Also, Miss Evans entered with keen interest and with joyfulness into all the pleasures of her girls, into the festivities of the holidays, entered into their contests, their games, their amusements with keen interest. . . . She tried to lead us, by helping us to hold up to a plane of character of effective, higher and better living."

The second of these remarkable women was Luette Bentley, an Ohio native and an 1865 graduate from Lake Erie Seminary, when she was immediately hired to teach. She served as assistant principal from 1878 to 1898, when she was appointed dean. Miss Evans and she together guided the college for over forty years. Students at that time described Miss Bentley as "our mother. We could weep on her shoulder and tell her our troubles. But Miss Evans was our inspiration."

The first building—for forty years the only building—on campus was Italianate in style, four stories high, 190 feet wide, and 60 feet deep, with a south wing added later. It housed the living quarters for students and faculty, classrooms, and a large room used as a chapel; the ground level was used as a gymnasium (with activities in and around the supporting pillars). By 1871 a gas well located on the campus began to supply steam heat to the building, though the girls still used oil lamps in their rooms. Prior to the steam heat each room had a small coal stove. Large closets were built into each dormitory room and were used as sanctuaries—later shortened to "sancs"—so that at given prayer times one girl could pray in the room and the other could retire to the closet/sanctuary for her devotions. These large closets also had washstands and slop jars, or potties.

The second building on campus was Memorial Hall, a chapel joined to the original College Hall. Rooms above were used for art classes and later dormitory rooms. Unfortunately this building, which had five beautiful Tiffany windows, burned in 1957. This building was followed by Bentley Hall, which contained all classrooms, and later buildings were a library and much-needed gymnasium, which had a swimming pool and a bowling alley. In 1927 a beautiful music building was built, and the campus was complete until the 1950s when a building spurt was begun.

An interesting sidebar to the Lake Erie history is the connection the college had with the Garfield family. President and Mrs. Garfield lived only a few miles from the campus, and Mrs. Garfield was a good friend of Miss Evans. Therefore, it happened that President Garfield spent his last birthday at Lake Erie, with the young ladies presenting a program of songs, poetry, and a fan drill. An etching of this occasion is in the college archives and history book. Two of the president's sons were also closely associated with the college. Architect Abram designed three of Lake Erie's early buildings: Murray Library, Ritchie Gymnasium, and Morley Music Building. His brother James R., who had been active in many government positions, including secretary of the interior under Theodore Roosevelt, was president of the Lake Erie board of trustees for forty years.

After Miss Evans, two other Mount Holyoke women came to Lake Erie as presidents, Vivian Small for thirty-two years and Helen Bragdon for ten. Then a radical change came with the appointment of Dr. Paul Weaver as president in 1951. Weaver, the first male administrator, according to Kim McQuaid, professor of history, was hired for economic reasons. "Bills weren't being paid," he said. "Debts were rising fast. Student enrollment was down to 125 from a previous peak of three to four hundred. Mission, now, had become secondary to the imperative of survival."

Weaver moved quickly to turn the college around. He integrated the curriculum, strived to improve community relations (he tore down the high wrought-iron fence that had isolated the college), and sought rich backers. One he found was James Lincoln, prominent Cleveland industrialist who became chairman of the board of trustees. During Weaver's tenure eight new buildings were erected. Nearly all of these were designed by one architect, Victor Christ-Janer. Several were award-winning designs but later proved to be impractical. Indeed, the beautiful Lincoln Commons, featured in several architectural magazines, has since been torn down and replaced by an attractive but less flamboyant and more practical building.

As early as 1935 men were present on the Lake Erie campus through Extension Courses in such subjects as world literature, modern European history, modern government, and contemporary social problems. These courses were taught by Lake Erie faculty members and college credit was offered. In 1959 Lake Erie had its first male graduate, who had gone through the community education program in regular night and summer classes.

Weaver began to integrate men into the campus with a program called Garfield Senior Center, which was designed to give graduates of two-year community colleges the courses necessary for a bachelor's degree. (This is the same as the current 2+2 Program.) These men and women were nonresidents who attended the same classes as the resident girls. This program existed until 1985, when Garfield Senior College ceased to exist and all students, men and women, became Lake Erie College students, with men now residents.

At the same time of these innovations, Weaver was spending freely, and the image of the college became somewhat of a debutante school with bridge tournaments, champagne parties, the popular equestrian program, and a college yacht. However, one innovative program Weaver established probably did more to save the college than any other. That was the institution of a winter term abroad for all juniors. The idea behind that was that many girls would come to Lake Erie for two years and then transfer to a university or other big schools. With this program, the first two years on campus were a preparation for the tour abroad, and then after that experience the girls were not likely to leave for their senior year only. This innovation prompted Eleanor Farnham, an alumna trustee to say, "Do you mind if I get up on the table and dance. The college is saved!" (Hence the title of the history of the college, *Dancing on the Table*.)

During Weaver's tenure the college also created the Lake Erie College Elementary School from what had been a multipurpose building housing a nursery school, adult education, rooms for seminars, and testing facilities. This was later named Phillips School. (In 1990 the building, along with the college gymnasium and maintenance building became what is now Phillips Osborne School, completely separate from Lake Erie.)

In 1958 the college acquired a 500-acre farm about five miles south of Painesville. The farm included the twenty-three-room Manor House and attached library–art gallery and rathskeller, three-acre lake, two tenant houses, three barns, and other buildings. Since that time the Manor House has been the home of college presidents, and the farm has been adapted for the Equestrian Program. Weaver's style, however, was essentially aloof to the students and faculty. He and his wealthy board members were acting on their own, and the college in the last two years of his tenure, when he was ill, was essentially leaderless.

When he left, according to an article in *Ohio* magazine, "Lake Erie was $2 million in debt, and a lethargic board of trustees seemed not to care; they had not mounted a major fundraising drive in twenty years. Lake Erie [had] conducted its financial affairs in strictest secrecy. The three wealthiest trustees quietly wrote checks so that bills could be paid. . . . They seemed fearful of letting anyone else know what bad shape the college was in."

Weaver's immediate successor, Dr. Charles Simmons, was a completely different sort of man. In the same magazine article Sue Gorisek said, "Weaver rode in a chauffeured Lincoln, he [Simmons] squeezed into a Volkswagon, which he drove himself. The college drydocked its yacht and sold off a third of its horses, to save the cost of feeding them. Dr. Simmons closed off part of the president's mansion, and would have rented it out for weddings and bar mitzvahs, but the trustees wouldn't hear of it." He was forced to raise money, and some of his ideas were really bizarre. He began holding bingo games in the new gymnasium, which netted the college about $100,000 a year for scholarships but also resulted in a fire that closed the facility for several weeks. The worst thing that happened during Simmons's administration, however, was his falling for a con man who cost the college thousands of dollars as well as its reputation. He was forced to resign.

Following Simmons's resignation the college hired Dr. Edward Q. Moulton, who came with excellent credentials. However, he chose to stay for only five months. Apparently his heart was still in Columbus, and he had kept his options open there and left to take a position with the Columbus Symphony Orchestra. Dr. Clodus Smith became the ninth president of Lake Erie College and faced huge challenges. He was able to stabilize the college financially through a three-year campaign that raised $10 million. With this money the budget was rescued and much-needed maintenance work was done. This was when Phillips School and part of Morley Farm land and some additional property in other locations were sold to garner more money. Faculty and staff salaries were increased, and a strong core curriculum was achieved.

The president's cabinet was reorganized with four vice presidents—for academic affairs, enrollment management, advancement, and administration. The board of trustees was expanded to broaden its background and areas of expertise. These programs helped to gain the college a 1990 *Money* magazine listing as "one of the best college buys in Ohio."

However, the F.B.I. and the U.S. Department of Education began to investigate the possibility of impropriety in use of government money. Federal regulations prohibit giving financial aid to colleges that show a deficit for at least its two most recent fiscal years. The investigations concluded that the college had corrected its financial problems, and thus the federal education officials saw no reason to impose sanctions on the school. But the college's reputation had suffered.

Smith resigned in 1992, and Dr. Harold F. Laydon became president. He had joined the college in 1990 as vice president for academic affairs and dean. Among his ten goals were balancing the budget, which he did; increasing the residential enrollment, which he achieved; and strengthening the academic programs.

Of course the curriculum of Lake Erie College has changed over the years, sometimes very slowly, but especially since the 1950s very rapidly. Indeed, what started out as a very rigid course of study, heavy on religion and the classics yet innovative in many ways, has changed until now a student at the college can almost determine his/her own four-year program or perhaps choose to get a degree in more than four years or even get a graduate degree. And the majority of the students are nontraditional nonresidents.

In the very early days of the seminary only a few of the women ever stayed the full three years of the program. This is probably a reflection of the times and the minimal regard for women in higher education. Yet alumnae records show that nearly all the women, whether they graduated or not, went into teaching when they left the seminary.

Not all students were completely satisfied with the curriculum at the seminary, and one wrote in an editorial of the March 1892 *Seminary Record,* "It might be helpful . . . [that] students should be intelligent in business matters that she may be able to invest her money wisely. If girls had more practical experience in simple matters of business and depended less upon the assistance of fathers and brothers, they would free themselves entirely from the helpless, bewildered feeling that takes possession of so many upon entering a bank or business office." Many years would pass before such business courses were available to Lake Erie women; yet in 2000 24 percent of undergraduates are majoring in business, and seventy-one were enrolled in the M.B.A. program.

One unique program at the seminary was the Conservatory of Music, which survived from 1898 until 1910, when it became the Department of Music at the college. It was originally open to both men and women, but women not from Painesville were expected to live in college housing and "share its privileges and duties." The conservatory catalog for 1901 noted that "the length of the course depends upon the native talent and the perseverance of the student. It is rarely less than four years."

In the early days the seminary was very aware of the need for the sciences, and early records note interest in physics, biology, and physiology. An 1896 edition of *Central Magazine* said, "The results are seen in the large number of graduates and students who have entered the medical profession and have become trained nurses. On Commencement day, three physicians representing the classes of [18]75, [18]76 and [18]84 were present from India, Massachusetts and Wisconsin . . . and as two of them were accompanied by their small sons, there was a pleasing certainty that the Seminary can train mothers as well as doctors."

During World War II the college necessarily had to make some curricular changes to adapt to the times. The president of the alumnae association volunteered to teach a course in statistics. First Aid courses were offered, and the home economics department offered a course that stressed the importance of nutrition for public health and national safety. And, most visibly, a course in aviation authorized by the Civil Aeronautics Authority was offered. At least one of the graduates of that course went on to serve in the Women's Air Force. At this time, too, the college facilities were used by Case Institute of Technology and Western Reserve University to teach local people from industry, banking, and others wartime-related courses paid for by the government.

In addition to the winter term abroad, Weaver instituted several other innovative programs that are still offered today: criminal justice, legal assistance, and environmental management. The college established an internship program through which students could move into the local, national, and international community to gain hands-on experience in a variety of social welfare, political, and research agencies. This program is still part of the college curriculum. In 1978 Lake Erie opened a weekend college to serve men and women over age twenty-five who found it more convenient to attend college on a weekend-only basis.

Teacher education has always been a large part of the Lake Erie curriculum. In the early seminary days nearly all students went into teaching whether or not they had completed their three-year program. Later the college granted certificates for secondary education, and then later the program was expanded to include elementary education as well. Education has continued to be one of the most popular majors, both in undergraduate and graduate school. However, since the 1990s the college is back to granting a degree in elementary education only.

Long before the full-fledged Equestrian Program became one of the top programs at Lake Erie today, riding was available to the young students. These riding opportunities were off campus and an alternative physical education activity. In the 1930s a few college horses were stabled at the Lake County Fairgrounds. Then in 1955, during Weaver's reign, came Laddie Andahazy, a Hungarian immigrant who had been active in Cleveland horse circles. On the recommendation of a prominent Painesville woman, Andahazy entered into an agreement to expand the equestrian program on a two-year trial. He brought twelve horses and tack with him and set up a small stable in the back of the campus. The women rode around the campus and had small horse shows at the fairgrounds. The program increased in popularity and began to receive area and even national publicity. After a brief stay at a local estate, when college acquired Morley Farm, the equestrian program was relocated there, and the women could learn riding, jumping, and other competitive skills. Until 1978 riding was still an adjunct to the physical education program. Since then it has been a full-fledged major at the college "Today's professional horse person must not only have the ability to handle horses but have a working knowledge of the most current scientific information to accompany their horse sense." Students can now receive a Bachelor of Science in Equestrian Facility Management, Equestrian Teacher/Trainer, or Equine Stud Farm Management, as well as a preveterinarian program.

The college established its first graduate program in 1971 with the Master of Science in Education degree. The Master of Business degree was started in 1981. The M.B.A. was designed to train middle- and upper-level management executives from a generalist's perspective, rather than preparing experts in narrow subfields of business, a program to fit everyone from the small businessman to a hospital administrator. Weekday and evening courses are available.

In addition to the weekend and evening courses on campus and in Willoughby, students may receive credit for prior learning for knowledge gained through work and life experience. The Lake Erie Adult Degree Program allows one to complete requirements for a degree outside the format of regularly scheduled classes. Another option is the 2+2 Program, which encourages students to transfer to Lake Erie without loss of credit from area community colleges.

Some form of physical exercise was expected of the Lake Erie students from its opening in 1859, and soon Athletic Field Days marked the beginning of an amazing period in the history of the college. From the first Field Day in 1898—with its wheelbarrow, sack, and bicycle races and "very interesting and scientific game of basketball"—through the 1960s, students participated in basketball, tennis, equestrian activities, field hockey, polo, dancing, swimming, baseball, volleyball, croquet, and archery. Until the 1960s the highlight of the spring calendar was the Field Day, an opportunity not only for intramural competition but, in the early days, also for long-distance competition with other women's colleges in the East. These were effected by comparing results among contests at the different colleges, with the winner chosen by comparing times and distances for various events. Lake Erie and Vassar were rivals. These early Field Days drew as many as a thousand spectators, and the Cleveland newspapers regularly covered the events and displayed full-page rotogravure pictures.

Now that the college is coeducational, various numbers and types of intramural and intercollegiate sports are offered: men's and women's soccer, basketball, and tennis; women's volleyball and softball; and men's golf. The "Storm" (college team name) is a member of N.C.A.A. Division III and also a member of the Allegheny Mountain Collegiate Conference.

President Laydon continues to keep a core curriculum of liberal arts and emphasize international understanding. Each student gets a passport when he/she becomes a freshman, and sometime during the four-year program he/she is encouraged to study abroad for a few weeks or a full semester. This usually happens during the second semester of the junior year and may be used to satisfy one of the general education requirements. In addition to the Academic Program Abroad, the college has developed a special relationship with the Universidad Interamericana in San José, Costa Rica, and a representative from that institution is now on the Lake Erie board of trustees.

The college is a charter member of the Ohio-Pennsylvania Academic Alliance, which includes Thiel College in Greenville and Westminster College in New Wilmington, Pennsylvania, and Youngstown State University and Walsh College, in Canton. The college now advertises itself as offering a "Career Oriented, Liberal Arts Education." The most popular courses are business, equestrian studies, teacher education, and the natural sciences.

Margaret Geissman Gross, *Dancing on the Table: A History of Lake Erie College* (Celo Valley Books, 1993).

Lourdes College

A Northwest Ohio Catholic Liberal Arts Institution in the Franciscan Tradition

NANCY J. BROWN

Who can say where the seeds of an educational ministry are planted? For the Sisters of St. Francis the fertile soil was spaded between 1870 and 1914 when there was a great immigration to the United States. Over one and a half million Polish people left their country for a variety of reasons. Those émigrés were the parents of the founding sisters, men and women who left poverty and subjugation with their infant daughters to settle in such U.S. cities as Rochester, Minnesota, and Toledo, Ohio, or in smaller farm communities like Wilno and Wells and Sobieski, Minnesota. No matter where these families made their homes, the environment was the same; traditional Roman Catholic values were nurtured and education was a priority. Young girls attended parish schools conducted by sisters who taught much more than the English language. Eventually a new congregation of women religious grew up to serve those Polish people and the Church.

By 1876 twenty-five families comprised Toledo's first Polish parish of St. Hedwig. By 1900 more than 600 families were attending services in that church. Eleven years later when the Reverend Joseph Schrembs was appointed the first bishop of the new Diocese of Toledo, there were several sisterhoods already in place. One of them was the Sisters of St. Francis, whose motherhouse was in Rochester, Minnesota. This community, founded by Mother Alfred Moes in 1877, staffed both the schools of St. Hedwig and of St. Peter and Paul.

Bishop Patrick Heffron, who was well acquainted with the Franciscans and was instrumental in helping Bishop Schrembs establish a Franciscan Province in the Diocese of Toledo, administered in Rochester, Minnesota, situated in the Diocese of Winona. He was deeply aware not only of Toledo's interest in serving the Polish community but also of the intense desire some of the Rochester Franciscans had expressed to teach in schools that served their national group.

In 1916 Bishop Heffron formally proposed the notion of a Toledo Province to the Council of Rochester Sisters. After the council visited St. Hedwig the decision was made in November to proceed. Twenty-three Rochester Franciscans of Polish descent, including older experienced sisters as well as novices, were selected to be the original province members. The newly appointed Provincial Superior, Mother Adelaide Sandusky, was forty-two years old.

The accommodations provided for the fledgling congregation left a great deal to be desired: "Bare, dirty floors, naked light bulbs, bars on newspaper covered windows . . . shoddy stoves and next to no furniture were the decor of this, the first home of the Province of the Immaculate Conception." Never ones to be defeated, and armed with $50 from Mother Leo of the Rochester community, Mother Adelaide and her partners set about making a convent from these humble beginnings.

The World War I years saw great growth in the size of the community; at the same time, war shortages and restrictions on building prevented an orderly process for housing all the new sisters. Three farms in Sylvania, Ohio, were purchased in 1917 using funds advanced by the Rochester community. Because money was extremely tight, the Dexter Street residence was still considered the provincial headquarters for a year or so.

Education during these early years focused on formation. As each candidate for the novitiate received her habit, her hours of formal instruction doubled, and those spent in private study increased. The study of Catholic doctrine was enhanced by study of Franciscan history and ideals. Latin was taught so students could understand the Office. Training in domestic skills like laundry, house cleaning, serving, sewing, and kitchen work helped the young women learn what was required and expected for service to the community. At the same time, as the number of children in the parish schools grew rapidly, teachers were needed, and the sisters were expected to fill those needs.

It was a decision time for the community. They had been busy establishing themselves, exploring ways to feed and clothe themselves and to farm their lands. Most of the farming enterprise, however, had rested on the shoulders of Sister Elizabeth, and in 1921 she was sent to Kentucky on another assignment. After her departure it became apparent that it was more useful for the candidates and young sisters to concentrate on education than agriculture.

During this time teachers were able to teach elementary grades with little education themselves beyond grade six; this factor allowed the sisters to fill the education needs of the parish schools in Toledo and its environs. By 1922, however, the Ohio State Department of Education had certified Provincialate High School. Gradually, then, as more sisters attended the high school and acquired secondary school teaching credentials, the curriculum was expanded. By the end of the provincial period, 1930, the original community of twenty-three had grown to more than 200 professed sisters, twenty novices, and twenty-two postulants.

The quality of normal school training received by the sisters who formed the nucleus of the provincilate was excellent. Montessori principles in primary methods were stressed as were the Herbartian process of preparation, presentation, assimilation, generalization, and appreciation in the preparation of older children. The first four students from Provincialate High School went on to attend the State Normal College at Bowling Green (now Bowling Green State University). Provincialate High School grew over the next few years adding courses in music, Polish literature, and spoken English. Some sisters were sent to attend summer sessions at other institutions. Because schools were growing, the demand for teachers with Polish backgrounds was constant.

In 1931 the Provincialate High School moved into new quarters on the campus, St. Clare Hall, and was renamed St. Clare Academy. In St. Clare Hall the postulants and novices were surrounded by the Old World beauty Mother Adelaide had loved and collected. "But of far greater value than the Piranesi etchings and wonderful Della Robbia ceramics" said one observer, "were the lessons taught by the group of religious women who comprised the faculty of the school. The candidates came from different schools and varied family backgrounds, but they were bonded to each other and to the sisters by the exhilarating experience of entering a world filled with people who gave them their best and expected the best from them." This spirit of learning as a dynamic exchange between "bests" is still the heart of a Lourdes College education today.

These congregations of women then integrated the best new teachers into a solid system of apprenticeship/internship and mentoring. Their main purpose was to provide teachers for the local parish community's parochial schools. With the large boom in Catholic immigration preceding World War I, the need for sister educators exploded. Immigrants loyal to the Church wanted their children educated in the church, but frequently they had little money to support their schools. Therefore, the communities of sisters stepped in to fill the need. These teaching sisters needed more and more education in content and pedagogy as the Catholic education system expanded beyond elementary school into secondary, postsecondary, and university education.

The founding of the Sister Formation Movement in 1954 brought more change to Catholic education. This national movement raised Catholic American education to its current level of respect in elementary, secondary, and higher education. The establishment of Lourdes Junior College was a direct result of this movement. Women religious educators came to understand that sending sisters into teaching too quickly was inhibiting religious growth. The Sister Formation Movement suggested that all teaching sisters should complete both their formation and their baccalaureate degrees before being allowed to begin teaching. This position would ensure two important qualities in women religious educators: one, the firm anchor in the faith that they would need to survive in the chaotic secular world of the community classroom; and two, a superior professional preparation.

To ensure the superior preparation, congregations began to send sisters from their small private colleges into larger, more secular colleges and universities. They, in turn, returned to their communities prepared to pass on their learning to their students. The result of the Sister Formation Movement was to make American sisters the most highly educated group of women religious in the Catholic Church and among the most highly educated women in the United States.

As Catholic higher education expanded and began admitting lay women and, in most cases at a later time, men, the faculty of Lourdes College also began to diversify. Lay faculty, women and men, have supplanted most women religious faculty members, and the number of student sisters has been integrated into the laywomen and men majority. The goal of combining liberal arts study with career preparation to form good citizens remains consistent with the goals for the sisters in the early days. Sister Mary Malloy, of the College of St. Teresa, then and others now, still believe that their colleges are charged with filling the needs of the church and the world. Although Lourdes graduates are no longer sisters, there remains a commitment to producing college graduates with a firm religious foundation cradled in conscience, a strong broad understanding of the world provided by the liberal arts, and practical preparation for career service.

Lourdes College, proud to have grown from seed brought from Minnesota origins, maintains the vision and commitment carried by the first Sisters of St. Francis who arrived from Winona, baggage in hand, to begin the work of creating a new, flourishing community. The sisters love retelling the story of their modest beginning on eighty-nine acres of yellow, sandy soil that would not produce strawberries or turkeys or peanuts. The enterprising leader of the school wrote to the School of Agriculture at Ohio State University and obtained a thousand evergreen seedlings. They were planted, and as they took hold the problem of winds and shifting sands was solved. That forest of pines is the most noted landmark of the Sisters of St. Francis and Lourdes College.

The campus grounds now present a pleasing mixture of contrasts: untamed woods on the west of the Portiuncula are home to deer and other wild life; to the right, where a pond once stood, is a neoclassic prayer garden with formal design. To the north and down the hill nestles a pond surrounded by a lush meadow and stately trees.

Mother Adelaide's eye for beauty was not limited to sculpturing only the grounds of the Lourdes College Campus. She knew art, and she knew value and she knew what she wanted. The stories of her worldwide bargain hunting are legendary. From the authentic Spanish wrought-iron grilles near the library to the small statues of saints and scholars imbedded in the walls of St. Clare Hall (formerly St. Clare Academy), Lourdes Hall, Mother Adelaide Hall, and the Duns Scotus Library, she lovingly handpicked and purchased each piece from many places around the country and the world. When salespeople were confronted by her zeal for art and her joyous nature, it is said that they practically gave away their treasures to her. An active and talented artist in her own right, Mother Adelaide's own paintings adorn the walls of the hall that carries her name. Active artists are still members of the congregation and of the faculty. Many of the more recent mosaic murals have been created by them and their students, a fitting tribute to the goals set some eighty years ago. In 1964, just two months before her death, Mother Adelaide was presented the Stella Maris Award from Mary Manse College for her overwhelming success at fulfilling her mission. Mother Adelaide was not noted just for the beauty she created, but also for her commitment to education. "Her aim," the citation continues, "has ever been to edify the minds, to elevate the spirits, and to ennoble the hearts of those in her charge. . . . Her schools have been the object of her careful guidance as she planned and worked to promote the cause of Catholic education in the United States."

Mother Adelaide was also a teacher and a highly competent administrator, and for forty-eight years she directed the progressive development of formal education. Before the founding of the Sylvania Congregation, she had been director of the

College of St. Teresa. She was its first graduate and a faculty member in the Department of Classical Languages and French; she attended Harvard and Columbia. Her responsibilities and skills grew at St. Teresa's, and her commitment to higher education was one factor in her being selected to establish the Sylvania Congregation. Here she immediately established the Provincialate High School (chartered by the state of Ohio in 1921), which became St. Clare Academy (accredited by North Central Association of Colleges and Schools in 1935) and then Lourdes Junior College in 1958 (accredited in 1964).

In 1942 negotiations with the College of St. Teresa led to the establishment of an extension of that college at the Sylvania campus. In 1957, when the Commission on Higher Education recommended that four-year colleges limit or reduce the number of affiliates, Sister M. Agnes, director of the Sylvania extension, was inspired by the Sister Formation Movement to establish a new, private, independent two-year college on the campus. Application to the Ohio State Board of Education resulted in a Certificate of Authorization, and in January 1958 Lourdes Junior College was born. Mother Justinian was the first president. True to the Sister Formation Movement's philosophy, Lourdes Junior College prepared future Sylvania Franciscan Sisters to continue their studies in diverse four-year colleges so that they would be better prepared to take part in the professional works of the religious community whose focus was education, health care, and social service.

Although Lourdes College's mission statement undergoes regular scrutiny and revision to stay current with the times, the college continues to focus on education, health care, and service to others. Its mission and its purposes remain central today in every student's program of study. A strong general education requirement provides the broad understanding of human history and values that only a liberal arts vision can give. Skills and theory classes prepare Lourdes's predominantly adult students to take their places in the world of work whether for a first job, a second career, or a long-awaited promotion.

The learning environment at Lourdes College is one that motivates and assists students "to integrate sound religious and philosophical values in their learning and relationships." It is also meant to inspire them to some type of human service, be it physical, social, psychological, or religious. Furthermore, the following attest to the integrity of the institution as it lives out its mission and purposes: the consistent growth of the student body, the expression of student satisfaction with their academic development, the relationships fostered among the members of the campus community, the reputation of Lourdes College in the greater civic community, and the interconnectedness of it all.

The whole that is Lourdes College is greater than any of its parts, and to be truly appreciated Lourdes's strengths must be experienced. Academically, Lourdes accomplishment is reflected in its accreditation history, which, although it spans just thirty years, has moved steadily forward. The North Central Accrediting Association of Colleges and Universities in 1964 accredited the college during the presidency of Sister M. Remigia (1962–72). Since that time the institution's growth has been significant in its physical plant as well as in its degrees offered. Ground was broken in 1963 for Mother Adelaide Hall, which houses classrooms, laboratories, the bookstore, and a planetarium, the first in northwest Ohio.

In the late 1960s two important things were happening to women. Fewer women were interested in pursuing the religious life, and those who chose to enter were older and already college educated. As a result, in 1969 the first laywomen were admitted to the junior college, and in 1973 Lourdes College became independently incorporated with "Junior" dropped from its name. Two short years later in 1975 during the presidency of Sister Rosaria (1972–81), the first men were admitted to the school. Also during 1975, educational opportunities were extended to students from St. Vincent School of Nursing in Toledo and the Providence Hospital School of Nursing, in Sandusky.

Not yet ready to rest, the college began preparations to offer four-year degrees. In 1977 meetings were held with the sisters and leaders in the business and education communities regarding the need for a Catholic college following the closing of Mary Manse College. These discussions led to a feasibility study in 1980. Under the guidance of Sister Marie Andree (1981–83) and Sister Ann Francis, acting academic dean, the first bachelor's programs, the Bachelor of Arts in Religious Studies and the Bachelor of Individualized Studies were developed.

Sister Ann Francis Klimkowski (1983–2000) went on to assume the presidency in 1983 and continued the work that her predecessors had begun. Focusing on her vision of "Life-Long Learning," a strong continuing education department was added, which offers courses for credit and continuing education units in several disciplines as well as noncredit enrichment classes. In addition, the college has a substantial membership in Eldervision, which specializes in educational trips to various points of interest, and a strong writer's workshop component. Recognizing that lifelong learning includes achievement of academic degrees as well as enrichment, careful attention has been paid to the specialized needs of the college's 80 percent adult student, 100 percent commuter population.

In the early days only a small group of students expressed an interest in a campus life, but as the number of students increased, interest in college spirit did too. As the college's student population leveled off and began to define itself, a dynamic, focused, and well-organized office of Student Services evolved. In earlier days the quiet halls testified to an "all business" atmosphere; today the halls team with activity and color. A well-placed snack bar offers sustenance to students on the run, while round study tables surround the planetarium, inviting students to sit and rest and chat if they have the time. Bake sales are frequent temptations in Mother Adelaide Hall, and bright posters announce the charity or organizational goal being pursued by the group sponsoring the fund-raiser. Bulletin boards on the walls of the various connected halls of Lourdes are peppered with colored posters announcing the next meeting of the Occupational Therapy Club or announcements of upcoming events.

Programs, services, and organizations emphasizing community service are especially successful. Of special note are Habitat for Humanity, Rotaract, and Campus Ministry. Other organizations foster family unity and professional development. In keeping with the mission the college wishes to foster leadership development, and the Student Leadership Advisory Council plays an important role in that development. In addition, Lourdes takes advantage of federal grants like TRIO, Upward Bound, and Title III to provide outreach to disadvantaged populations, a critical part of the mission of the college and of the Sisters of St. Francis.

In 1986 two more degrees were added: Bachelor of Arts and Bachelor of Science in Nursing. During 1993 Lourdes received authority to develop additional majors, and a full complement of majors within the Bachelor of Arts degree now exists. The two-year degrees have not been abandoned; the Occupational Therapy Assistant program leads to the Associate of Applied Science Degree. Students can select from a wide variety of concentrations such as art, criminal justice, liberal arts, or sociology, which will earn them the Associate of Arts degree. In 1999–2000 Lourdes College received authorization and accreditation to offer the Bachelor of Science.

Expansion of degree offerings led to an expansion of the size of the student body, which in turn led to the need to expand the physical plant. As the number of students in the college grew, the number of sisters decreased, and the college was able to draw from the already existing and architecturally harmonious buildings belonging to the congregation of the Sisters of St. Francis. Preferring always to restructure, rearrange, and reuse the old rather than replace with new, parts of Lourdes Hall and St. Clare Hall, Carmel Hall, the Learning Center (formerly the House of Prayer), and Assisi Hall have been converted to meet the needs of the college. Sleeping quarters have been converted to offices; meeting rooms have become classroom space; air conditioning and elevators have been added; and offices, laboratories, and classrooms have been rewired to accommodate computerization.

Every effort is made to let students at Lourdes College know that, no matter how much technology and art and nature abound, people are most important. True to its mission of service, Lourdes has a liberal admissions policy. Although students must meet standards with a combination of test scores, transcript, and a minimum grade point average, the underprepared student may still find admittance under one of the college's special programs, where they receive intensified counseling and special courses designed to help them address their academic deficiencies. Whatever their original status, students completing a program at Lourdes are prepared in their courses to think logically, communicate clearly and persuasively, analyze rigorously, and solve problems systematically. Ideally, by graduation they will have recognized their unique potential, defined worthy goals, and chosen a career that includes a measure of human service. Their life activities will be enriched through the achievement of the learning outcomes that the college views as flowing from its mission and purposes: communication competence, critical thinking ability, aesthetic awareness, ethical foundations, historical consciousness, cultural awareness, scientific literacy, quantitative competence, personal wellness responsibility, and a religious perspective. To whatever level of excellence Lourdes students may achieve these objectives, the greatest outcome the college hopes for is that in their lives they will be motivated by a continuing pursuit of truth and service to family, Church, and the global society.

Lourdes is convinced of the importance of continuing and strengthening the influence of Catholic education in northwest Ohio, the college's latest triumph being the acceptance by the State of Ohio of the teacher preparation program at all levels, early childhood through adolescent and young adult. The college is committed to the belief that Catholic education, including higher education, is vitally needed to provide the world with reasons for life and for optimism. The college works to change society by cooperating with individuals, groups, and institutions to effectively communicate Christian values as outlined in the *Ex Corde Ecclesia.* The college cannot, nor does it pretend to, compete with the large state universities. Today, liberal education is challenged to also prepare persons for a livelihood. Lourdes College is still unfaltering in its commitment to do for its lay student body as it did for its sisters at its beginnings. It is pertinent to argue that that the college can prepare students for a career and educate people how to live—before, after, and during work—and perhaps to live well.

On July 1, 2000, Dr. George Matthews passed through the campus's open gate to become the sixth president to lead Lourdes College. His assumption of the presidency marks a new renovation on the Lourdes campus. In 1989 the board of trustees revised the by-laws of the college to create the possibility of a lay president. Changing times dictate change, as the founders of Lourdes College understood so well. The current strategic plan, forged by the consensus and collaboration of the board of trustees, the faculty, administration, staff, students, auxiliary, and alumni in the spirit of change has assured an orderly transition into the twenty-first century.

Suggested Reading

The following are found in the archives of the Sisters of St. Francis in Sylvania, Ohio: Marya Czecl, "Formation and Education: An Historical Partnership" (Ph.D. diss., 2000); Sisters of St. Francis, *The Golden Link 1916–1966* (1967); M. Justinian, *Of Evergreens Rooted in Yellow Sand* (1967); Sisters of St. Francis, *Our Mother* (1959).

Malone College

Christ and/or Community?

JOHN WILLIAM OLIVER JR.

Malone, like most private colleges, was born out of a distinct religious tradition (Evangelical Friends, a branch of the Society of Friends, or Quakers). Yet unlike many independent colleges, Malone continues to advertise on Christian radio, employ churches as major tools to recruit students, and integrate religion into sciences, humanities, and student life. Malone professors attend conferences on integration of "faith, learning, and living." Students attend two mandatory chapels each week; volunteer for mission work overseas and in poverty areas in America; and participate in study programs in Washington, D.C., Los Angeles, England, Latin America, China, Russia, and the Middle East with faculty from the Council for Christian Colleges and Universities. Bible studies meet in every dorm. If mixing religion with education appears anomalous in a post-Christian age, schools where religion remains a pervasive part of a college experience represent a flourishing phenomenon in higher education.

Malone's history can be divided into two eras. The Bible college era began in 1892 when J[ohn] Walter and Emma Brown Malone opened an Evangelical Holiness Quaker school in Cleveland, which they called the Christian Workers Training School for Bible Study and Practical Methods of Work. The Christian college era started in 1957 when their son-in-law founded an evangelical Christian college in Canton.

As proponents of Wesleyan Holiness, the founders inherited a nineteenth-century heritage of reform—evangelism, free pews, abolition, temperance, and urban rescue work—and ascetic living sustained by revivalism, rules, and prayer. As Quakers they also embodied an even older tradition of holy living, nonviolence, and racial and gender equality.

As a boy in rural Ohio, Walter lived beside John Henry Douglas, the leading nineteenth-century Quaker evangelist. His mother established a school to teach children

Class of 1893

the doctrines of the Friends. As a young man Walter later said, "I hungered to be a preacher like my mother." Emma was first converted to evangelicalism by Dwight L. Moody and later to evangelical Quakerism by another evangelist, Esther Frame.

In Cleveland, faculty and students from the training school did evangelism and rescue work in a district around Public Square that had 400 saloons, forty houses of prostitution, opium dens, and most of the city's "gambling resorts and wholesale liquor stores," a district called, by a pastor of Old Stone Presbyterian Church, "the devil's throne." Urban vice shocked Quakers, who commonly came from rural meetings with strict moral codes. In Cincinnati, where Walter lived before coming to Cleveland, Quakers were "active in every public agency for poor relief." In Cleveland each student was assigned a neighborhood in a poor district to visit each day to evangelize and offer human services (food, medical care, etc.) paid for by the Malones.

Rescue work received mixed reviews, even from Friends. A Quaker "gentleman" complained that, with "Holiness band, Salvation Army, or Free Methodists" becoming Friends, I can no longer be proud of my Quaker ancestry." Another Friend, a father of a president of a college for wealthy women, scolded Walter after he called Quakers to "take in the poor people and go after the outcasts . . . with the expectation that we will be poor, despised people."

By 1900 students from the school had rescued women from prostitution, founded or worked in five orphanages, twenty shelter homes, and twenty-nine rescue missions. Cleveland's director of charities praised two of Emma's homes for unmarried mothers that offered free medical assistance, reunited mothers with their parents, and helped with adoptions as models of "practical Christianity." The school also ran an orphanage, with Walter Malone Jr. as superintendent. He later became vice president of McCormick Theological Seminary in Chicago and president of Millikan College in Decatur, Illinois.

As a boy in New Vienna, Walter's neighbor, John Henry Douglas, was the first general secretary of the Peace Association of Friends. Daniel Hill, the foremost Quaker peace activist in the nineteenth century, lived 100 yards south of his home. Hill led the Peace Association for years and edited two peace journals, *The Messenger of Peace* and *The Olive Leaf*. The latter was the first Quaker periodical for children in the United States.

The school condemned all lethal violence. War? A "system of murder, falsehood, robbery and desolation." Military personnel who claimed to be led by God were charged with "delusion" and told to "Get Out. Get Out." Suicide? "Self-murder." Capital punishment? "Willful murder." Abortion? "Prenatal infanticide" or "deliberate murder." The founders blamed the movement to legalize abortion on a "cultured and refined" class that devalues life and on men who desert women after they become pregnant. They chided an editor for reporting professional boxing and contended that football has "no rightful place in . . . athletics."

Openness to African Americans came from Walter's Quaker roots. His home in New Vienna had a hiding place for runaway slaves. As a young man he worshiped with Levi Coffin, leader of the "Underground Railroad," in a Cincinnati Friends Meeting and later worked with a former slave who became a Quaker evangelist in Ohio. The Malones praised Booker T. Washington and W. E. B. DuBois. Students who went as missionaries to South Africa were accused by whites of breaking down the "natural separation between the races" and making the black "think he is as good as a white man." African Americans attended the Malones' school from at least 1901, three decades before being admitted to any eastern Quaker college.

If Quaker women were "mothers of feminism," so were Bible colleges. Four of the first five had women presidents, three were coeducational, and two were for women only. From 1888 to 1903 Bible college women founded at least twenty hospitals and uncounted numbers of rescue homes.

Five women and two men were the first teachers at the Malones' school. Emma shared with Walter the title "principal" seventy-five years before a woman headed a coeducational university. Emma, a minister, was co-clerk of Ohio's Friends and of a national meeting of Quakers in 1897. Walter made a special appeal to women to pursue God's call to ministry. Thirteen women from the first class became ministers, twice the number in any large denomination in the 1890s. By 1907 the school had produced sixty-eight women ministers (more than any other school in the nation). A Malone journal credited Quaker growth "largely . . . to the preaching of women." Carole Spencer contends that this claim "could not have been voiced at any previous era in Quaker history other than its beginnings and probably has not been heard since." The decline of women ministers among evangelical Friends may be due to the retirement of the Malones in 1917 and because a married woman could saddle a church with the extra burden of finding a job for her husband. Also, as Quaker traditions crumbled, Baptists, Methodists, and Presbyterians who opposed women ministers persuaded some Friends.

Scripture, revivals, hagiographies, and mystical visions fueled holy living. Walter and Emma prayed for an hour on their knees before each class. To Quaker mystics, prohibitions against cards, dancing, "immodest dress," and theaters were seen as "hedges" to protect an "enclosed garden" in which to raise children and as spiritual disciplines to purify themselves for intimacy with a holy God. Christ appeared to Emma, an encounter so sacred that we have no record of it until Walter told the story as an old man. Witnesses said Walter's face glowed when, at the moment of death, he reported seeing "a great multitude gathered around a throne." He added, "I know a great many of them." Both saw and exorcised demons. This, Walter said, "opened our spiritual eyes to see unseen things . . . after this we knew what was opposing us."

Holy living required charity. A professor resigned in 1892 after a woman became pregnant with his child. After they married he became a frequent speaker at the school. In later years small groups gathered daily to watch Walter and Emma enter the school arm in arm—to one viewer it was "the most beautiful sight I ever saw." While most of their six children did not practice their ascetic lifestyle, all spoke of their parents as "saints." Former students tearfully recalled Walter's gentle whisper, "The Lord and I are counting on you."

The founders had only high school degrees: Walter from the prestigious Chickering School in Cincinnati, Emma from West High School in Cleveland. Some students had no high school education; others had college degrees. Professor William Pinkham had been acting president of Earlham College. Other teachers were simple soul-winners. When Friends colleges taught biblical criticism and Darwinism, this school opposed "modern thought" that undermined biblical authority and the uniqueness of humans as embodiments of "the Light of Christ." A critic reported women from the school "dressed in ancient Quaker garb and wholly in black spend evenings in missionary work, street preaching or slum visiting . . . [and] their days in Bible study under their leader." This, he said, "must cramp their minds." Yet the *Oberlin Review* called Willis Hotchkiss, a graduate who pioneered Quakerism in Kenya and represented the Student Volunteer Society, "more sought after by the colleges and universities than any other missionary." In the early twentieth century more than a thousand people heard Hotchkiss speak at Oberlin.

While one historian credits the Malones with saving Quakerism in the Midwest and West from near extinction, it is also true that in saving it they changed it. Hymns, gospel choruses, revivalistic preaching, and altar calls supplanted silent meetings. Displacing Quaker traditions with *sola scriptura* (biblical authority alone) set the stage for Evangelical Friends to assimilate with theological and social conservatives outside the Society of Friends.

After the Malones retired the school kept its Holiness ties but had less to do, by mutual consent, with theologically liberal Friends. All succeeding presidents in Cleveland were Holiness preachers. One led the National Holiness Association; another headed the National Holiness Missionary Society. Only the last, Byron Osborne, spent his entire life as a Friend, but he also served as director of education for the National Holiness Association.

The Malones welcomed homeless people to stay with them overnight, honoring them "as if they were Jesus." But in the 1930s, if not sooner, rescue works diminished. The neighborhood changed. Crime and urban blight made parents reluctant to send daughters to the school. In the 1940s the *Cleveland Bible College Messenger* ignored the poor. In the 1950s a dean, after encountering a destitute woman on the street, charged that "it is not merely unfortunate to be the victim of evil, it is wrong." Nevertheless, by the anniversary in 1952 the school's 1,200 graduates included forty rescue mission workers, eighty foreign missionaries, and 600 pastors, as well as two doctors, four founders of Bible colleges, twenty-five nurses, and forty college or Bible college professors.

In 1948 the faculty endorsed a letter from a "Committee to Oppose Conscription" at Antioch College. However, in 1955 (the Cold War era) the school advertised itself as "Ohio's West Point of Christian Service." Its radio program, carried on nine stations, called socialism "evil" and communism "a system modeled after the devil and his angels." Byron Osborne, last president in Cleveland and first in Canton, remained a pacifist. Young Friends did not. In 1958 the superintendent of the church, and later second president of the school in Canton, complained that "almost none of our young men are . . . conscientious objectors."

To guard holy living, catalogs in the 1950s instructed women to dress in "modest apparel, with shamefacedness and sobriety": elbows covered, skirts no higher than fourteen inches above the floor. Men had to wear "long trousers." Couples could receive permission to sit together in class, church, and the school parlor (Wednesday evening until 7:10 P.M., Friday until 11:00 P.M.) but not in parked cars. In 1949 an evangelist—innocently, to be sure—made an "inopportune gesture" directing a "bird circus" in chapel. The faculty sent "a statement of its disapproval," and the president sent a letter to the evangelist. Students advocating Darwinism or Calvinistic doctrines could be expelled (some feared the dogma of predestination would discourage soul winning).

In 1936 the school adopted a four-year degree program with new courses in liberal arts. In 1956, after the state seized part of the campus for an expressway, the school was invited to relocate in Canton, the nation's largest metropolitan area with no liberal arts college. Canton needed a college, and the Bible college needed a campus. Canton voters had rejected a levy for a community university. At the same time, the Friends could not staff or fund a Quaker or Holiness liberal arts college or draw enough like-minded students. A Friends pastor in Canton chaired the board of trustees. Canton was within thirty miles of one-third of all members of the supporting denomination. A trustee, a Canton businessman, presented an invitation from civic leaders to bid on a fifty-four-acre tract of land. A college wary of secularism; a community wary of sectarianism—the future for this oddly matched couple would not be boring.

In the Christian college era, Byron Osborne tried to preserve the Quaker-Holiness heritage of the institution. President from 1951 to 1957 in Cleveland and 1957 to 1960 in Canton, this son-in law of the Malones had lived with Walter for fifteen years, taught at the school for thirty-seven years, and prayed "the mantle of Walter Malone might fall on me." The eponymous name "Malone College," he said, is "not so much to honor the founders as [to reaffirm the] message and character . . . of the school."

To Osborne, church and college rested on three foundations: divine guidance (his *Malone Story* gives a providential history of the school), Scripture, and a discipline that from Ohio's first Yearly Meeting in 1813 forbade participation in war, dancing, or theaters, "practices [that] alienate the mind from the counsel of divine wisdom." Other Quaker schools influenced by modern thought had discarded these prohibitions. Swarthmore trained military units during World War II and had dances by at least 1910. Haverford had dances by 1921, Wilmington by 1932, Guilford and Earlham by 1933. Evangelical Friends, he believed, were different, for they had reinforced ascetic hedges by ties to the Holiness Movement.

Holiness hedges protected students from alcohol, dancing, theaters, and tobacco, and no military recruitment was allowed on campus. Most trustees had to be Friends. Most faculty and administrators were Friends, or from Holiness churches with undergraduate degrees from Holiness schools or Wheaton College in Illinois. A college creed said the "purpose of this Institution is to maintain and inculcate doctrines," including the "inviolable authority" of Scripture and a Wesleyan Holiness belief in "entire sanctification . . . as a definite, instantaneous experience" followed by "continuous victory over sin." Holy living was a Quaker concern. The expectation of instant perfection was a later innovation.

To Osborne, "spiritually underprivileged" students offered a God-given "opportunity to show perfect love." Chapel met five days a week, with revivals and altar calls to promote holy living. A picture in *Look* magazine in 1960 was captioned "Emotion overwhelms this [Malone] student as she kneels at the altar to pray for salvation."

Catalogs said the college allows "considerable liberty to young people," yet rules from the Bible college era were retained. Women's knees and elbows remained covered, and they were not to wear slacks on campus. African Americans comprised 10 percent of the first graduating class, larger than in any succeeding year. In 1958 the choir canceled a concert in Virginia after a Friends church told them their one African American member was not welcome. After Osborne retired in 1960, he continued to denounce lethal violence and sexual impurity in letters to a local newspaper.

Osborne's successor, Everett Cattell (1960–72), a former missionary and superintendent of Ohio's Evangelical Friends, called Malone "an experiment in which a church college attempts to preserve spiritual integrity while serving community needs." The "Malone Experiment"—religiously diverse students and an evangelical Protestant faculty—would serve "the interests of a very small church, admittedly conservative, narrow and thoroughly committed, and those of the community, which is heterogeneous, progressive, broad and undecided." Malone would be a "center for independent moral judgments," a prophetic "voice in the wilderness . . . crying out for national righteousness and denouncing evil."

Cattell's call resonated in the Cold War era when the locus of evil lay in a foreign enemy and goodness in the American political and economic system. A commencement speaker, a theologically liberal but economically conservative Friend, called free enterprise "God-centered economics." Under Cattell the college's position differed from that of earlier Quaker ascetics, who denounced acquisitive competition and praised communal assistance and plain living.

Cattell's blend of theological, political, economic, and social conservatism into a "Christian worldview" prevailed, except for an occasional professor in history and social sciences. In the early 1960s the college received a Freedom Foundation award for its "campus program in teaching Americanism." Freshmen wrote required essays to honor freedom and denounce communism. A professor wrote a guide on Americanism for schools. Faculty gave anti-Communist talks in schools, civic clubs, and churches. The college sponsored a concert by the Army Field Band, films by the House Un-American Activities Committee, and a rally "to awaken America to dangers of Communism."

In the sixties college and church changed in tandem. Ohio's Evangelical Friends dropped their prohibition against participation in war while expressing support for "members who refuse to bear arms for conscience sake." In 1963 the college invited military recruiters to campus. In 1964 the student paper called for "total war" in Vietnam. Students who seized recruiting materials had to write essays to explain why stealing, not killing, is immoral, to be approved by a religion professor who supported the war. This ambivalence was not unique. Another Evangelical Friend, Richard Nixon, called himself a "deeply committed pacifist, perhaps because of my Quaker heritage from my mother" while bombing Cambodia.

Other hedges fell. In the year the church revised its stance on war, it dropped its threat to disown members who attend theatricals and movies, asking only that they avoid those "of a demoralizing nature." One professor was surprised in the later 1960 to hear a colleague speak of going to a movie. He also attended, but added, "I wouldn't have talked about it." At the same time the church hardened its stance against dancing, singling it out as "defiling."

In hiring faculty Cattell focused on academic qualifications and "personal relationship with Christ," not convictions about rules. Numbers of new faculty came to escape sterner behavioral restrictions at Holiness or fundamentalist colleges, notably Asbury, Bob Jones, Cedarville, or Marion (now Indiana Wesleyan). Ideologically, the campus was influenced by a New Evangelicalism that arose after World War II to reassert biblical authority, oppose secular thought, and dispel "legalism." This "Evangelical mind" captured older colleges (Wheaton, Taylor) and new ones (Gordon, Malone) that had been Bible colleges.

In the later 1960s the student newspaper debated restrictions on alcohol, dancing, dress, and tobacco. A few professors—asserting that Christianity has to do with relationships, not rules—opened a coffeehouse off campus where students smoked in public. A leader of the Evangelical Friends responded to a question in chapel by saying, "The church doesn't care how you dress." Cattell, feeling undercut, or so he told a colleague, and weary of protests—some against restrictions, others against the college "becoming liberal"—looked for middle ground. While insisting that anyone at Malone who uses alcohol, tobacco, or dances "violates a sacred trust," he conceded that the college would no longer seek to enforce bans on off-campus behavior.

Every dean of students in the Osborne-Cattell years was a minister, either a Quaker or from another Holiness or peace church. No student was to marry during the school year without notifying the college two months prior to the wedding. After a performance of *The Man of La Mancha,* with a cautiously choreographed rape scene, future plays had to have prior approval from the administration. Unmarried pregnancies were rare; when they occurred, mothers, but not all fathers, left the college, with permission to reapply after one year. Some professors made special efforts to encourage and support these women.

Uncertainty grew about what, if anything, faith had to do with legislating behavior. Two religion professors left to protest the erosion of Quaker-Holiness norms. Four professors replaced them; two held a Holiness theology akin to the founders, but only one (an Anabaptist) opposed all violence. Graduates in religion had been encouraged to attend Holiness schools, especially Asbury Seminary. After 1967 broader-based evangelical schools (Fuller, Gordon-Conwell, Trinity Evangelical) were apt to be recommended as well. Chapel changed; neither of the two chaplains in the later 1960s was a Quaker, and neither was a proponent of Wesleyan Holiness or revivalistic preaching. The first brought evangelical scholars and writers to campus. The second recommended replacing chapel with small-group Bible studies. Chapel continued, but not as the high-powered emotional engine that fueled and sustained Holiness in the earliest days in Canton.

Faculty luminaries included a microbiologist and former dean at Ohio State University, a scientist who left to head the Ohio Geological Survey, and another who later chaired the history of science department at the University of Wisconsin. A son of Quaker medical missionaries taught African history before heading the Africa desk at the State Department and serving as ambassador to African countries. History majors from the 1960s and 1970s were accepted at Harvard, Johns Hopkin, and Princeton. The debate team sometimes defeated Ivy League schools. Socially, while everyone opposed racial segregation, an administrator privately reprimanded a historian for participating in an interracial marriage. Denied tenure, he left to teach at a state university.

In Cattell's last years debt rose and enrollment fell from over 1,132 to below 800. Cattell warned, "Malone is not for everyone. If you want to leave we will help you go." He also cut back in the liberal arts.

In the 1970s modern foreign languages were eliminated; literature, history, and social science courses were trimmed. A professional program, social work, was added for pragmatic reasons. Yet, in spite of cutbacks, the college hosted the Midwest Writers Conference that brought 350 writers and editors to campus in 1979. Annual "Christianity and Literature" conferences met until the late 1970s, and every year from the mid-sixties to the mid-nineties more than 100 students attended a "Faith and History" conference to hear visiting scholars, including two past presidents of the American Historical Association. Renamed the Conference on Faith and Learning, it was terminated in the 1990s amid concerns that too much attention was being given to the college's history after it examined the Quaker heritage of the founders. Also in the 1990s a book on Quakers was banned from the general curriculum.

Hedges were further trimmed in the 1970s. Lon Randall, president from 1972–81, although a minister in two Holiness bodies and son of a Pilgrim Holiness minister, had been influenced by New Evangelicalism's antipathy to legalism and by success in the corporate world (he sat on the board of Canton's First National Bank). After Title IX banned gender discrimination in federally funded programs, putting gender-based rules to protect women in a different context, the college gave resident women the same rights as resident men. The fall of the strict dress code was also facilitated by a shift in Holiness and Pentecostal churches, as these now gave less attention to "modesty" or "plain dress."

Plain living was modified. In 1972 the president's starting salary was more than four times what Osborne was paid in 1960. Randall lived in a college-owned stone home with six bathrooms, two elegant libraries, servant quarters, and an elevator. Osborne had lived in a two-bedroom cottage. The campus was upgraded, especially after the school bought land adjacent to the college where a barn was transformed into a campus center called by one Pulitzer Prize–winning poet "the most beautiful building I've ever been in." Administrative offices were air conditioned (some faculty had enjoyed air conditioning since 1966). A wing of the cafeteria in what is now Founders Hall was enclosed and remodeled to entertain guests.

In the 1970s a military veteran led Ohio's Friends for the first time in history. He also chaired the religion and philosophy department and asserted that Vietnam was a "just war." With worries about survival, the "Malone Experiment" (Christian versus non-Christian) became the "Malone Experience." The school described itself as simply a "College of Persons." Chapel continued, with more attention to "community building" and less to evangelism. Promotional materials said less about the Christian character of the college. Admissions counselors and coaches were careful not to give undue attention to religion when visiting public schools. Before resigning, Randall became chairman of the Christian College Coalition (now Council for Christian Colleges and Universities), which then included sixty liberal arts colleges with 75,000 students and 3,500 faculty. On leaving Malone he served briefly as director of international operations for the Peace Corps.

In the 1980s Gordon Werkema (1981–88) set about to rebuild enrollment. He required higher ACT scores for admission. At the same time he purchased a degree-completion program, the Malone College Management Program (M.C.M.P.), from Lon Randall, then with the National Teachers College (now Lewis National University). By 1985, with 125 students in M.C.M.P., the college's enrollment rose from 770 in 1981 to 1,039. Led by a music instructor, three of the first eight "primary instructors" were business professors, two were coaches, and the rest had degrees in religion, education, and communications. By the third millennium M.C.M.P. had graduated almost 2,000 students. Forty percent of undergraduates continue to be from this program. In spite of Werkema's cuts in liberal arts, entering students since the 1986–87 academic year consistently score one to two points above the national average on the ACT exam and higher than the four other colleges and universities in Stark County and well above neighboring state universities.

Werkema, founder of the Christian College Consortium and past president of the Christian College Coalition, advertised the Christian character of the school and cultivated relationships with Christian high schools. Visiting scholars instructed faculty on integration of faith, learning, and living. Professors received stipends to attend these lectures, which examined philosophical roots of Christian and secular thinking.

While theologically conservative, none of these scholars represented the economic and social conservatism that had prevailed in Cattell's era. At the same time little effort was made to apply this "Christian mind" to controversial issues in the larger culture.

In the 1990s the convergence of college, community, and culture accelerated. President Woody Self (1989–94) was from Holiness roots (Church of the Nazarene), and Ronald Johnson (1995–) spent his life as an Evangelical Friend and served as interim president as well as vice president, dean, and provost.

Under Self a new entrance and new buildings transformed the campus. A campus center was built in spite of the withdrawal of a promised gift of $1 million when the college refused to hire a Jewish professor. While new sports programs for women were established, and football for men, Malone is best known for its nationally acclaimed program in cross-country. Enrollment-building graduate programs were added in education, business (to draw from M.C.M.P.), and Christian ministries (including an innovative program in sports ministry), with courses in online learning.

By the first academic year of the new millennium, 77 percent of full-time faculty (82 of 106) had come to the college during the 1990s alone. In 2000, for the first time in forty years, there was no graduate in history. However, the college has hired bright young scholars to rebuild this discipline, with an Honors Program for gifted students. In 2002 there were nineteen graduates in history and social sciences, with forty political science and history majors in 2003.

Under Self a few Nazarenes joined the faculty, but not all were proponents of Holiness. Some left after a few years for one of their denominational schools. Diversity grew. The first Catholic was hired in the mid-1980s. Johnson, who may have looked for middle ground after supporting the release of a politiclly incorrect teacher, later released a professor who publicly converted to Judaism who offended some more liberal colleagues by focusing on Western Christian (male) writers. (He chairs the English department at a higher-ranked college, where he received the Governor's Award as one of that state's outstanding teachers.)

In 2000, the day before the college's first dance was announced at Yearly Meeting, the church withdrew its prohibition against dancing. Dancing, the college's president explained, is "a wholesome activity within a Christian setting." On Veteran's Day the chaplain (a Quaker minister and former army chaplain) honored veterans in chapel. The senior staff chaplain in the Gulf War praised soldiers for "making America great" and recounted challenging troops in Vietnam and Iraqi to fight enemies who do not believe humans are created "in the image of God." Ironically, this phrase had been used by the Malones to condemn killing, not condone it.

If redefined, religion remains vital at Malone. Students volunteer for service trips to Africa, Latin America, and inner cities in the United States. Hundreds gather on Thursdays for a worship celebration that attracts students from neighboring colleges and universities. Professors sing choruses and hymns at faculty meetings. Some lead Bible studies in their homes and in area churches.

To understand change at Malone, it is helpful to recall that Osborne's faith in the fixed character of the college was rooted in his belief in Scripture as a clear inerrant guide, a stable Book of Discipline, and a Quaker-Holiness *weltanschauung.* However, by 2000 there was little inclination to settle disputes by citing Scripture. The Discipline had proved more flexible than Osborne imagined. The president's decision to hold dances on campus preceded the revision of the Discipline. Practices at other Christian colleges and at Friends churches, not Osborne's bellwethers for divine guidance, were cited to support his decision.

By 2000, with greater focus on professional training, less attention to liberal arts, and more emphasis on "ministry" than on historic theology, sectarian distinctives from the training school and early Christian college eras were gone. The founders' focus on rescuing "sinners" from urban vice had been replaced by a faith with greater freedom to pursue one's own understanding of right and wrong. Cattell's call to be a "voice in the wilderness" denouncing evil faded with the Cold War. The college had become a community-oriented "Christian College of the Arts, Sciences, and Professions" akin to the community university Canton leaders had envisioned at midcentury, if with a heritage of nonviolence and care for the poor that continues to haunt some members of the college community.

Finally, the imposing heritage of this college lies in the vision of the Malones to prepare students to serve God and humankind. In the "Afterword" to *J. Walter Malone: The Autobiography of an Evangelical Quaker,* a grandson writes that "for those of us who knew [Walter] intimately, the benediction of his life has haunted us all our lives, and, we hope, will haunt our children all of their lives, and their children to the end of time." To the respected literary critic Lauren King, who "cannot remember a book I have read in all my reviewing and other reading that has moved me as has [Malone's autobiography]," this heritage lies not in rules but in the life-affirming spirit of the Malones.

SUGGESTED READING

J. Walter Malone: The Autobiography of an Evangelical Quaker, ed. John Oliver (University Press of America, 1993); David Johns, ed., *Hope and a Future: The Malone College Story* (Friends United Press, 1993); Byron Osborne, *The Malone Story: The Dream of Two Quaker Young People* (Union Printing, 1970); John Oliver, "Emma Brown Malone: A Mother of Feminism?" *Quaker History* 88 (Spring 1999): 4–21; John Oliver, "J. Walter Malone: The American Friend and an Evangelical Quaker's Social Agenda," *Quaker History* 80 (Fall 1991): 63–84; John Oliver, "Cleveland Quakers from 1892–1907: Evangelism, Gender and the Poor," Western Reserve Studies Symposium, 1994, Case Western Reserve University Library Website; John Oliver, "Walter and Emma Malone: Friends of Sinners and the Poor," *Quaker Studies* 6 (Mar. 2002): 195–210; John W. Oliver, "Evangelical Campus and Press Meet Black America's Struggle for Civil Rights: Malone College and *Christianity Today,*" *Fides et Historia* 8 (Fall 1975): 54–70.

Marietta College

Teaching the Useful Arts

JAMES H. O'DONNELL III

The seeds of higher education in the Northwest were planted in Marietta by the first settlers who arrived from the East in 1788. Inheritors of the Revolutionary legacies that fostered both love of country and desire for enlightenment, these pioneers sought to cultivate democratic civilization and learning on the banks of the Ohio. Devoted to the principles inherent in the Ordinance of 1787, these immigrants were committed to the idea that their descendants should not perish uneducated in the untamed wilderness. As the framers of the Ordinance wrote, "Religion, morality and knowledge being necessary to good government and the happiness of mankind, schools and the means of education will forever be encouraged."

Once the initial decade of overcoming basic survival needs had passed, the Marietta community turned its attention to the creation of the Muskingum Academy. Opened in 1797, the new institution offered instruction to the children of the West for the next thirty-five years. Among the teachers at the academy were graduates of Yale and Dartmouth.

The idea of a college also was present among the citizens of Marietta from the earliest days, but it did not find clear definition until the early 1830s with the opening of the Institute of Education organized by Luther Bingham, pastor of the First Congregational Church. Support for this institution came from those who were concerned about the general lack of collegiate education in the West, the need for qualified teachers in that area, and the hope for improving their community by locating a college in it. Two years later this school became the Marietta Collegiate Institution and Western Teachers Seminary. By 1835 the school was transformed into Marietta College under charter from the state on February 14.

As a state-approved, degree-granting institution, Marietta was to eschew all overt sectarianism. In the minds of the founders, however, its purposes were established on

Erwin Hall

Christian principles. During the first twenty-five years of its existence, more than 40 percent of its graduates entered the ministry, a number going on to study at Lane Seminary in Cincinnati, Ohio. Marietta College certainly was not alone in this respect. College-educated men had few career opportunities open to them, so it was only natural that the majority of them entered the ministry. Out of Amherst's 1831 graduating class of sixty, thirty-two entered the ministry; Dartmouth's 1836 class of twenty-four had sixteen dedicated to ministerial service. As one student of higher education in that time observed, "The ministry was the supreme ideal of Christian manhood."

The college's leader who firmly supported such a philosophy for almost half a century was Israel Ward Andrews, an 1837 graduate of Williams College who came to Marietta to teach math in 1839. Professor from 1839 to 1888, Andrews also was treasurer from 1850 to 1855 and president of the college from 1855 to 1885. The son of a Congregationalist pastor in Connecticut, Israel Andrews was a self-admitted conservative Puritan of the old school. Much like his father, who had helped found Hartford Seminary in protest against the liberalism of Yale, Andrews admitted this persuasion without apology. Indeed, he brought with him to Ohio many of the ideologies that had flourished in his home state during his adolescence. Clearly he did not subscribe to the more liberal interpretation of Calvinism advanced by the New Haven group, nor did he have any toleration for Roman Catholicism. As he confessed in 1841, moreover, he was a teetotaler, willing to be called a fanatic if his personal stance brought down that appellation.

The greatest obstacles to the success of Marietta College in the nineteenth century were much the same as they remain in the twenty-first century: money and students. During the early years of Israel Ward Andrews' service, the number of graduates never numbered more than four or five a year, while the student body ranged from forty to fifty-five. Any crisis would send students home after the first term, whether it be sickness, finances, or family pressure to help on the farm. An event as catastrophic as the Civil War would depress enrollment severely as young men of military age answered the call of patriotic duty.

During the 1850s student debates reflected the intense national issues of the day. In July 1854 the students engaged in a heated exchange about the Kansas-Nebraska Act, which they resolved to condemn as an insult to "national honor." With the coming of war in 1861, wrote one student, "games and recreation gave place to military drills; the campus became a drill ground." By 1864 enrollment had declined by 36 percent as Marietta College students enlisted, with the majority serving in the 36th, 77th, and 92d regiments of the Ohio Infantry. President Andrews's brother, Professor Ebenezer Baldwin Andrews, served as major, lieutenant colonel, and eventually colonel of the 36th Ohio. In the course of the war nineteen students gave their lives in the service of the Union. Given the proximity of the college to the South (western Virginia was just across the Ohio River), it is not surprising that seven graduates, seven undergraduates, and one academy student served the cause of the South. Henry Fitzhugh (Class of 1847) was appointed Confederate commissioner to England in 1864.

Throughout the nineteenth century finances were as uncertain as student enrollments. From the time of its founding, the college had no solid financial base. Money was so scarce that the faculty, including the president who was also a professor, often received promissory notes in lieu of compensation. President Henry Smith referred to money as "an unknown commodity." From 1835 to 1860 the college operated at large annual deficits, often spending $7,500 a year while receiving only $3,500. The presidents and other representatives of the college frequently traveled both regionally and nationally in search of funds to keep the college afloat.

Soon after he was elected the college's leader, Israel Ward Andrews journeyed by steamboat, stagecoach, and rail throughout southeastern Ohio between Marietta and Portsmouth meeting supporters, preaching in churches, and recruiting students. Most solicitations for funds resulted in minimal returns, with the majority of those canvassed citing recent reversals of one sort or another as keeping them from fulfilling commitments previously made. Early in Andrews's service the college had joined other schools in the common fund-raising venture known as the Society for the Promotion of Collegiate and Theological Education at the West. The brainchild of Lyman Beecher, who had left the comfort of pulpits in the East to lead Lane Seminary in Cincinnati, the society brought together several colleges in the West to raise funds jointly, thus avoiding duplication of effort. Led for many years by Theron Baldwin, the society often proved the difference between success and failure for the struggling schools, which found the sums assigned to them, whether $500 or $1,000, like the proverbial manna in the desert. Many college presidents warmly expressed their institutions' gratitude for this help at the annual meetings of the society during its lifetime from 1843 to 1874.

Another common factor shared by these schools in the West was the concern for signs of religious awakenings. Commitment to evangelism had crossed the mountains with many of the leaders, so it was expected that presidential reports would indicate the number in the student bodies who could be described as "hopefully pious." Good Calvinists that these leaders were, they could not assert salvation in explicit terms but could indicate the hopefulness of those who had turned their hearts toward religion. Whatever the actual religious condition of their students, presidents like Israel Andrews included descriptions of the previous years' revivals in their annual reports to the society. Religion was woven into the fabric of campus life at Marietta College, with the students expected to attend chapel twice daily and a local church on Sunday. A Society of Inquiry was organized in 1833, even before the school's charter was granted, with the purpose of promoting religious activity, encouraging missions, and being alert for any "special visitation of the Holy Spirit." Both Presidents Smith and Andrews were pleased by the frequent revivals and prayer meetings that marked religious activity on campus.

The other agenda promoted by the colleges supported by the Western Society was an offensive against the perceived Roman Catholic menace. Lyman Beecher, the moving spirit behind the organization, had declared his anti-Catholic crusade in his 1831 *A Plea for the West*. This antipathy was shared by most of the college presidents who went to the society for help; their sermons reflect this theme, as do the minutes of the annual meetings of the society. The Annual Concerts of Prayer for colleges sponsored on the campuses mirrored this crusade throughout the 1840s, in part a reflection of the national anti-Romanism of that time. Also, adversaries of a different sort were colleges whose founding principles seemed too liberal for the leaders of the society. Chief among these for a time was Oberlin, many of whose early faculty and students had once been at Lane Seminary, the Beecher-influenced school in Cincinnati. Oberlin's official history reflects the perspective that a principal reason for the founding of the Western Society was to keep donors from giving funds to Oberlin!

Its New England roots defined Marietta College's sense of purpose in its early days. Most students came intent on a career in the ministry. Given the difficulties of travel, the majority came from Ohio and West Virginia. There was the occasional student who came from the East with less than a dollar in his pocket, intent on pursuing education on the banks of the Ohio. Once enrolled, students literally had to request leave from the faculty for any absence from the campus. There were two long terms, broken briefly by a vacation, but the final classes of the year did not end until the last week in July with baccalaureate and commencement. Each member of the class offered an oration, and the president preached the baccalaureate. Requests from graduates finally persuaded President Andrews to allow the alumni to add their own celebration to graduation week. Since Andrews knew every graduate from 1840 to 1888, he must have come to appreciate these annual commencement celebrations.

Throughout the years from 1835 to 1890, the curriculum at Marietta College changed little. Based on long-held classical models, student courses for the class of 1839 differed little for the next sixty years. An entrance examination required candidates to pass tests in Greek, Latin, English grammar, arithmetic, algebra, and geometry. Hebrew, Greek, Latin, math, philosophy, natural theology and evidences of Christianity, political economy, Roman history, and rhetoric were long a part of the curriculum. All students, moreover, had to take a kind of senior capstone course. Taught for many years by President Andrews, the course focused on Andrews's interpretation of the U.S. Constitution. During the Civil War Andrews gave lectures on the importance of the Union that were published by the alumni in Cincinnati. The war motivated the president to write his *Manual of the Constitution* in 1874, and it was used as a text in several college courses at Marietta and elsewhere. As early as 1866 an Ohio education official had urged the Greek requirement be dropped because it discriminated against students whose high schools had no instruction in Greek, but it was not eliminated until 1875. Four years later mention of a "Philosophical Course" appeared in the offerings as a modification of the classical course by dropping Greek and allowing the substitution of history, French, German, natural science, or a critical analysis of the English language.

Although the curriculum remained conservative, science was not neglected at Marietta. The president's brother, Ebenezer Baldwin Andrews, came to Marietta College, graduated in 1842, and then went to Andover Theological Seminary. He returned to Marietta College in 1851 as professor of natural sciences. After teaching for a number of years, he enlisted in the 36th Ohio Volunteer Infantry during the Civil War as a major, ultimately receiving promotion to colonel. After the war he taught at Marietta College before his appointment to the Ohio Geological Survey in 1869. E. B. Andrews was the typical liberal arts teacher of his time, whose approach to science was general and concerned with the connection between science and religion. Like his father and brothers, Ebenezer Andrews also preached regularly.

By the 1870s Marietta College had overcome some of its earlier financial difficulties, thanks to the generosity of such local supporters as Douglas Putnam, secretary of the board of trustees from 1833 to 1894. A challenge gift from Putnam in the late 1850s brought more than $50,000 to the college in a short time. This did not solve all the college's woes, but it did help with the beginnings of an endowment. Even so, the enrollments of the postwar period were uneven, with the student body fluctuating in number between seventy and ninety.

Like many of its sister schools, Marietta passed through an era of change in the last decades of the nineteenth century. Two events indicative of these transitions were the admission of women in the 1890s and the advent of organized field sports during the same period. During most of the nineteenth century only rowing had been allowed for recreational purposes, a practice indicated by the first regatta in 1878. Prior to that students had to petition the faculty for a day off at the end of the semester to go fishing. Officially sponsored team activities came in the last decades of the century with the organization of both football and baseball teams. Another indication of increased campus commitment to athletics came in 1903 with the completion of Goshorn Gym with its adjoining tennis courts. A multipurpose structure, it served primarily as home to the men's and women's basketball teams for the next quarter-century. It was replaced in 1929 by the Ban Johnson Field House, named to honor B. Bancroft Johnson (Class of 1887), who started a building fund for the new structure with an initial gift of $25,000.

One positive change in enrollment patterns came in the late 1890s when Marietta College began to admit women. This dramatic makeover took place because a wealthy potential benefactor said he would give money only to coeducational colleges; if Marietta remained only a "boys school," he would give it nothing. Since many of Marietta's competitors (except Kenyon and Wabash) admitted women, Marietta chose to follow. Thus the board accepted the new arrangement over the protests of certain vocal alumni. Women actually had begun attending classes in the middle 1890s as part of an arrangement with Elizabeth College, a college for women founded in 1890, through which the Elizabeth students took Marietta classes. Before women were officially admitted, their presence on the campus reportedly helped the less industrious males to graduate. That parallel arrangement continued until 1898, when the college became officially coeducational. When enfranchisement became an issue after the turn of the century, placards at a rally for the Coed Suffrage Club suggested that the men could sew on their own buttons if they did not back the drive for giving women the right to vote.

Early in the new century Marietta College marked its seventy-fifth anniversary. Held in conjunction with the annual commencement exercises, this joint celebration was honored by the presence of President William Howard Taft, who received an honorary Doctor of Civil Law degree. Also present were the governor of Ohio, Judson Hudson; the president of Ohio State University, William O. Thompson; and the national president of Phi Beta Kappa, Edwin A. Grosvenor of Amherst College. Marietta's chapter of the national honorary was the sixteenth in the nation. Also in the platform party that day was Charles G. Dawes (Class of 1884), later cowinner of the Nobel Peace Prize in 1925 and U.S. vice president (1925–29).

By the First World War the males in the student body had exchanged their normal attire for the khaki of the Reserve Officers Training Corps. Complete with a corps band, the officers in training attended classes and also prepared for the eventuality of service overseas. With the coming of peace in 1918, life on campus once more could return to normal. More activities outside the classrooms emerged between the two wars as music, drama, and social activities involved numbers of students. Fraternities had existed at Marietta College since the 1850s, a legacy in part resulting from Andrews's undergraduate experience at Williams. President Andrews had belonged both to a fraternity and to a literary society, so he readily accepted these at Marietta. Literary societies and magazines were other ways for the rather conservative students to express themselves. The *College Olio* began publication under the sponsorship of the two literary societies in 1872, and the college yearbook was first published in 1878.

In the second half of the nineteenth century, moreover, the student body had become less focused on religion. Evening chapel had been discontinued in 1868, with compulsory Sunday church attendance lasting until 1878. Pressure for change increased after the *Olio* went into publication, as its editors kept discussing the matter of compulsory religion. The appointed hour for morning chapel was advanced from 7:30 to 8:00 and eventually to 11:00. The venerable Society of Inquiry was eliminated in 1884 when President Andrews, who had preached to it so often, permitted the Young Men's Christian Association to take its place. The YMCA movement was sweeping college campuses at that time, with a strong emphasis on missionary service. The creation of a Marietta College chapter would be acceptable to a mission-oriented individual like Andrews, who had been a member of the board of the American Board of Commissioners for Foreign Missions. He also welcomed speakers from the Student Volunteer Movement, the collegiate organization inspired by Dwight L. Moody to recruit students for missionary service. Several graduates in the 1890s became missionaries, including Edward Marsden, a Native American from British Columbia.

No doubt Israel Ward Andrews's retirement from the presidency in 1885 helped pave the way for a less rigid moralistic spirit throughout the campus. A personal philosophy hammered out on the anvil of New England Calvinism before 1825 was hardly in touch with the young men born during and after the Civil War. A further moderation of the religious atmosphere took place in 1891 when the faculty voted that Bible study become a subject of instruction rather than indoctrination; from that time on there would be graded examinations and recitations at the end of the term, just as in other courses in the curriculum.

President Andrews's death in the spring of 1888 came during an eastern trip that included a number of speaking engagements. One of his themes was the centennial of the Northwest Territory, a topic he had researched in connection with the centennial of Marietta. The city celebration itself had caused him difficulty. As the dominant academic citizen of the town, Israel Ward Andrews had been named to the centennial committee only to discover that there was a difference of opinion about the proper day for the celebration. President Andrews and the traditionalists wanted to mark the April anniversary of the pioneer landing. Other citizens, more concerned with weather conditions in early spring, pushed for postponing the date until the summer when more moderate weather might allow larger attendance. Some scholars see this as a struggle between the new business class of the Gilded Age and the more conservative members of the community. The division apparently was irreconcilable; Marietta celebrated her centennial twice in 1888, once in early April and again in July. Andrews in the meantime had gone East, where he was caught in a late-spring snowstorm that left him so ill that he died at his brother's house in Hartford, Connecticut.

Marietta College without Israel Ward Andrews entered a new era. A conservative leader, who had known each of the 562 alumni from 1840 to 1888, President Andrews had permitted change only when forced to do so. Although Andrews had regarded the college as religious in purpose, it had never had a denominational connection or a stipulated devotion to sectarianism. The school therefore benefited from its nonsectarian nature during its fund-raising efforts of the late nineteenth and twentieth century, when it was clear that prominent philanthropists shied away from denominational connections. Early in the nineteenth century two challenge gifts came from Andrew Carnegie, one of $40,000 in 1906 for building a library and another of $25,000 in conjunction with the seventieth-fifth-anniversary campaign in 1910. The first stipulated a matching amount; the second required that all the pledges of the drive be paid and the institution's debts paid before the Carnegie money would be granted. Welcome, although belated, assistance came also to the faculty in 1906 from the Carnegie Foundation for the Advancement of Teaching when Marietta College professors with fifteen years' teaching experience in an institution of higher learning were selected as eligible for pensions under the foundation's guidelines.

The 1898 class song that echoed the twin sentiments of coeducation and war indicated the ways in which the college reflected the changing American culture. End-of-the-century imperialism was an attitude shared by the earnest young men of America's colleges who abandoned the isolationism of their forebears to take up the burdens of empire. Given the long-time attachment of Marietta's leaders and students to the cause of missions, this commitment was really not a great departure. Admitting women to the campus was another way to measure the institution's willingness to change with the coming of the new century. Women quickly became part of the campus scene, whether in the classroom, in the laboratory, or on the playing field. If in that class song they claimed to have assisted the men in graduating, by 1914 they lobbied openly for the franchise.

In the post-Andrews era students at Marietta faced much the same dilemma as the society: cling to the familiar roots of the past or move toward the sounds of industry's siren song. This struggle between those who espoused the liberal arts and those who saw the college's chartered mission to teach all "the useful arts" as something more practical would never be resolved satisfactorily. A century later the argument would be between the liberal arts, however defined, and the so-called "professional programs," which by the early twenty-first century were accounting and management, petroleum engineering, and sports medicine.

Early in the twentieth century the college library began to receive a number of extensive collections of both printed and manuscript materials. Fortunately for historians of early Ohio and the Old Northwest, the papers of the Ohio Company of Associates had been donated to the library and formed the core of its manuscript collections. Beginning with President Henry Smith's book-buying in Germany before the Civil War, the library had slowly acquired a number of useful printed volumes. Between 1885 and 1910, however, several bequests pushed the holdings to a position of unusual strength. President John Eaton donated some 1,600 books, many of them reports and journals from the field of education that were extremely difficult to locate. Librarian Rodney Stimson, who had arrived as a penniless student, donated more than 18,000 volumes of important Americana worth approximately $30,000 in 1900. Perhaps the most potentially valuable gift came from Charles Goddard

Slack (Class of 1881), who gave his collection of American autographs, including signatures of fifty-four of the fifty-six signers of the Declaration of Independence.

The cultural life of the college also expanded during the 1920s and 1930s with the creation of choral music groups, a players club for drama, an orchestra, and a forensic organization. Thanks to the activities of the last-named group, Pi Kappa Delta, the national forensics honorary, chartered its Marietta chapter in 1925. The increasing activities of women on campus were reflected in the political cooperation of the sororities in 1931 to vote one of their own into the office of student body president. Although the men of that day pledged it would never happen again, it would happen again and with increasing frequency after the election of Mary Beth Rhodes in 1974. By the end of the twentieth century it was just as common to have a woman as president of the student government as a man.

With the coming of war in 1941, the campus again would know the presence of men in khaki. Although many of the regular undergraduate males joined the armed services and left the campus largely female, a sizable unit of U.S. Army Air Corps trainees came for several months of training, making the college temporarily a "military reservation." Some of these personnel returned after the war to attend as students, happily no longer in uniform. They came thanks to the GI Bill, bringing with them, in many cases, wives and children. The small campus was soon bulging as the administration sought to find housing for all these newcomers. Creative solutions to space needs included a floating dormitory on the Muskingum River, barracks erected on the campus green, trailers for families parked next to the field house, and a temporary building disassembled at Wright-Patterson Air Base in Dayton and brought to campus for reassembly. It served as classroom building, faculty offices, and bookstore until 1970. In the aftermath of the shootings at Kent State University, a party or parties unknown burned the building to the ground. No one was hurt, and the building's rubble was cleared, since it had been scheduled for demolition.

The postwar growth and demand for housing also prompted the college to renovate a nineteenth-century chair factory into a men's dormitory. Named for Douglas Putnam, the college's most prominent benefactor in the fifty years he served on the board from the 1832 to the 1894, the dorm served generations of freshmen before it, too, was taken down in the name of progress in the 1980s. The factory's solidly built five-story office building and warehouse also was acquired and transformed into a science building. The college observatory, originally constructed in 1882 and given to the school in 1892, was relocated to its roof.

Enrollment at Marietta College was boosted by the impact of both World Wars. The First World War increased the student body from just over 200 to more than 400. For the next twenty years the numbers remained at about 400, with a roughly two-to-one the ratio in favor of men. During the Second World War the national demand for enlistees dropped the numbers dramatically downward, with only women remaining on campus for the most part. After the war, however, thanks to a new eagerness for education and the support of the GI Bill, the number of students on campus reached new heights. In the twenty years from 1945 to 1965 the student body expanded from 400 to about 1,600, continuing to grow until it reached its peak at more than 1,800 in the late 1960s. That growth meant new buildings were needed, including two new dormitories in addition to the renovated chair factory as well as a new classroom structure and a fine arts building. The demography of the student body, which had begun to change after the First World War, became decidedly more eastern, with approximately 60 percent of the students recruited from the East Coast; the ratio of men to women shifted slightly, the numbers becoming five men to every three women. By the end of the twentieth century the numbers finally balanced, with approximately equal numbers of men and women being admitted. Since the retention rate for women tends to run higher than for men, the day is likely to come when the traditional ratio will reverse in favor of women.

In the twentieth century the college was led by a number of presidents, none of whom matched the longevity of President Andrews. Faculty leadership was established in the 1930s by a number of department heads that remained in power until the late 1960s. At that time the administrative team of President Frank Duddy and Dean Al Bosch, who came together from Westminster College in Utah, undertook the task of modernizing the faculty structure and the curriculum. Increased offerings in marketing, accounting, computer science, petroleum engineering, mass media, psychology, education, and sports medicine gave more options to the students but aroused the ire of the traditionally minded defenders of the pure liberal arts. The debate between the two camps would go on without resolution, but in the meantime increasing numbers of majors would be drawn to these areas of study. By the end of the twentieth century the majority of the college's students would find themselves completing degrees in one of these fields.

Fuel was added to the burning argument in the early 1980s when the college received a multimillion-dollar grant from the estate of Bernard P. McDonough, a wealthy industrialist from nearby Parkersburg, West Virginia. Initially it was believed the funding should go to expand the business offerings, but eventually it became the endowment for the Bernard P. McDonough Center for the Study of Leadership and Business. Under the leadership of former faculty Stephen Schwartz, the center has become a value-added attraction, bringing a new type of student to the campus. At the beginning of the twenty-first century, more than 40 percent of the entering classes have come to Marietta College in part because of the attractiveness of the Leadership program.

As Marietta College looks toward its bicentennial in 2035, it is in many ways a college still in search of itself. In part this is the nature of the academic enterprise, constantly examining oneself in search of renewal. At the same time, however,

Marietta's dilemma is compounded by its nineteenth-century history, wherein it was neither fish nor fowl. Although not a denominational college in any sense, it was until Andrews's death a religious institution. Indeed, the remnants of this legacy lasted until World War II. When a new instructor of history and political science was hired in the late 1930s, he was expected to address the college chapel from time to time in one of its twice-weekly meetings. The eminently practical minded veterans can be credited with the elimination of chapel when they arrived after the war.

Marietta's other great quandary from 1835 to 2001 has been sheer survival. It is rather difficult to rise above the mundane to think noble thoughts about an institution's educational purpose when always lurking in the shadows is the ghost of the future. The friends who wish the college to have a tercentennial celebration would do well to focus their energies on so undergirding her endowment that the question of survival would no more stalk her halls.

The college's new century opened with an auspicious start when the board named the first woman president of the institution. Jean A. Scott, a Harvard-trained historian with a wide range of experiences as both professor and administrator, was inaugurated the college's sixteenth president. A gracious southerner who knows how to say "no" to the most challenging faculty, she promises to give the school the direction it needs to move toward its bicentennial. She is complemented in her leadership style by Provost Sue DeWine, whose long experience as both professor and administrator in the field of communication stands her in good stead as she guides the academic life of the college. Under their leadership Marietta College will continue to prosper on the banks of the Ohio, as it has since 1835, teaching the useful arts to all who would come.

Suggested Reading

There is no scholarly history of Marietta College. Arthur G. Beach's *A Pioneer College: The Story of Marietta* (1935) is the useful, but sympathetic work of a long-time professor of English. The sequel to Beach's book is Vernon E. McGrew, *In the Various Branches of Useful Knowledge, Marietta College, 1935–1989* (1994). The town's story may be found in Andrew Cayton and Paula Riggs, *City Into Town* (1976). Scholars interested in primary documents may find them in the Marietta College Library's Special Collections. Especially important to the nineteenth century are the papers, including all of his sermons, of President Israel Ward Andrews.

College of Mount St. Joseph

An Educational Institution Rooted in Values

KIMBERLY J. M. WILSON

Situated on a high hill overlooking the Ohio River, the College of Mount St. Joseph has stood as a beacon of education, faith, integrity, respect, and character for its students for over eighty years. Founded as an institution of higher education for Catholic women in 1920 by the Sisters of Charity of Cincinnati, Ohio, the college has grown and developed into a coeducational undergraduate and graduate degree-granting institution still rooted in the mission and values of its founders.

In 1920 the College of Mount St. Joseph became one of a small number of Catholic colleges for women in the country to offer baccalaureate degrees. From the beginning the Mount provided a choice to women seeking an educational environment within the context of Catholic Christian values, as its original mission statement attested: "The College aims to inform the mind, to train the heart, to stimulate the will so that the result will be a true woman ready to take her rightful place in the social, the business, and the religious world. Throughout the course Religion prompts the knowledge, the discipline, the self-control, the fundamental principles of Christian culture. Through the entire period of college life, the true woman is fostered."

Dedicated to developing women of character, the Sisters of Charity provided the financial, moral, educational, and personal backing for the College of Mount St. Joseph for over fifty years. The Sisters not only led the way toward creative and responsive educational programming, but they contributed their services to the day-to-day operation of the college in unsalaried positions, ranging from maintenance duties to faculty and administrative appointments; wherever the Sisters recognized a need, it was addressed.

The first Sisters of Charity came to Cincinnati in 1829, after being asked by Bishop Edward Fenwick to organize and staff an orphanage and a free school. It was in

1849 that the Sisters on mission in Cincinnati learned that their community in
Emmitsburg, Maryland, planned to affiliate with the French-based Daughters of
Charity. This community decision prompted a break between the Cincinnati and
Emmitsburg Sisters, and in 1852 a separate and independent community of Sisters
of Charity in Cincinnati was established. Two years later, in 1854, the Sisters of

Charity were incorporated by the Ohio State legislature, which granted them the right to confer academic honors and collegiate degrees. That same year the Sisters opened Mount St. Vincent Academy for girls, the predecessor of the College of Mount St. Joseph. Mount St. Vincent Academy was eventually moved to the Sister's Delhi Township motherhouse in western Cincinnati and was renamed Mount St. Joseph Academy in 1906 when the Sisters relocated a boarding academy for boys, St. Aloysius, to Fayetteville, Ohio.

Mount St. Joseph Academy offered college-level courses (equivalent to one year of college credit) to any student interested in furthering her education beyond the traditional academy program. Students who chose to take advantage of these courses were usually those women who planned to become teachers or who went on to other institutions of higher education. It was customary at this time for area schools to accept academy graduates without examination. It was not until 1918 that the Mount learned from authorities at the State Department of Public Instruction that neither the Hamilton County superintendent nor the state itself fully recognized the academy as an institution of higher education.

This revelation came to the Sisters after a former academy graduate who had taken college-level courses at the Mount was denied state verification for her teaching license. After much distress, the student did receive her license once it was established that her coursework did meet the certification laws, but not before the episode brought to light problems with the Mount's college-level courses.

Not wanting another academy graduate to have to endure the scrutiny of the state, the Sisters made a visit to the Department of Public Instruction in Columbus and inquired about the procedures involved in gaining state recognition for the Mount's college-level courses. They were informed that before anything could be done, an inspection of the school and an evaluation of the Mount's teacher training, course of study, equipment, and physical conditions would have to be performed.

Following this initial meeting, the Sisters returned to Cincinnati and began preparations for the upcoming state inspection. In the fall of 1919 state representatives arrived at Mount St. Joseph and began a series of observations and inspections, which continued through the year. It was at this time that the Sisters, on the advice of a local priest, Father William Clark, inquired about earning a college rating for the school as well. When Mount St. Joseph Academy was officially recognized by the State of Ohio in 1920, the Sisters immediately submitted an application for a college charter to Senator Robert O'Brien of Cincinnati, who presented it to the Ohio legislature. On February 26, 1920, the community was notified that the application had been accepted and that the Sisters of Charity had been named as trustees of the College of Mount St. Joseph.

The Sisters of Charity officially opened the doors of the College of Mount St. Joseph to a charter class of twenty students on September 14, 1920. The college shared facilities and dormitories with the academy, operating out of Marian Hall in the community motherhouse until Seton Hall was built in 1927. The schedule included courses in education, English, French, Latin, mathematics, philosophy, religion, social service, sociology, and Spanish as well as offerings in art and music. Greek, home economics, physical education, public speaking, and the Normal Department (teacher training) were added the second year. Mother Mary Bertha Armstrong served as the ex-officio president of the college and Sister Leonita Mulhall as academic dean, overseeing the day-to-day running of the college.

Faculty for the new college was recruited from among seminary professors and local clergy with appropriate backgrounds and degrees, as well as members of the Sisters of Charity community who met the requirements for teaching at the college level. The college had eight departments and a full-time faculty of ten, which was comprised of three Sisters of Charity and seven Cincinnati archdiocesan priests.

Those students, who paid a tuition bill of $400 per year, including board and laundry (day students paid only $100), were instructed not only in educational endeavors but also on proper behavior for an educated Catholic woman. The Sisters insisted on proper behavior in speech, manner and dress, and etiquette from all students, and by doing so they made weekly etiquette classes mandatory. They claimed that their purpose for doing this was to encourage purity, simplicity, and elegance of language. Special attention to dress was also addressed by the Sisters, who felt that high necks and long sleeves were an obligation of respectable women in the 1920s. They also stated that students should wear cap and gown for daily chapel services.

Besides receiving speech and wardrobe instruction as a part of their education, students were also taught the meaning of "humility, simplicity, and charity" by the Sisters. In the early years students were expected to rise at dawn and attend chapel without complaint. Parents were encouraged to give their daughters a "modest" allowance for the school year, because the college discouraged anything that developed the habit of monetary extravagance. Obedience and hard work by students was paramount to the educational experience at the Mount.

In a quest for the expansion of the college, as well as recognition for the groundwork being put in place for the moral and spiritual growth of its students, the Mount underwent a series of transformations and sought accreditation from appropriate educational organizations. The first accreditation came in 1923, when the National Catholic Education Association recognized the Mount as a college that advanced the educational and catechetical mission of the church.

The college held its first commencement ceremony in 1924 as nine graduates earned their baccalaureate degrees. In 1926 the Mount introduced a five-year program leading to the baccalaureate degree in nursing in cooperation with the Good Samaritan Hospital School of Nursing diploma program. Also in 1926 the college broke ground for a new five-story building to accommodate a growing enrollment. The new building, named Seton Hall, adjoined the original college and academy building, Marian Hall. Seton Hall could accommodate an enrollment of 140 students. The new college building opened in the spring of 1927, with two floors for classrooms, labs, offices, a library, and a reception area and three floors for student housing.

This physical expansion of the college marked the beginning of the Sisters' unwavering long-range commitment to the growth of the Mount as an institution of higher education. In 1928 enrollment surpassed the 100 mark when 111 students from eight different states arrived on the Mount campus. The next year the Sisters applied for admission to the Ohio College Association, and by 1930 the Mount was recognized as a member of the organization.

By 1931 the burgeoning college on the Ohio River was being lauded for its academic programs and commitment to producing conscientious women. Invitations to join the Association of American Colleges and the American Council on Education were issued and accepted in 1931, and in 1932 the college was accredited by the North Central Association of Colleges and Secondary Schools. When the Mount celebrated its fifteenth anniversary in 1935, there had been an increase of full-time faculty members from ten to forty and growth in enrollment from twenty students to more than 250.

Although the college was experiencing tremendous growth in both enrollment and recognition in academic circles during the 1930s, the country was in the midst of the Great Depression. The Sisters continued to emphasize simplicity and restraint to students. Practical knowledge and vocational skills were taught in the classroom and advocated in the new college mission statement. However, the development of women of character still remained the main purpose of the college.

During the great Cincinnati flood of 1937, when the Ohio River rose to over eighty feet high, Mount students had the opportunity to apply the many lessons in character they were learning at the college in the local community. Because of its safe location on a high hill overlooking the river, and with its wells of pure drinking water, the Mount was a haven for flood refugees who lived in the surrounding communities. While the Mount supplied victims with shelter, water, and medical assistance, students contributed clothing and assisted the Red Cross in caring for victims. As if matters were not hectic enough, just as the flood was subsiding, a fire broke out in the boiler room and kitchen of the motherhouse, causing over $200,000 damage. Fortunately, there were no injuries and classes resumed the next day, but not before students were reminded of the grace of God by the Sisters. Immediately plans were undertaken to repair the damage, as current and former students bonded together with the Sisters to generate the necessary funding for the repairs.

At this time the students were also growing deeply concerned about the possibility of war in Europe. In an effort to have an open dialogue about world conditions, students organized a Clio Club in 1938 to encourage interest in foreign affairs; the group then sponsored a regional conference to found the Ohio Valley Student Peace Federation. Students also wrote editorials about the unease in Europe in the college newspaper, the *Seton Journal*. These editorials triggered similar editorials in Catholic college newspapers across the nation. As a result the Mount hosted the 1938 Catholic School Press Association meeting on the nature of fascism, communism, and democracy. By 1941 it was obvious to many people in the world that Hitler's blitzkrieg was not going to end anytime soon, and so the Mount initiated a national college drive for peace via prayers. This effort enjoyed the participation of both Catholic and secular colleges, earning Mount students the admiration of many for their initiative and concern for others.

After the United States entered the war in 1941, the Mount became one of the first colleges to change its academic calendar to a year-round trimester schedule, allowing students to earn their degrees in three rather than four years. This change was instituted to help fill the need for medical technicians and other skilled workers in the war effort. Students were instructed by the new mission statement that the college aimed to prepare them to take their places in a modern world "where the world of tomorrow is the problem of the world today." With their academic schedule set, these students and "citizens of the world at large" turned their attention to their extracurricular activities. Social events such as the prom were replaced with bond, stamp and scrap drives, growing victory gardens, and praying for peace. Students raised hundreds of thousands of dollars in these efforts, earning the college a citation from the USO for meritorious service to the country. When the war ended in 1945, the Mount returned to its normal academic schedule and focused on helping with various relief programs for European refugees.

The next decade at the college was filled with new programs and plans for another building. In 1950 the five-year nursing program was replaced with a new, four-year program, which received immediate accreditation from the American Nursing Association. In 1953 the Mount established an elementary education program to help relieve the critical teacher shortage across the nation.

By the early 1950s enrollment had grown to nearly 500 students. Seton Hall, built in 1927, had been designed for 140 students. So it was now time for the Sisters to plan for a new campus that would meet the needs of a growing student population. In May 1954 the college announced plans for a modern educational campus to be built on the seventy-five-acre tract of land that served as the Sister's turkey farm, located across the road from the motherhouse.

While the architect's plans were being drawn and ground leveled at the site of the new campus, the college administration was undergoing its own reorganization. For the first twenty-nine years of the college's operations, the Mother Superior, or General, of the Sisters of Charity had served as ex-officio president while a dean managed the day-to-day affairs. This changed in 1959 when Mother Mary Omer Downing named as president Sister Maria Corona Molloy, who had been the dean since 1933. Over the next thirty-four years as president, Sister Maria Corona shaped the college's growth and advanced its mission. Soon after taking her post, she began to build the college's partnership with the business community by forming the Associate Board of Lay Trustees. This marked the first time that the laity became involved in the administration of the college.

Groundbreaking for the new $15 million, eleven-building campus took place in 1960. In September 1962 the new campus opened its doors to welcome more than 700 students. The new campus was five times larger than the former college facilities. Students found forty-five new classrooms, twenty-three labs, dorm facilities for 650, a three-story library, an expansive theater, a modern art gallery, and a breathtaking chapel. By 1964 word had spread about the contemporary college in Cincinnati overlooking the Ohio River, which offered late-afternoon and evening classes and summer sessions along with regular classes. Enrollment soared with more than 1,000 students.

In addition to the new campus, the college initiated programs that served new populations of students. In 1969 the Mount began to admit male and female adult students into the Department of Continuing Education. This program was an instant success, enrolling 474 adult students in its first year. In 1971 the Mount began its Futurology Institute and Religious Studies Institute, which attracted nationally known speakers such as Henry Kissinger and Mother Teresa to the campus. By the end of its first decade at its new location, the College of Mount St. Joseph had become a place where new ideas were contemplated and students were encouraged to make personal judgments while developing their religious, moral, and social beliefs.

Despite the success of the new campus, the college encountered the same problem as the rest of the country in the 1970s: inflation. Since its inception, mostly Sisters of Charity had staffed the college. However, after the sweeping reforms of the Second Vatican Council and changes in the Sisters' community constitution, the Sisters no longer assigned community members to unsalaried positions at the college. As fewer women entered religious life and with increases in the costs of living, retirement, and social security, the Sisters looked ahead to ways to support their various ministries while remaining a strong and secure community. Because of their solid commitment to the mission of the college, as well as their desire to aid with its development, the Sisters turned the administration of the college over to a new board of trustees in 1972. This board, comprised of two-thirds lay membership and one-third Sisters of Charity, became legally and fiscally responsible for the newly incorporated College of Mount St. Joseph. While the Sisters retained ownership of the college, the academic, administrative, and fiscal policies were now to be determined by the board. According to the agreement, the board leased the college from the Sisters and assumed a capital debt of $12 million, which the Sisters deferred repayment of until 1977. As a result of this transition, Dr. Robert E. Wolverton was named the first lay president of the college.

However, by 1977 rapid inflation resulted in additional costs at the college, and the capital debt could not be repaid. Not wanting to close an institution of higher education dedicated to personal, religious, social, and academic values, the Sisters forgave the existing capital plant debt and formed a new lease agreement with the board of trustees, charging them one dollar per year to lease the plant. This move by the Sisters not only ensured the long-term financial stability and development of the college, but it also led to the appointment of Sister Jean Patrice Harrington to the college presidency in 1977.

Committed to building resources, Sister Jean Patrice directed the college's growth as an innovative academic institution while increasing its visibility in the Greater Cincinnati area. She joined local business and educational boards to extend the college's community relationships. On campus she supported the development of innovative programs that served the needs of the local community. In 1977 the Mount faculty launched a Weekend College program, the first of its kind in Cincinnati offering both men and women degree programs in a weekend time frame. The first master's degree program in education was begun in 1978. The Mount Annual Fund was begun and attracted strong support from alumni. By the 1980s Sister Jean Patrice had the Mount back on track financially and on the cutting edge of academic innovation under a mission that focused on meeting the needs of students of differing interests, plans, expectations, ages, and capacities.

In 1982 the college's mission expanded to meet the educational, cultural, social, and religious needs of the local community and its students. In response three new programs were introduced in Cooperative Education, Project EXCEL, and English as a Second Language (ESL). The Mount became the first liberal arts college in Cincinnati to offer Cooperative Education to students in all majors, which gave students an opportunity to earn academic credit while gaining valuable work experience in their fields of study. Project EXCEL was developed to assist students with learning disabilities succeed in college. In the ESL program international students were recruited to the Mount. These three programs expanded diversity on the growing campus while gaining local, national, and international recognition of the Mount's innovative academic programs.

In 1986 the Mount responded to national reports on the declining number of African Americans attending college by addressing the preparation of students at the high school level. Called Project SCOPE (Summer Collegiate Orientation Program and Enrichment), the Mount's program was designed to introduce Greater Cincinnati–area African American high school students to college life through a summer residency experience. Each summer a group of high school sophomores begin the program and then return each summer through their senior year. By the time they complete the program, which is fully funded by the college and with grant support, the students have experienced college classes, learned about career preparation, and become familiar with application, financial aid, and registration procedures. As always the college was quick to respond to the changing needs in the academic, professional, and social world with the development of this program.

As the new population of full-time and part-time students grew on campus, the Mount was still widely recognized as a women's college. By 1985 male enrollment had reached 12 percent. In 1986 the board of trustees formally established the college's status as fully coeducational. Male enrollment continued to grow, and by 1989 the Mount added male sports to the athletic program with the introduction of a football program.

In 1987 Sister Jean Patrice announced her retirement as president of the college after ten productive years. Credited with revitalizing nearly every aspect of the college, Sister Jean Patrice passed the reins of the presidency on to Sister Francis Marie Thrailkill, O.S.U. If Sister Jean Patrice is credited with the revitalization of the Mount, Sister Francis Marie is known as the leader who guided the college into the twenty-first century. A woman committed to mission and service, Sister Francis Marie led the campus community in the development of a long-range strategic plan called Vision 2000. The plan, adopted in 1991, was designed to direct resources and attention to providing a curriculum, technology, and learning environment to prepare students intellectually, spiritually, and morally as citizens of the new century.

The first part of the plan to fall into place came when the Mount received the largest grant in its history, $1.7 million, from the federal Strengthening Institutions Program (Title III) for implementation of its Vision 2000 program. The Mount followed this achievement with a campaign to raise $10 million to support new programs, technology, and scholarships and to build their endowment. By 1998 the Mount had doubled its original $10 million goal by raising $20.5 million. As a result of these substantial fundraising activities that supported strategic goals in academics, technology, and student services, the Mount transformed itself into a college of the twenty-first century with the support of alumni, constituents, and the Greater Cincinnati area community.

Under Sister Francis Marie's Vision 2000, there was a complete renovation of the Science Building, new apartment suites were added to the Residence Hall, and a comprehensive student activities and recreation center was built. Named in recognition of Sister Jean Patrice Harrington, the new student center featured a Student Leadership Suite, Wellness Center, Children's Center, bookstore, food court, gym, and racquetball court. In the area of academics, new majors such as mathematics/computer science and physical therapy were developed, a new Honors Program was initiated, and a new liberal arts and sciences core curriculum was introduced in the fall of 2000. The new curriculum was designed to help students integrate their intellectual skills with the knowledge they absorbed in their liberal arts and major courses. Developing skills such as appreciating the complexity of human behavior, knowing the relation among various ethical systems, and appreciating the relationship of Catholic Christianity to other belief systems were also facets of the program. As part of the new curriculum, the Mount launched a universal computing requirement, MERLIN (Media-Rich Learning Infrastructure). In the fall of 2000 the College of Mount St. Joseph became one of the first colleges in the nation to offer students classes in a wireless computing environment using portable laptop computers.

Socially conscious programs were also instituted under the Vision 2000 plan, most notably the Service Learning Program. A nationally recognized program, Service Learning was begun to help build character in students by allowing them to earn one free credit hour by participating in service projects. The program required students to donate thirty hours of community service at an agency or in a program that the Mount was committed to. Working with a faculty member, students were asked to reflect on and make connections between their service, the academic course, and the experimental learning taking place.

A rousing success, the Vision 2000 plan directed the Mount into the twenty-first century and placed the college in a very illustrious position in academic circles. Continually ranked by *U.S. News and World Report* among the top Midwest universities for academic quality since 1996, the Mount has also been ranked first in the State of Ohio for "best value" by the magazine and was also recognized for leadership in the field of student character development in *The Templeton Guide: Colleges that Encourage Character Development*.

The Mount enters the twenty-first century with forty-three baccalaureate degree programs, ten associate degree programs, four graduate degree programs, and an enrollment of 2,300 students. With both the facility and academic expansion of the college over the years, it is difficult to believe that just eighty-three years ago there were only twenty students enrolled in the eight-department college housed inside the Sisters of Charity motherhouse. Yet, although the number of students and location of the Mount has grown, the underlying mission has remained firm. There is, and has always been, a deep commitment to developing students who understand the meaning of discipline, integrity, respect, and faith. With a foundation that nurtures sound judgment and a passion for service, the Mount continues to help students recognize their obligations to God, themselves, and those around them. And in the end, men and women of character emerge from the small, Catholic college situated high above the Ohio River.

Suggested Reading

Helpful in the research for this essay were the publications by the Sisters of Charity: Judith Metz, *Women of Faith and Service: The Sisters of Charity of Cincinnati* (1997), and Benedicta Mahoney, *We Are Many . . . : A History of the Sisters of Charity of Cincinnati 1898–1971* (1982).

Mount Union College

The Experiences of "Integral Education"

JOHN SAFFELL

In the autumn of 1846 a young man of twenty-three who had just completed his freshman year at Allegheny College came to the little village of Mount Union (now part of Alliance, Ohio) to help care for a sister who was dying of "pulmonary consumption." That man was Orville Nelson Hartshorn, now remembered as the founder and first president of Mount Union College. While he was on this mission of mercy, a few youths of the small community asked the young undergraduate to establish a subscription school. It opened with six students on October 20, 1846, in the third-floor attic of a woolen mill. These were the humble beginnings of Mount Union College.

A couple of weeks before this opening day, in a speech that lasted an hour and a half, the neophyte educator had explained his educational philosophy at a public meeting attended by skeptical villagers. The views he explained that evening in the district school building have guided Mount Union through the hopes and fears of the more than 150 years that separate us from that meeting in early October 1846.

Some of the ideas that Hartshorn expressed reflected the spirit of a society just emerging from the rough and tumble of frontier life. Bold, confident, and individualistic, he had faith in the potentialities of the common man. "From the farmer's country home and the mechanic's or merchant's cottage," he declared, "rather than from the palace, come those of sound mind and body, who, by force of will, heart and thought prove themselves the pioneers and persevering laborers in the arduous and usually thankless work of true reform, national zeal, and human elevation." Mount Union was to be a school for the people, and Hartshorn promised to keep expenses low so that this objective could be realized. He went on to declare for co-education: "The sexes are designed properly to live together in the same community, and should be accordingly educated." In this same address Hartshorn advocated a

Chapman Hall

pedagogical technique he labeled "illustrative education." He sensed the value of laboratories, experimentation, specimens, and of what a later generation would label "visual education." Central, however, in the young leader's philosophy was what he called "integral education":

> Integral culture, that is, the education of the whole man, is necessary to the observance of the laws of our physical, intellectual, social, and moral being, consequently, to individual happiness and public welfare. All young of either sex, and of whatever rank or condition, have a natural and equal right, to the full and harmonious education of all their faculties. . . . We should begin and train not

merely the intellect, which is less than a third of the faculties, but each faculty and class of faculties, in their material order, so as to round out the character and fit the student for the varied duties of life.

Hartshorn's concept of "integral education" is a central theme in the history of Mount Union College.

The fledgling school faced a special crisis during the winter of 1847–48. Only some of the students were Christians, and many of the villagers scoffed at the Bible. "These infidels and worldly indulgers declared war against the 'select school,' unless the young president ceased reading the Bible and praying at Chapel exercises." Hartshorn, even though some local churchgoers were neutral in the controversy, stood his ground. He organized an association of Christian students and led a revival movement that resulted in the conversion of seventy-eight students and citizens. As the chronicles noted, "Hartshorn had achieved a signal victory. His school was definitely established. Not only had he helped to bring about a great moral and spiritual uplift in the village of Mount Union, but now the villagers understood quite clearly that his school was founded on Christian principles." It was a pivotal episode.

Hartshorn's religious enthusiasm did not at all preclude his endorsement of scientific studies. He made this clear in a speech delivered in 1850: "Science, no longer confined to a privileged few, has in earnest begun the great work of instructing our race. . . . Science is now studied as a mighty power of thought. It frees the mind from the old bounds . . . calls the past to account, and deems nothing too sacred for investigation."

Life was real and life was earnest at nineteenth-century Mount Union. Students were to arise at five o'clock. Daily chapel attendance and regular class attendance were required. Rules forbade card and checker playing, dancing, and the use of alcohol. Students were not allowed to smoke within the school enclosure or to spit tobacco juice within the building. There was even a touch of political correctness: students were prohibited from "the use of profane or unchaste language, injuring designedly the character or feelings of another." There were fixed study periods, eight or more hours a day. Probably the rule most resented was the one which stated that "students are prohibited, on pain of dismission, from visiting the other sex, or receiving visits from them, during any of the Late Hours at night, or during any of the Study Hours of any day in the week."

In spite of the strict regimen, the little school grew rapidly. Enrollment reached 211 in 1851, and before long it had doubled. Many factors explain the progress. Clearly, the leadership of Hartshorn and the dedication of his closest coworkers, Oscar Chapman and George Washington Clarke, were crucial. Trends of the time helped too. Alliance was becoming a railroad hub. This stimulated the economic vitality of the area and gave the little community easy tie-ins with the larger world.

Another trend helped: the demand for better-trained teachers induced by the drive for an adequate system of public education. Ohio, however, would not have a state-supported normal school for another half-century. Hartshorn, sensing a need, established a teacher training program in 1851. For a few years his school was known as Mount Union Seminary and Normal School; often half the students were in the teacher training program.

Advance continued. On January 9, 1858, Mount Union Seminary and Normal School, though its assets were appraised at only $7,500, received a charter of collegiate rank. It was a remarkable record; the little subscription school, which had started only a dozen years before, was now an institution of collegiate rank with an enrollment of more than 350 students. Plans for the construction of a major new building were soon under way. On July 4, 1863, the cornerstone was laid for the large brick structure that has become a symbol of the institution and that has been known for almost a hundred years as Chapman Hall. There was another success. In March 1864 the Pittsburgh Annual Conference of the Methodist Episcopal Church granted full patronage to Mount Union College. Though its early leaders were devout Methodists, the school was not founded under church auspices. Since 1864, however, the college has had a formal church affiliation. Hartshorn believed that these recent successes deserved an impressive celebration. By great persistence he persuaded Salmon P. Chase, former governor of Ohio and more recently secretary of the treasury in President Lincoln's cabinet, to speak at the affair on December 1, 1864. While at Mount Union Chase received the telegram announcing his nomination as Chief Justice of the United States Supreme Court. Hartshorn had achieved a public relations coup. Two years later another new building was ready for use—a dormitory and dining facility known since 1906 as Miller Hall in memory of Lewis Miller, benefactor and long-time trustee, who has a niche in American social history as cofounder of the Chautauqua movement.

The triumph of the great celebration of 1864 was followed by a decade of progress and apparent prosperity. This was the happiest period of the college's first fifty years. Mount Union was the second largest college in the state (Oberlin was first). Enrollment in the 1870s sometimes exceeded 800, a level it did not reach again until the influx of veterans after WWII. The commercial department, established in 1868, contributed substantially to the enrollment upsurge. A museum with an Egyptian mummy, a gorilla, and countless other exotic specimens caught the imagination of the public. Compared favorably with the Smithsonian by some loyalists, the museum gave evidence of Hartshorn's commitment to "illustrative education." The college adopted the elective system in 1870 and that same year began offering summer courses. Mount Union was among the first schools in the country to offer summer instruction. Several graduates of the period later achieved considerable recognition: William H. Hoover (Class of 1870), founder of the internationally known Hoover Sweeper Company of North Canton; Henry S. Lehr (Class of 1871), founder of Ohio Northern University; and Philander C. Knox (Class of 1872), secretary of state in the William Howard Taft administration.

Less happy days lay ahead. Heavy indebtedness burdened the college. Monies to pay for Miller Hall did not come in; interest costs mounted. Hartshorn's lavish expenditures for the museum drained away resources. At the same time the increasing enrollment brought a critical need for more space. To meet the need the president wanted to purchase the property of a failed rival institution. He spread a story that the facility he wanted was about to be purchased by the Northern Ohio Female Hospital and Retreat as an abode for wayward and diseased women. The story, he hoped, would so frighten local citizens that they would readily subscribe the money he needed. An aggrieved party in the complicated affair took Hartshorn to court; the judge condemned the scheme as "a stupendous humbug whereby to blindfold and deceive the people." The episode tarnished the image of the college, and though the president stayed on until 1887 his administration was crippled. Indeed, the college would not enjoy a great new forward thrust for two decades, until the selection of W. H. McMaster as president in 1908.

Meanwhile, the trustees looked for Hartshorn's successor. Their first choice took the train back to New York after a visit to the campus convinced him that Mount Union was a hopeless cause. Trustees then turned to a young man in his early forties, Tamerlane Pliny Marsh, a graduate of Wesleyan University who had held pastorates in and around Chicago. Early in his administration the school was saved from financial collapse primarily by the gift of $76,000 from three Canton industrialists; but finances remained precarious. Faculty salaries were minimal; church support was meager; efforts to raise endowment funds failed. Enrollment in 1898 was only about 400, less than half what it had been in the golden years of the 1870s.

However, all was not bleak. Campus tone improved. Marsh eased some of Hartshorn's rigid disciplinary rules. Religious emphasis was strong. It was during the Marsh years that the Union Avenue Methodist Episcopal Church was built. The president's intimate involvement in its construction was symbolic of his concern for the religious life of the campus. Too, he was a strong advocate of athletics and physical education. In his inaugural address he said, "We hear a great deal about brains. . . . Let us hear more about brawn as well." In spite of financial strains, money for the construction of a gymnasium was raised. Mount Union was among the first schools in the country to introduce basketball. By the mid-1890s there was a regular schedule of football, basketball, and baseball. Emphasis on athletics and physical education has continued.

Marsh tried to bring what he called a New Era to the academic program. He established a library, meager though it was. He worked to raise standards. He added three new departments: biblical, military, and elocution and oratory. The other departments were collegiate, preparatory, art, postgraduate, business, music, and normal. Only about one-fourth of the students were in the collegiate department. Nevertheless, during Marsh's tenure Mount Union became a member of the Ohio College Association. The academic offering that seems most remarkable in retrospect was the graduate program. There were no residence requirements. The candidate for a degree read a certain number of required books and took examinations thereon. During Marsh's tenure, the college awarded sixteen doctor's degrees and eleven master's degrees. The burden of making out the examinations and evaluating them fell mainly on the president, who also often taught twelve hours a week. Utterly exhausted after ten years, Marsh left office in 1898. It is all too clear that Mount Union in the 1890s was trying to do much too much with much too little. Neither trustees nor president knew how to raise money to support the programs they felt conscience bound to offer.

Fortunes did not improve under Marsh's successor, Albert B. Riker (1898–1908), who came to Mount Union from a pastorate in Charleston, West Virginia. He lacked the special touch that establishes easy rapport with students. Their frequent pranks enlivened the life of the campus but bedeviled his. On one night, for instance, Daisy, the president's cow, found a way to ascend the many steps that led to the third floor of Ladies' Hall. Riker did abolish the doctoral program, but there was no major academic reorganization. It should be said, though, that he made some wise faculty appointments, particularly that of John Brady Bowman, later dean of the college. Finances remained precarious, and it was Riker's pitifully unsuccessful efforts to raise funds that forced his resignation in 1908.

Looking back on these years it is easy for the institutional historian, especially when he paints with broad brush, to conclude that the three decades preceding 1908 were bleak and barren. It was a time of troubles, but this is only part of the story. Upon reflection, this writer, born and raised in the Alliance area, realizes that many of the community people whom he revered as a child and youth, people who enriched his life in many ways, were graduates and former students from these years that he has just described in unflattering terms. It is all too easy to forget that even in these years when the bitch-goddess success seemed to frown on Mount Union, there were able and dedicated professors, people like James A. and Amelia Brush, Joseph L. Shunk, and E. N. Hartshorn, the president's brother, who worked tirelessly to meet the high goals they set for themselves and for the institution to which they committed their lives. It is far easier to summarize trustee minutes than to calculate the impact of such personalities.

Riker's successor was William Henry McMaster, a graduate of the college in 1899 and, at the time of his selection, pastor of the Embury Methodist Church in Brooklyn. Handsome, magnetic and genial, he brought new vitality to a faltering institution. "Night is gone with doubt and fearing"—lines from the "Alma Mater"—had real meaning for students and alumni in those years.

Fund-raising efforts succeeded. Alumni quickly raised $150,000 so as to claim a $50,000 challenge offer from Andrew Carnegie. By June 1909, not much more than a year after McMaster took office, the check from Carnegie was in hand. About the same time, in 1911, Mount Union merged with Scio, a struggling college about forty miles south of Alliance. The East Ohio Conference of the Methodist Episcopal Church had been encouraging some sort of merger. Had it not been for new signs of life McMaster brought, it might well have been Mount Union, not Scio, that lost its identity.

New facilities appeared: Lamborn Science Hall, Elliott Hall, Hartshorn Stadium and, a little later, Soldiers' Memorial Hall. McMaster persuaded the local community to help with an elaborate campus beautification project. The writer's grandfather, a local farmer, came with his slip scraper and "team of good bay horses" to help excavate for the lakes. Soon the carefully landscaped campus, the reflection of the pillars of Elliott Hall in the lakes, and the domes and turrets of Chapman Hall made the campus a special place and gave Mount Union a touch of magic.

There were faculty members who added to the magic, only a few of whom can be mentioned here. Isaac Taylor Headland, who had for years headed the Christian University of Peking, China, was a well-known lecturer and writer who did not hesitate to remind colleagues that he alone among them had an international reputation. His wife, Mariam, had served as personal physician to the sister of China's Empress Dowager. Joseph M. Scott, who held a doctorate from Johns Hopkins, developed a pre-med program highly regarded by prestigious medical schools. Robert Stauffer, successor to the revered professor of Greek, J. L. Shunk, kept alive both the critical need for a new library and an interest in Greek culture. One of his students, Robert Scranton, went on to head the classics department at the University of Chicago.

These professors taught within a new academic framework. McMaster recognized that if the school were to gain recognition from accrediting agencies and raise endowment funds, an entirely new academic organization was required. In 1911 the faculty voted to discontinue the various departments that had offered below college-level instruction but which had heretofore made up the larger part of the offerings. Soon the old normal, commercial, and graduate departments were abolished. Dean John Brady Bowman, a towering figure in Mount Union history, led the conversion of the school to a strictly liberal arts college. It was an educational revolution.

Clearly, McMaster brought new life to an institution that had been floundering for decades, but as time passed some trustees became critical of faltering fund-raising efforts and signs of institutional inertia. McMaster resigned in 1937.

By the time McMaster's successor, Charles B. Ketcham, was inaugurated in the fall of 1938, war clouds were gathering over Europe. Alumni families were soon more worried about the fate of their sons than about the balance sheet of their college. Plans for revitalization were put on hold, and traditional college life succumbed to the needs of a nation at war.

Ketcham, a Phi Beta Kappa graduate of Ohio Wesleyan University, held advanced degrees from Drew and Columbia. He was serving as district superintendent of the Cleveland District of the Northeast Ohio Conference of the Methodist Episcopal Church at the time of his Mount Union appointment. An ardent spokesman for religion and the church-related college, he declared in his inaugural address "in religion lies our only hope of saving this generation from confusion and chaos." He encouraged church support of Ohio's Methodist colleges through his leadership of the Four College Commission and the Ohio Foundation of Methodist Colleges. His organizational plan for maximizing religious influences on a college campus received national attention. At one point he threatened to resign rather than accept a modification of the required chapel policy. He was determined that Mount Union be church related in more than name. Lucille Brown Ketcham, her husband's activist partner, pushed for the rights of African Americans years before the civil rights movement gained national attention. Her name is still cherished in the Alliance-area African American community.

The religious emphasis was clear during all the years of Ketcham's tenure, but special new energies appeared during his later years here (1946–53). The influx of World War II veterans brought change and vitality. Enrollment surged to levels not known since the 1870s. It exceeded 100 in 1946. Such numbers challenged schedule makers and strained facilities. Some of these young men had themselves carried heavy command responsibilities; many brought to a perhaps somewhat provincial college a new awareness of distant places and foreign cultures. Campus people who had not known the terror of battle were humbled, and thereby perhaps a little ennobled, as they glimpsed those among them who were able to walk to class only because of stainless steel and the miracles of orthopedic surgery.

There were other signs of new energies. An aggressive board of trustees, led by Dr. George L. King Jr., eye surgeon and prominent Methodist layman, was ready, once the war had ended, to launch a major fund-raising campaign. The board unveiled a long-range campus plan that provided for a new library, a little theater, a chapel and several new academic buildings and dormitories. Its grandiosity stunned old-timers. Mount Union had not had a major campaign for funds since the 1920s, and it had floundered. There had been no major new structure on campus in the last quarter-century. But the drive for funds was a resounding success. Money came in faster than expected. Even cash-strapped veterans made pledges. Dedication of the new library came in 1950, and plans were soon under way for the construction of a fine arts complex.

Dr. Ketcham died suddenly in 1953. Though at the time of his death Mount Union was experiencing financial strains, a mood of optimism about the long-range future prevailed. Indeed, the period from the end of World War II to the end of the twentieth century was to be a time of unparalleled advance, a new era of good times that dawned in the latter part of Ketcham's tenure.

Ketcham's successor, Carl C. Bracy, came to Mount Union from the chancellorship at Nebraska Wesleyan. It was soon clear that the new president's dynamism would make possible implementation of the ambitious plans forward-looking trustees had been formulating for almost twenty years. New buildings seemed to spring up like mushrooms after a rain. There were four new dormitories, a health center, a student center, and additional facilities for music and the sciences. The complete renovation of Chapman Hall was a massive undertaking. These were the most dramatic changes that had come to the campus in the last fifty years.

Bracy attempted equally dramatic changes in the educational program. In 1959 he brought in a new academic head, M. Francis Christie, a Vanderbilt Ph.D. in religion and philosophy. From his volcanic energy flowed academic revitalization. He raised admissions standards; some families who had sent their offspring to Mount Union for generations were stunned when rejection slips arrived. "We are not going to play school," Christie said. "We are going to have school." Not just nontenured professors were on trial. A popular tenured associate professor who had been with the college for fifteen years was suddenly out. Christie scoured the country for effective teachers. At one point students were required to return for Friday classes after the traditional Thursday Thanksgiving holiday. The pace was hectic. There was a new calendar. A new curriculum gave added emphasis to the humanities. It was the utopian phase of revolution. Soon there was a drift to normalcy. Mount Unionites, as heirs of Hartshorn's concept of "integral education," believed that students need some time for social life and the playing fields. Christie resigned in 1965 to accept the deanship of his alma mater, Hendrix College. He left his imprint. Many of the faculty he recruited remained for years and added to the intellectual vigor of the college. In addition, his push for greater faculty involvement in institutional life survived and grew stronger.

During the Bracy year ties with the church were close. Both Bracy and Christie were Methodist ministers. At one point the religion and philosophy department had five Ph.D.s; the English department had three; and some departments had none. An outgrowth of the close connection with the Methodist education office in Nashville was the formation of the Association of Colleges and Universities for Intercultural and International Studies, which aimed particularly at easing Cold War tensions. In 1961 trustees voted to establish a chaplaincy at Mount Union. During this period Mount Union began sponsorship of Methodist Invasion Day, when 300–500 high school students visited the campus for worship and a glimpse of college life. The program helped the college maintain connections with local parishes and served as a recruiting mechanism.

Unfortunately, Bracy's unhappy marriage set in motion events that led to his sudden resignation in October 1967. Bracy's successor was Ronald G. Weber, a Mount Union graduate who had served as vice president for business affairs since

1950. Though all Mount Union presidents have carried heavy burdens and faced perplexing problems, no other president has ever faced as many immediately threatening day-to-day crises. This was the period when African American students were making loud demands—sometimes threatening violence. They almost succeeded in breaking down the doors and taking over Chapman Hall. In the period of the Vietnam War and the May 4th tragedy at Kent State, Mount Union was caught up in the wave of student activism—public meetings, demonstrations, strikes and the threat of strikes, even a bomb scare. In spite of turmoil, the academic enterprise continued to operate; there was neither loss of life nor serious destruction of property. The dean of the college, DeBow Freed, later president of Ohio Northern University, was a tower of strength during the months of turbulence.

It was a time of soul searching. Weber in his inaugural address had described Mount Union as a college that believed "in the inherent worth and dignity of each individual as a child of God." Personal attention was a hallmark of the school. It was difficult, though, for the president and old-time faculty members to come to terms with the new "political personalism" of the 1960s. Weber was a loyal churchman, reserved, and formal in manner. (Student jokesters doubted that even his wife, in the couple's most intimate moments, had ever seen him without a necktie!) It is one of history's little ironies that he was the one who presided over basic changes in the fabric at Mount Union life—liberal visitation hours, fundamental changes in governance, beer on campus, and the end of required chapel attendance. The chapel issue was especially troubling for Weber, because the United Methodist Church, through the Crusade for Christian Higher Education, had just raised a million or so dollars earmarked for construction of a chapel at Mount Union. It was with great reluctance that the president recommended diversion of this money to a scholarship fund for Methodist students. It was not for "light and transient causes" that Mount Union gave way on such issues. The forces for change seemed overwhelming.

There were other significant developments at Mount Union during these years. The curriculum was expanded, and many new majors were offered, such as accounting, computer science, communications, and social service. By 1980 half of the students were enrolled in majors that had not been offered ten years before. Non-Western studies got added emphasis. Mount Union was gaining new visibility as an athletic power. There were remarkable successes in track and cross-country. Football records were on the upswing and presaged the national championships of the next decade. Weber's administration brought the construction or renovation of six buildings. The endowment tripled, to about $10,000,000. Finances were sound. There was a hefty reserve fund. Even the *Wall Street Journal* took note of Mount Union's fiscal probity. Faculty critics charged that Weber was more interested in building up reserves than in funding innovative programs. His many supporters, however, viewed him as an advocate of fiscal sanity in an age addicted to debt and applauded him as a defender of traditional values in a time of moral breakdown.

G. Benjamin Lantz Jr., dean of the college, succeeded Weber. An ordained minister, he was the first Mount Union president to hold an earned Ph.D. Though his presidential tenure was the shortest in Mount Union annals, his years brought significant changes. There was a shift from the term system back to the more traditional semester calendar. A major curriculum revision reversed the trend toward permissiveness fostered in the 1960s. Even though the drift toward careerism continued, over 40 percent of the graduation requirements were in the liberal arts. Lantz was responsible for establishing an orientation program that introduced incoming students to the liberal arts experience. It remains in place. There were significant additions to the physical plant: a new Field House was dedicated in 1981 and new science facility in 1983. The budget remained in balance, in spite of an ominous enrollment decline. Understandably, the college was stunned in the spring of 1985 when Lantz announced that he was resigning to accept a lucrative offer in the corporate world.

While trustees looked for a successor, Clifford Shields, longtime trustee and retired Sohio executive, took over for a year. An able, loyal, and generous alumnus, he had worked over the years to improve the budgeting process. Now, as acting president, he streamlined the administration and headed a highly successful fund-raising effort. It was a very good year.

Indeed, the last years of the twentieth century brought Mount Union to a level of prosperity only dreamt about a half-century ago. Endowment has reached $115 million. Among Ohio's private colleges, Mount Union ranks sixth in terms of endowment per student. Enrollment has more than doubled since 1984. The end of the twentieth century brought construction of three dormitories, a Center for Human Health and Well-Being, a new athletic facility, and an impressive renovation of the Student Center. The spring of 2000 was notable for the dedication of three new buildings, which dot a campus now somewhat insulated from the frenzy of the world outside by a master plan that restricts parking to lots on the periphery.

The person who glimpsed the need for this campus master plan and who has guided the college since 1986 is Mount Union's ninth president, Harold M. Kolenbrander. He holds a Ph.D. in biochemistry from the University of Iowa and came to Mount Union after having served as dean and provost of his alma mater, Central College (Iowa). Guided by his keen understanding of the Mount Union ethos and by his recognition of the college's potentialities, he has shown a remarkable capacity to energize a constituency that is understandingly proud of the national visibility that material advance and athletic preeminence have brought. (Mount Union's football team won four Division III championships in the 1990s.)

Just as Hartshorn more than 150 years ago was championing innovative instructional technique, so now Mount Union is moving aggressively into the computer age. In 1993 the college undertook a major $4 million project to update its computing and data communications systems. That earlier phase is completed, and now, in addition, the new Kolenbrander-Harter Information Service Center is in operation. It houses the latest information retrieval technology and is expected to become the intellectual hub of the college. Mount Union enjoys preeminence as one of "America's Most Wired Colleges."

Technological advance, victories on the playing field, and financial well-being have not dimmed Mount Union's commitment to its larger goals, in Kolenbrander's words, "to teach students how to learn, how to communicate, and how to live." Even though recent years have seen a drift to careerism, over 40 percent of graduation requirements are still in the liberal arts. Mount Union tries not to forget what John Milton called "those thoughts that wander through eternity." There is a multitude of options; about forty majors are offered. One can major in sports medicine or Japanese, in exercise science or philosophy. Provincialism belongs to an earlier day; there are many non-Western offerings. Mount Union has a sister-college relationship with Baika College in Japan. Sometimes there are as many as forty students from Japan; others come from as far away as Bangladesh and Kazakhstan. There is an aggressive effort to recruit minority students. All this underscores Mount Union's awareness of demographic trends.

In spite of the new directions, Mount Union's deep roots in the Judeo-Christian tradition remain intact. The formal tie-in with the United Methodist Church continues. Graduation requirements include two courses in religion philosophy. While chapel attendance is no longer obligatory, one of the three new buildings recently dedicated is Dewald Chapel, which will house, besides the sanctuary, a prayer and meditation room, offices for the various religiously affiliated campus organizations, and an office for the full-time chaplain. There are countless service projects each year. Mount Union appears on the Templeton Honor Roll for Character Building Colleges. The college has never marginalized morality. Many students do have a woeful lack of biblical knowledge—one faculty wit said, "These kids don't know but what Immaculate Conception has something to do with clean sheets at the Ramada!"—but there is another side. Many Mount Union students show every day that they cherish the tradition of hope and take seriously the moral imperative that underpins their Judeo-Christian inheritance.

Through all the years the college has held fast to what its founder called "integral education" and what Kolenbrander describes as the "education of each student as a whole person." Mount Union honors intellectual rigor and rejoices in the excitement that often comes with the search for truth, but it tries never to forget that all students have social, physical, moral, and spiritual potentialities that need nurture. This world cries out for people with a sense of responsibility, a capacity for empathy and compassion, and a feeling of awe and wonder about this mysterious universe. They are the ones most likely to prove wrong the spinners of Doomsday scenarios.

In 2000 Mount Union welcomed Kolenbrander's successor, Dr. John L. (Jack) Ewing. He has deep roots in the Judeo-Christian tradition and will guide Mount Union through the moral and ethical thickets through which the college and the larger society must pass on the way to the "broad sunlit uplands."

Suggested Reading

Newell Yost Osborne, *A Select School: The History of Mount Union College and an Account of a Unique Educational Experiment, Scio College* (Alliance, 1967); John E. Saffell, *Wake the Echoes: An Updated History of Mount Union College* (Mount Union College, 1996), covers the years 1946–96.

Mount Vernon Nazarene University

The Miracle on the Kokosing

PAUL D. MAYLE

Until 1968 a visitor to Mount Vernon, the county seat of Knox County, Ohio, might have passed the rolling farmland drained by Delano Run and the Kokosing River without ever imagining that a university campus would rise from the sprawling cornfields and pasturelands. Even as late as 1968 the working farm at the edge of the city limits was a county landmark. This was a farm with a distinguished history.

In 1871 Columbus Delano built a palatial farmhouse as the centerpiece of his 500-acre property and dubbed it Lake Home. Delano, a strong opponent of slavery, was elected to the U.S. House of Representatives in 1844 and delivered the speech in Chicago to second Abraham Lincoln's nomination for the presidency in 1860. After serving as secretary of the interior in the Grant administration, Delano resigned in 1875 and returned to his beloved farm to devote the rest of his life to his prize stock herds of Merino sheep, Jersey cattle, Percheron horses, and Berkshire pigs. How was a parcel of roughly 200 acres from Delano's estate transformed from pastureland and cornfields into a Nazarene university? In time the farm, renamed Lake Holm, then Lakeholm, came into the possession of industrialist Bert W. Martin. Martin gave the property to Ohio State University with "no strings attached as to its use" but expressed the hope that a branch campus would be developed. And that might have eventually happened had not events taken a different course.

That different course was set in motion by a seemingly unrelated incident in the Pacific Northwest. A bold proposal addressed to the delegates at the 1964 General Assembly of the Church of the Nazarene in Portland, Oregon, called for increasing the number of colleges established by the denomination. Bold is hardly a fitting description. From the birth of the Church of the Nazarene near the turn of the twentieth century, church leaders had demonstrated an unusual zeal for establishing institutions of higher learning. In 1964 there were already six Nazarene colleges—Eastern

Lakeholm Administration Building, 1997

(Massachusetts), Trevecca (Tennessee), Olivet (Illinois), Bethany (Oklahoma), North-west (Idaho), and Pasadena (California). With a number of institutions already oper-ating, it might have surprised a fair number of the delegates to learn about a plan to add to the list. It must have been even more surprising that the recommendation, even though based in part on rapid church growth, called for the founding of two new liberal arts colleges, designated for the time being as Zone A and Zone B, and a Bible college. Rather than a hasty or spontaneous act, however, this was a carefully conceived plan based on the findings of a 1960 education commission.

Early in its history the Church of the Nazarene espoused the value of higher edu-cation linked to spiritual development and specifically emphasized liberal arts. Church fathers identified Christ's redemptive work as all-inclusive and applicable to transforming the whole person. Rather than a threat to faith, education was regarded as essential in training believers to become more effective in service to the community, nation, and the world—and all to the glory of God. The *Manual*, the authoritative written guide for the denomination, states that higher education is critical in assisting the process of spiritual maturity and should contribute to the development of "thinking, loving servants of Christ" equipped to address world needs.

The Church of the Nazarene was organized to preserve the focus and thrust of the eighteenth-century revival movement of the Wesleys, John and Charles, and George Whitefield as well as the nineteenth-century holiness movement led by Phoebe Palmer, Charles G. Finney, and Asa Mahan. Here are shared roots with Wesleyan Methodists, Free Methodists, and the Salvation Army. In the 1890s the Church of the Nazarene was formed to meet the specific longing for a national holiness church in the United States.

What is distinctive about the Church of the Nazarene? First is the doctrine of holiness, or entire sanctification, "that act of God, subsequent to regeneration, by which believers are made free from original sin, or depravity, and brought into a state of entire devotement to God, and the holy obedience of love made perfect." One result of devotion and obedience is that the believer will be committed to serving others. It follows that education is therefore regarded as instrumental in preparation for meaningful service. Higher education should equip graduates for a lifetime of service to others, regardless of the area of specialization or discipline.

Another distinctive purpose of the church is its emphasis on addressing human needs, particularly those of the less advantaged of society. Taking to heart the admonitions of Old Testament prophets who railed against the failure to take care of the oppressed and poor, the turn-of-the-century reformers sought to direct the mission and resources of Christianity to provide spiritual, medical, and social services to those most in need. Here, then, was another reason to support higher education that could provide the necessary skills and training for service. Thus, the church founders pursued, as part of a deliberate strategy to bring all aspects of human society under Christ's sovereignty, the construction of liberal arts colleges.

The liberal arts college to be carved out of the population and financial bases that were previously parts of the Eastern, Trevecca, and Olivet regions was given the unexciting title of "Zone A Junior College" and assigned to serve Ohio, West Virginia, and eastern Kentucky. How Zone A Junior College became Mount Vernon Nazarene College still strikes many eyewitnesses as nothing short of miraculous.

In May 1966 the site selection committee of the newly formed board of trustees received inquiries from eighteen communities interested in attracting the new college. Most of the communities offered outright land grants as part of their invitation. Nevertheless, few could have believed that building a new college almost literally from the ground up would be easy. Tackling such a major task, said one of those present at the beginning, was "an audacious thing to do." The initial budget was a meager $5,000. Dr. Stephen Nease, elected as the first president, often quoted the portion of John 15.5 that read "for apart from Me you can do nothing" to remind audiences of the divine source of power and guidance for the ambitious project.

In September 1966 the board of trustees reviewed a list of possible sites. The board took into account such factors as the desirability of the community, reputation of the public school system, community culture, work opportunities, transportation, and housing for faculty. The ideal community would be located within a 150-mile radius of the heaviest regional population density and "Nazarene concentrations." Six communities located roughly within a fifty-mile radius of Columbus made the final list. One day was spent visiting Springfield, Marysville, and London. The following day was devoted to New Philadelphia, Coshocton, and finally Mount Vernon.

Newspaper editors fanned public interest in helping the college find a home. For example, the *Coshocton Tribune* observed that "any expense, any commitment would seem reasonable" to win the bid, while the *Madison Press* editorial summarized London's position as "Community Needs College—The College Needs Us." New Philadelphia's *Daily Reporter* urged readers to bear in mind that there "never has been any question that the Nazarene college would enhance this county's educational position in respect to attracting new business."

As the relative merits of the various sites were evaluated, it did not take long to reach agreement as to which site was the front-runner by a considerable margin. Each of the sites had potential and strengths relative to the others, but one site was the clear choice. According to the board minutes that recorded the decision to choose Mount Vernon, "It was noted that unanimous action had been characteristic of Zone A College Board since its inception and that God had evidenced Himself in every step thus far."

It was not just the appeal of the spacious and attractive Lakeholm property, with necessary utilities already in place, which swayed the site selection committee. Overall, the community of Mount Vernon greatly impressed visitors who were drawn to the small town atmosphere. In addition to the rural charm of the All-American City, Mount Vernon offered an inviting and safe environment in which to raise a family. And this was a community that was anxious to have a Nazarene junior college.

The only remaining roadblock was the fact that Mount Vernon's citizenry were proposing to give away property that was not yet in their possession. The community leaders therefore offered to purchase the Lakeholm estate from the Ohio State University board of regents. In turn they would donate a significant portion of the property to the college and set aside as much as eighty acres for the construction of a public high school and some twenty-two acres for a joint vocational school. The parcel designated for the college was plotted at 234 acres, and the OSU regents agreed to sell the entire estate for $1,000 an acre. Thereafter, community leaders undertook a feverish and spirited public campaign to raise the necessary funds in less than a week. When the deadline for completing the campaign and purchase arrived, the fund-raising, though Herculean, came up $25,000 short of the goal. Despite the hard work and considerable effort, the fund-raising resulted in pledges of $209,000 that could go toward the college. To have raised so much money in just three days only to miss the goal was, of course, discouraging and marked, or so it seemed, the end of the bid to place the new college in Mount Vernon. When a last-minute attempt to find some source for the revenue shortfall failed, it was clear to the fund-raisers that the community had given its very best effort and could not do more.

With obvious disappointment the committee prepared to inform the officials at Ohio State that the community was unable to raise the total purchase price. However, in preparation for sale, the board of regents had authorized its own land survey and determined that the original deed was inaccurate and that the parcel set aside for the proposed college actually totaled 209 acres. Some may call it a coincidence that the community had raised exactly the amount needed to meet the initial terms of the negotiations. But you simply will not convince any member of that original community committee, or the site committee, board of trustees, or anyone involved in the early years of the college, for that matter, that this was by chance or accident. That convergence of the funds raised and the surveyed acreage to the exact figure is still hard to explain, except to witnesses who insist, "God certainly had a hand in the project." Without this turn of events, it is unlikely that the negotiations would have continued.

On September 16, 1966, the *Mount Vernon News* reported that the decision to build a new college in the community had been sealed. The initial enrollment was estimated at 750 students. That was either optimism or a misprint! Readers were also informed that "the liberal arts college will be open to students of all faiths and will emphasize teacher training." The next day's paper included a warm welcome extended by Dr. F. Edward Lund, president of nearby Kenyon College, who "hail[ed] the decision of the Church of the Nazarene to establish a college in Mount Vernon."

But another roadblock loomed when a new surveyor's report added seventeen acres to the total estate. To purchase a larger estate than expected the community faced the unpleasant prospect of raising more money. This might have ruined the sale had not the board of regents agreed to accept $292,000 for the whole property. The *Mount Vernon News* reported that the total cost came to about $948 per acre, applauded the transaction and expressed the community's gratitude in this way: "Thank You, OSU."

On March 15, 1967, the transfer of the property to the community and then, in turn, to the college board of trustees was completed. In the final analysis, the community paid $195,055 for the 206.23 acres that were given to the college.

From the beginning it had been decided to undertake a modest building program and to use as many of the existing buildings on the estate as possible. After inspecting the massive barns one of the pioneer trustees remarked that it "seemed wasteful to tear them down." The mansion, a carriage house, and several barns, plus the icehouse, could be put to immediate use or renovated. Renovating the mansion proved to be something of a challenge. It had been remodeled in the 1940s but required substantial changes to make appropriate space for offices. One of the first tasks was to remove nearly twenty coats of paint. Torches were used to burn the paint away to bare wood. The wood and insulation burned quite as easily as paint, thus the fire department paid two calls when workmen raised the flames out of control and threatened to engulf the entire structure. Inside the mansion there were interesting revelations, including the servants' staircase hidden between the walls to provide access from the basement to the upper floors and a bathroom with a particularly unique inlaid linoleum floor featuring a can-can girl. The basement was reminiscent of a medieval dungeon, and the roofing timbers covering the upper floors occasionally sheltered bats.

The college office was housed temporarily in a medical arts building off campus until renovations were complete. A chair, one card table, and a picnic table made up the list of office furnishings for the president, director of development and business affairs, the receptionist (who also served as secretary and office manager), and the accountant/errand runner. The office equipment consisted of one typewriter. There were some in the community, apparently, who were not aware of the purpose of the office inasmuch as the occasional disappointed caller had to be informed that Dr. Nease was taking no new patients or scheduling surgeries.

In the midst of the many diversions and challenges, the staff pressed on to launch a new college. The second floor of Lakeholm mansion became the temporary residence for the president's family while their home was under construction. What had formerly been the carriage house, an oversized garage, was turned into a temporary faculty residence shared with a sizeable population of field mice. That carriage house eventually housed the first library. And the icehouse, which housed campus security, was affectionately called the "bear house." The dairy barn, pressed into temporary service as the first cafeteria, harbored roosting swallows on the roofing beams.

Some of the farm structures, although impressive from the outside, either had structural problems or were positioned where more appropriate facilities were needed. The caretaker's house and a number of barns would have to come down. The horse barn was sitting astride the location designated for the classroom building now known as Faculty Hall, but when workmen began the demolition they encountered a territorial mother duck and her nest. Not until the newly hatched ducklings were able to follow their mother outside and the nest was temporarily abandoned was the barn torn down.

The first phase of new construction, projected to cost $2.25 million dollars, was funded by M.V.N.C.'s "Founder's Offering," a program that raised $300,000 in pledges and was supplemented by a $1 million loan from a newly formed community association willing to venture capital on the proposition that something other than grain might be raised on the property. The architect, in keeping with Mount Vernon's identity as a "Colonial City," designed the campus structures in imitation of Colonial Williamsburg, Virginia. This decision was greeted with resounding approval as the *Mount Vernon News* noted that "the colonial will be in harmony with the architecture used in most of the public buildings and in several privately constructed buildings here." Originally there were plans to construct a chapel, but the initial construction phase had to be scaled back to match the available funds. The chapel would be built later.

Shovels stabbed at the frozen earth on January 6, 1968, at the groundbreaking for the Campus Center to house the cafeteria and the library, a dormitory (Pioneer Hall), and a classroom building (Founders Hall). Those present for this service huddled inside one of the remaining barns during the opening ceremony to shelter from the bitter cold as temperatures dipped to a few degrees above zero and the wind roared over the rolling landscape. Only someone who has never braved the wind in the dead of winter on the campus of Mount Vernon Nazarene University would dare to doubt that the weather conditions influenced the brief, but meaningful, spade work, as the dignitaries "got that over pretty quick."

Recruiting faculty, administrators, and staff for a new college meant seeking people willing to risk personal security and financial difficulties since the fledgling college would not be able to offer competitive salaries. The necessary positions, however, were all filled. The privilege and opportunity to serve outweighed any considerations of remuneration in terms of dollars and cents.

One of the most daunting tasks confronting the new faculty and administration was reaching agreement on adopting the college curriculum. What courses should be offered? Which and how many should count toward completion of a two-year degree? While the questions were not at all uncommon for a brand new institution to consider, the way the basic curriculum was first formulated was somewhat unique. Dr. Arthur Seamans, professor of English, was commissioned to travel across the country visiting campuses along the way to study various options and then bring back a report to the faculty. As might be expected, the report was not greeted with instant unanimity, and there was considerable disagreement and debate. There was nothing unusual about that. There existed, however, such a sense of camaraderie, common purpose, and, it must be added, divinely appointed mission that there was a "sense of oneness even in the midst of disagreement," followed by compromise, tweaking, fine-tuning, and harmony. One of the advantages of having a small faculty with an embryonic campus was the quick acknowledgement that success could only be possible if all worked together. But it was more than that. Talk to the first administrators and faculty members, and they will tell you, without exception, that there was a sense that all were in the venture together, and the recognition of the common cause created a family of coworkers.

The faculty and staff welcomed the first students, thereafter known as the Pioneer Class, 191 strong, on October 12, 1968. The local newspaper observed that October 12 had been the date in 1492 when Christopher Columbus first spotted the New World and marked 1968's "Day of Discovery." The Mount Vernon pioneers at least came better equipped than Columbus and his hardy crew. According to the *Mount Vernon News*, "cars wove their way over mud roads on the campus—laden with suitcases, cartons stuffed with 'absolute' necessities for dormitory life and those inevitable poles hung with clothing over the back seat."

Construction delays, mostly caused by inclement weather that drove locals to benchmark that fall as the worst in memory, had pushed the opening back from September. As might be expected, members of that first group love to tell the story of how difficult and challenging those first days were. Oft repeated are anecdotes about trudging through the mud and snow as the first winter descended upon the emerging campus where construction of walkways lagged behind more critical priorities, and residents were forced to make their own paths. There are, of course, differing memories concerning how thick the mud was and how deep the first snow. Another favorite theme was the adventure of mealtime. Students arrived before cafeteria seating was ready, so food was prepared in the kitchens and then carried across the road to an old dairy barn, where birds perched in the rafters above the tables. The unwary diner was subject to unwanted supplements to the cuisine. The pioneering founders often remind newcomers that beds had to be assembled the night before students arrived, that the first residence hall housed men in one half and women in the other, and that faculty monitors patrolled the hallways to encourage the development of appropriate study habits.

What attracted students to join that pioneer class? For some there was a sense of adventure and desire to participate in something historic. One young lady from Boston explained, "If I could have one wish, I think it would be to see a field of corn blowing in the breeze. I think that would so peaceful. I have never seen a field of corn!" And for a young man from California, the appeal was likewise the corn: "When I read in the M.V.N.C. catalog it was on a 200-acre farm with fields of corn, I thought how beautiful and peaceful that would be. . . . I want to know that peace." What marketing genius would have ever dared suggest using maize as the focal point of a recruiting strategy?

On January 2, 1969, the *Mount Vernon News* reflected on all that had happened at the site of Columbus Delano's farm: "We saw the new Mount Vernon Nazarene College move from the drawing boards to actual existence with a student body of some

200 students in a matter of six months—an accomplishment which future generations may regard as almost unbelievable." The goal was to become a four-year college as soon as possible. This was the mandate issued at the General Assembly in 1964. From the beginning the vision that this junior college would grow into a four-year institution was strong and vibrant. Work in pursuit of accreditation began almost immediately. The administration submitted a plan to North Central Association of Colleges and Schools for accrediting a two-year college with the understanding that the next step, establishing a four-year college, would be pursued vigorously. Following candidacy as a two-year institution authorized to grant associate degrees in 1970, accreditation was granted in 1972. In 1974 accreditation was extended to the offering of bachelor's-level degrees. And on August 1, 2002, a new chapter began as the institution was renamed Mount Vernon Nazarene University.

From the earliest period of the university's relatively short life, the mission of the institution was clearly and powerfully articulated. The by-laws committee of the board of trustees, chaired by Dr. Lawrence B. Hicks, a compelling and poetic orator, worked with President Nease to draft a document that would capture the purpose and vision of the new institution. In the words of the 1966 charter: "With an eye single to the Glory of God and as the avowed servants of the Lord Jesus Christ, we, the duly elected and constituted Board of Trustees of Mount Vernon Nazarene College, moved by the steadfast faith that all branches of education and instruction should be promoted with a firm Christian philosophy and perspective, do this day organize and set forth this corporation." At the leading of President Nease, the motto "To seek to learn is to seek to serve" was adopted. And that, in a nutshell, is the institution's mission. Or, as one of the first trustees commented, the school's "saying . . . covers it pretty well." The mission statement has been revisited from time to time and presently states that the institution "seeks to (1) provide a rigorous academic program that encourages scholarship, critical reflection, and problem-solving; (2) promote a distinctively Christian lifestyle within the Wesleyan evangelical tradition; and (3) offer a supportive environment that inspires students to achieve their highest potential spiritually, intellectually, socially, and physically, as they prepare not only for a career but also for meaningful service to God and humankind wherever their vocational choices under the leadership of God take them."

Ask the pioneers if the institution began with a clear mission, and they will quickly affirm that there was a common understanding that the purpose of the project from the first day the doors opened was, and remains, the preparation of students for service to God and mankind regardless of the career choice. Still, there has never really been an improvement on the motto: "To seek to learn is to seek to serve."

Since the beginning bricks have multiplied to provide needed classroom space, dormitories, and apartments. A chapel and a library have risen in colonial architecture where farmland once stood. A few of the original buildings remain to remind the visitor of what once stood on the grounds. That dairy barn used for the first meals on campus, the ice house, and, of course, Lakeholm Mansion remain to link the campus to its origins. And that is a large part of the charm of a university landscape that is attractive and pleasing to the eye. The beauty of the old has not been entirely destroyed or replaced but, in many cases, tastefully enhanced.

From the beginning there was a deep commitment to continuing the careful stewardship that had contributed to making the farmstead an outstanding example of ecological harmony. At the time the campus property was acquired, the administration retained the groundskeeper—a Hungarian refugee who fled his homeland at the time of the Russian occupation in 1945 and never learned much English—to tend the flowers, trees, and lawns. His legacy of hard and skillful service set the example for the dedicated staff that has grown over the years as the campus has expanded. Early on there was established the tradition known as Blue-Green Day. This is one day set aside in the spring when students, staff, faculty, and administrators join together to plant flowers and trees to beautify the campus.

Over the past thirty years Mount Vernon Nazarene University has experienced a steady growth in enrollment. It has grown in spite of dire national forecasts that a diminishing student pool would threaten the existence of small institutions lacking substantial endowments. At the turn of the millennium the enrollment passed the 2,000 mark. The curriculum has expanded to include the Executive Center for Lifelong Learning (EXCELL), a degree-completion program for nontraditional students with an Associate of Arts in General Studies and a Bachelor of Business Administration options and graduate programs in religion and education.

At each step the institution has maintained strong ties with the founding denomination. While faculty and staff need not be members of the church, they must affirm and support the "Agreed Statement of Belief," which states:

We believe (1) In one God—the Father, Son, and Holy Spirit;
(2) That the Old and New Testament scriptures, given by plenary inspiration, contain all truth necessary to faith and Christian living;
(3) That man is born with a fallen nature and is, therefore, inclined to evil, and that continually;
(4) That the finally impenitent are hopelessly and eternally lost;
(5) That the atonement through Christ is for the whole human race; and that whosoever repents and believes on the Lord Jesus Christ is justified and regenerated and saved from the dominion of sin;
(6) That believers are to be sanctified wholly, subsequent to regeneration, through faith in the Lord Jesus Christ,

(7) That the Holy Spirit bears witness to the new birth and also the entire sanctification of believers; and

(8) That our Lord will return, the dead will be raised, and the final judgment will take place.

Nearly a century after the denomination was founded, churches in the university's educational zone send approximately 800 students and contribute almost $2 million through local church budgets to the college each year. The board of trustees is composed of the superintendents of the various districts on the university zone, along with pastors and lay people elected by representatives of the individual churches in Ohio, West Virginia, and eastern Kentucky. Many of the faculty members completed undergraduate training at one of the Nazarene institutions. *Nazarene* is thus at the core of the college's identity.

There is little evidence that the university will drift from its mooring. Every member of the campus family is expected to model adherence to behavioral rules that include abstaining from drinking alcoholic beverages; sexual acts with anyone other than one's spouse; social dancing; entertainment that is promiscuous, pornographic, or occult; illegal drugs and misuse of legal prescriptions; and tobacco in any form. From a communal standpoint these lifestyle guidelines represent tangible ways of testifying to the pursuit of Christ-like character. Students and faculty are expected to attend chapel services three times a week. And the campus community is challenged to experience hands-on service through ministry courses, internships, community projects, and mission trips. The short-term mission program, "Joining Hands," involves training students and faculty for spring break and summer trips to Belize, Brazil, Costa Rica, Guatemala, Haiti, Hungary, India, Israel, Kenya, Romania, and Mexico as well as innercity ministry in New York City, Orlando, and Indianapolis. Increasingly graduates spend a short-term assignment serving, for example, in South Korea, Japan, the Philippines, China, and the Czech Republic.

The university is poised to implement the resolve of the board of trustees to facilitate continued growth. In 1970 the gift of Mary Starr added nine acres, part of which fronts the Kokosing River, to the college campus. In 1999 the university acquired the neighboring 128-acre Pinecrest Farm. There are plans to establish a center for global mission and ministry studies to provide training and consultation services with a specific emphasis on compassionate ministries around the world. And EXCELL has established branch campus facilities at Polaris, Newark, and Lima.

In the end, none of the physical elements of the college has meaning devoid of the dedicated people who have invested their resources, talents, and their faith. One donor faithfully sent five dollars a month for the "Chapel Fund" long before such a thing existed and died in a rest home without ever seeing the harvest of his giving. And there was a soft-spoken, gentle janitor who took a job on campus to pay for his son's education and ended up impacting students, faculty, and staff by his living example of glorifying God in every task, however menial. What the giants—those pioneers and their descendants who gave of themselves and their resources—seem to have in common is their ability to dream. They could envision an institution of higher learning where there were cornfields and grazing cattle. They were the visionaries who helped make the miracle.

Muskingum College

Persistence and Success

WILLIAM FISK

The origins of Muskingum College lie in the great migration of the Ulster Scots to Pennsylvania in the eighteenth century, the closely related development of Presbyterian denominations, and the impulse for personal improvement that was a strong current in American culture in the early national period. By the time of the American Revolution most of the Scotch-Irish had become indistinguishable from other English-speaking colonials. Evidences of ethnic origins survived, however, especially among leaders of the minor Presbyterian denominations, who, along with their Calvinist theology, preserved some folkways and Scotticisms in English usage well into the next century. The oldest of these denominations, the Reformed Presbyterian Church, cherished its memories of the seventeenth-century Covenanter rebellion against the Church of Scotland and the Stuart kings, so that two centuries later in America its members still called themselves Covenanters. In the early eighteenth century secession from the Church of Scotland against the influences of the Scottish Enlightenment created the Associate Synod, whose adherents became known as Seceders. Both denominations had adherents in Pennsylvania before 1750, and part of each body united in 1782 as the Associate Reformed Church. Small migrations from Ulster invigorated these sects throughout the nineteenth century.

Along with the Old School Presbyterians, these groups preserved allegiance to the stern Calvinist theology of the seventeenth-century Westminister Confession. Organizing churches first in southeastern Pennsylvania and then in southwestern Pennsylvania after the Revolution, they followed the frontier to the Ohio Country at the dawn of the nineteenth century. Despite the privations of their origins, they so venerated an educated ministry that in Pennsylvania they founded colleges and academies with high priority for training ministers. In Ohio the same pattern appeared when John Walker, a Seceder minister educated at Jefferson College in Canonsburg,

Academic Quadrangle

Pennsylvania, came to Harrison County. He first opened an academy and then Franklin College in New Athens, an institution that rapidly gained a reputation for excellence in eastern Ohio. In 1819 Old School Presbyterians opened Union Academy in their newly erected church building at Pleasant Hill on Zane's Trace, a mile south of the future site of New Concord. That school had an ephemeral existence, but its records were still extant when Andrew Black, a native of the New Concord area and a Franklin graduate, opened a classical school on New Concord's Main Street in 1836.

The flowering of the dream of a college for New Concord came from roots that ran deep in the village's Scotch-Irish heritage and its Presbyterian system of values and drew sustenance from its location in the New West at a time when Americans enjoyed the buoyant assurance of endless progress. When on July 9, 1836, citizens of the village met to plan for an academy, they were conscious of a variety of ways in which this legacy had recently impinged on their lives. They remembered the Union Academy at Pleasant Hill where David Findley, who laid out the village of New Concord, and other early citizens had served as trustees. Presumably New Concord's failure to acquire the Associate Reformed seminary had been a blow to village pride, and the Associate Reformed minister, Johnston Welch, had just left his Crooked Creek charge, close by New Concord, to become president of Franklin

College. Early in 1837 a citizens' group, styling themselves "the Friends of Education," petitioned the Ohio state legislature to charter a college in New Concord. While they awaited word of the approval of their petition, they met in the district schoolhouse on February 24 to hear a lecture on "The Science of Chemistry," and on March 1 about "The Rudiments of Literature."

Among these "Friends" were two clergymen, Samuel Willson and Benjamin Waddle. Samuel Willson's interest sprang from his role as minister to the Pleasant Hill Old School Presbyterians in whose building the Union Academy had operated. The debt Muskingum College owes to their informal partnership is immeasurable.

Both men were products of the West. Benjamin Waddle was born in 1802 and reared on a farm near Wheeling; he graduated from Wheeling Academy. Trained in theology at the newly founded Associate Reformed Seminary at Allegheny (Pittsburgh), he was licensed for the ministry in 1829. His first pastorate brought him to Perry County, Ohio, where he became pastor of Jonathan's Creek, Rush Creek, and Thornville, with residence at Mount Perry. From there he was called in 1836 at the age of thirty-four to the charge of Crooked Creek, Salt Creek, and Lebanon. Within six months of his arrival in New Concord, he was actively engaged in the affairs of the academy and plans for a college. He was called in 1859 to the United Presbyterian Church at Kenton, where he remained as pastor until his death in 1879. In 1872 and 1873 he served a term as Hardin County's representative in the state legislature.

Benjamin Waddle's ministerial colleague, Samuel Willson, had come to New Concord in 1832. Born in Westmoreland County, Pennsylvania, he grew up in Washington County and became a member of the Bethel Presbyterian Church (Old School). After briefly practicing medicine at Raccoon, Pennsylvania, he studied theology privately and was ordained to the Presbyterian ministry. At the age of thirty-three he came to Ohio and accepted a call to the Pleasant Hill–Norwich charge; he retained his pastorate there for thirty-seven years. Many years after New Concord was laid out, the Pleasant Hill congregation moved its building to the village where it has continued as the Westminster Presbyterian Church; its congregation worships in a building whose framing timbers are those of the original Pleasant Hill church and academy.

In addition to their other tasks, all the early presidents had to maintain good relations between the college and the town, an especially delicate matter amid the growing acrimony of the slavery controversy in national life. Waddle was a Free Soiler but not an abolitionist, while Samuel Willson grounded his acceptance of slavery in the extreme biblicism of the Old School Presbyterians. Waddle served as president during the 1837–38 year and again from 1855 to 1859. Willson was president from 1838 to 1845. Other early presidents, often men in their twenties, kept the college alive by not much more than a thread and, while despising slavery, hoped the slavery controversy would not consume the pathetically feeble college.

They had enough problems at home. The citizens of New Concord built the first building, a two-story structure, in 1838. Despite warnings that it was a firetrap, adequate repairs were delayed until the inevitable fire destroyed half the building in 1851. In a patched-up form it survived until 1899. The staff included the president and two professors, one of ancient languages and one of mathematics. During the first decade of the college's existence, both Waddle and Willson regularly filled both professorships themselves whenever there was a vacancy, and both maintained their continuous service to their congregations.

It is not easy to piece together the daily routine of these clergymen-professors, but enough is known of the Presbyterian minister's life in nineteenth-century America to make some inferences. As pastors of thriving congregations before agriculture had begun to decay in eastern Ohio, Waddle and Willson had respectable incomes from their charges. Further, hearing daily recitations in Greek and Latin from a dozen and a half boys in three or four small classes may not have taken much of their day or much preparation. The lectures in science, mathematics, and moral science, usually expository glosses on standard texts, seldom changed in an age when new discoveries and interpretations did not daily threaten professorial knowledge with obsolescence.

However, the demands of the congregation on its pastor were impressive. Weddings and funerals occurred in proportion to the size of the congregation and the shorter life span of Western man before Pasteur. Sermons had to be long, meticulously interlaced with scriptural references, and vigorously delivered. It becomes obvious that men with this schedule, who might find time to meet their classes regularly, could scarcely have been expected to find the time required to study the broader needs of higher education or to make intellectual or financial contacts outside their parishes. That they persevered so faithfully is enough to merit respect, and it is no wonder that by end of 1845 both were ready to resign their college duties.

Beleaguered by debt, the college barely survived the loss of its first two leaders. For the next decade a series of young men interrupted their theological seminary studies to accept the presidency of the struggling college, each for only a few years. The first of these, David A. Wallace, tarried long enough in New Concord to marry David Findley's granddaughter and to publish the first college catalog in 1846. From Andrew Black's seventeen students, the college had grown in a decade to fifty-seven—twelve in the collegiate department, twenty-two in the preparatory, and twenty-three in the scientific department. The geographical distribution covered the eastern Ohio counties, Preble County in southwestern Ohio, and three students from Washington County, Pennsylvania.

Because Wallace's immediate successors all served short terms, the trustees elected Benjamin Waddle as president again in 1855. The college had barely recovered from the 1851 fire when he confronted a student rebellion and bad blood between college officers and village. At one point the enrollment in collegiate courses shrank to nine, with only one solitary freshman. The trustees asserted their support of President Waddle and admonished all parties to the dissension to bury their differences. The local turbulence had religious and political overtones as well as dimensions of student unrest. In 1858 the Associate Reformed Church and the Associate Synod united to become the United Presbyterian Church. National officers of the new denomination encouraged incumbent ministers of local churches to resign their charges and make way for new ministers who would better represent the new denomination. Waddle reluctantly resigned his charge, as did the Seceder minister in New Concord, but old loyalties and old resentments in the church and college died a slow death.

The friction had a more subtle and sinister dimension. The slavery controversy dividing the nation similarly disturbed tranquil villages like New Concord. Benjamin Waddle, though a member of the Free Soil party, feared the tactics of some of the abolitionists. Accordingly college regulations denied the use of the college hall to "strolling lecturers," presumably extreme advocates of abolition. In New Concord the members of the Covenanter Church actively spirited slaves through the town along "the Underground Railroad." The United Presbyterian Church, though equally opposed to slavery, took a more moderate stance, but gradualist views on the elimination of slavery were yielding to the abolitionist position. The antislavery impulse came naturally to Muskingum.

Along with Presbyterian piety, Muskingum students had imbibed the strong expectation of national progress and improvement that was as much a part of the temper of the times as was their grounding in Calvinist cultural values. The first literary society actually antedated the founding of the college, and the presence of townspeople at literary society meetings showed the shared interests of town and gown in their essays and debates. All through the quarter-century before the coming of the Civil War, the literary society programs show what Muskingum students were thinking about in their more serious moments.

In 1838 the Union Literary Society debated the heated topic "Are free states implicated in the crime of slavery in the District of Columbia?" A year later the subject was "Should the American anti-slavery society be patronized?" "Does the avowal of infidel principles by the president forfeit his right to the presidential chair?" the Philomatheans asked themselves one night in 1848. On another evening the question was "Should Roman Catholics be deprived of the right of suffrage?" On this issue Muskingum students chose to disavow the Know-Nothing movement, for the division of the house on sentiment was in favor of the negative. The same year the sentiment of the house was negative on the question "Should foreign immigration be prohibited?" Shifting away from public controversy, the Philos reflected the optimism and faith in progress of the age by debating "Is there any limit to the improvement of human society?" Since hope for human perfectibility embraced widespread concern for reforming the evils of society, another timely topic of 1848 was "Is intemperance a greater evil than slavery?" Later a similar question was posed: "Should the vendor of ardent spirits be punished with imprisonment?" There can be no question about Muskingum students' interest in the contemporary development of the slavery quarrel. On July 26, 1850, the Philos debated "Is Clay's Compromise calculated to benefit the country?" The slavery question had cut deeply into church loyalty, and another topic asked whether the Free Presbyterian church, a splinter that had favored an extreme abolitionist position, was culpable in breaking off from the main body.

By 1861 the college had made efforts to broaden the thrust of its program, geared from the beginning toward ancient languages and mathematics, to include a scientific course for nondegree students and to open a female seminary in a converted residence a block from the college building. The college opened all college classes to women in 1863. But the absence of adequate funds hamstrung these efforts at growth, and the college's outreach remained parochial, its status essentially that of a poor relation of Franklin. And with the outbreak of the Civil War, the overwhelming loyalty of New Concord to the Union cause decimated the male portion of the student body. As a consequence the enrollment seldom numbered 100 in all departments. But the college never closed its doors. In fact, enrollment grew modestly between 1861 and 1865.

During the war years it made its first overtures toward a broader constituency, advertising itself in Zanesville newspapers as a school for the Muskingum Valley. For the first time it attracted Zanesville students. The petition for the original charter of the college announced that Christians of different denominations were joining in the launching of the college. In practice the self-perpetuating board prescribed a formula by which all trustees came from the Associate Reformed, Seceder, Covenanters, and Old School Presbyterian denominations. That formula was quietly dropped during the war, but the dissenting Presbyterian denomination would play a larger role in the life of the college for many more years than would the Muskingum Valley.

The strong support in the region from the three minor Presbyterian bodies and the Old School Presbyterians led to Muskingum's acceptance as the denominational college of the United Presbyterian Church. It was the era of denominational rivalry and the founding or adoption of denominational colleges. Over the next quarter-century five colleges became increasingly identified as United Presbyterian colleges and hence deserving of denominational benevolence. Westminister in Pennsylvania and Monmouth in Illinois began as denominational schools. Muskingum first came under the care of two individual presbyteries and then of the whole denomination. Then Tarkio in Missouri, Sterling in Kansas, and Knoxville in Tennessee (founded in the Reconstruction era as a college for freedmen) also all received denominational support. They all shared whatever advantages came from their place on the consciences of United Presbyterians, and the small denomination prided itself on the sponsorship of the colleges. For the hundred years of its denominational history to 1958, denominational magazines faithfully reported news of its colleges to its readers.

Postwar affiliation with the United Presbyterian Church began during the administration of David Paul, an influential United Presbyterian minister and Muskingum graduate who served as president from 1865 to 1879. He strengthened the reputation of the college and was recognized years later by having the new building built in 1873 and attached to the 1838 building named in his honor. Under Paul's successors growth became more sporadic. The faculty undertook to improve the teaching of science and to develop normal school courses for public school teachers. In 1899 the original college building was finally torn down before it fell down, and a second building added. These two buildings and a minuscule gymnasium constituted the total physical plant.

As Muskingum entered the twentieth century, change came about with the arrival of a new president in 1904. J. Knox Montgomery, a product of the Scotch-Irish United Presbyterian colonies in the lower Ohio valley in Illinois and Indiana, came to Muskingum from a successful pastorate in the Associate Reformed Presbyterian Church in Charlotte, North Carolina. President Montgomery incorporated the evangelical zeal of his ministerial calling with a boundless optimism about Muskingum's prospect, an equally strong gift of nervous energy, and what his daughter-in-law once described as "plain Montgomery nerve." It was an unbeatable combination for a college president at the time when America was entering the Progressive Era, with its motifs of reform in many phases of national life, not the least of which was education at all levels. For twenty-seven years he sold his vision for the college to students, alumni, and friends of the college. That vision was conservative in both religious and social outlook but never became trapped in the fundamentalist-modernist quarrel of the times. For example, when the two members of the Bible department developed irreconcilable views on the inerrancy of scripture, Montgomery simply divided the department into separate ones, Bible and religion, and gave each man his own domain long enough to staunch the quarrel.

Muskingum had enforced strict rules for student behavior from its earliest days, and to President Montgomery tobacco was anathema. In one famous incident he successfully defied the United States Army on the subject. During the First World War Muskingum hosted an army training unit whose officers were assigned offices in the basement of the newly built college chapel. The president informed them of the college's no smoking rule. When they refused to obey, the president told them that he would be on the next train to Washington to make his case before the War Department. The army capitulated, and New Concord long remembered the indomitable will of the president. Similarly, the college had long prohibited alcohol, and when the reforming impulse of the Progressives moved toward national prohibition during the First World War, the college enjoyed the enhancement of its long-standing position. Dancing and card playing also were forbidden, rules clearly supported by the more conservative elements of the United Presbyterian Church.

But conservatism in morals and manners only partially characterized Muskingum in these years. American universities were rapidly changing their roles as transmitters of the accumulated culture of the ages to a new emphasis on research. While the language of higher education now made frequent reference to "departments" and "chairs," one late-nineteenth-century professor at Muskingum, long accustomed to teaching in a variety of fields, commented that he occupied a sofa, not a chair. Gradually Muskingum moved away from the old terminology of classical and scientific courses into the structure of departments. Greek did not disappear as a requirement for a Bachelor of Arts degree until the First World War, but professors became more identified with individual departments and tried to keep up with changing developments in one field of knowledge.

President Montgomery staffed the departments with young professors from some of the country's most prestigious graduate schools; few completed doctorates, because either they were more interested in teaching than research or their burdensome teaching loads precluded time for other activities. The college also tried to balance its long-standing commitment to the religious nurture and classical education of its students with new viewpoints about the purposes of higher education. Modern languages became more popular than Greek or Latin, and a department of oratory, favored by the president for its benefit to the pulpit skills of prospective ministers, grew into a variety of speech and theater offerings. Intercollegiate football had made its debut in the 1890s, and instruction in physical education followed.

But the new variety in the cultural life of the college sounded the death knell of those bastions of nineteenth-century college social life, the literary societies. At Muskingum they died a lingering death after 1900 and finally disappeared as a casualty of wartime change. During these years newly formed social clubs absorbed the social function of the literary societies without any pretense of preserving their intellectual role. President Montgomery insisted that they should not be Greek-letter fraternities and sororities, which he remembered unfavorably from his student days at Indiana University.

Progressive educators like John Dewey, who taught at the University of Chicago during William Rainey Harper's presidency there, made the improvement of public education a major cause. As the State of Ohio began fitfully to raise standards for public school teachers, Muskingum began to build a strong program for both high school and elementary teachers. The market for teacher training courses enabled Muskingum to finance its basic purpose of instruction in liberal arts. Ohio particularly sought to lift the level of competence of elementary teachers. Between 1910 and 1940 beginning teachers had to have completed one, then two, then three, and finally four years of college. In the 1920s the enrollment of 600 or 700 students in the academic year swelled to more than 1,000 in summer school as elementary teachers sought to upgrade their credentials to keep their jobs.

On occasion the college's commitment to training public school teachers produced some points of conflict with colleges like Muskingum. In Ohio new normal schools were created in northwestern and northeastern Ohio, and Ohio University and Miami University added elementary education programs to their curriculum. Normal schools quickly became political footballs in many states as local politicians sought to make them pork barrel morsels. In eastern Ohio both Cambridge and Cadiz were being considered for normal schools. At the risk of incurring the ill will of boosters in both towns, President Montgomery successfully persuaded state legislators that Muskingum could meet the needs of eastern Ohio for normal school programs.

During the period between 1904 and 1918, the transition from the old classical curriculum to departmental courses also slowly accelerated. Biology, chemistry, and physics emerged as departments, and geology followed a few years later. Chemistry spawned a separate department of domestic science, while old offerings in zoology and botany merged into a biology department. On occasion ill-conceived innovations in the curriculum, such as a Department of Agriculture, arose and quickly vanished.

The students who encountered the changing curriculum reflected the nineteenth century's faith in progress and the Progressive Era's expectations of rapid improvement in national life. In 1905 a survey of the eighteen seniors, who ranged in age from twenty to twenty-eight, reported that eight supported the Prohibition party, seven were Republicans, and two were Populists. Twelve of the eighteen had earned part or all of their college expenses.

With the coming of the First World War in the spring of 1917, the college arranged for 130 men to finish the semester early in order to go to work on farms, an indication of the rural character of the student body. By October 1918, 155 Muskingum men had been inducted into the army. By that time the influenza pandemic of 1918 had disabled a third of the student body. When the armistice came, Muskingum professors and students echoed the national faith that the war had ended all wars. That idealism and the Progressives' reforming spirit were destined to erode quickly in the ensuing decade.

Muskingum's enrollment grew rapidly in the 1920s to 700 students. But the postwar era, with its modest trend toward loosening social restrictions, created tensions on the campus. College officials had to work harder to hold the line against student agitation to relax long-standing rules against dancing and card playing. The automobile in particular caused trauma for college officials, who touted Muskingum as a rural retreat safe from the temptations of urban life. Now students could easily get away from New Concord at a moment's notice and go dancing at nearby Moxahala Park—so long as the officers of the college didn't find out.

In 1929 the world both of restrictions and of students' dissent fell into ruins together. For a decade the Great Depression paralyzed change and growth of any kind at Muskingum. During the 1920s the college had built three substantial new buildings and begun work on a long-needed gymnasium. After the Crash the rusting girders of that unfinished building stood as a stark reminder that money had dried up. An even more somber note was added in 1931, when the unwaveringly optimistic President Montgomery died. His ambitious plans for the college included arrangements to continue his vision after he was gone. His son, Robert N. Montgomery, was being groomed to be his successor by way of two years' experience as president of Tarkio College, a struggling United Presbyterian college in Missouri. With only one dissenting vote the trustees endorsed his election. The new president, ably assisted by his talented wife, quickly won the acclaim of the college community. The surface discontent of the students vanished when the long-awaited approval of dancing came from the new administration. In many ways the president made his interest in students felt and won their respect as a friendly leader.

With his position thus enhanced, Robert Montgomery tackled the grave problems of college finances. By 1935 the enrollment of 700 in 1930 declined to fewer than 500 students, and small annual deficits were turning into a threatening indebtedness. Along with his brother, J. Knox Montgomery Jr., who had been installed as vice president and business manager, the new president won the undying gratitude of a generation of students by accepting deferred and partial payments on bills; and both men sometimes helped penniless students with money from their own pockets. The faculty shared in the students' endurance of the straitened circumstances. Salary cuts came one after another, reaching 50 percent in 1933 and, for one terrible semester at the time of the national bank holiday that year, 60 percent from the 1929 base. Not until 1947 were the cuts restored, and the president himself, who shared in them first, received a salary of $7,000 in the late 1940s.

One particularly skillful maneuver enabled the college to erase the specter of the unfinished gymnasium, as a Public Works Administration project of the Roosevelt New Deal resulted in one of the best physical education facilities in any Ohio college. But the debts kept mounting, in spite of what to a later age would seem unbelievably frugal policies. At the outbreak of war in Europe in 1939 the college undertook to refinance its debt, only to learn for a terrifying few days that panic in the international banking community prevented both the old and new lender from completing the transaction.

That crisis passed, but all too quickly the uncertainties of the Depression turned into the equally painful realities of war. The government's needs for manpower greatly reduced male enrollment, and once again in 1944 there were only 400–500 students, and proportionate tuition receipts. The college received temporary relief for its shrunken budget when in mid-1943, without much early notice, the government approved its application for an Army Specialized Training Unit and then just as quickly disbanded the unit the following March. Hiring and dismissing the teaching staff was an added annoyance of the dislocation of the war. The president's wife and a chemistry instructor found themselves operating the Muskingum House, a local restaurant, to serve the needs of the college for obligatory hospitality.

In 1945 the dearth of students gave way to the first intimation of the glut of customers for higher education to come. The passage in Congress of the famous GI Bill had unprecedented effects on the hunger of veterans for college education. By 1946 housing became acutely short, and the main floor of the new gymnasium, which had served as an army barracks three years before, now became a dormitory for freshmen men. The national housing shortage hit New Concord in an idiosyncratic way. For many years the college had counted on retirees moving to New Concord to board students as a supplement to their income. Suddenly that supply dried up. No longer did elderly United Presbyterians find keeping a rooming house as pleasant as they once had, and no longer were postwar students satisfied with the sometimes derelict furnishings their predecessors had once accepted.

At the same time that the Congress passed the GI Bill, it also provided colleges with no longer needed but usable barracks from army camps. For several years these buildings provided much-needed housing for both men and women. One enterprising group of women still housed in a barracks in 1960 even staged a "barracks formal" as a spoof on the social customs of the campus. A spate of student housing construction began in 1951 with the first residence hall for men, followed by five more dormitories, most financed with federal subsidies and generous interest rates. Winking at the potential for antidiscrimination suits, the government also made grants for housing for social clubs. The apogee of interest in both men's and women's social clubs came in the 1950s when as high as 90 percent of eligible students sought membership in them, a figure that gradually shrank to 40 percent by 2000.

Central to the intellectual history of the college in the postwar period was the transition in style and interests of the faculty. Between 1904 and 1962 both Presidents Montgomery relied heavily on the United Presbyterian Church for aid in recruiting both students and professors. Particularly in the first half of the century, the faculty evinced remarkably homogeneous patterns of educational and social philosophy. The union of the United Presbyterian Church with the main body of American Presbyterianism and the secularizing forces in American life eroded that homogeneity. In the quarter-century after the war, twenty Muskingum professors retired; all had taught at the college for twenty-five years or more, making the transitions in the various departments bumpier than usual. Although their successors often came with more extensive academic credentials, no one inquired whether the completion of an ostensibly research-designed degree was the best preparation the higher education establishment could design for teaching undergraduates. It was a question William Rainey Harper had pondered in his correspondence with David Paul about linkages that might be made between Muskingum and the research behemoth he was creating at the University of Chicago.

Muskingum could not escape wrestling with educational philosophy during and after the war years. Harvard and the University of Chicago both explored the tension between specialized and general education before the war. Indeed, when Robert M. Hutchens, Chicago's innovative new president, proposed a format for the university wherein students would enter after two or three years of high school and collect their bachelor's degree after four years and then enter a four-year master's program, he first described the idea in an address at Muskingum when the college sponsored a William Rainey Harper Memorial Conference as part of its centennial celebration in 1937.

In 1939 Muskingum joined several other colleges in a study of general education sponsored by the University of Chicago. Muskingum professors were encouraged to dream about innovative ways to repackage higher education into interdisciplinary courses, and by the end of the war Muskingum launched its own general education program to replace the rigidities of departmental offerings for the first and second years of college. Some of the most enthusiastic proponents of general education moved on from Muskingum after a few years, leaving the guidance of the program in less capable hands. It was also sabotaged by informal alliances between the more conservative senior professors and youthful additions to the faculty with shiny new doctorates. Few self-respecting historians would teach generalized courses in social studies for more than a few years, and no chemist wanted to participate in Muskingum's integrated course labeled "Our Scientific Heritage." By 1955 the general education courses were dead or dying. The debate about the virtues of integrated courses as opposed to beginning departmental courses as requirements for beginning students would continue for the rest of the century, and new interdisciplinary combinations would reappear for a few years and die again at about twenty-year intervals.

While the faculty chewed over educational philosophy, the college began to enjoy an unprecedented market. A brief shrinkage of enrollment after the end of the GI Bill era gave way to long years of growing numbers, peaking in 1968 with 1,400 students and then leveling off to 1,200 for the next fifteen years and then dropping to fewer than 1,000 by 1990. The college tried various gambits, including a master's degree in education, to compensate for the decreased enrollment and then in 1995 undertook a daring experiment in reduction of tuition by $4,000. It is much too early to make judgments on the long-range effect of the action, but the short-run results were an overwhelming success. Once again 1,400 students crowded the facilities, and the improved compensation for the faculty and the erasure of deferred maintenance in buildings and grounds increased morale.

As the fortunes of the college languished or burgeoned, presidential administrations kept watch over the changing scene. Robert Montgomery had endured the anguish of the depression years and enjoyed the good years after the war. His retirement in 1962 ended a regime of father and son of fifty-eight years, unmatched in American colleges. No one could have seen the aftermath, but his retirement set in motion a revolving-door presidency that escorted four presidents in and out of office in sixteen years. The times were anything but propitious for the success of any president, but these four able men came and went, largely the result of personal and family circumstances. Though each worked hard at his job, the incessant change damaged both the financial and programmatic stability of the college. In 1978 stability returned with the presidency of Arthur De Jong. Interested primarily in the financial aspects of higher education, he succeeded in stanching the flow of red ink that had plagued his predecessors and presided over a successful money-raising campaign. Like many college presidents of his generation, he did not think of the president's job as a longtime commitment and after ten years moved on to the presidency of a college in the Pacific Northwest.

Before leaving De Jong encouraged the board of trustees to choose Samuel W. Speck, a Muskingum graduate, as his successor. Speck had taught political science at Muskingum and then entered the Ohio state legislature, where he was the author of a long-overdue act to curb the ravages of strip-mining in eastern Ohio. Speck capitalized on De Jong's good stewardship of Muskingum's finances and added to the stability of the college. He installed a state-of-the-art telecommunications system in all college buildings. And confronted by a residence hall that had deteriorated from deferred maintenance almost to the point of no recovery, he deliberated a long time before deciding to renovate it, with impressive structural and aesthetic results. Then again after long deliberation and continued nudging by a strong administrative staff, he announced the tuition reduction plan. That strategy brought the college and its president national attention and enrollment results that would have been the envy of any college president. Finally, a well-planned and executed development program that coincided with the unprecedented national prosperity at the end of the century resulted in an endowment of about $50 million, modest by current standards but beyond all previous financial efforts at Muskingum. When Speck left the college in 1999, Muskingum's position among Ohio colleges had never been stronger.

Still, uncertainties remained. With the aggressiveness of the state university system in attracting private benevolence, would the private colleges' share of money given to higher education continue to shrink? Would Muskingum have the wisdom to decide on and maintain its most suitable level of enrollment? In a time when, unlike earlier generations, students increasingly elect to attend college close to home, how will Muskingum cope with the disadvantage of its location in one of the less prosperous regions of Ohio?

Suggested Reading

William Fisk, *A History of Muskingum College* (Muskingum College, 1978).

Notre Dame College

Respice Stellam, Voca Mariam

PATRICIA E. HARDING

April 1, 1921

Dear Mother Superior:

A school difficulty has come up for consideration repeatedly during the current year . . . . May we give our 1921 Graduates the promise that we can offer them work of College grade in the Fall Term—that is, may we open a college for our girls next Fall? Our students have pleaded repeatedly that we open a College. Cleveland is a very large city, we would have no difficulty in getting started or keeping up the College Department. . . . . We, the undersigned Sisters are one heart, one soul and one desire concerning the beginning of a College.

This simple request, sent to Mother Mary Cecilia Romen at the German Mother-house of the Sisters of Notre Dame, set the stage for a Catholic college for women directed by the Sisters in Cleveland, Ohio. Despite challenges and detractors, the Sisters would persevere in their dream to create a college for women based on their characteristic mission, one that would prepare lay and women religious for leadership, service, or economic survival in the twentieth century and beyond.

Notre Dame College owes its origin and development to the Sisters of Notre Dame, a Roman Catholic apostolic congregation from Coesfeld, Germany. These women are the spiritual descendants of Saint Julie Billiart (France, 1751–1816) and followers of the educational principles of Bernard Overberg (Germany, 1754–1826).

Even in childhood the teaching vocation of Julie Billiart was already apparent. Impelled by deep faith and love for the good God, Julie shared her faith with the children and women of her French parish. Although she was an invalid for most of her adult life, she devoted herself to teaching, traveling great distances to spread the good word during and after the French Revolution. A priest who recognized

Administration Building, 1961

Julie's extraordinary devotion to the word of God encouraged her to establish a religious institute whose focus would be the care, education, and vocational training of poor children, especially girls and young women. That congregation became the Sisters of Notre Dame of Namur.

Meanwhile, the German Catholic educational system had been reorganized according to the spirit of master teacher Bernard Overberg. He brought method to teaching, preparing teachers who would respect children and place knowledge of a loving God first in their own lives and, consequently, first in the hearts and minds of the children. By the mid–nineteenth century, in the town of Coesfeld, Hilligonda Wolbring (1828–1889) and Elisabeth Kuhling (1822–1869) were applying Overberg's principles to their work with orphaned and neglected children. Their parish priest encouraged them to establish a religious congregation to ensure continuity for their work. Looking for a congregation that would train these two teachers as religious, the priest chose the Sisters of Notre Dame of Amersfoort, Holland, a congregation that followed the mission (charism) and Rule of the Sisters of Notre Dame of Namur and whose religious and educational beliefs meshed well with the spirituality of

Overberg's emphasis on a loving God's provident care. From 1850 to 1855 Sisters from Amersfoort trained the Coesfeld women in the spirit of Julie Billiart. When political tensions in Germany forced the Coesfeld group to separate from the Amersfoort congregation, they took for themselves the simple name Sisters of Notre Dame. They rapidly developed a ministry that guided students from kindergarten through teacher education according to Overberg's psychological, pedagogical, and spiritual principles. Summer institutes and regular visitations from the Superior General promoted the primacy of religion; the thoroughness of instruction in all subjects; character training; physical, mental, and spiritual development; and the teacher's sacred duty to self, to the students, and to God.

During the political upheaval of Bismarck's Kulturkampf (1871–77), the state took control of Catholic schools, ultimately expelling teaching congregations from Prussia. At the same time in the United States, Cleveland was experiencing unprecedented growth in its German immigrant population. The need for teachers in Cleveland's Catholic schools was so great that Bishop Richard Gilmour wrote to Coesfeld's Mother Superior requesting that Notre Dame Sisters be sent to Cleveland. In a letter dated July 9, 1873, Bishop Gilmour assured the Mother Superior that "if your Sisters were here they would easily be employed . . . . Let them learn all the English they can. At present your Sisters would be employed in parochial schools. . . . You must send me first class teachers or I don't want them." When the first group of exiled Sisters of Notre Dame arrived from Germany on July 6, 1874, Bishop Gilmour immediately placed them in charge of St. Peter's School at East 17th Street and Superior in Cleveland.

By 1877 approximately 200 Sisters of Notre Dame had journeyed to America, each a graduate of a German normal school with teaching certification. In 1878 the Sisters opened Notre Dame Academy with fourteen students paying three dollars per month tuition. By 1910 growth had been so dramatic that the Sisters purchased property on Ansel Road overlooking Rockefeller Park to build a new academy and Provincial House. The Gothic brick structure, affectionately dubbed "Castle Ansel," was completed and dedicated in 1915. Within a year enrollment reached 500. Castle Ansel would eventually house a fledgling college and serve the Sisters of Notre Dame for the next fifty years.

The Cleveland Sisters had been discussing the need for a college for some time and wrote to Reverend Mother Mary Cecilia Romen to ask permission to establish a college at the academy in Cleveland. She approved, saying, "Do everything that is necessary to prepare a faculty and to qualify with both Church and State. . . . God Himself will help us." On March 26, 1922, Reverend Mother Romen explained to Bishop Joseph Schrembs that a college would allow the Sisters to be educated in their own institution to meet the increasingly stringent state requirements for teacher certification. She pointed out that more sisters would be needed to staff parish schools and that they hoped to attract aspirants to the congregation from the student body. Furthermore, she explained that the parents of academy students were asking for a college for their daughters so they would not have to attend non-Catholic colleges in the region.

Bishop Schrembs granted permission in April 1922, but only after assurances from the Sisters that they alone would bear the costs involved. Bishop Schrembs was named "Honorary President," and Sister Superior Mary Evarista Harks became the first college president, a part-time position because of her administrative responsibilities within the congregation. Sister Mary Odila Miller, procurator for the American congregation, served as treasurer, and Sister Mary Agnes Bosche was named the college's full-time dean and administrator. With the main responsibility for the fledgling college vested in the dean, it was up to Sister Mary Agnes to determine the philosophical foundations of the college, the high standards of its educational offerings, and the formulation of the procedures by which the college would operate. She gathered the faculty, shaped the curriculum, and worked with students to establish extracurricular life. Until 1950 the dean was responsible for the daily operation of the college.

In lieu of a catalog, an eight-page "Announcement" was printed for distribution, listing the "Aims of the College: to offer Catholic young women the advantages of a liberal education, to equip them with the requisites necessary to make them potent factors in the many and varied life-activities of the present, to direct them in the acquisition of those womanly virtues which will make them exponents of ideal Christian womanhood, thus enabling them to offer the highest type of service, whatever be the chosen field of labor." Four-year programs were established for the Bachelor of Arts and the Bachelor of Philosophy in Education degrees. Courses included religion, scripture, philosophy, history, English and American literature, modern language, physiology, politics, economics, sociology, mathematics, Greek, Latin, and education. The scholastic year was divided into two semesters of sixteen weeks each, with tuition of $75 per semester.

The hard work and long hours of discussion and prayer culminated on September 18, 1922, the first day of classes for eleven novices and thirteen young women from prominent Cleveland Catholic families. Bishop Schrembs celebrated the opening with a Mass in the Convent Chapel. The faculty numbered nine: three Sisters of Notre Dame, three priests, and three lay women.

The following January the president and the dean began the process of securing state approval, taking various legal documents and a tentative course of study to the State Department of Education in Columbus. On March 30, 1923, the Articles of Incorporation were filed for "the instruction and education of young women and to promote education, religion, morality and the fine arts and to confer the usual degrees and honors. . . . Special attention shall be given to the training of teachers and to facilitate that work a normal school department shall be conducted as a part of the college herein provided for." On May 4, 1923, the Ohio Department of Education approved Notre Dame College to grant the Bachelor of Arts, Bachelor of Commercial Science, Bachelor of Music, and Bachelor of Science degrees (in art, education, home economics, chemistry, and physics). Also approved was the normal training course for elementary school teachers. For the bachelor's degree, 128 semester credits were required; 74 credits were required for the teacher training course.

Enrollment in regular college classes in 1923–24 was sixty, with a faculty of fifteen. In 1924–25 eighty-one students were enrolled, with fifteen novices listed as "special" students and seventeen faculty members. At the Department of Teacher Training's first graduation in 1925, five students received Ohio elementary school certificates. In response to the demand for adult education, Notre Dame also opened a Department of College Extension with 170 women taking nondegree evening classes in English, French, child psychology, religion, mathematics, stenography, typewriting, china painting, and piano.

A pioneer spirit characterized the early years of the college. Under the direction of the dean, Sister Mary Agnes, the young women, busy with their academic studies, established college traditions reflecting the special spirit and identity of Notre Dame. She established policies promoting responsible social, spiritual, and intellectual development and encouraged the students to develop to the limits of their abilities, discover their goals, and develop lifelong friendships. Religion was paramount. Resident students were expected at Sunday Chapel in cap and gown; it was assumed that day students would attend their family parish. Attendance at daily services was required, and special devotions were regularly scheduled. Annual retreats were led by visiting priests. Father Daniel Lord, S.J., national director of all sodalities in the United States, led the first college retreat in 1923 and organized the college chapter of the Sodality of the Blessed Virgin in 1926, in which all students were automatically enrolled.

Student organizations and activities such as the League of the Sacred Heart, Students' Mission Crusade, Booster Club, Student Senate, Orchestra, Glee Club, Athletic Association, Newman Club (literary), Pate and Periwig Players, and Debating Club provided meaningful breaks in the academic routine. College publications included the *N.D.C. News,* later renamed the *Notre Dame News,* which provided coverage about the college and the academy, the Sisters, and the Ohio elementary schools under the direction of the Sisters. In 1925 the National Scholastic Press Association awarded the *News* an "All American" rating, the highest rating for a college newspaper and the first of many awards to come over the next twenty years. Parties, music, and sports filled leisure time. Upper classes "initiated" underclassmen, and Seton Hill College (Pennsylvania) was a frequent athletic rival. When Notre Dame musicians broadcast over Cleveland radio station WTAM, congratulatory telegrams were received that attested to the professionalism of the performers. Listeners responded from as far away as Wisconsin and Maine.

Growing enrollment in both the academy and the college necessitated frequent room reassignments for students and personnel. The need for a separate college facility was clear. Accrediting agencies looked askance at colleges and academies sharing the same facilities and faculties; those that did not separate found it difficult to differentiate themselves from finishing schools or junior colleges. In June 1923 the Sisters of Notre Dame signed a lease option for thirty-nine acres on Green Road in South Euclid, and in June 1924 an adjacent fifteen acres were purchased. All schools under the direction of the Sisters of Notre Dame sponsored events and activities to contribute to the college building fund. Notre Dame College students organized bridge games, theatrical events, and concerts, while children collected nickels and dimes. These modest activities funded the college; no wealthy benefactors stepped forward to lead the campaign to build Notre Dame College for women in the 1920s.

In 1925 the Sisters hired architect Thomas D. McLaughlin and Associates of Lima, Ohio, to design the college. McLaughlin's plan for the fifty-four-acre parcel in South Euclid consisted of fourteen buildings arranged around a quadrangle. The administration building would be built first, constructed by John T. Gill and Sons in fifteenth-century, English Gothic style using aged-crossed brick with sandstone trimmings. It would include administrative offices, guestrooms, classrooms, science and home economics laboratories, a dining hall, dormitory rooms, lounges, library, gymnasium, chapel, and service areas. Later development would include classroom buildings and separate buildings for an auditorium, gymnasium, library, powerhouse, and infirmary. The landscaping design by A. D. Taylor of Cleveland included an orchard and park surrounding a manmade lake, an athletic field and tennis courts, several shrine areas, and a parking area. Memorial gates on College Road would mark the main entrance to the quadrangle.

Meanwhile, 125 college students and twenty-five faculty members were scattered among six different academy buildings. From the college building fund, $12,000 was used to purchase a portable building with six classrooms and the necessary amenities, which was dedicated on December 8, 1925, as Immaculate Conception Hall. Salaries were not high for lay faculty, and the Sisters contributed their services. Faculty frequently taught in several departments, and no department head held a Ph.D. With an eye toward accreditation, a book drive was organized to acquire the 4,000 volumes still needed to meet the 9,000 volume requirement for entrance into the North Central Association.

A major challenge was to keep students through the senior year. Some students left because of the newness of the institution. Other students, under pressure from their parents, followed the two-year certificate course in teaching or business and then left to accept employment. The Sisters themselves often left school after two years to fill vacancies in the understaffed parochial schools. Sisters who were able to remain in the four-year program were encouraged to begin work on advanced degrees as soon as they could be released from duties to do so.

In 1926 Notre Dame began earnest attempts to obtain accreditation. Early concerns of the accrediting agency focused on the proximity and enrollment of the academy as compared to the college, the lack of accreditation for the academy, and the dearth of advanced degrees in the faculties of both institutions. The dean, Sister Mary Agnes Bosche, argued that the academy was not a part of the college and that land was being developed east of the city solely for the college. In February 1926 the North Central Association suggested that the academy reorganize some departments and grade levels; when it did so, the academy received its accreditation the following year. The college was informed that its evaluation could not be conducted until at least one baccalaureate class had graduated and until the department heads had obtained advanced degrees.

On June 9, 1926, the first baccalaureate degree candidates graduated from Notre Dame College. Receiving degrees and teaching certificates were the Misses Brennan, Carter, Fertig, Fournier, Hahn, Harrington, Leahey, Leonard, Mahan, Martin, McElroy, McGrath, Woodward, and Sister Mary Constance, O.S.A. Nine women received diplomas from the two-year Department of Teacher Training. The brand new Notre Dame College Alumnae Association held its first meeting the following day, June 10.

College life continued at Ansel Road: twenty-eight bachelor's degrees were granted and eleven teacher training diplomas were awarded in 1927. The first Founder's Day observance was held in memory of Reverend Mother Mary Cecilia Romen, who had died in 1925. The Alumnae Association formed a constitution to promote the welfare of the college, holding an event to raise a year's tuition for one deserving student. Alumnae and students attended college social events, creating a spirit of connectedness and "family" at Notre Dame.

No ceremony was held when ground was broken at the South Euclid site in late October 1926, but by December the base for the foundation of the Administration Building had been laid, with construction scheduled to continue after the loan had been made in the spring. On June 5, 1927, more than 2,000 friends and supporters attended the cornerstone-laying ceremony. The translated inscription on the cornerstone read: "Under the auspices of Mary, the first stone of the college of the Sisters of Notre Dame, an institution for [the] higher education of girls, is laid. AD 1927." By mid-1928 only the east and north wings of the new building were finished; the west wing ground floor housing the ever-popular Willow Room was enclosed and roofed with tarpaper. (Lack of funds would delay construction of the west wing upper floors until 1961.) In preparation for fall classes, equipment and furniture were purchased and set up in offices, classrooms, and residents' rooms. Food, books, and supplies were ordered. On September 17, 1928, eighty-two students arrived for the first day of classes in the new college building. The dedication and formal opening of the new college building occurred on November 25, 1928, when 3,000 guests were forced indoors by a raging storm. Congressman Charles A. Mooney observed that "in the past twenty-five years the position of woman has changed. Leadership is an added role for her today, and a Catholic leadership of virtuous and valiant womanhood is imperatively necessary."

The months preceding the 1929 Great Depression saw the publication of the college's first viewbook, yearbook, and *Faculty Bulletin*. The catalog suggested appropriate attire for college life: "dress lengths which cover the knees," long sleeves, and "fullness [so] that the body form is not conspicuous." With 142 women enrolled, Notre Dame was admitted to membership in the Ohio College Association, but the application for North Central accreditation was denied once again.

In an unsigned letter of February 15, 1929, to the university examiner at Ohio State University, the author pleads that the college be examined by North Central, even though there is only a slim chance that accreditation will follow. The writer states that "the strain that we are under in consequence of our non-affiliation with North Central Association is becoming almost unbearable. We feel that we want to put forth every effort to secure the recognition or know exactly why we cannot be on the official list." In March the North Central Association once again denied the application, citing lack of department heads with the Ph.D. degree and recommending consolidating the curriculum into eight departments from ten, merging the mathematics and science departments and including journalism in the English department program.

In the late 1920s other curricular modifications resulted from changes in the Cleveland diocese. After inspecting both Notre Dame and Ursuline Colleges, the State Department of Education recommended that training for elementary school teachers be consolidated elsewhere because of the scarcity of students and teachers in both colleges and the need for centralized supervision of student teaching. In the spring of 1928 the Cathedral Normal School (renamed Sisters' College in 1930, then St. John College in 1948) opened to provide certification for diocesan teachers. Sisters from all local congregations were expected to send their teachers-in-training to the Cathedral Normal School. As a result, Notre Dame closed the two-year elementary Department of Teacher Training but did retain its four-year program in high school teacher education.

During the Depression the diocese prepared for a college merger based on the European university method. Father Albert Fox of John Carroll wrote a proposal to create "the Corporate Colleges of John Carroll," incorporating the seminary, Cathedral Normal School (Sisters' College), Notre Dame, Ursuline, and the Catholic schools of nursing, with faculty members shared among the schools. The incorporation took place in December 1929, and Notre Dame became "Notre Dame College of John Carroll University." Barely five years later the State Department of

Education ruled that one incorporated body (Notre Dame College) could not be a part of another corporation (John Carroll University) and dissolved the incorporation in March 1934. While diplomas would no longer read "Notre Dame College of John Carroll University," the Catholic colleges of the diocese would continue joint commencement ceremonies until the 1940s.

The 1930s fostered growth at Notre Dame despite the worldwide economic setback. By January 1930 Notre Dame College had hired five faculty members with Ph.D. degrees for the Departments of Science, Modern Languages, History, Sociology, and Education. Two Sisters were candidates for the Ph.D. in June. The college's outstanding reputation in teacher training spread across the region. The library reported 10,000 volumes and 100 periodicals. Finally, after the March visit by North Central, the highly sought-after accreditation notice was awarded to Notre Dame College on April 4, 1931.

Newly accredited, the college demonstrated in its daily operations fidelity to its purposes. The statement of college objectives, called "Ideals" in the early catalogs, declared that "Notre Dame College realizes the obligation of developing Catholic womanhood of character, scholarship, power and charm. To attain this goal its curriculum includes the necessary philosophical, cultural and vocational courses which, if pursued with assiduity should secure the formation of a sterling Catholic character, a broadened and enriched background of the liberal arts, and if necessary, the power of maintaining economic independence." Initiative and leadership were to be inculcated through religious, scholastic, and social activities. The Students' Spiritual Council gave direction to the religious organizations of the college. The student council directed all matters pertaining to student life not under the jurisdiction of the faculty. An extracurricular activity point system prevented any one student from monopolizing the offices of too many student organizations. Student publications flourished, including the literary journal *Pall Mall* and the *Endameon,* a yearbook later renamed the *Pivot.* The *Notre Dame News* continued to win national awards for outstanding reporting and design. Chaperoned dances were growing in frequency, offering a fun but elegant respite from the bleakness of world affairs. Photographs attest to the popularity of raccoon coats and bobbed hair. Catholics were encouraged to improve race relations, for a Christian heart had no room for bigotry or segregation. In 1938 Betty Brown, an art and music major, was the first black student to graduate from Notre Dame College; she returned to the college in the 1950s as a faculty member in the art department. In 1939 the College Placement Service was established to test aptitude, assist students in obtaining part-time work, and to direct alumnae in finding possible positions.

The scholastic year was divided into two semesters of eighteen weeks each. Each student chose a major in one department and minors in two other departments. Two years of physical education were required of all students. The physical education department was recognized by the State Department of Education, making

Notre Dame the only Catholic college in Ohio to be certified for the health and physical education major. The State Department of Education also approved the training of home economics majors and recognized the music department. A successful door-to-door enrollment campaign was conducted in 1930, resulting in a 100 percent increase in the freshman class and a 1931 enrollment of 164 students. Twenty-three degrees were granted in 1932. By October, when Notre Dame celebrated her tenth anniversary, 1,287 students had registered since its founding. While continuing to stress the primacy of religion and of the liberal arts, the college also offered career preparation courses in advertising, dietetics, household arts, interior decoration, journalism, secretarial science, and social service "to enable young women to provide for their economic status" as the Depression continued.

During the 1930s students could earn part of their expenses under various federal work programs, offered to those students "whose health, scholarship, and reliability warrant such aid." Sister Mary Odila, treasurer, arranged for the students' brothers and fathers to work off tuition costs by constructing tennis courts. The farm on Green Road provided fruit, vegetables, dairy products, and meat for the Sisters and the students; the ground floor of the college building contained a canning area, and the kitchens used for the home economics classes did double duty. Other financial support came from the Alumnae Association's Scholarship Fund and the Notre Dame Guild's benefit chicken dinners, which continue to the present. In 1933 the Sisters exercised their option to buy the thirty-nine leased acres on Green Road and assumed the mortgage, but expansion of the physical plant would not occur for another twenty-two years.

With the outbreak of World War II, Notre Dame students organized a Defense Committee to study and discuss Christian principles of peace and help the students keep up with the issues and "-isms" of the day. The college participated in the rationing of gas, sugar, and fat, and a War Council Art Service produced posters and publicity. Blackout drills were scheduled, and the Tower was declared a safe place to escape poison gas attacks. By 1943 students had sold $30,953 worth of war bonds and stamps. Workshops were offered in air raid precautions and first aid, as well as classes in preflight aeronautics, applied mathematics, mechanical drawing, radio writing, and industrial drafting. From 1939 to 1950 a Bachelor of Science degree in nursing was offered to graduates of accredited nursing schools. Notre Dame became the first college in Cuyahoga County to establish a student chapter of the American Red Cross. As one of the first women's colleges in the United States to respond to the government's plea for accelerated classes to move graduates into defense work quickly, Notre Dame arranged for a four-year degree to be completed in three years, with three ten-week summer sessions. In 1944 Notre Dame became one of seven Catholic colleges in the United States to train medical, social service, and secretarial workers for the rehabilitation of Poland.

Of the 200 women enrolled in 1944, most were the first generation in their families to attend college, and nearly all were Catholic, Caucasian, and residents of northeastern Ohio, most close enough to commute. Religious activities continued to offer mandatory, but meaningful, experiences. For example, the Bishop Fulton J. Sheen Lecture Series was inaugurated in 1940. In order to win Cleveland's Bishop Schrembs's Gold Cross, seniors competed in essay contests on topics chosen by Bishop Schrembs, such as "Principles of Christ, the Only Sure Foundation of World Peace" and "Religion and the War." Catalogs of the 1940s describe extracurricular activities as "numerous and of a sufficiently wide range of interest to allow each student to find some field in which she can be an active participant." Social life "is marked by dignity and freedom." The Debate Club offered an annual tournament and coed intercollegiate debates. The Pall Mall Honorary English Society and the Pate and Periwig Players furnished opportunities for discussion and performance in literature and drama, and the Choral Club presented an annual major concert with other colleges. The Chamber Music Ensemble involved students from Notre Dame and John Carroll. Fewer dances were held because of the shortage of men created by military service; even then, many girls were escorted by their fathers or younger brothers until a favorite beau came home on leave. Smoking was banned, but a short walk north of the campus led to "butt alley." In the residence hall, "lights out" was the rule at a certain hour, but once the bed check had been completed, some read or talked long into the night. Late-night raids on the kitchen were common, and occasionally a Sister joined in. Because nylon was needed for the war effort and slacks were not an option, the students established a Silk Stocking Cooperative where they could buy hosiery and other sundries.

The alumnae released the first issue of the *Alum-News* in 1945. In December 1946 they celebrated Notre Dame College's first twenty-five years (1922–47) with a Jubilee Ball, and in April 1947 they held a Spring Festival for the building fund. In the late 1940s the alumnae changed from a dues system, in effect since 1926, to an annual giving program in an effort to "pay" for that part of their education not covered by tuition and fees. In the first year of the giving program, 349 alumnae contributed $3,704.

A historic first occurred in 1950 with the creation of the position of vice president, filled by Francis W. Grose, a faculty member since 1929. The year 1955 brought the first full-time president to the college, creating a definite administrative separation between the college and the Sisters of Notre Dame. No longer a part-time responsibility for the Provincial Superior, the presidency became a full-time position for a Sister who could devote herself exclusively to the needs of the college, particularly in the demanding areas of fund-raising and development of the physical plant.

Since the college's beginning, the board of trustees was comprised solely of Sisters of Notre Dame and the bishop of Cleveland. By 1952 the time had come to seek advice and support from the business community. William C. Connelly headed the new advisory board, made up of prominent Cleveland businessmen and professionals who advised the Sisters in such matters as finance, policy, and public relations. In 1974 a Notre Dame alumna became the first woman to serve on the advisory board. Further reorganization of the board took place in the 1990s.

Expansion was the theme of the 1950s. The front end of the baby boom created a need for more and better teachers, as did the national fear of Russian superiority. Notre Dame enrollment was climbing, with 300 students in 1952. The fourth-floor residence hall was crowded, and the Sisters were sleeping in their offices and classrooms to provide lodging for tuition-paying students. Housing was critical, so a new expansion program "for a Greater Notre Dame" kicked off during Alumnae Week in 1952. Harks Hall, a brick residence hall named in honor of the first president, was completed by the architectural firm of Horn, Rhinehart and Truthan in 1955.

With campus housing improved, college administrators directed attention to the unfinished Administration Building, which stood as a constant reminder of plans abandoned in 1928. Once the proposals were in, some favored the least expensive plan—a three-story addition with a flat roof for $518,240. Others favored an adaptation of the original McLaughlin design, for $927,000. The final choice was a nearly exact match between the east and west wings, with building code upgrades, costing $1.2 million. The manufacturer of the original brick was commissioned to produce 160,000 custom-made bricks to match the first unit. With a public relations program carefully designed to make the community aware of Notre Dame's reputation and its impact on the northeastern Ohio area, the campaign was placed under the patronage of St. Joseph, and the alumnae were asked to make the Rosary Novena for fifty-four days to ensure the success of the campaign.

Without wealthy benefactors, Notre Dame traditionally relied on the resources and contributed services of the Sisters of Notre Dame. In a letter dated May 18, 1960, the president wrote that "the survival of Notre Dame depends on building soon" and states that "students and parents are justified in not wanting to be affiliated with a college that is housed in an unfinished building." Forty freshmen were turned away because on-campus housing was still inadequate. In May 1960 the Sisters' Provincial Council agreed to co-sign loan papers for the west wing (reestimated at $877,000) and for a new residence hall ($476,000) but stipulated that the college alone should bear full responsibility for the repayment of the loans. Ground was broken for a new residence hall (Providence Hall) in August 1961, and the west wing construction was completed in September 1961. Enrollment was 341 in 1960; by 1968 it had more than doubled to 721, largely due to the construction of yet another residence hall (Alumnae Hall), and the Connelly Center dining hall, named for William C. Connelly, founder and first chairman of the advisory board.

The library had outgrown its location on the first floor of the Administration Building by the late 1960s. The dream for a separate library building was realized in

1969, with Cleveland industrialist Paul J. Fritzsche the major benefactor of a modern facility designed by Rowley, Payer, Huffman and Leithold. With a 100,000-volume capacity, the library opened in 1971, named in honor of Fritzsche's mother, Clara. To move the books from the Administration Building to the new facility, a human chain made up of enthusiastic students, faculty, and staff stretched from the old to the new, passing all of the books over by hand. Today the Clara Fritzsche Library boasts holdings over 88,000 volumes, and the admissions office occupies the former library site in the Administration Building.

As evidence of its apostolic commitment to Catholicism, the liberal arts, and its founding principles, Notre Dame has been a leader in educational developments. The 1960s through the 1980s brought approval by the State Department of Education for certificates for teaching the slow learner and for special education and for training teachers to teach the developmentally handicapped. Notre Dame was the first college in northern Ohio approved to prepare teachers for certification in learning disabilities and behavioral disorders. In 1979 the State Department of Education asked Notre Dame to develop a certification program to teach moderately, severely, or profoundly retarded children. In 1980 a diagnostic clinic opened, providing clinical experience for education majors and establishing a community service component for the identification and remediation of children's learning disabilities. In 1983 the teacher education program was the first in Ohio to be found in 100 percent compliance with standards set by the Ohio Department of Education.

Notre Dame also expanded its collaboration with neighboring colleges, working on interinstitutional planning, laying the groundwork for the transfer of credits, faculty exchanges, and library borrowing privileges for the decades ahead. Through a cooperative agreement, Jewish students from Yavne Teachers' Seminary (now Yavne College for Women) obtained liberal arts degrees and teacher certification through Notre Dame College. In a government-funded experiment that brought men to campus, the sociology department offered the Law Enforcement Education Program (LEEP). Twenty-five men earned the associate's degree between 1975 and 1980 but were not admitted to the baccalaureate degree program at NDC.

In the late 1960s and early 1970s demographic trends indicated that the body of traditional, white, eighteen- to twenty-two-year old students was declining. At the same time adult women were planning for careers or for career advancement. In response Notre Dame inaugurated an extensive series of afternoon, evening, and Saturday classes and workshops in 1970. In 1975 Executive Vice President Sister Mary LeRoy Finn established the Lifelong Learning Center for the ongoing education of mature women and to ease the return to college for women over age twenty-five. Within two years more than 400 nontraditional women had enrolled in Lifelong Learning workshops and classes, both credit and noncredit. Because potential students who were working full time or who had families found it impossible to take daytime classes, Sister Mary LeRoy designed the Weekend College (WECO) in 1978. Forty women enrolled in classes scheduled on six alternate weekends in three time slots: Friday evening, Saturday morning, and Saturday afternoon. Up to three different classes could be taken following this schedule, enabling the WECO woman to complete a bachelor's degree in four years. Since its first class graduated in 1982, WECO continues to be one of the most popular program options and, in turn, has brought new life, vision, and income to the college. By 2000 almost 700 WECO women had received their baccalaureate degrees from Notre Dame College.

In answer to Vatican II's encouragement to develop an active lay apostolate (1965), the Saint Julie Billiart Center for Catechetics was created in 1972 as an affiliate of the Virginia-based Notre Dame Institute for Advanced Studies in Religious Education. It was the first undergraduate program of its kind in the United States to prepare teachers in methods and content for religious education (catechism). In 1976 the Center launched a program in Lay Leadership in Pastoral Ministry, in which lay students and women religious enrolled to earn certification (sixty-five credit hours). In 1985 the Center for Catechetics and Ministry inaugurated the annual Eastern Church Traditions seminar, a several-day-long affair that attracts religious leaders from around the country to address concerns shared by the Eastern Orthodox, Byzantine Catholic, and Roman Catholic Churches. The center received the 1989 Unity Award from the Cleveland Catholic Diocese's Interfaith Commission. In 1999 the Coalition of Eastern Churches chose the college as the site for its Eastern Church Resource Center. Located on the first floor of the Clara Fritzsche Library, the center displays icons and offers materials about the Eastern Orthodox and the Byzantine Catholic religions.

After North Central reaccreditation in 1980, the college turned its attention to stronger marketing efforts. Tucked neatly in the center of fifty-four acres, the college buildings are nearly invisible to passersby, blocked from view by the gently rolling former farmland along Green Road. A new illuminated sign at the corner of Green and College Roads made Notre Dame more visible to the public. Public relations laid out a media plan featuring print ads, thirty- to sixty-second radio spots, and public service announcements. A Title III federal grant funded the New Development Concept, which attracted national attention in 1981 for its innovative, holistic method of self-directed "journaling" by a student through four years of growth. When the 1982 proposed federal budget planned to eliminate three student financial aid programs and decrease two others, Notre Dame's president testified publicly before the U.S. Senate Finance Committee. The Kellogg Foundation funded Project QUE (Quality Undergraduate Education), part of a highly visible national effort to help students understand basic relationships among what may seem isolated experiences. Lecture series, offering speakers of local and national importance, were opened to the public.

With a declining pool of Sisters of Notre Dame available to contribute their services at the college, more lay faculty and staff were hired during the 1980s, resulting in greater salary costs. Acting on the advice of both North Central and the Board of Trustees, the college implemented an accounting method by which the Sisters' salaries were listed as expenses on the books, while those dollars were rolled back into operating funds. Increased operating expenses, of course, resulted in higher student costs. A year's tuition and room and board cost $3,560 in 1980; ten years later it was $9,470; and in 2000 it was just over $19,000. In November 1984 President Ronald Reagan signed legislation that restored and extended the tax exclusion for employer tuition reimbursement plans, legislation that had a direct impact on the enrollment of nontraditional students at Notre Dame: WECO enrollment had been 172 in mid-1982 and increased to 305 in the fall of 1985.

In response to the needs of students, faculty, and staff, Tot Spot opened in 1984, providing care, education, and recreation for up to fifty children, from newborn through age ten. Licensed by the State of Ohio, Tot Spot is operated by a professionally trained staff, assisted by college interns and community volunteers.

Notre Dame College was one of the first colleges in Ohio to explore the feasibility of identifying and targeting the underserved Hispanic woman. A study conducted in two Cleveland neighborhoods determined that educational attainment for Hispanic women must be compatible with cultural and family attitudes and that improved math and communication skills were needed, as well as mentoring by successful Hispanic women. Between 1984 and 1988 thirty-nine Hispanic women enrolled; a few graduated, but most faltered, lacking the support of their families and culture. By 1989 the Hispanic Project was over, replaced by a Minority Affairs Office. Ironically, a decade later, a major university in Ohio would identify Hispanic women as an underserved group and take steps to study their situation and offer programming to fit their needs.

The 1980s was also a time for recognizing service to the college. The Sister Mary Cleophas Garvin Computer Center was named in honor of the retired chair of the mathematics department. The library dedicated the Multi-Media Learning Center in honor of Sister Mary Cesarie Miday, a Fulbright scholar and professor of French. The Instructional Media Center was dedicated to Cleveland Bishop Clarence Issenmann, and the Exhibit Room honored retired head librarian Sister Mary Genevieve Baker. In the Administration Building the Green Lounge was renamed the McHugh Room, in tribute to Sister Mary Inez McHugh, former college president. The decade also witnessed the creation of the Distinguished Faculty Award and the Outstanding Teaching Award. The nationally famous sculptor, Joseph Turkaly, was commissioned to fashion the Fidelia Award, given for outstanding service and loyalty to the college. To honor loyal staff, the Service Plaque recognition was established. In 1984 the Administration Building itself was placed on the National Register of Historic Places.

The campus reached its present appearance in 1987 with the dedication of the Joseph H. Keller Fitness Center, which serves both the college and the residents of the surrounding communities, who may purchase memberships. Within its first year 2,700 persons were using the Keller Center each month. A full time director was hired in 1988, and in 1989 Notre Dame awarded its first athletic scholarship. In 1997 the Coca-Cola Corporation provided funds for a softball field. The 1980s closed with the first-ever formal inauguration of a Notre Dame president, Sister Marla Loehr, and an enrollment of 827 students.

During the 1990s Notre Dame College took several key steps toward becoming more clearly separate from the founding congregation while retaining the spirit of collaboration in mission. In 1990 the six Sisters of Notre Dame who comprised the governing board of the college adopted a new constitution establishing a lay board of trustees for Notre Dame College. The congregation as the sponsoring order retained the power to modify the mission of the college but turned legal and fiduciary responsibility over to the board members, of whom 20 percent were Sisters of Notre Dame. When Sister Marla Loehr resigned as president in 1995, the bylaws were changed again to open the presidency of the college to any lay or religious man or woman. To devote adequate time to the historic selection of its first non–Sister of Notre Dame president, the college chose to appoint as interim president Dr. Robert Karsten, a Lutheran minister, who became the first male, the first layman, and the first non-Catholic to lead the college in its seventy-three-year history. In January 1996 Dr. Gay Culverhouse was named president but abruptly resigned in May for personal reasons. In August 1996 the college welcomed the current president, Dr. Anne L. Deming. With a doctorate in counseling psychology and experience as a faculty member and as a vice president for advancement, Dr. Deming brought a lifetime career in higher education and a personal commitment to the values of Notre Dame College to enrich the college in her role as president.

Technological advances and physical renovations made new fiscal demands in the 1990s. A challenge grant by the Kulas Foundation enabled the college to convert the former gymnasium in the Administration Building into a multipurpose auditorium and performing arts center, with an art gallery and reception area. Between 1990 and 1994 several grants, including a large matching grant from the National Science Foundation, enabled the science department to endow a science scholarship and to renovate and upgrade scientific and computer-assisted equipment, thus giving students the opportunity to conduct research in labs similar to those used in industry and government. When the $750,000 Science Research Center was opened for public viewing and dedicated during the week of March 10, 1994, leading scientists from across the country, including Notre Dame alumnae, attended or presented lectures and demonstrations.

Among the challenges of the 1990s was the necessity for rapid response to new demands by an increasingly diverse public. Notre Dame modified programs, procedures, and the physical plant in response to consumer demands but did so without changing its values or heritage. The board of trustees approved a series of important documents reflecting Notre Dame's contemporary stance: a revised Mission Statement and Statement of Purpose, a Catholic Identity Statement, and a Commitment to Minority Student Development and a Multi-Cultural Environment. Guided by a presidential task force, faculty researched and developed multicultural course content, Admissions actively recruited minority students, and the college sponsored a variety of multicultural programs. Throughout the 1990s, 30 percent of the Notre Dame students claimed a minority heritage. According to the 1990 self-study on Catholic identity, "the vision and goals of the administration, the mode of governance, the institutional policies, and the academic priorities reflect commitment to the ideals that inspire the mission of the College."

The entire academic program was evaluated for opportunities to blend the strong liberal arts core with career preparation. In the decade following 1990, new programs were in place: associate's degrees were offered in pastoral ministry (1990), paralegal studies (1992), and environmental technology (1997). Bachelor of Arts degrees were offered in graphic communication (1990), early childhood education (1992), dietary management (1992), sociology (1993), art history (1994), applied communication (1994), paralegal studies (1994), biology (2000), and chemistry (2000). Interdisciplinary minors were approved in women's studies (1992) and in ethics-driven athletic coaching (2000). Certificate programs were approved in gerontology (1990), paralegal studies (1991), business administration (1994), environmental technology (1997), and information systems (1999). Experiential learning requirements in the form of cooperative education programs, internships, or practicums were expanded to all majors in 1999.

The college continued its historic emphasis on teacher preparation by introducing certificates in early childhood education (1992), TEEC (Teacher Education Evening Certification, 1994), and severe behavioral disorders (1995). A master's degree in education (M.Ed.) was approved by the State of Ohio in April 1991, as well as graduate-level certificates in special education (1992) and "teaching to the multiple intelligences" (1994). Open to men and women, the M.Ed. program focuses on the skill of teaching rather than on school administration or subject specialization, aiming to train "master teachers," to keep them in the classroom doing what they do best. In 1994 the college opened the Center for Professional Development to sponsor seminars, workshops, staff development programs, and intensive graduate classes on topics recommended by the Ohio Board of Regents.

Notre Dame adapted to the technologies of the Information Age with the same flexibility that characterized its previous innovations, beginning with the renovation and automation of the Clara Fritzsche Library. The library's 88,000-volume collection was converted from Dewey to the Library of Congress classification system, and the holdings were online by 1997. Terminals and computers were installed throughout the library. A $250,000 Gund Foundation grant allowed Notre Dame College and four other area colleges to train their librarians in new technologies, join OhioLINK, and access materials at libraries statewide, with project headquarters at Notre Dame College. Today the Notre Dame community has access to local, national, and international databases and electronic journals. In 1997 the Tolerance Resource Center was dedicated in the Clara Fritzsche Library. Open to the public, the center offers materials and resources related to the Holocaust, diversity, and bias issues.

In addition, the Campus Computerization Project, aided by a volunteer team from Ernst and Young, studied the informational and equipment needs of the faculty and staff. Today all offices are computerized and networked, and a technology department assists students, faculty, and staff. In April 1997 the 2,800-square-foot John J. and Frances Dwyer Learning Center was dedicated. Located in the Administration Building, the million-dollar center is an interactive electronic classroom that consolidates the writing and language labs with the student computer labs into one all-purpose electronic resource center. The center contains fifty computers with the latest hardware and software, projection capabilities, and Internet access. Peer tutors and lab assistants are regularly available to assist students. In 1999–2000 Notre Dame's first distance learning course, "John Henry Newman's Theory of Knowledge," was offered online to reach the widest audience possible.

On February 12, 1999, fire struck the biology lab and adjacent areas on the third floor of the Administration Building. There were no injuries, but the smoke and water damage totaled more than $2 million. Offers of assistance poured in from the community. Classes were cancelled only on the day of the fire. For the next year the biology department operated out of makeshift quarters. The tragedy turned out to be a blessing, as renovation occurred on all floors. Upper-floor offices and classrooms were remodeled. Laboratories were renovated to meet new guidelines and safety standards. On the first floor, once the college's statuary collection was secured, the water-damaged Marian Room received a complete overhaul with new cabinetry and lighting. On April 5, 2000, city officials, safety forces from eighteen communities, and interested friends joined the Notre Dame community to rededicate the newly refurbished and enlarged science wing.

In August 2000 Notre Dame College announced that men would be admitted to all degree programs in 2001. Fall 2001 enrollment soared to 923 students, the highest in the history of the college.

With new initiatives to recruit international and home-schooled students, the college continues to serve a diverse population and enthusiastically embraces its mission to change the world, one student at a time, by educating students of all ages, races, colors, religions, national origins, and socioeconomic backgrounds. Many are, as have been throughout Notre Dame's history, the first generation of their family to attend college. Ninety percent receive some form of financial aid. Through the liberal arts and theology core, a Notre Dame education continues to be grounded in ethics and spirituality and embraces the diversity in the world. In small classes with a student-to-faculty ratio of 12:1, students are challenged to think and communicate critically and creatively in subjects within and beyond their area of interest. Participation in any of twenty-nine organizations or in athletics offers students the chance to become leaders or team players on a campus where the traditions of student leadership and active social life still flourish. The lifelong friendships formed at Notre Dame are evident in the active and loyal Alumnae Association, whose annual gatherings still bring to campus a few graduates from the 1920s. Many of the alumnae, outstanding in their respective fields, generously serve as mentors to Notre Dame students.

As it enters the twenty-first century facing many of the same challenges as other small private liberal arts colleges, Notre Dame will draw on its history of resourcefulness and creative dedication to mission, while the college community will "look to the Star [and] call upon Mary" with faith and expectation. *Respice Stellam, Voca Mariam.*

Suggested Reading

The following works will offer the general reader insight into the charisma and mission of the founders of the Sisters of Notre Dame of Namur and the Sisters of Notre Dame: Anon., *Letters of Reverend Mother Mary Cecilia, Third Superior General of the Sisters of Notre Dame* (1953); *The Educational Ideals of Blessed Julie Billiart, Foundress of the Congregation of the Sisters of Notre Dame of Namur,* translated from French by an anonymous Sister (1922); Mary Fidelis, *As Gold in the Furnace: The Life of Blessed Julie Billiart, Foundress of the Sisters of Notre Dame de Namur* (1957); Gerard Carroll Malachy, *The Charred Wood: The Story of Blessed Julie Billiart, Foundress of the Congregation of Sisters of Notre Dame of Namur* (1950); Mary Vincentia, *Their Quiet Tread: Growth and Spirit of the Congregation of the Sister of Notre Dame Through Its First One Hundred Years, 1850–1950* (1955).

The following volumes are written by a Sister from the Chardon, Ohio, Province and provide interesting documentation on the work of the Sisters in Cleveland, Ohio, including the founding of Notre Dame College: Mary Luke Arntz, *In Our*

Lady's Household, Vol. 4: *Sister Mary Evarista (1867–1943), Life and Times,* (1988); Vol. 6: *Three Memoirs: Sister Mary Odila, S.N.D., Sister Mary Bertilda, S.N.D., Sister Mary Fortunata, S.N.D.* (1991); and Vol. 7: *Remembering Sister Mary Agnes, 1885–1949* (1994).

For information on the incorporated colleges of Cleveland, read Donald P. Gavin, *John Carroll University: A Century of Service* (Kent State University Press, 1985).

Oberlin College

Early Decisions

GEOFFREY BLODGETT

The founding of Oberlin College in 1833 was a landmark event, of a piece with the early-nineteenth-century surge of missionary reform out of New England across upstate New York into the Middle West. This reformist awakening took many forms. It helped turn Brook Farm outside Boston from a colony of gentle Transcendentalists into a phalanx driven by the dreams of the French utopian Charles Fourier. The awakening also transformed broad stretches of upstate New York into a "Burnt-Over District," so named because of the blazing evangelical revivals, waged by Charles Grandison Finney among others, that repeatedly scorched the region. The Mormon Church of the Latter-Day Saints, founded by Joseph Smith in Palmyra near Rochester, New York, sprang from the same ferment. So did John Humphrey Noyes's "free love" community in Oneida, New York, and Lane Seminary in Cincinnati. And so did Oberlin.

For all their diversity, what these ventures shared in common was a post-Calvinist faith in the ultimate perfectibility of human nature, to be achieved in each case by some crucial social change—in family and sexual relations or the redistribution of labor and property or restrictions on clothing or diet or the abolition of slavery or female emancipation. Each community searched for its special latchkey to human perfection. Early Oberlin experimented with all of these changes, but it focused from the outset on seeking perfection through the cause of missionary education.

John Jay Shipherd, a radical Christian preacher from the Green Mountain country spanning western New England and upstate New York, founded Oberlin after migrating across the Burnt-Over District into Ohio's Western Reserve. His ambition was bold—to save the raw, young Midwest from the perceived sins of Jacksonian America. He named Oberlin after the renowned turn-of-the-century Alsatian educational reformer John Frederick Oberlin. The recruits he gathered for his ven-

First Church—Town

ture qualified for membership by signing the Oberlin Covenant, a demanding document packed with pledges of personal self-denial when it came to tobacco, tea, tight
dresses, and fancy homes. Enforcement of the covenant screened the sorts of men
and women who joined Shipherd's collegiate colony. They were a morally headstrong batch, with nothing otherworldly about them. They wanted to perfect
people's behavior here and now by training them for moral missionary service to a
region in urgent need of saving.

Four big decisions early on defined specific innovations impelling the Oberlin mission. The first focused on manual labor. Each student contributed several hours of
hard work each day to ensure the colony's survival. Women tended to housekeeping

while men farmed nearby. Manual labor as an educational reform did not last long. Male students were no match for local farmers when it came to raising crops and milking cows. James Fairchild, an early student who later served as college president, recalled that, "to discuss first principles became their pastime. They rested on their hoes in the cornfield to look into their inner consciousness, and the manual labor cause suffered in the interest of philosophy." But the cause lived on—in the solemn motto of the college, "Learning and Labor," in the concept of a sound mind in a sound body, the governing notion behind the establishment of physical education as an academic discipline at Oberlin from the 1890s to the 1970s, and in the popular program of dining cooperatives that have flourished since the 1950s.

The second big decision was to educate women along with the men. Surprisingly little controversy surrounded the beginning of coeducation. It was regarded at the outset as a way of producing as many Christian teachers and missionaries as possible rather than as an explicit feminist reform. It turned out to be a more daring departure than the founders intended. After the Civil War when universities like Cornell and Michigan decided to experiment with coeducation, they sent inquiries to Oberlin to discover how it was done, including how to teach biology. Oberlin fostered careful policies of sexual segregation to mollify more critical observers. Coed classrooms were separated by wide aisles—men on one side, women on the other—to keep all minds in proper focus. Two-lane wooden sidewalks prevented couples from holding hands while crossing the campus together. Separate hours for each sex governed library use till the 1890s, and chapel seating remained segregated until 1934 when the faculty finally caved in on that issue. Oberlin's commitment to teaching men and women together made its admissions policy distinctive until the 1970s, when coeducation swept through previously all-male eastern colleges and universities with which Oberlin traditionally competed for students.

The third big decision came in 1835 when Oberlin opened its doors to African Americans. Nineteenth-century fears about racial mixing combined with Oberlin's commitment to coeducation to make this a daring choice: white women, black men, black women, white men, all living together on the same campus. For many this prospect was frightening. But John Shipherd knew exactly what he was doing. His choice proved to be the college's salvation. By 1835, just two years after its founding, Oberlin found itself on the brink of collapse, hurting for students as well as money. When theology students at Lane Seminary in Cincinnati rebelled against official efforts to squelch their antislavery agitation, Shipherd invited them to transfer to Oberlin and then won from the abolitionist Tappan brothers, wealthy New York City clothing merchants, a promise to finance the exodus. The Tappans also offered to hire the famed evangelist, Charles Grandison Finney, to become head of Oberlin's theology department. Shipherd, Finney, and the Tappan brothers all insisted on one condition—that Oberlin launch a color-blind admissions policy. Reluctantly, by the narrowest of votes, college trustees finally agreed, and Shipherd's splendid deal went through. Thereafter, over the next century, the commitment to black admissions resulted in Oberlin producing more African American graduates than any other predominantly white college in the United States.

The fourth and final big decision of the 1830s was what became known as the Finney Compact—the principle of faculty control over the internal academic affairs of the college without trustee interference, a principle Finney insisted on after the trustees balked over the issue of black admissions. The Finney Compact, entrenched during Finney's presidency of the college from 1851 to 1866, made Oberlin unique among American colleges for a long time thereafter. It remained a touchstone of the college's governance until the 1990s, when growing numbers of faculty members—preoccupied with teaching and research as distinct from administrative duties—lost interest in the arrangement.

Back in the decade of the 1850s the sin of slavery posed the harshest challenge to Oberlin's perfectionist ideals, and abolition became its dominating moral cause. The so-called "Underground Railroad" passed through town, helping fugitives and free blacks on their way to the safety of Canada. Many chose to stay in Oberlin, raising the local percentage of African Americans higher than in any other town in the North. In 1858 Oberlinians prevented slave catchers from carrying fugitive John Price back to bondage by way of Wellington, a rail town ten miles to the south. Some twenty Oberlin men, college and town, black and white, spent three months in a Cleveland jail for the crime of rescuing John Price. The Wellington Rescue became a central legend in the Oberlin abolitionist tradition. The tradition was reinforced when several Oberlin blacks joined John Brown in his famous raid on Harper's Ferry in 1859. "Oberlin is abolitionism boiled down to the quintessence of bitterness," Cleveland's leading Democratic newspaper decided. "Its reputation in this respect is worldwide." Humorist Petroleum V. Nasby, explaining why the Civil War broke out, wrote that "Oberlin commenst this war. Oberlin wuz the prime cause uv all the trubble."

The Civil War thoroughly reshuffled Oberlin's priorities. The college now concentrated on fortifying its institutional strength and stability. The postwar student body doubled, the endowment tripled, and the physical campus was rebuilt almost from scratch. Prewar perfectionist values did not disappear. Abolition gave way to a Reconstruction drive to educate southern black freedmen, and a long crusade for prohibition, aimed at both tobacco and alcohol, got under way. "The moral village of Oberlin is again on the rampage against the evils of society," a newspaper in a neighboring town noted. "This time tobacco has to suffer." In 1893 the Anti-Saloon League, ultimately the main force behind the prohibition movement of the 1920s, was founded in Oberlin. Meanwhile the community dispatched its first missionaries to China—a

Pacific Rim linkage that outlasted the Boxer Rebellion, two world wars, and Communist revolution, and survives throughout Asia to the present day.

Beginning with the presidency of James Harris Fairchild (1866–89) and even more decisively under that of Henry Churchill King (1902–27), improvement got under way in the rigor and quality of the Oberlin educational experience. The Conservatory of Music, joined to the college in 1865, was grounded thereafter in the European musical tradition at Leipzig, where many of its faculty trained. The conservatory soon rivaled Eastman and Juilliard as the nation's best. In the college itself a rising percentage of thoroughly secular young Ph.D.s replaced reverend clergymen in the classroom. The curriculum was overhauled and modernized with the arrival of the elective system pioneered by Harvard's president Charles William Eliot. Across the 1890s the new social sciences emerged one by one, along with modern languages, contemporary literature, and regular lab work in the physical sciences. With the advent of electric lights, reading after dark became a major undergraduate industry. In the early twentieth century the library acquired one of the two or three largest college collections in the country, and the college art museum became the finest of its kind. The ethic of discovery now charged the campus: the notion that some things were known and some were unknown, and the trick was to push back the unknown. This was an enormously exciting idea, and it transformed the meaning of a college education.

In the nineteenth century Oberlin graduates proceeded in large numbers into the ministry or school teaching. Now a rising percentage went on to graduate school to prepare for careers in law, medicine, and, above all, a higher education. Since 1920 Oberlin has been a larger source of students headed for the Ph.D. than any other college in America. It also became the most cosmopolitan college in the Midwest in terms of the far-flung origins of its students. Geographical variety was matched by ethnic and religious variety starting with the depression decade of the 1930s, when Oberlin's low-cost, high-quality education attracted more and more students from big eastern cities.

As a result of all these twentieth-century shifts, Oberlin became more famous for its cosmopolitanism and academic excellence than for its early moral and ideological commitments. However the reformist tradition lived on. Inspired by the Social Gospel movement, the first undergraduate socialist club was founded in 1911, and leftist enthusiasms have enlivened the campus ever since. The college became a powerful pacifist stronghold in the 1930s and contributed passionate force to the antiwar movement of the 1960s. In more recent decades it has globalized its curriculum to combat Eurocentrism and embrace the Third World. In compliance with national trends it has earnestly adopted the identity politics of multicultural diversity. Thus the tension between the main priorities of twentieth-century Oberlin and those of early-nineteenth-century Oberlin—a tension between the head and the heart, analysis and enthusiasm, knowledge and hope, between trying to understand the world and trying to save it—remains intact and will probably never go away. It has always been a creative tension, forever generating rival visions of what Oberlin was, is, and ought to be.

Suggested Reading

John Barnard, *From Evangelicalism to Progressivism at Oberlin College, 1866–1917* (Ohio State University Press, 1969); Geoffrey Blodgett, *Oberlin Architecture, College and Town: A Guide to Its Social History* (Kent State University Press, 1985); James H. Fairchild, *Oberlin: The Colony and the College, 1833–1883* (1883); Carol Lasser, ed., *Educating Men and Women Together: Co-education in a Changing World* (University of Illinois Press, 1987).

Ohio Dominican University

Its Mission and Identity

CAMILLA MULLAY

In July 2002, Ohio Dominican College became Ohio Dominican University. Announcing the change, President Jack P. Calareso affirmed the institution's continuity with its founding mission: "The change to Ohio Dominican 'University' will not change our founding mission. . . . In fact, our expanded 'university' identity will broaden and diversify the ways we express our Dominican values of contemplation of truth, preaching, . . . community, service, and educational excellence. . . . Ohio Dominican 'University' moves us boldly and with confidence from our distinguished past to our exciting future."

At the entrance to Ohio Dominican's main academic building, carved in stone, is this translation of the Dominican motto: "To contemplate truth and to share the fruits of this contemplation." Moving into the new millennium, Ohio Dominican College was well positioned for the future. The North Central Association Report of 1997 shows why. Among the strengths of the college are these achievements: a "concerned and committed Board of Trustees," the "extraordinary commitment" of the faculty, administrators, and staff to the mission of the college, a strong significantly improved financial situation, "acquisition of technology and its integration into the learning environment," a "clearly . . . sufficient number" of students, and the college's "visibility and leadership in Columbus through a variety of programs."

In addition to the commitment "to contemplate truth," the college's Catholic focus could be seen in its special concern for the kinds of students often denied access to higher education: first-generation college students, minority students, students from families of modest means, and adults returning to school. In 2000 the enrollment was 19 percent American minorities, with Ohio Dominican having one of the highest graduation rates for African Americans in the state of Ohio. ODC also modeled community service by its outreach programs, especially those for

middle and high school students in the area where many residents are economically poor and educationally deprived. The school has won national recognition for these and other innovative programs.

With an enrollment of more than 2,100 students, 130 faculty, excellent financial management, and a carefully cultivated growing endowment, Ohio Dominican is well known in the community and is financially healthy. It is also a good neighbor. Probably the earliest indicator of its new era is not the latest computer network linking all the campus components and connecting them to the outside world, but the act of taking down, in 1981, the long fence that for years had separated the campus from the rest of the world.

To understand the transformation, one must appreciate the past that was prologue. This history began with a shared vision from which sprang a mission rooted in faith and hope and carried out with charity and sacrifice in the face of great hardship. From the beginning, the institution's features were trust and collaboration, fidelity and hard work. In 1830, four Dominican Sisters came from the hills of Kentucky to Somerset, Ohio, where they opened an academy for girls. When a fire destroyed their buildings in 1866, they accepted a gift of land and bricks to build on this property on the east end of Columbus. They named their new motherhouse and academy St. Mary of the Springs. These Sisters were members of the Dominican Order, founded by St. Dominic in 1216 to preach and defend the truth of the Catholic Faith. Considering all truth to be one and to lead to God who is Truth, Dominicans studied all branches of knowledge, not only theology or sacred truth. In this spirit, the Dominican Sisters conducted St. Mary of the Springs Academy and taught in other schools elsewhere in Ohio and across the eastern United States.

In 1911, the school (which later became Ohio Dominican) was chartered by the Dominican Sisters as the "Ladies Literary Institute of St. Mary of the Springs" to offer college classes. It formally opened as a four-year Catholic liberal arts college for women in 1924 with ten students and five faculty members—two Dominican Sisters, two lay women, and one priest. The president and the dean were Dominican Sisters. That first year the college offered courses in apologetics (a branch of religion), philosophy, languages, hygiene and physical education. In May three examiners from the State Department of Education reported the spirit of the new college to be "refined and serious, with a decided emphasis on the cultural and philosophical side. It is like a world apart and secluded."

Realizing that the college needed growth space, Mother Stephanie Mohun, Mother General of the Dominican Congregation of St. Mary of the Springs, and her General Council decided to embark on a building program and change the name of the corporation to College of St. Mary of the Springs. A large elegant dining room was completed in 1928, and by the fall of 1929 two other large buildings were ready for occupancy, an academic building and a residence hall. To finance this construction, the Sisters had floated a bond issue for $800,000 in early 1929 with the congregation's property as collateral. The Great Depression hit before a year was up. With income from student tuition and music lessons greatly reduced and with significant decreases in the Sisters' small stipends for teaching in the parochial schools, the congregation was unable to meet the second payment on the principal and the interest on the debt. Both the congregation and the college were facing foreclosure! As the Sisters struggled for survival, the unstinting efforts of a Columbus attorney, James I. Boulger, managed to get the debt refinanced.

In the first decade, 1924–34, the administration focused on securing accreditation and increasing enrollment. In the crucial days that it faced foreclosure, the college was blessed with Sister Jane de Chantal Magruder as academic dean. Her administrative talents and winning personality were especially needed because, for the first seventeen years, the president was part-time, since she also served as the religious superior of the convent. When the number of college students had dropped drastically in 1932 because of the Depression, Sister Jane and Mother Stephanie arranged that those qualified young women entering the congregation would be enrolled as full-time students so that the college's enrollment would reach the required 100 for NCA accreditation. With the help and support of the president, Sister Bernardine Lynam, and of Mother Stephanie, Sister Jane managed to achieve North Central Accreditation, given unconditionally in April 1934.

By 1934 the college had become a member of the Ohio College Association, the National Catholic Educational Association, the Association of American Colleges, the American Council on Education and the American Library Association.

Both sufficient enrollment and competent staff were required for accreditation. Instrumental in achieving both these requirements were three priests on the faculty: Richard B. Bean, who also taught at Pontifical College Josephinum; Joachim M. Bauer; and Matthew M. Hanley. These three scholarly and beloved professors were also the chief recruiters.

Of these three Father Bauer served the longest, from 1930 to 1965. Not only did he teach philosophy and religion and serve as chaplain, but also he took charge of landscaping the campus and directing an impressive annual public lecture series. Bauer brought to campus speakers with national and international reputations, such as Anne O'Hare McCormick, famed writer for the *New York Times*; Monsignor Fulton J. Sheen, able apologist, author, and TV personality; and Ralph Bunche, UN secretary general. These lectures helped make the college better known in Columbus. Lay teachers were also vital to the college. Two of these were Clemence Plique, assistant professor of French, and Sara Macdonald, instructor of German, both of whom contributed a portion of their salaries during 1936–37, as did other generous lay teachers in subsequent years.

During the 1920s, the catalog stated the aim of the college in two sentences: "The educational work of the Sisters of St. Mary's combines the best features of the present pedagogical system with the higher requirements of the convent college. The student is prepared . . . for the responsibilities of our complex modern life, she is thoroughly imbued with lofty ideals and is armed with the Faith, which is both her shield and her support." The meaning of these sentences was unequivocal to the congregation of Dominican Sisters, who had been teaching young women in Ohio for almost 100 years. The aim was clear also to those who would enroll their daughters in the new school.

During the 1930s and 1940s the spirit of St. Mary of the Springs College (SMC) continued to be religious and intellectual. In this period, the college administration further elaborated three main objectives:

1. To know the God-given purposes of life, since the primary purpose of the curricula offered . . . is to enable each student to grow in her Faith through a broad knowledge and a deep love of God.
2. To prepare for life and a work in life . . . to enable her to take her place in the home, in the classroom, in the field of social service, and in such professional careers as are open to women.
3. To be a woman living the Catholic life, inspired by her Faith and strengthened by Catholic philosophy to accomplish her chosen work.

Scholastic philosophy was the chosen means of correlating the courses and integrating the professional courses with the liberal arts. In addition to scholastic philosophy, religion permeated the college in the persons of the white robed Dominican Sisters and priests on the faculty and other clergy, in the code of conduct expected of the students, required religion classes, and the three-day annual retreat for Catholic students. Even non-Catholics were required to attend chapel exercises unless individually excused. Besides daily Mass, there were other religious ceremonies for the campus such as daily benediction before dinner, campus observance of the Church holy days, which were also free days, the celebration of the feast of St. Thomas Aquinas, patron of Catholic schools, and the activities of student groups like the Sodality of the Blessed Virgin Mary. The spiritual atmosphere, combined with the scholastic, was unmistakable.

In those days the National Catholic Educational Association (NCEA) used to ask its members for statistics on the numbers of Catholics and non-Catholics among the students and the faculty, full time and part time. In 1947–48 of the 259 students, fourteen were not Catholic; of the thirty-two full-time faculty, only two were not Catholic; and of the nine part-time faculty, four were not Catholic. Ten years later, out of an enrollment of 287, only two students were not Catholic. There were no full-time non-Catholic faculty, and only one of nine part-time faculty was not Catholic.

The religious spirit of the college was evident, but financial difficulties continued to plague the institution through the 1940s and 1950s. During the 1940s the North Central Association (NCA) required a financial report almost every year. But during those difficult years, the students had no idea of the college's financial straits. Life for them was happy. Most were residents, and there was a familial spirit in the campus community since, because of the small numbers, everyone knew everyone else. The atmosphere was intellectual, cultured, and genteel. A Sister-teacher lived in each section of the dormitory, and the Sisters' relationships with the residents were friendly.

From the first the college focused on developing leadership in the women who attended. A few of the many examples of the success of this effort are these alumnae. Martha Sliter Sheeran (Class of 1935) worked her way up in several companies and, becoming director of corporate communication for Nationwide Insurance, was the first woman to be named a department director at Nationwide. She has held leadership positions also in numerous cultural, religious, and service organizations. Ann DeCain Blackham (Class of 1949) has been president of her own realty company since 1968. In addition to contributing her talents to many civic groups, she has received a Broadcaster's Award for Civic Leadership in 1962, was named New England Business Owner of 1995 by the New England Business Owners Association, was appointed to the President's Task Force on Women's Rights and Responsibilities, and served as the New England regional director of the National Federation of Republican Women. She also organized a pilot childcare program in the basement of the building housing the U.S. Department of Labor in Washington, D.C.

A 1957 graduate, Gretchen Wagner Gooding became professor and vice chair of the Department of Radiology at the University of California in San Francisco and chief of the Radiology Service for the Department of Veterans Affairs Medical Center, the first woman to hold this position. Speaking about what led her to this career, she singled out Sister Suzanne Uhrhane, head of the chemistry department, and Sister Margaret Ann McDowell, head of biology: "[They] enjoyed what they did. They were enthusiastic and curious about the adventure of life." Dr. Gooding felt that her education was extraordinary because of the personal consideration all the Sisters had for their students. "They looked after us and touched our lives in a way that isn't possible at a large university."

Looking back to her student days at SMC, Joanne Luckino Vickers (Class of 1963) also recalled that the atmosphere was intellectually nourishing and at the same time encouraging and supportive. "The teachers never said to a student you couldn't or you can't do whatever you hoped to achieve." Pat Semple Fitzharris (Class of 1966) credited the college with giving her the strength to follow her dreams and recalled that "women learned to be leaders; the school fostered self-esteem in women." Writing in 1963, Sister Camilla Smith, dean of women at SMC, pointed out that women become the principals on campuses "designed specifically for them." She observed that, "homogeneous as it may seem, the woman's college is a microcosm . . . her associates, professors, and college personnel are selected representatives of the human race. Her milieu is, as it always will be, the Mystical Body of Christ."

In the minds of the Sisters of this era, the purpose of the school was first and foremost religious because they believed this purpose gave meaning to and enhanced education in all the subject areas. Responding in 1949 to a question about the college's religious life and interests, the dean wrote: "This institution by its very nature makes ample provision for the development of the students' religious life." Administrative Council minutes from the 1950s attest that the rules for enhancing the students' religious life were as strictly enforced as those intended to maintain an atmosphere of study and good decorum. Students who skipped conferences during the annual retreat were penalized by not being allowed to serve in any capacity of honor such as membership on certain prestigious committees. One student who returned to the dorm "under the influence of alcohol" was sent home for a week. Another student who persisted in dating a married man after learning that he was married was barred from attending her commencement exercises and taking part in other graduation events. During these years, students regularly attended an early-morning Mass—although some of the students wore coats to cover their pajamas! By the end of the 1950s 140 students from the college had chosen to enter the Dominican Sisters' congregation.

In the mid-1950s four events somewhat alleviated the money worries of President Sister Angelita Conley: the college joined the Ohio Foundation of Independent Colleges in 1955, ensuring it of a steady stream of unrestricted income: in 1956 and 1957 SMC received a total of $108,000 from the Ford Foundation; the congregation was able to pay off the debt on the college buildings in 1956; and enrollment steadily increased so as to crowd the main residence hall and make it necessary to house freshmen in an area dubbed College Hall in the convent building. By the end of the decade the college had the largest number of incoming freshmen and the largest total enrollment in its history, 340 women.

Meanwhile, Sister Angelita called on the Sisters of the congregation to help the college: "Each Sister of the Community should continue to be a 'recruiting officer,'" keeping in mind that "we desire good academic students with high moral integrity." Ever since the founding, the Sisters had sacrificed for the college. They had given up gifts they had received individually, patched their clothing time and time again, made beautiful handmade articles to sell, solicited books for the library from their relatives and friends, and even begged at churches. As Mother Stephanie had often reminded them, it was *their* college.

In 1960–61 St. Mary of the Springs College was still "the Sisters' college." The catalog objectives were the same as for the past twelve years. However, a purpose statement preceded the objectives: "As a college conducted by Dominican Sisters, whose motto is *Veritas*, the College . . . has been conceived to educate young women and inspire them ever to seek that Truth which alone makes men free. To achieve this, the faculty endeavors to inculcate such a love of Truth that the three ends of the Dominican Order . . . To Praise, To Bless, and To Preach, will be realized in the lives of its students." By further "Dominicanizing" the statement on the aim of the college, the Sisters made explicit what had been implicit from the beginning.

During the presidency of Sister Angelita Conley (1947–64), the College of St. Mary of the Springs reached the apogee of its original purpose as a Catholic college for women. Two circumstances paved the way for the great change the 1960s brought to the college. First, the college dormitory space was already overcrowded and certainly could not continue to house the increasing numbers of resident students. Second, Father Edward Sanford's visit, provided by the Association of American

Colleges at no cost to the college, gave the Sisters valuable recommendations about the organizational and financial structure of the college. The most important of these was to separately incorporate the congregation from the college with financial reporting distinct from the finances of the Sisters' convent and the academy. These two circumstances led the governing body of the congregation and the administration of the college to plan important changes that belong to the 1960s.

In August 1964 Sister Angelita, ill with cancer, resigned, and Sister Suzanne Uhrhane was named president. Within the space of six years, the College of St. Mary of the Springs had undergone significant changes. In 1963 it became financially and legally separated from the congregation of the Dominican Sisters. In 1964 it turned coeducational and shortly afterward was renamed Ohio Dominican College. Soon enrollment was 1,000 students with a ninety-member faculty, the majority of whom were lay. The college built a large new residence hall and planned a library and a campus center. In 1964 North Central paid its first accreditation visit since 1934 and followed it up with another visit three years later. In 1969 the Sisters completely restructured the board of trustees and gave over ownership and control of the college, though retaining sponsorship. Why and how all these changes happened is a complicated story of strong centripetal forces impacting the college within a relatively short time.

Sister Angelita had pointed out the need to build another residence hall. To apply for a government loan, the college would have to know with accuracy financial data it did not have under its present arrangement. This need, coinciding with the congregation's need for an accurate budget for planning a residence for the large number of young Sisters studying for the Bachelor of Arts degree, led to the legal separation of the college from the motherhouse and the academy in 1963.

The decision to go coed was spurred by the Bishop of Columbus, who told the Sisters that he wanted the Catholic men of the diocese to have access to a Catholic college within the diocese. If the Sisters' college would not go coed, he would bring in the Jesuits to establish a college for men. Reading the handwriting on the wall, the Sisters decided that St. Mary of the Springs College should become coeducational for the fall of 1964. To provide more space for the college, the congregation next closed its academy, which for thirty-five years had occupied the southern half of the main academic building, with the college occupying the northern half. North Central in 1964 had expressed concern that the college library and science facilities did not have sufficient space. Concluding that the need for the college was greater than the need for St. Mary of the Springs Academy for girls, particularly in light of the five new diocesan coed high schools in the city, the governing board of the congregation decided to close its academy.

In the first year of coeducation, the enrollment jumped from 539 to 728. The next year it increased to 948, with the number of men going from 81 to 235. The 1960s brought huge increases in college enrollments across the nation with the baby boomers arriving at the doors and many of the men wanting student status in order to avoid being drafted to fight the Vietnam War. Into all the political and social turmoil of the sixties there erupted what historian Philip Gleason has called "a spiritual earthquake in the American Church." Considering the wake of the Vatican Council II (1962–64), Gleason noted that "the old ideological structure of Catholic higher education . . . had been swept away," leaving Catholic colleges and universities "uncertain of their identity." The climate of pervasive questioning and uncertainty in the sixties, plus the need for government funds to accommodate the big increases in enrollment, led Catholic college and university presidents to look at the question of restructuring their boards. Mother Francis de Sales Heffernan of the Columbus Dominican Sisters, chair of the board of Ohio Dominican College, heard the question of restructuring discussed at every educational or religious meeting she attended at the time. Superiors whose congregations had colleges or universities were asking how they could ensure the Catholic character and mission of their colleges if they gave up control.

As Mother Francis de Sales and her General Council of Sisters sat in their capacity as governing board of Ohio Dominican College, they pondered and debated this question. (The presidents of both the colleges sponsored by the congregation also participated in these deliberations on restructuring their boards.) Strong differences arose among the Sister trustees over questions of how to preserve the Catholic character of the colleges and whether there should be built-in control by the congregation. Finally, in March 1969, they voted unanimously to adopt a new board structure for ODC having no Sister majority, no two-tiered setup, no inner control group, no veto or reserved powers. The congregation gave over, without recompense and without condition, the land and the buildings with all their furnishings and equipment but continued its sponsorship with one-third membership of the board. So with full deliberation and hopeful confidence in Divine Providence, the Sisters entrusted Ohio Dominican College to the new board. The college had come of age.

Sister Suzanne guided ODC through this whole process of coming to age. Having come into the presidency after Sister Angelita had been ill for almost two years, she had her agenda cut out for her. It was spelled out in detail in the North Central Reports from the visitations in 1964 and 1967. Changes, though necessary, had been "too much, too soon" for the college that had been a small intimate place used to relying heavily on the oral word and a multiplicity of exceptions to the rule. Written policies needed to be developed and promulgated in a number of areas (for example, a new faculty handbook). Other weaknesses lay in the areas of financial organization, development, planning, inadequacies in the physical facilities, and communication. How hard the president and her staff worked on these concerns can be gleaned from the report from NCA's return visit in 1967, which listed the college's greatest strength as "the willingness of its leaders to accept constructive criticism and to implement suggestions for improvement." Student and faculty morale was good. By then the proportion between lay and religious faculty was fifty-fifty. The report affirmed: "The examiners detected no friction between lay and religious faculty, or between Catholic and non-Catholic, either at the student or faculty level . . . the non-Catholic and/or the less religious are not made to feel uncomfortable by their positions and are not put under pressure to conform. All of this contributes to high esprit de corps and strong institutional loyalty."

Finances, however, continued to be a serious problem. A large factor in the solvency of the operations of the college was the substantial portion of the total income from the contributed services of the religious on the faculty and staff. In 1972 the NCA review team noted the financial condition of the college as "grave, but not yet critical."

One of NCA's commendations's that year highlighted the "extraordinarily good atmosphere for blacks and other minority groups. There appears to be a real sense of community between the races at this institution, with less friction than at any other institution with which the examiners are familiar." This atmosphere was the result of the strong commitment to social justice that belonged to ODC's heritage. At the same time a major factor in creating the inclusive atmosphere in which minorities felt welcome was the teachers' respect and concern for each individual student in their classes, knowing each by name and helping each to succeed. On a standardized campus morale scale for 1971, ODC rated a score of 85 for professors going "out of their way to help students," whereas the published mean for 100 colleges was only 49.

With the appointment of the first lay dean of students in 1969, major changes occurred in the rules and regulations, particularly for the residents. The women's dormitory, built in 1966 became coed. By 1974 visitation hours were continuous on weekends until 11:30 P.M. on Sundays. Students of legal age for drinking were permitted alcoholic beverages in their rooms. This was a far cry from the rules of the fifties! And Sisters no longer monitored the residence halls. But North Central was pleased with student life at ODC, which by this time had become largely a commuter college.

By the time NCA visited in April 1978, it was evident that a remarkably favorable change had taken place at the college. The team concluded its report by saying: "The college meets fully its commitment to do what it says it is doing. While it has future financial concerns as well as areas to which it needs to turn its attention, the quality of the programs and the strong sense of academic quality which existed among all elements in the institution led the team to believe that it can continue to be a strong College in the future." They commended the "good academic programs and student life, dedicated and able administration and faculty, excellent Board and well-ordered financial affairs," and one of the many strengths listed was "college-wide understanding and agreement on goals of the institution."

All the faculty, staff, and administrators rejoiced with Sister Suzanne when word arrived of the ten-year accreditation. It was great news after the previous decade of being subjected to reaccreditation every two to five years. Major helps to Sister Suzanne in the interval between 1972 and 1978 were the contributions of Sister Mary Andrew Matesich as academic vice president and dean and Thornton N. McClure as financial director and vice president for business affairs, plus the advantage of a much more active and involved board of trustees, particularly blessed with Dean Jeffers, chairman and CEO of the Nationwide Insurance complex of companies.

Thornton McClure, having recently retired from directing finances for the University of Rhode Island, came to ODC in December 1971 as a part-time financial consultant for six months. It was a fruitful love match, and he remained until 1983. Dean Jeffers, a Methodist, committed himself to helping this small Catholic college to surface from its grave financial condition. The day he saw a young paraplegic being wheeled into the academic building and attended with care, Jeffers decided to say "yes" to the invitation to serve on the board. His stature in the city and in the nation, coupled with his lengthy service on the board, greatly assisted ODC to a new level of community recognition as well as financial health.

At this critical point in the college's history, Sister Mary Andrew was able to bring not only a vision for the future but an excellent grasp of what was needed to move the college toward it. Receiving two substantial grants, the college was able to develop a new mission statement with participation by the entire campus community, as well as alumni and board members, and to design a new liberal arts core for the curriculum. These two changes followed an action taken by the faculty in 1969 before Sister Mary Andrew was dean. They had voted to change the curriculum to a system in which the normal student load would be four four-hour courses each semester. This change, initiated to enable the students to concentrate on fewer subjects in greater depth, necessitated a complete revamping of the academic program. With all courses being four credits, it was necessary to reduce the requirements for philosophy and theology in order to fit all the liberal arts general distribution requirements into the 124 credits needed for graduation. The new requirements included a twelve-credit sequence: one course in philosophy, one in theology, and a third in either discipline. This was a major change form the previous fifteen credits in philosophy and sixteen in theology required of Catholics. The change effectively ended the college's Thomistic core curriculum. Elsewhere many Catholic institutions of higher learning had abandoned the Thomistic synthesis that had been their hallmark. What replaced this synthesis at Ohio Dominican was the new Humanities Program, a sixteen-credit curriculum based on a type of freshman "Great Books" course that would be integrated with writing courses.

Why a Humanities Program? In the mid-1970s the college had committed to increasing diversity in the student body, so at this point 16 percent of the study body was black. There was also an increase in international students. In 1976 forty-six students from twenty-five different countries were enrolled, the majority from the Middle East. Still another aspect of the new diversity consisted in admitting a greater number of students of lesser academic achievement than in previous years. Considering this diverse student population now coming to Ohio Dominican, the task force worked to structure a core program to try to provide entering freshmen with a common content and vocabulary for intellectual discourse together with the critical skills needed for college.

This Humanities Program, which went into effect in 1978–79, was closely tied to the college's new mission statement. A grant from the Exxon Foundation in 1976 funded a two-year process involving extensive and intensive participation by all the college's constituencies to set goals and to revise the mission statement. The revised statement opened with emphasis on the Dominican motto: "As a Catholic liberal arts college with a Dominican tradition, Ohio Dominican College is guided in its educational mission by the Dominican motto: to contemplate truth and to share with others the fruits of this contemplation." It spoke of truth as "the basis of human freedom and the source of human effectiveness."

In earlier years mission statements contained a more explicit expression of the school's Catholic and Dominican character. The 1964–65 catalog had stated clearly that "the end of education is the knowledge of God." The preface to the statement of the college's objectives read: "The philosophy of education at the College of St. Mary of the Springs is Thomistic philosophy.... Following in the Dominican tradition, Thomistic philosophy seeks *truth*, which leads to the knowledge of man's last end." The new statement of 1977 focused on the search for truth without stating the meaning of the object of the search.

This same year, 1977, Sister Suzanne, having served as president for thirteen exceptional years, announced her retirement effective the following year, and for the first time the board of trustees conducted an open search for a new president. With faculty and student involvement and after months of committee meetings chaired by Dean Jeffers, the board unanimously elected Sister Mary Andrew as president.

As had her predecessors, the new president applied her energies to addressing the concerns the North Central team had expressed in its latest visit. Determined that ODC would not only survive but thrive, she attended first to developing the college's financial base. Before the end of the decade both a new science building and an athletic facility had been completed, and the endowment was growing.

The 1987 NCA Report was laudatory. Regarding the mission, the team wrote: "The rich Dominican background of the College is strong and inherent in the educational programs. It bodes well for the continuity of a sound educational program which is built with humanities as a central core." Under the evaluation category of Institutional Effectiveness, the report complimented the college on having met the changes of the past decade and having "emerged a stronger institution both educationally and fiscally." It predicted a bright future, and the subsequent paragraph noted: "Leadership has been strong, sustained and effective. The faculty, well-trained and motivated, has been flexible enough to meet the changing needs and the entire institution is well-anchored by a nucleus of Dominican sisters who both teach and serve as administrators. Most of all they are a strong presence."

In 1987, although the academic dean was no longer a Sister, twenty-three Dominican Sisters served as faculty or staff, 20 percent of the total, full and part time. Their annual contributed services exceeded $200,000. Since 1981 the congregation had given two six-figure capital gifts to ODC. Referring to the congregation's contributions, the college's self-study report for the 1987 visit by NCA said: "Most important to all, they [the Sisters] have given Ohio Dominican its motto, tradition, distinctive character and vision."

The decade following the 1987 NCA report brought further changes to Ohio Dominican. The administration initiated and managed change by rewarding those faculty and staff who contributed to its planned implementation. This strategy spurred the institution to a remarkable transformation in the 1990s. Decisions about any new program, however, required first applying the mission statement as an evaluative measure.

Have the changes in the character of the college altered its essential identity as a Catholic liberal arts college with a Dominican tradition? In 1998 Joanne M. Burrows studied Ohio Dominican in a comparison of five Catholic colleges and, by means of interviews, analyzed how fourteen of ODC's faculty members were interpreting the meaning of "Dominican" and "Catholic" in the opening sentence of the mission statement. She discovered that while "liberal arts college" was the dominant concept in their descriptions of the college's academic identity, "all participants use[d] the Dominican motto, 'To contemplate truth and to share the fruits of this contemplation with others,' to construct ODC's religious identity." The college's emphasis on "the Dominican tradition," which is an intellectual tradition, seemed to have had an interesting effect on the interpretation of its mission by many of the faculty, perhaps the majority. Actually, the Dominican Order was founded to preach and teach the truth of the Catholic faith. The order and its tradition have their identity within the broader context of Roman Catholic identity. Burrows's interviews found a decoupling of the concepts of Dominicanism and Catholicism at ODC, whereby Dominicanism provides a "common belief system that is accessible to individuals holding a wider range of views." Dominicanism, given an inclusive and elastic interpretation, had become "the overarching category," and Catholicism, "a particular expression to which only a limited portion of the campus community subscribes."

Today the Catholic identity of the college appears far less clear than its Dominican identity. The eleven Catholic participants in the Burrows's study expressed a wide range of views about the Catholic faith and the Church. As far as the atmosphere at ODC, there are fewer than half as many Sisters and priests on the campus as there were a decade ago. There are no statistics on the percentage of Catholics on the faculty. Of the students who indicated their religious affiliation in 1999, not quite a third were Catholic. Burrows's study reports that "religious activities are limited and few students take advantage of these opportunities."

Lack of clarity about what it means for any college, in this case for Ohio Dominican, to be Catholic dates from the sixties. ODC's student body, faculty, and board of trustees became much larger and more diverse than the founders of the college had envisioned. No longer were the majority Roman Catholic. The sixties ushered in a period of soul-searching questions and unsettling changes within the Roman Catholic Church and the sponsoring congregation of Dominican Sisters. Beginning in the late 1960s the congregation experienced a severe drop in new vocations as well as the departure of existing members. Some of these were college teachers. This period was a time of lengthy dialogue among Catholic religious, church, and college and university leaders about what constitutes a Catholic institution of higher learning. These dialogues and the documents they produced eventually led to Pope John Paul II's apostolic constitution *Ex Corde Ecclesiae* in 1990. When the U.S. bishops asked Catholic college and university presidents to react to this document, Sister Mary Andrew invited faculty input. Some of ODC's faculty again began seriously discussing what makes a college Catholic. The discussion is ongoing.

President Sister Mary Andrew and her administrators were strongly committed to maintaining the Catholic as well as the Dominican character of the college. However, in light of how the institution has developed, it is hard to envision that the faculty would espouse the term "Catholic" in the way they have come to own "Dominican." One reality is very clear: the sponsoring body no longer has control over the legacy it bequeathed to the college. When Sister Mary Andrew announced that she would be stepping down after twenty-two years as president in June 2001, the board of trustees elected Dr. Jack P. Calareso, president of Briar Cliff College in Sioux City, Iowa, to succeed her. As the college's first lay president endeavors to build on the achievements of his predecessors and continue faithful to ODC's mission, a new era has begun.

In the course of its growth, Ohio Dominican College developed a life of its own, much broader than that which characterized it before the 1960s. It was inevitable that the great changes during the sixties and subsequent changes in the constituencies of the college would result in a new mission statement that would reinterpret the mission and tradition given the college by the sponsoring congregation. Certainly there were, and are, strong continuities. In accord with its tradition, ODC reaches out to educate those who especially need what it has to offer. This outward reach to fill a need is not new. One reason for founding the college was to provide a good Catholic education for women in a geographical area where it was not available to them. The other reason, perhaps even more important than the first, was to educate the Sisters of the congregation to teach in Catholic elementary and high schools across the nation. Always the Sisters had welcomed into their schools students of different backgrounds and religious faiths and, even during the Depression, took in some students who could not afford the tuition. ODU's atmosphere is still warm, welcoming, and caring, and the tuition is the lowest of any comparable private college or university in the area. Professors still give students individual attention, devoting their energies more to teaching than to research, publishing, or the lecture tour. In academic and disciplinary matters, the student gets the benefit of the doubt. Overall at ODU there is still a pervasive charity—"doing the truth in love."

From the beginning the Dominican Sisters read the signs of the times and discerned those societal needs they could effectively address in carrying out their mission in the Church. Throughout its history the school introduced programs needed at the time—for example, in 1944 a degree in nursing in collaboration with area hospitals, then library science certification when no other institution in the area offered it, and, in the aftermath of Vatican Council II, a certification program in religious education to assist the diocese.

Sister Suzanne's letter to the Sisters of the congregation in 1967 telling them about the college's name change gives a good insight into the heritage. Taking the Catholic character as a given, she wrote, "'Dominican' specifies the whole name. It connotes a long tradition of learning, sanctity and culture." The letter concluded: "The College of St. Mary of the Springs would not exist today were it not for the vision, dedication, and sacrifice of the Dominican Sisters. The name *Ohio Dominican College* is a constant reminder of this debt. We feel that the name best expresses what we are."

Another vigorous element of continuity in the history of ODU is collaboration with clergy and laypersons, without whose help the Sisters could not have founded or continued the college. Before the college was built the Sisters consulted the bishop of Columbus, set up a lay advisory board, and relied on excellent clergy and lay faculty members and staff to further its mission. Nor have all its collaborators been Catholic. Another blessing for the tuition-driven college has been the benefactors who assisted it through periods of financial hardship.

At Ohio Dominican today there are other important continuities. These vital elements of the heritage are still strong—the conviction that the life of the mind is important, that truth is freeing, and that there is an obligation to serve, to reach out to others and "share the fruits." And there are faculty, lay as well as religious, who continue to sacrifice for the mission of the university and to hope that their students will learn to know and to contemplate not only truths, but Truth.

Alice Gallin, Preface to *American Catholic Higher Education: Essential Documents, 1967–1990* (Notre Dame University Press, 1992); Philip Gleason, *Contending with Modernity: Catholic Higher Education in the Twentieth Century* (Oxford University Press, 1995), and "Neoscholasticism as Preconciliar Ideology," *Catholic Historian* 7 (1988): 401–11; George M. Marsden, *Soul of the American University: From Protestant Establishment to Established Unbelief* (Oxford University Press, 1994).

Ohio Northern University

"Roots and Wings"

PAUL M. LOGSDON

A casual observer could easily have overlooked the slight, twenty-eight-year-old man as he stepped off the train at the Ada, Ohio, depot. In March 1866, Henry Solomon Lehr was a recently discharged Union veteran, and he had come to northwestern Ohio in search of a site for his projected university. That same observer might well have smiled at Lehr's ambition since neither he nor the rough village of Ada showed obvious promise.

Lehr, however, impressed the members of the Ada school board sufficiently for them to hire him as their schoolmaster. This was with the understanding that he would be able to use the facilities after classes to teach a "select school" for those wishing education beyond that offered during the day. As his reputation grew throughout the area, the number of select school students increased, and in 1870, Lehr felt sufficiently well established to approach the citizens of Ada for funds to purchase land for a campus and an academic building. Lehr was to contribute $4,000; the citizens were to provide the campus and a $4,000 loan. A village committee was formed to raise subscriptions from its citizens, and Lehr and two colleagues, John G. Park, and B. F. Niesz, raised the funds pledged by Lehr toward this endeavor. In August 1871, the Northwestern Ohio Normal School, later Ohio Northern University, was launched. Lehr, John G. Park, George W. Rutledge, and Frederick Maglott, all teachers in the institution, were the sole owners and proprietors of the Northwestern Normal School in 1878. In 1885 the institution was chartered by the State of Ohio and a board of trustees was created. Lehr and his associates appointed themselves to the board.

The period after the Civil War saw dramatic changes in American higher education as a reunited nation was transformed by industrialization and urbanization. A more educated populace was needed and the sciences and modern languages rose in importance in college curricula to equal footing with the humanities, religion, and

Hill Memorial

classical languages. Lehr was receptive to the needs of the new era, and he crafted an institution with those needs in mind. He also bore in mind his own educational experiences, both as a student and teacher, and this, in turn, shaped his philosophy.

Coming from a poor family, young Henry's schooling was formed by his need to support himself. He worked on neighboring farms, attending school when time and finances permitted. In 1854, with the encouragement of his teacher and a loan from one of his brothers, Lehr was able to attend Alfred Holbrook's academy at Marlborough, Ohio. This educational background was sufficient to permit him to teach in the local county schools.

Later, at Northern, he strove to keep tuition as low as possible, and as a country schoolmaster, realized that in order to be accessible to most Americans, his institution's calendar and curriculum would require considerable flexibility. The curriculum offered was clearly and unabashedly practical. As the school's first catalog noted: "It is the design of the Institution to provide . . . an education that will fit the rising generation to discharge life's duties with credit to themselves, honor to their parents, and benefit to humanity."

While a student at Mount Union College, Lehr absorbed the concept of education as a democratizing force. Sidestepping the debate over whether women should be admitted as students, Northern, from its inception, was coeducational in both its student body and faculty. It is also worth noting that, although Lehr was a man of strong religious convictions, the school was not established with a specific denominational affiliation, nor has it subsequently sought to limit admission according to church membership.

Lehr realized that to succeed, Northern would have to adapt its curriculum to society's needs. Although founded as a normal school, an institution for training teachers, Ohio Northern had, by the mid-1880s, added programs in pharmacy, engineering, law, and business. The early curriculum was also distinguished by a willingness to experiment, although some efforts, like the College of Agriculture, failed to take root. This experimental approach and a willingness to adapt the curriculum to contemporary needs has long been a hallmark of Ohio Northern.

Northern's earliest years were a trial for both the institution and its founder. Classes began at the new institution on Monday, August 14, 1871, though not without difficulties. Because of delays in finishing the Normal School Building, the 147 students enrolled found themselves temporarily relegated to downtown stores and local churches. Not until October 16 were the first classes taught in the building, and even then the interior was incomplete. Lehr had recently rushed to finish his own degree at Mount Union prior to the start of classes. He also had to pressure the contractor to fulfill his obligations, recruit a faculty, and see to the furnishing of the classrooms and the printing of the school's catalog. Lehr was, in short, creating an educational institution literally from the ground up. While serving as chief administrator of the new school and ensuring funding and buildings, in that first year he also taught elocution, arithmetic, grammar, geography, advanced algebra and trigonometry, beginning and advanced geometry, Latin, Cicero, analysis of sentences, advanced rhetoric. He started at 4:00 or 5:00 A.M. and ended late in the evening.

By the 1880s, with the problems attending its founding largely behind it, Ohio Northern entered a period of growth and curricular diversification which gave permanence to Lehr's original vision. This happy situation was reflected by the trustees' decision in the spring of 1885 to change the institution's name from the Northwestern Ohio Normal School to Ohio Normal University. The catalog for that year cited the growth of the curriculum as the first reason for the change. Student recruitment also was no longer limited to the northwestern corner of the state.

The 1880s saw the creation of several major programs. During this period the commercial course of the 1870s emerged as a separate college. The title page of the 1881–82 catalog cited a "Business College" at the Normal. The Civil Engineering Department, first of the institution's professional programs, appeared in the 1881–82 catalog. The existence of a law department was noted in the catalog of 1884–85, and the following year the catalog listed for the first time a "School of Pharmacy." Medical classes and courses in chemistry and botany were offered. The decision to expand these into an actual college was prompted by the passage of Ohio's first pharmacy licensure act in 1884.

The expanding curriculum and student body placed pressures on campus facilities that were difficult to meet. The first two buildings had been constructed by local funding. When, in 1883, Lehr and his colleagues again asked for assistance, their appeals were ignored. Despite a threat to relocate the institution, Lehr and his fellow trustees were finally forced to erect a modest frame building at their own expense. This decrease in local support foreshadowed more problems in the coming decade.

Throughout the 1890s, it became increasingly apparent that major changes would be required in the way in which the institution was administered. Outside funding eluded Lehr and the other trustees because of their continued control of the institution. Lehr's policy of keeping tuition low, commendable as that may have been, left the institution chronically underfunded. At the same time, larger enrollments and an expanding curriculum made finding funds for additional buildings all the more pressing. In addition, President Lehr, the guiding force behind the university, was fifty-two years old at the beginning of the 1890s. Although a dedicated teaching staff assisted him, he was beginning to have concerns for the future of the institution. What would become of the university if illness removed him?

In trying to secure greater permanence for Northern, Lehr tried two approaches. In 1897, he first sought state support for the institution. When this tack failed, he agreed to sell the university to the Methodist Church. The sale was plausible given that at that time 75 percent of ONU students were Methodists. In June 1898 Lehr received a visit from one of his faculty members, Simeon Fess, and the pastor of the local Methodist Church, Revered S. L. Boyer. They asked if President Lehr and the other trustees would be willing to sell the university to the Central Conference of the

Methodist Church. The answer, after a meeting of the trustees, was affirmative. The asking price was $24,000. The actual transfer of assets was completed in 1899 and Dr. Leroy Belt, 1900–1905, and Dr. A. E. Smith, 1905–30, succeeded Lehr as president.

Lehr believed that he would be allowed to continue at Northern in some managerial capacity, though this proved unfeasible. The catalog for 1998–99 showed a two-tier administrative arrangement. The board of trustees had been reconstituted with Lewis Dukes, a wealthy Hancock County farmer as president. Leroy A. Belt, a Methodist minister and trustee at Ohio Wesleyan was vice president, and, as events unfolded, the real power on the board. The board had an executive committee and committees for finance, buildings, and instruction. Lehr was on all three. In addition, a local board of management was created to exercise day-to-day control of the institution. Of all the flaws in this complex arrangement, perhaps the most serious was the impossibility of fixing responsibility for most university operations. Lehr resigned in frustration at the conclusion of the 1903 academic year.

The period between 1900 and 1930 saw the institution transformed administratively, physically, and pedagogically. As rapidly as their contracts expired, faculty members were organized in a more standard departmental fashion. Under Lehr, a number of programs such as law, art, pharmacy, stenography, music, and oratory were conducted on a semiautonomous basis. Tuition collected in these courses was divided among the faculty with only a percent being remitted to the university. Under President Belt, all funds were sent directly to the ONU treasurer, who then paid individual professors a stipulated salary. The practice of faculty members renting books and equipment to students was also curtailed. Finally, individual professors were placed under the supervision of department chairmen.

Meanwhile, at the trustee meeting of July 28, 1903, the university's name was changed from Ohio Normal University, a name that it had borne since 1885, to Ohio Northern University. Tradition recounts that President Belt was petitioned to make the change by a group of engineering students headed by Thomas J. Smull. As participants in a professional program, they felt that their degrees' value was diminished by having been awarded by a "mere" normal school. This move also reflected major academic changes under way.

The curriculum was extensively revamped again during this period with an eye toward contemporary needs and trends. In 1904 an attempt was made establish a joint medical program with the Fort Wayne College of Medicine in Indiana. Although this concept had potential, it proved to be short-lived. Another innovation was the creation of a College of Agriculture in early 1911. By the fall term, nearly 300 students had enrolled in the college, and the college's farm eventually consisted of ninety acres. Although the failing Agriculture College was disbanded in 1923, the university wisely retained ownership of the former farm that later formed the core of Northern's west campus.

The curriculum adapted to contemporary developments by removing as well as by adding programs. In 1925, the university's preparatory department was abolished. Since President Lehr's day, the department had served as a bridge between high school and the university. This practice had merit as long as there were few high schools, but by the 1920s, they were common in Ohio. Moreover, the practice of admitting high-school-age students to the university now detracted from the institution's academic reputation. Today the postsecondary option program updates this earlier program. In 1921, the Military Department, established under Lehr, had also been discontinued, thus freeing resources for the rising star of varsity athletics.

President Smith was a fund-raiser of considerable ability and stamina. During his long administration, the local newspapers were peppered with articles announcing his departure on trips to visit potential benefactors. The student body, which found itself occasionally at odds with Smith over his regulations, may well have breathed a collective sigh of relief each time his train pulled out of the Ada depot. There is, however, little doubt that his frequent journeys benefited the university. He was, for example, instrumental in creating the university's first endowment fund and raised roughly $500,000 for it.

President Smith was less successful in dealing with his exuberant and irreverent students. Although fraternities were first introduced under President Belt, Smith viewed these organizations with considerable suspicion, seeing them as a challenge to his authority, especially where the university ban on dancing was concerned. The use of alcohol and tobacco by students, both on and off campus, was also forbidden. President Smith apparently visited the Ada train station to catch intoxicated students returning from the fleshpots of Lima. The students were, at least in some cases, able to bribe the conductor to stop outside town for a hasty departure.

Had the university's economic situation remained stable, the next change would have been to further strengthen its academic program. The desirability of doing so had been noted in the 1920s, especially in terms of gaining recognition from regional accrediting bodies. It was unfortunately necessary to delay this step for almost two decades as the Great Depression and the Second World War buffeted Ohio Northern.

Like many institutions, Northern was heavily dependent on tuition income, and the arrival of economic hard times slashed enrollments. Although the Methodist Church provided strong moral support and encouraged Methodist students to attend ONU, direct financial assistance from the church remained modest. The number of students attending dropped from a pre-Depression high of 1,056 in 1928–29 to 529 in 1935. From that point, enrollments grew until, immediately prior to the Second World War, they were approaching those of the late 1920s.

President Williams (1929–43) and the trustees enacted several measures to improve the university's finances, perhaps the most significant of which was to reduce the number of staff employed. In 1928–29, for example, Ohio Northern had sixty faculty members, but by 1934–35 this number had been reduced to thirty-two. By the latter date, many of the administrative staff was also listed with the faculty, suggesting that the administrators were pressed into the thinned faculty ranks.

The curriculum was revised with an eye toward greater efficiency. The overall effect was to consolidate various independent academic programs into the College of Liberal Arts. One of the first units to be abolished was the College of Music. It had been formed at the end of President Smith's administration, and, given the modest size of the program, demoting it to a department in the College of Liberal Arts was a sensible step. In 1930, the College of Education was similarly reduced to the division of teacher training. Both the School of Fine Arts and School of Oratory met similar fates. Indeed, even the School of Commerce, a product of the Lehr era, became the department of economics and business administration within the College of Liberal Arts.

As American entry into the war became more likely, the university sought to minimize its impact by participating in several government programs. In early 1940 students began flight training under an Army Air Corps program. With the international situation growing more threatening, a ground school was added to teach nonpilots the rudiments of various aviation-related subjects. By April 1942, the Navy had approved Northern for officer training. Just as it had during the First World War, the federal government turned to schools such as Northern to provide engineering expertise. Anticipating wartime needs, the Federal Security Agency created a program to train nonstudents in war-related industries. Later in the war, this program was consolidated under the Engineering, Science, and Management War Training program (ESMWT). By mid-1943, the university was conducting ESMWT classes in fifteen cities in the region. Between the program's beginning in January 1941 and its end on June 30, 1945, more than 5,400 individuals were enrolled in classes taught by Northern. Despite these efforts, the size of the student body dropped below the worst levels of the Depression. In the fall of 1943 only 156 students were enrolled.

Various emergency measures were enacted to deal with the crisis. The school's yearbook, the *Northern,* ceased publication with the 1942 issue. Next year, the student newspaper, the *Northern Review,* closed. The last full-sized university catalog was printed for the 1942–43 academic year with thirty-page pamphlets issued thereafter. At least one building, Presser Hall, was closed for most of the war. A sure indication of the seriousness of the situation was the decision, in 1943, to cancel intercollegiate sports for the balance of the war. Several changes were made to the university's calendar to accommodate wartime requirements. Restrictions were lifted regarding when students could enter Northern. Incoming students could begin their studies during any quarter, just as they had in Lehr's time. Course offerings were increased for the summer session, thus making the university effectively a year-round institution.

The following year brought the first good news that had been heard on the Ada campus for several years. The Serviceman's Readjustment Act of 1944, dubbed the "GI Bill of Rights," was enacted. Under Title II of the act, qualifying veterans enrolled at a college or university could receive tuition assistance. This promise of future income would be invaluable if Northern could survive into 1945 when the returning servicemen arrived.

The university was also fortunate to have a core of faculty and administrators who were dedicated to the university's survival. For his part, President McClure (1943–49) served his first year in office without pay. Others followed his example on the faculty, some of whom served either without pay or at considerably reduced salaries.

The opening of fall quarter 1945 found the university trying to cope with a sudden influx of students. With peace only one month old, an initial group of thirty veterans had enrolled. By the beginning of spring quarter, an estimated 325 ex-servicemen were on campus, and the enrollment for the following fall was projected to be 750. By winter quarter 1946, over 900 students were enrolled, and the fall 1948 class numbered 1,209. This sudden growth strained the local housing market, and Northern, which at that time had no dormitories, acquired, courtesy of the federal government, an assortment of trailers and prefabricated dwellings. By the beginning of fall quarter 1946, the university had in place 114 trailers and five barrack-style dormitories for single men to house the returning veterans and their families.

By the start of President McIntosh's administration in 1949, enrollment had stabilized to the extent that the institution's efforts could shift from mere survival to long-desired improvements in academic programs. For two decades the university had been handicapped by lack of accreditation from any regional or national agencies; by 1958 this problem had been corrected. The professional programs, however, had won recognition earlier, with the College of Law gaining American Bar Association accreditation in 1948. The College of Pharmacy's accreditation by the American Council on Pharmaceutical Education followed in 1951, and the Accreditation Board approved the College of Engineering's programs for Engineering and Technology three years later. The process was completed when, in 1958, the North Central Association of Colleges and Secondary Schools accredited all undergraduate programs. When the news reached campus, a joyous crowd gathered at McIntosh's home to celebrate. For his part, President McIntosh declared a free day for the campus and went out of his way to recognize the efforts of the faculty, administration, and students in securing accreditation.

It would be comforting to believe that, with its obvious crises past, Ohio Northern University then entered a period of unruffled calm. In the ensuing years, however, the university has been a changing part of a vibrant and changing society. While the core liberal arts and professional programs have remained strong, new disciplines such as biochemistry, computer science, public relations, telecommunications, international business, and computer engineering have grown along side them. Recruiting an increasingly competent faculty for those programs and providing appropriate facilities has been a major challenge. Numerous academic buildings have been added including the science complex, chapel, library, sports center, and performing arts center. The new classrooms and laboratories have also required increasingly sophisticated and expensive equipment, and the advent of computers and networking has emphasized this trend. Literally all of the earlier structures have been renovated. A total of eight residence halls were constructed and additional private homes and a senior citizens complex were acquired to house the student body that grew from about 850 in 1951 to more than 3,000 in 1998. Further expansion of the campus was made possible in 1989 when an additional 120 acres south of the main campus were purchased and again in 1999 when twenty-two acres west of campus were obtained. Whatever else Ohio Northern University may run short of, new challenges are not among them.

Ohio Northern University is a difficult institution to categorize. Although located in one of the more rural parts of the state, it is not isolated. It is connected to the rest of the world by the Internet and satellite links. Information is rapidly disseminated on campus through a well-developed computer network and via the university radio and television stations. While still known for its core professional programs in law, pharmacy, education, business, and engineering; the sciences, social sciences, humanities and music, the visual and performing arts have all been strengthened. Northern has been, and remains, a work in progress.

Throughout its history, that work has been reflected in the accomplishments of a long and growing list of notable alumni. In the field of politics, Northern's graduates include men such as U.S. Senator Frank B. Willis, who also was a faculty member, served in the Ohio General Assembly and as governor. Congressional Representative Simeon Fess, who also served as president of Antioch College, would also have to be included in this group. Anthony Celebreeze, a graduate of Ohio Northern's School of Law served in the U.S. Senate, was elected to four terms as mayor of Cleveland, and served as Secretary of Health, Education and Welfare in the Kennedy and Johnson administrations. In recent years, Northern graduates, like U.S. Senator Mike Dewine and State Senator Robert Cupp have continued this tradition of public service.

Ohio Northern's alumni have also contributed in the sciences. One early graduate, Benjamin F. Finkel, was an educator and founder of the American Mathematical Society. George W. Crile is known both as the founder of the Cleveland Clinic and as a pioneer in the area of trauma medicine. His groundbreaking work in the area of blood transfusion was a major medical breakthrough.

Northern's former students have enjoyed considerable success in the area of business. George Franklin Getty, an 1878 graduate, later founded the Getty Oil Company. Benjamin Fairless, who studied engineering before the First World War, went on to become president of U.S. Steel. Clayton Mathile, a 1962 graduate, established the Iams Company, a major producer of pet foods.

The course of Ohio Northern University's development is perhaps best summarized by the administrations of her two most recently retired presidents. At his inauguration in 1965, President Samuel Meyer spoke of the institution's bequest to its students of "roots and wings." His vision for Ohio Northern was that of a university capable of supplying its graduates with the educational "roots" necessary for them to make their way in the world. However, he also saw the need to offer the spiritual "wings" which Northern, as a church-related institution, was able to provide and strove to provide both to Ohio Northern's students.

Under President Meyer a long list of badly needed buildings were completed. These included the Heterick Memorial Library, the Tilton College of Law, the Taggart Law Library, Wesley Center, Young Building for Philosophy and Religion, Biggs Engineering Building, the Robertson-Evans Pharmacy Building (begun under President McIntosh), King-Horn Convocation Center, Park Hall, McIntosh extensions (White Bear and Wishing Well), the refurbished Taft Building, the Wilson Art Center, and the later-renamed Meyer Hall of Science. By the end of the Meyer administration in 1977, all of the private residences lying between the original campus on Main Street and the new west campus had been removed, and the intervening space completely landscaped.

As President Meyer noted in his comments at retirement, the extensive building program was a visible manifestation of the intangible improvements to the university's educational program. The size of the faculty was increased by over two-thirds and the curricula were modernized. In addition, chapters of five national honorary societies were established to recognize academic achievement and leadership, a number of student living groups and social groups were formed and intercollegiate athletic teams were expanded.

The work of strengthening the academic program and the physical facilities of the campus was continued under President DeBow Freed who, along with his wife, Catherine, quietly exemplified a spirit of Christian care and concern. His low-keyed and civil approach to campus leadership was much appreciated, as was his concern for Northern's students.

Changes in the curriculum and the continued growth of the student body required improved academic facilities. In 1982 an addition to the law library was dedicated. Three years later, the music building, Presser Hall, was renovated and enlarged in 1985–86. A second addition to house student practice rooms and faculty offices was added in 1998.

Due to the purchase of 120 acres south of the campus, space was available for the Freed Center for the Performing Arts. This facility included two theaters, their support facilities, broadcasting studios, and a classroom wing. It was opened in

1991. Even before the Freed Center was completed, work began on a 62,000-square-foot field house with an additional fitness center and improved exercise equipment.

In the 1990s, additions were also made to Dukes Memorial, the pharmacy building (the Pierstorf addition), the Wilson Art Building and the university gained the use of the Metzger Nature Center in Tuscarawas County for student and faculty environmental and biological study. A senior citizen complex where seniors and students live as neighbors in small housing was also acquired in the 1990s. In 1996, ground was broken for an annex between the Biggs Engineering Building and the Meyer Hall of Science. The groundbreaking, in summer 1998, for the Heterick Memorial Library expansion and a new president's home on campus, marked Dr. Freed's final building projects on this extensive list.

Along with the buildings, continued strengthening of academic programs in the colleges through improved equipment and staffing, growth in co-op and internship opportunities, increased scholarship assistance, increased faculty development opportunities, increased library holdings, and a number of international partnerships with universities abroad became reality. Strategic planning became a way of life during Dr. Freed's tenure, and through two decades (1982–2000), this planning resulted in an evolving plan for program development. The current document is "Strength for the 21st Century" (October 1998), and ongoing review continues.

These improvements were underwritten in part by two ambitious fund-raising campaigns. In the mid-1980s, an $18 million campaign was announced. At its conclusion, over $23.5 million had been committed. Only five years later an even more ambitious enterprise, the $30 million "Campaign for the 21st Century" was launched and successfully completed.

The major improvements to the university's physical plant were joined by another development in the 1980s. It was subtle and easily overlooked but arguably as significant as the erection of any building. The use of computers, once the province of a small circle of faculty and students, began to spread throughout the institution. This change was driven by the advent of personal computers in the early 1980s, which provided an alternative to Northern's centralized mainframe machines. This was followed, in 1990–91 by the installation of a fiber-optic network on campus. Over the next four years, most buildings, residence halls included, were connected. This local network was, in turn, linked to the Internet in 1992. The university joined OhioLINK, the Internet consortium of public and private college and university libraries in Ohio in 1995. In 1998 the first distance learning courses were offered in pharmacy.

A new president, Dr. Kendall L. Baker, joined the university in August 1999 as its tenth president. Energetic and outgoing, he and his wife, Toby, ate their meals in McIntosh Dining Hall with students in August and lived in the Freed Center until moving into temporary housing. Dr. Baker met with focus groups of faculty, students, and staff across campus working on health plan questions, the budget, salary plans, and their visions for the university. Inaugurated in December 1999, Baker did what ONU presidents do: get to know the ONU people on and off campus, continue and update the program and building plans of the university, and develop new goals. In 2000, an update of the campus master plan is under way, an undergraduate honors program will begin in 2000–01, new student apartments are being constructed for fall 2000, new initiatives are being explored by all colleges.

Although courses, methods of instruction, faculty and staff, and students may change, the constants at Ohio Northern University are close student-faculty relationships, Lehr's practical (practice) learning, a commitment to values and service, the NCAA Division III ideal of the "scholar-athlete," and institutional flexibility. The more Ohio Northern University changes, the more it remains the same.

Suggested Reading

George Eugene Belch, "Tempered by Crisis: The Centennial Year History of Ohio Northern University" (Ohio Northern University, 1971); Sara Lehr Kennedy, *H. S. Lehr and His School: A Story of the Private Normal Schools*, 2d ed. (Ohio Northern University, 1983); Henry Solomon Lehr, "History of the O.N.U.," edited by Kelly A. Wacker, foreword by Paul M. Logsdon (Ohio Northern University, 1994); Edie Mae Hamilton-Herrel, "Heritage of a Noble Quest" (Ohio Northern University, 1997); Charles A. Heller Jr., ed., "Strength for the 21st Century" (Ohio Northern University, 1998); *Ohio Northern Magazine and Alumni Journal* 1–60 (1940–2000).

Ohio Wesleyan University

Continuity and Change

RICHARD W. SMITH

In a hymn written for an English school, Charles Wesley urged the union of "knowledge with vital piety." His words had broad implications for Methodist higher education. As the Republic matured, thoughtful members of the Methodist Episcopal Church recognized the growing wealth and social status the denomination was acquiring. Aspiring young Methodists who could help shape the Republic needed "collegiate instruction, without imbibing ideas at variance with the religion of their fathers."

The Ohio and Kentucky Methodist Conferences founded the first, semipermanent Methodist College in Augusta, Kentucky, in 1821. The principal factor that weakened Augusta was the slavery controversy. By the end of the 1830s the Ohio Methodist constituency was ready for a new start in collegiate education. Edward Thomson, a noted cleric, issued a strong call for a college in 1840. The next year the Reverend Adam Poe rallied the town of Delaware behind the cause. The Mansion House, formerly a hotel, was purchased and made available to the Church. During the ensuing deliberations Charles Elliott, of Cincinnati, led the movement in the Ohio Conference to accept the offer. In 1842 Ohio Wesleyan was chartered as a university. The document, presumably written by the Reverend Joseph Trimble, stated that it "is forever to be conducted on the most liberal principles, accessible to all religious denominations and designed for the benefit of our citizens in general."

One observer wrote in 1844 that Northern and Southern elements were pouring into the Ohio Valley "forming there a third type that will . . . remold American civilization." It was, indeed, a good environment for the fledgling school. The trustees first reorganized an academy that met in the Mansion House. In November 1844 Edward Thomson, the first president, convened the faculty and the students to inaugurate the college division of the university with 110 students. The first college degree was awarded to William Godman in 1846. He studied calculus, four

Ohio Wesleyan Univesity, 1860

sciences, and the classical languages; other courses included political economy, German, logic, and mental philosophy. Godman memorized books for daily recitations. He wrote no original papers.

President Thomson moved promptly to broaden the program to meet the diverse interests and perceived needs in the Buckeye State and by 1849 opened college preparatory and general scientific divisions, both two-year programs. To enhance the school's appeal to prospective students, the 1850 and 1851 catalogs included an etching of Elliott Hall (the Mansion House). A rising reputation and cheap tuition vouchers increased enrollment to 511 by 1854. Wesleyan was competitive as three new buildings were constructed. There were three literary societies on campus, and some members interacted with Louis Kossuth, the Hungarian statesman, during an 1852 visit. The first fraternity, Beta Theta Pi, arrived on campus in 1853. Seven years later the academy enrolled 35 percent of the students, the preparatory unit 16 percent, the scientific division 12 percent, and the college 37 percent.

Everyone involved in the new enterprise was determined to make the Methodist mentality and value system a reality within the accepted liberal arts framework of the antebellum period. Accordingly, the only layman of professorial rank was ordained after five years of teaching. The 1844 catalog declared, "The government of the Institution will be . . . parental . . . [seeking to cultivate] . . . in the student a taste for intellectual and virtuous habits." The university thereby accepted a broad custodial role over the youthful students. They attended daily chapel services and Sunday services in a Delaware church. Thomson's Sabbath Lectures were regarded as challenging and inspirational. Copies of the *Western Christian Advocate* were available. The student rules included a ban on smoking in a university building. Within weeks of the opening of the college, however, a student threw a wash basin down a three-floor stairwell in Elliott Hall. At least two cases of intoxication surfaced. The custodial role, obviously, would require alertness.

Most students knew the history of Bishop Francis Asbury's battle to abolish slavery in the denomination. In 1844 acrimony over the issue led to the division of Methodism into the Methodist Episcopal Church and the Methodist Episcopal Church, South. At Ohio Wesleyan, President Thomson and Frederick Merrick, professor of natural science, were strong, vocal antislavery men. During the antebellum years only seventy slave state students enrolled, and fifty-six of them were from the Border South, where the moral position of the Methodist Episcopal Church had support. Student debates regarding the overriding issue of the era largely reflected Northern political lines.

The assault on Fort Sumter galvanized patriotic action in the university and the town. Nevertheless, two local clergymen, one a former member of the Board of Visitors, were dismissed for opposition to the Union war effort. On the campus, Peace Democrats were subdued as the Unionists erected a flag and conducted drills. During the course of the war, approximately 300 students served in Federal uniforms. These men, including several generals, were scattered through dozens of regiments. Wesleyan also sent two generals to the Confederate army.

During the savage Battle of Franklin, Confederate brigadier general Ortho Strahl (withdrew 1856) was killed. Capt. M. B. Clason (Class of 1858) expressed the idealism of the period in a letter to his wife: "We are just as determined as the South are desperate. God cannot permit this contest to be a failure. . . . His Providence . . . must work for the destruction of a people who wish to perpetuate . . . human bondage." He died at Kennesaw Mountain a few days later.

During the war the Zetagathian Society removed Jefferson Davis from its membership. Enrollment fell to 360 in 1863, and a faculty salary cut was effected. That year the Ohio gubernatorial contest was the Union's most vituperative wartime election. In that atmosphere the students disagreed on the significance of the Battles at Shiloh and Stones River. Unionists and Peace Democrats vociferously defended their positions. With victory assured, President Abraham Lincoln wired the Unionist leader, "Ohio has saved the Union." Later, Lincoln's death brought overwhelming grief to the campus.

Despite wartime turmoil and financial difficulty, the university had weathered the Republic's greatest crisis. As an institution grounded on Christian verities most persons thought that continuity would be the theme for the future. One wonders how often the leadership considered Heraclitus's maxim, "The only constant is change." In 1867 a student newspaper, the *Western Collegian*, was started. No one recorded the interplay between the genteel tradition and the behavior of the veterans. For the students the rigid academic routine was mitigated in the rooms of the literary societies. As early as 1853, the Chrestomathian Society had 1,700 books while the university library had 3,000. It was a heady environment where ideas were exchanged and papers written for presentation. The students formally debated such topics as, "Was Hamlet Insane?" "Should the Government Own the Railroads?" and "Are the Probabilities against a Perpetual Republic?"

The smoldering criticism of the social fraternities ignited a battle. In 1870 there were 417 students enrolled in the university when President Frederick Merrick unsuccessfully sought to ban the fraternities. During the struggle a science building had to be finished with endowment money. Later, the rivalry between the fraternity men and the independents intensified and became a fixed part of campus life.

Another turning point for the institution was union with the Ohio Wesleyan Female College. Founded in 1853, it was located on a hill less than a mile from Elliott Hall. On the Monnett campus, named for a student donor, Mary Monnett, a mix of courses in the traditional subjects and the arts was offered. Two of the diplomas awarded were Mistress of Liberal Arts and Mistress of Music. Clionian was the first of several active literary societies. There were 210 women registered in 1870. After the war Elizabeth Hyer, a student, recalled, "We caught the new responsibility assumed by women for reform and social welfare." Regional and local pressure for coed instruction forced university leaders to gradually move toward union. The *Collegian* declared the merger question, "A hackneyed theme as early as 1870." Opposition among university leaders such as Merrick continued until 1877 when Charles Payne secured an affirmative vote as the new president.

The union enriched the institution with the addition of Schools of Art and Music. During 1877–78 five women taught in various disciplines in the university. Even before the merger, male collegians chose either German or French for their programs. In line with the Harvard model electives were introduced, especially in the Bachelor of Literature degree. Off campus, several fraternities acquired houses that gave more stability to the system. A cultural anomaly appeared during those years. Greek oratory and theater were studied in the original language. In 1882 the faculty approved an intercollegiate oratorical contest. The students, nevertheless, were forbidden to see theater productions at the city auditorium in 1884. Eleven men were suspended for doing just that the next year. One year later the *Transcript*, the student paper, asked about "the naughty students who attended theater this week." The rule was not enforced.

The theater question was but one facet of a complex problem. The Methodist concern for piety and morality was well defined. It was a constant challenge for the institution to make an appropriate response to incidents involving that code. Dancing, cosmetics, and other particulars were more easily regulated than was the use of alcohol and tobacco. Reasonable flexibility evolved as the response to both "undesirable" drugs. In reality there was less drunken behavior than might be expected in the period. The temperance movement "made sense" to a vast majority of students.

In 1871 Merrick hired the first Ph.D., but departmental specialization came twenty years later with President James Bashford. Physics separated from chemistry and geology from biology, while history, Bible, economics, and English were created. The new pedagogy mandated classroom lectures with supplementary laboratory or library assignments. Bashford, who had examined German universities, endorsed the innovations. They were implemented as the senior faculty retired. Modernity necessitated new buildings, and four were constructed.

Dr. Bashford was the embodiment of Christian liberalism. The faculty was urged to teach evolution, and he began to consult them on appointments. His administration apparently enrolled the first African Americans. He also started a drive for $5 million to facilitate the "providential work of the twentieth century," but the campaign was thwarted by the 1893 depression.

The first women who studied in this combined institution were overwhelmingly native daughters. The earliest to receive the B.A. degree were Inez White (Class of 1879) and Kate Blair (Class of 1880). In 1891, of the 1,156 undergraduates on campus, 47 percent were in the college, 2 percent in a normal program, and 10 percent in music and art. "Forced to recognize" the inadequate schooling of many, the university trained 41 percent of the total in the college preparatory division. By 1896 the school was sensitive to the "competition of the state universities."

The call to religious service was strong at Wesleyan. The domestic ministry attracted over 450 men by 1900. Before 1861 a Female College Preceptress was the first to undertake a foreign missionary career. Later Galdino Gutierrez (Class of 1888) returned to Mexico. Fuchow, China, was the center of work for several graduates. Sarkis Yenovkian (Class of 1891), a pastor in Maras, Turkey, came for a degree. A Japanese graduate went home to teach in a Methodist school. As a medical doctor serving the Korean royal family, Horace Allen (Class of 1881) had an unequaled impact. The first Protestant missionary there, he organized the first hospital and made "possible Korea's first railroads, . . . waterworks, . . . city lighting and . . . modern mine."

Organized intramural baseball appeared at Ohio Wesleyan very early. The popular sport moved to an intercollegiate level in the 1880s. When the Eastern game of football swept into vogue, the faculty approved an intercollegiate football schedule in 1890. Although women initially were limited to croquet, basketball for both women and men arrived in the 1890s. The women displayed both their athletic and dramatic skills in 1896 by transforming traditional May Day revelry into Monnett Day. The celebrations, which soon included a queen, became a meaningful point of identity for campus women.

In 1894, when Wesleyan celebrated her fiftieth anniversary, there was ample reason for pride in alumni accomplishments. Worthy of note were Amos Dolbear (Class of 1866), who may have invented a telephone before Alexander Graham Bell; John White (Class of 1868), professor of Greek at Harvard; and Lucy Booth (Class of 1881), the first woman to earn a Ph.D. When former president Payne addressed the crowd, he was positive about the Christian college. It was the leader in producing "the [person] prepared for complete living, the symmetrical [person]," individuals who will not "leave society as they find it."

In 1904 Bashford became a bishop, and Herbert Welch was named president. The period from 1900 to 1917 was one of enhancement and splendor. Two buildings, including an innovative swimming pool, gave Wesleyan superior facilities. The hallmark of the faculty was personalized mentoring of the students. The mixture of required courses and specialized electives formed a strong curriculum. Student creativity and independence were enhanced so that the literary societies declined and eventually ceased to exist. In 1913 there were 1,094 undergraduate students enrolled; that year the faculty abolished the Greek requirement. The percentage of women taking the B.A. degree did not change in the next four years. The preparatory division was phased out in 1916. In a sharp break with tradition the faculty allowed the student council to handle all charges of academic cheating from 1911 to 1931. The Women's Student Government Association created in 1914 gave women limited control over their own rules. The administration established a faculty and staff pension plan in 1912.

Wesleyan was in an eminent position. Phi Beta Kappa came to the campus in 1907. E. R. Lloyd (1905) and E. E. Lincoln (1909) were named Rhodes Scholars. The university led the nation with fourteen graduate students at Harvard in 1905. The traditional strength in pre-law and medicine was accelerated. Four persons had served as governors of states. Two alumni were elected to the United States Senate, and one of them, Charles Fairbanks (Class of 1872), served as vice president under President Theodore Roosevelt. Myron Herrick (Irr. Prep. 1875) served as ambassador to France. Eight men became bishops in the church. The European manager of the United Press was Edward Keen (Class of 1891). Throughout the years more students had entered education than any other profession. In addition to public school teachers, several college presidents and distinguished faculty persons were graduates of the institution.

In 1916 Welch was made a bishop. John Hoffman quickly assumed the presidential mantle. The new president was a football booster who arranged in 1916 for the first football homecoming. Three months later the *Transcript* reported "strong alumni sentiment" for a new sports program that would "bring honor to Ohio Wesleyan."

Hoffman was still adjusting to his new position when President Woodrow Wilson and the Congress took the nation into World War I. In the excitement, some thought near-hysteria, many coeds turned to Red Cross work, and student drill teams were formed. About 850 Wesleyanites joined the service. Much as was the case in the Civil

War, the men were scattered in various units of the service. The old 4th Ohio, as the 166th, in the 42d Division, was commanded by Col. Benson Hough (withdrew 1898), who led the unit to an excellent fighting record. There were nearly eighty Wesleyanites in the 147th Field Hospital, 37th Division. It was active in supporting the Meuse-Argonne offensive. Transferred to the Ypres area in late October 1918, William Frazier (Class of 1921) found it "the most dismal spot in the world . . . desolation everywhere." The war claimed the lives of eighteen men. A leading civilian administrator was Leon Marshall (Class of 1900) on the Council of National Defense.

In the fall of 1917 there were 550 women on campus compared to 353 men. The wartime years were difficult. Mobilization hurt the stability of the fraternities and disrupted many extracurricular activities. In the crusade "to end all wars," an anti-Teutonic spirit swept across the land and the campus. A national drive to project unity muted the pro-German sentiment. It was a short period of dislocation, for by the summer of 1919 all could anticipate a return to normalcy.

The postwar university asserted that "it is in no sense sectarian." Under a liberal charter "it seeks to be Christian in spirit and policy." In the period before Pearl Harbor the implementation of that policy brought several new departures. The student body was increasingly urban in orientation and included more non-Methodists. A major concession to the rising secularism was made when Sunday church attendance was no longer required. Veterans, as one might expect, did not appreciate traditional student rituals. The war also advanced women's rights. In response to the Nineteenth Amendment many coeds were active in the presidential campaigns of the 1920s. The suffrage triumph, the passage of the Prohibition amendment and other social currents gave campus women a sense of power and achievement. A seismic break with established customs occurred when coeds began to bob their hair and wear short skirts. New dorms, one built with endowment funds, provided fine accommodations. Sororities, which had been quashed in 1886, were brought to the campus in 1923, with Alpha Delta Pi the first to arrive.

After the war students and alumni avidly supported intercollegiate athletics. Football victories raised the morale of the university, especially the wins over Syracuse and Michigan. The Battling Bishops were also strong in basketball. Both sports brought out large crowds and zany cheers. Women at that time were particularly active in seven intramural sports.

In academic matters Robert Smith (Class of 1920) won a Rhodes. Dean William Smyser offered a curriculum based on "a new . . . educational theory." The central concerns were "the life needs . . . of the students." New departments such as political science, zoology, and psychology were welcomed. Business-related work attracted greater interest. Among alumni Bishop McConnell (Class of 1894) headed an investigation of the steel industry. The work of the Interchurch World Movement led to the abandonment of the twelve-hour day. President Hoffman launched an important capital campaign. The university, however, collected only one quarter of the $8 million goal. The shortfall destroyed plans for two essential buildings, a men's dormitory and a social science hall. Nevertheless, a stadium was started with a designated gift, but the total project required endowment money.

After President Hoffman's resignation in 1928, the circumstances of the Great Depression carried the university to the brink of collapse. Endowment values fell and President Edmund Soper struggled as undergraduate enrollment plunged from the high figure of 1,925 in 1926 to 1,295 in 1933. Faculty lore held that nearly every time Professor Rollin Walker prayed at a faculty meeting a salary cut ensued. Book and equipment acquisitions were slashed, but every discipline made the best of the situation. Cultural and sporting events gave relief from the gray mood. For many women smoking was all the rage. At least one full-pay student was allowed to return regardless of grades. In 1935 student leaders cited "liberalism and constructive advancement" as the themes for the year. Soper's insistence on formal faculty dinners elicited a mixed response. The despair was softened by the New Deal's National Youth Administration, which provided money for student assistance. By 1937 there was a measure of recovery noticeable, a circumstance which made it less worrisome for President Soper to retire.

When President Herbert Burgstahler and his assistant, Abbie Probasco, arrived in 1939, the continued recovery seemed to warrant a grand centennial celebration. The Sino-Japanese war and the early stages of World War II, did not affect the university to any great degree. Isolation and intervention were seriously debated, but the fighting was "over there." Some junior faculty became disenchanted as they were forced to bargain with Probasco over salaries. Simultaneously, there was an affirmative consensus on the issue of curriculum revision. In 1941–42 the faculty implemented the Havinghurst Report, which established the Humanities Books courses and abolished the foreign language requirement. Meant to be progressive, the latter action seemed more in line with isolationist sentiments.

Pearl Harbor produced a moderated excitement. There was no dissension on campus, and there was grim determination to make a contribution. The school felt it proper to proceed with centennial plans. It netted 70 percent of a $1 million campaign goal. In the spring of 1942 the Federal Council of Churches, guided by Walter Van Kirk (Class of 1917), and the university sponsored an international forum on the churches and peace. Some 375 delegates helped marshal opinion for work toward economic and social improvements and a United Nations.

More than 5,000 people attended the June centennial festivities. In the major address Lord Halifax, the British ambassador, reviewed John Wesley's "inspiration . . . to the humanitarian movement," especially "the abolition of slavery." He stressed the need to defeat the "evil madness now loose in Nazi Germany." It was not known that, as foreign minister, he advocated a settlement with the Axis in the spring of 1940.

Wesleyan contributed to the Allied war effort about 2,650 men and women. Those in combat fought in every theater of the war, while Wesleyan women were active in several of the services. A Navy Cross, eleven Silver Stars, and twenty-six Distinguished Flying Crosses were won. No statistics exist indicating service to the Axis powers, but a later graduate who had served as a Japanese office gave the library peace bell to the university. Ninety-two alumni became casualties. On the home front, too, Wesleyanites contributed significantly to the total effort.

During the war academic standards were not eased. In 1945 news of President Franklin Roosevelt's death stunned the campus. The postwar environment was marked by new attitudes. Planning a career in industry became popular. In 1948 Arthur Flemming (Class of 1927) became president.

Aided by federal legislation known popularly as the GI Bill, returning veterans, many of whom were married, immersed themselves in their courses. The faculty appreciated the dedication. In 1953 research revealed that between 1946 and 1951 Wesleyan was not as strong as De Pauw, Wooster, or Oberlin in the per capita production of Ph.D.s or advanced doctoral students. The data were in line with the varied career goals of the graduates.

When the question of race splintered the Democratic party in 1948, the issue became a central one for the university. In 1948 an interracial fraternity, Beta Sigma Tau, was formed. An African American attendant was in the queen's court at one Le Bijou dance. The number of black students began to rise. The Greek system removed restrictive clauses in keeping with a trustee resolution. Branch Rickey (Class of 1904), meanwhile, integrated professional baseball.

In other developments, the 1953 catalog stated that students at Wesleyan had an "opportunity for growth in religious thought and life." The YWCA remained a vital organization until the late 1970s. Continuing a thirty-year trend, however, the YMCA lost much of its influence. President Flemming initiated a program for academic- and student-orientated buildings. Fraternity pressure limited the dining facilities in the first men's dormitories. A third building had complete facilities. An innovative student union became the center for all types of campus and alumni activities. The president strengthened the faculty committee system. A funded pension plan was available after 1951. In 1953 William McCoullough was named a Rhodes Scholar. As for finances, the university reported an endowment of $5.6 million in 1955.

When another armed conflict, the Korean War, took students into the armed services, it was closely monitored by those on the campus. Three Wesleyan men died in the bitter fighting, which reaffirmed the college's ties to that nation. In 1956 the *Transcript* had to report that the school had not received a Ford Foundation "accomplishment grant" for faculty improvement. Flemming left the university in 1958 to serve in the Eisenhower cabinet. Five persons have since held the office: Dr. David Lockmiller, 1959–61; Dr. Elden Smith (Class of 1932), 1962–68; Dr. Thomas

Wenzlau (Class of 1950), 1969–84; Dr. David Warren, 1984–93; and Dr. Thomas Courtice, 1994. During those years the transformation in the lives of Americans defies complete understanding. No one associated with this Protestant school could have anticipated the multiple dimensions of the new age.

Flemming and Dean Clarence Ficken developed a genuine dialogue between the administration and the faculty personnel committee. When President Lockmiller turned to "intuition" in making personnel decisions, the faculty successfully resisted. The critical function of shared institutional government was preserved. Changes in student life came as the GIs and their spouses made social drinking acceptable, a new tradition the university finally recognized. Another social sea change took place as postwar attitudes toward casual sexual relations eventually led to the sexual revolution. Indeed, factors such as greater student diversity and increased secularism on campus led to the abandonment of required chapel in 1965. On the academic side there was a restoration of the foreign-language requirement. The centrality of the library was recognized and a new structure was erected. During those years Wesleyan students won twenty-four Woodrow Wilson Fellowships.

Wesleyan continued its visiting lecturer tradition, which over the years hosted such notables as Mark Twain, Jane Addams, Booker T. Washington, Eleanor Roosevelt, and William McNeill. Some of the artists featured as part of the music series were: Madame Schumann-Heink, Paul Robson, Isaac Stern, and Vladmir Ashkenazy. Students and visitors waited in line to obtain seats for Paul Tillich's Merrick Lectures. The first mock political convention on campus was held in 1884 (Blaine vs. Cleveland). In the twentieth century, political speakers such as Senators Robert Taft and Margaret C. Smith broadened student horizons.

The college was firm with the first students to use "street drugs." However, it soon backed down. It was, perhaps, no more of a turning point than earlier decisions regarding other drugs. The university had learned not to expect perfection, for it could not be attained.

The missionary tradition of the nineteenth century was refocused. In addition to an extremely high Peace Corps participation ratio, many students worked in the civil rights crusade. The national "student unrest" movement came to Wesleyan and was centered on the Vietnam War, the ROTC unit, and curricular revisions. Vehement arguments over the war rocked the college and the town. ROTC was continued after a debate and vote by all concerned, part of the spirited student and faculty antiwar agitation. The Peace Accord of 1973 left an unresolved division over the nation's role in collective security actions. Few of the course proposals occasioned by the war were accepted. The close town-gown relations soured, however, leaving the college's liberalism as a sore point for much of the city.

The Vietnam War involved scores of Wesleyanites. They participated with dedication to the cause; twelve died in the fighting. Amidst an essential continuity, the postwar changes are recognized in our increasingly homogenized society. The institution surrendered its custodial controls of student life. Currently, student misconduct goes to well-organized student courts and, when necessary, to the city courts. Women's studies and gender issues are being taught and addressed. The campus has a House of Black Culture and a Black World Studies program. In 1979 the university declared, "Consistent with our Methodist tradition, Ohio Wesleyan encourages concern for all religious and ethical issues."

Every administration encounters the Sisyphean task of keeping buildings and equipment up to date. From the start the faculty had an interest in publishing when possible, now it is the prime goal for many. For the period 1920–80 Wesleyan was fifteenth in absolute numbers among 867 liberal arts schools in the production of business leaders. It was seventeenth on the list for Ph.D.s. The diversity among the American students gives the university a cosmopolitan atmosphere, which is enhanced by the large contingent of international students. Independents and the Greeks mingle on campus in an easy fashion. In athletics the women now have twelve varsity teams. The men have won NCAA Division III national championships in football, basketball, and soccer, and the women have won the soccer championship. Nonetheless, student attendance at sports, artistic, and lecture events is spotty. Comparative enrollment figures show 2,277 on the campus in 1963, 1,687 in 1984, and 1,731 in 1994. The endowment was above $120 million as the new millennium began.

Methodist traditions were evident at Ohio Wesleyan throughout the years. The leaders did not insist on superior, scholarly achievement as the highest priority. For over one hundred years the constituency has articulated the "well rounded" theme. Strong academics have been emphasized with the corollary that service in a calling is of a higher order. The graduates are a blend of inspiring teachers and outstanding scholars in diverse specialties, as well as leaders in law, homemaking, social service, and the arts. The institution's alumni files include many nationally and internationally known persons. Their accomplishments include Nobel Prize, Sherwood Rowland (Class of 1948); Lasker Medical Prize, David Smith (Class of 1953); Pulitzer Prize, Philip Meek (Class of 1959) and Susan Headden (Class of 1977); Guggenheim, Edwin Cady (Class of 1939), Ezra Vogel (Class of 1950), Lloyd Gardner (Class of 1956), Sherwood Rowland, and David Smith; education, Helen Kim (Class of 1924); president of Ewa University, Korea, Wilma Player (Class of 1929); religion, James Charlesworth (Class of 1962), Norman Peale (Class of 1921), and Ralph Sockman (Class of 1911); business, Robert Bauman (Class of 1953), George Conrades (Class of 1961), and John Sagan (Class of 1948); law, Charles Ritchey (Class of 1945) and Alice Batchelder (Class of 1964); Asian affairs, Ezra Vogel; radio-TV, Frank Stanton (Class of 1930); American Academy of Arts and Sciences, Sherwood Rowland; medicine, Edward Miller (Class of 1964); politics, Clarence Dill (Class of 1907) and Daniel Koinange (Class of 1929), cabinet minister in Kenya; drama, Ronald Leibman (Class of 1958).

Given all the accomplishments of the institution, Emerson's dictum that "an institution is the lengthened shadow of one man" is too simplistic. At every turn in its history many persons have contributed meaningfully to the success of the school. The work of distinguished and much-admired faculty members cannot be detailed here. Since 1960 the faculty has influenced more policy matters and has, at certain junctures, determined the course of events. The presidents and a small group of trustees and administrators, nonetheless, have been the dominant players since 1844.

The evolution of Wesleyan has resulted in a collegiate entity that would stun its founders. The same would be true should any thoughtful person of the age of Van Buren, Clay, and Calhoun examine contemporary American society. The transformations have come about as the university developed within the changing religious, intellectual, and societal structure of America and the world. Wesleyan's leaders, while seeking divine inspiration, recognized that it was a human institution. Within the limits of their power they encouraged or permitted the shifts and modifications they felt were appropriate.

SUGGESTED READING

Interested readers will find valuable accounts in the following: Edward Nelson, ed., *Fifty Years of History of the Ohio Wesleyan University* (1895); Henry Hubbart, *Ohio Wesleyan's First Hundred Years* (W. B. Conkey, 1943); Barbara Tull, *150 Years of Excellence...* (Ohio Wesleyan University, 1991); Bernard Murchland, ed., *Noble Achievements: the History of Ohio Wesleyan from 1942–1992* (Ohio Wesleyan University, 1991).

Otterbein College

From a Christian Liberal Arts College to a
Comprehensive Liberal Arts College

Elizabeth MacLean

Typical of many small denominational colleges that emerged in the antebellum era, Otterbein College grew out of the perfectionist, egalitarian, and democratic spirit of the Jacksonian Era and Second Great Awakening. Its founders, ministers in the United Brethren Church, designed an institution to benefit the church and the nation. Their objective was a "general diffusion of knowledge," especially among United Brethren parishioners, families of modest means from the farms and villages of central Ohio. Yet they opened the doors of the infant institution to all who had a "thirst for knowledge" and sought "to be useful to their country and age," regardless not only of denomination, but of gender and race as well. Through a common course of study within a Christian environment, combining the classics with a strictly defined social and moral code, Otterbein's founders hoped to "produce strong, accurate thinkers, diligent students, and practical men and women."

Over 150 years later, Otterbein continues to be related to, but no longer is controlled by, the Church. The college today, moreover, imposes no specific social or moral code, but it remains committed to a "value-centered" education. The founders' mission to serve students of modest means, educating them for a practical role in society, also has been maintained, while the egalitarian pledge of inclusiveness has been expanded beyond the founders' imagination.

The college traces its origins to Philip Otterbein, a product of the German Reformed pietistic movement. Otterbein journeyed to America in the mid–eighteenth century just as the first Great Awakening was reaching its height. Among his fellow colonists in Lancaster, Pennsylvania, he preached a message of experiential piety. Otterbein's own transformation into a zealous evangelist owed much to his first encounter with the dynamic revivalist and former Mennonite, Martin Boehm. Pro-

Towers Hall

claiming *"Wir sind Brueder,"* Otterbein joined Boehm in founding the Church of United
Brethren in Christ. The new church embraced the Methodist doctrines of free will
and individual responsibility. Preaching the revivalist message of a loving God, imparting a strict moral code in a warm and tolerant spiritual environment, the brethren followed the settlement of German farmers into the democratic frontier of the
Midwest, expanding church membership into eight states as far west as Iowa.

In the first decades of the nineteenth century, as its organization matured, an effort to establish an institution of higher learning under the auspices of the church
gained momentum among United Brethren ministers in Ohio. Because of its growing
population and central location, Ohio already had been selected for the establishment
of *The Religious Telescope,* the official publication of the church. Located first in Circleville

and later in Dayton, hubs of United Brethren activity, the editorial offices reinforced the status of both villages as prime candidates for the site of a future college.

Just above the state capital in the village of Westerville, however, lay an abandoned eight-acre site, on which stood the two buildings of Blendon Young Men's Seminary, a defunct enterprise of the Methodist Episcopal Church. In the fall of 1846, while shopping in Harvey Coit's clothing store in downtown Columbus, Randal Arnold, a seminary trustee and Westerville citizen, apparently overheard two United Brethren ministers discussing the proposal for a college. Calculating the potential benefit of freeing the budding village of Westerville of the seminary's debt while gaining an institution of higher education, he and his fellow citizens sent the town's most prestigious representatives to exert their influence over the crucial Scioto Conference of United Brethren ministers meeting in Circleville. The effort paid off, as the conference delegates ultimately settled on the Westerville site, purchasing the Blendon property for $1,300, a sum covering the seminary's entire debt.

Success in getting the infant institution off the ground and in overcoming fears of a potential "priest factory" owed much to the determination of two of its first trustees, Bishop William Hanby and the Reverend Lewis Davis. As editor of *The Religious Telescope,* Hanby had guided that vulnerable enterprise through the depression of the late thirties. Circuit riding through the Scioto Valley, he had preached in camp meetings and in the barns and cabins of pioneer farmers. What he saw convinced him of the need for an expansion of educational opportunities among United Brethren parishioners. William Hanby's good friend Lewis Davis then trudged through snow and muddy swamps in the heart of winter to solicit funds to make possible the assumption of the seminary debt. He later would serve as president of the college, providing essential leadership in its first critical years. The Hanby and Davis families eventually built homes next to each other, facing the campus.

Bishop Hanby's life and the principles by which he lived helped set the tone of the college. After escaping indentured servitude under a brutal Pennsylvania master, he had found freedom in pioneer Ohio, where he joined the United Brethren Church and rededicated his life to humanity and to the brotherhood of man. He favored the advancement of women's rights and, supported by what was a nearly unanimous condemnation of slavery among the church brethren, became an active participant in the Underground Railroad.

Given that many colleges and universities in the antebellum era were elitist institutions for sons of the wealthy, Otterbein and other small denominational colleges made a statement of democratic principles by reaching out to the sons and, in the case of first Oberlin and then Otterbein, the daughters of families of moderate means. The motives of the founders, however, were not entirely unselfish displays of democratic spirit. The farms and villages of central Ohio represented the available market in potential students as well as the heart and soul of United Brethren parishioners.

Their enrollment would not only fulfill Hanby's mission of providing them an education "within the influence of the church, but also would benefit the church through the training of ministers. The combination of democratic ideals and demographic realities guided Otterbein's initial enrollment policy and continues to do so today.

William Hanby's dream of an educational institution for United Brethren came to fulfillment as Otterbein University opened its doors in September 1847. The mere handful of students who attended the opening ceremonies, about to receive what for several years to come would be for all practical purposes a preparatory education from an unspecialized faculty of United Brethren generalists, seemed to mock the founders' decision to call the budding enterprise a "university." Although not clearly defined at the time, the title seemed to have a more impressive sound than "college," and it also certified the serious intent of the brethren. By the mid-1850s, Otterbein caught up with similar institutions of higher learning in offering not a university-level graduate program, but an undergraduate classical education in philosophy, history, the classical languages, mathematics, and the natural sciences. Because most students attending college during the nineteenth century trained for the ministry or anticipated careers in teaching, law, politics, or medicine, oratorical skills were also considered a sine qua non. In line with the tradition of other higher institutions of the day, therefore, Otterbein organized male and female literary societies, where contemporary issues became the focus of discussion and debate.

Education of the mind went hand in hand with development of character in a value-centered Christian environment. Before graduating, every student enrolled in what later would be known as a "capstone" course, integrating "Mental and Moral Philosophy" with "Political Economy." Offered by the president of the college, it provided a common experience for all. By applying clearly defined ethical principles to contemporary issues, the course also reflected the fusion of personal and social morality so characteristic of the perfectionist spirit of the Second Great Awakening.

The college's location in a rural environment, free of the city's temptations, was an appropriate setting to facilitate the inculcation of moral values, which seemed all the more critical in light of the still novel experiment in coeducation. A high priority was placed on defining appropriate social relationships between male and female students, with one president going so far as to order that when students of the opposite sex were walking, they should be separated by at least ten feet, as measured by a pole. The United Brethren set taboos on dancing, games of chance, profane language, and the use of alcohol. Instruction in moral values was facilitated by attendance at lectures given by Otterbein faculty, many of whom were United Brethren ministers, by annual revivals, nightly prayers, and mandatory daily chapel.

The strict adherence to traditional moral values undoubtedly contributed, as it had at Oberlin, to the success of the democratic experiment in coeducation. Not only were women accepted at Otterbein from the beginning, constituting over a third of the student body in its first years, but the college's first two graduates were women, and a woman served on the first faculty. Otterbein, however, was not engaged in some feminist venture. Women enrolled in the "Ladies Course," and while some went into teaching after graduation, the majority assumed traditional roles as homemakers. The college insisted that the women students were not only "scholarly" but also, significantly, "just as lady-like" as young women attending traditional female institutions.

Broadening the principles of brotherhood and democracy to students of color proved far less successful, despite the open-door admissions policy of the United Brethren founders. On the most divisive issue of the antebellum era, the abolition of slavery, the church and the college were united in opposition to the "Peculiar Institution"; the United Brethren Church was not torn apart as were some other denominations of the day. Bishop Hanby, whose barn was used as a hiding place for escaped slaves, colluded with his neighbor, President Davis, in helping escapees. Hanby's son, Benjamin, an Otterbein student, memorialized the plight of one runaway earlier given refuge in his family's home. Benjamin Hanby's song "Darling Nelly Gray," upon publication, reached a wide audience in America and Europe.

The college's unified stand broke down, however, as it attempted to fulfill in practice its forward-looking principle of open admissions. Davis's egalitarian policy sparked opposition within the board of trustees, while a prominent Westerville citizen advised that it would be in the president's best interest to leave town. Even before the first student of color enrolled, rumor had it that every student at Otterbein University was "obliged to sign a paper agreeing to accept a colored student as a roommate and sleeping companion." Davis remained steadfast, but when William Hannibal Thomas was admitted in 1859, his presence proved so unwelcome that members of the faculty and trustees offered Thomas financial aid if he would leave Otterbein and enroll at Oberlin, which had opened its doors to students of color some years before. Thomas withdrew before completing a single term. By the end of the century, however, William Henry Fouse, a son of slaves, worked at odd jobs to finance his education, graduated, and went on to a career in teaching. Joseph Hannibal Caulker, a tribal prince from Sierra Leone, where Otterbein-trained United Brethren clergy engaged in missionary work, found a receptive atmosphere at the college. Several members of his family subsequently attended the college. Otterbein's attempt to put its principles of racial democracy into practice, though meager at first, stood out in contrast to the sanctioning of de facto segregation in much of Ohio after 1890.

Otterbein's second moral and social crusade won far more support from Westerville citizens, but ultimately opened both the college and the town to ridicule. The consumption of alcohol among pioneer farmers in the antebellum era had put temperance and prohibition high on the agenda of social concerns not only of

United Brethren ministers, but of a wide spectrum of concerned citizens. Otterbein's founders, not surprisingly, made the use of alcoholic beverages grounds for expulsion. In the 1870s, when one Henry Corbin attempted to establish a saloon in the heart of the town, faculty and students joined forces with Westerville citizens in their most famous crusade to keep the village dry. When peaceful demonstrations and exhortations, vigilance committees, mass meetings, and boycotts failed to dislodge the saloon, anonymous persons demolished the building in a series of explosions. Corbin retaliated by forcing former Bishop Hanby among others to stand trial for the deed, but all were acquitted. Several years later, another explosion destroyed Corbin's second effort to establish a saloon. The culprits were never found, but in 1923, an anonymous individual implicated an Otterbein student of having taken violent action "to save his roommate from the temptation of drink."

Otterbein utilized a variety of other channels to promote its antialcohol message. Women students were active in the Women's Christian Temperance Union, while one president, Reverend Henry Thompson, was a leading figure in the Prohibition party. Westerville's reputation as a dry town was assured when in 1909 the Anti-Saloon League located its headquarters and publishing house there. Reverend Walter Clippinger, who became president of the college that same year, served as president of the Ohio branch of the League. Anti-Saloon leaders built homes within a block of the college on a street later dubbed "Temperance Row." Today some of their residences, ironically, have been refashioned into fraternity houses. The campus and the town, nevertheless, officially remain dry.

During the last decades of the nineteenth century, meanwhile, the benefits offered by small classes and close contact between students and teachers helped Otterbein weather the competition created by the establishment of large land-grant colleges that appealed to a similar market of students. The recurring threat that the trustees might move the college to Dayton finally fizzled at the turn of the century as Otterbein successfully retired its nagging debt and the citizens of Westerville, for their part, went all out to upgrade the town's infrastructure and bring it into the modern world. Equally important was the completion of the college's administration building. With its upper-story stained-glass windows and impressive wood-paneled literary society headquarters, the new centerpiece of the campus, later known as Towers Hall, symbolized the renewed sense of confidence with which the college entered the twentieth century.

Propelled by the forces of modernization generated by the industrial and technological revolutions of the late nineteenth century, Otterbein followed the lead of other institutions in transforming its classical curriculum into a modern liberal arts program with a diverse set of offerings in the sciences, modern languages, English literature, and the fine arts. Traditionally described as a "Christian" institution, the curricular innovations led Otterbein to redefine itself as a "Christian liberal arts" institution. In so doing, it set the tone of its academic mission for much of the next century. Following the lead of Harvard, in 1918 Otterbein adopted the system of majors and minors, and in the twenties, in response to the enormous research being done in the social sciences, moved toward separate departments for each of those disciplines. English literature also expanded to incorporate the discussion of contemporary issues, once the preserve of the literary societies.

Reaffirming its mission to produce students who would play a practical role in society, Otterbein also introduced a set of specialized nondegree programs to better prepare students for careers in teaching and, for the first time, in business. As a result, within a few decades, some 20 percent of graduates were choosing careers in business, while about a third moved into teaching fields. A large contingent (18 percent in 1930) still selected the ministry, while well into the 1940s, some 30 percent to 40 percent went on to graduate school.

In 1917, meanwhile, Otterbein finally had clarified its status as an undergraduate institution by adopting the title of "college." A bare minimum of courses had been offered at the graduate level and the primary responsibility of the faculty had always been teaching rather than research. The lack of specialization, with some faculty teaching across as many as three disciplines, and the limited number holding doctoral degrees (as few as 17 percent in 1930) made that clear. Even after World War II, when President Gordon Howard made known his desire to increase the number of doctorates, salary scales, which fell below other denominational colleges, frustrated efforts to hire new faculty with Ph.D.s. As late as the mid-fifties, fewer than one-quarter of faculty members held doctoral degrees. The college encouraged the completion of doctorates while teaching, but that was a tough assignment, given the heavy teaching responsibilities, which prevented many even from taking advantage of the sabbatical program offered since 1910. The demanding teaching load was said to have caused a few faculty to experience physical suffering and near breakdown.

At the same time, student evaluations, first recorded in the twenties, had propelled faculty into an ongoing campaign to develop creative pedagogical techniques to supplement the traditional lecture format and to introduce what later would be known as "critical-thinking" techniques. Applying those approaches to reach students representing a wide spectrum of academic abilities was then, and remains today, one of the primary challenges faced by Otterbein's teachers. The effort to meet that challenge, along with a faculty-student ratio of one-to-fourteen or better for much of its history, gained Otterbein the reputation of being dedicated to effective teaching and close student-faculty contact.

Meanwhile, successive college presidents, almost all ministers, passed down to each new generation of students the perfectionist and democratic principles of the founders by reiterating their original charge to develop good citizens with a Christian understanding of life and a commitment to unselfish service. Members of the United Brethren Church (renamed the Evangelical United Brethren Church after its 1946 merger with the Evangelical Church) still represented the largest contingent of students, followed closely by Methodists and then Presbyterians, the two denominations that had originally settled the Westerville area. Daily attendance at chapel services remained obligatory until the sixties, with more than five absences per semester constituting grounds for adding hours to the requirements for graduation. The religious—and political—values of most students tended to be conservative, often fundamentalist.

Some students in each generation, meanwhile, attempted to modernize the college's strict social and moral code in the face of a determined and principled opposition on the part of the church and the trustees. In the wake of World War I, as literary societies declined, students pressed for official recognition of fraternities and sororities. The response of the church brethren was hardly surprising. Bishop William Hanby himself had long before denounced secret societies because of their detrimental impact not only on the church, but on the members of such societies as well. The United Brethren argued that fraternities and sororities smacked of elitism and exclusiveness, while also serving as potential havens for immoral conduct. The conflict ultimately was resolved, however, in favor of the students. Accepting the inevitable, the trustees imposed a variety of restrictions and sufficient faculty oversight to satisfy their gravest concerns.

More significant was the impact of the post–World War II wave of GI Bill veterans, who inundated the campus, bringing with them not only a standard of academic excellence (30 out of 39 men on the honor roll in 1946 were veterans) but a far more cosmopolitan social and moral code than practiced by the traditional undergraduates. In 1947, when the alliance of traditional students and veterans succeeded in eliminating the century-old prohibition against dancing, which even the self-proclaimed "modern" generation of the twenties had failed to crack, Walter Winchell felt compelled to broadcast the event on his radio news. The administration, conscious of concerns among some of the trustees, chruchmen, and alumni, kept a watchful eye over the proceedings in the form of four faculty wives serving as chaperones in a new on-campus social center. Less than five years later, the *New York Times* gave some indication of the ongoing liberalization of the social code as it announced that some 150 Otterbein students had inaugurated "the first panty raid" in American history.

Otterbein's original mission to admit students regardless of race made little headway during the first half of the twentieth century, despite the changes in demographic patterns sparked by two world wars. The college had a long way to go before becoming seriously committed not just to the admission, but to the recruitment and retention of students of color. Otterbein's mission to educate women, on the other hand, was far more resolute, although the college, reflecting the values of the larger society, made little effort to address many of the issues related to women's independence and professional aspirations until well after the sixties. During World War I and World War II, women temporarily assumed leadership positions in a variety of student organizations or joined the WACS or Waves. Ultimately, the career of choice of a large percentage of women graduates, however, continued to be homemaking. Reflecting the ongoing transitional status in women's roles in the middle years of the century, the administration, seeking to offset declining enrollments during the Korean War, tried to entice more women to apply by offering new courses, significantly, in home economics and secretarial studies, but also in medical technology, chemical analysis, and radio journalism.

By 1960 Otterbein had weathered the multiple crises of the Great Depression, two world wars, and the Korean War. In each case, enrollments had plunged and faculty salaries had suffered. Nevertheless, the college had always bounced back as had the enrollment figures. By the end of the fifties, some 1,200 students attended the college, the overwhelming majority of whom were traditional undergraduates. The campus infrastructure also had steadily expanded. Despite federal grants and a modest endowment, however, the college remained heavily dependent on student fees and the financial support of the church.

Hoping to take advantage of the potentially huge enrollments anticipated as a result of the post–World War II baby boomers reaching college age in the 1960s, Otterbein undertook the most radical change in its academic program and governance structure since the end of the Gilded Age. Determined to establish a new level of academic excellence, the college reevaluated and ultimately redefined its entire curriculum, the requirements for graduation, and the calendar itself. It eliminated the traditional semester system in which students registered for six or seven courses meeting two or three times a week, and adopted instead a new "3/3 plan," based on three ten-week terms, which allowed students to focus more intensively on only three courses at a time, each meeting five days a week.

To upgrade the liberal arts program, the faculty introduced a totally new set of common interdisciplinary courses in the humanities, social sciences, arts, and natural sciences. Required for graduation, what later became known as the Integrative Studies courses, became the central core of every student's program beyond the individual major. Based on a common theme, the nature of man, the I.S. Program expanded on the original mission of Otterbein's founders to educate the mind within a value-centered framework in order to better prepare students "for a responsible role in society." Through a four-year program of progressively complex interdisciplinary courses, students, engaging in dialogue with their professors, would enlarge their awareness and understanding of the world and of the diversity of human nature and experience. Instituted in 1968, the Integrative Studies Program won national recognition and established a pattern followed by other institutions.

The new level of dialogue between faculty and students generated by the I.S. courses expanded into other areas, producing a major reorganization of the college's governance structure. At the heart of the reorganization was the new College Senate, which included representatives of the trustees, the administration, faculty, and students. With the exception of the board of trustees, which retained final power over all decisions, the College Senate had, and continues to have, the last word on all curricular proposals and a wide range of issues concerning the college's social and academic life. Equally significant, since 1968, students have served with faculty on every important college committee, ultimately including even the personnel committee and the board of trustees. At a critical time when many institutions were facing multiple crises generated by the controversial issues of the late sixties, the new governance structure, singularly democratic and inclusive in nature, went a long way in institutionalizing channels of communication among the various constituencies in the college. Winning national recognition, it succeeded, according to observers, in part because of what was seen as a traditionally friendly environment, but perhaps as well because of the existence of a relatively homogeneous student population, the overwhelming majority of whom shared the same social and political values.

Faculty development, considered a crucial facet of the effort to achieve a new level of academic excellence, proceeded meanwhile at a slow but steady pace. In response to increased enrollments generated by the baby boom, additional faculty positions were created, giving the college a complement of ninety-four full-time faculty by 1969–70, but still under 40 percent held doctoral degrees. At that time, on the other hand, ten-week sabbaticals every seven terms became a requirement for every tenure-track faculty member. While most at first used the time to design and modify courses, ultimately the mandatory program provided opportunities also for research and writing. With the exception of the interdisciplinary Integrative Studies Program, the specialization process proceeded apace as nearly all faculty taught courses in only one discipline. Teaching loads, however, remained heavy, and despite efforts to raise compensation, salaries continued to rank only in the middle range when compared to other denominational institutions in Ohio.

Ultimately as significant as the reforms in the academic program and governance structure were the changes inaugurated in the relationship between the Evangelical United Brethren Church and the college. In 1968, the E.U.B. Church united with the Methodist Church to form the United Methodist Church. For over a century Otterbein had been one of only six colleges sponsored by the church, and it had held a special place among those colleges as the first institution of higher learning established by the United Brethren. As of 1968, however, Otterbein became one among seventy-seven other institutions under the Methodist umbrella, four of which also were in Ohio (Ohio Wesleyan, Ohio Northern, Baldwin-Wallace, and Mount Union). Over the next three decades both the involvement of the church and its financial commitment would progressively decline, fewer church members would serve on the board of trustees, the proportion of United Methodist Church members in the student population would decrease, and fewer graduates would choose the ministry as a career. Otterbein continued to describe itself as a "Christian Liberal Arts" college, but after 1968 it was only "related to . . . not controlled" by the church.

If the church's institutional role was on the decline, the ideal of brotherhood and the spirit of service, so much a part of the founders' mission, was not. Following the pattern established during World War II, when many students (if not Westerville as a whole) welcomed Japanese American students from the internment camps on campus, Otterbein students in the sixties sought opportunities to experience a multicultural environment through study abroad, through friendships with the small contingent of foreign students and black students on campus, or by enrolling in Otterbein's first course in Contemporary Black Thought. Black students took the initiative to improve relations among the races at the college through membership in a mutual support organization known as SOUL.

The ideal of service had been in evidence over previous decades in a variety of Christian umbrella associations on campus, which had long focused on community service, the most notable being the Otterbein branch of the YMCA organized before the turn of the century. Such efforts found new avenues of expression in the sixties. While the vast majority of students remained politically and socially conservative, the civil rights movement and the social idealism of the sixties may have been a catalyzing agent for many and certainly for a determined activist minority (some of whom later joined the faculty), who increasingly raised concerns about contemporary issues, welcomed civil rights and environmental speakers on campus, and took the lead in an array of new student-sponsored, service organizations, focused primarily on the inner city. The best known included SCOPE (Students Concerned Over People Everywhere), the Community Explorations Project, and the Concord Project, a phone-counseling service, still in existence today, dealing with a wide array of problems, including drugs. That so many graduates in the sixties chose service-oriented careers (over 60 percent selecting teaching and another 3 percent government service or the Peace Corps), while under 10 percent chose business, may have been a reflection of the spirit of those years.

The baby boomers, meanwhile, had continued to push enrollments up. By the end of the seventies, however, enrollments leveled off at 1,680 and in the early eighties declined by another hundred students. The bonanza was over, just as the college was coping with the withdrawal of the federal government's largesse. Left in a critical financial state, Otterbein was forced into a major reassessment that, in turn, led in the early 1990s to a redefinition of the college's century-old liberal arts mission.

In place of the traditional undergraduate student, a potentially huge market was increasingly evident in the adult population of suburban Ohio, especially in the population of women, seeking to complete their undergraduate education or to obtain degrees in professional fields. How to tap into that market while maintaining the best of Otterbein's traditions became the key question. Westerville's transition from a provincial rural town into a modern suburb in an area of central Ohio that was growing by leaps and bounds gave Otterbein tremendous potential to take advantage of the new market by combining a modernized and more professionally oriented curriculum with the college's traditional drawing cards of small classes and close faculty-student contact. So concluded the new president, Brent DeVore, and many administration and faculty colleagues. Adults seeking an opportunity to continue their education, but hesitant to take the plunge after years out of school, might find what generations of rural undergraduates had earlier discovered. A small institution with an attractive campus, still located in a semirural setting, Otterbein could serve as a psychological as well as geographical mean between the suburban and metropolitan worlds.

Efforts to tap the adult market had begun as early as 1975, when the Adult Degree Program had been established, offering a Bachelor of Science in Nursing. In the next two decades, the program significantly expanded with the establishment of Weekend College and new degrees at the master's level in nursing, teaching, education, and, more recently, business administration. Enrollments averaging more than 400 nontraditional graduate students in the last few years suggest the level of success of the new programs. Inaugurated in 1996, the Professional Accelerated Continuing Education program (PACE) offered six new undergraduate majors, in business administration, organizational communication, business psychology, human resources management, leadership and the liberal arts, and management and leadership. By 1998 PACE enrollments reached 103, nearly doubling to 205 by the fall of 2000. Keyed to the needs of adults with full-time jobs or full-time family responsibilities, the program's flexible scheduling on evenings and weekends allowed students, literally, to set their own pace. For 150 years Otterbein had been a campus for traditional undergraduate students. The demographic changes in the student body at the end of the century, with some 37 percent of students in the nontraditional categories, constituted one of the most significant developments in the college's history

Meanwhile, the college applied a similar prescription to the traditional undergraduate market. While professional programs in education, pre-law, and pre-med had long been offered, to reach the expanding suburban population, programs in a variety of new areas were created, including equine science, public relations, broadcasting, and sports medicine. Enrollments of traditional undergraduate students rose from 1,114 in 1984 to an all-time high of 1,832 in the fall of 2000. Today's freshman class of 550 constitutes the largest in Otterbein's history. Not surprisingly, programs such as accounting, communications, sport and wellness management, and computer science have seen some of the most substantial increases, while business, education, and nursing continue to attract large numbers of majors. Ironically, the Integrative Studies Program, intended originally to upgrade the liberal arts, facilitated indirectly the creation of more professional programs, as courses in the interdisciplinary liberal arts required for graduation constituted less than a third of a student's curriculum.

The official redefinition of Otterbein's mission statement came in 1993 in the midst of the transition. The college reaffirmed its traditional status as a "private, church-related, four-year coeducational" institution, but broadened its dedication to "the liberal arts as 'the broad base of learning,'" to include "professional education at Baccalaureate and Master's levels." No longer defined as a Christian liberal arts college, Otterbein identified itself as a "comprehensive liberal arts college." In fact, the college had always had an undefined mission to provide professional programs. What had once been a limited set of offerings to prepare students for careers in law, medicine, the ministry, teaching, and eventually business, had simply mushroomed into the diverse set of offerings today.

The choice of careers by graduates in recent years illustrates the change. In 2000, for example, nearly half of Otterbein's graduates chose business-related careers, while only 17 percent went into teaching and less than 1 percent selected the law or the ministry. Some 23 percent entered careers in science or health-related fields, the social services, or government, while 6 percent, benefiting from Otterbein's renowned theater and music programs, continued in those fields. About 12 percent went on to graduate school, primarily in psychology, sports medicine, and health education. A majority of graduates ultimately chose to take an advanced degree, most often in business or professional fields.

Certainly the economic prosperity of the nineties and recent increases in the population of eighteen-year-olds have had much to do with the college's positive enrollment picture, which today is more than 3,000 students. Nevertheless, the success of the college's new mission that has ranked Otterbein nationally for ten consecutive years among the top ten comprehensive liberal arts colleges—as well as "one of the 'Best Buys in Independent Higher Education'"—owes much to a multipronged effort to attract students that has emphasized modernization while preserving Otterbein's heritage. The creation of new professional programs has been the most visible part of that effort, but those programs alone cannot account for the record high retention rates of over 92 percent of upperclassmen. What has accompanied those programs has been equally important.

At the top of the list stands the four-year Integrative Studies Program, expanded to include a course in non-Western cultures. Separate from, but closely aligned with I.S., is a new team-taught senior-year capstone in contemporary issues. Through the I.S. Program, as well as the strengthening of the liberal arts majors, many of which represent the backbone of the program, the liberal arts has remained a vital part of every student's college experience from freshmen through senior year. In recent years history and political science, significantly, have seen some of the largest increases in enrollments.

Meanwhile, flexible scheduling has benefited traditional as well as nontraditional students. Upgraded meal plans and modernization of residence facilities, including the establishment of Otterbein's first apartment complex, have made the campus environment more attractive to undergraduates, while the construction of Roush Hall, the college's first multipurpose academic building, has benefited the entire campus community.

The college's traditional emphasis on good teaching, still the primary factor in hiring and promotions, has been balanced by a new commitment on the part of the administration to faculty development. Advanced degrees and research, once viewed as peripheral to good teaching, are now regarded as keys to effective teaching. In 1984 only 41 percent of faculty members had Ph.D.s or other terminal degrees, but today the figure has risen to over 91 percent of a total full-time faculty of 144 members. Support for scholarship has been demonstrated by an ongoing commitment to the sabbatical program, by funding for travel and research, and by the upgrading of scholarship criteria for promotion. A new emphasis on salary equity and on the modernization of facilities through significant investments in technology have paralleled those developments.

Meanwhile, for the first time in its history, Otterbein has marshaled its resources across the board to carry out the principles of its founders to open its doors to all those interested in learning, regardless of denomination, gender, or race. The college's historic and ongoing commitment to students of modest means has been a crucial element in that mission, and today, along with a large number of scholarships, about 80 percent of students receive financial aid based on need. What has changed is the diversity factor, in terms of religion, and even more significantly in terms of ethnicity and race.

What once was a college dominated by United Brethren students, followed by Methodists and Presbyterians, now, while still largely Christian, is more diverse. In 1969 United Methodists constituted 54 percent of the student body. Today they represent 17 percent of students, while Catholics are a slightly larger group with 18 percent. Baptists, Lutherans, and Presbyterians together account for 15 percent.

Meanwhile, a concerted effort has been made to fulfill Otterbein's historic egalitarian mission in terms of ethnicity and race. During the eighties, all levels of the college community became engaged in a major reassessment of the curriculum, the faculty, and the overall culture and climate of the campus. The college hired an African American associate director of admissions and a decade later created an Office of Ethnic Diversity, with an African American assistant dean of student life dedicated to making students of color "feel more a part of campus." The result has been a multiplicity of programs and organizations reaching out to students of color, including an African American student union, a black student newspaper, black sororities and fraternities, an integrated gospel choir, a policy of "rainbow casting" for actors in the theater department, and special awards and scholarships. Similar efforts on behalf of Asian students has led to the establishment of an Asian Student Interest Association, the International Students Association, and an annual weeklong international festival. New or modified courses focusing on diversity and multiculturalism supplement the creation of a black studies minor and the new I.S. requirement in non-Western cultures. Meanwhile, the nineties has also brought a recognition of gays and lesbians through the organization on campus of the Bisexual, Gay and Lesbian Alliance and Friends.

In 1988 only 3 percent of the student body represented students of color, while today the figure has risen to almost 12 percent. International students come from about thirty different countries. Once a homogeneous student body, the college has moved steadily and persistently since the mid-eighties to more accurately reflect the diversity of the nation's population. Far more than in the past, students of color at Otterbein believe that they are a part of the campus, and they have more confidence that the college is making a genuine effort to deal with the problems of race. Meanwhile, persons of color represent 11 percent of the faculty, but little progress has been made at the highest levels of administration and the board of trustees.

Attention also has been paid in the most recent decade to creating a more genuinely egalitarian environment for women through, among other things, recruitment of women faculty, the addition of a women's studies minor, and attention to the special concerns of women students, and in particular the needs of women students of color. In 1993 the college appointed its first woman vice president of academic affairs, and today 73 of the 144 faculty members are women, while women serve as almost half of department chairs.

The college's emphasis on diversity has been matched by more concerted efforts to broaden the founders' original mission of service. Paralleling a growing commitment to service on the part of students nationwide, students at Otterbein have found multiple avenues for involvement, from participating in Habitat for Humanity to tutoring at middle schools, volunteering in literacy programs and nursing homes, and creating the AIDS Task Force. Through "Community Plunge," freshman students join faculty in a day of community service. The new Senior Year Experience (SYE) course requires students to participate in the larger community. Outlined in

The Templeton Guide's profile of outstanding college programs, the SYE course, by merging contemporary issues and ethics, has carried on the tradition of the first president's common course. Thus, the SYE has helped reinforce Otterbein's historic commitment to a value-centered education as it challenges students to "live 'the examined life.'"

The college has tried in other ways to maintain and broaden many of the goals of its founders. Its pledge of inclusiveness is still best identified with the governance system created in the sixties. By bringing all elements into the decision-making process, that system smoothed the way for the institution of the MBA program, the acceptance of the faculty-inspired all-tenure-track promotion system, and an environment more conducive to the discussion of issues concerning budgets and salaries. Also important has been the commitment on the part of the present administration to a more open dialogue as well as a reinvigorated faculty spurred on by a short-lived chapter of the American Association of University Professors pressing for change. Ironically, inclusiveness has had its costs. Student voices have been diffused somewhat by participation in an all-campus College Senate as opposed to an organization composed solely of students. The need for consensus, moreover, can produce a reluctance on the part of some to express controversial opinions. The success of the governance structure has bred a certain disinterest, a tendency to take it for granted, especially when few hot-button issues are at stake. Still, the positives of inclusiveness outweigh the negatives in the minds of most of the campus community. One exception to the trend, the practical impact of which is still unclear, has been the recently revised constitution of the board of trustees, which, in downsizing its membership, has also reduced from six to four the number of student and faculty representatives on the board.

With the near-doubling of the student population as well as the campus itself in the last two decades, one of Otterbein's greatest challenges has been to preserve a sense of cohesion and common experience, so much a part of the college in the days when students, lacking cars and off-site living arrangements, focused their social as well as academic lives on the campus. Although few students would call for a restoration of the chapel requirement, it was a common experience, bringing the entire college community together once a day. The diversity of college life today precludes 100 percent participation in any activity, but efforts to recreate that sense of common experience for large segments of the campus community have proceeded at several levels, one of the most significant being the Common Book Program, which originated in 1994 out of a grant from Mary Burnham Thomas, a former student. Selected each year by students and faculty and given to all incoming freshmen and all faculty, the common book, each of which focuses on a contemporary issue, serves as the focus for discussion during freshman orientation and is used in all introductory I.S. classes. Each fall, the author of the common book spends two to three days on campus, the high point being an all-campus convocation with the author as featured speaker.

The most recent and visual testimony to Otterbein's effort to maintain its traditions while furthering the process of modernization has been the renovation of Towers Hall, the oldest building on campus and central focus of college life since 1872. Given its condition, Towers might have been destroyed. Instead, a year-long renovation produced the most modern facility on campus, with the latest technology in every classroom, while at the same time reviving the aesthetic charm and historic interior of the venerable old structure. Completed in 1999, the restored Towers Hall serves as a tribute to Otterbein's respect for its heritage as it moves into the next century.

Suggested Reading

The best sources for Otterbein's early history are the Reverend Henry Garst, *History of Otterbein University* (United Brethren Publishing House, 1907); *The Religious Telescope,* the weekly paper of the U.B.C. church (1834–); *Minutes of the Otterbein Board of Trustees* (1847–); the annual catalogs (1848, 1853–); and the *Otterbein Record* (1880–85). For the twentieth century, see Willard Bartlett, *Education for Humanity: The Story of Otterbein College* (Otterbein College, 1934), and several campus publications, including the *Otterbein Handbooks* (1883–), the *Otterbein Aegis* (1890–1916), *Sibyl* (1901–), the *Otterbein Weekly* (1906), the *Tan and Cardinal* (1917–), and *Quiz and Quill* (1919–).

Harold Hancock, *The History of Otterbein College, 1930–1972* (Otterbein College, 1972), is an excellent analysis based on a wealth of primary sources, including many listed above as well as three other college publications, *Towers Magazine* (1939–), *Otterbein Miscellany* (1965–), and the annual reports (1967–). Most recently, in celebration of Otterbein's sesquicentennial, Daniel Hurley created a limited-edition pictorial history of the college's 150-year story, *Otterbein College: Affirming Our Past Shaping Our Future* (Otterbein College, 1996), which merged the primary and secondary sources noted above with a host of personal interviews.

The University of Rio Grande

The Unending Quest for Identity in Appalachian Ohio

IVAN M. TRIBE

The University of Rio Grande—known as Rio Grande College until 1989—has survived for a century and a quarter in the heart of the Ohio hill country. For the first seventy-five years of its existence it had a Baptist affiliation and later was an independent liberal arts college. In addition, since 1974, the public has provided some funding through a contract with Rio Grande Community College by which the older private institution provides educational services. This gives the school a complex uniqueness. But in the eyes of the general public, Rio Grande remains best known for its early fifties basketball hero Bevo Francis and its link to Bob Evans Farms.

One of the most amazing things about Rio Grande is that it has survived at all. Throughout most of its existence it has operated on a proverbial "shoestring" budget with an understaffed, underpaid, and sometimes underqualified faculty and staff. Only sheer dedication on the part of personnel enabled the college to keep its doors open, particularly in those times of financial hardship; all in that portion of the state that places a lesser value upon formal education than in more affluent areas.

Rio Grande's origins—in the abstract—were first conceived within the fertile mind of a struggling Free Will Baptist minister Ira Z. Haning. He was born on June 9, 1825, as the seventh in a family of twelve children. The Hanings came from pioneer stock, having moved to the "Donation Tract" of Washington County in 1792 and to southern Athens County in 1797 or 1798. Ira's parents, James and Gertrude Brooks Haning, adhered to the Free Will Baptist denomination. Young Ira experienced conversion at eighteen and soon felt the call to preach. Licensed in February 1846, he spent the remaining thirty-two years of his life spreading the faith as he knew it. Through a series of revivals, he founded several congregations in Athens, Gallia, Meigs, and Vinton Counties, at least three of which still flourish (in Albany, Cheshire, and Rio Grande). Haning's two major converts—in terms of Rio Grande's

Atwood Hall

history—a childless middle-aged couple, Nehemiah and Permelia Ridgway Atwood, farmed extensive acreage and kept a prosperous tavern on the stagecoach line midway between Gallipolis and Jackson.

Nehemiah Atwood had been born in Shenandoah County, Virginia, on December 7, 1792, and had passed through southeastern Ohio as a soldier in General Harrison's army during the War of 1812. Afterward he returned and settled near Raccoon Creek in Gallia County, where he married fifteen-year-old Permelia Ridgway on May 7, 1818. Born in South Carolina on December 30, 1802, Permelia and her parents came to the area in 1805 with the first wave of settlers in the Raccoon Creek Valley. After the Atwood's conversion and baptism at a Haning revival in 1851, they manifested an interest in Christian educational philanthropy. Not only did they donate $2,000 toward the building of Calvary Baptist Church in the nearby hamlet of Rio Grande (named for the post office established in 1846), but in the mid-1860s they contributed $3,500 for an academy in Reverend Haning's hometown of Albany, which thereafter bore the name Atwood Institute. However, the aging philanthropist determined that the bulk of his fortune should go to endow a school in the locality where his monies had been accumulated. Atwood died intestate on December 18, 1869. According to "the authorized centennial history of Rio Grande" (but not mentioned in three earlier histories), the words "Permelia, build the college," ranked among his last. Whether Nehemiah Atwood actually uttered those words on his deathbed cannot be determined, but they evidently represented his intentions.

Permelia Atwood spent the remainder of her life as the principal benefactor of what became Rio Grande College. On November 2, 1870, she married Harrison Wood, who served as one of the college's first trustees until his death on February 12, 1877. He apparently objected to his wife's 1876 will in which she named "I. Z. Haning and George Eagle in trust for Rio Grande College" as the sole beneficiary of her estate. By the time Permelia Atwood Wood died on March 9, 1885, her college had been in operation for nearly a decade. During that period, Mrs. Wood also served as a trustee, donated 113 acres of land, furnished $17,000 for the construction of Atwood Hall (the main building), gave another $13,000 for construction of a boarding hall and, according to Ben R. Evans (the most reliable of the early Rio Grande historians), "paid the expenses of the college and the salary of the instructors beyond the income from student fees as they came due."

Meanwhile Ira Haning and George Eagle (who served as treasurer until March 1891 and as sole executor of the Atwood estate after Haning died on September 28, 1878) endeavored to get buildings erected, personnel hired, and students enrolled. Articles of incorporation were drawn up on November 1, 1875. By that time construction on what later became known as Atwood Hall had already been underway for some weeks, as the *Gallipolis Journal* on November 1, 1875, reported that "the sign above the door reads as it were in 'letters of gold' Rio Grande College on the front of the building. . . . In all probability [it] will be completed about the middle of December." A little over a month later, the same newspaper reported "plastering done at the college[;] it was done by some colored men from Gallipolis and is pronounced a good job."

Although Rio Grande's *Journal* correspondent thought that the building could house a functioning Preparatory Department in the spring of 1876, it did not happen. The trustees hired Reverend Ransom Dunn, a Free Will Baptist minister, as president and planned a dedication ceremony, which took place on August 30, 1876. This event featured a picnic, speeches by Haning, Dunn, newly hired mathematics professor Albanus A. Moulton, and entertainment by the Naomi Band of Gallipolis.

The press noted that a second building, the "Boarding Hall . . . is almost ready for its mansard roof." Classes began on September 13, with fifteen students paying tuition rates of six dollars per term. For an additional dollar, students could get twenty lessons in their choice of penmanship, bookkeeping, or vocal music. Room charges in the new Boarding Hall—when finished—varied from 25 to 35 cents weekly. The trustees managed to hold boarding fees to two dollars a week until 1906. In keeping with the time, college officials made and enforced strict rules of behavior. When the fourth term began on April 24, 1877, enrollment had increased to seventy-five, and members of the Shakespearean Literary Society anticipated a "lively" election of officers at their upcoming meeting.

Ransom Dunn provided leadership for the first two years of Rio Grande's existence. A native Vermonter born in 1818, Dunn came to southeastern Ohio from Hillsdale College in Michigan—at the time another academic haven for Free Will Baptists—on a leave of absence. He guided the school without totally relinquishing his Hillsdale connection. He also initiated a long-standing tradition of nepotism by hiring his son-in-law George Slayton as professor of natural science and Latin. An early Rio Grande historian commented, "His advice, executive ability and force of character helped to win . . . from the very beginning a high degree of public favor." Once Dunn thought he had the fledgling school on a firm foundation in 1879, he resumed his full-time connection with Hillsdale, eventually becoming president of the Michigan institution in 1884. The leadership at Rio Grande then fell on the shoulders of Professor Moulton.

Albanus Avery Moulton, unlike Haning and Dunn, felt no call to preach but remained a zealous Free Will Baptist. An 1871 graduate of Yale, the Massachusetts native held a master's degree from Michigan and had practical experience as a railroad surveyor. The general impression of Moulton is that of an able instructor-administrator who managed to write a mathematics textbook, despite steadily worsening tuberculosis. In 1885 he took leave of Rio Grande for the presumably healthier climate of the Colorado Rockies. After two years in the West he resigned and then died a year later at the age of forty. His widow had his remains returned to Rio Grande and interred in the Calvary Baptist Cemetery where the Atwoods and Ira Z. Haning already rested.

Throughout the early period enrollments at Rio Grande fluctuated from one term to another as well as from year to year. Students in the Preparatory Department—secondary-level classes—typically outnumbered those in the Collegiate Department. Newspapers sometimes reported enrollment numbers from such vague phrases as "a goodly number of students in attendance" to such specifics as "fifty" in April 1879, "sixty" in October 1879 , and "130" in June 1882. At that latter date, the Rio Grande Library reported having 100 volumes and apparatus valued at $100. Beyond the literary society, little is known concerning student life in the early years. The college-level curriculum consisted of two alternatives, the classical and the scientific. Of the two the classical included a much higher proportion of literature from antiquity such as Livy, Tacitus, Horace, Cicero, Homer, and Xenophon.

Enrollments fluctuated in part because students often dropped out of school temporarily to work and then return. As a result no one received a bachelor's degree until 1883. Thomas Davis, a son of local Welsh immigrants who ultimately moved to Nebraska, Gertrude Rebecca Haning and Ida Belle Haning, daughters of the late cofounder who soon became faculty members, and Ira W. Jacobs who taught at the school for some years prior to his move to Vinton, comprised the first four graduates. Subsequent graduating classes were often smaller. In fact, the eight graduates in 1892 remained the largest until 1920. Through 1900 a total of fifty-three students took their bachelor's degrees, while another nine received a master's. Those awarded master's degrees were recipients of the bachelor's degree who had waited three years and, in the opinion of the faculty and administration, deserved further honors.

After President Moulton's resignation in 1887, the leadership at Rio Grande passed to John Merrill Davis, a forty-one-year-old Civil War veteran who was a native of Harrisonville, Meigs County. After the war he briefly attended Franklin College (the predecessor of the Atwood Institute) in Albany before enrolling at Ohio University, where he was graduated in 1873. Prior to graduating, he taught in Ohio's preparatory school. Between 1874 and 1878 Davis taught at Ridgeville College in Indiana, serving for part of that period as acting president as well as pastor of the local Free Will Baptist Church. In 1878 he came back to the Ohio hill country as head of the Wilkesville Academy. Moving to the Rio Grande faculty in 1879, Davis served as acting president from 1885 until Moulton's resignation. He held the presidency until 1911 and remained on the faculty for another eight years. Perry D. Woods, the first Rio Grande historian, wrote of Davis's forty years of service, "the Atwoods gave their money, he his life." In addition to his efforts for Rio Grande, Davis remained active in Free Will Baptist circles.

During the first decade of the Davis era, the Ohio judicial system finally terminated the Atwood endowment question. In 1889 a coterie of Atwood and Ridgway relatives filed a civil suit in the Gallia County Court of Common Pleas to break Permelia Atwood's will. Judge Hiram Sibley denied their request and on November 10, 1896, the Ohio Supreme Court reaffirmed Sibley's decision. The Atwood estate—valued at $77,102—became the core of the Rio Grande College endowment. Compared to the philanthropy of a Vanderbilt, a Stanford, or a Duke, this indeed seems like a minuscule amount, but it helped keep the tiny college's doors open for people in an area sorely in need of additional educational attainment.

A glimpse of student activity in the Gay Nineties may be gleaned from the June 5, 1893, program of the Shakespearean Society. Musical events ranged from vocal and violin solos to a brass band number. Other students recited both prose and poetry and conducted a debate concerning the McKinley Tariff. Society president J. W. Davis (son of the president) gave his farewell address on "Future Battles," and the society adjourned after a benediction.

John Merrill Davis, aided by dedicated long-term instructors like Clarence O. Clark, who had been the last principal and instructor at the Atwood Institute, kept Rio Grande together through the depression and into the new century. Seven miles from a railroad and in a relatively poor condition, the little Baptist college continued plodding along as the hard times of the mid-nineties evolved into McKinley prosperity at the turn of the century. As the twentieth century began, the full-time faculty in addition to President Davis in psychology, Bible, ethics, and Latin and Professor Clark in English, physics, and chemistry included John D. Holcomb in mathematics; Ruth Brockett in German, botany, and geology (she also served as "Preceptress," or guardian of female student virtue); Stella Fulton in English and Latin; George Bohannon in music; and, for one year only, Carrie Davis in zoology and English. After the latter's departure, Mrs. Chestora McDonald Carr began a long tenure as instructor in elocution. In more than a quarter-century at Rio Grande, Carr also directed numerous plays and dramas, including the 1926 Golden Anniversary Pageant. Usually she taught only part of the year at Rio Grande, as she spent the winters touring on the Chautauqua circuit as a lecturer and entertainer.

During the first decade of the new century the college continued to change. In 1906 a summer term was added to accommodate the increasing numbers of public school teachers who needed college credits to maintain their certificates. Summer enrollments often exceeded those of the regular terms. Until 1907 students enrolled at the collegiate level had the option of either the "classical" or the "scientific" courses. From that time, only the scientific remained. In 1909 the Preparatory School was discontinued and incorporated into Raccoon Township High School. However, from then until 1930 several faculty members taught at both institutions and the college rented out classroom space for high school use.

The year 1911 also marked significant modification at Rio Grande. The Free Will Baptists merged with the Northern (later American) Baptist Convention. The amount of funding from this source remained small. President Davis, having reached the age of sixty-five, stepped down as executive although he continued teaching for eight more years. Simeon H. Bing—a Methodist who had received his bachelor's degree only in 1910—took his place. Bing was the first of two Gallia County natives and Rio Grande alumni to lead the school. The thirty-five-year-old Bing who had finished his degree through the summer school, had some years of one-room school teaching experience and high school principalships at Bidwell and Procterville in his background. Although some later presidents still came from a Baptist clerical heritage, one suspects that for the next several decades, Masonic ties may also have had an influence on presidential choices as not only Bing, but also Lewis, Charles Davis, Lyne, Christensen, Quick, Hayes, and Smith held membership in this fraternal organization.

Under Bing's leadership more changes took place. In 1914 the State Department of Education approved Rio Grande's "normal" program for elementary teacher training. Some years later the curriculum for secondary teachers also received state approval. On the early morning of February 17, 1917, the Boarding Hall burned to the ground; fortunately, the forty inhabitants escaped with but one minor injury. Bing moved quickly to get the building replaced with a combination theater-gymnasium known as Community Hall, which was dedicated on May 5, 1918. Thereafter, the vast majority of students who did not commute, roomed and boarded either with private families or faculty members who lived in the little village. After President Emeritus Davis died in 1921, trustees obtained use of his home to house female students—as Davis Cottage—and eventually purchased the house, situated across the street from the campus block.

In the second half of the Bing presidency, Rio Grande enjoyed relative growth, especially during the summers. Ten seniors received bachelor's degrees in 1920, and the numbers increased to eleven, eighteen, and seventeen in the next three years. In 1918 and 1920 President Bing won election to the lower house of the Ohio General Assembly as a Republican from Gallia County. In 1921 he sponsored a major piece of legislation, the "Bing Law," which required all children in the state between the ages of six and eighteen to attend school, unless they had already graduated or obtained a working certificate after reaching age sixteen and completing the seventh grade. Perhaps because of this and the modest improvements made at Rio Grande, in 1923 Bing accepted a faculty appointment as professor of education at Ohio University, where he taught until his death in 1937.

Following Simeon Bing's departure, the trustees chose as president Horace Houf, a Missouri-born Baptist minister—most recently at Granville, site of the Northern Baptist Convention's other Ohio Baptist college, Denison—as president. During the latter Bing years and the Houf tenure, Rio Grande College enjoyed unprecedented prosperity as the number of students increased, especially after 1920, when two six-week summer terms were incorporated into the school year. Ben R. Evans, a student himself during that decade, recalled that in some years, the enrollments approached 500. A breakdown for 1919–20 showed: 117 in the college, 85 "special students in education," 29 in music courses, 10 in elocution, 141 in the high school or preparatory, and 211 enrollees in summer school. With "each name counted once" the total came to 459. In 1925, twenty-four persons received their degrees, and in 1928 the number of graduates passed the 100 mark (this included twenty-eight degree recipients and seventy-six two-year "normal graduates"), a number not surpassed until 1961. Most students in the 1920s aspired to be teachers, with many being in that field already. A study of the thirty-seven graduates in the class of 1929 revealed that all of them subsequently taught school for a minimum of five years, some for more than thirty years. That same year another sixty students received two-year diplomas that enabled them to teach in the elementary grades. At that date one-room schools still dotted the landscape in much of southeastern Ohio to employ them. Furthermore, until the latter part of 1923 the highway that passed through Rio Grande remained unpaved. In much of rural southeastern Ohio the forces of modernization came at a slow pace.

In 1926 Rio Grande College celebrated its golden anniversary as an institution. Professor Carr organized a pageant that a large cast of faculty, staff, students, alumni, and townspeople presented to the public on June 7 and 8. Many people connected with the early days of the college returned for the celebration, including the surviving children of Ira Z. Haning and Albanus Moulton, as well as J. Boyd Davis, who had been a leading trustee since 1921. Perry D. Woods, minister at the local Calvary Baptist Church, authored *The First Fifty Years of Rio Grande College*. Most significant, however, President Houf launched a successful fund drive for a new classroom building, Anniversary Hall, dedicated in 1927 and still in use at the dawn of the twenty-first century.

President Houf's wife, Ruth, left a fine written impression of Rio Grande in the mid-twenties which emphasizes the rural nature of the still struggling college:

> The years between 1923 and 1928 at Rio Grande were still of the old dispensation. There were no sororities or fraternities—or dancing. There were parties and pranks and jolly times shared by students, professors and towns people as well. The Annual Bean Dinner was an example of college and town cooperation. The Eisteddfod [Welsh Singing Competition] was still being held at the college. Much emphasis was laid on music as there were many Welsh in the community, and they enjoyed singing. Mrs. Chestora Carr came from Columbus each spring and directed some plays. These were well done and were of much interest to both audience and participants.
>
> It seems impossible now to think that radio was comparatively new between the years of '23 and '28. Mr. and Mrs. Howard Gross gave the college its first radio. There was great excitement and much noise, but only now and then a word or scrap of a sentence could be understood. Perhaps with a regular electric current the reception would have been much better, but only generators furnished electricity in Rio Grande then, and very few people had them. For lighting people mainly used oil lamps or acetyline [*sic*] gas. Fire was a terrible hazard in those days as there was no public water system. The fire department was a bucket brigade. Improved roads led into Rio Grande in 1923.
>
> During the years between '23 and '28 the college was still small enough that professors and students were well acquainted.. There was a distinct air of friendliness in and out of the classroom. Neither students [n]or faculty had much money.

Teachers taught heavy schedules for very small salaries, but throughout the faculty and student group there was a sense of dedication. It was an era in which professors were attempting to stimulate intellectual curiosity and to hold before the young people nobility of character and service to fellow man. It has been through the devotion, effort and sacrifice of faithful teachers, administrators, trustees and friends that Rio Grande College has continued to live and help supply to the field of education, trained and dedicated teachers.

Perhaps less provincial than his predecessors, Horace Houf realized that in spite of Rio Grande's relative prosperity in the roaring twenties, competing with better-endowed private colleges and the expanding state universities would make survival difficult. The school still operated on an extremely tight budget. The proposed expenditures for the 1925–26 school year were only $40,000. Houf's idea was to concentrate on the first two years of collegiate studies, which would for all practical purposes convert the school into a junior college. By the spring of 1928 the regular enrollment totaled 225, taught by a faculty of fourteen. President Houf, however, left before the reductions could be fully implemented. In that year President Elmer B. Bryan of Ohio University invited him to join their faculty of religion and philosophy. Houf remained at Ohio University and in Athens for the remainder of his life, writing a popular textbook, *What Religion Is and Does,* and continued serving Rio Grande as a trustee for some years. Ruth Houf later reminisced, "There remained a corner of his heart which belonged to Rio Grande."

The conversion of Rio Grande into a virtual junior college became an accomplished fact during the 1928–31 presidency of Willard W. Bartlett. Ironically, although neither Houf nor Bartlett could have predicted the stock market crash of October 1929 and the Great Depression that followed, the retrenchment they initiated proved well suited for the ensuing decade. Bartlett won some praise for supervision of the downsizing and broadening the variety of student activity, while coming under criticism for nearly bankrupting the school. A New Yorker by birth, Bartlett came to Rio Grande from Carleton College in Northfield, Minnesota, after a varied career as teacher and missionary. He held degrees from Colgate and Columbia University Teacher's College. The three years he spent at Rio Grande proved unhappy ones, and he left to pursue a doctorate at Ohio State. After receiving it he joined the faculty at Otterbein where he spent many years. One of Bartlett's most severe critics wrote, "He came with great ideas from a big city: urban life to country rural life. In his attempt to change the culture of R.G.C. he also spent Rio Grande College's money faster than it could be made."

Bartlett's departure led to a recall of a key figure who had been on a leave of absence in pursuit of a doctorate at New York University. If John Merrill Davis constituted the first person to give "his life" to Rio Grande, then William Allen Lewis must have been the second. Lewis had been born in Harrison Township, Gallia County, on January 22, 1877. He began teaching in one-room schools in 1897 and from 1905 slowly pursued a degree at Rio Grande during summers, taking until 1915 to complete it. He joined the summer faculty almost immediately and became a full-time faculty member in 1918. With the exception of the time away from campus in pursuit of advanced degrees, Lewis gave the rest of his life in service to his alma mater. He received a master's degree from Ohio State in 1927 and spent the 1930–31 school year at New York University laboring toward a doctorate but answered Rio Grande's call to the presidency in 1931. He held the office until 1940, when he resumed the deanship he held prior to his sojourn in New York. In his four decades at Rio Grande, Lewis held the following positions at one time or another: janitor, bookstore manager, bell ringer, librarian, summer school director, dean, president, registrar, professor of psychology, and three brief stints as acting president, in 1944, 1951, and 1954. In addition, prior to 1930 Lewis also taught some classes at the local high school. Usually referred to by his preferred title, there is no doubt that Dean Lewis earned the sobriquet "Mr. Rio Grande."

Undoubtedly Lewis had his work cut out for him. Rio Grande in the thirties had little money, few students, and many problems, but he did his best with what he had. Actually Rio Grande never relinquished its authority to grant four-year degrees, but for several years offered no junior- and senior-level work. From 1931 through 1939 the school awarded only two-year elementary teaching diplomas, although in 1937 it presented 105 of these. Finally in 1940 Lewis's last year as president, trustees bestowed two B.A. degrees and eighty-one two-year diplomas.

Lena Kronk Smith, who attended Rio Grande in the depth of the Great Depression, has vivid memories of student life in that era. As valedictorian at Minford High School, she had a tuition scholarship, lived in Davis Cottage, washed dishes to pay for room and board, and received a one-dollar weekly allowance from her parents. Most of her fellow students had a similar modest economic status. No one smoked on college property, drinking remained virtually unknown, and girls could date no more than once a week (which consisted of walking around, conversing, and no contact beyond, perhaps, hand-holding). Most other students roomed in private homes within walking distance, although a few commuted from Vinton, and several carloads—mostly of boys—drove out from Gallipolis. Virtually no students who lived in Rio Grande owned automobiles. Paul Lyne coached all the athletic teams and taught a full course load in subjects far removed from physical education. Lena remembers Dean Lewis's psychology courses as especially challenging and that, although respected as a leader, he exhibited an intensely "sarcastic" attitude in class. She had no prior experience in the subject and described herself as "afraid of him" for some time.

Troubles continued to plague the Lewis administration, although virtually none of them were of the president's making. On November 19, 1937, Atwood Hall burned to the ground, leaving nothing standing but "four grim-looking brick walls." Lewis immediately contacted the trustees asking if the school should continue or close its doors. Getting a "thumbs-up" decision, Lewis had earlier conceived a "self-help" plan titled "Forward Movement" to keep the institution afloat. This included purchase of a farm—what later became known as the Bob Evans Homestead Farm—and a student labor building program. He drew his ideas from what had worked at such other schools that catered to poor students from highland areas: Berea College in Kentucky and College of the Ozarks in Arkansas. The Northern Baptist Convention advanced funds to start the program. The farm never quite met expectations, but the building program in the next decade constructed three brick edifices: Science Hall (later renamed Haning Hall), a cafeteria (later a student center with a board room on the second floor), and a student center (that later headquartered a music program, ROTC building, and more recently a day care center). In 1935 the college had obtained title to a brick store and hotel known as the Varney House, which provided a college-owned facility to house students in addition to Davis Cottage.

In 1940 William Lewis gave way as president and returned to the deanship and the classroom. The new leader, R. Lloyd Pobst, was a Baptist minister originally from upstate New York. One gets the idea that the Northern Baptist Convention may have favored one of their own, because Lewis was a Methodist. At any rate, Pobst began his presidency by displaying a remarkable degree of optimism. Soon he had to deal with World War II, which depleted most of the college's male population, a circumstance that later led a writer for the *Gallipolis Daily Tribune* to write, "the bombs which fell on Pearl Harbor left . . . Rio Grande College . . . in a worse shambles." To again quote Francis Burdell, "President Pobst's optimism continued until one day [in 1944] he told some of us he was resigning." In short, he had exhausted his supply of optimism. Much of the problem derived from losses encountered by the college farm. With almost no male students, the college had to hire laborers at higher rates, and the man from whom the purchase agreement had been made—ironically a trustee—refused reducing payments, and the whole agricultural operation lost some $5,000 to $6,000 yearly.

When Reverend Floyd W. McDermott, the last Baptist preacher president, took the helm at Rio Grande in the fall of 1944, only thirty-three full-time students were enrolled. The football team canceled its schedule because the student body lacked eleven boys. The junior class numbered all of three. Farm losses continued, but financial prospects improved when the war ended and the GI bill brought some increase in enrollment. By 1947 the student numbers reached 218 but fell to 200 in 1948. As deficits mounted only the contributions of board chairman Dr. Charles Holzer and Don Allen, an alumnus who had become a successful Chevrolet dealer in Buffalo, New York, kept the doors open. Salaries remained quite low. McDermott received $4,000 in 1950–51, Dean Lewis $3,500, and the highest-paid professors

$3,000. At one point in 1949 the administration tried to settle with creditors for one cent on the dollar. The education leadership of the newly renamed American Baptist Association, moreover, became increasingly disenchanted.

By the time Baptist dissatisfaction reached its climax, McDermott had departed, being replaced by Charles E. Davis, a Jackson County native and 1926 Rio Grande alumnus who had a background that included several years as a semipro football player and an even longer career in public school administration. After some years of relative drift, many trustees saw their new president as a man of action. Certainly Davis had a keen awareness of the task he faced, particularly after what transpired in his first year. The one bright spot came with the purchase of the farm by affluent alumnus Don Allen, who then sold it to emerging agribusiness tycoon Bob Evans in 1953.

In mid-January 1952 the American Baptist Association served notice that they would terminate their relationship with Rio Grande College on May 1, 1952. Their criticisms of the school focused on financial instability, rapid turnover of frequently underqualified faculty, and a 1948 crisis in which the State Department of Education temporarily "withdrew accreditation for teacher certification" from Rio Grande, but it reluctantly extended it for three more years after a strong appeal from students and prominent local citizens. The Baptist board based its decision on a document known as the Rivenburg Report, which scathingly outlined the academic and financial inadequacies under which the institution operated. The spark that ignited the report seems in part the result of one of Rio Grande's best students being denied admission to Andover-Newton Theological Seminary because his alma mater lacked North Central Accreditation. Among other deficiencies, the library had only 11,000 volumes, valued at less than one dollar per book. The enrollment had dropped to 135. College income for 1950–51 amounted to $68,880. To those friends of Rio Grande such as Charles Holzer and Don Allen, whose philanthropy, coupled with the tireless efforts of Dean Lewis and others who had kept the doors open for years, the Rivenburg Report must have appeared bleak indeed. With this cloud of gloom hanging over the little campus, the enrollment declined to 125 in the fall of 1951 and to 94 the following autumn.

Then an extremely unusual phenomenon occurred; some people might even term it a miracle. Athletics at Rio Grande had seldom been in the forefront. Football had never been a major sport, largely because of the small enrollment. Between 1917 and March 1950, when R.G.C. dropped the game for the final time, they had occasionally been competitive, but were better remembered for a record losing streak more than anything else. In basketball the Redmen fared somewhat better, at least sometimes. In 1941 for instance, their team star, Jack Duncan, had set some enviable records in small college ranks and in the late forties a feisty little guard named Newt Oliver had gained some renown for his free throw prowess. In the summer of

1952 President Davis had offered Oliver the basketball coach's position, knowing full well that it could well be the last year that Rio Grande College would even exist. Oliver could best be described as a physically small young man with big ideas. According to his own account, Oliver received $3,000 from Don Allen for basketball scholarships and recruited some decent athletes, most notably a talented tall youth from Wellsville, Ohio, Clarence "Bevo" Francis, whom he had earlier coached in high school. What happened over the next two years is a Cinderella story that is virtually unique in the annals of college sports. While opinions vary widely and are controversial, the publicity generated by the circumstances may well have rescued Rio Grande from probable extinction.

Oliver's plan called for building his team around Francis and gave him the opportunity to do most of the scoring. The resultant publicity that accompanied his high point totals would ultimately bring more fame and fortune to Rio Grande than it had heretofore obtained. In the broad sense, he succeeded—probably to even greater extent than his own immodest predictions—as the Redmen went 39-0 in his first year as coach, with Francis amassing an average of 50.1 points per game, including 116 in a single contest against Ashland Junior College. Since the Rio Grande schedule included some games against two-year schools, military bases, and freshman teams of larger colleges, however, many of the Francis achievements were disallowed. The headlines engendered more publicity for Rio Grande than they ever had before. In the second, and final, season of the Francis era, the enrollment jumped to 128, and the team went 21-7, with Francis averaging 46.5. This time only one contest was with any other than four-year schools, and while Rio Grande did not do as well, they more than held their own against what might be labeled "big name" schools and proved competitive, if not invincible. Francis scored 113 points in a game against Hillsdale, a college that had been often entwined with Rio Grande in past years. In both years Francis appeared on the All-America Second team of many sportswriters and press groups. The team had indeed played in numerous major venues, including Madison Square Garden, and Rio Grande's share of the visiting team revenue brought in thousands of dollars to the strapped treasury. However, after the season Francis withdrew from school never to reenroll. Oliver resigned as coach, followed by President Davis a few weeks later, and a sea of controversy nearly engulfed the still-struggling college.

In essence, much of the dissension resulted from a power struggle between Davis and Oliver, who often tended to act independently. Davis, with urging from some faculty and trustees, as well as considerable pressure from the Ohio College Association, feared that Rio Grande was fast becoming the focal point of a media circus that they were ill equipped to handle. Nonetheless, the fame engendered from the Francis era undoubtedly helped the college to reap modest benefits for the remainder of the decade and well into the sixties.

Paul R. Lyne, a former Rio Grande coach and professor (1923–29, 1932–38), returned from a high school principal's job in Cambridge to assume the presidency. Under Lyne Rio Grande College enjoyed modest if unspectacular growth. By the spring of 1959 enrollment had climbed to 296, about 20 percent larger than in the final year of the Houf presidency. In 1961 a total of 120 degrees were granted, a new record. In 1957 the Davis Family of Oak Hill provided funds for a new dormitory to house 118 girls, and Don Allen, who became the college's leading benefactor following the death of Charles Holzer in 1956, contributed money in 1958 for a new administration-classroom building, named Allen Hall, on the site of the long-burned Atwood Hall. In 1961 construction began on Moulton Hall, a dormitory housing seventy-eight men, financed through an FHA loan. Some scholars with solid academic credentials joined the faculty. Eugene Murdock—with a doctorate from Columbia and a subsequently published dissertation on Tom L. Johnson—taught history from 1952 to 1956 before moving on to Marietta. By the time he retired Murdock had achieved a national reputation for his books on the Civil War draft and the history of baseball. A husband-wife team, David and Anne McCarrell, each with a Ph.D. from Duke University, also taught at Rio Grande for several years in history and political science. Less credentialed but with long-standing reputations, teachers such as Clara Poston and Robert Ewing in English, Zelma Northcutt in history and music, and Francis Burdell in the sciences provided continuity with an earlier era. Dean Lewis remained with Rio Grande until his death in October 1956. After eight years at the helm, Lyne retired, leaving the college in much better condition than when he arrived.

Still Rio Grande College had many problems. In particular it lacked North Central accreditation. Alphus R. Christensen who became president after Paul Lyne's retirement, placed accreditation at the top of his wish list, pointing out that the college had never sought this validation prior to 1963. Christensen came to Rio Grande from South Dakota with a Ph.D. in speech and communications from the University of Minnesota. In some respects he resembled the typical pipe-smoking academic stereotype of the pre-Vietnam era. While disliked in some circles, he too led the institution forward and helped move it away from the provincial backwoods image it had acquired. John Graham, associate professor of speech, and Ruth Thomas, assistant professor of English, share credit with Christensen for making the accreditation effort a success. Finally, after one failed attempt, Rio received its long-coveted accredited status in March 1969. In the meantime enrollment more than doubled, and additional buildings went up on campus. Student numbers increased nearly everywhere in the 1960s partly because of the general prosperity of the decade and partly from an influx of persons hoping to avoid the draft. By 1968 the out-of-state students numbered 134, more than the entire enrollment only fifteen years earlier. In 1963 Rio had 398 students; by the fall of 1968 821 were enrolled. The number of graduates peaked at 205 in 1971. Two new dorms, Holzer Hall and Boyd Hall, went up in 1966 and 1967 and a new dining hall in 1966, relegating the old student-labor-built dining hall to become a student center largely for the growing commuter traffic. Most significant of all, trustees dedicated a new library named for Jeanette Albiez Davis in January 1966. The Paul R. Lyne Physical Education Center opened in the fall of 1969, providing the college with a new gymnasium and swimming pool.

Like most schools, Rio Grande did not avoid the student unrest that enveloped colleges in the later sixties. However, in retrospect, these years turned out to be far less disruptive than in most places. Most of the disruption at Rio Grande took place in the spring of 1969, and the usual counterculture elements—antiwar, antipoverty, and pro–civil rights—had a presence. Local issues, however, seemed at the heart of the discontent, especially a decision by President Christensen to deny a contract renewal to William Christopher, a young English professor with a degree from Dartmouth and an obvious sympathy with the protest movements. Abbie Hoffman made a brief visit to the campus, but in the end little came of it. Christopher and another faculty dissident, sociology instructor Eugene Newman, were dismissed, twenty-nine students were reprimanded, and another ten were exonerated. By the mid-1970s the incident was nearly forgotten.

An enrollment peak of 850 in the fall semester of 1969 was followed by the inevitable downsizing that occurred after introduction of the Nixon-initiated draft lottery and later the all-volunteer army. By 1972 it had fallen to 667. By this time Alphus Christensen had developed his second major contribution to the history of Rio Grande College, a four-county community college district for which Rio Grande would provide services through a contractual arrangement. Working out specifics of such an arrangement took some time, as commissioners of the four counties, Rio Grande trustees, and the Ohio Board of Regents had to be in agreement. Then final approval would be dependent on voter approval of a 1 mill tax levy in the four counties. According to Christensen, it came as something of a surprise to Regents chairman John Millett that voters approved the levy, on the first try, on June 11, 1974, by a vote of 4,220 to 3,730. Gallia and Jackson supported the levy by sufficient margins to overcome a sixty-two-vote deficit in Vinton County and a larger one of 612 in Meigs (much of which is closer to Ohio University in Athens). By the fall of 1974 Christensen's last year in the presidency, numbers had partially recovered to 747. Some of that rebound resulted from a one-time-only $1,000 scholarship credit given to recent high school graduates in the four-county district. The Regents also required conversion to the state-mandated quarter system as well as development of two-year technical programs. Many old financial debts were also settled. By the fall of 1975, when the community college operation began, enrollment hit a new high of 949. At that time first- and second-year students in the four-county district paid a fee of $13 per credit hour, while those from elsewhere in Ohio paid $17 per hour. When a student in a four-year program passed ninety-five credit hours, private college fees became $52 per credit hour. In this manner Christensen hoped that enough students would remain in the private college to keep it viable—an assumption that has proved correct for a quarter-century.

In 1975 Paul Hines succeeded to the presidency of Rio Grande but remained for only a year. Hines, a native of Kansas City, had prior experience as president of Barton County Community College in Garden City, Kansas. However, this background apparently failed to benefit him in creating harmony between the private college board and the community college board. After a frustrating year, he accepted a vice presidency at Marshall University.

While both sets of trustees sought a new president, Thomas Quick, a recently retired official in the Ohio Department of Education, served nearly a year in the interim. Quick generally maintained a competent but low profile until Paul C. Hayes took over in the spring of 1977. His prior experience had been as a school administrator and then as departmental chair in graduate education at the University of Akron. In many respects Hayes could be best described as an academic version of the eighteenth-century "Enlightened Despots." He often angered faculty, staff, and sometimes students with his arbitrary manner, but he got the job done. He developed a working relationship between the two boards and often virtually coerced faculty committees into hiring new people with doctorates; for many years it had been a common phrase in southeastern Ohio education circles that "all you needed to teach at Rio Grande was a master's degree," and sometimes those with M.Ed. degrees taught liberal arts subjects. Hayes made progress in this area, despite complaints from older, insecure instructors that "Ph.D.s can't teach" and "people with Ph.D.s will never stay here." By the time he left, there were several new faculty members with doctorates from such distant locales as the University of Chicago, the University of Arizona, George Washington University, and the University of Illinois, as well as products of the relatively new Ph.D programs in the Mid-American Conference schools such as Ohio University, Bowling Green State University, the University of Toledo, and Ball State University. Some of the younger faculty without terminal degrees took leaves of absences to pursue graduate study at schools ranging from West Virginia to Florida. Although some of the old provincialism had waned, enough of the "old Rio family" attitude remained to preserve some of the friendly, relaxed atmosphere of past decades.

More building construction took place in the Hayes era too, much of it with state funding. James Rhodes spent his second tenure as governor during the Hayes presidency, which proved beneficial to the college, since the governor loved building and the new president had a good working relationship with him. The E. E. Davis Career Center housed the new technical programs. Community Hall came down in the late seventies and a new Fine Arts Center went up in its place. A new student center named for the "bricks and mortar governor" opened early in 1983. Since the Rhodes Center contained a new cafeteria, the old one became Florence Evans Hall and housed the growing school of business. Although Hayes had retired for the first time before completion of a new math and science building, it ultimately replaced Haning Hall (which then became a parking lot). In one the president's more astute moves he succeeded in 1980 in making the heretofore independent Holzer School of Nursing a part of Rio Grande College. Hayes also attracted more philanthropy by renaming the business department the Emerson Evans School of Business and enticed a major contribution from the aging Ohio Valley banker. When Paul Hayes stepped down in 1983, retiring to his home in Wilmington at age sixty, the enrollment had reached 1,300.

Growth continued at a slower pace during the brief three-year presidency of Clodus R. Smith, a former official at Cleveland State University, in a period best described as anxiety filled. Smith quickly developed a habit of hiring new people in administrative positions and then casting them aside when he needed a scapegoat. He apparently trusted few people outside his inner circle and did not hide it well. A switchboard operator was exiled to a pole barn–type storage building because Smith thought she was tapping his phone line. When the president became embroiled in controversy with trustee James Dailey, Smith tried to get the trustee's wife's courses (she taught in the communications department) deleted from the catalog. At that time the state legislature, at the behest of House Speaker Vernal Riffe, moved to create a four-year school in Portsmouth known as Shawnee State University. Smith launched an effort to stop it only after it had become a virtual certainty, thus wasting what little rapport he still had as a lobbyist. When one anonymous critic put out a mimeographed satirical sheet titled "The Boss Clod Fan Club Newsletter," he tried to have copies confiscated. On a more positive note, he secured funding for an annual faculty teaching prize, the Edwin A. Jones Award, but it hardly compensated for a multitude of weaknesses. Finally, after a faculty vote of confidence went against him 38-12, Smith began seriously searching for another position. He found one in August 1986 at troubled Lake Erie College, where he had another tumultuous tenure. The Rio Grande board of trustees quickly asked Paul Hayes to return from retirement, and he came back for another five years.

Perhaps because of the anxiety engendered by the Smith regime, the second Hayes period witnessed years of less tension and continued modest growth. At the end of 1988 Wood Hall, a new classroom building opened primarily for classes in the liberal arts and social sciences. More new faculty were hired with doctorates from such schools as the University of Chicago, Indiana University, Oregon State University, SUNY-Buffalo, University of Missouri, Texas Tech State University, and Pennsylvania State University, along with additional alumni from Ohio State and the Mid-American Conference institutions. By 1995 eighteen faculty members had obtained their bachelor's degrees from Rio, it represented a smaller percentage than in past generations, an indication that much of the older "inbreeding" and provincialism continued to decline. The one major fiasco associated with the second Hayes term came in a botched effort to create a branch in Japan. The president hastened too quickly to get the project off and running before he retired. Then, when so many American colleges opened branches there and the Japanese economy hit a mild recession, Rio Grande–Japan, along with many other Japanese branches, closed. The fact that the Japanese investors in the program were far more interested in turning a profit than they were in providing quality education did not help much. On the local front Hayes fostered efforts to raise more money for scholarships, chief among them the Atwood Awards, which provided four years of tuition remission for recipients. Also—for better or worse—in 1989 Rio Grande College became the University of Rio Grande. While many other Ohio institutions of similar size—Ashland, Findlay, and Urbana among them—did the same thing, some pondered the wisdom of such a move and thought it presumptuous. As one faculty cynic remarked, "It would still be a good place to start a college." By the time Hayes ended his second term as president, the student body numbers eclipsed the 2,000 mark. In both his stints at Rio Grande, Paul Hayes, like Lyne and Christensen before him, left the institution in much better shape than it had been before.

In 1991 Barry Dorsey, who had past experience in the Virginia state college system, assumed the Rio Grande presidency. Through the remainder of the decade the enrollment remained stable—sometimes up a little, sometimes down a little. The fall quarter of 2000 had a head count of 2,107. McKenzie Hall, located behind the math and science building, provided permanent quarters for the nursing school. Another new cafeteria and another dorm were built, and in 1999 a groundbreaking occurred for a new building to house the School of Business. Regular classes also began at a Meigs County Center. From the mid-1990s on a number of students from area high schools took classes on a regular basis as part of the Post-Secondary Option Program (PSO). Sometimes nearly a hundred of these youths participated in the process, and while it could not be termed a universal success, many of those remained at Rio Grande and have compiled fine academic records. One young lady, by attending summer classes, managed to earn an associate's degree and accumulate some 106 hours of credit. Others compiled hourly totals in the sixty- to-ninety-hour range and became recipients of the coveted Atwood Scholarships.

As the twentieth century drew to a close, the University of Rio Grande began preparations to celebrate its 125th year. While a degree from Rio Grande might still be less prestigious than those from the more elite private schools such as Denison, Marietta, Muskingum, or Oberlin, none could deny that the college had made forward strides, particularly in the years since Bevo Francis made his first headlines in the nation's sports pages. From its beginnings as a tiny Free Will Baptist institution until 1923, Rio Grande has served a constituency from what many Ohioans would consider the backwaters of the Buckeye State.

For several decades most of its alumni became schoolteachers, the majority of whom worked in the same area, where pay scales lagged behind other parts of Ohio and student attitudes ranged from apathy to outright hostility. Unlike the alumni of more elite schools, they lacked the affluence to donate millions back to their alma mater. Yet these people, like Dean William A. Lewis, who had inspired so many, often learned to do the best they could with what they had. In doing so they earned the admiration of some outside observers like Charles Otis Gill and Gifford Pinchot, who in their 1919 church-reform-oriented book voiced strong criticism of southeastern Ohioans. *Six Thousand Country Churches* found the only bright spot in an otherwise dismal picture as "the area immediately affected by the admirable and effective work of Rio Grande College."

Rio Grande continues to serve this clientele, although perhaps with something less than the Baptist zeal of an earlier era; today they make up for it by being better equipped. Many of those who attend the school are youth with real ability and potential who lack the confidence and/or funds to attend larger or more distant institutions. One recalls in the late seventies a pair of aging hill-folk parents looking over the campus with their daughter in tow. They stared at two-story brick buildings such as Allen Hall and Davis Library as though they might have been Manhattan skyscrapers. Their clothing seemed some two decades behind the times. A student such as this might well be lost in the complexity of Ohio State University or even Ohio University. Yet at Rio Grande she showed real ability, became an effective teacher, and went on to obtain a master's degree. Another earned a 3.653 GPA despite a dysfunctional family background. One young lady of modest means scored a 26 composite on the ACT, received an Atwood Award, wrote an article for a scholarly journal, coauthored a chapter published in a University of Illinois Press book at the age of twenty, and finished her senior year with a 3.655 GPA. Sometimes at a graduation one can see parents arriving in battered pickup trucks to see their son or daughter receive a degree. Other students could be classified as "late bloomers" and do well in spite of low achievement in high school. Nonmonetary rewards such as working with students like these can compensate for some of the deficiencies and less-than-overwhelming salaries at Rio Grande. Not many Rio Grande students pursue graduate work in fields other than education, but the attainments of those who succeed are a source of satisfaction. Of course, other enrollees compile average and even lackluster records, as is found in all colleges and universities. Unfortunately, Rio Grande still suffers from an identity problem. Part of this derives from the tendency of administrators constantly to "reinvent" the institution. Mission statements change almost with the season. New presidents often give the impression that they think little—or nothing—was there prior to their arrival. And many people in southeastern Ohio express reluctance to identify with the area's Appalachian characteristics unless federal grants are involved. Programs are sometimes initiated on the basis of insufficient data and then abandoned if they do not immediately draw the expected numbers. As a result the school sometimes strives to be both more than it is and also less. To paraphrase the venerable Dean Lewis, one must endeavor to provide Rio Grande students with as much of a quality education as they would receive at a larger and more elite institution, yet one must also work with the students at the level one finds them. Balancing these two extremes has been, and remains, a challenging task. However, it is the position that the Rio Grande instructional and administrative staff continues to encounter. Sometimes—but not always—it has been done well.

As Ben R. Evans wrote after the school's first sixty-three years, the school had been "serving the needs of hundreds of students who would otherwise have not been able to attend an institution of higher education." More than another six decades has passed since Evans's observation, but the primary purpose of the school known as "the lamp of the hills" remains the same. The future challenge is to keep the light burning.

Suggested Reading

Until recently, no adequate history of the University of Rio Grande existed. Three earlier efforts do contain considerable factual information: Perry Daniel Woods, "The First Fifty Years of Rio Grande College," *Bulletin of Rio Grande College*, n.s. 15 (April 1926); and Benjamin Rees Evans, *A History of Rio Grande College* (Martin Printing Co., 1939), are both pamphlets, the latter written as a master's thesis in education at Ohio State University. James Sherman Porter, *Lamp of the Hills: The Authorized Centennial History of Rio Grande College* (ca. 1978) is longer but proved so inadequate that it never went on sale, although numerous copies circulated. One hopes that Abby Gail Goodnite and Ivan M. Tribe, *Rio Grande: From Baptists and Bevo to the Bell Tower, 1876–2001* (Jesse Stuart Foundation, 2002), will stand as definitive.

Anna C. Smith Pabst, ed., *The Haning-Atwood Vision: Rio Grande College, Rio Grande, Ohio* (Delaware, 1969), is a random collection of newspaper articles and a variety of primary documents by a former faculty member that contains much useful information. The Bevo Francis episode has received considerable attention, most completely and sympathetically by Juanita Evans Dailey, *His Records Stand: The Incredible Bevo Francis* (1995), based on a master's thesis at Marshall University. Newt Oliver, as told to Dan Hoyt, *One Basketball and Glory* (1969), is the coach's somewhat egocentric viewpoint on the events. Two other studies—Danny Fulks, "Bevo's Odyssey," *Timeline* 9 (Feb.–Mar. 1992): 2–19, and Debbie McGuire, "Bevo Francis: Burning Up the Hardwood at Rio Grande College, 1952–1954," *Buckeye Hill Country: A*

Journal of Regional History 1 (1996): 12–24—offer a more detached historical perspective. Fulks, a Rio Grande graduate of 1960, more than the others, views Charles Davis as caught in an academic crossfire between Dean Lewis and Newt Oliver.

Numerous primary source material in the form of trustees meeting minutes, catalogs, school newspapers, yearbooks, photographs, tape recordings, and archival data may be found in the Heritage Room on the top floor of the Allen House.

Tiffin University

Risk and Gain

MICHAEL A. GRANDILLO

Tiffin University's motto, "Without Risk, There Is No Gain," has served it well through its 115-year history. From its founding as the for-profit Commercial College at Heidelberg College to its transformation into a modern independent university, Tiffin University has endured times of instability as well as three physical moves, all of which have served to strengthen and unify its academic culture. Tiffin University has survived and prospered because of the commitment of its founders to recreate itself to respond to the needs of students. George W. Williard of Heidelberg College, Franklin J. Miller, Alfred Reichard, and George Kidd Jr. all advanced the institution through artful risk taking. And it is this story of risk taking that needs to be told.

Institutions providing instruction in business and commerce in the United States developed rapidly between the Civil War and World War I, spurred on by the transition of the American economy from one dominated by local family businesses to one characterized by large corporations and national and international markets. Business, or "commercial," education became a movement in the 1880s, arising from the growth of the American economy and the public need that accompanied it. Although early ideals of education and business were dramatically opposed, American businessmen turned to private commercial colleges as a source for trained business employees.

Unlike in Europe, no significant tradition of clerical or commercial apprenticeship existed in the United States. Following their initial appearance in the 1850s, commercial colleges specializing in business education were numbered at twenty-six by 1870 with more than 5,800 enrolled students. Commercial colleges were usually proprietary or for-profit institutions. Although the institutions varied in quality, and most were modest operations, courses in elementary bookkeeping and ornamental penmanship were augmented by courses in stenography, typewriting, and secre-

Higher Accounting class, 1920

tarial training. Graduates of these colleges quickly filled the need of a growing business community for trained individuals. Their success in commercial ventures of the day speaks to the rapid development of commercial colleges between 1870 and 1900. By 1900 more than 400 commercial colleges enrolled more than 110,000 students, including 65,000 men and 45,000 women. Education and business were firmly brought together, clearly recognizing the utility of their mutual interests.

Heidelberg College, founded in 1850 in Tiffin, Ohio, was one of the few liberal arts institutions to recognize the direct benefit of business education in a college environment in the nineteenth century. During the 1880s higher education was greatly broadened and began to include specialized academic divisions, which included the introduction of new scientific, technical, and arts curriculums. Heidelberg quickly joined this educational movement and expanded its offerings to include a Conservatory of Music, Department of Art, Department of Polytechnic, and, most notably, the College of Business, or Commercial College. Soon the college administration and trustees sought to change the status of the institution from college to university, and legislation to effect that passed in 1890. Heidelberg's new charter as a university boldly included the "new" discipline of business in its official structure.

The genesis of Tiffin University can be traced back to the interest of the Heidelberg College faculty who wished to connect with a school in nearby Carey, Ohio, for the purpose of adding commercial programs to its curriculum as early as 1886. As discussions and negotiations continued throughout the 1886–87 academic year, the addition of a Business College at Heidelberg received a strong boost from President George Williard, who lent his full endorsement to the program in June 1887, agreeing with the faculty that it would be a very attractive offering for the young people in the region and that it would help the college many ways. Although he repeatedly presented the faculty proposal to Heidelberg's board of trustees, he never received a clear direction on how to proceed.

Eventually, despite a lukewarm response from the board, Williard and the faculty independently secured the appointment of Mr. E. W. Keen in the fall of 1888. Keen established a commercial department in the college and served as its first principal. The Department of Commerce quickly enrolled students, and attendance grew to more than sixty by the end of the second year. Williard also secured space for the new department in the first building constructed on the campus, presently called Founders Hall. This building, built in 1851, had recently been overshadowed by the new College Hall, dedicated in 1886.

Keen served as principal and lead instructor in the department for three years (1889–92). Vice Principal A. G. Barone assisted him during this period. The Heidelberg College catalog for the 1889–90 academic year lists a business course of study that included bookkeeping (single and double entry), penmanship, shorthand writing, and typing and typewriting. The success of the program and high demand for its progressive approach to business education resulted in increased enrollments and an annual request by Keen for more room on the Heidelberg campus. At its height the business program made up a quarter of the total enrollment at Heidelberg. The 110 students enrolled strained the modest space allocated the commercial department and prompted Professor Keen to endeavor to define the department's exact status within the institution and to seek assurances that the commercial college's sacrifices would be rewarded in the future.

It is important to note that during thirty years of existence, the Department of Commerce, or the Business School or the College of Commerce (different references were used throughout its history), at Heidelberg operated as an independent unit but at the same time was under control of the trustees and the university's administration. This relationship appears to have been defined by the necessity of the moment. For example, when Heidelberg needed the Department of Commerce for financial reasons, it was fully included. Conversely, when the department advertised its program, it emphasized its association with the college, and Heidelberg's facilities provided needed academic space. This rather ad hoc arrangement led to complications. For example, the board of trustees of Heidelberg College appointed the department's principal and allocated space on campus. Despite this close administrative control the department was an independent financial entity. Yet once when the department attempted to disassociate itself from the university or sell the property and goodwill of the department, the trustees blocked such moves. On many occasions Heidelberg showed no interests in financial transactions from principal to principal. Business students were not considered undergraduates, because the course of study was generally one year, and admissions were less competitive. These inconsistencies aggravated the relationship between Heidelberg University and the College of Commerce and eventually led to the resignations of Keen and Barone.

Unable to secure the necessary classroom space they felt was needed for growth; Keen and Barone finally submitted their resignations in 1892. As a part of the split they sought to personally sell the property and goodwill of the department to the highest bidder. However, the board refused to recognize the action and began the search for their successors. From 1892 to 1896 the trustees appointed a series of three principals who were singularly unsuccessful in making the newly named College of Commerce a financial success. Although the enrollment averaged about thirty-five students throughout the four academic years, lack of space and competition from another commercial school in Tiffin, Tiffin Business College, owned by Charles Clinton Kennison, contributed to the overall stagnation of the College of Commerce.

In 1895 Professor Kennison had offered to sell Tiffin Business College, which was located in downtown Tiffin, to Heidelberg. The university first declined, but a year later accepted the offer and sought to move the College of Commerce to downtown Tiffin to attract more students. Instead, the colleges were combined on Heidelberg's campus as an effort to increase enrollment. Kennison was subsequently named principal of the merged school on August 27, 1897, where he and the College of Commerce remained until 1903. Kennison proved to be an able leader. He added faculty, started a night school, and revised the curriculum. Enrollment rose to a high of seventy-two, once again reviving the calls for building maintenance and increased space. But a new commercial school opened in nearby Fostoria in 1902, and while enrollment in the College of Commerce remained steady through 1903, attendance dropped precipitously in 1904, and Principal Kennison resigned that same year.

The university catalog of 1903–4 included an announcement that "Heidelberg Commercial College" was to open under the new management of John F. Sterner, an expert accountant with twelve years experience as an instructor and principal. Under Sterner the college expanded, averaging eighty students a year during his eight years (1904–12) as principal. He, along with W. H. Holland, who served as coprincipal from 1908 to 1910, reorganized the curriculum to include a more practical approach to higher accounting, bookkeeping, shorthand, and penmanship. The $45 yearly tuition also entitled students of the Commercial College to take subjects taught in the preparatory department of Heidelberg University. The Commercial College became a financial success under Sterner, allowing it to acquire some of the best office equipment of its time in the region. Sterner, however, had his sights on political office. In 1912 he was seeking a buyer of the College of Business so he could devote time and resources to run for county auditor. The next owners were to change the course of academic history in Seneca County, Ohio.

Franklin J. Miller and Alfred Martin Reichard became associated in the summer of 1909 when Reichard became associate principal and instructor of Ottawa Business College in Ottawa, Ohio, which had been owned and operated by Miller since 1904. This was the foundation of a lifetime partnership that would lead to the formation of the future Tiffin University. After two years in Ottawa Reichard decided to pursue a master's degree, and Miller was determined to have him return to Ottawa upon completion of his degree. Noting the small population of Ottawa and the proximity of strong, competing schools, Reichard began to send letters of introduction to other business colleges in the region seeking possible employment. Dr. Charles Miller, then chancellor of Heidelberg University, received one of the letters and suggested that Reichard contact Sterner directly. Sterner's letter of reply made it clear that he wanted to relinquish his principalship and proffered a sale. Reichard forwarded the letter to Miller in Ottawa, and they met in Tiffin to review the offer. Before their first visit was over, Franklin J. Miller owned Heidelberg's Commercial College.

Although the amount Miller paid to purchase the school almost drained him financially, he and Reichard set out to build the college, establishing college traditions and raising standards. Taking along the single bicycle they mutually owned, they rode trains and the interurban as they worked the countryside recruiting prospective students. Historically, high school graduation had been officially required for admission, but this was seldom enforced. Miller and Reichard gradually changed that, and a graduation from a "first grade" high school was required for matriculation. The new owners of Heidelberg Commercial College had close competition to contend with. Both nearby Fostoria and Fremont had for-profit business schools. But after two years of aggressive recruitment, Miller bought the Fostoria school and opened a night school to fend off any new competitors; and the Fremont school simply closed.

Miller's and Reichard's hard work and entrepreneurial spirit paid off: During the five years Miller was principal and Reichard was vice principal (1912–17), the Commercial College of Heidelberg University was never more successful. Enrollment grew from 91 the first year to a high of 166, and this growth was supported, in part, by the addition of a Spanish American Department, which recruited a sizeable number of Cuban students. A Cuban native, Armando A. Perez, who was a graduate of Defiance College, taught these students in Spanish.

Professor Miller's aggressiveness in promoting the College of Commerce fulfilled the board of regents's wishes and at the same time caused some friction. He took rightful pride in the increased enrollments and improved quality as he continued to push for recognition of the importance of commercial education. However, even with his charisma and with the proven success and evident progressive approach, Miller could not achieve what others before him had tried and failed to do: the acting chancellor and the board of regents of Heidelberg University rejected Professors Miller's and Reichard's request for more space to increase enrollment in June 1916.

Moreover, Chancellor Miller and Principal Miller did not agree on the manner in which the Commercial Department would and did function. At the June 1916 meeting of the board of regents, members voted to discontinue the commercial department at the end of the 1916–17 academic year. The shortage of academic space on campus, the addition of the Cuban students, and the emphasis on lucrative job placements after graduation exacerbated relations between the two organizations. Without more space, Principal Miller feared, expansion was impossible.

However, Miller and Reichard were looking forward; for some time they had been considering founding a business school that mirrored the newly popular junior college of the day. Although years of planning and research were in place, the thoughts of securing a new location and the necessary equipment dissuaded them. With negotiations with the Heidelberg board failing, Miller and Reichard felt the time was opportune to embark on moving the Commercial College away from Heidelberg's aegis and establishing a new institution devoted to raising the standard of business education.

On Friday, January 14, 1918, the Commercial College of Heidelberg officially closed. Approximately eighty students from Heidelberg transferred to the new Tiffin Business University, where classes began on Tuesday, January 18, 1918. F. J. Miller rented four rooms on the second floor of one of downtown Tiffin's largest and most modern buildings, the Remmele Building. Only one day of class was lost for the move. On December 10, 1917, with a $10,000 personal investment of Mr. Miller, Tiffin Business University began operating as an incorporated institution. Miller and Reichard chose to include "university" in the name to signify their commitment to raising the academic standards of the school. With the $10,000 stake, they equipped the Remmele Building with the finest equipment available to accommodate more than 200 students. New courses of study were adopted, dropping all courses under two years of study; new faculty were added; and a new catalog was developed featuring higher accounting and management. This was a progressive departure from the typical one-year courses previously offered.

With a paternal fervor and an entrepreneurial flare, President F. J. Miller set out to build Tiffin Business University into the quintessential business college of the twentieth century. The 1920s were a time for physical, academic, and enrollment growth. Miller and Reichard were determined that their students would not only have the best facilities possible but the strongest possible academic program. The move to the Remmele Building proved to achieve this for the reorganized institution. The new facilities were a source of pride. The new catalog featured pictures and descriptions boasting that the facilities were "modern to the minute." Finally Miller and Reichard were not constricted by space, and the founders now turned their sights to advancing the academic stature of the university.

By the opening of the 1920–21 academic year, all programs were two years in length. Students could choose among accounting, business administration, executive secretarial, or commercial normal course, newly approved by the State of Ohio. The 1920s saw commercial education become a significant offering at the high school level, replacing what earlier commercial colleges offered. The teacher education program offered by Tiffin Business University provided its graduates the opportunity to teach in any four-year Ohio high school, as well as those in thirty-five other states. One of the first of its kind in the United States to receive authority to educate secondary school business teachers, Tiffin's Commercial Normal Course prepared its graduates to earn a teaching certificate awarded by the State of Ohio Department of Education.

The ultimate aim of Miller and Reichard was to offer a traditional four-year degree. In 1924 the university applied to the State Department of Education for authority to confer a Bachelor of Commercial Science degree with majors in Higher Accounting and Business Management and Commerce and Finance. This authority was quickly granted, and four graduates in the Class of 1925 were the first to be conferred this degree. The Commercial Normal Course was also elevated to a Bachelor of Science in Education degree. In addition, many four-year college features were added, including fraternities and sororities, orchestra, a college newspaper, and many other social activities. By the end of the 1920s, with the university's long waiting list for matriculation, President Miller expanded the physical plant to the entire second and third floors of the building. It was truly a decade of much advancement.

By the mid-1930s Tiffin Business University had grown far beyond a typical commercial college of the day. It was both a junior college and an institution empowered by the State of Ohio to grant four-year degrees. In addition, it held a small but substantial endowment and had no debt. Although the institution was officially a for-profit institution since its inception in 1888, its shareholders operated it as an educational enterprise devoted to students, one never strictly concerned with matters of profit. Modest dividends were awarded every few years, averaging four dollars a share, a token bonus.

In recognition of the growth and natural development of the institution, Franklin J. Miller, Alfred M. Reichard, and E. M. Huth, the sole owners of the outstanding stock of Tiffin Business University, devised a plan to change the for-profit status to a nonprofit status in the late 1930s. They believed that this change was essential to maintaining the highest standards for an institution of collegiate rank. After a year of conducting its affairs in a nonprofit manner, the board of trustees voted unanimously on November 10, 1939, to perpetuate the ideals and purposes of Tiffin Business University as a nonprofit institution. Their petition to the State of Ohio for nonprofit status included a new set of by-laws for the institution and a new name: Tiffin University.

Although many Ohio colleges' enrollments shrank during World War II, Tiffin University's swelled when it answered a call from the federal government. In 1943 the War Department was in dire need of trained typists, stenographers, and clerical workers. Because of Tiffin University's reputation as a first-class business school, it was selected as the only institution in the Midwest to train more than 800 women for the Air Technical Service Command (ATSC). This highly selective, intense program lasted fourteen weeks, with classes running six days a week, eight hours a day. Students came to Tiffin University from ten states. Adding to the desire to serve their country at a time of war was a generous salary, tuition and textbooks, and automatic job placement at Wright Field upon successful completion of the rigorous program.

A. M. Reichard remained actively affiliated with the institution for thirty-five years as secretary of the board of trustees and principal of the accounting department until he retired in 1947. President Miller announced his retirement on June 10, 1953, and was named president emeritus in honor of his forty-one years of service. The board chose one of its own, Richard C. Pfeiffer, to succeed Miller. An alumnus and successful accountant, Pfeiffer quickly hired the university's first academic dean, Dr. Olive Paramenter, to offset his lack of experience in academic endeavors.

By 1956 the Remmele Building's second and third floors had been home to the college for nearly thirty-nine years. Its ground floor was used for retail purposes. In college catalogs and promotional material, the building was often pictured surrounded by billowing clouds blocking out the first retail floor. Tiffin University was appropriately nicknamed the "Campus in the Clouds" by alumni and friends of the era. That was soon to change, however.

Over a July golf game with a member of the Tiffin board of education, President Pfeiffer learned that the local city schools were auctioning one of their historic school buildings. Pfeiffer then moved to bring the campus out of the clouds and place it on the ground, where it is truly a campus. The university's bid for the building was accepted, and on December 18, 1956, students, faculty, and administrators joined to move to this new collegiate home. An historic and architecturally significant structure in a residential neighborhood, "the Main" classroom building was to become the signature building in the center of the modern campus.

The campus grew to include more than a dozen buildings, most of which were residential houses purchased throughout the 1960s. One building purchased in 1968 was constructed 1872 and later would become Seitz Hall, the university's administration building. After a series of unsuccessful fund-raising efforts, the university successfully raised enough funds to construct its first building, a much-needed library. The board authorized its construction on June 26, 1967, and Pfeiffer Library was dedicated ten years later in honor of President Pfeiffer's twenty-five years of service as president.

Tiffin University averaged 200 full-time students and graduated an average class of sixty-two throughout the 1960s. Most of the students enrolled in the two-year program, however, and the trustees and President Pfeiffer feared that this trend threatened the future of the institution. Yet, expanding the curriculum and developing the physical plant seemed a daunting task.

But the 1970s brought new challenges—namely, growing competition from newly formed community colleges and the need to secure proper academic accreditation, both of which compounded Tiffin University's growing financial instability and threatened college's survival. It was obvious to many that the school had to rethink its academic offerings. Criminal Justice was added as a major in 1970, and on May 15, 1970, the Ohio Board of Regents certified that Tiffin University's two-year standard junior college course could be upgraded to an Associate's in Business Technology degree, thus reaffirming the university's ability to offer the four-year Bachelor of Commercial Science. This allowed the university to fully participate in the newly initiated federal and state financial aid programs, in turn serving more veterans returning from the Vietnam War.

The early 1970s were characterized by low enrollments and annual operating deficits. However, the advent of returning veterans would temporarily change that. Enrollment quickly increased from 1973 until the university posted its largest enrollment to date (624) in 1976. Concurrently, financial concerns and the lack of terminal degrees among the faculty stopped Tiffin University from securing proper academic accreditations. A lack of residence halls forced prospective students away, and by the end of the 1978–79 academic year, 60 percent of the 300 full-time students were enrolled in the evening program.

A milestone occurred when President George Kidd Jr. assumed the presidency in April 1981. When he became president there was talk of folding the school or merging it with another institution. He sought to change the perception that the university's mission was to train people to work for others. Asking stakeholders to raise their sights, Kidd set out to become like other universities. Referred to as "the founder of modern Tiffin University," Kidd found a willingness among the twenty faculty and staff to change and take risks, which allowed the institution to survive long enough to become part of the fabric of higher education in Ohio. Kidd quickly launched the most explosive growth in the institution's 115-year history. In his tenure as president, Kidd transformed this small, financially troubled business school into a comprehensive university.

Indeed, the transformation Tiffin University experienced was remarkable. Through a combination new academic and cocurricular programs and physical expansion, President Kidd launched a series of five-year plans that outlined growth in every academic and nonacademic area. Long-sought accreditation by the North Central Association of Colleges and Schools was received in 1983, recognizing President Kidd's ability to attract faculty to teach in baccalaureate-level programs. In 1980 no members of the faculty held terminal degrees, and the majority of students were in the two-year programs. By 2000 80 percent of the faculty held terminal degrees, and only 6 percent of the students were enrolled in the two-year programs. In 1983 the Bachelor of Commercial Science program was changed to Business Administration, while at the same time planning was begun to broaden the academic offerings, resulting in the addition of the Bachelor of Criminal Justice and Bachelor of Arts (1995) degrees. In the 1990s Tiffin University added is first graduate degree programs. The first Master of Business Administration (MBA) class graduated in 1992, and a Masters of Criminal Justice (MCJ) was added in 1996.

Word of mouth about the changes at Tiffin University became the best recruiter. Students began enrolling from beyond the traditional fifty-mile radius. With enrollment skyrocketing, many needed a place to live. The three-acre campus of 1980 would expand to eleven acres in 1990 and more than 130 acres in 2000. President Kidd led an effort to develop a total residential student experience, adding professional student personnel and residence halls. He constructed seven residence halls in a sixteen-year period: Friedley (1984), Zahn (1985), Miller (1992), Craycraft (1990), Huggins (1994), Kirk (2000), and Benner (2000). The Gillmor Student Center was dedicated in 1988 and became the largest construction project to date. Housing a gymnasium, as well as a complement of student service amenities, its size doubled in 2001 when it was expanded to include a theater and a new dining hall. The four intercollegiate athletic teams in 1980 quickly expanded to sixteen, including football added in 1985. Tiffin University was accepted into the National Collegiate Association of Athletics (NCAA) in 1999 and now competes at the Division II level. In 1992 the university added eighteen acres of modern athletic fields and locker rooms.

The academic transformation mirrored the physical growth. The university grew into its name, realizing the dreams of F. J. Miller and A. M. Reichard, by reorganizing its academic divisions into schools. In 1996 Tiffin University divided into the Schools of Business, Arts and Sciences, and Criminal Justice and a Graduate School. At the turn of the twenty-first century Tiffin University enrolled 1,600 in undergraduate and graduate degree programs offered at its main campus in Tiffin, at several locations in Ohio, at the University of Bucharest in Romania, and online. Tiffin University is truly a comprehensive university.

George Kidd Jr. announced his retirement in 2001 after twenty-one years of transformational leadership of Tiffin University. On July 1, 2002, Dr. Paul B. Marion became the fourth president of Tiffin University. The former president of Franklin College in Indiana, Marion arrived at Tiffin with thirty-four years of successful experience in higher education, including seventeen years as a chief executive officer. Tiffin University looks forward to reaching new levels of success under his leadership.

Suggested Reading

The Annual Report of Tiffin University (1995); Carl G. Klopfenstein, "TU: Our Beginnings," *Challenge Magazine: Centennial Edition* (1988); E. I. F. Williams, *Heidelberg College: A Democratic, Christian College* (Heidelberg College, 1950).

Urbana University

Persistence through Adversity

LISA ODA FEDE

One hundred and fifty years ago a group of men with the charge of educating their children according to their religious beliefs founded Urbana University. Among the leaders was Col. John H. James, a well-to-do settler of the Urbana community. Fellow members of the Ohio Association of the New Church, known later as Swedenborgians, including noted leaders James Parke Stuart and Johnny "Appleseed" Chapman encouraged him to donate ten acres of land he owned in Urbana as the site of a New Church University. James, Stuart, and Chapman believed that a Swedenborgian education could fill a void they believed existed in the nation's educational system during the early to mid-1800s. They believed the existing system fell short because it failed to emphasize the importance of spiritual and moral values in human development.

The teachings of Emanuel Swedenborg, the fifteenth-century Swedish scholar and inspiration for the religion, emphasize open discussion and the pursuit of truth in both academic and spiritual quests. Those who followed Swedenborg's teachings were encouraged personally to seek life's answers. Such a self-examination encouraged open thinking and openness to the discovery process—spiritually, nonspiritually, and academically. Indeed, freedom to pursue the truth is the foundation of Swedenborg's philosophy. For this reason the founders sought in their original goals to make sure that students were encouraged to pursue truth by open inquiry in any subject, be it religious or secular in content. In order to guarantee this process to all, the founders unanimously agreed that Urbana University would be a coeducational institution, making it only the second college in Ohio to include women.

On March 7, 1850, the Ohio legislature officially approved Urbana University's original charter as Colonel James had written it. The charter authorized "the creation of

The 2002 graduating class, nubering 289

an institution of learning designed to encourage and promote the diffusion of knowledge in all branches of academic, scientific, and evangelical instruction, and to combine therewith instruction in the productive arts and the practice of rural economy."

In the deed granting his property for the campus of Urbana University, Colonel James set forth several "conditions" to provide for the early financial stability and educational foundation of the university. According to the *New Jerusalem Magazine* of July 1849, James valued his ten-acre tract at $1,000 and stipulated that others shall contribute the sum of $2,000 within one year and that a building suitable for an institution of learning be constructed within three years. He also insisted that no part of Urbana University grounds be used for reasons other than education. In its 150-year history the school has overcome various difficulties, including low enrollment and financial hardships, by adhering to James's "conditions."

Throughout its history Urbana University has provided thousands of students with a liberal arts education that maintained its founders' goals of pursuing truth by means of open and independent inquiry. It has also encouraged an educational curriculum that emphasizes the importance of moral and ethical values in human development.

The person recognized as Urbana University's first president is Milo G. Williams. Although a relatively young man, Williams was a renowned educator. Born in 1804 in Cincinnati, he had established primary schools there and in Dayton. In 1822 Williams met Adam Hurdis, leader of the Swedenborg Society in Cincinnati, and was impressed with the church's doctrines of self-directed education and open inquiry, which mirrored his own educational philosophy. Williams, with fellow Swedenborgian David Pruden, opened the Dayton Manual Institute in 1833, one of the earliest institutions based on vocational education in Ohio. He served as headmaster of the public high school in Springfield, Ohio, from 1835 until 1839, when the opportunity became available to establish a Swedenborgian school in Cincinnati. Although the school was educationally sound, Williams faced financial difficulties in its operation, and the school was forced to close in only three years. Williams then moved to Dayton and opened the Dayton Academy, which proved successful. In 1850 Williams was chosen by Urbana University's board of trustees and founders to be the first president of the institution. He never accepted the official title, however, feeling unqualified to carry the distinction of "president." Instead he claimed the titles of dean of the faculty and president of the board of trustees.

Williams served the university until his death in 1880 but relinquished his duties in 1858, weary from the responsibilities of the new institution. At Urbana University's commencement exercises in 2000, Williams's school bell, which he used to call pupils to class throughout his distinguished educational career, was rung to call the commencement ceremony to order in honor of Williams, the university's founders, and the university's sesquicentennial anniversary. The ringing of the bell has since become a traditional event to call future commencement ceremonies to order.

In 1858 the Reverend Chauncey Giles was elected president of Urbana University, but ministerial responsibilities with the Swedenborg Church in Cincinnati prevented him from moving to Urbana. Since he held the position in the absentee role, he relied on those holding the position of dean, or principal, to handle the everyday affairs of the university.

The Civil War forced Urbana University to close from 1861 until 1866, when the university reopened in 1866 with a new principal, Alonzo Phelps. Phelps managed to expand enrollment from thirteen on reopening day to more than 100 in just two years. Phelps's adoption of an open-door admissions policy, while profitable, led to strife with the faculty, who were dedicated to academic standards and developing a highly regarded reputation for the university based on those high standards. This, together with Phelps's decision to more-or-less discontinue coeducation at the university by sending female students to a seminary off campus, led to a lack of confidence in his vision for the young university among faculty and members of the board of trustees. The move to separate men from women may have stemmed from increasing disciplinary problems, most likely attributed to nondiscriminatory enrollment, but it was looked on as a direct violation of the teachings of the Swedenborg church, which encourages open learning for all people.

With the appointment of the Reverend Frank Sewell as president in 1870, the board of trustees hired a leader who would be available to the university at all times. The board required the new president to move to Urbana and maintain regular office hours on campus. Under Sewell's leadership Urbana University made significant strides toward balancing its academic, moral, and ethical purpose and its need for financial stability.

Sewell encouraged self-improvement and open learning at the university by instituting such student activities as the annual "Spring Exhibition," which included presentations, orations, dramas, and musical numbers for students to publicly display their skills. The exhibitions were also well attended by the Urbana community. This reinforced the foundation for the university's long-awaited and hard-fought reputation as an institution noted for academic excellence. Extracurricular activities inspired by academic motivation not only greatly reduced the disciplinary problems but enhanced student educational opportunities toward open inquiry and personal reflection on moral and ethical values. Accordingly, students actively participated in musical, theater, and literary societies. Most notable was the first Urbana University student newspaper. First published in 1877, the *Courant* was such an outstanding exhibition of the literary and journalistic talent expressed by Urbana students that subscribers in twenty-five states and eleven foreign countries recognized it.

President Sewell's academic mission was coupled with a vision for financial stability in the undertaking of the university's first substantial endowment drive with an ambitious goal of $50,000. Unfortunately, due to lackluster growth in enrollment, the funds raised in this effort had to be used to cover operational costs. Sewell resigned in 1886.

Urbana University marked its fiftieth anniversary at the dawn of the twentieth century. Through continued efforts to deal with fiscal issues and administrative organization, the university enjoyed strengthened academic programs and new interest in athletic competition. Tennis and golf were popular sports, and the university fielded teams in baseball and football.

The presidency of the Reverend Russell Eaton was one of the most progressive in the university's history. Upon accepting the presidency in 1912, Eaton oversaw improvements in nearly every avenue of the university. A large bequest of $100,000 by Sarah Putnam Ropes of Salem, Massachusetts, came at a time when the university's aging facilities were in need of attention. The bequest was joined by a successful capital building fund from which repairs and renovations were made to Oak, Bailey, and Barclay Halls. The campus grounds were attractively improved with a new fence, walkway, tennis courts, and track. A basketball court was built in Barclay Hall. Inspired by the improved facilities, students became even more active in extracurricular activities, organizing athletic and academic groups. The first university glee club was formed.

At the commencement in 1916, John Worchester Spiers from Virginia became the university's last bachelor's degree recipient for more than fifty years, as the country was about to enter World War I and the university was about to change its curriculum to a two-year, junior college program. Russell Eaton resigned as president in 1917.

On April 5, 1920, a devastating fire occurred. Flames could be seen rising from the recently renovated Barclay Hall. Students and faculty risked their lives to rescue books and laboratory equipment from attached Bailey Hall, fearing the fire would destroy both buildings. The students were able to rescue the university's library, and the Urbana fire department saved Bailey Hall with minimal damage. No one was injured, but Barclay Hall, with its new gymnasium and roof, was a total loss.

Again the university received financial aid from a large bequest, this time from Thomas Coleman DuPont, an 1879 graduate whose family had amassed one of the largest fortunes in the United States. DuPont contributed $150,000, and another $125,000 was raised from other contributors to the fund. The DuPont donation allowed for repairs to Barclay Hall and for the university to continue operation despite low enrollment.

The 1924 course catalog was printed with the name "Urbana Junior College" on its lime-green cover. (That name would be used until 1967, when the four-year curriculum was reinstated and the name Urbana College was used. In the late 1970s the university again was called by its chartered name, Urbana University.) It was during this time that students again enjoyed expansion of student activities. In 1925 a student council was organized, and the university's new basketball team had a successful season, including two wins over Bowling Green State University.

Thanks to its earlier benefactors, the university survived the Great Depression with few difficulties. The 1930s brought new resurgence to the university's purpose of instilling open thought and the importance of moral and ethical values, along with self-discovery of the meaning of these values in one's own life. A new reputation was also being developed by the university among its students and constituencies, which still exists today: Urbana University is a friendly place to learn. Students and faculty developed friendships that remained through their lifetimes. This reputation, coupled with the academic reputation the faculty had developed, created a strong bond between the students and the institution. Urbana University continues to have reputation as a "family-oriented" campus where everyone knows everyone and a caring relationship exists between students and faculty.

Change in leadership and new organization within the administration led to prosperity in the early 1960s. President Ralph Gauvey set lofty goals to not only increase enrollment but also to set forth a new direction in the university's educational philosophy. Gauvey implemented a challenging new curriculum in English, sociology, history, mathematics, and science that focused on the philosophical and conceptual nature of the disciplines rather than on traditional memorization and rote-based principles. This curriculum incorporated a learning environment that encompassed the founding ideals of the university of open thinking and self-directed learning through personal exploration.

Gauvey initiated a ten-year plan of development that included financial stability, rapid growth in physical facilities, and enrollment expansion. The president also set forth plans to reinstate the four-year college program, with lofty goals of someday offering graduate degrees at the university. By the time Gauvey resigned in 1963, many of his goals had been achieved, and the plan was in place to achieve many more. Two new dormitories had been built and a successful fund-raising effort had been accomplished.

Gauvey's successor, Ronald Jones, continued plans for growth. Between 1965 and 1970 six new dormitories were constructed. Funds were raised, and the Swedenborg Memorial Library and University Community Center (now known as the Warren G. Grimes Center) were built. Leading the fund-raising efforts were community leaders Lewis and Jean Moore. Lewis Moore was mayor of Urbana, and his wife, Jean, was a member of the university's board of trustees. Their leadership and the support of Urbana University students has been a remarkable asset during the past thirty-five years.

The resurgence of the four-year program led to more liberal extracurricular activities on campus, including theater, choir, and band. The athletic program also was enhanced, due to both the four-year program and the construction of the University Community Center, which included a gymnasium, an Olympic-size swimming pool, racquetball courts, locker rooms, and exercise facilities, as well as classrooms. For the first time Urbana University teams played their home matches on campus rather than at local high schools. In 1969, after a fifty-three-year hiatus, bachelor's degrees again were awarded to forty recipients.

During the 1970s Urbana University began participating in a state and federally funded program to offer educational degree programs at two Ohio prisons, the London Correctional Institute and the Ohio Reformatory for Women in Marysville.

The prison education programs were looked on by critics as offering free education to criminals at taxpayer expense. But university trustees saw the program as an opportunity to honor the philosophy of the university by offering an education to all who seek to know the truth and look to better themselves through educational advancement, no matter what their position in life may be. In the early 1980s Urbana University (as it was once again officially known) boasted the highest enrollment in the school's history, although nearly half of its students were incarcerated.

President Paul Bunnell enjoyed the financial windfall and spent funds on main campus programs that benefited the declining number of main campus students. By 1988 Bunnell boasted an enrollment increase of 55 percent and an annual budget increase of 52 percent, most of which was attributed to the prison education program. Despite a lofty budget, when the city of Urbana condemned Barclay and Bailey Halls because of wiring and asbestos insulation problems, Bunnell could find no funds to repair the historic structures and recommended that they be destroyed. A few years earlier, Bailey Hall was awarded distinction on the National Historic Registry. An architect presented a proposal to the board of trustees to stave off the demolition by converting the buildings into a student union center, but the board decided that the $500,000 needed to renovate the structures would be better spent on new facilities for classrooms and science laboratories. Still, the board refused to approve the demolition of the buildings.

Since that time both halls have been reopened, and a capital campaign is under way for the renovation of the historic buildings. The $1.5 million renovation will allow the buildings to house the Johnny Appleseed Educational Center, university archives, and educational classrooms. Locating these programs in the buildings where their tradition and legacy will be preserved will honor the relationship between Johnny Appleseed and the university's founders.

Francis Hazard assumed the presidency in 1992 and addressed issues of enrollment and fiscal stability. He set forth a master plan to control spending and stimulate enrollment growth, similar what Ralph Gauvey achieved three decades earlier. While the university enjoyed strong academic programs and a highly regarded reputation as an academic institution, Hazard also sought to reaffirm the university's dedication to its founding principles. With faculty approval, the university established an educational mission based on its founding ideals.

The establishment of several national honorary societies on campus stimulated the academic mission. The curriculum was pruned, then expanded, particularly in the form of service to nontraditional adult students in degree-completion programs. The university began offering classes for nontraditional students at off-campus sites in Bellefontaine, Piqua, Dayton, and Columbus. Hazard also gave approval for the establishment of the Johnny Appleseed Museum on campus, which honored the Swedenborgian missionary who influenced the founders to establish the university.

In 1995 the Urbana University board of trustees unanimously approved the most significant change in governance in the university's history. Members of the Swedenborgian Church relinquished their position as majority seat holders on the board in favor of a governing body that could be more locally controlled by civic and business leaders and university alumni members. The new governing body was now comprised of no fewer than five members of the Swedenborgian Church, no fewer than five alumni, and as many as fifteen at-large members. The restructuring of the board allowed for more active membership in the university's governance from those in the immediate area served by the university.

Throughout the university's history the Swedenborgian Church has maintained an informal relationship with the university in sharing educational philosophies and ideals of its founders. The denomination, however, was never imposed on its students, in favor of the full freedom of religious opinion and faith consistent with its educational philosophy. Although now officially a private, independent, liberal arts institution, Urbana University still holds an informal relationship with the Swedenborgian Church.

A capital campaign was begun with assistance of Lewis and Jean Moore that culminated in the construction of the multimillion-dollar Lewis and Jean Moore Center for Mathematics and Science, which opened in 1996. Through the construction of this technology facility, students were given access to new, state-of-the-art science, laboratory equipment, and computer facilities.

Hazard also initiated enrollment programs with a goal of increasing main campus enrollment to 1,000 students through steady, yet manageable enrollment growth. Dormitories, which had been half-full only two years earlier, were nearly full by the beginning of the 1999–2000 academic year. The substantial growth in enrollment required construction of a new residence hall in 2000, the first built on campus in thirty-two years. A resurgence in on-campus students allowed for increases in student activities and programs on the main campus. The Cultural Awareness Organization became an active student group, bringing speakers to campus who motivated the student body to explore and respect individuals of all races and cultures, the same ideals the founders had wanted their children to be taught and early faculty members sought to instill in their students.

The Johnny Appleseed Society moved from its original location at The Dawes Arboretum near Newark, Ohio, to Urbana University. With students and alumni members, as well as members from all over the United States, the society is dedicated to preserving the ideals and legacy of the famous first farmer. The society's founder, Robert R. Williams, was the great-great-great-great-nephew of Johnny Appleseed. Williams saw the move of society to the university and the establishment of the Johnny Appleseed Museum on campus to be an ultimate tribute to his ancestor's legacy.

Along with success in attaining Hazard's goal of sustaining educational programs came continued growth in athletic programs. And in 1998 Gauvey's vision was finally fulfilled when the Master's of Education degree program for classroom teaching was established with twenty graduate students. Urbana University celebrated its sesquicentennial in 2000. It was poised to embark on the new millennium with an established pride in the institution's accomplishments and in its commitment to maintaining the educational philosophies upon which it was founded. In the 2002–3 academic year, the university enjoyed an enrollment boom. Over a two-year period, enrollment rose 28 percent to a total of 1,450 students. In September of that year the university celebrated a new partnership with the Community Hospital School of Nursing in nearby Springfield. The partnership allows nursing students to complete a dual degree consisting of a two-year nursing diploma from the nursing school and an associate's degree in health sciences from the university. The partnership was an initial plan to grow in the area of health science education.

Robert L. Head was inaugurated as the twentieth president of Urbana University in October 2001. His background includes twenty years in banking and nine years in higher education. His experience in strategic planning and budgeting will be key to helping the university meet its goals and in moving the institution forward. Head also brings experience in building community relationships and has worked to enhance the involvement of the university in the surrounding community. Pride in the institution's accomplishments and a commitment to the founding ideals were themes expressed in his inaugural address: "Our future is dependent upon three priorities: our ability to serve students well academically, to serve the community well, and to be keenly aware and adaptive to our greater societal involvement."

The coming years for the university will surely include changes in the way this educational philosophy is implemented, as technological advances are made and the computer age continues to call for more technologically based educational programs. However, Urbana University's founding educational philosophy will endure throughout the ages because it is based on the hope of all human beings for the freedom to seek the truth and be given the opportunity to learn from our own educational pursuits.

SUGGESTED READING

Frank Higgins, *The Will To Survive: Urbana College, 1850–1957* (Urbana College, 1977).

Ursuline College

Leader in the Education of Women

ANNA MARGARET GILBRIDE

Standing at the dawn of a new century, and a new millennium, one tends to look to the future and not to the past. On the campus of Ursuline College today, new challenges, new programs, and new buildings heighten excitement. On a campus with the oldest buildings constructed only a little over thirty years ago, it would be easy to forget that Ursuline College will soon be 132 years old and that its roots are much older still. To look back on the beginnings of Ursuline College is to trace a journey involving two continents.

The story of Ursuline College traces its beginnings to 1535 when Saint Angela Merici founded the first teaching order of religious women in Brescia, Italy. She named her community the Company of Saint Ursula after an early Christian martyr who was recognized as a leader of young women. The members of Angela Merici's religious order then came to be known as Ursulines. From the beginning the mission of the Ursulines was to lead and teach girls and young women the basics of a good Christian, educated life. This was at a point in history when education for girls was not even considered.

In time the movement spread from Italy to France where many schools for girls were established and staffed by the Ursuline nuns. A foundation in Paris became the center from which a number of other schools were founded. One of these was in the northern city of Boulogne-sur-Mer on the shores of the English Channel. Because of the school's reputation and its closeness to England, some English families sent their daughters to the Ursuline academy in Boulogne-sur-Mer in order to benefit from the Ursuline method of education. Three of these young women from England were Mary Beaumont, Theresa Young, and Arabella Seymour. A few years after completing their studies at the academy, Mary Beaumont and Theresa Young entered the convent and became Ursuline Sisters themselves. Meanwhile, Arabella

Original site of Ursuline College in downtown Cleveland, 1871

Seymour, who had converted to Catholicism while at the academy, started a school of her own in Lille, France. By 1850 these three women would help found the first Ursuline school in Cleveland, Ohio.

Three years earlier Bishop Amadeus Rappe had been named the first bishop of the new Diocese of Cleveland. Prior to this time, Cleveland had been part of the Diocese of Cincinnati, which encompassed the entire state of Ohio. As a young priest in France, Father Rappe had been the chaplain at the Ursuline Academy in Boulogne-sur-Mer before volunteering as a missionary in the Toledo area. He knew well the educational work of the Ursulines. With the large influx of Catholic immigrants in the 1840s, especially the Irish who were fleeing the famine in Ireland, Bishop Rappe turned to his friends in France and begged them to open a school in Cleveland. Permission was granted and a small group led by Mother Mary of the Annunciation (Mary Beaumont), set out from France for America, accompanied by Bishop Rappe. Three other members of the group were Ursulines—Sisters Theresa Young, Victoire Boudalier, and Sylvia Picquet—and the fourth was Arabella Seymour, who had been urged by Bishop Rappe to accompany the Ursulines. She agreed to come and brought numerous items from her school in Lille. They arrived in Cleveland on August 8, 1850. Soon after their arrival Arabella entered the Ursuline Community and received the name Sister Mary St. Austin.

To prepare for the arrival of the Sisters, Bishop Rappe had purchased a two-story home on Euclid Avenue in downtown Cleveland. In time a third floor was added, along with two curved wings for classrooms, which extended to the front edge of the property, almost to the street. The academy flourished. Young women also came to the Sisters in the evening to learn English and other skills.

Twenty-one years after their arrival in Cleveland, Mother Mary of the Annunciation Beaumont recognized the need for higher education of women and founded Ursuline College. In those days, opportunities for women to receive a college education were severely limited, due to the prevailing attitude that higher education was for men only. In 1837 Oberlin College had begun to accept women as well as men; and one of the Ursuline Sisters, Mother Ascension Smyth, had attended Oberlin before entering the Ursulines in 1865. Knowing the strong Ursuline mission to educate women and realizing the need, Mother Mary of the Annunciation obtained a charter from the state of Ohio on November 17, 1871, making Ursuline College the first chartered college for women in Ohio. The academy continued to exist as a separate entity, while Ursuline College provided higher education for women under empowerment from the state to grant degrees. Emphasis in the curriculum was placed on the liberal arts, and the degree conferred on graduates was the Bachelor of Arts.

In the beginning enrollment in college classes was extremely small, so classroom space was not a problem. After twenty-two years, however, it became evident that a move from downtown Cleveland was going to be necessary. The increase in commercial buildings on Euclid Avenue was crowding Ursuline College; and since the land was in great demand, a decision was made to move to another area.

A good location was found away from the center of the city at the corner of what is now East 55th Street and Scovill Avenue. The Sisters engaged the services of a noted architect in Cleveland, Charles F. Schweinfurth, to design a new and larger building that would meet the needs of Ursuline College, Ursuline Academy, and the Ursuline Convent. After spending forty-three years in downtown Cleveland, they moved the entire educational enterprise in 1893.

The next two decades witnessed the opening of an increasing number of parochial schools across the city, which placed demands on the Ursulines to staff them. Their numbers had grown as students who had been taught by the Sisters began to enter the community in Cleveland. In order to meet the needs, more and more time and efforts of the Sisters teaching college courses had to be spent in preparing the younger Sisters as teachers for the parish schools. This situation continued for a number of years and became the focus and priority of their teaching. After graduation in 1902, the college temporarily discontinued the granting of the Bachelor of Arts, a situation that lasted for over twenty years.

In 1922, however, Ursuline College had a major resurgence. In response to numerous requests to reopen the college to laywomen, Mother Mercedes Keegan, superior at the time, resumed the privileges of the college charter given in 1871. A new opportunity arose for Ursuline College to have its own campus, separate from the convent and academy. A building at University Circle, next to what is now Severance Hall, became available for renting to the Sisters. It belonged to the Catholic Diocese of Cleveland and had been used as a residence for the faculty of Cathedral Latin High School and later as a house for young men preparing to enter the seminary.

When the college reopened at this new site, twenty-six freshmen and four sophomores enrolled. Close to the building on Euclid Avenue was Western Reserve University. Officials there graciously allowed the Ursuline students to use their library to supplement the small one at Ursuline. As a result, numerous friendships were formed between the young women at Ursuline and the young men at Western Reserve.

Mother Mercedes assumed the role of dean and began the task of reorganizing the college and its curriculum. During the first academic year she obtained an affiliation with the Catholic University of America in Washington, D.C., and the college also became a member of the Ohio Classical Conference. The revised four-year course of study could lead to Bachelors of Arts, Science, or Letters degrees. The curriculum included languages, both modern and the classical, history, literature, religion, mathematics, the sciences, and the arts, especially music and painting. In 1924 Ursuline College was approved by the State of Ohio Department of Education for the training of high school teachers. Priests from the diocesan seminary had joined the faculty and taught theology, philosophy, and ethics.

The young women who enrolled as students were quite feisty and had a great deal of initiative. Their interests were not limited only to academics. In a short time, a basketball team was formed. Because there was no gym at Ursuline, games had to be played at other sites. This did not hinder the team, though, because it had many victories. In 1926 Ursuline College's basketball team won the citywide championship in Class A basketball, going through the year without a single loss. They played women's teams at hospital schools of nursing, other colleges, and Protestant churches. The championship game was won against the Central YWCA team. Other sports included track, field hockey, tennis, and ice skating at Wade Park. The main social event of the year was the all-college prom held at the Mid-Day Club downtown.

Case School of Applied Science extended hospitality to the Ursuline students when the Newman Club gave a bridge party for the juniors and seniors in 1925. Three young women and four Sisters were graduated that year, and seventeen young women the next. Fifteen received the degree Bachelor of Arts and two the Bachelor of Letters. The graduations were held at Wade Park Manor. Eleven of the 1926 graduates had fulfilled the requirements of the State Department of Education and received their four-year provisional certificates for teaching in high school. Added to that enrollment, another 200 more Sisters of various religious communities in Cleveland were enrolled in extension courses. A large number of Sisters also took courses on campus during the summer of 1924, the first time that Sisters of other communities were able to attend a Catholic college in Cleveland.

In April 1926, only four years after its reopening, word was received that the building which housed Ursuline College would be sold to Western Reserve University. With the demands of enrollment growth and expansion, it was also becoming apparent that more space would be needed, so it was time to move again. The building that housed Ursuline College from 1922 to 1926 is still standing today. It became Hitchcock Hall at Western Reserve and is now part of the expanded student center at Case Western Reserve University.

A new site was located at the top of Cedar Hill at the corner of Overlook Road. This area was considered the gateway to Cleveland Heights and was not far from the previous site on Euclid Avenue at University Circle. One class was held at the new location during the first semester, but the actual move took place between semesters in December 1926 and January 1927 during a severe blizzard. Two mansions separated by a driveway became the main buildings of the campus. One was designated as the administrative and academic building with lecture rooms, offices, assembly room, chapel, and dining room. The other building housed the library, music studios, and rooms for a limited number of boarders, plus quarters for the Sisters on the top floor. A third building behind the two houses became the science hall, with a gymnasium in the middle of the structure, while the left and right wings were given over to biology and chemistry laboratories. In time the second floor became the home economics department. Classes were soon in full swing, and things began to settle down. It seemed as if Ursuline College had found a lasting place. As events unfolded, however, the college would stay there for forty years before moving again.

In 1929 the first two African American students, Grace and Melvina Lomax, received their degrees from Ursuline College. Commencement was held in the Music Hall of the Public Auditorium. During that same year Ursuline became a member of the Ohio College Association and began the process of applying for accreditation from the North Central Association of Colleges and Schools. Mother Mercedes sought advice from other colleges and was always grateful for the counsel and assistance given to her by Bland L. Stradley of the Ohio State University, who remained a sincere adviser and friend for years to come. Among the recommendations that emerged during the accreditation process were calls for many more books for the library, more space, better science equipment, and more faculty with doctorates. This spurred the alumnae and friends of the college in their efforts to increase the library holdings with donations of books and money for science equipment. Meanwhile, two more Sisters were working on doctorates, one at Catholic University and the other at St. Louis University. Priests from the seminary had higher degrees, and additional lay faculty members with doctorates were hired to meet the standards required. Word of Ursuline College's accreditation by the North Central Association arrived in March 1931. Everyone rejoiced at the news and continued efforts to improve in every area.

In the meantime life on campus was busy not only with classes but also with guest lecturers and dramatic entertainment at weekly assemblies. Students were active in various clubs—such as the French Club, Latin Club, Spanish Club, Choral Club, Drama Club, Bio-Chem Club, Aquinas Study Club on world problems, Booknook Club, Bridge Club, and the Florentine Art Club—and basketball continued to be the favorite intercollegiate sport.

In 1931 Ursuline College, Notre Dame College, and John Carroll University held a joint commencement at Music Hall of the Cleveland Public Auditorium, along with the Catholic nursing schools in Cleveland. The three Catholic colleges had entered into an informal agreement to combine their Departments of Education, with Dr. Hugh Graham, chair of the education department at John Carroll, teaching on the faculty of the other two colleges. This arrangement seemed to satisfy the Ohio Department of Education in regard to teacher training in secondary schools. Ursuline College then became a participant in what was called the "Corporate Colleges of John Carroll University." This plan lasted for less than three years, however, partly because the legal and financial implications led lawyers for each institution to advise discontinuation of the arrangement. At the request of the bishop of Cleveland, though, the three Catholic colleges continued to have joint commencements for ten more years. Each college granted its own degrees with Bishop Schrembs presiding, but the ceremony took place on the campus of John Carroll, with the exception of 1939, when all Catholic educational institutions had a common graduation at Cleveland Stadium. In 1943 Ursuline College held its own separate commencement at Severance Hall for the first time. Severance Hall still hosts the annual Ursuline graduation, allowing each year's class to see the building next door, which housed the college from 1922 to 1926.

During the thirties Ursuline students continued with their academic programs but took time to socialize with other colleges. They still had bridge parties with Case Newman Club, and the seniors at Ursuline and Notre Dame entertained each other at an annual tea. John Carroll students presented entertainments at assemblies and attended various dances sponsored by Ursuline. They also shared intellectual pursuits through intercollegiate organizations on different topics; for example, the French Club of Ursuline entertained the French Club of John Carroll at the Statler Hotel in 1931. Spiritual development was nurtured through liturgies, speakers, and annual retreats. Students prepared Thanksgiving baskets for the poor each year and gave Christmas parties for underprivileged children.

In 1932 Mother Mercedes stepped down as dean of Ursuline College due to failing health. From the beginning of the college, the general superior of the Ursulines had served as president. Mother Mercedes had reopened the college while she was the general superior and had taken over as dean when her term as superior was over. Then, with more time given to the running of the college on a daily basis, she had immediately formed an advisory board to assist her. An English scholar, an able administrator, and a teacher of music and the dramatic arts, she had served as the leader of Ursuline College for ten years. The Mercedes Forum, a study group for students who gave presentations on current events, was established in her memory.

Sister Gonzaga Haessly took over as dean at the beginning of the academic year in 1932. Dean Haessly had been a faculty member teaching Greek and Latin. For many years she was active in the Ohio Classical Conference and attended meetings with colleagues and students at various Ohio colleges such as Oberlin, Marietta, the University of Akron, and the College of Wooster. Others attended numerous meetings of different associations that met in Ohio during those years. As numbers of participants grew, these meetings tended to move to larger space at hotels, but there are happy memories of meetings at other Ohio colleges, with the beauty of each campus and the gracious hospitality of those who hosted the meetings.

Students also enjoyed visiting other colleges. Ursuline students participated in a debate tournament with twelve other colleges held at Case School of Applied Science. Members of the Bio-Chem Club at Ursuline later visited the Case Observatory, where they viewed the telescope and heard a lecture on the sun. Later on they also visited the seismological laboratory at John Carroll.

With news of war and disruption in Europe, students and faculty planned programs for peace, such as an intercollegiate symposium on peace and war. One of the students presented a paper on the ethics of war. Students represented Ursuline College at the Ohio Valley Conference of the Carnegie Endowment for International Peace held at the Ohio State University. A large number of students also attended a lecture entitled "A Constructive Program for World Peace" by Dr. Charles Fenwick at Severance Hall. The situation in Europe remained a constant topic for conversation and class discussion, gaining greater momentum when the United States entered the war in 1941. Three months later Ursuline College announced the beginning of an accelerated program to meet the urgent need for women with degrees to fill positions of men who had entered military service. Courses would be offered in the summer during two separate sessions in order to accelerate the academic program so that students would be prepared to qualify for those positions.

Ursuline students also participated in various other efforts. Committees were formed to promote the sale of war bonds and defense stamps. After two years it was announced that Ursuline College had exceeded its goal and that year's quota with 100 percent participation of the student body. In a report compiled by the U.S. Treasury Department on the efforts of women's colleges during the Second World War Loan Drive, Ursuline College, in proportion to its enrollment, ranked first in Ohio and fourth in the United States. First aid classes were taught, and students made posters urging everyone to participate in some patriotic effort. The junior class contributed proceeds from the prom to purchase a pilot radio for the reception of air raid signals. With the opening of the 1942 fall term, the U.S. Office of Civilian Defense called on colleges and universities to mobilize civilian defense on their campuses. As a result organizations of faculty and student defense units were formed at Ursuline. The college also participated in a drive sponsored by the National Council of Catholic Women to purchase ambulances. Enough funds were raised to purchase nine ambulances, which were formally presented to the United States Army. Four representatives of the college attended the presentation.

Some of Ursuline's graduates participated in the war effort in a different way. One received a position as interpreter of French with the American Red Cross and was sent to France. Other individuals joined the WACS, the WAVES, and the Marines. There was great jubilation when the war ended in both Europe and the Pacific. Every family was touched by it because everyone had someone in the armed forces.

The postwar years brought continued emphasis on fieldwork in certain majors. Much like the education major whose student teaching experience prepared her for the classroom, a student majoring in sociology and aspiring to a career in social services could do some type of fieldwork at various local children's agencies. In some cases students attended informal hearings in Juvenile Court. Visits to Hudson Boys' Farm and Blossom Hill School showed rehabilitation programs in operation. Parmadale's Children's Village and the DePaul Home illustrated the care given to dependent babies and children. Those majoring in dietetics were able to do internships in hospitals in various parts of the country.

At the time of the move to Overlook Road, a carriage house behind the main buildings had been turned into a charming art studio. Although art courses had always been taught, there was no major in art until 1947, when Sister Gonzaga asked Sister Kilian Hufgard to establish a Department of Art after she returned from teaching art at Catholic University. Professor Hufgard established an art department on the first floor of a small building behind the residence hall. That same year the first Founder's Day was inaugurated at Ursuline College to honor Mother Mary of the Annunciation Beaumont.

Life at Ursuline College was pleasant during the fifties, as it was in most colleges throughout the country. The war was over, students were serious about their studies, faculty worked hard to teach their classes, and activities were supported enthusiastically. Clubs remained active at Ursuline, and some increased their outreach to the poor. The Red Cross Unit at Ursuline had many projects to help others in need. For a number of years the Choral Club presented an annual spring concert in the auditorium of the Cleveland Museum of Art. In 1957 Ursuline College became a member of the Ohio Foundation of Independent Colleges, an organization that would become a significant source of financial support for many years to come.

The decade of the sixties began with excitement. John F. Kennedy was elected president, and young people began showing an interest in politics. (An Ursuline student, Mary Rose Oakar, attended his inauguration in Washington. Some years later she became a member of Cleveland City Council and was then elected to the U.S. House of Representatives, where she served her Ohio congressional district for many years.) Vatican Council II had opened in 1962 and brought a breath of fresh air into Catholic life. Students became involved in ecumenical activities and the civil rights movement. The war in Vietnam, however, had a chilling effect on campuses throughout the nation. When the war was coming to an end, an Ursuline graduate, Ursula Gallagher, assisted in the airlift of orphans out of Vietnam. She was working for the Children's Bureau of the former Department of Health, Education, and Welfare and had helped to develop standards for services and laws related to adoptions. An estimated 14,000 children were transported to the United States where families waited to adopt them.

Meanwhile, based on studies of children who would reach college age in the sixties, colleges and universities in Ohio had been looking ahead to plan for an expanding enrollment of baby boomers in the next decade. Ursuline was no exception. The Ursuline Sisters were building a new convent at this time in Pepper Pike, and a college building fund was started to plan for the eventual move of Ursuline College to the same property. In a few years it would be time to move again.

When the college had reopened to the public in 1922 at University Circle, Mother Mercedes and the advisory board knew from the start that they had not yet found a permanent home for Ursuline. With the purchase of the property at the top of Cedar Hill, the problem was solved temporarily, but there was still concern about finding a campus for the future. In the meantime the Sisters at the motherhouse and Ursuline Academy, the high school at East 55th and Scovill, were also looking for a place to relocate. In 1927 Mother Eusebia Kelly, general superior, had purchased fifty acres of property on Fairmount Boulevard near Lander Road. It was hoped that the space could one day accommodate both a motherhouse and the college. Two years later saw the onset of the Great Depression. The Ursuline Sisters held on to the property, though, and never gave up their dream.

Almost twenty years later a fire destroyed a building on the grounds of Villa Angela Academy where many of the Sisters had been living since the move from East 55th Street. Now they were even more aware of the need for new space and new buildings. An opportunity to buy more land adjacent to the property in Pepper Pike presented itself in 1949. A little over sixty-two more acres were purchased at a sheriff's auction. This additional property faced Lander Road. The land, at least, was in place.

Fund-raising efforts then began in earnest. Under the leadership of Mother Marie Sands, general superior and president of Ursuline College at the time, a new mother-house was planned to house administrative offices, infirmary, classrooms, novi-tiate, and living space for the Sisters. This had to be the first priority, since many Sisters had been displaced after the fire. The building opened in 1958. Even while it was under construction, though, plans were under way to move Ursuline College to the property. Alumnae of the college had started fund-raising events for a new resi-dence hall. A new advisory board was deeply involved in the planning and fund-raising efforts. It was the first time in its history that Ursuline College had a public campaign for funds.

When Mother Marie presided each year at honors convocations and granted awards, she would give regular reports to the faculty and students on progress to-ward the new campus. As it happened, this was also at a time when Case Western Reserve University was looking for more space to build residence halls, and the Ursuline property became of interest to them.

Initial plans for the new campus included an administrative and academic build-ing with classrooms, offices, chapel, and theater; a science building with laborato-ries for biology, chemistry, and home economics; a residence hall; a dining hall; and a temporary library. Mullen Academic Building was named for Monsignor Jo-seph J. Mullen, who had taught at Ursuline from 1923 to 1966. Although it was ex-citing to anticipate the move to Pepper Pike, emotions were mixed for students, faculty, and alumnae as they prepared to leave the place that Ursuline had enjoyed for forty years. The move took place in the summer of 1966. When classes started in October that year, it was the first time that Ursuline had a campus with brand new buildings, and a whole new era opened for the college.

Other changes began to occur. A new general superior was elected, Mother Annunciata Witz. Whereas the general superior had always been the president of the college, with a dean in charge of daily operations, Mother Annunciata made a significant change. She appointed Sister Rose Angela Johnson, who had been serv-ing as academic dean, as the first president of Ursuline College who was not also the general superior. The system of dual roles had served well when the college was small, but as enrollment increased so did the complexities of administration. Now, with the move to a new campus, it seemed wise to make the change. Two years later the college was separately incorporated from the motherhouse with its own board of trustees, composed of both laypersons and Ursuline Sisters. Herbert E. Strawbridge, president of the Higbee Company in Cleveland, was elected the first chairman. One of the board's early decisions was to drop the phrase "for Women" in Ursuline's title so as not to discriminate against men, a few of whom were seeking admission to classes on the new campus. Although Ursuline has remained a college primarily for women and its mission to educate women has not changed, some men have opted to enroll in certain programs, initially in music and business. The first male student was graduated in 1975.

In the summer of 1969 Sister Kenan Dulzer became the first president elected by the new board of trustees, a position she held for the next seventeen years. During those years remarkable growth took place in enrollment, new programs, and new buildings. Sister Rose Angela returned to Ursuline in 1970 and began a program in continuing education for adult women returning to college, one of the first in Ohio for nontraditional-aged students. The following year Ursuline celebrated the hundredth anniversary of its founding in 1871. Numerous events were planned for the entire year in recognition of Ursuline's centennial, which included a series of women's conferences, opening with Ohio governor John Gilligan as keynote speaker.

That same year an innovative tripartite College Council of fifteen members was instituted, composed of five administrators, five faculty, and five students. Administrators were elected by others in administration, faculty members by their colleagues, and students by their peers. The president of the college attended each meeting, gave reports on what was happening, and answered questions. Proposals were submitted for discussion and input, after first being submitted to the respective group's representative body, and some were approved for implementation. The College Council was one of the first such groups in the country that included students in decision making, providing them a forum and the opportunity to discuss issues and make decisions with administrators and faculty.

During the late sixties and early seventies the Choral Club had annual concerts with other choral groups from Catholic men's universities, such as Georgetown University, the University of Notre Dame, Mount St. Mary's, John Carroll, and Holy Cross. A new physical education facility opened in 1974 with a gymnasium, a swimming pool, and classrooms for teaching dance. It soon became a favorite gathering place for students.

A major change for Ursuline, however, would happen the following year. In the fall of 1974 it was announced that St. John College in downtown Cleveland was closing. St. John's had been founded in 1928 by the Diocese of Cleveland in order to centralize and strengthen teacher training for the Catholic elementary schools. A nursing program was added in 1947, and St. John's was then authorized to confer two degrees, Bachelors of Science in Education and in Nursing. By the early seventies, however, enrollment in the education program had decreased significantly; and although the nursing program was doing well, the school required a substantial diocesan subsidy. Unable to continue this financial commitment, the diocese determined that St. John's would have to close at the end of the 1974–75 academic year. The bishop of Cleveland, James A. Hickey, asked Ursuline College to take on the nursing program in order to save it. After studying for weeks the impact on Ursuline that such a merger would entail, especially the financial implications, the Ursuline board of trustees voted to accept the nursing program with all of its students and faculty members, a sizable addition of almost 400 people. Many challenges ensued with the merger of two student bodies, two faculties, and two curricula. The program retained the name of St. John College for a few years until Ursuline gained its own accreditation for the program.

In December 1980 all at Ursuline College were shocked and saddened to hear that Ursuline Sister and graduate Dorothy Kazel had been murdered with three other missionary women in El Salvador. Each year on the anniversary, luminaria and candles are lit on campus in memory of her martyrdom. Twenty years after her death, Sister Dorothy was inducted into the Ohio Women's Hall of Fame for her profound dedication to justice and compassion for the poor.

Under the leadership of Sister Kenan, Ursuline College grew in a number of ways. It was time for new options. The Florence O'Donnell Wasmer Art Gallery was built in 1980; and ushering in an age of graduate programs on campus, a Master's in Educational Administration for Nonpublic Schools was approved in 1982. Also, in 1985 a new library was built and named after Ralph M. Besse, who had worked tirelessly to raise funds for Ursuline College when the Pepper Pike campus was built. Clearly it had been a busy and energetic time since the move from Cedar Hill. In 1986 a second graduate program was established, a Master's in Art Therapy, currently the only approved graduate art therapy program in Ohio. That same year Sister Kenan stepped down and Sister Anne Marie Diederich became president.

President Diederich soon began a process of strategic planning. Everyone in the college community was included in discussions on the mission statement, and committees were formed around issues, which included a revision of the curriculum. A task force presented a model for a core curriculum based on the values associated with Ursuline's identity as a Catholic liberal arts college for women. The new program gained national attention as the only one in the country to be based on the research into women's learning reported in *Women's Ways of Knowing,* by Belenky, Clinchy, Goldberger, and Tarule. Called the Ursuline Studies Program, it created an interdisciplinary liberal arts core that encourages students to relate learning to life, to make connections between their experiences and those of others, and to work collaboratively with faculty and peers throughout their college careers. Also, as part of the strategic plan a comprehensive campaign was launched in order to raise funds for an endowment, renovation of buildings, and initial computerization of the campus.

The beginning of the nineties saw the establishment of a master's degree in ministry, a program that promotes and fosters professional ministerial development by providing a blend of academic, formational, and practical experiences for persons involved in or preparing for church-related ministry. A master's in education was later inaugurated as a teaching apprenticeship program in conjunction with University School.

In 1992 the college celebrated Mother Mary of the Annunciation Beaumont's induction into the Ohio Women's Hall of Fame for the influence she had on women and education in Ohio. By association the honor was also a tribute to those pioneer women who came with her from France to Cleveland to start a system of education in the Ursuline tradition. These religious women and those who became their followers as Ursulines were intelligent, talented, dedicated, and prayerful leaders of women.

Sister Diana Stano was inaugurated as the sixteenth president of Ursuline College in 1997. Identifying strategic issues and a vision for Ursuline based on the mission statement, she immediately pursued an innovative accelerated program in business management designed especially for professional women and men. The program meets the needs of a diverse clientele by providing flexible scheduling and a variety of approaches to learning. Under President Stano's leadership the college also offered enhanced technological instruction with Web courses and initiated an effort to gather information on factors affecting women and their career selections, student population demographics, trends in higher education, and employment trends. The results indicated the expansion of women's roles into leadership and executive positions, increasing competition for students, increasing diversity, and advances in technology. Among the recruitment initiatives proposed in response was recognition of the need for an intercollegiate sports program that would expand the college's pool of prospective students. After study the board of trustees approved the establishment of a sports program with basketball, volleyball, soccer, and golf.

In 1998 Ursuline began a Master's of Science in Nursing, the first in the nation to offer students the option of specializing in palliative care. A second option in the program is case management, which combines nursing and business theory. Two years later a Master's in Liberal Studies began to be offered. A new Student Learning Center was built and opened in 2001, after a long process of planning involving the entire college community and a successful fund-raising campaign. With its lighted tower, new technology, and a stained-glass window highlighting the spiritual nature of the college, the building has become the focal point of the campus and is viewed as the first step in a new master plan.

Reflecting the parable of the mustard seed, Ursuline College has grown from its small beginning in 1871. As it moves ahead into the new millennium, the college will continue to maintain its focus on women while welcoming all students into an academically challenging and values-based environment that fosters the lifelong learning of the total person while preparing leaders for society. Judging from its legacy, Ursuline College will fulfill its mission, remaining ever old and ever new.

Rosemarie Carfagna, *Educating Women at Ursuline College: Curriculum, Collaboration, and Growth* (Mellen, 1998); Cynthia Glavac, *In the Fullness of Life: A Biography of Dorothy Kazel* (Dimensions, 1996); Michael Francis Hearon, *The Broad Highway* (1951); Luciana Mariani, Elisa Tarolli, and Marie Seynaeve, *Angela Merici* (Enitrice Ancora Milano, 1989); and materials in the Ursuline College Archives.

Walsh University

The Youngest Catholic Cradle of Conscience

JOSEPH TORMA

The education of students is to combine academic and professional development with formation in moral and religious principles and the social teachings
of the church.

—Pope John Paul II, "The Apostolic Constitution on Catholic
Universities," *General Norms,* Article 4, No. 5

Walsh University, Ohio's youngest four-year Catholic college, received its first class
in 1960 under the name of Walsh College. It was established by the Brothers of
Christian Instruction, an international congregation of Roman Catholic Teaching
Brothers founded in France in 1819 primarily to provide education for the poor.
The latest edition of the Brothers' Rule of Life still states that "the Congregation
fulfills its apostolic mission primarily by the human and Christian education and
instruction of youth, especially of the lowly and the poor." From France some of
their number went to Quebec and eventually to the northeastern United States,
where they founded elementary and secondary schools, especially for the needy. In
the 1950s they founded Lamennais College in Alfred, Maine, primarily to prepare
their student Brothers for teaching careers.

Soon, however, because of their interest in more effectively extending their educational services to able college-level young men of limited means who might join
the Brothers, they were willing to move their college to a diocese in which they
could do this. The Catholic diocese of Youngstown, Ohio, agreed to assist the Brothers financially in opening a college in North Canton, if they would help start and
staff St. Thomas Aquinas High School, a new Catholic high school on the east side
of neighboring Canton. At first the Brothers called their new institution Canton
College but soon found that a small business college had prior rights to that name.

Saint Francis, Peace Park, 1996

They then christened the school Walsh College after the bishop of the Youngstown Catholic diocese, Bishop Emmett M. Walsh. The college's identity evolved over time.

The school opened in 1960 on 123 acres of land with two buildings—one donated by the diocese—and a small freshman class of sixty-seven young men, including a number of student-Brothers. Seven idealistic and energetic Brothers made up the entire administration and faculty, while the students did most of the janitorial work. The school grew by about 100 students a year until it reached 1,000 in 1970.

During the 1960s Walsh College was a traditional Catholic college with strict behavioral standards for the residential students, extensive requirements in theology and philosophy, high visibility of the Brothers, a mostly Catholic faculty and staff, and a priest-chaplain supplied by the diocese. The Brothers, however, were not able to continue to train and provide Brothers who had terminal degrees.

The end of the baby boom and the opening of the Stark County campus of Kent State University in 1968 began to affect enrollment, because Walsh was primarily dependent on students from the area. The coeducational nature of Walsh's primary feeder system within the Catholic high schools led the college to become officially coeducational in 1972, but the numbers continued to decline to about 600 in 1976.

During this time the Brothers added laymen, mostly businessmen, to the board of trustees, and eventually the board became one that was relatively independent of the Catholic hierarchy. The Brothers also gave up majority control on the board in 1975. This transfer of ownership, called "alienation of property" in Church law, happened in most Catholic colleges after the Second Vatican Council and occurred in most cases, including that of Walsh College, without the ecclesiastical permission required by Canon Law. According to Stanislaus Woywod, O.F.M., "The disposal of the ecclesiastical goods is invalid if any formality was neglected which is prescribed under pain of invalidity. . . . Since the disposal of it was invalid, the possessor did not acquire title to the property" (*A Practical Commentary on the Code of Canon Law,* 239). One effect of the attempt to transfer ownership from the Brothers to an independent board was that the school began to become more dependent on the secular community than on the official Church community.

Nevertheless, Walsh kept a clear Catholic identity during most of the 1970s. Most students continued to be recruited from Catholic high schools (with scholarships for a gifted student from each Catholic high school in Ohio). All students took three or four courses in theology. The Brothers along with the Catholic faculty and staff were in the majority, even though non-Catholic faculty and staff had been added. Support for diocesan schools came in the form of assistance in training Catholic schoolteachers, even though the college was not yet coeducational and most of the teachers were women. Help from the diocese came in the form of a priest-chaplain supplied by the diocese. The college also provided space for the annual diocesan Catechetical/Liturgical Day, an in-service conference for hundreds of people serving in diocesan, parish, and school catechetical and liturgical ministries. The annual Theology/Philosophy Symposium, which usually featured key Catholic speakers, was begun in 1976. This symposium was, and continues to be, the only regularly scheduled annual lecture at Walsh.

While its Catholic identity remained strong, the college did not develop many partnership ties to individual parishes of the diocese of Youngstown or the parishes of the contiguous counties belonging to the Cleveland, Columbus, and Steubenville dioceses. For many, if not most, denominationally related schools constituent congregations serve as a source of new students, new faculty, new staff, and new revenues. The lack of such a source for Walsh may have contributed to the decline in enrollment. Also, because the school was young and had not developed much endowment and because the post–Vatican II decrease in numbers of Brothers had necessitated the hiring of more expensive lay faculty, the decline in enrollment led to a financial crisis.

In 1978 Brother Francis Blouin, a theologian and former provincial-superior of the Brothers, became Walsh College's third president. As provincial he had overseen the attempted transfer of ownership of the college from the Brothers to an independent board of trustees. Now he helped Walsh College survive its economic crisis through selling seventy acres of college land and securing an emergency loan from the Brothers. Eventually the college reduced the number of full scholarships offered select Catholic students and attempted to broaden its student base by offering partial scholarships to a larger number of students with a wider range of ability, providing more aid to an increased number of varsity athletes, and initiating professional programs such as nursing, counseling, and business. As a result of these steps student enrollment increased steadily during the 1980s.

Although there also was a larger number of lay faculty with terminal degrees, the corps of Brothers remained strong. They were supported by a half-time Brother and a full-time Sister who had joined the chaplain in campus ministry because the president continued to be concerned, as he was in 1979, that the religious identity of the college "had become blurred, and that a concerted effort was needed to create at Walsh the Christian community of learning and service which had been envisioned by its founders."

He did not seem to perceive that the continued "blurring" might have been at least somewhat related to his preference for the word "Christian" instead of "Catholic" in the context of his statement that "all religious traditions make contributions to the understanding of man. . . . We at Walsh College are proud to have members of many different religious denominations on the faculty and among our students."

Additionally, the connection to the diocese weakened. It was no longer involved in the training of Catholic schoolteachers at Walsh, nor was its Catechetical/Liturgical Day held on campus. Also the college did not act on the diocesan plan to co-sponsor lay ministry training at Walsh. In 1984 the diocese decided to ask Ursuline College of Cleveland to provide theology courses in the Canton area.

Immediately an emergency meeting between representatives of Walsh and the diocese was held at the diocesan offices in Youngstown. Walsh inquired as to what it could do for the diocese. The diocese explained its most pressing need was an associate's degree program in pastoral ministry to prepare part-time lay pastoral ministers for service in the parishes. Diocesan leaders anticipated that by the year 2000 the diocese would have only about one-half of the priests it had at that time. As a result the college developed both associate's and bachelor's degree programs in pastoral ministry. However, for some reason it failed to advertise the programs or provide the diocese with promotional materials, and it did not add the necessary personnel. In 1990 the college canceled the associate's degree program but retained the bachelor's degree program for the few students who were interested.

There were other signs of weakening Catholic identity. Crucifixes were absent from classrooms in the science building because of the perceived requirement to ban religious symbols from places that benefited from federal funds. Some thought that theology courses should not to be taught in the science building for the same reason. Theology requirements were reduced by one course, and courses in Judaism and Eastern religions could now count toward the theology requirement. A professor trained only in philosophy was hired to teach theology. Promotional materials no longer emphasized the religious identity of the college, nor was careful attention given to the potential "fit" of the students, particularly athletes, for a "Catholic" institution. While faculty, administration, and staff were screened for professional credentials, little attention was given to church relationships. By the end of the decade there was no longer a "critical mass" of knowledgeable and dedicated Catholics. When a Peace Park was established on campus and named for Brother Francis in 1993, dedication speakers included a Protestant congressman and a Jewish Rabbi, but no representative of the Catholic diocese.

At the same time the president was responsible for other things that reaffirmed the college's Catholic identity. A Peacemakers Chapel that could seat more than 100 replaced a chapel that held twenty. Campus ministry was given a room to nurture Christian community, and the Brothers established Peacemaker Scholarships for students to work in campus ministry. The Brother responsible for international students, who lived in a student dormitory, also worked half-time in campus ministry. He facilitated numerous projects, including the Peace Academy and the campus chapter of the Pledge of Resistance, a movement of public opposition to U.S. policy in Central America organized by the Sojourner Community in Washington, D.C. In keeping with this Central American commitment, the Brothers also helped provide sanctuary for an El Salvadoran political refugee. Speakers on justice and peace, including Coretta Scott King and four Nobel Peace Prize winners—Mother Teresa, Willy Brandt, Adolfo Perez-Esquivel, and Elie Wiesel—visited campus each semester.

An Institute for Justice and Peace (IJP) was started in 1985 to "evaluate social issues in the light of Catholic social thought." A theology professor was given extra-curricular responsibility for the Institute and, in time, paid part-time help and work-study students. IJP sponsored special events such as weeklong summer workshops and the Bread for the World musical *Lazarus*. Later on the Institute organized a "Peace Goods" display (for the sale of justice- and peace-related items) in the bookstore. Most of the day-to-day activity of the Institute involved keeping social issues before the consciousness of the Walsh community through display racks of social justice literature, the maintenance of social justice bulletin boards and a social issue video series, and periodic speakers (often in conjunction with the diocese). The Institute also sponsored a monthly community discussion of a Catholic social document—the only regularly scheduled general discussion at Walsh of any Catholic teachings. These discussions were critical to Walsh's Catholic identity because they symbolized the uniqueness of Catholicism as stated by the prominent American ecclesiologist the Reverend Richard McBrien: "Unlike his brother Christians, the Catholic accords antecedent attention and respect to the stated positions, past and present, of the Church's college of bishops, whether expressed collectively or through its spokesman, the bishop of Rome."

The most visible initiative of the Institute, however, was the Peace Park, mentioned above, which was meant to embody the university's commitment to the Church's requirement that Catholic education include "formation in . . . the social teachings of the church." The park, which occupies a substantial portion of the area between the administration and science buildings, is described in a brochure as "a monument to the traditions of peace and justice that have helped to shape the spirit of Walsh University." It includes a Peace Pole Garden with stones commemorating the visits by the Peace Prize winners, a Shalom Pavilion with a statue of a man beating a sword into a plowshare (Isaiah 2:4), an Earth Flag and a United Nations Flag, a statue of St. Francis of Assisi, and an Armillary Sphere on a column with words from the Second Vatican Council: "God has willed that all people should constitute one family."

As the 1990s dawned Brother Francis felt he had done all that he could for the school. Although he had saved it from fiscal difficulty, increased enrollment to 1,550 students, and professionalized faculty and staff, he had two consistent frustrations: raising money in the community and seeing many students without apparent growth in moral stature. Also, he did not feel that he could effectively lead the institution closer to its founding mission. Although the board encouraged him to stay on, he resigned in 1992.

The Brothers had been very concerned about the Catholic identity of the school. But it may be that, unconsciously, they equated that identity primarily with the commitment of the Brothers rather than with the commitment of the members of the institution as a whole. For the first time the president was not a Brother of Christian Instruction but a Franciscan priest trained as a psychologist, Father Richard Mucowski. He recruited two other Franciscan priests who, together with a Franciscan Sister already in campus ministry, seemed ready to replace the Brother of Christian Instruction presence with a Franciscan one.

The new president immediately initiated a change of name from Walsh College to Walsh University, promoted the deans to vice presidents, and added new deans. He brought football to the athletic program, built a new dormitory, and added an accelerated degree program in business as well as a physical therapy program. All these changes involved expenditures that required an increase in tuition that may have moved the university increasingly out of its working-class market niche. The ensuing diminution of numbers let to an overextension of the university's budget and the president's premature departure after about four years. Before leaving, however, he had begun to deal with the issue of Catholic identity that had been raised in 1990 by Pope John Paul II's "Apostolic Constitution on Catholic Universities" (*Ex Corde Ecclesiae*), which was based on the teachings of the Second Vatican Council and Canon Law. The document contained statements clarifying the Pope's understanding of the identity and mission of the Catholic university as well as the norms that follow from this understanding. The guidelines for implementation of these norms were to be worked out by the nation's bishops. When the guidelines were approved by the Vatican, they were to be put into place at each college and university.

The first version of the guideline suggested by the American Catholic bishops was presented to the Catholic college and university presidents in 1993 for reaction. The presidents in general felt that the guidelines were too "juridical" and would compromise their academic freedom, so they asked for a revision. In the meantime the presidents were asked to educate their constituencies about *Ex Corde Ecclesiae.* There are three positions taken by *Ex Corde Ecclesiae* that are especially notable here:

1. "The education of students is to combine academic and professional development with formation in moral and religious principles and the social teachings of the church" (General Norms, Article 4, No. 5)
2. "The responsibility for maintaining and strengthening the Catholic identity of the university is shared in varying degrees by all members of the university community and therefore calls for the recruitment of adequate university personnel . . . are both willing and able to promote that identity" (General Norms, Article 4, No. 1)
3. "Bishops have a particular responsibility . . . even when they do not enter directly into the internal governance of the university, bishops should be seen not as external agents but as participants in the life of the Catholic university" (Identity and Mission, No. 28)

The president delayed educating the Walsh University community about these principles and, instead, requested that the university review and revise its mission statement. Various constituencies contributing ideas for drafts. A critical moment came in October 1993 when the provost sent "Draft No. 7," which had originated in the president's office, to the Academic Assembly (an organization of faculty and administrators with "faculty status"). The provost wrote, "The Mission draft you are now receiving has been read and revised several times at a variety of levels. We are asking that you review it once again before it is considered by the Board of Trustees." This draft began with "Walsh University is an independent, coeducational institution that was established in the Catholic, liberal arts tradition with a global perspective." Although the statement retained references to the "Judeo-Christian tradition" and "the example and teachings of Jesus Christ," the relationship to the specific "Catholic" and "liberal arts" traditions was consigned to the past ("*was* established in the Catholic, liberal arts tradition"). Underlying this could have been the understanding that if you claimed that Walsh "is" Catholic, then you would be admitting accountability to the juridical Church, which claims proprietorship over the name "Catholic" when it is used by institutions.

According to the minutes of that Academic Assembly meeting, a professor "suggested that the members of the Assembly examine the draft line by line, discuss revisions, and reach consensus before adjourning. The members accomplished this task in a spirit of cooperation and enthusiasm. The result of this undertaking is attached hereto as Draft 8." Draft 8 restored the present-tense reference to Catholicism—"Walsh University is an independent, coeducational, Catholic, liberal arts university"—and was then presented to the board of trustees, which retained this sentence, even though they rewrote other parts of the draft.

With the official retention of a Catholic identity, the president appointed a theology professor to be the university's first "Mission Effectiveness Officer." In turn, the officer organized a committee to work with him from 1995 to 1997. They educated the various university constituencies regarding the Apostolic Constitution and derived from them a large number of practical ideas for enhancing Walsh's Catholic identity. The entire process, however, was not without controversy, especially among the faculty. One professor argued that Catholic identity should be developed from within the university and not imposed from without. He had difficulty with the juridical connection of the university to the Catholic Church. The same was true of the chair of the board of trustees, the last Brother-president. When he was at the university for a board meeting he attended an *Ex Corde Ecclesiae* meeting of the Academic Assembly. In a final comment he stated that he had trouble referring to "Catholic values" and preferred "Gospel values" instead.

Soon after the revision of the mission statement, the board of trustees reviewed the *Faculty Handbook*. They inserted into the "Equal Employment Opportunity" section this sentence: "Walsh is a Catholic University and, thus, may prefer individuals who are Catholic or who demonstrate adherence to the ideals of Catholicism." During an Academic Assembly discussion of this sentence in October 1995, one of the Brothers, a lawyer, stated that the language was legally allowable. The theology professor who was the university's Mission Effectiveness Officer expressed the opinion that this was the minimum required by *Ex Corde Ecclesiae*. Nevertheless, the minutes of the meeting record that "there was almost unanimous dissent about the clause preferring Catholics. Most Catholics who voiced an opinion wished to go on record that they were Catholic and feel the preferential hiring and treatment of Catholics to be offensive. . . . Overall speakers felt the section was not in keeping with Walsh's tradition and mission statement."

Despite the attention and discussion given to the institution's religious identity, by the mid-1990s the university's top management, with the exception of the president and his assistant, was non-Catholic. This applied to the vice presidents for academic, student, and business affairs and enrollment management and development. Since the second-level management and the faculty were also largely non-Catholic, the only constituency with a small majority of Catholics was the student body.

In 1995 the Catholic Diocese of Youngstown had not replaced the departing diocesan priest-chaplain with another diocesan priest or supplied the funds for his replacement. One of the Franciscan priests hired by the president was appointed to do half-time work in campus ministry (replacing the full-time priest) and half-time teaching in the theology department. The half-time Brother in campus ministry, who organized social concern activities, was not immediately replaced when he left Walsh to study for the priesthood. This 40 percent decrease in campus ministry personnel was accompanied by a 40 percent decrease in campus ministry office space. At the same time the campus ministry became directly accountable to the vice president for student affairs (who was not Catholic) rather than to the president. In the meantime, too, the number of Brothers employed full-time by the university decreased from twelve in 1990 to just four in 1999 (none of them members of the theology faculty).

What may have been the most significant academic event of the late 1990s, as far as Catholic identity was concerned, was the restructuring of the academic core. Instead of trying to satisfy the objectives of *Ex Corde Ecclesiae* and increasing the minimal theology requirements (which at the time were two to three courses for the B.A. and two courses for the B.S.), the requirements were reduced to two courses for the B.A. and one to two for the B.S. At the time of the Academic Assembly discussion about the proposed core changes, the Mission Effectiveness Officer suggested that any discussion about the core should include reference to *Ex Corde Ecclesiae* and the requirements that would seem to flow from that. This was not done, and the proposed reductions were voted on and passed without any reference to the Apostolic Constitution. Some students could now graduate from Walsh with only one course in theology (the prerequisite Scripture course). While Catholic identity declined, the university started a Jewish studies program. A Jewish rabbi who taught the courses in the program on an adjunct basis was given special assistant professor status, and a Walsh professor became the director of the Jewish studies program.

What is probably a good summary of the impression that Walsh gives to the outside world can be found in a recent reference work called *Ohio Cum Laude: The Whole Ohio College Catalogue*. After indicating that "Walsh is affiliated with the Roman Catholic Church and was founded by the Brothers of Christian Instruction," it observes that

> the Catholic connection is not nearly as strong at Walsh as it is at other church-affiliated schools. . . . The school catalogue proudly states, "Spiritual enrichment for all students, no matter their faith and background, is an important aspect of life at Walsh." A handful of Catholic brothers continue to live on campus . . . . theology classes . . . are said to be non-denominational. The school also offers a full program of religious activities, including Sunday Mass, weekly liturgical services, retreats, Bible study, service opportunities, ministry experiences, and prayer groups. Still attendance isn't required of students for any of the activities, and the majority of the services are ecumenical.

The school's foundation with the church is also evidenced by the presence of the Institute for Justice and Peace, which "aims to evaluate contemporary social issues in light of the tradition and teaching of the Catholic Church." The institute's work is displayed by the Peace Park, a spot in the middle of the suburban campus neatly decorated with benches, monuments, and flower beds. (283)

The question of Walsh's Roman Catholic identity was one of the concerns of Bishop Thomas Tobin, the new bishop of Youngstown. Aware that *Ex Corde Ecclesiae* gave ultimate responsibility for the university's Catholic identity to the bishop, he addressed this issue specifically in his installation homily on February 9, 1996: "Every person or agency that bears the name 'Catholic,' whether it be . . . a Catholic university . . . is called to be authentically Roman Catholic embracing everything that noble name implies . . . that we are united to the Universal Church; . . . that we are proud of our Catholic heritage and anxious to pass that heritage on to future generations." Because the priest-president of Walsh had recognized the canonical relationship of Catholic bishops to Catholic universities, he had invited both the Latin Rite bishop of Youngstown and the Romanian Byzantine bishop of Canton to be part of the Catholic identity discussions when those discussions first began at Walsh in 1993. The bishop of Youngstown and the Byzantine bishop were part of the preliminary discussion.

When in 1996 the Mission Effectiveness Officer invited the new bishop of Youngstown to become involved, the bishop stated: "As you know, perhaps, the NCCB [National Council of Catholic Bishops], at its recent meeting, approved a proposal for the implementation of *'Ex Corde Ecclesiae'* in the United States. It is my understanding that this proposal now requires the approval of the Holy See. When that final documentation is received, it will be very important for me to become more familiar with and involved in the discussion of *'Ex Corde Ecclesiae'* at Walsh University." In contrast, when the Franciscan chaplain replaced the original Mission Effectiveness Officer, the Byzantine bishop was not invited to continue with the discussions. Nevertheless, he continued to be involved at Walsh as a member of the advisory board of the Institute for Justice and Peace.

In 1997 Walsh named economist Dr. Kenneth Hamilton as its first lay president. He had not been educated in Catholic institutions of higher education, but he was a Catholic and had served as a professor and administrator in two Jesuit colleges. Although the immediately preceding interim president had been a non-Catholic, the board of trustees had required that the new president be a Catholic and work to enhance Walsh's Catholic identity. Among the changes made immediately were the inclusion of explicit references to Catholicity in all promotional material, the addition of pictures of the Pope and the bishop of Youngstown in prominent places, and the placement of crucifixes in all classrooms. The contributions of the Brothers were highlighted in official publications and at various community gatherings. The Franciscan priest who was director of campus ministry was also appointed chair of the theology department and to the president's staff as Mission Effectiveness Officer. The Institute for Justice and Peace also came under his purview, because responsibility for it was transferred to the theology department from the office of the vice president for academic affairs. Coordination of service projects was included again in campus ministry. In direct gestures to the diocese, the university established closer ties to the diocesan education department and agreed to host the first Diocesan Eucharistic Congress.

At the same time, however, the renewed emphasis on juridical accountability to *Ex Corde Ecclesiae* had the potential to create tensions. Some in the university, and especially among the faculty, had difficulty with *Ex Corde Ecclesiae's* idea, in Article 49, that "all the basic academic activities of a Catholic university are connected and in harmony with the evangelizing mission of the church." As his first major appointments the president replaced four non-Catholics and one Catholic with five non-Catholics in the vital roles of vice presidents for business affairs, enrollment management, and development and assistant dean of students and registrar. Although the bishop had stated in 1996 that he would become involved at Walsh only after the Vatican approved the guidelines for application of *Ex Corde Ecclesiae*, after three years he could wait no longer. He arranged for a four-and-a-half-hour visit at Walsh in which some of the implications of the document were discussed with key officials, theologians, and campus ministers.

In light of the Brothers' primary concern for education and the poor, the subsequent status of Catholic identity at Walsh might well be indicated by a case study of the recent experience of the Institute for Justice and Peace. When the Institute was begun in 1985, it enjoyed the active support of the president, the academic dean, the campus ministers, and the members of the theology department. This situation continued until when, in 1992, the Brother-president resigned and the academic dean returned to the teaching faculty. At that time support for the Institute began to weaken. The weakening continued with the departure of the Brother in campus ministry, who had been directing social concern activities, and the naming of the Franciscan chaplain as director of campus ministry.

In 1997, when the first lay president was being interviewed for the job, he stated that he felt that the American bishops had received bad advice when they wrote their landmark 1986 pastoral letter on economics and that they should have kept to general principles and away from specific applications. And, immediately after he became president, he began to withdraw institutional support for the Institute's mission of academic examination of social issues. His spokesperson wrote, "While

I have called for student involvement in service to others, you have suggested that your role and the role of the Institute should be primarily academic."

The Institute's advisory board (which included a bishop, diocesan officials, a former missionary priest, and various Walsh personnel and alumni) met with the president and communicated their conviction, as stated later in a letter from two diocesan members, that "the Institute . . . effectively promotes the Catholic identity of Walsh University through social justice education." The president replied that the Institute could pursue its social education goals "only if it did not use tuition dollars." And, subsequently, he wrote that "neither office space, funding for staff salaries or general budget line funding will be provided to the Institute" and that "the Institute exists now as a concept only."

At this point it could have been concluded that the relatively secularized condition of Walsh University would make the continued strengthening of its specific denominational identity difficult but not impossible. Walsh had a significant record of contribution to the mission of the Church, especially in the area of justice and peace when this was not popular in the Canton area. And there is no doubt that the university sincerely wished to continue its service, especially in regards to cultural opportunities and the training of teachers for roles in Catholic education. Moreover, Catholic colleges and universities, unlike many of their non-Catholic counterparts, do not have the liberty to declare themselves free of responsibility to the juridical Church. This fact evidenced itself when, in the spring of 2001, the president, under pressure from members of the board of trustees, set up an ad hoc committee to deal with "Mission Fulfillment." The committee was to be chaired by Richard Jusseaume, the vice president of the board, who was a CEO of a small company and a former Brother of Christian Instruction who had served two terms as dean of students at Walsh. The first meeting of the committee was delayed until finally half of the committee was able to meet on June 5. The meeting was relatively uneventful, except that the chair revealed to one of the members that he had just resigned as CEO of his business and was offering his services to the church.

This fact became significant almost immediately. That very evening the president died suddenly. Within two weeks Jusseame was asked by the board to serve as president. Immediately he became involved not only in continuing the building and educational projects begun by the former president; but in the spirit of the committee on mission fulfillment that he had chaired ever so briefly, he also began to address the issue of Catholic identity. He extended the services of the university to the diocese even more than before and began to hire people who were noted not only for their professional credentials but also for their ability to contribute to the Catholic identity of the university. He made a commitment (especially significant in the light of increased student interest in religious careers) to establish or strengthen pastoral ministry programs at every level and to increase the presence of the Brothers at Walsh. And he reactivated the Institute for Justice and Peace.

The previous spring two freshmen who had been involved in the protest against the School of the Americas at Fort Benning in Columbus, Georgia, expressed an interest in getting involved with the Institute for Justice and Peace. During orientation they had heard from the professor who had directed the Institute about the essential nature of justice and peace education in a Catholic university. Now they were informed that the Institute existed "in concept only." However, in the fall they asked the new president if they could become work-study students in the Institute. After brief research into the history of the Institute, and with the agreement of the professor who had been the director to again direct the Institute and serve as their supervisor, the president reactivated the Institute. He provided office space, ad hoc funding, and promise of continued support.

The reactivation of the Institute is just one development among many others. The establishment of a prayer garden with religious statuary, the creation of an Institute of Catholic Studies, the expansion of the theology faculty and plans for a graduate degree, and a program of religiously oriented speakers all point to a future more characterized by the founding Catholic mission of the Brothers of Christian Instruction.

Suggested Reading

Other sources of information about Walsh University include James A. Baumann, *Ohio Cum Laude: The Whole Ohio College Catalogue* (Orange Frazer Press, 1997). Materials available at Walsh University's Library include Walsh College and Walsh University catalogs, back copies of *The Spectator* (student newspaper), and back issues of the university publication *WalshWorld* (now *Walsh University Times*). See also Cynthia Wise Staudt, "The Brothers of Christian Instruction at Walsh College: Catholic College Builders in a Non-sectarian Era (1958–1992)" (Ph.D. diss., University of Akron, 2000).

Wilberforce University

Black America's Oldest University

ERVING E. BEAUREGARD

Wilberforce University proudly presents itself as the oldest private institution in the United States of America for the higher education of members of the Negro race. Both black and white parishioners of the Methodist Episcopal Church cooperated in the founding of the institution named in honor of the great abolitionist, William Wilberforce. The torch of the founders passed on to dedicated persons who continued the mission of service under the African Methodist Episcopal Church.

By the 1850s antislavery ministers of the Cincinnati Conference of the Methodist Episcopal Church believed that an institution of higher learning for the education of Negroes would help greatly in eradicating slavery. They felt their view was reinforced by Bishop Daniel A. Payne of the African Methodist Episcopal Church who preached inside and outside his denomination that the "Negro be educated to plead his own case."

On October 31, 1855, a committee of the Cincinnati Conference sought to raise $10,000 for establishing "The Ohio African University." The site would be Tawawa Springs, Greene County, Ohio. The committee chose that spot because of its reputation as a health resort. The mineral springs attracted many visitors and the water was transported for therapeutic purposes. Moreover, facilities shone at Tawawa Springs: a magnificent building of 200 rooms for possible classrooms and dormitory and cottages for faculty and employees.

On August 26, 1856, a Cincinnati Conference committee renamed the institution "Wilberforce University" and secured recognition from the authorities of Greene County, Ohio. (Tawawa Springs would become the village of Wilberforce.) Twenty-four persons comprised the board of trustees, four of whom were "colored": Bishop Payne, Lewis Woodson, and Alfred Anderson of the African Methodist Episcopal

Original buildings of Wilberforce University, 1856

Church and Ishmael Keith of the Baptist Church. Wilberforce University "was to afford facilities for the liberal education of the colored youth of the country in general"; "was organized in a spirit of enlarged Christian benevolence"; should allow "all equal opportunities and the utmost freedom of opinion"; was to remain under the control of the Methodist Episcopal Church; and a majority of the trustees "shall always be members of the Methodist Episcopal Church."

Wilberforce University opened in October 1856. The elected president, Frederick Merrick, refused the office. The Reverend M. P. Gadis Jr. of the Methodist Episcopal Church was the principal. The other faculty members were the principal of the Normal and Preparatory Department, the matron, the music teacher, and additional teachers deemed necessary by the trustees.

On June 30, 1858, a product of Wesleyan University, Richard S. Rust of the New Hampshire Conference, Methodist Episcopal Church, was unanimously elected president. The faculty consisted of: George M. Wendell (A.M., Ohio Wesleyan University), classical languages and natural science; Mary J. Allen (Wesleyan Academy), French and mathematics; Sarah Jane Woodson (Oberlin College), English; and Adelaide Warren (Oberlin), music. Within two years the enrollment increased from fewer than fifty students to more than 200. Curriculum revision and extensive planning occurred. Quickly Rust converted Wilberforce from a primary school into a college featuring the classics, French, mathematics, and theological studies.

By 1859 there were 207 students. Most were natural children of Southern planters. The latter would arrive each summer to enjoy the mineral waters of Wilberforce village. A number of families came also, and the slave mothers and children were manumitted; broad farmlands were purchased, homes were established, and liberal funds were provided for their maintenance. Moreover, Negro students were recruited from the free states of California, Ohio, and Pennsylvania. After their education at Wilberforce University most of the students taught in several of the western states and, after the Civil War, entered the South as teachers of freed persons.

By 1860 indications pointed to an excellent future for Wilberforce. However, the outbreak of the Civil War proved calamitous. Serving the Confederacy, the Southern planters and slaveholders no longer sent their children as students. Thus, financial collapse ensued. In October 1862 the trustees closed Wilberforce University.

On March 10, 1863, Bishop Payne, on behalf of the African Methodist Episcopal Church purchased the property of Wilberforce University for $10,000. The sum of $3,000 was to be paid within three months. Within that period Payne, assisted by Principal John G. Mitchell of the Eastern District School, Cincinnati, a graduate of Oberlin College, and the Reverend James A. Shorter, pastor of the African Methodist Episcopal Church, Zanesville, raised the $3,000. On July 10, 1863, a new charter was granted. The charter stated that the university was "to furnish the educational means of a thorough course of education to the colored race." The institution was to "forever remain under the management, direction and control of the African Methodist Episcopal Church and for that, a majority of the Board of Directors and Trustees shall always be members of the African Methodist Episcopal Church." The charter also provided that no one, "officers, faculty or pupils," shall be excluded "on account of merely race or color." The trustees numbered 130: 115 denominational, nine honorary, and six ex-officio bishops. The trustees elected Payne president of the university, Mitchell treasurer, and Shorter principal.

Mitchell, who had immediate direction, opened the new Wilberforce University in the first week of July 1863. There were "six pupils in primary English studies; having but one teacher." Enrollment gradually increased. Soon the principal's wife, Fannie, joined the faculty, and in the spring of 1864 Esther T. Maltby, graduate of Oberlin College, became lady principal and teacher. In 1865 Greek, Latin, and lower mathematics were added for the more advanced students.

President Payne devoted himself to financial matters. Visiting all seven of the African Methodist Episcopal Annual Conferences, he secured pledges of $2,000 from each for Wilberforce. He contacted also wealthy persons for funds for the institution's continued operation. However, five conferences failed to raise their quotas, and only the Baltimore and Ohio Conferences fulfilled their full pledges. Yet within two years, Payne, Shorter, and Mitchell had paid the full amount of the debt.

However, before the agents made the final payment on the property, disaster struck. On April 14, 1865, fire set by a bitter Southern sympathizer destroyed the main building. Some thought the institution would close, but Payne and his coworkers redoubled their efforts to raise funds for operation. Erecting classrooms in cottages, Professor Maltby continued instruction for the few students who remained, but the burden undermined her health, and she resigned in 1866. For awhile Joseph P. Shorter, one of the advanced students, did much of the teaching.

President Payne worked strenuously for Wilberforce University. As patrons of the institution he obtained U.S. Chief Justice Salmon P. Chase, Senator Charles Sumner, Maj. Gen. Oliver A. Howard, and Gerrit Smith. Payne secured appropriations from the U.S. Congress. He got financial support from private organizations like the American Unitarian Association but failed to raise funds abroad. Payne built a brick structure to replace the frame one destroyed by the 1865 fire.

Payne held strong views. He stressed class work and examinations. He was a strict disciplinarian and favored minimum student social life. Payne's philosophy of education, "Christianity and Culture," dominated the lives of faculty and students. He made religious instruction a rock of the university. He instituted twice-daily chapel attendance. (This continued until 1891 when the trustees permitted the faculty to omit one of the daily periods.) Payne also ordered two prayer meetings during the week, one obligatory for students and one optional. He urged the African Methodist Episcopal Conferences to send young men to Wilberforce for ministerial training and young women for preparation for Christian education. He stressed preparing teachers for public schools and the development of music education. Payne made physical culture a required course for men and women.

Payne expanded the curriculum. In 1866 the classical and theological departments began, the scientific followed in 1867 and the normal in 1872. Payne's Wilberforce consisted of six divisions: subacademic, covering two years; law, two years; normal, two years; academic, three years; scientific, four years; and theological, four years. In the academic division instruction stressed Greek, Latin, and Hebrew. In 1870 the first degrees were conferred.

President Payne gathered a competent and satisfied faculty. He strongly opposed the annual election of teachers. Black faculty members were Professors Josephina Jackson, Thomas H. Jackson, Benjamin F. Lee, Fannie A. Mitchell, Samuel T. Mitchell, Emma J. Parker, Benjamin K. Sampson, and Mary J. Woodson. (The latter two were graduates of Oberlin College.) White faculty included Professors W. B. Adams of Amherst College; Alice M. Adams of Mount Holyoke College; Roswell Howard and William Kent of Oxford University; John Little, Mary McBride, and Esther T. Maltby of Oberlin College; and Theodore Suliot of the University of Edinburgh.

To advance Wilberforce University President Payne founded organizations. He established the Wilberforce University Endowment Association to raise funds for scholarships and professorships. He organized the Society of Inquiry of Missions to gather data about Christian missionaries and to inculcate the missionary spirit in theological students. Payne founded the College Aid Society in order to promote the mutual helpfulness of the community's married women and the university's more advanced female students. He promoted the Solalian Literary Society and other student groups involved with cultural development of students.

President Payne resigned in 1876. He took pride in the granting of twenty-five degrees. He also noted the attendance of scores of other students. They entered several professions in various parts of the country. In 1876 the Reverend Benjamin F. Lee became president. A graduate of the Wilberforce Class of 1872, he had been professor of theology and ecclesiastical history at his alma mater and then an African Methodist Episcopal pastor. Now he headed Wilberforce, which had hostility from a large segment of the African Methodist Episcopal ministers. Lee sought funds in vain from the Church's Conferences. As a result the faculty accepted low salaries so the university would operate.

Difficulties arose between Lee and the faculty. Alice Adams, the able principal, and the respected S. C. Bierce (graduate of Oswego Normal School), head of the normal department, resigned over disagreements with the president. Suitable persons could not be found to replace them. Eventually, the board of trustees begged Lee and Bierce (now married to Professor William Sanders Scarborough) to harmonize their disagreement, and she resumed her position. Adams did not return.

President Lee's administration showed little advancement for Wilberforce. Although the president gave much attention to the matter of instruction, the curriculum remained static. Low enrollment in the law department caused demands for its abolition. The Bierce-Lee imbroglio caused a severe setback for the teacher training department. Nevertheless, Lee's tenure had some assets. The university had enrolled 1,179 students, including five Haitians, and graduated forty-one. The Wilberforce Concert Company, organized in 1881, through its tours advertised the university and thus helped increase the student body. Shorter Hall was completed. And because of Professor S. C. B. Scarborough's advocacy, a museum was purchased. Ware Art Room was fitted. Bethel African Methodist Episcopal Church of Philadelphia furnished music rooms. President Lee hired Professor Williams Sanders Scarborough, an Oberlin graduate, who would leave his mark as classical scholar and administrator.

In June 1884 President Lee resigned. He had been elected editor of the *Christian Recorder*, the leading African Methodist Episcopal Church newspaper. Wilberforce now faced a bitter presidential election. Choosing the new president deeply divided the trustees. John G. Mitchell received seventeen votes, T. G. Steward twelve, and John T. Jenifer two. Since sixteen votes sufficed, Mitchell was declared president. However, Steward's followers would not concede. A day after the election the trustees met and passed a motion to rescind the election. Thereupon Samuel T. Mitchell, a brother of John G. Mitchell, was elected and ordained in the African Methodist Episcopal ministry to preserve an "inviolable tradition."

President Mitchell, Wilberforce alumnus (Class of 1873) and professor, proved an excellent choice. A dynamic speaker, he attracted private donors, thus being able to increase income 50 percent. Furthermore, in 1887 he made an unprecedented arrangement with the Ohio legislature. The state would finance a "Combined Normal and Industrial Department at Wilberforce University," the university providing buildings and teacher training resources. For 1887 and 1888 the state pledged $5,000 per annum. Thereafter the department's trustees (three named by the governor of Ohio and three by the Wilberforce board of trustees) would make annual estimates of expenses for presentation and review by the legislature. Each legislator from all of Ohio's eighty-eight counties was permitted to send one student tuition free. Mitchell also secured state funds for a female dormitory.

During Mitchell's regime the regular college curriculum, four years for a bachelor of arts, was the typical college curriculum of the time: the classics, mathematics, biological and physical sciences, philosophy, and religion. There was a "scientific" curriculum for a bachelor of science. The curriculum of the normal course consisted of two courses: the elementary English course of two years and an advanced English course of three years. The degree-granting Law Department included mock courts. In 1894 the U.S. government established the Department of Military Science and Tactics (the first at a "colored" school). The trustees in 1891 converted the theology department into Payne Theological Seminary, executive power residing in its dean. (Bishop Payne became the first dean.) Because of the state appropriations for the Combined Normal and Industrial Department, the African Methodist Episcopal Church authorities decided it best to place the work in theology in a separate institution. Thereafter A.M.E. Church funds were apportioned between Wilberforce's collegiate and preparatory divisions on the one hand and the seminary on the other. The latter conferred a Bachelor of Divinity degree.

In 1896 an unfortunate action took place. The state trustees of the Combined Normal and Industrial Department prevailed in making the department's superintendent its de facto president. The office, a political appointment by the governor, received a salary larger than that of the Wilberforce president as well as several perks at the state's expense. Thus, the Combined Normal and Industrial Department became a separate entity.

President Mitchell's term included a transcontinental event. In 1894 Bishop Reverdy Ransom of the A.M.E. Church sponsored the enrollment of the first South African students at Wilberforce. By 1918 fifty students had arrived and about twenty-five had graduated. On a campus of about 400 students they were conspicuous. The very month the first South Africans arrived, Wilberforce was visited by a self-styled "African explorer," who showed astonished students the scars that established her as a "blood brother" of a particular "tribe." Sermons, essay contests, and monthly missionary meeting all dwelt on Africa. Groups of church women "adopted" a number of the South Africans, despite the fact that most were well into their twenties.

Wilberforce had a powerful impact on its South African students. "Shielded as they were from the more intractable realties of Afro-American life, they left the school with all the articles of their nineteenth-century creed—their devotion to 'civilization,' their beliefs in education and progress, their faith in the essential reasonableness of the colonial order—intact." These students helped in forming and spreading the African Methodist Episcopal Church in South Africa. And they became politically prominent. One participated in founding what became the African National Congress and also the Industrial and Commercial Workers Union. Three Wilberforce graduates belonged to the Johannesburg Joint Council, which brought together enlightened whites and blacks to discuss South Africa's racial problems. Another was a stalwart in the Joint Conferences of Europeans and Bantu. The Wilberforce graduates presented their grievances with moderation and decorum.

Some controversies occurred in President Mitchell's term. In 1891 Mitchell had serious trouble with the Reverend Dr. Thomas H. Jackson (Class of 1870), professor of Hebrew and theology and affectionately known to the students as "One-eyed Jack" because of blindness in one eye. (In 1882, as a member of the board of trustees, Jackson had opposed the retention of Mrs. Scarborough because he believed she would not work in harmony with President Lee.) The trustees refused to reappoint both Mitchell and Jackson until they agreed in an open meeting of the board to harmonize their differences. Upon compliance they were rehired. The board's minutes do not specify the cause of conflict in this case.

In 1892 a dispute broke out between Jackson and William Sanders Scarborough, professor of classics. On May 6, 1892, in a letter to the *Cleveland Plain Dealer* Scarborough attacked Jackson's character. (Jackson had proposed the abolition of the classics department.) Scarborough accused Jackson of mistreating his own family, consuming "spirituous liquors," keeping a mistress in Xenia, and misbehaving with female students. The board appointed a committee that accepted Jackson's side of his marital problems and his statement that drinking "spirituous liquors was for medicinal purposes"; the committee judged the mistress allegation as rumor and believed forty "lady students" whose signed statement denied improper relations with Jackson. Nevertheless, the board, without allowing Jackson to appear before it, condemned his character (Jackson was himself a board member) and took no further action against Jackson. In that same year Jackson left the Wilberforce faculty to occupy the presidency of Shorter College; however, he retained active membership on the Wilberforce board. In 1912 Jackson became professor of practical theology at Payne Theological Seminary, keeping that position until death.

President Mitchell's administration witnessed a feud between Scarborough and Joseph P. Shorter. The latter, Wilberforce's only graduate in the Class of 1871, was professor of mathematics for twenty-three years, vice president from 1884 to 1892, treasurer for many years, superintendent of the Combined Normal and Industrial Department from 1892 to his death in 1906, and trustee for more than twenty years. Between Scarborough and Shorter lay a longtime battle of personalities and educational ideals. According to one authority, "Scarborough was interested in scholarly progress, especially in the classics, while Shorter . . . sought to get the faculty to seek state funds to establish a normal and industrial department."

In 1892 a conflict erupted between President Mitchell and Professor William Sanders Scarborough. The latter had written a letter making damaging statements about the president's handling of university funds. After an inquiry the board acquitted Mitchell and dismissed Scarborough. However, the very next day the latter joined the faculty of Payne Theological Seminary. In 1897 Scarborough returned to Wilberforce as professor of classics and vice president.

In 1894, after study at the University of Berlin, W. E. Burghardt Du Bois joined Wilberforce's faculty. He taught Greek, Latin, German, and English, and he claimed that he sought in vain to add sociology to the load. Du Bois left in 1896. Writing forty-four years later, he affirmed, "I was not kicked out, but that was only because I moved before the inevitable swing of the boot." Du Bois claimed his bête noire was Bishop Benjamin M. Arnett, the powerful chairman of Wilberforce's board of trustees. Du Bois believed the animosity could be traced to his successful opposition to Arnett's attempt to impose his unqualified son, Benjamin Jr., as Wilberforce's professor of literature.

Mitchell retired in 1900 and died a year later. His successor was the Reverend Joshua H. Jones. A Wilberforce graduate, he had done much for his alma mater in the A.M.E. Church Conferences and in getting aid from the state. He had become a wealthy businessman. Jones sought financial security for Wilberforce. In 1901 he bought a forty-seven-acre farm with funds from the dining hall, hoping to supply many products for the latter and eventually make enough profit to pay for the farm and assure some much-needed productive endowment. In 1902 he purchased a $110^1/_2$-acre-farm for the same reasons. A year later Jones bought for $10,000, out of his own funds, another farm for the university and operated it for profit through the dining hall; he paid himself 6 percent interest on his investment. This transaction aroused the trustees, who censored him for arbitrary action. Finally, Jones was required to purchase the farms from the university.

President Jones desired organic unity and centralization of authority within the university. There existed three autonomous units. Work in theology resided in Payne Theological Seminary under its board of trustees. Another unit was the Combined Normal and Industrial Department, whose trustees elected a superintendent of the department (instead of a superintendent of industries as provided by law) and invested him with executive powers in addition to the fiscal authority provided for in the law creating the department. Thus President Jones's administrative powers lay only in the College of Liberal Arts. He made no headway in his attempt at centralization of authority.

Despite Jones's immense popularity with faculty and students, the trustees dropped him in 1908. The factors were animosities engendered by his campaign to become an African Methodist Episcopal bishop; Professor W. S. Scarborough's ambitions for the presidency; administrative misunderstandings over Jones's attempt to unify Wilberforce's administration; and perennial disagreement over the purchase of the university farms.

In 1908 Professor William Sanders Scarborough was elected Wilberforce's first lay president. An Oberlin College graduate, he was an eminent classical scholar. Scarborough brought Wilberforce to wide public notice. His acquaintance with scholars and his membership in numerous learned societies led to contacts with philanthropists and multiple agencies. He traveled a great deal in the East. Scarborough obtained funds for a new girl's dormitory and balanced the budget by obtaining help from persons he persuaded to become Wilberforce's patrons. Gradually he reduced the standing debt to $25,000, made investments, increased the endowment fund, and worked to get state appropriations increased from $3,500 annually to $5,000.

Scarborough's administration stood for the separation of Wilberforce Academy from the College of Liberal Arts; instruction at a high level; and closer institution-alumni relations. Also there occurred a revision to the curriculum, a doubling of the college's faculty, an updating of the accounting system, and a phenomenal increase in enrollment. In World War I Wilberforce took the lead in war service among the "Negro colleges."

In 1920 President Scarborough retired, thus ending the long feud between him and former president Joshua H. Jones, who had been elected a bishop of the A.M.E. Church in 1912 and president of Wilberforce's board of trustees. Sentiment prevailed that Jones forced Scarborough's retirement in order to secure the election of his son, Gilbert H. Jones, to the presidency. However, after two days of wrangling in 1920 the board elected the Reverend John A. Gregg, then president of Edward Waters College. President Gregg, a graduate of the University of Kansas, enjoyed a successful regime. The Victory Rally of 1920 disposed of all debts. In 1922 Shorter Hall burned, but it was rebuilt. The building program took care of almost 1,000 students annually. In 1924, on his election as an A.M.E. bishop, Gregg left Wilberforce.

The new president was a layman, Dr. Gilbert H. Jones, who had been dean of Wilberforce's College of Liberal Arts for ten years. He worked closely with his father, former president Joshua H. Jones, who from 1912 to 1924 headed the Wilberforce board of trustees and, from 1924 to 1928, was vice president of the board and member of the executive committee. Both father and son lived in Wilberforce village.

In 1930 the College of Liberal Arts ceded its courses in education to the Combined Normal and Industrial Department. Thereupon the college reorganized. Curricula in journalism, library science, and social administration were organized, and the combined curricular courses, in arts-journalism, arts-commerce, and arts—home economics, and arts-agriculture were abandoned. Four-year courses in agriculture, commerce, and home economics appeared in the Combined Normal and Industrial Department.

President G. H. Jones worked avidly to improve Wilberforce. The alumni organized a promising endowment drive, but the trustees vetoed it. In 1929 Jones launched a million-dollar drive, but the Great Depression torpedoed it. The College of Liberal Arts obtained State of Ohio funds for providing liberal arts courses needed for teacher training work in the Combined Normal and Industrial Department. Leaves of absences were given to faculty, and forty-eight of seventy-two faculty took advanced training. Jones got Wilberforce accepted by the Association of American Colleges and the New York State Board of Regents. The large debt caused by rebuilding Shorter Hall was a major factor in nonaccreditation by the North Central Association of Colleges and Schools.

The year 1932 marked change in the control of Wilberforce. The powerful Bishop Joshua H. Jones was expelled from the bishopric by the A.M.E. General Conference. Bishop Reverdy Ransom, as head of the Church's Third District, became president of Wilberforce's board of trustees. He asked the board to replace Gilbert H. Jones as president. Jones resigned. (Later he became professor of political science at Wilberforce.) "The long reign of the 'Joneses' came to an abrupt end and the reign of the 'Ransoms' began." In June 1932 the board elected the Reverend Charles H. Wesley. An effective public speaker, he had been professor of history at Howard University. After thirty days Wesley resigned the presidency over the poor financial condition of the university and because there was no presidential residence.

Bishop Ransom drafted the Reverend Richard R. Wright Jr. as acting president. Wright had been editor of the *Christian Recorder,* the leading A.M.E. periodical. Wright initiated the *Book of a Million Years,* which listed all donors to the university; after moderate success the campaign was discontinued. To gain accreditation consultants were employed and the faculty made extensive studies. Curricular reorganization, library expansion, and reform of the accounting system occurred. The North Central Association denied accreditation, but its reports for meeting accreditation requirements gave Wright hope that Wilberforce would meet them soon. In 1936 Wright left to become "perhaps the most distinguished of the A.M.E. Church's twentieth-century bishops."

The trustees elected president the Reverend D. Ormande Walker, a West Indian. He had pastored a Cleveland A.M.E. parish. Walker obtained Wilberforce's conditional accreditation by the North Central Association, which called Walker's administration "the most dynamic and progressive and his achievement as phenomenal." A strong personality, Walker believed in presidential authority. In the beginning the trustees supported him, dismissing the deans of liberal arts and education, five departmental heads, and several teachers. Walker completed the enlargement of the library building, made several physical improvements, unified the registrar's office, reduced the heavy indebtedness to half its original size, and introduced a tenure system that the church board (Wilberforce University) adopted but the state board (Combined Normal and Industrial Department) would not.

Walker became embroiled in a bitter struggle. He sought to harmonize two camps at Wilberforce; the Booker T. Washingtonians who stressed industrial education and the W. E. B. Du Boisians who emphasized the liberal arts. The university should have a unified program, Walker believed. Many faculty members expressed concerns about the quality of education in the Combined Normal and Industrial Department. Moreover, they pointed out the marked enrollment decline in that department while the College of Liberal Arts grew substantially. Walker's decision on action caused an explosion.

Walker argued that the state board of trustees undermined his attempt at a liberal arts–industrial arts cooperative program. He viewed those trustees and their control over industrial education programs within the Combined Normal and Industrial Department as a political football. He accused Ohio's Republican governor of seeking to control Wilberforce as a means "to pay off political debts to loyal supporters." The state trustees maintained that Walker, a Democrat, sought to control Wilberforce's industrial education programs via political campaigns and subsequent board appointments. One state trustee claimed that Walker's dictatorial activities had caused a student uprising.

The Republican establishment acted firmly. The legislature in 1939 gave the governor power to appoint six of the nine members of the state board, the others being appointed by the African Methodist Episcopal Church. Without the consultation of the Wilberforce University board of trustees, in 1941 another law raised the status of the Combined Normal and Industrial Department to that of the College of Education and Industrial Arts. Also in 1941 Governor John W. Bricker demanded Walker's resignation or dismissal. In July 1941 Bishop Ransom and former president Bishop Wright got the university's board to support the state board's demand for Walker's dismissal. The university board had concluded that it needed the state's financial support. The departing Walker became an A.M.E. bishop in 1948.

In 1941 Bishop Wright was reappointed president until a person satisfactory to both boards was found. Until that year the church board had been electing the president who served as president of the entire institution, comprising both church and state units. Such a president may not be, and often was not, the choice of the state board and who may have been the very person the state board did not care to have. This naturally resulted in habitual friction between the two units. The report of the Special Committee of the North Central Association made in 1941 demanded a unified administrative control in fact and not merely in name as had been the case until Dr. Walker's election to the presidency in 1936. The association felt that this would solve the many difficulties facing the institution for several years. To meet this demand the two boards created in 1941 a third board called the Joint Executive Board, consisting of three members from the church board and three from the state, thus recognizing for the first time equal partnership between the church and state boards in the election of the common executive officer. However, the customary power of the university to dismiss a president was not removed.

As the period of Bishop Wright's presidency expired in 1942, he joined with the Joint Executive Committee and recommended to the church board the name of Dr. Charles H. Wesley, dean of the graduate school at Howard University, as his successor. Thus came Wesley's second and highly controversial term. In the early years there were some achievements: improving the external relationship of the institution; securing large appropriations from the State of Ohio for postwar buildings for the College of Education and Industrial Arts; promoting the debt reduction campaign; and receiving the College of Education and Industrial Arts' accreditation by the American Association of Teachers Colleges. But Wesley also gained foes for many reasons: mistreating former President Walker; acquiescing to the state board's arbitrary dismissal of faculty who had supported Walker; summarily dismissing the dean of women; instituting the summer session, where faculty taught six to eight hours a day; allowing students to acquire twenty quarter hours in six weeks; dismissing a professor who protested the president's actions regarding the summer school; kowtowing frequently to students; losing good students because of his wishy-washy stands; abandoning the *Negro College Quarterly* (started by President Walker as *Wilberforce University Quarterly*); allowing some students to enroll for twenty-five hours a quarter; raising student grades; admitting unqualified students; duplicating courses and top-sided curricular programs; overlooking deplorable conditions on campus; enjoying a large salary and lavish lifestyle paid by the university; ignoring faculty welfare; using the A.M.E.'s treasury to get the press on his side; and falsely claiming credit for the erection of the Student Union Building.

Since June 1944 Wesley's presidency had been continually questioned by the university trustees. Indeed, in August some A.M.E. bishops advocated replacing Wesley with former President Walker, but the move failed. In 1946 the faculty voted no confidence in Wesley. In 1947 the North Central Association withdrew accreditation. It put the blame for withdrawal on the conflict between the university and state boards as well as on the hiring of young and immature teachers and the employment of an inordinate number of relatives.

In 1947 Governor Thomas J. Herbert got the legislature to pass the bill giving the state-supported board the right to select the president of the College of Education and Industrial Arts and raise the ratio of the state-appointed board members from six to eight, leaving only one member to be selected by the African Methodist Episcopal Church. Herbert asserted that certain Ohio State University officials wanted a well-equipped state school where black students would go instead of "crowding" Ohio State University.

In 1947, fed up with Wesley, the university board, voting sixteen to five, dismissed Wesley. He refused a compromise involving one year's pay for his resignation. The next day, commencement, he announced that he would remain as president of the state-supported unit, the College of Education and Industrial Arts, and invited all likeminded to follow him to that new state college, free of any connection with the African Methodist Episcopal Church.

Wesley greatly harmed Wilberforce University. He moved from Shorter Hall to Bundy Hall as president of the "College of Education and Industrial Arts at Wilberforce, Greene County, Ohio," a name ordered by the Court of Common Pleas at Xenia. (The institution became Central State College in 1951 and Central State University in 1965.) Wesley invited faculty and students of the old institution to join him, enticing them with mentions of larger state appropriations for his college. He took the records from the Wilberforce University president's office, three secretaries, and the personnel deans and their records. He spirited away the Wilberforce University catalog about to go to press and seized the university registrar's records. Wesley stripped many items from the university library and the president's office, even the pencil sharpener. He also stole the university's alumni list and sought to prevent any contact between students of his new college and Wilberforce University.

Battered, Wilberforce survived. The trustees elected president the scholar, preacher, philosopher, and theologian Charles L. Hill. The dynamic and popular new president, with the wise guidance of Bishops Ransom and Wright Jr., stabilized the scattered forces of Wilberforce. Despite enticing offers from Wesley's institution, Wilberforce's six Ph.D.s remained, and some faculty who had deserted with Wesley returned. The faculty numbered 47 (a drop from 120) and students 400 (a drop from 1,400). The students had come without any advertisements and despite propaganda from the secessionist camp that the church university would soon collapse for lack of funds. Amazingly the university "paid full two month salaries to all its summer teachers, something Dr. Wesley," with all his state backing, was never able to do. However, the trouble caused by Wesley's defection made it impossible for Hill to get reaccreditation. In 1949 Hill merged the Colleges of Education and Business Administration with the Liberal Arts and Sciences.

During Hill's presidency Wilberforce became immersed in a case involving a blacklisted person during the McCarthy era. Hans Freistadt, a young physicist and

Communist party member while doing graduate study at the University of North Carolina, gained national attention in 1949. He lost his Atomic Energy Commission fellowship when Senator Bourke Hickenlooper (R-Iowa) used highly publicized hearings before the Joint Congressional Committee on Atomic Energy to latch onto Freistadt as a symbol of the agency's laxness. In 1950 Wilberforce hired Freistadt, who claimed he had "taken special pain to inform the president [Hill] of my [Communist] membership and he had already secured approval of my appointment by the Board of Trustees (or so he told me)." Three months later, at the term's beginning, the board cancelled the appointment.

In December 1955 a heart attack felled Hill. In 1956 the trustees elected the Reverend Rembert E. Stokes president. He was an alumnus of Wilberforce and was much influenced by President Walker. Stokes had pastored A.M.E. parishes and for five years was dean of Payne Theological Seminary. The university progressed markedly under Stokes. His first ten years concentrated on reaccreditation. Stokes hired experienced and more capable faculty to fulfill the catalog requirements, and faculty salaries were raised to stimulate faculty retention. Now 25 percent of the faculty had doctoral degrees. President Stokes changed the composition of the board of trustees of the university by admitting persons from business, industry, and education. The curriculum was restructured. In order to prepare the university for accreditation review, everyone in the university was involved in series of workshops on accreditation. In 1962 the university regained accreditation and became a member of the Ohio Foundation of Independent Colleges in 1963.

Consultants were used frequently to provide guidelines on what needed to be done for improvement. The Committee of Visitors served as consultants on curriculum revision and improvement in other university functional areas. The university concentrated on liberal arts and science and Christian theology, the major objective being teaching students how to think, express, interpret, and act clearly. A very close relationship was maintained with Payne Theological Seminary.

The catastrophic burning of Emery Hall in 1958 created new problems for the university. Yet it was a blessing in disguise because it brought new donors who helped the university meet its financial commitments.

In 1964 Stokes introduced the Cooperative Education Program. Grants for its establishment came from the Ford Foundation and an anonymous donor. Despite some opposition, Stokes made the program mandatory in 1967. It involves the student alternating periods of academic study on campus with similar periods of paid employment in positions related to his/her academic, career, or personal interests. The program caused a significant increase in student enrollment. It also facilitated the enrollment of white students. Today Wilberforce is one of two four-year institutions in the nation operating a mandatory co-op program.

Stokes approached Central State College for interinstitutional cooperation. In

1958 there came reciprocity wherein Wilberforce opened its philosophy and religion courses to Central State students and Central State opened its elementary education and business courses to Wilberforce students. Many Wilberforce students took advantage of the arrangement, but Central State students did not.

Stokes continued his hard work in his remaining presidential years, 1966–76. His goal was to build "a new Wilberforce University" by moving to a new site in Wilberforce village in order to have room for expansion needed for the expected increasing enrollment. New residence halls for men and women were constructed. The period was a turning point in the life of the university. Increasing enrollment and great improvement in the university's financial conditions led to continuous decline in the accumulated deficit. The enrollment more than tripled. The faculty doubled in size and its quality was very satisfactory. There was a respectable student-faculty ratio of about one to twenty. New academic programs were introduced, and some of the previous programs were modified to prepare students for the keen competition in the world. Consultants were employed to provide feedback on actions taken and strategies used on various university issues. The team of consultants from General Motors Institute and General Motors Corporation reported that the mission of the university was its greatest strength and that the university's leaders showed ability for change and growth.

After Stokes's first decade of the presidency, the quality and morale of the faculty rose sharply, though faculty salaries were relatively lower than national averages. In September 1967 twenty-nine new faculty members were hired, ten having doctoral degrees. The faculty numbered forty-one. In the 1967 trimester nine faculty members received National Teaching Fellowships.

During his last decade in office President Stokes sought prompt action on various issues. An integration program was embarked on to make the university multiethnic but without much success because of its limited resources. The University Fountain, the institution's symbol, was moved to a permanent location on the new campus in 1974 as one of the creative strategies used by the university to raise funds. The university received recognition as the most promising liberal arts college in the country, and the architectural design of its classroom building was rated as first in the nation. The generosity of many donors and the hard work and dedication of President Stokes and his staff made it possible for the university to move parts of its functions to the new campus.

Many notable events took place during Stokes's tenure. Changes happened in the board of trustees: one faculty member and one student were elected by their constituents. Students were placed on university committees. New admissions strategies were developed in preparation for the accreditation in 1967 and 1972. The university started participating in the Black Executive Program, sponsored by the National Urban League. Through this program black executives were borrowed from business and industry to add practical dimensions to classroom theory. Every week a different lecturer was on campus for two days, visiting and interacting with students and faculty in classrooms and other meetings. Moreover, the General Education Program was revised; a new business administration program debuted; the pre-law curriculum obtained development; and a dual-degree program with the University of Dayton bowed. A Student Exchange Program with the University of Hull in England was set up (William Wilberforce was born in Hull), and the United Negro College Fund admitted Wilberforce.

In 1976 President Stokes departed to become a bishop in the African Methodist Episcopal Church. His successor was a layman and, at thirty-two, the youngest president in Wilberforce's history. Charles E. Taylor had been vice president for Operations within the Academy for Contemporary Problems and had been responsible for overseeing the academy's financial operations and administrative and personnel management. While president of Wilberforce, Taylor joined the African Methodist Episcopal Church.

Under President Taylor Wilberforce's "Old Campus" was sold for $600,000 to the State of Ohio "to relinquish outstanding university debt." Also, Life President H. Kamuzu Banda of Malawi, graduate of Wilberforce Academy, visited the campus and donated $3,500,000, the university's largest individual gift. The Timken Foundation aided the construction of apartment-style student housing, and the university received numerous other gifts, grants, and corporate sponsorships. Emphasis was placed on community outreach, resulting in increased university visibility with and support from the Columbus and Dayton areas. Taylor made decisive moves. His policy of "Excellence in Education" called for a managerial approach to academic program review. He eliminated the teacher education program and abolished intercollegiate basketball and track. Moreover, he ruled for a cut in enrollment: the university would accept only 750 students instead of the usual 950.

Taylor roused the faculty. Discontinuing the teacher education program led him single-handedly to terminate faculty, including tenured persons. He hired new faculty at better salaries than the old faculty and provided no clear guidelines on promotion and other personnel matters. In 1978 the faculty reacted, and the campaign of the Wilberforce University Faculty Association for a faculty union triumphed, winning 90 percent in the faculty vote. That association would affiliate with the national American Association of University Professors (AAUP). A court ruled that the establishment of the Wilberforce union did not violate the U.S. Supreme Court's Yeshiva decision concerning collective bargaining in private collages and universities; therefore, the Wilberforce board of trustees had to bargain with the union. After nine months of negotiation, in 1979 the board recognized the faculty union.

The union improved conditions. Certain terminated, tenured faculty received reinstatement while others received compensation. Formalization of faculty-administration relationships took place, helping to eliminate arbitrary decisions by the administration. A grievance procedure ensued. Faculty participation in promotion and tenure decisions improved, as did salaries. The union advanced the lot of the female faculty. Faculty morale rose. The founding of the union has been called "a unifying event for both black and white professors."

In 1984 President Charles E. Taylor departed for the business world. His replacement was Wilberforce's only female president, Yvonne Walker-Taylor. Daughter of President D. Ormonde Walker, she had held numerous administrative positions at Wilberforce under Presidents Stokes and Taylor. The Walker-Taylor administration displayed activity. The endowment grew from $1,949,523 to $4,211,401, and the declining enrollment trend reversed, with revised admissions criteria producing better-qualified admits. The student retention program was launched. An Adopt-a-Student mentoring program appeared (with a student selecting a person from the faculty or staff for guidance and help), and the default rate in the Federal Perkins Loan Program dropped from 69 percent to 17 percent. Moreover, additional construction happened on campus. Other developments included the addition of a computer literacy program; a second dual-degree option of computer science; a computer information systems major in the Business Division; and a gerontology emphasis curriculum in the Social Science Division. Also, a community articulation program for Cuyahoga, Harrisburg-area, and Muskegon Community Colleges was established, and the university joined SOHIO's College Science Instruction Improvement Program. Before her retirement in 1988, Dr. Walker-Taylor brought Wilberforce national exposure in both print and television.

Advancement continued under her successor, President John H. Henderson. The board of trustees was restructured: it consists of thirty-five members from various vocations, chooses its chair, and fills its vacancies from names presented by its nominating committee, whose head is the chancellor, the bishop of the Third Episcopal District (Ohio, Pennsylvania, West Virginia) of the A.M.E. Church. The completion of the Wolfe Administration Building created one campus after twenty-three years as two. Other construction occurred, including a teacher collaboration and research center. Applause came for faculty and staff salary adjustments and an improved benefits package. Advisory boards were created for the Co-op Education Program and for each of the academic divisions and a university-wide program to assess student learning. The Cooperative Education and Natural Science Division established a dual-degree forestry program with the University of Vermont. The Wilberforce University Institute of African American/Israel Exchange Program was founded as was the Study Abroad Program in Egypt. The William Wilberforce Award and the David Alexander Payne Award were set up. Intercollegiate basketball returned.

The Henderson administration engaged in community service. In 1994 the Wilberforce University Family Life Center was established as a portion of the Minority

Male Consortium Grant Program sponsored by the U.S. Department of Health and Human Services. The center provides year-round programming via tutoring, academic classes, enrichment activities, and personal skill enhancement training in concert with area public schools. Targeted youth with high-risk exposures to violence, academic deficiencies, and low self-esteem are enrolled in the in-school, after-school, or summer enrichment programs. Aptly titled the Partnership in Education with Parents and Schools (PEPS), the center's staff offers activities both on the Wilberforce campus and in the targeted schools and communities. These activities include such diverse opportunities as attendance at academic classes taught by the Wilberforce University faculty, field trips to museums and other cultural sites, personal health and wellness opportunities, parenting workshops and training, and violence prevention strategies and techniques taught by professionals from the fields of communication, medicine, child development, and education. All the services are provided free of charge to the students, parents, and schools.

A notable contribution by President Henderson, who resigned June 30, 2002, was the inauguration of Credentials for Leadership in Management and Business (CLIMB). The program is designed for adults who have already completed a minimum of two years of college. The CLIMB program offers bachelor of science degree majors in organizational management, health services administration, and information technology. Each major consists of ten modules, totaling thirty-three semester hours. The majors help experienced adult learners develop management skills through a curriculum that is both analytical and application oriented. These courses, which are designated as modules, are taught in seminar style following an intense program of classes and individual study. The ten modules give special attention to the individual behavior of managers, decision making and conflict resolution in groups, accounting practices, technological applications, personnel procedures, interpersonal communication, ethics, and legal aspects in business. A distinctive component of these undergraduate programs is a major research project on a work-related topic. The research project integrates skills in report writing, problem solving, and research design. The courses are offered at nine satellite campuses.

Wilberforce University is an institution presenting an intriguing story in the histories of Ohio, the United States, and South Africa. Created by the Methodist Episcopal Church in the era of slavery, it provided education for African Americans. During the Civil War the African Methodist Episcopal Church took control. That power has passed and Wilberforce, under a self-perpetuating board of trustees, is today an affiliate of the African Methodist Episcopal Church. The ideal of freedom within the atmosphere of Christianity survives. The mission of developing education among African Americans remains. Also alive is the charter's prohibition of "all distinction based on race or color."

Wilberforce's perpetuity illustrates strength of character in African American life. Numerous crises—the Civil War, repeated financial woes, fire, inadequate enrollment, squabbles involving trustees, administration and faculty, machinations of Ohio politicians, and the secessionist establishment of a state-owned predominantly black college—have been devastating. Nevertheless, institutional life carried on through the hardworking efforts of certain bishops of the A.M.E. Church, enterprising presidents, self-sacrificing faculty, dedicated alumni, and loyal students.

Wilberforce's near-miraculous existence springs greatly from ingenuity. The university's authorities have displayed adaptability and, indeed, innovation. The new campus is an attractive asset. Various campaigns resulted in appropriations from private donors, corporations, and governmental agencies. The board of trustees has been broadened to include members from business, industry, and education. Outside consultants have invigorated old programs and initiated new ones. Curriculum revision does not flag. The cooperative education program attracts students, and the CLIMB program has been very popular among diverse groups, including whites, on satellite campuses. The computer literacy program gained faculty and student support. Also, dual programs with other universities have been established, and exchange and study abroad programs have widened student outlooks. Community outreach gains applause from neighborhoods. Recruiting of qualified faculty emerged. A cosmopolitan faculty—African Americans, Caucasian Americans, Africans, Asians—appeals to students. The faculty union is almost unique in American private higher education. (In that domain it is the only one in Ohio.)

Wilberforce University has made notable contributions to society. Alumni have entered the realms of teaching, politics, law, business, the arts, and other fields. The university has furnished bishops and ministers to the African Methodist Episcopal Church and also clergy for the Baptist, Episcopal, and Methodist Episcopal Churches. Wilberforce graduates fought for the Allies in World War I, and the university introduced and promoted courses and programs for the war's efforts. Wilberforce did much for the Allied cause in World War I. It provided a center on campus for examination of applicants for the officers training camp at Des Moines, Iowa. Black soldiers were trained on campus, and many male students left school to assist in food production. Also, professors and students went to Howard University for intensive preparation for service as clerks in France, and President Scarborough served in four agencies in the prosecution of the war. Graduates participated in the U.S. civil rights movement and the antiapartheid cause in South Africa.

Wilberforce University's multifaceted past provides guidance and hope for the future. And while adequate financing and enrollment increase linger as formidable problems, success, this observer predicts, will prevail.

Frederick A. McGinnis, *A History and an Interpretation of Wilberforce University* (Brown Publishing Co., 1941); David Smith, *The History of the Development of Wilberforce University* (Adline Publishing Co., n.d.); Hallie Q. Brown, *Pen Pictures of Pioneers of Wilberforce* (Aldine Publishing Co., 1937); Arthur P. Stokes, "Daniel Alexander Payne: Churchman and Educator" (Ph.D. diss., Ohio State University, 1973); Francis P. Weisenburger, "William Sanders Scarborough: Early Life and Years at Wilberforce," *Ohio History* 71, no. 3 (1962); *The Autobiography of W. E. B. Du Bois* (International Publishers, 1991); W. E. Burghardt Du Bois, "The Future of Wilberforce University," *Journal of Negro Education* 9, no. 4 (Oct. 1940); Timothy A. Dortch, "The Development of Curriculum and Instruction at Wilberforce University from 1941 to 1947" (Ph.D. diss., University of Akron, 1997); "The Wilberforce Dilemma: A Critical and Objective Evaluation of Dr. Wesley's Administration," *Wilberforce University Bulletin* 32, no. 4 (Jan. 1948); Gabriel Adebayo Babarinele Omolewu, "The Presidency of Bishop Rembert Edwards Stokes at Wilberforce University: 1956 to 1976" (Ph.D. diss., University of Akron, 2000); James T. Campbell, *Songs of Zion: The African Methodist Episcopal Church in the United States and South Africa* (University of North Carolina Press, 1998).

Wilmington College

Liberal Quaker Education for Practical Idealism

LARRY GARA

"Peace, social justice and nonviolence are at the very heart of our mission," said Wilmington College president Daniel DiBiasio, speaking in 1998 to participants in the annual Westheimer Peace Symposium. Although Wilmington's early football teams were called "Fighting Quakers," a philosophy as DiBiasio stated it has influenced the college for decades. Specifically, Wilmington College has advanced the goal of preparing "practical idealists," a phrase that Dean and later Provost Sterling Olmsted borrowed from a student.

In its early years Wilmington College was much more traditional, emphasizing personal morality as understood and practiced by the Quakers and most mainstream Protestants. Yet even from the start there was some attention to integrating personal morality and outward service as parts of a liberal arts education. In 1872 John Henry Douglas, one of the college's founders, predicted that the school would become "a great means of advancing the cause of education in our land and promoting the cause of morality and Christianity." Three years later Wilmington's second president, Benjamin Trueblood, told the first graduating class, "The design of education is character building." But he also added, "Knowledge is for use and not merely for display. It is to feed and strengthen your power of doing good."

Wilmington did not start out as a Quaker institution. Its roots go back to a project of three brothers, Hugh, James, and Thomas Garvin, who hoped to create Franklin College in Athens County. When they learned that Ohio University was already serving Athens County, they decided to establish their college in Wilmington, where they purchased the Clinton County Fairgrounds. On July 4, 1866, the Garvins began construction of Founder's Hall and offered free tuition to disabled Civil War veterans and "ladies of good moral character without sufficient means." Such generosity may have contributed to the institution's downfall, since the Garvins were unable to pay the

College Hall

brick masons for their work on the partly completed Founder's Hall. The masons went to court for their pay and Franklin College went on the auction block.

At the same time, several Wilmington-area Quakers were hoping to establish a college. In 1870 representatives of three quarterly meetings of the Religious Society of Friends bought the Garvins' college at public auction for $11,334. After completion of the first building, renamed College Hall, Wilmington College became a reality. After major renovations in 1970, College Hall remains in use today. The Quaker founders, affiliated with Indiana Yearly Meeting, soon realized that having their own college suggested having their own yearly meeting as well. In 1892 they established

Wilmington Yearly Meeting comprising three quarterly meetings. Wilmington College remains under the care of Wilmington Yearly Meeting today. During its first thirty-five years the institution also included a preparatory or high school that was larger than the college. While Quaker influence has remained strong throughout its history, a number of the college's presidents, as well as many faculty members and students, have been members of other denominations.

The Society of Friends, or Quakers, do not have a clearly defined creed or stated rules of conduct that members are required to accept and follow. Instead, each yearly meeting has "testimonies" that provide guidelines for personal conduct as well as statements of religious faith. All of them grow out of a fundamental belief that in every person there is a spark of the Divine. Belief in this spark, usually referred to as "the Inner Light" or "the Light Within," compels Friends to consult their consciences in applying Quaker principles to their own lives, and leads naturally to testimonies against war, social pretensions, and racism. In earlier times, deviation from basic tenets, for example joining the military or marrying a non-Friend, led to an individual's being "disowned" by the local meeting. In recent decades disownment has rarely, if ever, been practiced.

Yearly meetings, the highest bodies within the loosely structured Society of Friends, are autonomous. Each yearly meeting publishes its own *Book of Discipline*, which contains "queries," or challenging questions that provide guidelines for personal and corporate behavior. Queries from the Discipline of Wilmington Yearly Meeting, besides references to basic faith and worship, ask Friends if they avoid and discourage the use of tobacco and alcohol, if they observe simplicity and moderation in their manner of living, if they observe the testimony against military training and service, and if they recognize and promote racial equality. These historic testimonies, along with concerns for various social justice issues, have affected programs and student life at Wilmington College.

Changing times have brought practices that contrasted with and openly challenged Friends' stated principles, often causing considerable controversy. Early examples were the introduction in 1907 of sororities and fraternities and the gradual abandonment of strict rules for women living in the dormitories. The subject of relationships between the sexes was a favorite one in President Unthank's required daily chapel talks. Mary Mills, who taught English during Unthank's presidency, reported that he "frowned upon romance," while the highly popular teacher Ellen Wright "glorified affection." As late as 1970 the Wilmington College catalog warned that any student intending to be married during the school year must notify the dean of students no later than one week before the wedding. Failing to do so, the student could be asked to withdraw from the college and apply later for readmission. In recent years, despite a Quaker testimony against the use of alcohol, students have been permitted to drink on campus under strictly controlled conditions, though such conditions are frequently bypassed. However, the use of given names rather than formal titles is still practiced by all members of the college community. Decisions of faculty and board meetings are still reached by "sense of the meeting," a kind of consensus. Members of the faculty who are unfamiliar with Quaker tradition sometimes question the practice, but it has never been supplanted by Roberts Rules of Order.

Like most other religious groups, the Quakers have experienced many divisions throughout their history. In seventeenth-century England Quaker meetings for worship were unprogrammed, with individuals speaking out of the silence as they were moved to do so, and that practice continued in the United States. As Quakerism expanded into the Midwest, however, some meetings took on a form more like other Protestant churches, with music in the service and a hired pastor. Most young Friends who attend Wilmington College are from a pastoral background and when they attend a place of worship it is usually Wilmington Friends Meeting that follows the pastoral model. In the late 1940s, a small group of faculty, staff, and students began holding regular, unprogrammed worship in the traditional manner. In 1954 the group became Campus Friends Meeting, a constituent member of Wilmington Yearly Meeting. The need to provide religious support for students led in 1988 to the hiring of a college pastor with partial funding from Wilmington Yearly Meeting. The college pastor holds services, keeps the college community informed of the need for special prayers or concerns, acts as a personal and religious counselor to students, and plays an important role in keeping the Quaker element visible on campus.

From its beginning, Wilmington College was coeducational, with most of its graduates trained for teaching. In its early years the college was forced to compete with Lebanon National Normal University, a 2,000-student private school in Warren County. By 1917, however, Lebanon University had fallen on hard times and its administration proposed a merger with Wilmington College. When that change was accomplished, Wilmington's teacher training program benefited through the acquisition of excellent teachers and students.

In the 1950s, when the college assumed a stronger liberal arts character, there was considerable questioning of the emphasis on teacher education. The solution was to keep teacher training but provide potential educators with a solid liberal arts background as well. The college set a record in 1958 when 75 percent of its graduates entered teaching. Today, though it cannot approach that figure, Wilmington continues to have a strong education department that trains many students for the teaching profession.

The Quaker peace testimony has always played an important part in the history of Wilmington College. Benjamin Trueblood, the second president, was also secretary of the moderate American Peace Society and editor of its journal, *The Advocate of Peace.* The nearby community of New Vienna was the center for that organization's publications. One recent president was a conscientious objector during World War II and another refused to register for the postwar draft. Never in its history has Wilmington had an ROTC unit, and when certain government funds required a loyalty oath, Wilmington College refused those funds at considerable financial sacrifice.

During World War II, when some Quaker colleges hosted military units, Wilmington College abstained. With low wartime enrollment this too had a price tag and was not a totally clear decision. The chairman of the board of trustees was also state chairman of Selective Service, while two board members belonged to the Daughters of the American Revolution. When he received an official request for the college to host a navy unit, President S. Arthur Watson replied that it would be acceptable only if recruits took regular college courses but received no military training on the campus. Watson wrote later that a naval officer visited Wilmington and expressed regret at having caused an "embarrassing and difficult situation." Had officials known that Wilmington was a Quaker college, he said, they would not have made the request. The manner in which the incident was handled suggests that the use of college campuses for military training was as much a matter of public relations for the war effort as it was fulfilling a clear need.

Though unwilling to welcome a military unit, Wilmington College gladly accepted a Japanese American student when individual Nisei were released from relocation camps to pursue an education. President Watson, concerned about possible negative reaction in the community, requested a female student, believing a woman would be less controversial than a young man. The young woman who came to the college was well received and encountered no difficulties on the campus or in the city of Wilmington. At the same time, adherence to the Friends peace testimony has never meant discriminating against veterans or members of the military. Many young men studied at Wilmington College under the GI Bill of Rights, and from time to time some graduates have entered the military. However, when a faculty member agreed to teach a course at nearby Wright-Patterson Air Force Base and requested faculty approval, a heated discussion led to rejection of the request.

Closely related to its peace testimony has been Wilmington's international emphasis, which began immediately after World War II under President Samuel Marble and evolved during the administration of James M. Read. Marble attracted students from Central and South American as well as Caribbean countries and added an international component to the core curriculum. In 1948 Wilmington held the first in an annual series of International Folk and Music Festivals. The festivals, drawing on the special expertise of international students, featured music, dance and discussions as well as renowned speakers and an all-Ohio high school chorus. Carl Sandburg, Eleanor Roosevelt, Pearl Buck, and Clement Atlee were among the keynote speakers. The unique festivals were dedicated to "peace through international understanding." In 1950 nearly a thousand people participated.

The international festivals continued on an occasional basis and in a modified format until the early 1980s. In the fall of 1967 the college hosted a folk festival featuring a concert of international music by Joe and Penny Aronson and another by Judy Collins. Demise of the festivals did not mean the end of an international emphasis, which James Read strongly supported during his ten-year presidency, 1960–70. Among many other activities under his leadership was a special celebration on the occasion of Kenya's independence. International students continue to attend Wilmington College and American students are encouraged to study abroad. For a number of years a term in Vienna proved to be a popular option. Other students have studied for shorter periods in Mexico, Kenya, and Nicaragua. In 1990 and 1991 a Wilmington professor took groups of volunteer students to Mexico to work on projects for Habitat for Humanity. In 1991 Wilmington instituted a global issues requirement with designated faculty members teaching in rotation.

During the years of the Vietnam War, the historic Quaker Peace Testimony inspired numerous campus antiwar actions that were always carried out in a spirit of nonviolence. There was never any vandalism, rioting, or shouting down of visiting speakers. A tiny minority attempted to foment some form of violent actions but met no success. Students organized the Committee for Peace and Freedom, which planned and coordinated most of the antiwar events with some faculty and staff participation. Beginning in October 1966 the group met weekly under a sign proclaiming: "A silent vigil to express our protest and our sorrow for the people of Vietnam, our brothers. Every Wednesday at noon."

As with all issues, members of the college community held differing views. While some were moved to oppose the war, others believed that peace vigils were an affront to the young men who had been drafted to fight. In October 1967 a countervigil appeared with signs that read: "We support our men in Vietnam and back our government." In an interview, one of the leaders said she thought peace vigils hurt the morale of the men in Vietnam but insisted that her group was not opposed to other organizations nor to anyone's grooming or dress. "We want peace as do the anti-war demonstrators," she emphasized. "These people do not realize their efforts only help to prolong the war." On that chilly day, many joined the vigil of their choice. More than two hundred participated, the two vigils divided about equally in number. The mood was serious and the silence profound. At the end of the hour vigil participants scattered quickly to warm up as rain began to fall. The vigil in support of the troops lasted only a few weeks, and then several of its members joined the other line.

The demonstrator's comment about dress was significant, for appearance was one of the issues dividing the campus. The more conservative students tended to join fraternities and sororities, which during that era were in a minority. They resented President Read's insistence that every student be considered for membership in one or another of the Greek organizations, and their anger grew when three fraternities were placed on probation because of a snowball fight that got out of hand. The campus was increasingly divided between so-called "straights" and the "grubs" or "hippies." Fraternity members believed themselves the victims of discrimination by the college administration, even as a besieged and neglected minority. One evening a small group, probably under the influence of alcohol, marched around campus shouting, "It's our Campus too." They made threats and ended the event by burning in effigy the figure of a "grub."

Antiwar activity was not restricted to the campus. Students took to the streets of Wilmington as early as 1965 when a group carrying antiwar signs marched silently from the campus to the center of town. The walk took them past the American Legion Hall. Psychology professor Robert Halliday went along as an observer, in part because his own son was in the march. As they passed the Legion Hall a veteran attacked Halliday, knocking him to the ground. Although he was not hurt and no fight ensued, Halliday met later with members of the American Legion, pointing out that he himself was a veteran of World War II and attempting to explain the concerns of the students. He recalled later that the wall of misunderstanding had not been broken but he believed, nevertheless, that the effort had been worthwhile.

In May 1968 eight members of the Committee for Peace and Freedom challenged a Wilmington ordinance making it illegal to leaflet downtown without a permit from the city government. They had requested permission but were denied by the mayor, who said that leafleting against the war would further divide the community. After consulting with the ACLU on the constitutionality of such a policy, the students returned downtown to distribute informational leaflets about conscientious objection. While some local citizens angrily refused to accept a leaflet, several surprised the students by expressing sympathy for their cause. Next they handed out leaflets at the local high school. In neither instance did the city attempt to enforce the ordinance, which was effectively annulled by the students' action.

Even more controversial was a large support vigil in downtown Wilmington for James Wessner who was arrested for refusing to report for induction. Wessner, a graduate student at a California university, was under the jurisdiction of the Clinton County Draft Board because his home was in nearby Blanchester. Local news organizations reported the demonstration as if it were an invasion from outer space.

Wilmington students also sent contingents to the many antiwar demonstrations in Washington, while smaller, local actions provided an opportunity for those unable to make the trip to express their concern as well. The largest local demonstration was in 1969, organized to coincide with the massive Moratorium in Washington. Many who had never participated in demonstrations joined a vigil line that reached completely around the Clinton County Court House. Students also collected money to send through the Canadian Friends Service Committee to buy medical supplies for hospitals in North Vietnam and held an overnight reading of the names of young Americans who had been killed in the war. Several students and faculty members also participated in weekly anti–Vietnam War vigils at the gates of nearby Wright-Patterson Air Force Base, vigils that started on Christmas Eve 1971 and continued every Saturday until the end of the conflict.

Wilmington's peace activist students initiated a protest that was observed at few other colleges. For some years local citizens and a few students had held Tax Day Vigils outside the post office, the principal federal building in town, to call attention to and protest the large percentage of tax money being expended for war and the military. In addition, one tax was specifically earmarked for war, the federal excise tax on telephone service, a tax that was increased to 10 percent to support the Vietnam conflict. As a "witness for peace," staff members at *The Witness*, the student newspaper, deleted those charges from the office telephone bill. Their war tax resistance had deep roots in Quaker tradition from at least the eighteenth century when John Woolman practiced and advocated refusal to pay war taxes as a matter of conscience.

Like many other colleges and universities, Wilmington faced a serious crisis following the killings at Kent State University on May 4, 1970. In a hastily called all-campus meeting, students, faculty, and some administrators suggested a march to Columbus to protest the action by the National Guard and to demand an explanation by Governor James Rhodes. Of course the rally was also another witness against the war. While thousands of Ohio students met in Columbus for the rally, the Wilmington delegation was the only one to walk the entire route, with Dean Sterling Olmsted joining the march to lead it to the grounds of the Ohio State House. One Wilmington student who took part in the protest, himself a member of the National Guard, was emotionally shaken to realize that he could have been one of those ordered to the Kent State campus. The killing of four students in Ohio and two students at Jackson State in Mississippi a few days later united the student body as never before. Divisions between the more conservative fraternities and sororities and the antiwar group were for the time being set aside. Although classes continued to meet as usual, many students received approval for such alternative activities as workshops, films, and discussions related to urgent national and international problems.

Reaction in the city of Wilmington, however, was far from sympathetic. Many merchants and political leaders placed a full-page advertisement in the *Wilmington News Journal* saying, "Thank You National Guard." Adding to the uproar was the 1970 college yearbook, which pictured anti-Vietnam actions, some modestly photographed nudity, and a call to revolution. A full-page photograph showed Wilmington's mayor standing across a street to watch a peace demonstration, with the image of a "hippie" superimposed over the mayor's picture and a quotation from the *Declaration of Independence* under the photo. Furious, Mayor Dale Minton protested inclusion of his photo in the yearbook, saying the political message under his picture bothered him more than the nakedness on other pages.

Kent State and the ensuing demonstrations brought to the surface much of the simmering anger some Wilmington residents felt toward the college and its administration. Many, already resentful of the college's perceived reputation for promoting radical thought and action, reached near-hysteria about the yearbook. Soon after its appearance, a pamphlet that reprinted most of the "offensive" pictures and carried an accompanying angry letter was mailed to parents, trustees, donors, and other friends of the college. The letter, purportedly from a nonexistent "Wilmington Citizen's Council," carried the names of the mayor and chief of police along with many of the town's business and political leaders. Suddenly a trickle of angry letters to the *Wilmington News Journal* became a flood. "This book is an affront to every decent person in this community," said one reader, while another wrote, "I want to disassociate myself from the trash and filth that was published in the Wilmington College yearbook."

An editorial in the *News Journal* described the yearbook as a "crummy, offensive, stupid, inexcusable piece of trash" but suggested that readers should keep it in perspective. "Let's not close ranks against Wilmington College," the editor wrote. "It's much bigger and lots more important to us than a crummy yearbook." The editor made a good point. At that time the college was the county's largest employer. Yet a well-reasoned letter from the chair of the college's board of trustees did little to calm the waters. For several years afterward the new president, Robert Hinshaw, had to devote precious time and energy to fending off criticism of the 1970 yearbook.

One of the requests made by Wilmington students in the aftermath of the Kent State disruptions was that the college add peace studies courses to the curriculum. In 1969 a grant from the National Endowment for the Humanities had enabled the college to implement an experimental program called, in the vocabulary of the time, "Man in Focus," which aimed to introduce students to pressing social and economic problems then facing the nation and the world. A section of the program that dealt with war and peace remains in the course listings today, though in greatly modified form. In 1978 the college adopted a peace studies major and hired a peace studies coordinator who also taught in the religion and philosophy department. However, as few students chose the major, it was eventually dropped in favor of an "enhanced minor" and an "Applied Peace Studies Certificate."

Since 1974 the Wilmington College Peace Resource Center has also played an important role in peace education and research. The center is a unique institution, housing one of the most complete collections anywhere of source materials relating to the atomic bombing of Hiroshima and Nagasaki. Barbara Reynolds, a Quaker peace activist, gathered the collection during her more than fifteen-year residence in Hiroshima, a city that made her an honorary citizen. When she returned to the United

States seeking a home for her collection, Wilmington College agreed to house it and made Barbara the first director. In 1975, as part of an observance marking the thirtieth anniversary of the destruction of the two cities, incoming president Robert E. Lucas formally accepted transfer of the collection to the college. The center and college also hosted a week of peace studies and workshops on the campus with Japanese and American participants. Over the years the center has attracted numerous Japanese visitors, including the mayors of Hiroshima and Nagasaki as well as scholars engaged in researching the bombing and its aftermath. Since its founding the center's collection has expanded to include materials on conscientious objection and other aspects of war and peace. Its tapes, films, and books, available for purchase or rent, have been used by individuals and organizations around the world, giving Wilmington College an international reputation. The center's current emphasis is on promoting nonviolence and conflict resolution in elementary and high schools.

Since 1991 the college has hosted the annual Westheimer Peace Symposium, a one-day event named for Charles and Mary Westheimer, who established an endowment to ensure its future. Each year the symposium focuses on one aspect of such peace and justice concerns as the nuclear threat, the environment, and human rights. Speakers have included Helen Caldicott, George McGovern, Colman McCarthy, and Julian Bond. In addition to providing Wilmington students an outstanding educational experience, this special day attracts visitors from many other parts of Ohio.

In April 1999 the college officially hosted a reunion of seven of the authors included in *A Few Small Candles: War Resisters of World War II Tell Their Stories,* edited by Emeritus Professor of History Larry Gara and his wife, Lenna Mae Gara. The unique event included an evening symposium that was taped and later broadcast on C-Span's "BookTV," bringing national attention to the support at Wilmington College for the Peace Testimony of Friends.

A unique aspect of Wilmington College is its agriculture department, established in 1948, making it the only private college in Ohio to offer such a program. In 1967 President James Read announced a joint venture with the U.S. Peace Corps that was to combine the agricultural program with the college's long-standing interest in peace. The plan was to train volunteers for agricultural development work in Latin American countries, combining two years at Wilmington College with two years of field service. However, when only 125 students applied for the program, Peace Corps administrators, afraid it would not produce a sufficient number of qualified volunteers, canceled the program before it could get under way. Nevertheless, a number of the Peace Corps applicants remained at Wilmington where their presence added an element of idealism that has permeated the college.

Although a majority of the college's trustees are required to be members of the Society of Friends, a crisis in 1959 threatened to eliminate much of its Quaker emphasis. Over the years Wilmington Yearly Meeting had willingly approved presidents chosen by the college's board of trustees, but appointment by the trustees of G. Richard Gottschalk of Syracuse, New York, alarmed the Quakers. The decision had been made by a majority vote of the board rather than through the traditional practice of reaching consensus. Moreover, the president-elect was an industrialist with little or no knowledge of Quakerism and no previous experience in educational administration. When the Permanent Board of Wilmington Yearly Meeting in effect overrode the trustees' decision, Gottschalk resigned without ever having assumed the post. That series of events caused deep divisions in the college community, among Ohio Quakers, and in the city of Wilmington. It was the skill of newly appointed president James M. Read that enabled a healing process to begin and the college to return to its Quaker roots.

Read had served as a conscientious objector in World War II and came to the college after ten years in Geneva, Switzerland, where he was UN Deputy High Commissioner for Refugees. His strong interest in peace and international relations, along with a program of welcoming innercity and international students, led to a number of programs consistent with traditional Quaker values. For several years he continued support for the International Festival. He worked out a plan to bring visiting historians from other countries to teach a year in the college's Department of History. The visitors came from England, Denmark, Wales, Japan, Spain, and India and provided a broadening academic experience for Wilmington College students. Read also devised a program called Goals for America, which focused on specific aspects of world problems, bringing to the campus international experts and scholars. And because of his work with the United Nations, Reed had many valuable contacts that he used to invite speakers for the series. These visitors were asked not only to speak but also to remain on campus for at least a day to interact with students, faculty, and staff. Eleanor Roosevelt, John Hope Franklin, and Sir Herbert Read were only a few of the visitors who brought an exciting atmosphere to Wilmington College.

President Read's international emphasis and open support for the Quaker Peace Testimony, including encouragement to students and faculty who participated in various peace actions, fueled opposition from a conservative faction in the city of Wilmington. False rumors that the college did not display the American flag led Read to take action. While a flagpole in the middle of campus had always flown the U.S. flag, Read, in 1967, had two poles erected at opposite ends of the new gymnasium, one for the Stars and Stripes and the other for the blue-and-white flag of the United Nations. Wilmington is still one of only a few colleges that flies the UN flag.

Even before completion of the new gymnasium, when the building's donor learned from local citizens that Read was a pacifist and had been a World War II conscientious objector, he refused to attend the building's dedication, saying that had he known of Read's past he would not have approved the grant. His contact person, of course, had known about and approved the college's Quaker affiliation as a peace church college. In his ten years at Wilmington College, James Read never retreated from his peace position. Shortly before leaving the college he expressed the hope that it would remain "a center for the cultivation of inquiring minds and sensitive spirits, where the young learn the ways of peace and how to achieve a world where nations not only tread on the moon, but do not learn war any more."

Not only peace but also social justice and racial equality were Quaker concerns, though with the latter the record has been flawed. In the 1920s Wilmington had many of the characteristics of a southern town, and strict racial lines existed in places of public accommodation. City elementary schools remained segregated until 1952, and that change occurred only after a prolonged challenge from black parents. The college was drawn into the dispute when some students and staff members supported the black parents, causing cries of "outside agitators and communists" to cloud public discourse. The Wilmington school superintendent defended board policy, while college trustees and administrators, trying to avoid further controversy, demoted a faculty member and pressured students to drop their actions. When the school board finally closed the segregated building, it cited economic reasons for its action. The episode left some bitterness in Wilmington and on the campus.

During much of its history the college did not accept students from the substantial African American population of Wilmington. That changed during World War II when a local African American student was accepted at Wilmington College. After the war students from Africa and Haiti began arriving on campus, and the color barrier fell. With the advent of the civil rights revolution, some Wilmington students held support vigils on the campus, and one, Carol Kornfield, participated in the Mississippi summer of 1964. The students, whose objective was to help blacks in the South to prepare for and register to vote, trained at Western College for Women in Oxford, Ohio. While in Oxford Carol and two friends drove to Wilmington, where one of them, Andrew Goodman, attended Campus Friends Meeting. Kornfield, Goodman, and Michael Schwerner then drove to Mississippi. A few days later word came that the two young men, along with James Cheney of Mississippi, were missing. Their brutal murders shocked the nation and the world. Carol Kornfield's participation in the Mississippi summer gave Wilmington College a bit part in that tragic drama and underscored the possibilities for heroism in the use of nonviolence.

Another active focus on social justice grows out of the traditional Quaker concern for prisoners and prison reform that Wilmington College expressed in its educational programs for prison inmates. Beginning in 1975 course offerings at the Lebanon Correctional Institution developed into an associate's degree program called Project Talents. Nine years later the State of Ohio granted authority to Wilmington College to award baccalaureate degrees in designated majors to prison inmates. Eventually the college also offered classes to inmates of the Warren Honor Camp and the Warren Correctional Institution when they opened.

The Wilmington prison program spawned a number of related projects and research studies, one of which clearly demonstrated that prisoners who completed college-level courses were far less likely to return to prison than those who had not. Other programs provided training and service to prisoners not enrolled in college courses as well as to those who had been released. Several hundred inmates of the Franklin Pre-Release Center for Women participated in vocational and skill-building programs provided by Wilmington College. Again, the value of educational programs was demonstrated, for a survey of former inmates found that 60 percent of those who had enrolled in the Franklin program were either in school or gainfully employed at the time of their response. Nevertheless, all the college's prison programs were affected and sharply reduced after Congress eliminated all federal funding for the education of prison inmates. However, the experience and expertise generated by its prison work has prompted the college to enrich its program by adding a popular major in criminal justice.

In 1971 a dramatic incident helped illuminate the Wilmington College commitment to Quaker nonviolence. Newly installed President Robert E. Hinshaw was an anthropologist with a special interest in developing a multicultural campus. Among other factors, the number of African American students at Wilmington began to increase. From their ranks came an organization called Concerned Black Students in which both men and women assumed leadership roles. When black students experienced discrimination and prejudice from some white students, open conflict erupted on the basketball court during an intramural game. An all-black team walked off the court, charging the referee with racism. The administration reacted quickly to form a task force on racism at the college. During a meeting of that group a leader of the Concerned Black Students confronted administration representatives with eleven nonnegotiable demands. President Hinshaw wrote a well-reasoned, five-page response and met again with African American student leaders. Coincidentally, this was taking place during the week of inaugural events to honor Hinshaw, a week the anthropologist president had termed an "Un-inaugural." It included a performance by an African dance troupe and a seminar featuring distinguished scholars and guests from other institutions. In the midst of this important event, word came that the black students had seized College Hall, the oldest and best-known building on campus.

Early in the morning of April 23 a select group of the faculty and guests met at the president's home to plan a strategy. There were ample grounds for concern. Events relating to the Vietnam War had seriously strained town-gown relations and there were disturbing signs of possible violence from young outsiders. Someone suggested cutting off all utilities to the building, another wanted a hard-line ultimatum, and, of course, one person favored sending in the police. A visiting scholar suggested a softer approach and Wallace Collett, chair of the board of trustees, challenged the group by asking, "Has anybody thought about getting some food for them? They must be hungry."

Arrangements were made to send food through other African American students at the college, and instead of calling the police the college summoned Arthur Slater of the U.S. Justice Department. Slater, an African American with considerable experience in conflict resolution, acted as negotiator in a meeting between college officials and the students. After two and a half hours an agreement was reached and the students left College Hall in essentially the same condition they had found it. There were a few nail holes where they had placed plywood, and they had knocked a lock off the switchboard to get at the phone. There were no cigarette butts or other litter in sight. Several years later, when College Hall was being renovated, Sterling Olmsted noticed some words scratched on one of the building's handrails: "College Hall Liberated April 23, 1971." Olmsted hoped to preserve that part of the rail for his own collection or for the college archives, but it was destroyed before he could retrieve it. The entire incident revealed a lot about the board and administration, about the students themselves, and about Quaker nonviolence at Wilmington College.

Suggested Reading

Much of the material for this article was based on thirty-eight years spent teaching at Wilmington College, with various college publications used to check my memory. I am deeply indebted to Ina Kelley, Wilmington College archivist, for providing material and checking the manuscript for accuracy, though of course any errors are my responsibility. The 1970 march to Columbus after the tragedy at Kent State is described by Emeritus Provost Sterling Olmsted in "Wilmington Students Protest the Cambodian Decision, the Deaths at Kent State University," *The Link: Alumni Magazine of Wilmington College* (Summer 1970): 12–13. Olmsted also described the occupation of College Hall in an unpublished essay that is in the possession of the author. The section on the college's early history was based on the 1959 history of Wilmington College written by Professor Oscar Boyd. Several chapters in *Partners in Education: Wilmington College and Wilmington Yearly Meeting of Friends* (1992) also proved very useful. The description of the symposium of April 13, 1999, is based on *A Few Small Candles: War Resisters of World War II Tell Their Stories*, ed. Larry Gara and Lenna Mae Gara (Kent State University Press, 1999).

Wittenberg University

Commitment to an Idea

RICHARD T. ORTQUIST

Lutherans in America were determined to establish colleges, and by 1959 some twenty-nine colleges and universities affiliated today with the Evangelical Lutheran Church in America (E.L.C.A.) had been founded with twenty-seven of them coming into existence during the nineteenth century. The first such school was Gettysburg College in Pennsylvania, founded in 1832, and the third one was chartered as Wittenberg College in 1845 in Ohio. By the year 2000 Wittenberg ranked among the leading institutions in the Lutheran circuit and was a highly respected liberal arts college nationally. Wittenberg's founding came at roughly the same time as that of several other church-related colleges in Ohio: Baldwin-Wallace (1845), Otterbein (1849), Capital (1850), and Heidelberg (1851). The early years of Wittenberg's history provided the foundations for the later institution.

Initially the intent of the Ohio Synod was to establish a college in Ohio as a western outpost of Lutheranism with an "Americanist" influence. It would provide theological training for clergy in English as well as German and embrace the revivalism and social reform movements that were part of the times. In 1842 the synod asked Ezra Keller, a graduate of Gettysburg College, who stressed the "Americanist" approach and was serving as a minister in Maryland, to help found a Lutheran college in Ohio.

Originally it appeared that Wittenberg, named after the university in Germany where Martin Luther had tacked up his Ninety-five Theses, would be located in Wooster, Ohio. The board of directors met there first in 1843, and in 1844 classes were held in Wooster while the board applied for a charter from the state. Keller, who would become the first president of Wittenberg in 1846, favored a more centrally located site for the school; after some exploration of locations further south, he discovered that both Springfield and Xenia were interested in having Wittenberg

Hollenbeck Hall, 2000

located in their city. Promoters in each city offered incentives in an effort to attract the college. Springfield came up with $4,667 and the choice of an eight-acre plot of land or a seventeen-acre plot owned by a cemetery association; Xenia offered $4,281 in cash and the choice of five smaller plots of land. Keller selected Springfield, which was located along the National Road, making it accessible and beneficial to the school in terms of enrollment and expansion. As the future site of the college, Keller chose the seventeen acres of land located just north of Buck Creek and donated by the cemetery association. Begun on that tract in 1845, in the year 2000 the campus totals seventy acres of rolling hills.

Following the model of eastern schools already established, Keller instituted a classical curriculum that included language, history, philosophy, literature, religion, mathematics, and science. This curriculum became the foundation for the liberal arts tradition that would be so essential to the Wittenberg story. A faculty of three, including the college president, taught all of the courses offered in the four-year cycle of a student's path to a degree. In the early years of the college's history there was a preparatory school, called the Wittenberg Academy, and a religion department that later developed into a seminary. During the early years the college's administration was comprised of the president and the Prudential Committee, a small body of seven that included members of the board and the faculty.

At the time Wittenberg was founded, national events and issues provided considerable controversy. The Mexican War and the growing antislavery movement were proving to be the hot issues of the day, and the college president did not avoid the issues. Although Keller was opposed to the Mexican War and slavery, he also rejected extremism and did not get involved in protests against the war nor did he become an abolitionist.

A hardworking, determined young man, Keller traveled around the state raising money for the college; he also managed to obtain an annual contribution of several hundred dollars (a substantial part of the operating budget) from the Society for the Promotion of Collegiate and Theological Education in the West. He oversaw the beginning of the construction of the first building on campus, Myers Hall, which was not completed until 1851, three years after his death. Until the building was ready, the first classes met in the basement of First Lutheran Church in Springfield. In mid-December 1848 Keller contracted typhoid fever and died at the age of thirty-six. In his brief tenure as president Keller had considerable accomplishments; he had fulfilled the goal set by the Ohio Synod of founding a college to provide instruction in the English language, established a lovely site in Springfield as the college's location, crafted a classical curriculum that attracted eastern financial support and served the liberal arts direction of the college, and started the construction of the first building on the campus.

Keller's successor was Samuel Sprecher, who also was a graduate of Gettysburg College. Sprecher followed in the footsteps of Keller, leading Wittenberg in the directions set by the first president. A number of potential problems did surface. In 1850 a group of Ohio Lutherans who were dissatisfied with the innovations surrounding Wittenberg (the Americanist approach) founded a rival Lutheran college, Capital University in Columbus, where a Lutheran seminary, which had its origins in 1832, already existed. In spite of the evidence that there were some Ohio Lutherans who were moving away from the innovations of the Americanist emphasis, Sprecher continued to hold to the path of aligning Lutheranism with American culture.

During the 1860s and 1870s Wittenberg encountered problems that threatened its continued existence as originally designed. The Civil War had an adverse effect on enrollment as some of the students left school to fight in the war and others who might have enrolled joined the military forces. Women were not yet admitted. In 1874 two changes were instituted: the first African American student was admitted, at the order of the board of directors and in opposition to the positions of the majority of the faculty and student body; and the board approved the admission of women, hoping that such action would ease some of the enrollment problems left over from the war. During the ensuing years not many women enrolled. The first three female graduates were the daughters of longtime mathematics professor Hezekiah Geiger. It was only with difficulty that the college managed to survive and continue a classical education in the liberal arts.

In the early 1870s a problem for the Wittenberg administration surfaced when some of the key citizens of Springfield seemed to forget about the school's needs in their efforts to obtain Ohio's land-grant college. At the time Springfield was a leading industrial city, manufacturing farm machinery. Local Springfield leaders believed that because of the city's prominence in the manufacturing of farm machinery and its selection in 1870 and 1871 as the host of the Ohio State Fair, the city stood a good chance to become the site of the agricultural institution. The local industrial leaders were keenly disappointed when, with the full weight of Governor Rutherford B. Hayes behind it, the city of Columbus won and was selected as the site of what eventually became Ohio State University.

Having lost out to Columbus, Springfield community leaders next turned their attention to Wittenberg. They began a campaign to raise local funds to provide chairs in agriculture and mechanics to change the Wittenberg curriculum, thus changing the nature of the academic program at the college. The Wittenberg board of directors, however, resisted that effort and continued in the liberal arts direction that had been pursued by Keller and Sprecher.

The depression ushered in nationally by the Panic of 1873 caused economic problems for the college, resulting in the reduction of faculty and a cut in the salaries of those who remained. The financial crisis also eroded the endowment pledges of $100,000. The board asserted itself and indicated to the Springfield community leaders that they had better help raise the necessary funds for a new building, or the college would be moved to another location. The board asked that the citizens of Springfield and Clark County raise $100,000 in order to keep the college in Springfield. At the end of the campaign only about 20 percent of that figure was raised, so the board lowered the figure to $75,000 to be used for a new college building; if that figure was not met in two months, the Board would consider moving to another location. A board committee reviewed proposals from other Ohio communities, including Bryan, Defiance, Kenton, Lima, and Mansfield. The Mansfield proposal was met with a great deal of enthusiasm and was discussed by the board but was rejected. Finally, despite the fact that only $60,000 of the $75,000 was raised by the deadline, this was enough to ensure the new building and ended any consideration of moving the college out of Springfield.

Several issues of the 1870s relating to student life on campus created some points of tension. As mentioned previously, the admission of the first African American student, Broadwell Chinn, was controversial. The faculty consulted the student body about the application, and the students overwhelmingly voted against it. The faculty rejected Chinn's application, but the board of directors overruled the faculty, and Chinn was admitted. He eventually became the first African American to graduate from Wittenberg.

The same board voted to admit women students, as long as they followed the same curriculum as other students. Although few women came in the first coeducational years, the presence of women meant that the male students had to behave and dress in a less casual or sloppy manner. This result, no doubt, pleased the administration. During Keller's and Sprecher's presidencies, strict discipline with respect to student life and behavior had been enforced. In the years following the Civil War, students chafed under the tight rules and regulations, and the trend was toward a looser, more casual behavior. One of the vestiges of this was greater interest in Greek letter fraternities. Following an antifraternity petition from thirty-seven students presented just prior to 1874, the board had censured fraternities but had not absolutely prohibited them, taking the position that students should voluntarily avoid joining and perpetuating them. The board's resolution on the matter proved rather hollow since it did not absolutely prohibit fraternities and came too late; by that time fraternities had existed on campus for nearly a decade. In spite of the controversy and debates about their presence, fraternities were there to stay.

Wars and economic depressions took their toll on Wittenberg over the years, but American participation in World War I was exceptionally frustrating for the college. Although there had been a significant revival of interest in German culture in the United States of the late nineteenth and early twentieth century, during the war the American people demonstrated extreme intolerance toward German Americans and German culture. The famous violinist Fritz Kreisler, for example, was booed off the stage at one of his performances. Wittenberg did not escape this. It is somewhat ironic that Wittenberg, which was founded by Lutherans who wanted to stress the Americanization of the clergy and the church and opposed the German orientation of the traditional Lutherans, would become one of the victims of this prevalent anti-German sentiment. It is true that the college did not abandon all aspects of its German heritage associated with the Lutheran Church, and the college did share in the nation's revived interest in German culture, but there was no evidence of a pro-German disloyalty to America. Nevertheless, the public associated the college with the German roots of Lutheranism, and the name, Wittenberg, added to a growing hostility to the college. The eastern press erroneously labeled Wittenberg "pro-German" and Springfield a "German-American" community.

Wittenberg most noticeably experienced the anti-German hostility in terms of retention and enrollment. In 1916, for example, 169 freshmen had enrolled, but only 95 returned the next year, and only 86 new freshmen entered the college. President Charles G. Heckert made every effort to counter the negative attitudes toward the college by advising the Wittenberg community to get involved in doing good works. This meant working on bond drives and in Red Cross activities, helping to collect clothing and supplies for newly recruited troops, and providing religious services for troops located in nearby camps. Heckert got students involved and took a leadership role himself, devoting time to bringing the gospel to soldiers stationed nearby and getting other pastors to do the same. He managed to obtain some significant outside help in convincing the doubting public about Wittenberg's loyalty. As a member of the Clark County War Chest Committee, he invited former president Theodore Roosevelt to come to campus to address students and local residents. Roosevelt came to the campus in June 1918 and gave a spirited speech in which he endorsed the college's Americanism.

Wittenberg survived the problems associated with World War I and moved into the 1920s with confidence. The college, like many others in the decade, experienced good times and the prosperity generally shared with other sectors of American society. But once again the economy and involvement in war hurt the college in terms of enrollments and resources. The stock market crash and the ensuing Great Depression nationally ushered in more faculty position and salary cuts. American participation in World War II during the early 1940s cut into the male student enrollments. Dr. Rees Edgar Tulloss, who became president of Wittenberg in 1920, managed to offset the wartime enrollment drop by obtaining a contract with the federal government to provide educational services to Army Air Corps personnel. In 1943 700 Army Air Corps cadets showed up on campus ready for special classes. Their presence and the government contract, which brought them to campus, helped to keep the college economically viable during those difficult years.

Tulloss, an ordained minister before becoming Wittenberg's seventh president, was also a sharp businessman. He owned rental property in Springfield and served on the board of a local bank at the same time he was president of Wittenberg. Many Springfield residents admired and respected Tulloss, but others resented his business practices, which, because of his position at the college, were viewed as Wittenberg actions and led to considerable ill will in the community. It would take many years, however, and actions of several future presidents to overcome the negative attitudes toward Wittenberg that had cropped up during the Tulloss era.

Despite the criticism leveled at Tulloss for creating tensions between the Springfield community and Wittenberg, the seventh president must be credited with developing a professional management approach to running the college and for successfully steering the college safely through the perilous economic difficulties brought on by the stock market crash, the Depression, and the war. His efforts paved the way for his successor.

In many respects the period following World War II marks the beginning of the modern era for Wittenberg. The college grew in terms of enrollment and in its physical plant, the endowment was increased, the college instituted the beginnings of a program to recruit talented faculty, the intercollegiate athletic program became highly successful, the ties with the Lutheran Church were strengthened, and Wittenberg officially became a university. Dr. Tulloss's successor in 1949 was Dr. Clarence C. Stoughton, who at the time he was invited to become Wittenberg's eighth president was serving as executive secretary of the Lutheran Layman's Movement for Stewardship and had held the post of secretary for stewardship of the United Lutheran Church in America (U.L.C.A.) since 1945.

Before his work with the Lutheran Layman's Movement and the U.L.C.A., Clarence Stoughton had been associated with Wagner College, a Lutheran institution in New York City, first as a faculty member teaching English and for ten years as president of the college. During his tenure as president of Wittenberg (1949–63), he managed to effect a number of significant changes and set into motion a number of advances for the college. President Stoughton (or "Prexy," as many called him) sought to attract and retain highly qualified faculty by raising faculty salaries. He was a seasoned and experienced fund-raiser who relied on his concept of stewardship and his unswerving belief in it. More than one observer reports that he did not hesitate, or flinch, when he confronted a prospective donor by saying, "I expect you to give $100,000 to Wittenberg," or even, "I want you to give the college a million dollars."

The physical plant went through a major period of growth during his presidency as the number of college buildings went from fourteen to thirty. He managed to repair any hard feelings that the Springfield community harbored toward the college as he involved himself in many civic activities. Stoughton was determined to build strong ties with the college and the Lutheran Church. It was during his presidency that the college appointed the first campus pastor. It was one of Stoughton's goals to make Wittenberg into the leading Lutheran college in the country. He believed that hiring and keeping outstanding faculty would elevate the academic programs and bring Wittenberg to the level of the Ohio colleges generally considered the chief rivals and competitors for students, namely Ohio Wesleyan, Denison, and Wooster. He was convinced that the school would receive national attention from the successes of its athletic programs, primarily in football and basketball, and from the publicity surrounding the Wittenberg Choir, which toured annually. He also believed, apparently like other college officials around that time, that there was more prestige in becoming a "university," and he wanted Wittenberg to be the top Lutheran university. Some of the elements of what comprised a university were present, and in 1959 Wittenberg College officially became Wittenberg University: Hamma Divinity School, although it had its own board of directors and administrative officers; the School of Music, which had been established in the nineteenth century; the School of Community Education (the evening school); and the School of Professional Studies, which included degrees offered by Departments of Education, Business Administration, Nursing, Home Economics, Christian Education, Medical Technology, and Fine Arts. The university even offered programs at the graduate level, including a master's degree in education and bachelor's and master's degrees in divinity.

It is fair to say that despite the good intentions of those who dreamed big, Wittenberg never became the leading Lutheran university. It has been a university largely in name only, and by 2000 several of the "schools" that were part of the original university were no longer in existence. The School of Professional Studies vanished in the early 1960s as degrees (and the related departments that offered them) in nursing, medical technology, home economics, and Christian education were discontinued and degrees in education, business administration, and fine arts were offered through the Departments of Education, Business Administration, and Art. The School of Music became the Department of Music, and Hamma Divinity School merged with Trinity Lutheran Seminary in Columbus in the late 1970s. All that remains is the college, which always was the heart of the university, and the School of Community Education.

Like many other colleges at the time, Wittenberg underwent a major curriculum and calendar change in the mid-1960s. Before the changes, the school had offered students degrees with majors in astronomy, biology, chemistry, economics, English, French, geography, geology, German, history, mathematics, philosophy, physics, political science, psychology, religion, sociology, and Spanish for the B.A. and majors in biology, chemistry, geology, mathematics, and physics for the B.S. (Before the School of Professional Studies was discontinued, students could earn a B.S. degree in business administration, education, home economics, medical technology, nursing, and Christian education and a Bachelor of Fine Arts degree in art.) The General Education, or Basic Studies, Program was typical of the ones offered by most liberal arts colleges and included courses in the humanities, social sciences, and the sciences. Under the traditional semester system, most courses carried three semester hours of credit.

At the same time that the college underwent a major curriculum change, it adopted a new calendar. A number of colleges during that period of time abandoned the semester system with its "lame duck" session after the Christmas break and moved toward more innovative calendars, like the 4-1-4, the 4-4-1, or the 3-3-3. Wittenberg opted for the 3-3-3, which meant that each student took three courses in one ten-week term (plus one week of final exams). Since the academic year included three terms, a student usually took nine courses each year and thirty-six courses to graduate. Each course usually met five times a week for one hour, and each course earned the same credit as every other course.

The faculty played a major role in effecting these changes with a faculty committee appointed by the president. The committee devoted considerable time to researching and examining alternatives and then presenting recommendations to the faculty, who would vote on them, adopting most of the committee's recommendations. The president who set these changes in motion was Dr. John N. Stauffer, who had succeeded Stoughton in 1963 as Wittenberg's ninth president. John Stauffer had been a member of the faculty in the Department of Psychology and was serving as dean of the college prior to his selection as president.

President Stauffer sought to strengthen the college's academic program by recruiting and retaining some of the young new Ph.D.s (and about-to-be Ph.D.s) from the best graduate schools in the country. It was also his idea to enlarge the role of the faculty in college governance. He not only gave the faculty a leading role in the changing of the curriculum and calendar, he also enlarged faculty participation in decisions related to promotions and tenure through the creation of a Faculty Personnel Committee. Previously department chairs, the dean, and the president made decisions regarding promotions and tenure, with the latter having the largest voice, and this was especially true during the Stoughton presidency. Of course, according to the college's charter and the bylaws, the board of directors had the final say in such decisions, acting on the recommendations of the president. For the most part, however, the board followed the president's recommendations. What John Stauffer did was to create more relative power for the faculty in several areas of college governance. Unfortunately, just a few short years into his presidency, the act of granting greater power to the faculty came back to haunt Stauffer.

Wittenberg may not have been at the leading edge of the manifestations of the social and political unrest associated with the turbulent 1960s in the United States, but neither was it immune. The war in Vietnam had generated protests on college campuses, and antiwar sentiment on the part of some Wittenberg faculty led to conflict with the president. In the summer of 1967 President Stauffer announced that Wittenberg would invite the U.S. Army to establish an ROTC program on the Wittenberg campus. The president indicated that he had consulted individual faculty members of the Faculty Executive Committee (who held the responsibility of acting for the faculty when school was not in session) and had not been met with any objections. When school began in the fall and the faculty was at full strength, opposition to the ROTC program developed, eventually leading to a vote by the faculty, which registered its disapproval of the idea.

The faculty opposition was led by those who were anti–Vietnam War and who claimed a military presence was unacceptable on a liberal arts campus like Wittenberg.

The president defended his action in seeking the program by arguing that it would give Wittenberg graduates an opportunity to fulfill their military obligation after graduation as officers, and that the presence of the program would help to increase the number of male students. There is reason to believe that the board, especially the chairman, who was inclined toward micromanaging the college from his position, was behind the president's move.

President Stauffer, disappointed by the faculty vote and with some feeling of betrayal by those he had sought to empower, submitted the application to the army despite the opposition. Not wishing to organize an ROTC program on a campus where there was open hostility to it, the army turned down the application. At the end of the academic year President Stauffer submitted his resignation and accepted the invitation to become the president of his alma mater, Juniata College in Pennsylvania. Many believed that his decision to resign came as a result of his frustration over the ROTC issue. Others believed that more likely he was dissatisfied with the frequent interference of the board chairman.

The departure of John Stauffer created a leadership vacuum for the college for several years. During academic year 1968–69 a three-man administrative team ran the day-to-day affairs of Wittenberg while the search for a new president was conducted by a search committee comprised of board members, administrators, and faculty. The committee was chaired by the board chairman who, using his two chair positions, forced his choice on the committee over the objections of faculty, some board members on the committee, and several administrators of the college. The choice was G. Kenneth Andeen, a clergyman who had taught at Augustana College in Rock Island, Illinois, and who had served as president of Bethany College in Lindsborg, Kansas. Andeen, a nice man who was not a strong enough leader to command the respect of the faculty and other administrators on campus, resigned in 1974.

It was during the year that the three-man administrative team was running the college that another one of the sixties issues rose up to confront Wittenberg officials. While the protests against the war in Vietnam had been taken up by college students on many campuses across the country, so, too, had the issues identified with the civil rights movement as African American students sought to increase the number of black students in colleges, the number of black faculty members, and the inclusion of black studies programs in college curricula. In 1969 black students at Wittenberg, who had organized as Concerned Black Students (CBS), presented a number of "demands," held a brief sit-in at Recitation Hall where the administrative offices are located, and then initiated a walkout. They left campus and traveled twelve miles south to Yellow Springs, Ohio, the site of Antioch College, where they were housed during the negotiations that took place between the CBS leaders and the college administrators plus the Faculty Executive Committee. The resolution of the incident came when college officials promised to increase financial aid and the number of black students, to increase the number of black faculty, and to provide black students with a center for them to gather and socialize. The Black Culture House was quickly established, and financial aid programs were put in place and admissions strategies were developed to increase the number of African American students on campus, but the number of black faculty remained quite small. The percentage of African American students at the time of the walkout was less than 1 percent of approximately 2,400 total students, while in the year 2000 they make up about 5 percent of the 2,174 student body.

Following the resignation of G. Kenneth Andeen as president in 1974, a search committee, which included board members, administrators, faculty, and a student, selected William A. Kinnison as Wittenberg's eleventh president. Kinnison, an alumnus of the college, had worked in the admissions office, completed a Ph.D. in higher education at Ohio State University, and was appointed assistant to the president, first under John Stauffer and continued in that position under Andeen. An energetic leader, President Kinnison initially had the full confidence of the board and the faculty. He brought to the office of president a commitment to strengthen Wittenberg's liberal arts program and its relative position with respect to other Ohio colleges with whom the college wished to be favorably compared and to other colleges in the Lutheran circuit. He also wished to strengthen the relationship between Wittenberg and the Lutheran Church. Another one of President Kinnison's goals was to get a Phi Beta Kappa chapter established at Wittenberg. He instituted a managerial style of leadership that was influenced by the Management by Objectives (MBO) program that was currently popular and his participation in Harvard's Institute for Educational Management (IEM). He also sent most of his administrative officers to take advantage of the IEM program. Kinnison used the technique of creating commissions to include faculty, administrators, board members, and, on occasion, students to help identify the mission and goals of the institution, to improve the status of the faculty, and to identify ways to increase minority student enrollments.

During his twenty years as president, Kinnison brought about a number of positive changes. He managed to raise faculty salaries in his early years as president to a position comparable to those salaries at some of the other Ohio schools, such as Wooster, Ohio Wesleyan, and Denison. That was a goal that President Stoughton had pushed earlier and one that accompanied the objective of President Stauffer to increase the number of Ph.D.s on the faculty. By the late 1960s, with a full-time faculty of around 150, the percentage of Ph.D.s stood at 75 percent; by 2000, with a full-time faculty of 134, it was 86 percent.

President Kinnison worked with the faculty to bring a Phi Beta Kappa chapter to Wittenberg, and after many years of making unsuccessful applications for a chapter, their efforts were rewarded with success in 1992. He encouraged the faculty to rework and modify the curriculum, which resulted in changes that included a one-course common learning experience for all freshmen, a writing component, and a community service requirement. None of the changes were in conflict with the liberal arts core that has been a constant in the long history of Wittenberg. By 1995 the curriculum changes were accompanied by a return to the semester system with credit hours replacing the course system of credit. Also, the General Education portion of the curriculum included a strengthened language requirement and an emphasis on learning goals. Other changes in the academic program came in 1978 when the Hamma Divinity School merged with Trinity Lutheran Seminary in Columbus; in 1983 when the School of Music was discontinued as a separate school and became the Department of Music; and in 1993 when the physical education major was dropped from the curriculum.

Another feature of Wittenberg during the modern era was its programs in intercollegiate athletics. Although intercollegiate athletics first appeared at Wittenberg in the late nineteenth century, it was during the mid-1950s and after that the school became a small college power in football and basketball. A member of the Ohio Athletic Conference (OAC) from 1909 until 1989 (except for 1928–34), Wittenberg won fifteen conference titles in football from 1955 to 1989 and five national championships. In basketball the college won sixteen conference titles and two national championships. The OAC included a large number of schools and specifically included the Ohio colleges with whom Wittenberg competed for students and with whom it wished to be compared favorably academically—schools like Ohio Wesleyan University, Denison University, and the College of Wooster—and colleges that Wittenberg respected for their national academic reputations, like Oberlin College and Kenyon College. In 1983 the five schools mentioned left the OAC and, along with Allegheny College in Pennsylvania and Case Western Reserve University in Ohio, formed a new athletic conference, the North Coast Athletic Conference (NCAC). Wittenberg was not invited to join at this time, and many at the college were disappointed by what was considered to be a snub prompted by resentment over the school's athletic successes, which other Ohio colleges in the NCAC incorrectly assumed could only have come at the expense of a quality academic program. Nevertheless, in 1989 Wittenberg was invited, along with Earlham College in Indiana, to join the NCAC, and the two colleges accepted the invitation.

Those at Wittenberg who wished to be in an athletic conference with the schools the college competed with academically and for students were pleased with joining the NCAC; others who were strong supporters of the football and basketball programs were less than enthusiastic about the change, which would end traditional rivalries with OAC schools like Baldwin-Wallace, Capital, and Otterbein. Differences in opinions between the athletic department and the administration led to conflicts that ultimately resulted in President Kinnison firing the athletic director (a former successful football coach at the school).

Many of the supporters of the athletic program at Wittenberg viewed the football and basketball programs as the primary ones and the ones that should receive the largest share of the athletic budget. Two significant developments in the 1970s challenged that position. Title IX meant that colleges and universities across the country were required to work toward a parity in funding support for men's and women's sports, and Wittenberg was not excepted from this expectation. Furthermore, President Kinnison wished to see the school's athletic programs broadened to include more participation by the students enrolled. He was interested in having Wittenberg add intercollegiate sports like lacrosse, soccer, volleyball, field hockey, and women's softball to the traditional sports of football, basketball, baseball, track, golf, tennis, and swimming. This was a part of the conflict between the athletic director and President Kinnison. The president won the battle, although his firing of the athletic director led to tensions between many alumni who were supporters of the traditional athletic program and the college administration. Wittenberg continued to be competitive in the NCAC, winning six football championships and seven basketball championships since it joined the conference. Also the women's basketball team won seven championships, and women's teams in field hockey, volleyball, and softball have proved very successful as well.

Wittenberg's relationship with the Lutheran Church remained strong over the years, even though a number of changes were occurring during the modern period. It should be noted that the Lutheran Church did not encroach on the classroom by insisting on the presentation of its views or doctrines. And there was no policy of hiring only Lutheran faculty. Increasingly, the Lutheran Church's monetary contributions declined in terms of the percentage of the operating expenses. The departure of Hamma Divinity School from the campus also removed a visible presence of the Church. A major reorganization of the board of directors of Wittenberg reduced the number of clergy members elected by the synods. As of the mid-1960s the board numbered seventy-six members, although the main work of the body was conducted by an executive committee of twelve, most of whom were businessmen or professionals. In 1987 the board was reduced to a more workable size of thirty-seven members.

Nevertheless, the college continues to recognize in its publications the importance and strength of its ties to the Lutheran Church. The college continues to have a Lutheran presence on campus by holding chapel services during the week, maintaining a Lutheran campus pastor and a director of church relations, and holding Lutheran worship services in the chapel on Sunday mornings, even though only about 20 percent of the student body is Lutheran. The president of the college still must be a Lutheran as stated in the by-laws.

Wittenberg was prominent in a significant merger of church bodies that took place in the 1980s. President Kinnison was one of the leading figures in effecting the merger of the Lutheran Church in America (L.C.A.), the American Lutheran Church (A.L.C.), and the Association of Evangelical Lutheran Churches (A.E.L.C.) to form the Evangelical Lutheran Church in America (E.L.C.A.). The merger meant that the two Lutheran colleges in Ohio, Wittenberg (L.C.A.) and Capital (A.L.C.), were now affiliated with the same national church body.

As Wittenberg approached the end of the twentieth century, a number of the goals set by the founders had been clearly met. Some were very obvious, like the fulfillment of the English-language education for the Lutheran clergy and the location of the college in Springfield. The college does have a strong and distinctive connection with the Lutheran Church. Very importantly, despite challenges along the way and the inclination toward flexibility, Wittenberg has held on stubbornly to its liberal arts roots.

Wittenberg has also addressed some of the hopes set forth by those who came after the founders. In line with educating the whole person, the college has managed to develop a strong academic program and also a strong athletic program. The faculty, 134 full-time persons in 2000, is a highly qualified body of teacher-scholars with 86 percent holding the Ph.D. The college does have a chapter of Phi Beta Kappa, making it one of 258 colleges out of over 3,000 four-year institutions with such a group. The college may not have reached the rank as the top Lutheran college or university in the country, but it is considered one of the top five schools in the Lutheran circuit. It has not equaled or surpassed such outstanding Ohio colleges as Oberlin and Kenyon, but in terms of its faculty, academic programs, and student profiles Wittenberg has maintained its position as being comparable to Ohio Wesleyan, Wooster, and Denison. Enrollments at Wittenberg have stabilized at around 2,100 to 2,200 students without any decline—and in some cases improvement—in board scores or class ranks.

The amazing thing is that these accomplishments have come in the face of limited resources, resulting from financial decisions made in the 1980s, some of which were on the conservative side. During that time the board committee, which managed the college's investments, pursued a very conservative policy. At one point in the 1970s Wittenberg was ranked at the top of all of the Lutheran colleges with an endowment of $20,000,000 (in 2000 it ranked third or fourth). Also in the 1970s it was ranked very near the top compared to some of the good Ohio schools. In the year 2000 even with an endowment of about $100,000,000, Wittenberg ranked near the bottom of the list of Ohio schools with whom it likes to be compared. At a time when a major capital campaign could have enlarged the endowment during the period when stocks were growing at rapid rates, the college opted not to engage in a major campaign, and this put the school considerably behind in its fund-raising. Also, the operating budget was placed under terrific strain as Wittenberg sought to compete with its peer schools for highly qualified students. The declining pool of students that began in the 1970s meant that in order to maintain enrollments with highly qualified students, Wittenberg had to offer increasingly more in financial aid. This was done at the expense of faculty salary increases, which meant that Wittenberg faculty salaries lost ground to those of the peer schools and also at the expense of maintaining some of the facilities.

These problems faced Wittenberg's twelfth president Dr. Baird Tipson, who was appointed to succeed William Kinnison in 1995. Dr. Tipson had taken his undergraduate degree at Princeton University and his Ph.D. in religious studies at Yale. At the time of his selection as Wittenberg's president, he was serving as provost of Gettysburg College, the college from which the first president, Ezra Keller, had received his degree. Tipson came to Wittenberg with a firm commitment to the liberal arts and a desire to upgrade the school's offerings and capabilities in technology. He also wished to maintain the strong Lutheran connection.

In Keller's time Wittenberg had a campus of seventeen acres and the first building, Myers Hall, was completed in 1851. By Tipson's time the campus had seventy acres and twenty buildings, the newest being Hollenbeck Hall, a magnificent three-story building housing the history, philosophy, religion, English, languages, and political science departments. Perhaps symbolically, Hollenbeck, completed in 2000, sits at the top of the highest hill on campus overlooking the campus and Myers Hall, the first and oldest building.

In the year 2000 Wittenberg undertook a major capital fund-raising campaign, seeking $70,000,000 to pay for classrooms, technology, renovation of Myers Hall, and an increased endowment. The campaign was entitled "Defining Moments: Wittenberg at the Millennium," and perhaps it will be just that for Baird Tipson and Wittenberg.

Suggested Reading

There are not many accounts of Wittenberg's history in published works. Two early histories are G. Gerlaw Clark, *History of Wittenberg College, Springfield, O.* (1887) and Harold H. Lentz, *A History of Wittenberg College, 1845–1945* (1946). The Clark volume is interesting in that, although relatively short, it contains brief biographical sketches and pictures of some key faculty and administrators, at least up to 1887. The Lentz history is longer and larger in coverage, but it is limited to the first 100 years of the college's history and is fairly detailed and quite pedantic, as are most centennial histories. By far the best histories in print are the two works written by William A. Kinnison, the college's eleventh president. The first is a pamphlet published by the Clark County Historical Society as *Wittenberg in Clark County, 1845–1970* (1970); the second is a volume entitled *Wittenberg: a Concise History* (1976), written and published during his presidency. The two Kinnison histories contain not only factual information about the college's history but also make some attempt to interpret the meaning and significance of that information. Neither of these works covers much beyond the 1940s, as the author has chosen to leave the more modern period to future historians.

The College of Wooster

The Quest for Significance

JAMES A. HODGES

One dominant theme of the College of Wooster has been its persistent quest from its beginning in 1866 to the new millennium to be a significant institution for its students, faculty, and society. At its centennial year in 1966 it was no accident that its president, Howard Lowry, chose "the pursuit of significance" as the year's theme. To Lowry—a 1923 graduate, a faculty member in the 1920s and 1930s, and president from 1944 to 1967—Wooster's hope had always been to be a college that made a difference in students' lives and one that prepared them to lead whole and useful lives in the greater society. Lowry believed that a college could create its own values and at the same time compete in the larger world of academic excellence with some degree of success. Wooster's history before and after Lowry gives credence to his firm faith that a college could thrive if it had a reason to be and a loyal constituency that believed it to be a unique and loved place worthy of support.

Only dreamers and nineteenth-century American optimists could have imagined a significant university in the small county seat town of 5,000 that was Wooster. One of them was the Presbyterian minister James A. Reed, who, on a ride in September 1865, stopped on the northern hill overlooking the town to the south, paused for prayer, and decided that the place would be a splendid site for a university. Fortunately, Reed's prayer coincided with those of New Light Presbyterians in Ohio who wanted an institution of their own. Ephaim Quinby, a local banker and a member of Reed's church, owned the land and was amenable to donating it as the first section of the current campus. Businessmen of Wooster and Wayne County, seeing the opportunity for entrepreneurial gain to be made from a new university, joined the church leaders' efforts. After a spirited burst of fund-raising, the Ohio Synod of the Presbyterian Church incorporated the University of Wooster in December 1866. The founders began with slender resources but large ambitions. "What we desire,"

Wooster faculty of 1874

said the first board of trustees, "is to make Wooster the great education center of Ohio as Oxford and Cambridge are in England and the universities are in Germany and France."

What the first trustees would create as classes opened for the first time on September 7, 1870, was a huge brick building, "Old Main," six stories high with an imposing mansard roof; two wings were added in 1891. It was certainly large enough for the thirty-four students who showed up on the first day to be taught by President Willis Lord (1870–73), professor of natural and revealed religion, who had assembled five other professors. The trustees incorporated a medical school in Cleveland and planned to open a school of law and a theological school in Wooster to complete the university. The faculty, in fact, did soon begin a postgraduate program that awarded a variety of M.A. and Ph.D. degrees for directed nonresidential study, and by the 1880s a music conservatory enlivened the school, though it fell short of a separate school.

Rather than being an Oxford or a Cambridge, the first faculty wanted to become the "Princeton of the West," and the B.A. curriculum they designed followed popular models of the time: a three-term year with two courses of study from which a student chose either the classical course (with three divisions) or the scientific course. Actually, most students followed in the first two years a closely laid out course sequence and only in the last two years selected a few electives that allowed limited specialization. The classical course of study proved the most popular, and by 1881 the university abandoned the scientific course, replacing it with a separate literary course of study. The science courses, always strong and popular by themselves, became part of the classical course of study requirements.

From its beginnings Wooster has held central values about education that underlay its curriculum. First and foremost its leaders had created a Christian university. President Lord believed that "the temple of learning" had to be connected to "the temple of God." "It is," he said, "a Christian college. It is a Presbyterian college, and its foundations were laid out in prayers and 'everything pertaining' to it has been solemnly dedicated to Christ and his kingdom." Within that Christian tradition, the university followed rather broad ideas of religious freedom, accepting students of all creeds or no creed. Not only did Wooster's scientists and theologians accept Darwinism, but also President Charles Wishart (1919–44) carried that standard into a winning battle against William Jennings Bryan for the moderatorship of the Presbyterian Church (U.S.A.) in 1923.

The university quickly became the sum of the men and women who taught there. The trustees had resolved that the university would be open to all religions, sexes, or races. The presence of women, said President Lord would, "conserve order, increase decorum, and in every way, cherish and stimulate manliness, honor, truth, and right." Emily Noyes graduated in 1874 as the first woman graduate, and Annie Irish became in 1881 the first woman faculty member. In the 1880s the first African American student, Clarence Allen, came to the university, but black student enrollment would not reach significant numbers until the late 1960s. The university's history would be made by its always dedicated faculty, such as the venerable Jonas Notestein in classics (who came to Wooster as a student in 1873 and stayed fifty-five years); the powerful Elias Compton (classics, English, and psychology); and William Zebina Bennett (the chemist who claimed he could quote sixteen straight hours of Shakespeare), and Orange Stoddard (science). Already an experienced natural science teacher when he came in 1870, Bennett established a strong laboratory science tradition.

Professors of the 1870s to the early 1900s were nineteenth-century people, often ministers, deeply religious, and trained in places such as Wooster. A second generation followed from 1900s to the early 1920s that had roots in the first generation but which was increasingly more leavened by the young Ph.D.s of the new graduate universities and by increasing numbers of female professors. By the 1920s and 1930s the third generation emerged, more centered in disciplinary work and a national professorate. Nevertheless, the early presence of a faculty that defined the university and thought it stood for a sharply defined mission, that had a sense of itself as an executor of the mission, and that considered the University of Wooster a distinct place and community became a lasting heritage for successive faculty members.

During the years of its first three presidents, Willis Lord (1870–73), Archibald A. E. Taylor (1873–83), and Sylvester Scovel (1883–99), the University of Wooster sought to survive and become a lasting enterprise secure on its own terms. Soon the 34 students had grown by 1874 to 139 students with another 35 students in the preparatory school (closed down in 1918). The trustees spoke with confidence in 1878 in one of the better-known recruiting boasts of Wooster: "It is better to give a son a complete education than to give him a farm. He will then be able to earn far more in a year than his farm would produce, and may besides yield a great influence for good. The well-educated young man will rise to leadership in the days to come." By 1880 the university enrolled 250 students from more than sixteen states with more than seventy women in the class; and, cognizant of its founding mission, in that year it had more graduates in Princeton Theological Seminary than did any other college in the country. The university was, of course, at all times chronically underfunded, but periodic forays by the presidents and faculty to Presbyterian churches and donors raised the money to supplement tuition and to modestly increase the anemic endowment and pay for faculty growth and campus expansion in the form of a handsome chapel and a library that held 20,000 books. The university had also made progress toward its first goal—to be a school of distinction that graduated useful citizens. In its first twenty years it had graduated 507 men and 95 women. More than 200 students had become ministers, 90 lawyers, 40 physicians, and 19 journalists, and others had entered numerous occupations. At the fifty-year mark, Wooster alumni had spread all over the country and the world. Thirty-two had become college or university presidents, and 175 were college teachers. More than 900 served as schoolteachers or administrators. Some 400 ministers served the Lord, and 112 had gone abroad as missionaries. Two students had won Rhodes Scholarships; others had distinguished careers in law, medicine, and other roles in life. Arthur Compton (Class of 1913) won the Nobel Prize in physics in 1927.

Wooster's stability, however, masked some undercurrents of disappointment. President Scovel, although admired by the faculty and students for his strength of character, had, with faculty support, banned intercollegiate athletics (after one of its first football teams had in 1889 defeated Ohio State 64-0). For good measure he also banned social dancing and theater on campus. A Wooster graduate of the 1890s argued that the faculty had been too devoutly pious. "They were not," he wrote, "a frolicsome faculty," and they did "painfully little to amuse us and often fell short of faint praise." When Scovel resigned in 1899 to enter a fruitful decade of teaching at Wooster as the Hoge Professor of History, Morals, and Sociology, the university gladly welcomed the thirty-nine-year-old Louis Edward Holden, a Princeton Theological graduate who had made his first career at Beloit College. Holden, although ministerially trained, threw himself into the role of the professional president and proclaimed, "I mean business," as he found an academic community that at the turn of the century needed fresh leadership.

Until the end of his presidency in 1915, President Holden needed every leadership skill he possessed. In the early hours of December 11, 1901, Old Main burned down. At dawn's light, the faculty met, prayed, and announced the continuation of classes and the date of final examinations. Holden energetically set out to raise money for a new Wooster. Telegrams were sent to "men of wealth." The one Holden sent to Andrew Carnegie began, "Yesterday I was president of a university. Today I am president of a hole in the ground." Holden, aided by the faculty and numerous small donors, improbably raised $290,000 in sixty days; $100,000 came from Carnegie after a direct appeal by Holden at the philanthropist's New York City mansion. Louis H. Severance of Cleveland, a former Rockefeller associate, also gave 50,000 dollars for a chemistry building. Over the next eleven years Severance became a financial angel for Wooster, giving two more buildings, the stadium, and generous amounts to the endowment that grew from 200,000 dollars to $1 million by 1910. Four new buildings, all in vaguely English collegiate gothic style and all in "white vitrified brick" (actually light tan in appearance) quickly arose, and the largest freshmen class ever, seventy-eight in total, entered the buildings in September 1903. These totally renovated buildings (one twice!) still form the modern campus, and they have dictated ensuing campus architecture to create a remarkable architectural unity.

Holden also presided over changing faculty as the first university-trained Ph.D.s came to teach at Wooster. The deep attachment of the early faculty to Wooster merged with the newer faculty's engagement with disciplinary learning. That early-twentieth-century faculty taught, so Arthur Compton claimed, "the best we know, on which we could willingly bet our lives." The pietistic grip of Scovel loosened, but, in the major change, Wooster abandoned the university model. The curriculum had evolved in 1906 from the old course of study tracks to a familiar curriculum with a core of general education courses, majors and minors, adding up to 124 credit hours for graduation. In 1914 and 1915 Holden won a bitter fight with some trustees and faculty members, and he shut down a summer school for teachers that drew close to 1,000 teachers to the campus. As part of that fight, with little fanfare, the University of Wooster in 1914 changed its name to The College of Wooster, a college of the liberal arts, which it really had always been.

Ready to move on, Holden resigned in 1915 and was replaced by John Campbell White, a Presbyterian minister and missionary who never established credibility with the now more professional and independent faculty. In 1919 the trustees called to the presidency the forty-nine-year-old Charles Frederick Wishart who had an established career as a seminarian and Presbyterian preacher in Pittsburgh and Chicago. If Holden was a great bricks-and-mortar president, Wishart, an accomplished speaker and a warm personality, became the great consolidator.

Wishart presided over a curriculum that accommodated the modern disciplines. He significantly expanded the campus by purchasing adjoining lands and built five new buildings. He began regular capital campaigns that established a certain financial stability. By 1938 student enrollment had doubled from 578 in 1919 to more than

1,000, and the faculty had grown from forty to eighty-four. The college had weathered not only the challenges of the Great Depression, but it would also ride out the enrollment crisis of World War II. Students and faculty alike knew him as "Prexy"; he called himself a "preacher-president" and presided over a college that appeared to be content in its sense of self as a "good liberal arts college" that did well for its students and one that enjoyed the respect and support of its alumni. It enjoyed the reputation as a place of some distinction and as one of the best Presbyterian colleges in the country. Nevertheless, its development paralleled that of many other similar colleges in educational values, faculty development, and patterns of growth.

When Wishart retired at age seventy-four in 1944, the trustees apparently had decided to follow the college's tradition of a Presbyterian minister as president, but key faculty members protested and pushed for the appointment to go to Howard Foster Lowry. A 1923 graduate of the college, the forty-three-year-old Lowry had never cut his ties to his beloved alma mater, teaching there off and on until he earned his Ph.D. in English at Yale. In the 1930s he taught at Wooster and emerged as a major scholar of Matthew Arnold, the English critic-poet. During that time he also became the general American editor of the Oxford University Press, often commuting weekly on the Pennsylvania Railroad from Wooster to New York City. In 1940 Princeton appointed him to a Sterling Professorship of English, and he joined the Wooster board of trustees. Lowry, an eloquent speaker at academic rituals (he was given sixteen honorary degrees), church events, civic clubs, and after-dinner occasions, impressed people with his warmth, rich humor, and wisdom gleaned from wide reading. Until his death in 1967, he worked tirelessly to take the "good" liberal arts college he led and create for it a national identity as a college with a fully articulated vision of the liberal arts college in the Christian tradition, one that would be a "true place of higher learning, advancing first-rate scholarship and matching the best of secular colleges and universities."

On coming to Wooster in September 1944, Lowry announced that the college would create a "credo" for the years ahead at a time when the large public universities threatened liberal arts colleges. But the new Wooster would not abandon the "scholar-teacher" model he so loved for the university-research professor ideal. A liberal arts college, he argued, had to have some faculty members deeply oriented to research if only to give the college credibility, but scholar-teachers were a liberal arts college's lifeblood. "What we want here," he said, "are men who both know their trade and something more than that—men of learning who respect knowledge but who know that beyond the world of fact lies a world of value, and, beyond that, some internal loyalties." Lowry wrote that the "college will never judge its teachers by the weight of their annual bibliographies. . . . We believe that research and scholarship may often, and at the best, consist not merely in the discovery of new facts but also in the fresh and creative relationship of facts already known." Wooster was only "the lengthened shadow" of its great teachers.

To counter the research-professor ideal of the multiuniversities, Lowry prevailed on the trustees to establish a generous leave program that allowed many to take a research leave every fifth year and some a study year every seventh. The leave programs would become a cherished part of faculty life at Wooster, and the college has increasingly advertised the publication success of its faculty while at the same time clinging to the merit of teaching. By the end of the century, though, tenure would be hard to achieve without some record of research activity.

Working with faculty members, Lowry, by December 1945, summed up the new Wooster's educational scheme in a document he largely wrote, in pamphlet form and in the catalog in brief, *Wooster: Adventure in Education*. Amended in some ways, it has remained the educational foundation of the college ever since. In its review the student newspaper announced, "Wooster has ceased to be an educational factory. Wooster today is an idea." Lowry supported the usual balanced general education program along with electives of a student's choice, but he focused on the courses that made up the curriculum. A liberal education should provide a student with a method and content. The method part consisted of courses helping students learn "how, under any given situation, to find the necessary facts, to associate and evaluate them, to draw just conclusions from them, and to present the results in clear and attractive form." But method was not enough. Courses had to have content that "consists of leading ideas and facts that form the mind and nature of man. There are certain great questions worthy to be asked by all men, and there is a great body of classic answers to these questions . . . that a human will be the poorer for not knowing."

The first two years of a Wooster education distributed general education equally among the sciences and math; history and social science; language and the fine arts; and religion, philosophy, and psychology, with two required courses in religion, the Old Testament and the New Testament. Lowry lavished his attention on the upper-class program. He saw the capstone of liberal education to be a four-course program in a student's major in what Wooster would call independent study (I.S.). The junior-year student would in two semesters select some special topic, begin investigation in the laboratory or library, and write three or four papers under the direction of a faculty member in one-on-one weekly conferences. In the senior year the student would write a senior thesis, once again under the weekly direction of a faculty member. Both years were bracketed with comprehensive examinations in the major field. Lowry wrote, "Independent Study is not reserved for the intellectual elite alone. . . . Every man and woman is potentially an honors candidate." Students would own their I.S. work, "a creative adventure in self-discipline and self-discovery that ought to be the first of such creative adventures throughout life."

Independent Study, reduced in 1970 to one course in the junior year and the two-course senior thesis, has become the trademark of a Wooster education and pervades the culture of the college as it works its way into other courses. In 1956 the faculty, prodded once again by Lowry, began a two-semester required first-year course, Introduction to Liberal Studies, built around a common core of reading, introducing students to some great questions of the humanities and sciences and, through discussing and writing, increasing the power of students to attack these questions in the course and, subsequently, in the curriculum to come. Enrollment in each class was limited to fifteen students. The required first-year seminar (later reduced to one course) would stand alongside I.S. as another persistent characteristic of Wooster. Lowry also called for continual experimentation with interdepartmental courses at all levels of the curriculum, and since the 1940s such courses come and go, change, and thrive at Wooster.

Lowry never lost sight of the larger aim of the college. The college, while preparing students for lives of "action and service to others," should "raise a standard to which those who would like to be wise and just can repair." Lowry wrote that "the pursuit of a significant life—the enhancement of our capacity to confer a meaning of life, the power to seek the significance with clarity, with range, with patience, with commitment, and perhaps with some touch of distinction, is the gift of education." Lowry annually gave baccalaureate talks and defended the Christian college. In *Wooster: Adventure in Education* he made the case that there was "no real incompatibility between a Christian education and liberal education." He wrote, "The Christian college is not a plot against the human mind."

Despite his eloquent defense of the Christian college, secularization crept into the college. In 1969 the Synod of Ohio released ownership to a secular board of trustees, and the college acknowledges its religious heritage with the statement in the catalog that it is a "college of the church." Students of all faiths enroll at the college, the religious diversity of the faculty has become pronounced, and the religious requirement of two courses has become a one-course requirement with a wide choice of several different kinds of religious study courses. The college advertises a "religious dimension" that has stayed alive with a Presbyterian church on campus, numerous speakers who address spiritual values, and the maintenance of a vital religious study department.

Lowry also presided over an expansion of the college. The enrollment went to 1,200 (well over his sense that the ideal liberal arts college had only 1,000 students), then to 1,500 as a goal after a selective admissions procedure. Two buildings were gutted and totally renovated and twelve new buildings built, the most important to him being a new library. At his death in 1967 a new physical education center and student union building were under construction; he had successfully completed a $20 million capital campaign, and the endowment had grown from $3.5 to $12 million.

In the 1960s, just as the Lowry era ended, the college had to accommodate itself to a changing student culture. Student life at Wooster followed patterns similar to that of other universities and colleges. At first Wooster was not even residential, with the first dormitory built in 1896 for women and one for men in 1913. National fraternities and sororities, however, came at the beginning to Wooster. But in 1913, amid controversy, the college banned them. But by the 1920s the separate staircases dividing the men's dormitory, Kenarden Lodge, had facilitated the emergence of local clubs known as "Sections." By the middle 1930s the Sections, named One through Eight, had assumed the identifying features of national fraternities with Greek letters, "Hell Week," and numerous parties. At the same time women's clubs with names like "Sphinx," "Peanuts," and "Imps" had established themselves. In 1936 the faculty belatedly recognized the existence of Sections and women's clubs and created a scheme of regulation. As late as the 1960s more than 90 percent of the men belonged to a Section, although that percentage had dropped by the 1990s to below 20 percent. Oddly, in 1985 the college recognized them for the first time as local fraternities and established a Greek Life Committee.

The students over the years led a well-regulated life following rules set by the faculty. Daily chapel attendance, required church attendance at a church of their choice, no drinking, and from 1883 until 1932 no dancing on campus bound their lives, but as students everywhere they amused themselves with a variety of such things as literary clubs, sports, pranks, campuswide events, and courting rituals. Some, of course, amused themselves by breaking the rules.

The cultural battles of the 1960s and 1970s created what might be called a new college of student life to contrast with the old college that had existed for so long. In the old college deans guided by an elaborate set of specific rules and penalties regulated residential life. Women were particularly singled out for close supervision by stringent rules of access to and from the residential halls. Parents expected the college to exercise a paternalistic oversight over students. By the 1970s the old college came apart. Students argued that they should be treated as adults, responsible for their own environment and their own actions; they pressed to be more actively involved in the rule-making process and in the government of the college as it affected their lives, particularly outside the direct academic process, the classrooms, and laboratories.

President J. Garber Drushal (1967–77), a likable, effective, and pragmatic successor to Lowry, who was a romantic Victorian hopelessly out of touch with the 1960s, quickly responded, first to the challenges of the Vietnam War and then to the so-called student movement. Drushal pushed through in 1969 a new lean standard of student life standards called the Code of Conduct (later the Code of Social Responsibility), which abandoned in locus parentis and set up a new system of campus government called the Campus Council, a tripartite body of administrators, students, and faculty, that over the years created its own bristling set of rules and standards for a community that lived in close quarters. The faculty gave up any direct control of student life, a control that had been omnipresent in the nineteenth century and early twentieth but episodic since the 1940s. Students became young adults subject to the usual civil codes. The college ended daily required chapel, moving first to twice weekly voluntary "convocation" and then to one convocation a week; by the 1980s it had dropped all-campus meetings altogether.

Aided by a faculty committee, Drushal replaced Lowry's maxims with a new Wooster reason to be, "Risk and Commitment." In many ways, ironically, the document printed in the catalog reaffirmed the Lowry curriculum, though Drushal spearheaded a turn to the quarter system as a way to offer more and different courses. The college abandoned the old course hour requirement and required 34–36 courses to graduate. Drushal, a key faculty member in the creation of Independent Study, reaffirmed the college's support of the expensive program, which soaked up 20 percent of the instructional budget.

When Drushal retired in 1977 at age sixty-five, the forty-three-year-old Henry J. Copeland, a Georgia native and Cornell University–trained French historian, came to the presidency. Copeland, who had served as history professor and dean of the faculty, was determined to make clear Wooster's commitment to being a distinctive institution. In 1977, in his inauguration address, he summed up his conviction that Wooster would remain "an autonomous center of ideas, values and standards, which, while rooted in the present, transcends in its concerns the here and now; which, rather than reflects the world, challenges it; which, rather than assuming all of the tasks that require doing, assumes one and does that superbly; which, rather than accepting the inevitable, creates a tension between what is and what could be; which, rather than being a mirror to society remains a place apart with its own character and purpose." Copeland realized that Wooster had to be a place that made a difference for the students in an educational world in which the all-purpose, large university had triumphed. Copeland envisioned Wooster as "a place apart," deeply concerned for standards, with a faculty that maintained "rigorous standards of craftsmanship," demanded "performance and achievements," and at the same time was concerned for values beyond the curriculum.

Copeland's Wooster faced sharp challenges—some subtle, but threatening nevertheless. The declining number of seventeen-year-olds in the pool of prospective students, caused by the end of the postwar baby boom and sharply increased cost of private education in the 1970s and 1980s, meant that Drushal's expansionist plans to go to 2,000 students would have to be abandoned if the student quality indices were kept at acceptable levels (at one point Wooster enrolled more than 1,900 students). The college revitalized the admission's procedure and with angst and concern among the faculty stabilized the enrollment at between 1,600 and 1,650 with increased selectivity. The faculty, which while still supporting the Independent Study program and the first-year required seminar, embraced the new knowledge by establishing twelve new departmental or interdepartmental majors, ranging from archaeology, black studies, and computer science to theater, urban studies, and women's studies. Throughout the last thirty years the college, through its courses, student life programs, visiting speakers, and key events, addressed the problems of American society at large, particularly international relations and the vexing issues of race, class, and gender.

Copeland supported faculty-driven changes in the curriculum such as a return in 1983 to the semester system, but he had a firm conviction that Wooster had too few resources to support the kind of college it wanted to be. He believed to some degree that to be small and good, you had to be wealthy (or at least have a steady income). Wooster's need to see itself as a significant place became even a harder task when in 1988 the influential *U.S. News and World Report* on higher education moved Wooster away from its top-ten regional college list to a "national" liberal arts college ranking. By its own honest self-analyses comparing indices of quality such as student profile scores, endowment per student, and faculty salaries, Wooster fell short of the top schools in the nation. Nevertheless, a recent study measured some fifty of the top colleges in three areas—educating scientists, educating leaders in international relations, and educating business leaders—Wooster was one of only twenty-one colleges to have a place in all three groups. Several studies over the years always placed Wooster well into the top-twenty colleges or universities in the country in the undergraduates' origins of Ph.D. production in the various disciplines. The college, led by Copeland and two outstanding chairmen of the board of trustees, J. W. Pocock (Class of 1938) and Stanley Gault (Class of 1948), labored mightily to try to pay for a curriculum that Copeland worried Wooster could not support. Gault, who generously gave millions to the college, led two separate capital campaigns, one for $36 million completed in 1985 and another in the 1990s for over $60 million. By Gault's retirement as chair of the board of trustees in June 2000, the college had raised $180 million since 1983, built or renovated a dozen buildings, and equipped a state-of-the-art computer-ready campus. The endowment stood over $220 million, and its annual budget exceeded $45 million. Copeland, ever modest about his achievements, on his retirement in 1995 said that he distrusted charismatic leadership and that Wooster's ability to meet the contemporary challenge to a liberal arts college depended on its core of supportive alumni and faculty members and trustees who won through a "triumph of conviction over adversity," through a conviction that Wooster offered a value-added approach to educating students toward high achievement and a life of significance.

In May 2000 the Wooster faculty produced a new educational statement that it called "A Wooster Education," arguing for a community of "independent learners" who enjoyed a curriculum "rich in content and intellectual rigor" that would prepare them for "lives of responsibility in a pluralistic society and instill a breadth of understanding, concern, and commitment." It featured new programs of interdisciplinary learning across the disciplines and writing across the disciplines that, along with I.S. and the Wooster first-year seminar, would hopefully keep Wooster a tangible place that had emotion, meaning, and that nurtured a purpose in life. President R. Stanton Hales (1995–) recognized the challenges in April 2000 for himself and the faculty. Since 1990–91 33 senior faculty members of the 140-member faculty had retired. Only 54 percent of the 1990–91 faculty remained at the college. He concluded that Wooster is "at all times a very old college and a very new college." The trick would be to keep it a college in touch with its heritage of high expectations.

Suggested Reading

For the history of the college from 1866 to 1944, one should turn first to the charming and informative two-volume study by Lilian Notestein, *Wooster of the Middle West* (Kent State University Press, 1937, 1971). See also James Hodges, Gordon Tait, and John W. Pocock, "Only Dreamers Could Have Seen a College," *Wooster* (Fall 1991): 18–25; James Blackwood, "The Ivory Tower Half a Century Later," *Wooster* (Fall 1991): 26–29; Henry Copeland, "An Improbable College," *Wooster* (Fall 1991): 30–33; J. W. Pocock, "Presidents Are People," *Wooster* (Fall 1987): 4–9; Jonas O. Notestein, "Wooster in the Seventies," *Wooster Alumni Bulletin* (Jan. 1926): 12, 16; A. T. Foreman, "Wooster in the Eighties," *Wooster Alumni Bulletin* (Feb. 1926): 6–7; Elizabeth E. Coyle, "Today's Picture of College Life," *Wooster Alumni Bulletin* (Fall 1926): 9–10; J. V. Stone, "Wooster in the Nineties," *Wooster Alumni Bulletin* (Mar. 1926): 89; Jonas Notestein, "Early Days at Wooster," *The Wooster Quarterly* (July 1914): 95–116; W. Dean Hopkins, "1910, Wooster, 1914: A Study in Ebb and Flow," *Wooster Alumni Magazine* (Feb.–Mar. 1971): 10–11; G. Pauline Ihrig, "In Those Days," *Wooster* (Spring 1988): 3–9; Melcher P. Fobes, "The Good Old Days," *Wooster Alumni Bulletin* (Jan. 1951): 103–5; William H. Snoddy, "The Price of Change," *Wooster* (Winter 1999): 11–16; Karen Taylor, "Participating in a Radical Tradition: Women on the Faculty, 1880–1960," *Wooster* (Winter 1992): 15–23; J. W. Pocock, "The Making of a Board, 1957–1986," *Wooster* (Fall 1989): 12–17; and "The Ohio Six," *Time*, Sept. 30, 1956.

Henry Copeland's collection of speeches, *An Improbable College and Other Convocation Addresses* (1977–95) has several speeches that address the college's history, and the 2000 catalog has a sketch largely written by him. See also Howard Lowry, *College Talks*, ed. James R. Blackwood (Oxford University Press, 1969); James R. Blackwood, *Howard Lowry: A Life in Education* (College of Wooster, 1975); James R. Blackwood, *The House on College Avenue: The Comptons at Wooster, 1891–1913* (Massachusetts Institute of Technology, 1968).

Xavier University

Its Jesuit Tradition

John LaRocca

In 1821 the Roman Catholic Church entrusted Bishop Edward Fenwick with the care of the Catholics in Ohio, Indiana, Michigan, and Wisconsin when the Pope appointed him the first bishop of the new Diocese of Cincinnati. Fenwick knew that the work of his diocese would be hampered if he did not have a seminary for the training of priests and for the education of Catholic youths. Without the seminary his diocese would be dependent on the work of European priests, whom he feared would not be numerous enough; on a practical level, he feared that he would have to support them for two to three years as they learned the English language and American customs. A native clergy would both know the area and would be inured to the rigors of life in the West. Fenwick wanted to find about seven or eight young men who had finished their studies to join his seminary so that they could teach the rudiments of Latin to young men between the ages of fourteen and sixteen. He realized that his seminary/school would give him influence in the education of youth that would greatly aid the cause of religion in the state. In doing this he realized that, like the bishop of Bardstown, Kentucky, who had done this before him, he might have to provide room and board for the seminarians and the lay students with them.

On May 11, 1829, Bishop Fenwick's new seminary opened in an old frame church in Cincinnati that stood next to the cathedral at the intersection of Sixth and Sycamore Streets. The seminary was placed under the patronage of St. Francis Xavier, S.J., the great missionary whose example Fenwick hoped would inspire his seminarians as they worked in his far-flung diocese.

Fenwick died of cholera in September 1832, a month before the opening of a separate college division, the Athenaeum, which was the second part of his plan for the education of youth. In December 1832 there were sixty students registered in the college, most of whom were not Catholic. The pastoral demands of the diocese

The Academic Mall

made it impossible for Bishop Purcell to keep priests in Cincinnati to teach young men. As early as 1838, therefore, he began to offer the institution to the Society of Jesus that was receiving requests from American bishops for priests to do mission work and to open schools. The General of the Society could not accept all of the offers made to him to undertake educational work in the United States. In the summer of 1840 after the General of the Jesuits decided to accept Bishop Purcell's offer, negotiations opened between the Belgian Jesuits in St. Louis and Purcell. The *Catholic Telegraph* announced the transfer of the school to the Jesuits on September 6, 1840.

Catholic educational institutions were essential in the mid–nineteenth century to the preservation of the Catholic community in the United States. In an age of both nativism and anti-Catholicism, educational institutions existed in a Protestant culture whose approach to religion was pro-Protestant and anti-Catholic. Archbishop John Hughes experienced both in New York City, where Know-Nothing crowds surrounded Old St. Patrick's Cathedral; he was also unable to obtain permission for Catholic children in schools to receive Catholic religious education in the classroom. As a result of that Hughes began a movement to remove religious education from public schools. That situation would lead the American Catholic bishops late in the century to decide that when a parish was founded, the school should be built before the church.

By 1840, therefore, St. Xavier College existed to produce educated Catholic young men, some of whom, the bishop hoped, would join the clergy. The Jesuits realized that they shared the goals of the bishop and that their school would improve the moral and the intellectual atmosphere of the city. Both the bishop and the Jesuits also realized that a system of Catholic education was necessary to keep the Catholic community in existence and safe from the attempts to convert youth in schools to Protestantism. Those were the reasons for the existence of St. Xavier College. The needs of the church, the apostolate of the Society of Jesus, and the opportunities and challenges of American culture shaped the mission of Xavier University in 1840 and would continue to shape and change the mission of Xavier University as they changed and developed.

To meet the needs of the population of Cincinnati, the college opened a night division to teach German to young men who wanted to learn the language after business hours. For the same reason the college ran a bookkeeping class at night. The college had opened a boarding school to provide for those outside of Cincinnati. The success of the division showed the need for education offered by the Jesuits. In the last year in which the boarding division was open (1852–53) there were seventy-seven boarders; thirty-two of them were from the southern states or Latin America. Most of those from the South were French-speaking Creoles whose presence raised the question of whether they should be allowed to speak French while living at the school. The boarders were usually equally divided between Catholic and Protestant. The Jesuits admitted that if they had only Catholic boarders there would be more students at exercises of piety, but they consoled themselves and others with the number of conversions. The unspoken subtexts indicate the need for a college in the area and the financial need of the institution as the reasons for the presence of the non-Catholics at St. Xavier College. Their presence there, however, demonstrates the accuracy of Fenwick's vision. His college would have influence in educating youth. The administration of the college closed the boarding division in 1853 because of the dreaded summer recurrences of cholera.

In the 1840s the college students who watched antislavery riots in Cincinnati were living in a city where many inhabitants were part of the "Underground Railroad." It is not surprising, then, that St. Xavier students debated the morality of slavery, debated whether Indians or Negroes had more to complain of because of treatment they had received from whites. While the debate topics are listed, the side that won is not listed. The one topic that the students refused to debate was whether the employment of women in factories was beneficial.

During the pre- and postwar years the student body of the college changed. Prior to the war the majority of the students were native born. As the potato famine in

Ireland and the *Kulturkamf* in Germany ran their course, the number of foreign-born and first-generation Americans increased. The college introduced immigrants and the sons of immigrants to higher education and to American culture.

With moral and political issues in the news again the tone was set for the debates carried on in the school in the 1860s. Students argued whether or not secession could be justified by the Constitution, whether or not Negroes should be granted citizenship, and whether white soldiers fighting in the Civil War were superior to black soldiers.

One Xavier faculty member dared to bring Xavier's presence to the attention of the Ohio College Association when it met in Cincinnati in December 1877 and he presented a paper on "The Jesuit System of Teaching the Classics." The paper was well received and brought the Jesuit *Ratio Studiorum* to the attention of the members of the association. Changes in American education over the next thirty years would result in the separation of the high school division from the college division. Because of this the college began a new graduate division in 1894 and regularly granted the master's of arts degree to those who had successfully completed their course of studies. The educational changes that were going on at Harvard under President Charles W. Eliot had no effect on the curriculum at St. Xavier College. At Harvard under Eliot there was only one required course. At St. Xavier, however, all the courses were required and all textbooks were specified. It would take ten years for the changes in American education to affect Xavier (thus proving the truth of Mark Twain's statement that if the world were to end tomorrow he would go to Cincinnati, because everything happens there ten years later). The high school and college divisions were finally separated in 1907.

The twentieth century not only witnessed educational changes at St. Xavier College but also witnessed the move of the college from its downtown location to a new and suburban location in Avondale. It also witnessed the opening of the School of Commerce in 1911 that held classes in the evening. Once again the college was responding to the needs of the community in which it was located.

St. Xavier College existed in part to serve the needs of the church. In February 1911 the Ohio legislature passed the Morris Education Bill, which approved state teaching certificates without examination for those who had completed high school and college. At the time the archdiocese had 110 parish schools with an enrollment of 30,000 pupils. The majority of those teaching in those schools were religious sisters who needed to qualify for teaching certificates if the parish schools were to be recognized by the state. In response to that problem, St. Xavier College began holding extension classes for the sisters.

The year 1917 not only witnessed the United States's entry into the Great War but further American influences on St. Xavier College. When the Jesuits took over responsibility for the college, they followed the European academic week of classes on Monday, Tuesday, Wednesday, Friday, and Saturday. The Thursday holiday was dropped in favor of the Monday-to-Friday workweek. It is not clear if the change was made because of an adaptation to American educational practice or because of an anti-European feeling that gripped the country during the war. The war took men out of the classroom and placed them in the trenches. Because women were needed in the business world to take their place and students were needed at Xavier, the college thus opened commercial courses, summer classes, and evening classes.

The postwar years saw the college take root and grow in Avondale. The growth of the college resulted in the change of the name of the institution from St. Xavier College to Xavier University on August 4, 1930. The depression and the Second World War were difficult for the new university, as they were for most small higher educational institutions. The postwar years saw the growth of Xavier University and presented many challenges. The GI Bill not only provided an opportunity for all returning GIs who wanted to go to college to go, but also the opportunity to do so. That opportunity allowed the new university to grow and provided one of the elements that would change the existence of Catholic higher education—the end of the ghettoization of Catholics in the United States.

The postwar years also witnessed the expansion of higher education in the United States. State university systems like those in California and New York grew and multiplied, and some Catholic institutions also grew and developed at an amazing rate. Xavier, however, remained small. The civil rights movement and the Vietnam War shook the American Catholic education. At Xavier the shock was not that great. The university confronted segregation in 1962 when the football team was to go to the Sugar Bowl in New Orleans. The student government asked the university president to get the team out of its contract with the Sugar Bowl if the seating arrangements would be segregated. The university president refused, saying that while he did not approve of segregation it was the law; he thought it would be more important to go to New Orleans and to exchange ideas with the people there. Vietnam does not seem to have been one of the issues that students cared about at Xavier; it is not mentioned in the history of the university.

The 1960s and 1970s witnessed the election of John Kennedy and the Second Vatican Council, and the number of Catholics who had taken advantage of the GI Bill and were becoming economically and socially prominent moved Roman Catholics into the mainstream of American life. Those events posed the greatest challenge to Catholic higher education in the United States since the initial economic problems that faced the founders of colleges and nativism of the Know-Nothing movement of the mid–nineteenth century, for in the 1970s the reason for Catholic education seemed to have disappeared. If the Catholic Church were to open up windows to let the world into the Church, if it were to embrace the world, if it were to take non-Catholic religions and ecumenism seriously, then what was the purpose of Catholic,

Jesuit education? In addition to that, the 1960s and 1970s saw the mass exodus from the religious orders and congregations that had traditionally sponsored those institutions. The problem appeared to be increased when the religious orders gave control over the institutions to lay boards of trustees either for financial reasons or out of conviction and when universities began hiring faculty for the strength of their terminal degree and not for the strength of their religious convictions. All of these and economic difficulties affected Xavier University. To offset a drop in enrollment the university admitted women to the day colleges for the first time in 1968.

Jesuit higher education began facing these questions on a national level in 1977 in a movement called Project One, which began conversations on Jesuit campuses across the country. Xavier, like its sister Jesuit institutions, began asking questions about its Jesuit and Catholic future and providing answers to those questions. By the mid-1980s the Jesuit community at Xavier University sponsored Ignatian Programs, a set of emphases designed to introduce new faculty and staff to the history and tradition of Catholic and Jesuit higher education. These programs are now under the direction of the vice president for religious development, which was founded in 1991 as a way of ensuring the ongoing Catholic and Jesuit nature of education.

In the late 1980s the president and academic vice president of the university invited the faculty to review the general education requirements for the undergraduate degree. The review process took three years and led the faculty to look at the tradition of Jesuit Catholic education and the needs of our students as they approached a new millennium. Requiring nine hours of theology, nine hours of philosophy, and nine hours of laboratory science preserved the Jesuit tradition of higher education, and grounding the general education requirements in the liberal arts also preserved it. New areas were instituted: a cultural diversity course and nine-hour ethics, religion, and society requirements. The general education requirements are the basis for a rigorous undergraduate education that introduces students to a cultural tradition and teaches them to think critically.

In the 1990s religious development introduced service learning semesters that allow students to take courses and live in Nicaragua, Nepal, or Cincinnati's Over-the-Rhine. These semesters are an attempt to allow students to study and to experience cultures caught in the trap of poverty and to reflect on an affective and cognitive level on poverty and its results in our world. It gives students an opportunity to serve and to be served, to teach and to be taught in nontraditional ways. The emphasis on service and connectedness with the poor and marginalized comes out of a 1975 meeting of Jesuits in Rome that dedicated the Society of Jesus to the service of faith through the promotion of justice. That thrust has had a great influence on how Xavier University has and will continue to define its Jesuit and Catholic nature.

The Superior General of the Society of Jesus addressed a group of administrators, faculty, students, and staff from all twenty-eight Jesuit colleges and universities at

Santa Clara University in October 2000. In his address he outlined a vision of Jesuit higher education that places service learning at the heart of Jesuit Catholic education, because, by coming in contact with the poor and marginalized, the heart may pull the mind to form Jesuit graduates who will not only take part in service activities to alleviate their lot but who will use the academic training they have and the intellectual gifts they have to work to change the structures of society to ease the grip of poverty on so many human beings. The questions that now face Jesuit Catholic institutions are how to educate students so that they realize their decisions affect not only themselves but all of humanity.

In addition to the demanding academic program, Xavier now offers opportunities for service. The university students take part in service programs, protest at the School of the Americas that trains Central American armies, run a Habitat for Humanity chapter, tutor in the inner city, and work in soup kitchens and a variety of situations in the area. In doing that they help Xavier live out the goals of Ignatius Loyola: the improvement of the moral and cultural life of the city. Xavier is probably more self-consciously Catholic and Jesuit now than it has ever been in the past, when the religious nature of the school was seen as the preserve of the Jesuits and not the concern of the faculty. In the words of Xavier's new president, Michael Graham, S.J., "Xavier's mission is to form students educationally, morally, and spiritually with rigor and compassion to lead lives of solidarity and service."

Suggested Reading

Lee J. Bennish, *Continuity and Change: Xavier University 1831–1981* (Loyola Univ. Press, 1981); Gilbert J. Garraghan, *The Jesuits of the Middle United States,* vol.3. (American Press, 1938).

Appendix

Defunct Ohio Private Colleges and Universities

Erving E. Beauregard

Ohio can claim an enormous number of colleges and universities that are no longer in operation. The sheer number of institutions of higher education in Ohio proved an obstacle to survival. At least 136 institutions have had a claim to imparting some undergraduate nonprofessional education of the four-year type, all but thirteen being private. Of those 136 institutions, eighty succumbed. Every one of the eighty was private. In addition to the eighty that closed, thirty-five were chartered but never opened. The histories of the once-operating colleges and universities reveal notable insights into the story of the Buckeye State.

Religion played a decisive role in the founding of many colleges and universities that later succumbed. At some time in Ohio practically every denomination operated a college or university: African Methodist Episcopal, Associate Presbyterian, Associate Reformed Presbyterian, Baptist, Brethren, Christian Connexion, Churches of God in North America, Congregational, Cumberland Presbyterian, Disciples of Christ, Episcopal, Evangelical Lutheran, Free Presbyterian, Lutheran, Mennonite, Methodist Episcopal, Methodist Protestant, Nazarene, New Jerusalem, "New School" Presbyterian, "Old School" Presbyterian U.S.A., Reformed, Reformed Judaism, Reformed Presbyterian, Roman Catholic, Society of Friends, United Brethren, United Presbyterian, Universalist, and the Young Men's Christian Association. In some instances control of the institution passed from one church group to another.

Generally, the religiously oriented colleges and universities did not invoke a strictly denominational stance. They favored Christianity but not in a dogmatic way. For example, Franklin College at New Athens, founded by an Associate Presbyterian minister, specified in its charter that "no religious doctrine peculiar to any one sect of christians [*sic*] shall be inculcated by any professor."

At times religion and politics intersected to bring forth an institution, as in the cases of Providence College at New Athens and Iberia College at Iberia. In the 1830s Franklin College at New Athens had become a bastion of antislavery advocacy, with the administration, faculty, and students demanding the immediate and uncompromising abolition of slavery. As a result a number of people in that community—members of the Associate Reformed Presbyterian Church, Methodist Episcopal Church, and "Old School" Presbyterian Church U.S.A.—founded Providence College at New Athens in 1842 in order to forward the gradual abolition of slavery. A dozen years later Free Presbyterians at Iberia established Iberia College (later renamed Ohio Central College) to promote the instant end of slavery.

In two instances a single congregation founded a college. At Bloomfield in 1873 the local Associate Presbyterian ("Seceder") Church organized McCorkle College. At Hopedale in 1879 trustees of the First Congregation of Disciples of Christ (Christian Church) set up Hopedale Normal College to offer degrees in arts and sciences.

Sometimes a combination of religion and other factors led resolute individuals to found colleges. The Reverend John Walker (1784–1845), the pioneer Associate Presbyterian clergyman in eastern Ohio, founded New Athens in 1817 to establish a classical school that would "coordinate factors in civilizing, humanizing, and Christianizing the inhabitants of the land." Thus he established in 1819 Alma Mater Academy, soon renamed Alma Academy. In 1825 Walker converted that institution into Alma College, renamed Franklin College in 1826. Alfred D. Lee, an ardent Methodist, founded a degree-granting college known as Rural Seminary at Harlem Springs in 1859. He wrote, "This rural locality was selected on account of its retirement, its healthfulness and the morality of the community." In 1867 Lee relocated the institution to a more accessible area twelve miles away at New Market (soon renamed Scio) because of the railroad there. In 1868 Rural Seminary would come under the auspices of the Methodist Episcopal Church's Pittsburgh Annual Conference. Eventually it became New Market College, then "One Study" University and, finally, Scio College.

Another resolute person brought forth a nondenominational institution that would achieve eminence. Alfred Holbrook, a leading educator, became the bulwark of South Western Ohio Normal School at Lebanon in 1855, a school renamed National Normal School, then National Normal University, and, finally, Lebanon University. Although Lebanon closed its doors in 1917, its last president, Dr. Holly Estil Cunningham, sought to revive it as Alfred Holbrook College at Lebanon in 1933. The following year he moved his creation to Manchester, Ohio, but the school lasted only until 1941.

The imprint of personality surfaced elsewhere. A once-thriving teacher education institution, which also conferred degrees in arts and science, began because of a husband-wife team. McNeely Normal School of Ohio at Hopedale owed its founding to Cyrus and Jane Donaldson McNeely. Members of the Christian Church (Disciples of

Christ) and dedicated abolitionists, they contributed to the school throughout their lives. McNeely Normal School of Ohio may claim uniqueness in still another manner. Although willing to continue support, Cyrus and Jane McNeely felt unable to maintain the school. Therefore, in 1855 they offered the institution as a gift to the State of Ohio. When the latter declined, Cyrus offered the place, valued at more than $100,000, to the Ohio State Teachers' Association for normal school purposes on the condition that it raise $10,000 for support of the institution. During negotiations Cyrus liberalized his offer by giving the association five to ten years to raise the $10,000. In 1855 the Ohio State Teachers' Association accepted the McNeely offer. McNeely Normal School of Ohio became the first institution in Ohio to use the name "normal school." Moreover, it was the first institution of higher education in eastern Ohio to admit female students.

When Rural Seminary departed from Harlem Springs in 1867, a new institution was founded in that Carroll County village. President Alfred D. Lee sold the seminary's property to Professor Robert H. Howey, a member of Rural Seminary's faculty. Howey opened and operated Harlem Springs College until it closed in 1889. Twenty years later the Reverend C. W. Milan, a Methodist Episcopal minister, reopened the college. In 1909 Milan sold the college to William Dunlap of Harlem Springs, who placed it under Professor and Mrs. A. C. Ackerman until Harlem Springs College closed permanently in 1914.

Another college displayed change. In 1854 the sole synod of the Free Presbyterian Church U.S.A. opened Iberia College at Iberia to all without distinction of sex, race, or color. In 1868 the institution passed to the care of the Presbytery of Mansfield, United Presbyterian Church. The name changed to Ohio Central College. In 1875 the Presbytery of Mansfield transferred the college to a joint stock company. This company provided "that the college be positively christian [sic] in its management, but not sectarian. Nine trustees, belonging to three different dominations, were chosen." Ohio Central College closed in 1894.

Alteration also occurred at McCorkle College. Opened in 1873 at Bloomfield by the local Associate Presbyterian congregation under the leadership of its pastor, the Reverend William Ballantine, its lack of resources forced closure in 1880. The same body brought back the college in 1882 but shut it down in 1885. Then in 1889 the same congregation reopened McCorkle as a normal school, but it could only continue into 1890.

Another intriguing episode of operation involved Hopedale Normal College. During 1879–81 it was owned by the First Congregation of Disciples of Christ in Hopedale. In 1891 that body leased to the college's president, Elmer E. Henderson, the buildings and grounds for two years with an option for ten years in all. In 1893, however, Henderson returned the college to the First Congregation of Disciples, which closed the institution in 1895. In 1899 trustees acting for the same First Congregation of Disciples reopened Hopedale Normal College but ceased its operation in the spring of 1901.

The prize for change of college operation apparently belongs to Richmond College at Richmond in Jefferson County. Owned by a private company from 1843 to 1850, it was taken over in 1850–51 by the Steubenville Presbytery of the Presbyterian Church U.S.A., controlled by its original corporation 1851–54, run by the Pittsburgh Conference of the Methodist Episcopal Church 1854–72, and operated by a private group of trustees 1872–78. In 1878 another private corporation assumed power but closed the college in 1880. In 1886 Richmond College reopened under a different private corporation of sixteen trustees but closed, finally, in 1913.

The precarious existence of institutions founded by religious bodies often involved denominational divisions. Invariably a national headquarters would not support a college or university. In the Protestant realm the backer might be a regional body such as a Lutheran synod, a Methodist conference, or a Presbyterian presbytery. In the Roman Catholic world the sponsor would be the local archdiocese, diocese, or religious order. Thus finances were greatly limited among denominational institutions. Furthermore, there were overwhelming burdens where single congregations tried to operate colleges like Hopedale and McCorkle.

The State of Ohio itself presented formidable problems for private colleges and universities. In the charters of Mühlenberg and Judson Colleges at Jefferson (later Germano), the state required that each raise $10,000 before the conferring of degrees, a considerable sum for the day. Financial restraints increased in 1876 when the Ohio legislature taxed "all institutions with leaseholds and those operated on a tuition basis." At the same time, moreover, the state established normal schools and universities that provided stiff competition to private institutions. Additionally, municipalities founded universities that drew students away from the private sector, and eventually the municipal universities joined the state system of higher education.

The demise of colleges and universities resulted from a wide variety of causes, including a lack of zeal after the founder's departure (Harlem Springs), cholera (Ripley), nepotism in the founder's family (National Normal University), a financial agent's confidence operation (Alliance), a president's financial misdeeds (Franklin at New Athens), departure of distinguished faculty members (Scio), competition within a village (Providence versus Franklin at New Athens), remoteness (Beverly and Judson), fire (Lebanon and Willoughby), and the oil boom that occupied the village with oil derricks and resulted in the influx of undesirables (Scio). Rapid turnover in an institution's presidency definitely threatened survival, an example being Scio College, which had fourteen presidents, some for just a few months during 1877–1911. At Scio and other schools the president could not devote his full time to the job because he served also as pastor of a church, to say nothing of the classes he often taught.

The inadequate finances that contributed immeasurably to the extinction of colleges and universities were largely a result of the difficulties found in securing endowment. The financial panics of 1837, 1857, 1873, and 1893 severely harmed fund-raising. Boards of trustees often were local citizens and clergymen who lacked financial sophistication. Many college presidents had little time for or expertise in fund-raising; they were also teaching and oftentimes serving a congregation. As a result the financial management of a number of institutions often passed to incompetent or self-seeking financial agents and business managers. Also, tuitions deliberately kept low to aid poor students were inadequate to maintain institutional upkeep.

The history of defunct colleges and universities also demands discussion of the thorny subject of mergers. Indeed, there are universities that trace their founding back to a predecessor absorbed by the present institution, but true mergers were quite rare. One occurred in 1914 when Baldwin University and German Wallace College united as Baldwin-Wallace College. Another happened in 1967 when Case School of Applied Science joined Western Reserve University as Case Western Reserve University. An intriguing episode occurred when Scio College merged with Mount Union College in 1911. Mount Union-Scio College became the official name of the institution; however, that title "provoked an outburst of complaint and dissatisfaction" on the part of the Mount Union alumni. After a vigorous alumni campaign of petitions and open letters, the trustees restored the name Mount Union in 1914 as the official designation for the college, "with understanding that on the catalogs and diplomas issued to the alumni the phrase 'Uniting Mount Union and Scio Colleges' should be used to perpetuate the fact of the merger." Overwhelmingly, mergers simply were pseudorelationships. One category involved an institution that would buy the property of another whose alumni/alumnae it would adopt. Such included the University of Akron's takeover of Buchtel College, Miami University's absorption of Oxford College for Women and also Western College, and Xavier University's acquisition of Edgecliff College. In response to the desire of Fenn College graduates, Cleveland State University, which had absorbed Fenn, retroactively granted and issued new Cleveland State University diplomas to all Fenn graduates from the first class of 1927 through the last class of 1965. Another class of merger merely meant an institution's willingness to accept the alumni/alumnae of another college. This happened in both Franklin College and Ohio Central College, which were adopted by Muskingum College, and Lebanon University, which was adopted by Wilmington College.

Peculiar situations at three of Ohio's defunct private colleges relate to other states. In 1861 the Reverend President Randall Ross closed Sharon College at Sharon and entered the Union army as a regular soldier. In 1866 he returned to Ohio, but a year later he moved to Missouri, where he resurrected Sharon College as Lincoln College. In 1880 Geneva Hall's authorities moved the college from Northwood to Beaver Falls, Pennsylvania, where it continues as Geneva College. In 1916 the student body of West Lafayette College was transferred to Adrian College, Adrian, Michigan.

The historian should exercise care in using the term "failed" for extinct Ohio private colleges and universities. To show the worth of eighty defunct colleges and universities would be a daunting task. To depict the impact of their thousands of graduates and attendees would require infinite hours of research and writing. Nevertheless, ample evidence does surface that several institutions exerted profound influence on humanity.

A phenomenal number of students attended defunct campuses. The variously named Scio College admitted more than 20,000 students. In less than half a century McNeely Normal School of Ohio and its successor Hopedale Normal College educated about 18,000 students. Countless students paid homage to the care, guidance, and learning they had received at McNeely or Hopedale. That variously named institution known as South Western Ohio Normal School, National Normal School, National Normal University, and Lebanon University admitted more than 2,000 students between 1885 and 1893, while full-time students ranged between 800 and 1,000. Between 1853 and 1953 Western College, originally Western College for Women, counted 10,768 students.

Franklin College at New Athens produced a significant impact on society. It figured prominently in the movement for immediate and uncompromising abolition of slavery. (This is commemorated in the Franklin Museum at New Athens, site of the last college building.) It became the first institution of higher education in Ohio to graduate an African American. Known affectionately as "Old Franklin," the college also proved a significant player in the anti-Masonic movement. In addition, records show that the proportion of Franklin's graduates going into the ministry was larger than any other Presbyterian college. At one time 55 percent of the nation's ministers in the United Presbyterian Church were graduates of this Franklin College. Furthermore, its graduates became leaders in denominations. Graduates of "little" Franklin College became important in national politics. One cast a decisive vote in the Senate in saving President Andrew Johnson from conviction of high crimes. Franklin-educated John A. Bingham was the author of the crucial Fourteenth Amendment, adviser to President Abraham Lincoln, prosecutor of Lincoln's assassins, prosecutor of President Andrew Johnson, and the longest-serving United States diplomat to Japan.

The oft-renamed Scio College served admirably in its brief half-century. Scio's graduates entered the ranks of the ministry, medicine, dentistry, pharmacy, chemistry, engineering, education, law, business, and the U.S. Navy. An alumnus rightly noted, "Scio College was always poor in purse but rich in achievement. It did a great work on a small capital." Additionally, Scio College pioneered in the "one study plan" of instruction. Operating during 1867–77, the curriculum provided "that in each term each student will have but one class, to which he will devote his whole time." The system's proponents claimed it accomplished "more thorough scholarship, more rapid advancement, study made a greater delight, a fuller mental development, and the proportion of graduates to those entering college increased five fold." The essence of Scio's one study plan was used at Hiram College between 1934 and 1958. In referring to Scio's experiment, President Kenneth I. Brown of Hiram College trenchantly remarked, "The operation was successful but the patient died." President Lee of Scio also instituted the "one study plan" at four other colleges he founded: Barnesville, Coshocton, Leesville, and Steubenville.

Graduates of many deceased colleges and universities worked ably in many fields. They hailed from institutions such as Alfred Holbrook, Buchtel, Edgecliff (originally Our Lady of Cincinnati), Fenn, Mary Manse, Oxford College for Women, St. John of Cleveland (originally Sisters' College), and Western.

In the final analysis, the demise of the eighty private colleges and universities in Ohio raises speculation about private institutions of higher education in the twenty-first century. Will every nonpublic college and university continue? Can the living learn from the dead?

Suggested Reading

An overall view is Charles Dominic, *Ohio's Antebellum Colleges* (UMI, 1987), but he omits many institutions. Steven Richard Mark, "Ohio Colleges and Universities during the Gilded Age: Institutional Evolution, Elective Curriculum, Graduate Education and Commercial Programs, 1865–1901" (Ph.D. diss., Bowling Green State University, 1991), should be used with caution, because several institutions that he states never opened actually did. Helpful are William L. McClelland, "Ohio Presbyterians and Their Schools, 1804–1966," in E. B. Welsh, ed., *Buckeye Presbyterians* (1968); Edward A. Miller, "The History of the Educational Legislation in Ohio from 1803 to 1850," *Ohio State Archaeological and Historical Publications* 27 (1919); Nelson L. Bossing, "The History of the Educational Legislation in Ohio from 1851 to 1925," *Ohio State Archaeological and Historical Publications* 39 (1930); Donald G. Tewksbury, *The Founding of American Colleges and Universities* (Archon Books, 1965); William Oxley Thompson, "Universities of Ohio," in E. O. Randall, ed., *Ohio Centennial Anniversary Celebration* (Fred J. Heer Press, 1903); and John M. Versteeg, *Methodism: Ohio Area (1812, 1862)* (Ohio Area Sesquicentennial Committee, 1962). Interesting accounts of individual institutions are Chester A. Roush, *The History of Alfred Holbrook College* (1980); George W. Knepper, *New Lights for Old: One Hundred Years of Urban Higher Education at the University of Akron* (University of Akron, 1970), which treats Buchtel College; G. Brooks Earnest, *A History of Fenn College* (Fenn Educational Fund, 1974); Karl J. Kay, *History of the National Normal University of Lebanon, Ohio* (Wilmington College, 1929); Mary S. Steele, "McCorkle—The College Which Fell by the Wayside" (1958), typescript, Muskingum College Library; R. H. Eckelberry, "The McNeely Normal School and Hopedale Normal College," *Ohio Archaeological and Historical Quarterly* 40 (Jan. 1931); Olive Flower, *The History of Oxford College for Women* (Miami University Alumni Association, 1949); Joseph B. Doyle, *20th Century History of Steubenville and Jefferson County, Ohio* (Richmond-Arnold, 1910) for Richmond College; Newell Yost Osborne, *A Select School: The History of Mount Union College and an Account of a Unique Educational Experiment, Scio College* (Mount Union College, 1967); Narka Nelson, *The Western College for- Women 1853–1953* (Western College, 1954); and Alvin W. Skardon, *Steel Valley University: The Origin of Youngstown State* (Youngstown State University, 1983). Erving E. Beauregard has written *Old Franklin: The Eternal Turch* (University Press of America, 1983); *Bingham of the Hills* (Peter Lang, 1989); *Reverend John Walker: Renaissance Man* (Peter Lang, 1990); *Notables of Harrison County, Ohio* (Mellen, 2000); "The Other Mühlenberg College," *Lutheran Quarterly* 13 (1999); and "A Collegiate Outpost of Gradual Abolition [Providence College]," *Upper Ohio Valley Historical Review* 14 (Spring/Summer 1985).

DEFUNCT PRIVATE COLLEGES AND UNIVERSITIES IN OHIO

INSTITUTIONAL NAME (FINAL)	LOCATION (FINAL)	LIFETIME
Albany Manual Labor University	Albany	1853–62
Alfred Holbrook College	Manchester	1933–41
Alliance College	Alliance	1866–71
American Female College	Glendale	1854–57
Baldwin University	Berea	1846–1914
Baptist Literary and Collegiate Institute	Huron County	1837
Barnesville College	Barnesville	1871–72
Belmont College	College Hill	1884–90
Beverly College	Beverly	1842–43
Buchtel College	Akron	1872–1913
Case School of Applied Sciences	Cleveland	1871–1967
Central College of Ohio	Blendon	1842–92
Central Ohio College	East Liberty	1883–93
Cincinnati College	Cincinnati	1819–25, 1836–46
Cincinnati Wesleyan College	Cincinnati	1842–94
Cleveland University	Cleveland	1851–53
Clifton College of the Sacred Heart	Clifton	1916–35
College of Ripley	Ripley	1830–32, 1840–49

INSTITUTIONAL NAME (FINAL)	LOCATION (FINAL)	LIFETIME
Coshocton College	Coshocton	1871–73
Crawfis College	Ottawa	1888–89
De Sales College	Toledo	1936–42
Edgecliff College	Cincinnati	1935–80
Farmers' College	College Hill	1846–70, 1873–84
Fayette Normal University	Fayette	1881–1905
Fenn College	Cleveland	1923–65
Franklin College	New Athens	1825–1921
Franklin College	Wilmington	1863–70
Geneva Hall	Northwood	1848–79
German Wallace College	Berea	1863–1914
Glendale Female College	Glendale	1854–57
Granville Female College	Granville	1867–98
Harlem Springs College	Harlem Springs	1867–89, 1909–14
Hillsboro College	Hillsboro	1857–1919
Hopedale Normal College	Hopedale	1879–95, 1899–1901
Judson College	Germano	1849–54
Lebanon University	Lebanon	1855–1917
Leesville College	Leesville	1871–75
Lima Lutheran College	Lima	1893–1908
McCorkle College	Bloomfield	1873–80, 1882–85, 1889–90
McNeely Normal School of Ohio	Hopedale	1854–78
Madison College	Antrim	1837–59
Mansfield Female College	Mansfield	1858
Mary Manse College	Toledo	1924–76
Miami Valley College	Foster's Crossing	1869–84
Mühlenberg College	Germano	1847–48
Oakland Female College	Hillsboro	1839–57
Ohio Central College	Iberia	1854–94
Ohio Female College	College Hill	1848–74
Ohio Wesleyan Female College	Delaware	1853–77
Oxford College for Women	Oxford	1867–1929
Oxford Female College	Oxford	1854–67
Oxford Female Institute	Oxford	1849–67
Poland Female College	Poland	1858–60
Providence College	New Athens	1842–43
Providence University	Oak Hill	1901–11
Richmond College	Richmond	1843–80, 1886–1913
St. Clairsville Collegiate Seminary	St. Clairsville	1837
St. John College	Cleveland	1931–75
St. John College	Toledo	1898–1936
St. John's College	Cincinnati	1845–52

INSTITUTIONAL NAME (FINAL)	LOCATION (FINAL)	LIFETIME
St. John's College	Cleveland	1854–56
St. Joseph College	Somerset	1850–61
St. Joseph's College	Cincinnati	1873–87
St. Joseph's College	Cleveland	1875–79
St. Louis College	Louisville	1866–73
St. Peter's College	Chillicothe	1855–56
Scio College	Scio	1859–1911
Sharon College	Sharon	1852–61
Shepardson College for Women	Granville	1859–1927
Springfield Female College	Springfield	1841–66
Steubenville College	Steubenville	1871–72
Twin Valley College	Germantown	1886–94
West Lafayette College	West Lafayette	1900–1916
Western College	Oxford	1853–1974
Western Reserve University	Cleveland	1826–1967
Willoughby University of Lake Erie	Willoughby	1834–59
Woodward College	Cincinnati	1836–51
Worthington Female College	Worthington	1839–74
Xenia College	Xenia	1854–88
Youngstown University	Youngstown	1888–1967

OHIO PRIVATE COLLEGES AND UNIVERSITIES CHARTERED
BUT UNOPENED

INSTITUTION	LOCATION	CHARTER
Bellefontaine, Ohio, College	Bellefontaine	1843
Calvin College	Cleveland	1883
Cambridge College	Cambridge	1850
Carnegie College	Rogers	1900
Chillicothe Female Seminary	Chillicothe	1833
Cincinnati Metaphysical University	Cincinnati	1888
Cincinnati University	Cincinnati	1807
College of Southern Ohio	Georgetown	1881
Columbus Academical and Collegiate Institute	Columbus	1845
Delaware Female College	Delaware	1843
Edinburgh College	Portage County	1848
Elizabeth College	Marietta	1889
English Lutheran Theological and Collegiate Institute	Wooster	1844
Fort Meigs University	Perrysburg	1845

Germania College	Columbus	1843
Glover Collegiate Institute	West Liberty	1894
Jackson Center College	Jackson	1889
Lafayette University	New Carlisle	1842
Lincoln College	Rogers	1901
Logan College	Bellefontaine	1838
Marietta Female College	Marietta	1847
Medina College	Medina	1848
Mount Hope College	Rogers	1893
Mount Washington College	Mount Washington	1849
Newcomerstown College	Newcomerstown	1871
Newton College	Hamilton County	1848
Northwood College	Logan County	1830
Protestant University of the United States	Cincinnati	1845
Union College	Jackson Township	1851
University of Southern Ohio	Cincinnati	1884
Weethee College	Mount Auburn	1861
Wesleyan Collegiate Institute	Olmstead	1837
Western Female College	Cincinnati	1846
Western Normal University	Tremont	1881
Worthington College	Worthington	1819

Contributors

DAVID R. ANDERSON is John S. Kenyon Professor of English at Hiram College. A 1964 graduate of Hiram, he received his M.A. from the University of California-Berkeley and Ph.D. from Case Western Reserve University. He has published on Washington Irving, nineteenth-century American architecture, the pedagogy of interdisciplinary teaching, and coedited *Anthology of Western Reserve Literature* and authored "Classic Hill: The Sesquicentennial History of Hiram."

ERVING E. BEAUREGARD, Professor Emeritus of History at the University of Dayton, is the author of seven books and 150 articles. He received the Distinguished Service Award from the Ohio Academy of History and the Robert Kennedy Award for outstanding contributions to academic freedom from the Ohio Conference of the American Association of University Professors.

GEOFFREY BLODGETT, a political and architectural historian, was Robert S. Danforth Professor of History at Oberlin College. His books are *The Gentle Reformers: Massachusetts Democrats in the Cleveland Era, Oberlin Architecture, College and Town: A Guide to Its Social History*, and *Cass Gilbert: The Early Years*.

NANCY J. BROWN is associate professor of English and chair of the Department of Language and Literature at Lourdes College. She wishes to acknowledge the contribution of Sister Cabrini Warpeha, retired vice president for Academic Affairs, to the development of her chapter.

RANDALL BUCHMAN is Professor Emeritus of History at Defiance College. His articles have appeared in journals such as *Ohio Archaeologist, American Antiquity*, and *Ohio History*. He is the author of *Historic Indians, Woods Journal*, and *The Confluence: The Story of Fort Defiance*.

JAMES L. BURKE, Professor Emeritus of History at Capital University, taught for forty-two years, the last thirty-four at Capital. He has written many articles on Ohio history, coauthored the textbook *Ohio's Heritage*, and written the history of Capital University, *Chronicles of Change: Capital University, 1950–2000*.

PERRY BUSH, professor of history at Bluffton College, received his A.B. from the University of California-Berkeley and Ph.D. from Carnegie Mellon University. A specialist in the history of American evangelicalism, he is the author of *Dancing with the Kobzar: Bluffton College and Mennonite Higher Education, 1899–1999* and *Two Kingdoms, Two Loyalties: Mennonite Pacifism in Modern America 1935–1977.*

JOHN CARRIGG, a native of Buffalo, New York, graduated from Canisius College in 1943. A veteran of World War II, he received an M.A. and a Ph.D. from Georgetown University and taught in the history department at Franciscan University of Steubenville for fifty-one years.

G. WALLACE CHESSMAN taught history at Denison University for thirty-one years, to 1983. He received his B.A. and Ph.D. from Harvard University. He published histories of Denison in 1957 and 1981, biographies of Theodore Roosevelt in 1965 (New York governorship) and 1969, and is the author of books and articles on leaders and institutions in the Granville/Newark, Ohio, area.

NORMAN J. CLARY, Professor Emeritus, headed the Humanities Division and the Marting Humanities Lecture Series at Baldwin-Wallace College. He holds a Ph.D. from Ohio State University. His research areas include democratic liberalism, French anti-Semitism, and National Socialism.

LISA ODA FEDE served as director of University Relations for Urbana University. She currently works in communications for Madison County Hospital in London, Ohio.

WILLIAM FISK graduated from Muskingum College in 1941 and received a Ph.D. in British history from Ohio State University in 1946. He served as professor of history and vice president for Academic Affairs at Muskingum and is now Professor Emeritus of History. He is the author of *A History of Muskingum College.*

LARRY GARA, historian, teacher, and part-time peace activist, lives in Wilmington, Ohio, where he is Emeritus Professor of History and Peace Studies at Wilmington College. A member of Campus Friends Meeting in Wilmington, he is the author or editor of six books.

ANNA MARGARET GILBRIDE, O.S.U. (Order of St. Ursula), is assistant to the president at Ursuline College. She received her Ph.D. in higher educational administration from Kent State University in 1979. Her dissertation traced the origins of the community college movement in Ohio. She is currently writing a book on the history of Ursuline College.

MICHAEL A. GRANDILLO is vice president of Development and Public Affairs and adjunct professor of political science at Tiffin University. A Ph.D. candidate at the University of Toledo, he holds an M.S. degree from the University of Dayton and a B.A. in political science from Ohio Northern University. He held administration positions at Heidelberg College and Ohio Northern and has written articles on the history of Ohio's independent colleges, with special attention to the impact of local boosterism on their founding and development in the nineteenth century.

MARGARET GROSS, a graduate of Lake Erie College, is the author of *Dancing on the Table: A History of Lake Erie College.*

PATRICIA E. HARDING is archivist and records manager at Notre Dame College. She received her B.A. and B.F.A. degrees from Lake Erie College and pursued graduate work in advertising, marketing for nonprofits, and communication at Cleveland State University. She has written for campus publications at Lake Erie College and Notre Dame College.

DENNIS HARRISON has been the archivist of Case Western Reserve University since 1985.

He is a former president of the Society of Ohio Archivists and currently serves on the Council of the Society of American Archivists. His published work is in the field of labor history.

JAMES A. HODGES is the Michael O. Fisher Professor of History (Emeritus) at the College of Wooster and past president of the Ohio Academy of History. He is the author of *New Deal Labor Policy and the Southern Cotton Textile Industry, 1933–1941*, two chapters in two separate books about southern labor history, and numerous articles and book reviews. He taught courses in recent American history, the American South, and labor history.

DAVID GERARD HOGAN is associate professor of history at Heidelberg College. He is the author of *Selling 'em by the Sack: White Castle and the Creation of American Food* and is currently writing about the history of higher education.

MARYANN JANOSIK is dean of the Social Science and Business Division at Oakton Community College in Des Plaines, Illinois. She was associate professor of history at Lake Erie College, adjunct lecturer in education at John Carroll University, and director of education at the Rock and Roll Hall of Fame and Museum in Cleveland. Her area of research focuses on the Catholic imagination in American popular culture.

RICHARD KERN is Emeritus Professor of History at the University of Findlay. He is the author of *John Winebrenner: Nineteenth-Century Reformer* and *Findlay College: The First Hundred Years* and coauthor of *A Pictorial History of Findlay/Hancock County*.

HELGA KITTRELL, former vice president for Development at Franklin University, currently serves as director of the university's centennial celebration.

GEORGE W. KNEPPER is Distinguished Professor of History (Emeritus), former university historian at the University of Akron, and former president of the Ohio Historical Society. He is the author of *Ohio and Its People* and six other books dealing with Ohio topics.

JOHN LAROCCA, professor of history with a Ph.D. from Rutgers University, specializes in English history and in the history of the Society of Jesus (Jesuits). He serves as director of the Honors B.A. Program at Xavier University.

PERRY LENTZ, a 1964 graduate of Kenyon College, completed his graduate work at Vanderbilt University. In 1969 he joined the Department of English at Kenyon and is now the Charles McIlvaine Professor of English.

PAUL M. LOGSDON is the director at Ohio Northern University's Heterick Memorial Library, where he has served in various capacities since 1978.

ELIZABETH MACLEAN is professor of twentieth-century American history at Otterbein College, where she served as department chair from 1991 to 1997. She is the author of *Joseph E. Davies, Envoy to the Soviets*. MacLean served as president of the Ohio Academy of History from 2001 to 2002.

PAUL D. MAYLE, professor of history and chair of the Department of History and Division of Social Sciences at Mount Vernon Nazarene University, received his Ph.D. in American diplomatic history from West Virginia University in 1982. He is the author of *Eureka Summit: Agreement in Principle and the Big Three at Tehran, 1943*. In 1988 he was a Fulbright-Hays scholar in India. He is director of MVNU's Semester in Hungary program.

CAMILLA MULLAY, O.P., was professor of history at Ohio Dominican University and historian for the Dominican Congregation of Saint Mary of the Springs, founder and sponsor of Ohio Dominican University. Her Ph.D. is from the Catholic University of America. Her publications include *The Barren Fig Tree: A Reappraisal of the Sandinista Revolution*.

MURRAY MURDOCH, is professor of history and chair of the Department of Social Sciences and History at Cedarville University, where he has been since 1965. He is author of the *Biography of Robert T. Ketchum: Portrait of Obedience* and *The Centennial History of Cedarville: A Century of Commitment*.

JOHN L. NETHERS, Professor Emeritus of History, taught for thirty years at Ashland University and served as chair of the Department of Social Science. He holds a Ph.D from the Ohio State University. He has written many articles on Ohio history, with special attention to the Amish, and is the author of *Simeon D. Fess: Educator and Politician*.

KELLI NOWLIN is director of communications at Franklin University.

JAMES H. O'DONNELL III is Andrew U. Thomas Professor of History at Marietta College, where he has taught since 1969, and past president of the Ohio Academy of History. A graduate of Duke University, his research specialty, Native American history, is reflected in his *Ohio's First Peoples: Native Americans in Ohio, 1450–1843*.

JOHN WILLIAM OLIVER JR. taught history at Malone College for thirty-two years and was adjunct professor of history at Walsh University and the College of Wooster. He is the author of many articles on Quaker history, editor of *J. Walter Malone: The Autobiography of an Evangelical Quaker* and coeditor of *Historical Dictionary of the Friends (Quakers)* and of a forthcoming history of America's Quaker colleges. A former member of the executive board of the Ohio Academy of History and clerk/convener of the biennial Conference of Quaker Historians and Archivists, he serves as coordinator of the North American chapter of the Orthodox Peace Fellowship.

RICHARD T. ORTQUIST, Professor Emeritus of History at Wittenberg University, received his B.A. degree from Hope College and his M.A. and Ph.D. from the University of Michigan. He taught for thirty-five years at Wittenberg and retired in 1999. His publications, including *Depression Politics in Michigan, 1929–1933*, center on the era of the Great Depression and the New Deal.

KIMBERLY ROUSH graduated from Heidelberg College with a history degree in 2002. She is currently a graduate student in history at Bowling Green State University.

JOHN SAFFELL is Professor Emeritus of History at Mount Union College, where he taught for thirty-four years. He received his Ph.D. from Western Reserve University. He is the author of *Wake the Echoes: An Updated Hitory of Mount Union College*.

SCOTT SANDERS has been the Antioch University archivist since 1997. He earned his M.A. in archival and historical administration at Wright State University. He has written articles about Antioch's history for the Ohio Historical Society publication *Timeline*, assisted Irwin Abrams's centennial edition of *The Nobel Peace Prize and the Laureates: An Illustrated Biographical History 1901–2001*, and written on Nobel Peace Prize research in the journal *Peace and Change*. He is a member of the Society for American Baseball Research.

RICHARD W. SMITH, Professor of History (Emeritus) at Ohio Wesleyan University and former president of the Ohio Academy of History, centered his teaching and scholarly reviewing on the slavery controversy and the Civil War era.

JOSEPH TORMA, professor of theology at Walsh University, has a Ph.D. from the University of Ottawa. He chaired the pastoral studies department at Saint Bernard's Seminary, Rochester, New York, and directs the pastoral ministry program at Walsh. He has been a consultant to dioceses and parishes in most areas of ministry and has a special interest in the social responsibility of the church in the modern world.

Ivan M. Tribe holds a Ph.D. in American history from the University of Toledo and has taught history at the University of Rio Grande since 1976. He has written extensively on Appalachian cultural history and industrial communities in southeastern Ohio. His latest book, in collaboration with Abby Gail Goodnite, is *Rio Grande: From Baptists and Bevo to the Bell Tower, 1876–2001.*

Kimberly J. M. Wilson earned a B.A. in history and communication arts from the College of Mount St. Joseph in 2002 and is pursuing an M.A. in history from Miami University. She serves as an assistant archivist for the Sisters of Charity in Cincinnati.

Index

Abbey, Henry, 97

Ackerman, Professor and Mrs. A. C., 560

Ada, and Ohio Northern University, 380, 383, 385

Adams, Alice M., 492–93

Adams, W. B., 492

Adelbert College, 97, 100, 101, 104. *See also* Case Western Reserve University

African Methodist Episcopal Church, 495; and Wilberforce University, 489–94, 496, 499, 505–507

Agnes, M., 259

Akron. *See also* University of Akron: Buchtel College in, 65–67, 76, 96

Alfred Holbrook College, 559

Allen, Clarence, 541

Allen, Don, 431–32, 434

Allen, Harvey L., 165–66

Allen, Horace, 396

Allen, Ira, 16–17

Allen, Mary J., 490

Alliance, Ohio, 299, 301, 304. *See also* Mount Union

Alliance College, 561

Alter, Karl J., 126–28

American Lutheran Church. *See also* Lutheran Church: and Capital University, 85, 87

American Unitarians, and Antioch, 18–19

Anabaptism, and Bluffton College, 52–53, 56, 58–61

Andahazy, Laddie, 251

Andeen, G. Kenneth, 532–33

Anderson, Alfred, 489

Andree, Marie, 260

Andrews, Ebenezer Baldwin, 278, 281

Andrews, Israel Ward, 3, 278–80, 282–83

Andrews, Lorin, 228–29

Anspach, C. L., 28

Antioch College, 3–5, 8–22, 9, 135

Arinze, Francis Cardinal, 184

Armstrong, Mary Bertha, 291

Arnett, Benjamin M., 496

Arnold, Randal, 406

Aronson, Joe and Penny, 514

Asbury, Francis, 394

Ashland Theological Seminary, 33, 36

Ashland University, 3, 23–38, 24

Atlee, Clement, 513

Atwood, Nehemiah and Permelia Ridgway, 422–23, 425

Auburn, Norman P., 76

Austria, Franciscan University branch in, 184

Avery, Charles Austin, 244

Avondale, Xavier University in, 554–55

Badger, Joseph, 10

Bailey, Silas, 146

Bailey, Steven Kemp, 211

Baker, Kendall L. and Toby, 390–91

Baker, Newton D., 102–103

Baldwin, John, 39, 41–42

Baldwin, Theron, 279

Baldwin University, 562

Baldwin-Wallace College, 3, 39–51, 414, 523, 534, 562

Ballantine, William, 560

Baltazar, Eulalio R., 126–27

Banda, H. Kamuzu, 504

Baptist Bible Institute of Cleveland, 112–13

Baptists, 418, 490; and Cedarville College, 112–16; and Denison University, 144–48, 152–55; denominations of, 112, 426; and the University of Rio Grande, 421–22, 424–25, 431–32

Barbic, Hugo A., 127

Bareis, George, 199

Barney, Eliam, 148

Barone, A. G., 444–45

Bartlett, Willard W., 429

Bashford, James, 396–97

Batchelder, Alice, 402

Bates, Miner Searle, 211

Bauer, Joachim M., 367

Bauman, Robert, 402

Bean, Richard B., 367

Beaumont, Mary of the Annunciation, 462–64, 469, 474

Bedell, Gregory Thurston, 229

Beecher, Lyman, 279

Bellamy, George, 212

Bellefontaine, Urbana University program in, 459

Bellows, Anne Foster, 18

Bellows, Henry W., 8, 15, 18

Belt, Leroy, 384–85

Bennett, William Zebina, 541

Bentley, Luette, 246

Benz, G. William, 32

Berea, 43, 49; and Baldwin-Wallace College, 39–41, 45

Berea Seminary, 39–41

Bernardin, Joseph L., 128

Bernlohr, Fred and Bill, 83

Beverly College, 561

Bexley Hall Seminary, 229–30, 237

Bierce, Lucius V., 71

Billiart, Saint Julie, 338–39

Bing, Simeon H., 426–27

Bingham, John A., 564

Bingham, Luther, 276

Birch, Hugh Taylor, 20

Bixler, Raymond W., 28

Black, Andrew, 325

Blackham, Ann DeCain, 368–69

Blackmore, Josiah, 88–89

Blair, Kate, 396

Blandy, Henry, 68

Bloomfield, McCorkle College in, 559–60

Blouin, Francis, 478, 481

Bluffton College, 52–63

Bodine, William, 230

Boehm, Martin, 404–5

Bohannon, George, 426

Bolton, Frances Payne, 103

Bonaventure, Sister, 178

Bond, Julian, 518

Bonds, Alfred B., Jr., 3, 48–50

Bonnette, Dennis, 127–28

Booth, Almeda, 210

Booth, Lucy, 397

Borgman, Jim, 240

Bosch, Al, 286

Bosche, Mary Agnes, 341–42, 344

Boudalier, Victoire, 463

Boulger, James I., 366

Bowman, John Brady, 304, 305

Boyer, S. L., 383

Bracy, Carl C., 307

Bragdon, Helen, 247

Brandt, Willy, 480

Breslich, Arthur L., 45, 47

Brethren Church: and Ashland University, 23–25, 27–29, 36; Church of United Brethren in Christ, 404–408; Evangelical United Brethren Church, 411, 413

Bricker, John W., 499

Brockett, Ruth, 426

Brothers of Christian Instruction, and Walsh University, 476–79, 481, 484, 488

Brown, Betty, 346

Brown, Charles Ira, 164–65

Brown, Kenneth I., 153–54, 212–13, 216, 564

Brownlee, Paul, 178

Brush, James A. and Amelia, 304

Bryan, Elmer B., 429

Bryan, Ohio, 526

Bryan, William Jennings, 541

Buchtel, John R., 66–70, 72–73, 77

Buchtel College, 64–77, 65, 96, 562. See also University of Akron

Buck, Pearl, 513

Bunche, Ralph, 367

Bunnell, Paul, 459

Bunte, Frederick J., 188–89

Burdell, Francis, 431, 434
Burgstahler, Herbert, 399
Burrows, Joanne M., 376–77
Burton, Nathan and Sarah, 149
Byers, Noah, 55–57

Cady, Edwin, 402
Caillet, George J., 121
Calareso, Jack P., 377
Caldicott, Helen, 518
Calvinism, 279, 283, 324
Campbellites, 208–10. *See also* Disciples of Christ
Canfield, H. L., 73
Canfield, Henry, 66
Canton, 78, 150; colleges in, 194, 263, 268; Walsh
    University in, 476
Canton College, 476
Capital University, 3, 78–90, 79, 523, 525, 534, 536
Caples, William, 238
Caris, Albert C., 136
Carr, Chestora McDonald, 426, 428
Carter, Pashal, 146
Casaletto, Thomas J., 127, 129
Case, Eckstein, 105
Case, Leonard, Jr., 91–92, 92, 97, 104
Case School of Applied Science, 92–93, 96–100, 103–
    105. *See also* Case Western Reserve University;
    collaborations by, 102, 250, 465; merger of, 562
Case Western Reserve University, 4, 91–107, 562
Casey, Robert, 182
Cassell, William, 206–7
Cathedral Normal School, 345
Catholic Church, 219, 418, 463; changes in educa-
    tion, 374, 377; and coeducation, 221–22; and
    College of Mount St. Joseph, 288–89, 291; col-
    leges and universities of, 5, 126–28, 219–22, 345,
    481–87, 555–57; discrimination against, 124,
    278, 280, 552, 555; education by/for, 254, 340–
    42, 344, 371, 378, 476–78, 551–54; education in
    Cleveland, 464, 465–66; education in Toledo,
    254, 256–57; and Franciscan University, 172–76,
    179–81, 183–85; and John Carroll University,
    217, 219, 222–25; and Lourdes College, 256, 262;
    and Notre Dame College, 338, 341, 350–51; and
    Ohio Dominican University, 364, 368–70, 372–
    77; reform of doctrines of, 125-29, 481–87, 555–
    57; and University of Dayton, 120-23; and
    Ursuline College, 463, 472–73; and Walsh Uni-
    versity, 476–88; and Xavier University, 551–57

Cattell, Everett, 269–71, 274
Caulker, Hannibal, 408
Cedarville University, 109–19, 110
Celebreeze, Anthony, 388
Central Mennonite College, 54–55
Central State College, 501, 502–503
Central Theological Seminary, 201
Chalmers, Gordon Keith, 232, 234, 237
Chamberlain, Clark W., 152–53
Chaminade, William Joseph, 120–23, 131–32
Chapman, Johnny "Appleseed," 453, 459–60
Chapman, Oscar, 301
Chaput, Charles, 184
Charlesworth, James, 402
Chase, Philander, 226, 228
Chase, Salmon P., 302, 492
Cheney, James, 520
Chinn, Broadwell, 527
Chrisman, John M., 125–27
Christensen, Alphus R., 427, 434–36
Christian Church, 139. *See also* Disciples of Christ;
    and Defiance College, 135–37; and McNeely
    Normal School, 559–60
Christian Connexion, and Antioch, 8–10, 12–13,
    16, 18
Christian Education Society, 19
Christian Movement, and Antioch College, 4–5
Christie, M. Francis, 307
Christ-Janer, Victor, 247
Christopher, Wiliam, 435
Church, Augustus B., 75–76
Church of God, and the University of Findlay,
    159–66, 170
Church of the Nazarene, 312–14; and Mount
    Vernon Nazarene College, 314–16, 321–22
Church of United Brethren in Christ, and Otter-
    bein College, 404–8
Cincinnati: and College of Mount St. Joseph, 288–
    90, 292, 295; Xavier University in, 551, 554
Clark, Clarence O., 426
Clark, William, 290
Clarke, George Washington, 301
Clason, M. B., 394
Clay, Henry, 227
Claypole, Edwin, 71
Clayton, Glenn L., 3, 28–30, 35
Cleveland, 86, 114; and Case Western Reserve Uni-
    versity, 94–98, 106; Catholic education in, 340-
    41, 467; and John Carroll University, 217;

Christian Workers Training School in, 263–65; and
Cleveland College, 102; and Notre Dame College, 338, 348–49; Ursuline College in, 463–64
Cleveland College, 100, 102–103
Cleveland Heights, Ursuline College in, 466
Cleveland State University, 103, 105, 562
Cleveland-Marshall Law School, 44
College for Women (Flora Stone Mather College), 100
College of Mount St. Joseph, 288–97
College of St. Mary of the Springs, 366. *See also* Ohio Dominican University
College of St. Teresa, 258–59
College of Steubenville, 172
College of Wooster, 523, 539–50; status of, 529, 534, 536
Collett, Wallace, 521–22
Collier, George F., 45
Collins, Judy, 514
Columbus, 78; Capital University in, 78–81, 86; Franklin University in, 186; Ohio Dominican University in, 366–67; university programs in, 86, 459
Community College Alliance, 189, 192
Community of United Christians, 39–40
Compton, Arthur, 542–43
Compton, Elias, 541
Cone, Orello, 73–74
Congregationalists: Christian Church merging with, 137; in United Church of Christ, 139
Conley, Angelita, 370
Connelly, William C., 348–49
Conrades, George, 402
Cooper, Peter, 15
Copeland, Henry J., 548–49
Copeland, Henry Jefferson, 3
Corbin, Henry, 409
Coshocton, vying for Nazarene college, 315
Courtice, Thomas, 401
Covenanters. *See* Presbyterian Church
Coy, James, 56
Craig, Austin, 13
Cramer, George Washington, 25
Crile, George W., 388
Crosby, John, 184
Culverhouse, Gay, 353
Cunningham, Holly Estil, 559
Cupp, Robert, 388
Cutler, Carroll, 100
Cuyahoga Community College, 103, 105

Dailey, James, 437
Darby, James M., 128
Davis, Carrie, 426
Davis, Charles E., 427, 432–33
Davis, David, 229
Davis, J. Boyd, 428
Davis, J. W., 426
Davis, Jefferson, 394
Davis, John Merrill, 425–27
Davis, Joseph M., 129
Davis, Lewis, 406, 408
Davis, Thomas, 425
Dayton, 409. *See also* University of Dayton; university programs in, 86, 459
De Jong, Arthur, 336
Defiance, bid for Wittenberg University, 526
Defiance College, 3, 134–42, 135
Delano, Columbus, 312
Delaware, Ohio Wesleyan University in, 392
Dell, George, 90
Deming, Anne L., 353
Denison, William S., 147–48
Denison University, 1, 4–5, 144–56; status of, 529, 534, 536
Devlin, Columba, 178, 182
DeVore, Brent, 415
Dewine, Mike, 388
DeWine, Sue, 287
DiBiasio, Daniel, 509
Diederich, Anne Marie, 473
Dieska, Joseph L., 125–28
Dill, Clarence, 402
Diller, Phyllis, 58
Disciples of Christ. *See also* Christian Church: and Hiram College, 210; and Hopedale Normal College, 560–61
Dixon, Paul, 116–18
Doctorow, Ed, 240
Doherty, James, 17
Dolbear, Amos, 397
Dombro, Richard J., 126–27
Dominican Sisters, and Ohio Dominican University, 365-72, 374–76, 378
Donnell, Mr. and Mrs. O. D., 166
Dorsey, Barry, 438
Douglas, John Henry, 264–65, 509
Douglass, David Bates, 228
Doure, Paul, 89
Dow, Herbert H., 99

Downer, Samuel, 16
Downing, Mary Omer, 294
Drushal, J. Garber, 547–48
Du Bois, W. E. Burghardt, 496
Dublin, Franklin University campus in, 190
Duddy, Frank, 286
Dukes, Lewis, 384
Dulzer, Kenan, 472–73
Dunathan, Homer, 166–67
Duncan, Jack, 432
Dunlap, William, 560
Dunn, Ransom, 423–24
Dunshee, Norman, 208
DuPont, Thomas Coleman, 457
Dwight, Holden, 42

Eagle, George, 423
Eaton, John, 284
Eaton, Russell, 457
Edgecliff College, 562
Egan, Daniel W., 172–78
Eisenhower, Dwight David, 138–39
Eisenmann, John, 99
Eliot, Charles William, 100, 362, 554
Elliott, Charles, 392
Ellis, A. Caswell, 102
Ellis, John Tracy, 221
Engle, Harold, 112–13
Episcopal Church, 3, 229; and Kenyon College, 226–28, 230–31, 233
Evangelical Church, 139, 411
Evangelical Friends. See Quakers
Evangelical Lutheran Church, 78
Evangelical Lutheran Church in America, 85, 87, 523, 536; Theological Seminary of the Evangelical Lutheran Synod, 78
Evangelical United Brethren Church, 411, 413
Evans, Ben R., 423, 427, 440
Evans, Bob, 432
Evans, Mary, 246
Ewing, John L. (Jack), 311
Ewing, Robert, 434
Ex Corde Ecclesiae, 481–86

Fairbanks, Charles, 397
Fairchild, James Harris, 362
Fairless, Benjamin, 388–89
Farnham, Eleanor, 248
Fay, Eli, 12, 17

Felicetti, Daniel A., 89
Fenn College, 105, 562
Fenwick, Edward, 288–89, 551, 553
Fess, Simeon D., 19, 383, 388
Ficken, Clarence, 401
Findlay, 159–61. See also University of Findlay
Findley, David, 325
Finkel, Benjamin F., 388
Finn, Mary LeRoy, 350–51
Finney, Charles Grandison, 314, 360–61
Fishel, Leslie H., 205–6
Fitz, Raymond L., 130–31
Fitzharris, Pat Semple, 369
Fitzhugh, Henry, 278
Flemming, Arthur, 400–401
Flexner, Abraham, 102
Flora Stone Mather College, 100
Fostoria, 446
Fouse, William Henry, 408
Fox, Charles Trout, 163–64
Fox, H. Clifford, 167
Francis, Ann, 260
Francis, Clarence "Bevo," 433
Franciscan University, 172–85, 173
Franciscans: and Lourdes College, 254, 256; at Walsh University, 481, 483–86
Franklin, John Hope, 519
Franklin College, 325–26, 329, 509–10, 558–59, 561, 563
Franklin Pre-Release Center for Women, 521
Franklin University, 2, 186–93, 187
Frasch, Joseph F., 188
Frazier, William, 398
Frederickson, Theodore, 89
Free Will Baptists. See Baptists
Freed, DeBow and Catherine, 308, 389–90
Freifield, Samuel, 176–77
Freistadt, Hans, 501–502
Fremont, 446
Frick, Ivan, 168
Fritzsche, Paul J., 350
Fulton, Stella, 426
Furry, W. D., 27

Gable, John, 160
Gadis, M. P., Jr., 490
Gallagher, Ursula, 470
Gambier, and Kenyon College, 226–28
Gambier, James Lord, 227–28

Gara, Larry and Lenna Mae, 59, 518

Gardner, John W., 105

Gardner, Lloyd, 402

Garfield, James A., and family, 209–10, 247

Garvin, Hugh, James, and Thomas, 509–10

Gault, Stanley, 549

Gauvey, Ralph, 458–59, 461

Geiger, Hezekiah, 526

Geiger, John O., 130

General Conference Mennonite Church, 54, 57

Geneva Hall, 563

Gerhart, Vogel, 197

German Reformed Church, and Heidelberg College, 194–97, 200–201

German Wallace College, 44–45, 562

Getty, George Franklin, 388

Gibbs, Wolcott, 96

Gibson, Thomas, 109

Giles, Chauncey, 455

Gill, Charles Otis, 438

Gill, John T., 343

Gilligan, John J., 129, 472

Gilmour, Richard, 340

Gilruth, James, 39

Gladstone, John, 224

Gleason, Philip, 129, 220–21, 372

Glennan, T. Keith, 104–6

Glynn, Edward, 224

Godman, William D., 43, 392–93

Going, Jonathan, 145–46

Good, Jeremiah, 196

Good, Reuben, 196

Goodale, Lincoln, 80

Gooding, Gretchen Wagner, 369

Goodman, Andrew, 520

Gorisek, Sue, 248

Goshen College, 55, 58

Gottschalk, G. Richard, 519

Gould, Samuel, 20

Graber, Martha, 58

Graham, Hugh, 467

Graham, John, 434

Graham, Michael, 557

Grant, Philip A., 129

Granville, and Denison University, 144–45, 147

Granville Literary and Theological Institution, 145–46

Greater Cleveland Associated Foundation, 105–106

Greeley, Andrew, 219

Greeley, Horace, 67

Green, John, 182

Gregg, John A., 497

Grinnell, Moses, 15

Grose, Francis W., 348

Gund, Graham, 240

Gutierrez, Galdino, 396

Guyer, William Harris, 165

Haessly, Gonzaga, 468–69

Hagedorn, Robert, 128

Hahn, Scott, 184

Hale, Edward Everett, 18

Hales, R. Stanton, 550

Halifax, Lord, 399

Hall, Jeremiah, 146–47

Halliday, Robert, 515

Hamilton, Kenneth, 485

Hanby, Benjamin, 408

Hanby, William, 406–409, 411

Handy, Truman P., 98

Haning, Gertrude Rebecca, 425

Haning, Ida Belle, 425

Haning, Ira Z., 421–23

Hanley, Matthew M., 367

Harkenrider, Edward W., 127

Harks, Mary Evarista, 341

Harlem Springs, 560; Rural Seminary in, 559

Harlem Springs College, 560–61

Harner, Nevin C., 204

Harrington, Jean Patrice, 295–96

Harris, Fred, 48–49

Harris, James T., 142

Hartshorn, E. N., 304

Hartshorn, Orville Nelson, 299–303

Harvard, 362; electives at, 395, 554; as model, 99, 100, 410

Harvey, James, 50

Hayden, Amos Sutton, 208

Haydn, Hiram, 100–101

Hayes, Paul C., 427, 436–38

Hayes, Rutherford B., 69, 229, 232, 526

Haywood, Bruce, 237

Hazard, Francis, 459–61

Head, Robert L., 461

Headden, Susan, 402

Headland, Isaac Taylor and Mariam, 305

Heald, Henry T., 105–106

Heckert, Charles G., 528

Heffernan, Francis de Sales, 372

Heffron, Patrick, 254–55

Heidelberg College, 3, 194–207, 195, 523; and Tiffin University, 442–47

Heisman, John, 72

Henderson, Elmer E., 560–61

Henderson, John H., 505–506

Henry, Terence, 184–85

Herbert, Thomas J., 501

Herrick, C. Judson, 150

Herrick, Clarence Luther, 149–50

Herrick, Myron, 397

Hickenlooper, Bourke, 502

Hickey, James A., 473

Hicks, Lawrence B., 320

Hicks, Lewis E., 149

Hill, Charles L., 501–502

Hill, Daniel, 265

Hill, Thomas, 4–5, 18

Hines, Paul, 436

Hinsdale, Burke Aaron, 210

Hinshaw, Robert E., 517, 521–22

Hiram College, 208–18, 209, 564

Hirschy, Noah C., 54–55

Hitchcock, Henry Lawrence, 95–96

Hitchcock, Reuben, 243

Hobart, John, 227

Hoffman, Abbie, 435

Hoffman, John, 397–99

Holbrook, Alfred, 40–42, 559

Holbrook, Dwight, 41

Holbrook, Josiah, 40–41

Holcomb, John D., 426

Holden, Louis Edward, 3, 542–43

Holgate, William C., 134

Holiness, Evangelical, 267–68, 271. *See also* Quakers

Holiness movements, 314

Holland, W. H., 445–46

Holzer, Charles, 431–32, 434

Hoover, William H., 302–303

Hope, Bob, 30–31

Hopedale, McNeely Normal School in, 559–60

Hopedale Normal College, 559–61, 563

Horn, Rhinehart, and Truthan, 349

Horsch, John, 57

Hotchkiss, Willis, 266–67

Houf, Horace, 427–29

Hough, Benson, 398

Howard, Gordon, 410

Howard, Oliver A., 492

Howard, Roswell, 492

Howe, Charles S., 104–5

Howe, Frederick C., 44

Howe, Samuel Gridley, 12

Howey, Robert H., 560

Hudson, David, 91–92, 92

Hudson, Western Reserve College in, 93, 96–97

Hufgard, Kilian, 469

Hughes, John, 552

Hulet, Fletcher, 43

Hunt, Emory W., 151–52

Hurdis, Adam, 455

Huth, E. M., 449

Hyer, Elizabeth, 395

Iberia College, 559–60

Irish, Annie, 541

Jackson, Josephina, 492

Jackson, Thomas H., 492, 495

Jacobs, E. E., 27

Jacobs, Edward, 23

Jacobs, Ira W., 425

Jagow, Elmer, 214

James, John H., 453–55

Janney, Allison, 240

Japan, University of Rio Grande branch in, 438

Jay, Eli and Mahala, 14–15

Jeffers, Dean, 374

Jenifer, John T., 493

Jeremiah, James T., 112–17

Jesuits, 221, 554; and John Carroll University, 217, 219–20, 224; rethinking role of, 556–57; and Xavier University, 551–53, 554–55

Jewett, Mary, 73–74

John Carroll University, 217–25, 218, 467; and Notre Dame College, 345–46

John Paul II, Pope, 183

John XXIII, Pope, 125

Johns Hopkins, 102

Johnson, B. Bancroft, 281

Johnson, Clifford, 115

Johnson, John L., 40

Johnson, Ronald, 273

Johnson, Rose Angela, 471–72

Johnson, Tom L., 102

Johnston, W. Noel, 139

Jones, Gilbert H., 497–98

Jones, Joshua H., 496–98
Jones, Ronald, 458
Jordan, Philip, 239
Josephson, Clarence E., 202–204
Judson College, 561
Juncker, Henry, 122
Jusseaume, Richard, 487–88
Justinian, Mother, 259

Kamm, Jacob, 48
Karsten, Robert, 353
Kazel, Dorothy, 473
Keegan, Mercedes, 465–66, 468
Keelan, Kevin, 174, 178–80, 182
Keen, E. W., 444–45
Keen, Edward, 397
Keeney, Betty, 58
Keith, Ismael, 490
Keller, Ezra, 523–25, 537
Keller, John, 58
Kelly, Edward, 177
Kelly, Eusebia, 470
Kennison, Charles Clinton, 445
Kenny, Henry, 128
Kent, William, 492
Kent State University, Stark County campus of, 477
Kenton, bid for Wittenberg University, 526
Kenyon College, 1, 3, 5, 226–41, 227; status of, 534, 536
Ketcham, Charles B. and Lucille Brown, 305–306
Kidd, George, Jr., 442, 449–52
Kilpatrick, Walter, 111–12
Kim, Helen, 402
King, Coretta Scott, 480
King, George L., Jr., 306
King, Henry Churchill, 362
King, T. Starr, 14
Kinnison, William A., 533–37
Kissinger, Henry, 294
Klassen, John Peter, 63
Klimkowski, Ann Francis, 260
Kluge, P. F., 240
Knapp, A. Blair, 153–55
Knight, Charles M., 69, 71, 74
Knobel, Dale T., 156
Knox, Philander C., 303
Kohlenbrander, Harold M., 309–11
Koinange, Daniel, 402
Kolbe, Carl, 69

Kolbe, Parke Rexford, 76
Korea, John, 177
Kornfield, Carol, 520
Kornhauser, Sidney I., 152
Kossuth, Louis, 80, 393
Kost, John, 198–200
Krason, Stephen, 184
Kreider, Robert, 52, 60–61
Kreisler, Fritz, 527
Kreuner, Harry H., 154
Kuhling, Elisabeth, 339
Kuzma, Hank, 178

Ladd, Silas Trumbull, 243
Ladley, Derostus F., 16
Lake Erie College, 243–53, 244
Lakeside Hospital Training School for Nurses, 103
Landes, Carl, 58
Lane Seminary, 360
Langevin, Thomas, 85–87
Langhirt, Francis, 126–27
Lantz, G. Benjamin, Jr., 309
Latchaw, John R. W., 135
Latchaw, John Roland Harris, 161–63
Laydon, Harold F., 249, 252
Lebanon, trying to get college, 10–11, 146
Lebanon College, 561
Lebanon Correctional Institution, 520
Lebanon National Normal University, 512
Lebanon University, 559, 563. See also National Normal University
Lee, Alex, 211
Lee, Alfred D., 559–60
Lee, Benjamin F., 492–93
Lee, Patrick, 184
Lee, President, 564
Lehmann, William F., 81
Lehr, Henry S., 303
Lehr, Henry Solomon, 380–84, 386
Leibman, Ronald, 402
Leibold, Paul F., 129
Lewis, William Allen, 427, 429–32, 434, 438, 440
Lima, bid for Wittenberg University, 526
Lincoln, Abraham, 394
Lincoln, E. E., 397
Lincoln, James, 247
Lind, Jenny, 80
Lindsay, Vachel, 212–13
Lisska, Tony, 156

Little, John, 492
Lloyd, E. R., 397
Locher, Ralph, 58
Lockmiller, David, 400–401
Loehr, Marla, 353
Lomax, Grace and Melvina, 466
London, vying for Nazarene college, 315
London Correctional Institute, 458–59
Loomis, Elias, 93–95
Lord, Daniel, 342
Lord, Samuel, 237
Lord, Willis, 540–41
Lourdes College, 254–62, 255
Lowell, Robert, 240
Lowry, Howard Foster, 3, 539, 544–47
Loy, Matthias, 82
Lucas, Robert E., 518
Ludwig, Marvin J., 141–42
Lumpp, Randolph F., 127
Lund, Franz Edward, 237–38, 316
Lutheran Church, 418, 536; American Lutheran Church, and Capital University, 85, 87; and Capital University, 80–81, 85, 87–89; colleges of, 523, 529–30, 536; Evangelical Lutheran Church, 78; Evangelical Lutheran Church in America, 85, 87, 523, 536; and Wittenberg University, 523–25, 527, 529, 535–37
Lutheran Church in America, 85, 87
Lynam, Bernardine, 367
Lyne, Paul, 429, 434
Lyon, Grace, 149

Mabery, Charles Frederic, 99
Macdonald, Sara, 367
Maglott, Frederick, 380
Magruder, Jane de Chantal, 366–67
Mahan, Asa, 314
Malicky, Neal, 50–51
Malloy, Mary, 257
Malone, John Walter and Emma Brown, 263–68
Malone College, 263–75
Maltby, Esther T., 491–92, 492
Manchester, Alfred Holbrook College in, 559
Manchester, Charles, 164
Mann, Horace, 3, 11–18, 21
Mansfield, bid for Wittenberg University, 526
Marble, Samuel, 513
Marianists. See Society of Mary
Marietta College, 1, 5, 137, 276–87, 277

Marion, Paul B., 452
Marquette University, 221
Marsden, Edward, 283
Marsh, Tamerlane Pliny, 303–4
Marshall, Leon, 398
Martin, Bert W., 312
Martin, Regis, 184
Mary Manse College, 260
Marysville, vying for Nazarene college, 315
Mason, E. G., 28
Matesich, Mary Andrew, 374–75, 377
Mathile, Clayton, 389
Matthews, George, 262
Matthews, Stanley, 229
McBride, Mary, 492
McBrien, Richard, 480
McCann, Kevin, 3, 138–39
McCarrell, David and Anne, 434
McCarthy, Colman, 518
McCarthy, Donald, 128
McChesney, Welbert Renwick, 111
McClellan, Earl, 113
McClure, Thornton N., 374, 387
McCollester, Sullivan, 68–70, 72
McCollum, Hugh, 109
McConnell, Bishop, 398
McCorkle College, 559–60
McCormick, Anne O'Hare, 367
McCullough, William, 400
McDermott, Floyd W., 431–32
McDonough, Bernard P., 286
McDowell, Margaret Ann, 369
McGovern, George, 518
McIlvaine, Charles Pettit, 228–29
McIntosh, President, 387
McKinley, William, 164
McKinney, David, 109–11
McLaughlin, Thomas D., 343, 349
McMaster, William Henry, 303–305
McMillan, H. H., 109
McNeely, Cyrus and Jane Donaldson, 559–60
McNeely Normal School of Ohio, 559–60, 563
McQuaid, Kim, 247
McReynolds, Peter W., 135–36
Meadville Theological School, 8–9
Meadville/Lombard School, 8
Meek, Philip, 402
Mees, Otto, 3, 82, 84
Mennonites, and Bluffton College, 52–57, 60–63

Merici, Angela, 462

Merrick, Frederick, 394–96, 490

Merrifield, Alpheus Marshall, 12–14, 16–17

Messenger, George, 66

Methodist Church, 394, 405, 413, 559. *See also* African Methodist Episcopal Church; Methodist Episcopal Church; United Methodist Church; and Baldwin-Wallace College, 44–47; and Mount Union College, 305–308, 310; and Ohio Northern University, 383–85; and Ohio Wesleyan University, 392–95, 402; at Otterbein College, 411, 417

Methodist Episcopal Church, 302–303, 489–90, 559, 561

Meyer, Leo, 120–23

Meyer, Samuel, 389

Meyers, Michele Tolela, 155–56

Miami University, Oxford College for Women and Western College absorbed by, 562

Michel, F., 81

Michelson, Albert, 96, 99–100

Milan, C. W., 560

Miller, Charles E., 3, 200–203

Miller, Edward, 402

Miller, Franklin J., 442, 446–49

Miller, Henry, 65–66

Miller, J. Allen, 26

Miller, Lewis, 302

Miller, Mary Odila, 341, 347

Miller, Richard, 49–50

Millett, John, 435

Millis, John S., 105–106

Mills, Mary, 511

Mills, William, 10–11, 15–16

Milner, 114

Minton, Dale, 516–17

Miravalle, Mark, 184

Mitchell, Fannie, 492

Mitchell, John G. and Fannie, 491, 493–94

Mitchell, Samuel T., 492, 493–96

Mohun, Stephanie, 366–67

Molinari, Todd, 183

Molloy, Maria Corona, 294

Monnett, Mary, 395

Montgomery, J. Knox, 330–33

Montgomery, J. Knox, Jr., 333

Montgomery, Robert N., 333, 336

Mooney, Charles A., 345

Moore, Lewis and Jean, 458, 460

Moores, Harry C., 192

Morey, Carroll A., 167

Morgan, Arthur E., 19–20

Morley, Edward W., 95–96, 99

Morse, Robert, 106

Morton, J. F., 109

Mosiman, Samuel, 55–58

Moulton, Albanus Avery, 423–25

Moulton, Edward Q., 249

Mount Gilead, not chosen for Buchtel College, 65

Mount Holyoke Seminary, 244

Mount St. Joseph, College of. *See* College of Mount St. Joseph

Mount Union College, 5, 299–311, 300, 382, 414, 562

Mount Vernon Nazarene University, 312–22, 313

Mucowski, Richard, 481

Muhlenberg College, 561

Murdock, Eugene, 434

Muskingum Academy, 276

Muskingum College, 1, 324–37, 325, 563

Musselman, Vivienne, 58

Mussio, John King, 172, 177

Nasby, Petroleum V., 361

Nase, Stephen, 315

Nast, Wilhelm, 44–45

Nast Theological Seminary, 45, 47

National Normal University, 559, 561, 563. *See also* Lebanon University

Nease, Stephen, 315, 320

Neufeld, Elmer, 52, 60, 62–63

New Athens, 325, 558–59, 561, 563

New Church. *See* Swedenborgians

New Concord, 328; Muskingum College in, 325–27, 332–34

"New England Plan," 145

New Philadelphia, vying for Nazarene college, 315

Newark, Denison University extension center in, 150

Newman, Eugene, 435

Newman, Paul, 240

Niesz, B. F., 380

Nilson, Birgit, 178

Nixon, Richard, 270

Northcutt, Zelma, 434

Notestine, Jonas, 541

Notre Dame College, 338–56, 339, 467

Noyes, Emily, 541

Nugent, Georgia, 240

Nye, Jean, 169

Oakar, Mary Rose, 470

Oberlin, John Frederick, 358

Oberlin College, 15, 137, 280, 358–63, 408; and coeducation, 221, 360, 406–407, 464; Schauffler
College in, 139–40; status of, 302, 534, 536

O'Brien, Robert, 290

O'Connor, John Cardinal, 184

Oden, Robert, 239–40

Ohio Academy of History, 1

Ohio Central College, 559–60, 563

Ohio Dominican University, 364–78, 365

Ohio Northern University, 2–3, 380–91, 381, 414

Ohio Protestant Episcopal Church, 3

Ohio Reformatory for Women, 458–59

Ohio State University, 312, 315–16

Ohio Wesleyan University, 1, 4–5, 392–403, 393,
414; status of, 529, 534, 536

Ohio-Pennsylvania Academic Alliance, 252

Ohl, Ferris, 205

Old School Presbyterians. See Presbyterian Church

Oliver, Newt, 432–33

Olmsted, Sterling, 522

O'Reilly, Bernard P., 124

Osborne, Byron, 267–69, 272, 274

Otterbein, Philip, 404–405

Otterbein College, 4, 404–20, 523, 534

Otto, Paul J., 189

Overberg, Bernard, 338–40

Owen, President, 148

Oxford, not chosen for Buchtel College, 65

Oxford College for Women, 562

Packer, Ezra, 24

Painesville, Lake Erie College in, 243–53

Palmer, Francis A., 17

Palmer, Phoebe, 314

Paramenter, Olive, 449

Park, John G., 380

Park, R., 109

Parker, Emma J., 492

Parmenter, Charlie and Fred, 70

Paul, David, 330

Payne, Charles, 395, 397

Payne, Daniel A., 489, 491–94

Payne, Henry, 97

Peale, Norman, 402

Pedersen, Charles J., 125

Peirce, Cyrus, 12

Peirce, William Foster, 3, 226, 229–38

Pennell, Rebecca and Calvin, 12

Pepper Pike, Ursuline College in, 470–71, 473

Perez, Armando A., 447

Perez-Esquivel, Adolfo, 480

Perkins, Grant, 19

Perkins, William Lee, 243

Peters, John Abram, 198, 200

Pfeiffer, Richard C., 449

Phelps, Alonzo, 455–56

Phillips, John, 10

Picquet, Sylvia, 463

Pierce, George Edmond, 93, 95

Pilarczyk, Daniel E., 128

Pinchot, Gifford, 438

Pinkham, William, 266

Piqua, Urbana University program in, 459

Player, Wilma, 402

Plimmer, Walter, 178

Plique, Clemence, 367

Pobst, R. Lloyd, 431

Pocock, J. W., 549

Poe, Adam, 392

Poston, Clara, 434

Pratt, John, 145–46

Presbyterian Church, 559–61; and Cedarville University, 109–11, 113–15; and the College of Wooster, 96, 539–42, 544, 546; colleges of, 96, 329–30;
denominations of, 111, 324, 328–29; and Franklin College, 558, 563; and Muskingum College,
324–27, 329–30, 334; at Otterbein College, 411,
417–18

Price, John, 361

Priest, Ira, 74–75

Probasco, Abbie, 399

Protestants, 5, 219. See also specific denominations

Providence College, 559

Providence Hospital School of Nursing, 260

Pruden, David, 455

Purcell, John B., 121–23, 552

Purinton, Daniel B., 149–51

Putnam, Douglas, 281, 285

Pytte, Agnar, 106

Quakers, 512; and antiwar activities, 514–16; and
Malone College, 263–74; and Wilmington College, 509–13, 518–22

Quick, Thomas, 427, 436

Quimby, Ephraim, 539

Quiring, Jacob, 57

Ramseyer, Lloyd, 52, 59–60, 62
Randall, Lon, 271–72
Ranney, Rufus P., 97–98
Ransom, Reverdy, 494, 498, 501
Ranson, John Crowe, 237
Rappe, Amadeus, 463–64
Rasmussen, Glen R., 169
Read, James M., 513–14, 518–20
Reed, James A., 539
Reformed Church, in United Church of Christ, 139
Reformed Presbyterian Church. *See* Presbyterian Church
Reichard, Alfred Martin, 442, 446–49
Remigia, M., 260
Research: applications of, 131–32; vs. teaching undergraduates, 335, 410, 417, 544–45
Research universities, 234–35, 240
Rexford, Everett L., 72–73
Reynolds, Barbara, 517–18
Reynolds, William M., 80
Rhodes, James A., 76, 436–37, 516
Rhodes, Mary Beth, 285
Richmond College, 561
Rickey, Branch, 400
Rickly, S. S., 195
Riemenschneider, Albert, 47
Riffe, Vernal, 437
Riker, Albert B., 304
Rinderly, Allen V., 127
Ripley College, 561
Ritchey, Charles, 402
Roberts, Henry, 241
Rockefeller, John D., 98, 202
Rockwell, Timothy, 243
Roesch, Raymond J., 126–29
Romen, Mary Cecilia, 340–41, 344
Ronk, Albert T., 29
Rooney, Arthur, 178
Roosevelt, Eleanor, 513, 519
Roosevelt, Theodore, 528
Ropes, Sarah Putnam, 457
Rosaria, Sister, 260
Ross, John, 9
Ross, Randall, 563
Ross, Stanley M. and Richard M., 192–93
Rothweiler, Jacob, 44–45
Rowe, H. D., 50
Rowland, Sherwood, 402
Rowley, Payer, Huffman and Leithold, 350

Rumbaugh, M., 160
Rural Seminary, 559–60
Rust, Richard S., 490
Rutledge, George W., 380

Sagan, John, 402
Sampson, Benjamin K., 492
Sandburg, Carl, 513
Sands, Marie, 471
Sandusky, Adelaide, 255–56, 258–59
Sanford, Edward, 370
Scanlan, Michael, 180–84
Scarborough, S. C. Bierce, 493, 495–96
Scarborough, William Sanders, 493, 496–97, 507
Schauffler College, 139–41
Schmidt, Wilhelm, 78–79
"Schneider plan," 20
Schonborn, Cristoph Cardinal, 184
Schreck, Alan, 184
Schrembs, Joseph, 254, 340–41, 348
Schuh, L. H., 82
Schultz, Arthur L., 31
Schutte, C. H., 82
Schwartz, Stephen, 286
Schweinfurth, Charles F., 464
Schwerner, Michael, 520
Scio College, 559, 561–64; merger with Mount Union, 305, 562
Scott, Jean A., 287
Scott, Joseph M., 305
Scovel, Sylvester, 541–43
Scranton, Robert, 305
Seamans, Arthur, 318
Second Vatican Council (1962–65), 125, 222, 225, 294, 351, 372, 470, 478, 481
Seiberling, Frank A., 202
Self, Woody, 273
Selle, Lewis, 202
Seman, Paul J., 127
Severance, Louis H., 543
Sewell, Frank, 456
Seymour, Arabella, 462–63
Sharon College, 563
Sharp, S. Z., 24–25
Shaull, Henry, 196
Shaw, Avery A., 153–55
Sheen, Fulton J., 367
Sheeran, Martha Sliter, 368
Sheldon, Henry, 39–40

Shepardson, Daniel and Sarah, 149
Shepardson College, 149–50
Shields, Clifford, 309
Shipherd, John Jay, 358–61
Shorter, James A., 491
Shorter, Joseph P., 492, 496
Shultz, Joseph R., 30
Shunk, Joseph L., 304, 305
Sibley, Hiram, 425
Silloway, Thomas W., 67
Simmons, Charles, 248–49
Sinclair Community College, 130
Sister Formation Movement, 257, 259
Sisters' College, 345
Sisters of Charity, and College of Mount St. Joseph, 288–95
Sisters of Notre Dame, 338–44, 346–49, 352–53
Sisters of St. Francis, 254; and Lourdes College, 258-59, 261
Slack, Charles Goddard, 284–85
Slater, Arthur, 522
Slayton, George, 424
Small, Helen, 247
Smith, A. E., 3, 384–86
Smith, Albert, 99
Smith, C. Henry, 56–57
Smith, Camilla, 369
Smith, Clodus R., 249, 427, 437
Smith, David, 402
Smith, Elden, 400
Smith, Gerrit, 492
Smith, Henry, 279, 284
Smith, Jim, 178
Smith, Lena Kronk, 429
Smith, M. K., 165
Smith, Robert, 398
Smith, Rowland, 402
Smull, Thomas J., 384
Smyser, William, 398
Smyth, Ascension, 464
Social Gospel movement, 362
Society for the Promotion of Collegiate and Theological Education at the West, 279–80
Society of Mary, and University of Dayton, 120–27, 130-31
Sockman, Ralph, 402
Soper, Edmund, 399
South Western Ohio Normal School. See Lebanon University; National Normal University

Speck, Samuel W., 336
Spencer, Carole, 266
Spielman, Christian, 80
Spiers, John Worchester, 457
Sprecher, Samuel, 525–26
Springfield: vying for Nazarene college, 315; Wittenberg University in, 523–24, 526–28, 536
Sprunger, Benjamin, 61–62
St. Clare Academy, 256, 258–59
St. John, Samuel, 93–94
St. John College (Cleveland), 345, 472–73
St. Mary College (Dayton), 123–24
St. Mary of the Springs (to be Ohio Dominican University), 366–67, 370, 378
St. Mary's Institute (Dayton), 122–23, 131
St. Vincent School of Nursing, 260
St. Xavier College, 553–55. See also Xavier University
Staley, Cady, 99
Stanford, Regis, 172, 174, 176
Stanley, Thomas A., 129
Stano, Diana, 474
Stanton, Edwin, 229
Stanton, Frank, 402
Starr, Mary, 322
Starvaggi, Michael and Angeline, 177
Stauffer, John N., 531–33
Stauffer, Robert, 305
Stegemoeller, Harvey, 87–88
Stellhorn, William F., 82
Sterling, Theodore, 230
Sterner, John F., 445–46
Steubenville, Franciscan University in, 172–74, 176-77, 181–82
Steward, T. G., 493
Stimson, Rodney, 284
Stockwell, John Nelson, 98–99
Stoddard, Orange, 541
Stokes, Rembert E., 502–4
Stone, Amasa, 97–98, 104
Stone, Marsena, 149
Storms, Albert, 47
Stoughton, Clarence C., 529, 531, 533
Stradley, Bland L., 466
Strahl, Ortho, 394
Strawbridge, Herbert E., 471
Stuart, James Parke, 453
Suliot, Theodore, 492
Sumner, Charles, 492
Swedenborg, Emanuel, 453

Swedenborgians, and Urbana University, 453, 455–56, 459–60
Swiss Mennonite Church, 55
Sylvania, Lourdes College in, 255, 259
Synder, Ellis, 82
Synder, Jacob, 69
Synder, Lee, 62

Talbot, Samson, 148–49
Tappan brothers, 360–61
Tarlton, German Reformed Church school in, 194–96
Tawawa Springs, Wilberforce University at, 489
Taylor, A. D., 343
Taylor, Archibald A. E., 541
Taylor, Charles E., 504–5
Taylor, Peter, 240
Tensing, Robert, 128–29
Teresa, Mother, 178, 294, 480
Theological Seminary of the Evangelical Lutheran Synod, 78
Thomas, Mary Burnham, 420
Thomas, Ruth, 434
Thomas, William Thomas, 408
Thompson, Henry, 409
Thomson, Edward, 392–94
Thrailkill, Francis Marie, 296
Thresher, Ebenezer, 148
Thwing, Charles F., 100–102, 105
Tickerhoof, David, 180
Tiffin, Heidelberg College in, 194, 196–98, 201, 443
Tiffin Business College, 201, 445
Tiffin University, 201, 442–51
Tight, William Dexter, 150
Tipson, Baird, 537
Tobin, Thomas, 485
Toepfer, Louis A., 106
Toledo, Catholic education in, 254, 256–57
Trueblood, Benjamin, 509, 512
Tulloss, Rees Edgar, 528–29
Turkaly, Joseph, 352

Uhrhane, Suzanne, 369, 372–75, 378
Ulrich, Lawrence P., 126–27
Unitarian Association, 8–10
Unitarians. See also American Unitarians: and Antioch, 16, 18–19
United Church of Christ: and Defiance College, 139–40; formation of, 139; and Heidelberg College, 205

United Methodist Church, 413, 414
United Progressive Mennonites, 56
Universalists, and Buchtel College, 64–68, 70, 72–76
Universidad Interamericana, collaboration with Lake Erie College, 252
University Circle (Cleveland), 98, 464–66, 470
University Heights, John Carroll University in, 217
University Hospitals (Cleveland), 103
University of Akron, and Buchtel College, 64, 76, 562
University of Chicago, 331, 335
University of Dayton, 120–33, 121
University of Findlay, 158–70
University of Rio Grande, 421–40, 422
University of Wooster, 96
Unthank, 511
Urbana University, 453–61, 454
Ursinus School of Theology, 201
Ursuline College, 345, 462–74, 463, 479
Ursulines, 462–66, 470–71, 474

Vagnozzi, Egidio, 127
Van Kirk, Walter, 399
Varacalli, Joseph, 184
Vatican II. See Second Vatican Council (1962–65)
Vayhinger, Ira D., 112
Vickers, Joanne Luckino, 369
Vickery, Willis, 44
Vinson, Robert, 102, 105
Vogel, Ezra, 402
Volpe, Ronald, 89

Waddle, Benjamin, 326–28
Wade, Jeptha, 97
Wadsworth Institute, 54
Waldron, John A., 123
Walker, D. Ormande, 498–500, 505
Walker, John, 324–25, 559
Walker, Rollin, 399
Walker-Taylor, Yvonne, 505
Wallace, David, 327
Wallace, James, 42–43
Walsh, Emmett M., 477
Walsh University, 252, 476–88, 477
Warren, Adelaide, 490
Warren, David, 401
Warren Correctional Institution, 520
Warring, Fred, 178
Watson, S. Arthur, 513
Watterson, Bill, 240

Weaver, George, 72
Weaver, Paul, 247–48
Weber, Gustav, 101
Weber, Ronald G., 307–309
Webster, Leonard, 114
Welch, Herbert, 397
Welch, Johnston, 325–26
Welker, Michael, 183
Wendell, George M., 490
Wenzlau, Thomas, 400–401
Werkema, Gordon, 272–73
Wesley, Charles H., 314, 392, 498, 500–501
Wesley, John, 314
Wessner, James, 515
West Lafayette College, 563
Western College, 562
Western Reserve Eclectic Institute, 208–10, 214
Western Reserve University, 91–93, 97–100, 100–105, 112, 562. See also Case Western Reserve University; collaborations of, 250, 465
Westerville, 190; Otterbein College in, 406, 408–409, 411
Westheimer, Charles and Mary, 518
Weston, J. B., 19
Wheeler, James, 42, 44
White, Inez, 396
White, John, 397
White, John Campbell, 543
White, William, 227
Whitefield, George, 314
Whyte, William H., 49
Wickenden, William E., 104
Wickham, William Terry, 204–205
Wieland, Frank, 70
Wiesel, Elie, 480
Wilberforce, William, 489
Wilberforce University, 489–507, 490
Wilcox, Aaron, 243–44
Williams, Arthur, 114
Williams, Milo G., 455
Williams, President, 385
Williams, Robert R., 460
Williamson, Samuel, 98
Williard, George W., 197–98, 200, 442, 444
Willis, Frank B., 388
Willoughby College, 561
Willoughby Female Seminary, 243
Willson, Andrew, 65–66

Willson, Samuel, 326–27
Wilmington, vs. Wilmington College, 515–17, 519–20
Wilmington College, 509–22, 510, 563
Wilson, James, 15
Wilson, Ollie James, 167–68
Winebrenner, John, 159
Wishart, Charles Frederick, 111, 541, 543–44
Wittenberg University, 523–37, 524
Witz, Annunciata, 471
Wolbring, Hilligonda, 339
Wolverton, Robert E., 295
Wood, Harrison, 423
Woods, Perry D., 425, 428
Woodson, Lewis, 489
Woodson, Mary J., 492
Woodson, Sarah Jane, 490
Woolman, John, 516
Wooster, 3, 111, 539–40. See also College of Wooster
Woywod, Stanislaus, 478
Wright, Ellen, 511
Wright, James, 240
Wright, Louis C., 48
Wright, Richard R., Jr., 498–501
Wright State University, 130

Xavier University, 551–57, 552, 562
Xenia, bid for Wittenberg University, 523–24

Yale, 4, 71
Yates, William Nelson, 163
Yavne College for Women, 350
Yellow Springs, 11, 13–14, 21
Yenovkian, Sarkis, 396
YMCA: and Antioch, 19–20; Franklin University sponsored by, 186, 188
Yochum, Harold L., 84–85
Young, Charles A., 95
Young, Teresa, 462–63
Young, W. L., 83
Young Ladies' Institute (Granville), 149
Youngstown State University, 252

Zachos, John C., 15–16
Zanesville, Denison University extension center in, 150
Zehler, Maximin, 122–23, 130
Zeis, Emma Carter, 177
Zirkle, Kenneth E., 169–70
Zoric, Joseph, 183